Lecture Notes in Computer Science 4717

Commenced Publication in 1973
Founding and Former Series Editors:
Gerhard Goos, Juris Hartmanis, and Jan van Leeuwen

John Krumm   Gregory D. Abowd
Aruna Seneviratne   Thomas Strang (Eds.)

UbiComp 2007:
Ubiquitous Computing

9th International Conference, UbiComp 2007
Innsbruck, Austria, September 16-19, 2007
Proceedings

 Springer

Volume Editors

John Krumm
Microsoft Research
Redmond, WA 98052 USA
E-mail: jckrumm@microsoft.com

Gregory D. Abowd
Georgia Institute of Technology
5th Street NW, Atlanta GA 30332-0280, USA
E-mail: abowd@cc.gatech.edu

Aruna Seneviratne
National ICT of Australia (NICTA)
Eveleigh, NSW 1430, Australia
E-mail: aruna.seneviratne@nicta.com.au

Thomas Strang
German Aerospace Center
82234 Wessling/Oberpfaffenhofen, Germany
E-mail: Thomas.Strang@dlr.de
and
University of Innsbruck
6020 Innsbruck, Austria
thomas.strang@deri.org

Library of Congress Control Number: 2007934832

CR Subject Classification (1998): C.2, C.3, D.2, D.4, H.4, H.5, K.4

LNCS Sublibrary: SL 3 – Information Systems and Application, incl. Internet/Web and HCI

ISSN   0302-9743
ISBN-10   3-540-74852-0 Springer Berlin Heidelberg New York
ISBN-13   978-3-540-74852-6 Springer Berlin Heidelberg New York

Springer is a part of Springer Science+Business Media

springer.com

© Springer-Verlag Berlin Heidelberg 2007

Typesetting: Camera-ready by author, data conversion by Scientific Publishing Services, Chennai, India
Printed on acid-free paper   SPIN: 12121083   06/3180   5 4 3 2 1 0

Preface

The Ubiquitous Computing conference series provides the premier forum in which to present original research results in all areas relating to the design, implementation, application and evaluation of ubiquitous computing technologies. It is a well-established platform to introduce and discuss research that enables new capabilities, appropriate security and privacy, improved user experiences and simplified and powerful development and deployment practices.

These proceedings contain the papers presented at the Ninth International Conference on Ubiquitous Computing (UbiComp 2007) in Innsbruck, Austria, in September 2007.

Our call for papers resulted in 150 submissions, each of which was assigned to a primary and a secondary member of our Program Committee. Every primary and secondary member was responsible for assigning one or more additional qualified reviewers with specific expertise in the field. After double-blind reviews and an online discussion, we had a two-day face-to-face meeting with 38 of the 40 Program Committee members attending the PC meeting held just before the Pervasive 2007 conference in Toronto, Canada, in May 2007. We are grateful to Khai Truong , Jeremy Knight and Alex Varshavsky of the University of Toronto for providing facilities and support for this meeting. At the PC meeting, about 80 of the submissions were individually and extensively discussed in one of the three subgroups *sensors*, *experiences* and *systems* as well as in the calibration and decision panels. The PC finally selected 29 papers for publication in these proceedings. Most of the accepted papers underwent a shepherding process by a reviewer or a member of the Program Committee to ensure that the reviewers' comments were accounted for in the published version. We feel our selective review process and shepherding phase has resulted in a high-quality set of published papers. Five of the 29 accepted papers were nominated at the PC meeting panel as candidates for a best paper award. These are marked accordingly in these proceedings to indicate their particular level of quality. Out of these five papers a subcommittee discussed and finally selected one paper as the best paper of UbiComp 2007. A similar award was given at the conference to the best full paper presentation as well as the best 1-minute-madness presentation, both for the first time at a UbiComp conference.

We extend a sincere "thank you" to all the authors who submitted papers, to our hard-working Program Committee, our thoughtful reviewers, our conscientious shepherds, as well as our sponsors.

September 2007

John Krumm
Gregory Abowd
Aruna Seneviratne
Thomas Strang

Conference Organization

General Conference Chair

Thomas Strang, University of Innsbruck and German Aerospace Center

Honorary Conference Chair

Manfried Gantner, Rector of the University of Innsbruck and Vice President of the Austrian Rectors Conference

Program Committee Co-chairs

John Krumm, Microsoft Research, USA
Gregory Abowd, Georgia Tech, USA
Aruna Seneviratne, NICTA, Australia

Workshops Co-chairs

Henk Muller, University of Bristol, UK
Anne Bajart, European Commission, Luxembourg

Late-Breaking Results Co-chairs

James Scott, Microsoft Research, UK
Minkyong Kim, IBM Watson, USA

Demos Co-chairs

Paul Lukowicz, University of Passau, Germany
Sung-Kook Han, Won Kwang University, Korea

Video Co-chairs

Nobuhiko Nishio, Ritsumeikan University, Japan
Flavia Sparacino, Sensing Places and MIT, USA

Doctoral Colloquium Co-chairs

Claudia Linnhoff-Popien, University of Munich, Germany
Jakob Bardram, IT University of Copenhagen, Denmark

Challenge Chair

Matthias Kranz, Technische Universität Braunschweig, Germany

Student Volunteers Chair

Jacek Kopecky, DERI, University of Innsbruck, Austria
Nick Noack, UC Irvine, USA

Local Arrangements Chair

Reto Krummenacher, DERI, University of Innsbruck, Austria

Public Relations and Outreach Co-chairs

Matthias Kranz, Technische Universität Braunschweig, Germany
Roberta Hart-Hilber, DERI, University of Innsbruck, Austria
Andreas Klotz, DERI, University of Innsbruck, Austria

Program Committee

Ken Anderson, Intel Research
Louise Barkhuus, University of Glasgow
John Barton, IBM Almaden
Christian Becker, University of Mannheim
Michael Beigl, TU Braunschweig
A.J. Brush, Microsoft Research
Roy Campbell, University of Illinois
Sunny Consolvo, Intel Research Seattle
Eyal de Lara, University of Toronto
Anind Dey, Carnegie Mellon University
Paul Dourish, University of California, Irvine
James Fogarty, University of Washington
Adrian Friday, Lancaster University
Hans Gellersen, Lancaster University
Beki Grinter, Georgia Tech
Mike Hazas, Lancaster University
Eric Horvitz, Microsoft Research
Stephen Intille, MIT

Yuri Ismailov, Ericsson Research
Shahram Izadi, Microsoft Research
Bob Kummerfeld, University of Sydney
Anthony LaMarca, Intel Research Seattle
Marc Langheinrich, ETH Zurich
Sang-Goog Lee, Catholic University of Korea
Jen Mankoff, Carnegie Mellon University
Joe McCarthy, Nokia Research
Henk Muller, University of Bristol
Max Ott, NICTA
Aaron Quigley, University College Dublin
Heather Richter, University of North Carolina, Charlotte
Mahadev Satyanarayanan, Carnegie Mellon University
Bernt Schiele, TU Darmstadt
Chris Schmandt, MIT
Albrecht Schmidt, Fraunhofer IAIS and b-it University of Bonn
Abigail Sellen, Microsoft Research
Joao Sousa, George Mason University
Khai Truong, University of Toronto
Andy Wilson, Microsoft Research
Woontack Woo, Gwangju Institute of Science and Technology
Daqing Zhang, I2R

Reviewers

Daniel	Abramowicz	The Royal Institute of Technology, Sweden
Jaime	Adeane	University of Cambridge
Manfred	Aigner	TU Graz
Ryan	Aipperspach	University of California, Berkeley
Morgan	Ames	Stanford University
Ian	Anderson	Bristol University
Zahid	Anwar	University of Illinois at Urbana-Champaign
Jorge	Aranda	University of Toronto
Sebastien	Ardon	National ICT Australia
Rajesh	Balan	Singapore Management University
Won-Chul	Bang	Samsung Advanced Institute of Technology
Jakob	Bardram	IT University of Copenhagen
Genevieve	Bell	Intel
Marek	Bell	University of Glasgow
Mike	Bennett	University College Dublin
Martin	Berchtold	Telecooperation Office (TecO), University of Karlsruhe
Nilton	Bila	University of Toronto

Mike	Blackstock	University of British Columbia
Julian	Bleecker	University of Southern California
Barry	Brown	UC San Diego
Lorna	Brown	Microsoft Research
Vinny	Cahill	Trinity College Dublin
Scott	Carter	FX Palo Alto Laboratory
Fang	Chen	NICTA
Guanling	Chen	University of Massachusetts at Lowell
Tanzeem	Choudhury	Intel Research
Elizabeth	Churchill	Yahoo! Research
Angus	Clark	University of Bristol
Adrian K.	Clear	University College Dublin
Norman H.	Cohen	IBM T.J. Watson Research Center
Ben	Congleton	University of Michigan School of Information
Katherine	Connelly	Indiana University
Scott	Counts	Microsoft Research
Lorcan	Coyle	University College Dublin
Anthony	Cozzie	University of Illinois at Urbana Champaign
Scott	Davidoff	Carnegie Mellon University
Rogerio	de Paula	Intel
Marco	de Sa	LaSIGE & University of Lisbon
David	Dearman	University of Toronto
Christian	Decker	TecO, University of Karlsruhe
Matt	Duckham	University of Melbourne
Frank	Duerr	University of Stuttgart
Paul	Duff	University of Bristol
Hakan	Duman	BT
Maria	Ebling	IBM T.J. Watson Research Center
Keith	Edwards	Georgia Tech
Jason	Flinn	University of Michigan
Andrea	Forte	Georgia Institute of Technology
Mike	Fraser	University of Bristol
Jon	Froehlich	University of Washington
Krzysztof	Gajos	University of Washington
Benoit	Gaudin	University College Dublin
William	Gaver	Goldsmiths College, University of London
Nathan	Good	University of California Berkeley
Saul	Greenberg	University of Calgary
William	Griswold	UC San Diego
Tao	Gu	Institute for Infocomm Research
Alejandro	Gutierrez	University of Illinois at Urbana Champaign

Joerg	Haehner	Leibniz Universitaet Hannover
Jonna	Hakkila	Nokia Research Center
Malcolm	Hall	University of Glasgow
Marcus	Handte	University of Stuttgart
Richard	Harper	Microsoft Research
Albert	Harris	University of Illinois at Urbana-Champaign
Beverly	Harrison	Intel Research Seattle
Lonnie	Harvel	Georgia Gwinnett College
Urs	Hengartner	University of Waterloo
Steve	Herborn	NICTA
Jeffrey	Hightower	Intel Research
Debby	Hindus	Rapport, Inc.
Steve	Hodges	Microsoft Research Cambridge
Paul	Holleis	Nokia Research Center, Finland
Dongpyo	Hong	GIST U-VR Lab
Jason	Hong	Carnegie Mellon University
Joon Sung	Hong	Samsung Electronics
Eva	Hornecker	The Open University
Elaine	Huang	Social Media Research Labs, Motorola Labs
Vincent	Huang	Ericsson AB
Scott	Hudson	Carnegie Mellon University
Dugald	Hutchings	Bowling Green State University
Giovanni	Iachello	McKinsey & Co.
Seiie	Jang	Nagoya University
Moongu	Jeon	GIST
Rui	Jose	University of Minho
Simon	Julier	University College London
Peter	Kahn	University of Washington
Judy	Kay	University of Sydney
Joseph "Jofish"	Kaye	Cornell University
Nicky	Kern	Marc Brandis GmbH
Florian	Kerschbaum	SAP Research
Julie	Kientz	Georgia Institute of Technology
Tim	Kindberg	HP Labs, Bristol
Scott	Klemmer	Stanford University
Stephen	Knox	University College Dublin
Alfred	Kobsa	University of California, Irvine
Antonio	Krüger	University of Münster
Matthias	Kranz	TU Braunschweig
Boris	Krassi	Technical Research Centre of Finland
H. Andres	Lagar-Cavilla	University of Toronto

Mathew	Laibowitz	MIT Media Lab
Koen	Langendoen	Delft University of Technology
Jong-Ho (John)	Lea	Samsung Advanced Institute of Technology
Jonathan	Lester	University of Washington
Yang	Li	University of Washington
Michael	Liljenstam	Ericsson Research
Brian	Lim	Institute of Infocomm Research
James	Lin	IBM Almaden Research Center
Beth	Logan	Intel Digital Health
Paul	Lukowicz	University of Passau
Zakaria	Maamar	Zayed University, United Arab Emirates
Blair	MacIntyre	Georgia Tech
Samuel	Madden	MIT
Scott	Mainwaring	Intel Research
Julie	Maitland	University of Glasgow
Lena	Mamykina	Georgia Tech
Natalia	Marmasse	Google
Stefan	Marti	Samsung
-	Mausam	University of Washington
Walterio	Mayol-Cuevas	University of Bristol
Rene	Mayrhofer	Lancaster University
Michael	McCarthy	University of Bristol
David	McDonald	University of Washington
Robert	McGrath	University of Illinois, Urbana-Champaign
Florian	Michahelles	ETH Zurich
Alex	Mihailidis	University of Toronto
David	Minnen	Georgia Tech
Iqbal	Mohomed	University of Toronto
Suvda	Myagmar	University of Illinois Urbana-Champaign
Hyun	Myung	Samsung Advanced Institute of Technology
Jin	Nakazawa	Keio University
Carman	Neustaedter	University of Calgary
Mark	Newman	Palo Alto Research Center
Jeff	Nichols	IBM Almaden Research Center
Yoosoo	Oh	GIST U-VR Lab.
Nuria	Oliver	Microsoft Research
Benedikt	Ostermaier	ETH Zurich
Tim	Paek	Microsoft Research
Joe	Paradiso	MIT Media Lab
Shwetak	Patel	Georgia Institute of Technology
Donald J.	Patterson	University of California, Irvine

Eric	Paulos	Intel Research
Jamie	Payton	University of North Carolina at Charlotte
Daniel	Peek	University of Michigan, Ann Arbor
Eranga	Perera	NICTA
Henrik	Petander	National ICT Australia
Matthai	Philipose	Intel Research
Jeff	Pierce	IBM Research
Claudio	Pinhanez	IBM Research
Vahe	Poladian	Carnegie Mellon University
Cliff	Randell	University of Bristol
Anand	Ranganathan	IBM T.J. Watson Research Center
Stuart	Reeves	University of Nottingham
Waqas ur	Rehman	University of Toronto
Matt	Reynolds	Georgia Institute of Technology
Till	Riedel	TecO
Matthias	Ringwald	ETH Zurich
Tom	Rodden	Nottingham University
Jennifer	Rode	University of California, Irvine
Yvonne	Rogers	Open University
Michael	Rohs	Deutsche Telekom Laboratories, TU Berlin
Ioanna	Roussaki	National Technical University of Athens
Christine	Satchell	University of Melbourne
Adin	Scannell	University of Toronto
Hedda	Schmidtke	Gwangju Institute of Science and Technology (GIST)
Jean	Scholtz	Pacific Northwest National Laboratory
James	Scott	Microsoft Research
Shondip	Sen	CSIRO
Choonsung	Shin	GIST U-VR Lab.
Chetan	Shiva shankar	UIUC
Irina	Shklovski	Carnegie Mellon University, HCII
Ian	Smith	Intel Research
Timothy	Sohn	UCSD
Mirjana	Spasojevic	Nokia
Sarah	Spiekermann	Humboldt University Berlin
Graeme	Stevenson	University College Dublin
Martin	Strohbach	NEC Europe Ltd.
Jing	Su	University of Toronto
Youngjung	Suh	GIST
Jay	Summet	Georgia Institute of Technology
Laurel	Swan	Microsoft
David	Symonds	University of Sydney

John	Tang	IBM Research
Alex	Taylor	Microsoft Research
Lucia	Terrenghi	LMU University of Munich
Niraj	Tolia	Carnegie Mellon University
Tammy	Toscos	Indiana University
Vlasios	Tsiatsis	Ericsson Research
Kristof	Van Laerhoven	Darmstadt University of Technology
Alex	Varshavsky	University of Toronto
Harald	Vogt	SAP Research
Rainer	Wasinger	University of Sydney, USYD
Allison	Woodruff	Intel Research
Christopher R.	Wren	MERL
Maomao	Wu	Lancaster University
Juan	Ye	University College Dublin
Hyoseok	Yoon	GIST U-VR Lab
Franco	Zambonelli	Universita' di Modena e Reggio Emilia
Manli	Zhu	Institute for Infocomm Research

Shepherds

Ken	Anderson	Intel Research
Louise	Barkhuus	University of Glasgow
Christian	Becker	University of Mannheim
A.J.	Brush	Microsoft Research
Sunny	Consolvo	Intel Research
Anind	Dey	Carnegie Mellon University
Paul	Dourish	University of California, Irvine
James	Fogarty	University of Washington
Adrian	Friday	Lancaster University
Eric	Horvitz	Microsoft Research
Shahram	Izadi	Microsoft Research
John	Krumm	Microsoft Research
Marc	Langheinrich	ETH Zurich
Rene	Mayrhofer	Lancaster University
Joe	McCarthy	Nokia Research
Aaron	Quigley	University College Dublin
Bernt	Schiele	TU Darmstadt

Sponsors

Silver Sponsors

Intel Research
Saltlux
Siemens

Bronze Sponsors

Microsoft Research
transIT
Nokia
KDubiq

We would also like to extend our thank you to the supporting local institutions such as the Digital Enterprise Research Institute (DERI), Semantic Technology Institutes International (STI2), University of Innsbruck, German Aerospace Center (DLR) and the Congress Innsbruck.

Table of Contents

A Statistical Reasoning System for Medication Prompting

Sengul Vurgun[1], Matthai Philipose[1], and Misha Pavel[2]

[1] Intel Corporation
[2] Oregon Health and Science University

Abstract. We describe our experience building and using a reasoning system for providing context-based prompts to elders to take their medication. We describe the process of specification, design, implementation and use of our system. We chose a simple Dynamic Bayesian Network as our representation. We analyze the design space for the model in some detail. A key challenge in using the model was the overhead of labeling the data. We analyze the impact of a variety of options to ease labeling, and highlight in particular the utility of simple clustering before labeling. A key choice in the design of such reasoning systems is that between statistical and deterministic rule-based approaches. We evaluate a simple rule-based system on our data and discuss some of its pros and cons when compared to the statistical (Bayesian) approach in a practical setting. We discuss challenges to reasoning arising from failures of data collection procedures and calibration drift. The system was deployed among 6 subjects over a period of 12 weeks, and resulted in adherence improving from 56% on average with no prompting to 63% with state of the art context-unaware prompts to 74% with our context-aware prompts.

1 Introduction

A context-based prompt is a message delivered to a person because their physical context satisfies some pre-determined criterion. Such prompts have long been considered a service that could be provided by ubiquitous computing systems. A key part of any context-based prompting system is the reasoning module, which infers high-level user context based on sensor data and determines when to issue prompts. Much has been written on how to infer relevant context and how to integrate it into a reminder system, but little empirical work has tested these ideas over long periods of time on non-researchers to solve particular problems. In this paper, we describe the design, implementation and use of a reasoning engine that prompted 6 elders in their home to take their medication over a deployment of 12 weeks, based on two carefully chosen kinds of context. Although the reasoning system was deliberatly simple in design, we believe the pragmatics of developing and using it to (successfully) complete its mission should be of direct interest to the Ubicomp community.

A real-world deployment of a reasoning-system may be valuable in many ways. First, although many techniques have been proposed for context-awareness, there

J. Krumm et al. (Eds.): UbiComp 2007, LNCS 4717, pp. 1–18, 2007.

is not much evidence whether they yield sufficient performance for practical applications. Applying such systems directly puts their utility to test. Second, techniques proposed have varied widely in their degree of sophistication and infrastructure use. A realistic deployment allows us to evaluate empirically the design space of solutions and determine whether various technical capabilities are worthwhile. In particular, real-world data often contains peculiarities that could serve either as a challenge or a justification for advanced techniques. Third, pragmatic difficulties in using techniques are often underplayed unless they are used at scale. A deployment should reveal major challenges of this kind. Finally, such deployments may reveal fresh challenges that either motivate new techniques or demand ad-hoc solutions of potential interest to practitioners.

We use our deployment experiences to make the following contributions:

1. We show that that simple reasoning techniques, when operating on data from fairly conventional wireless sensors, can indeed produce a useful end-result in an important application. In particular, average adherence rates across our subjects increased by 32% relative to no prompting at all, and 17% relative to state-of-the art time-based prompting.
2. Starting with a conventional statistical representation (the Dynamic Bayesian Network (DBN)) for processing time series data we present a detailed quantitative exploration of the design space for the structure of the DBN. As an extension of the exploration, we show that temporal reasoning does contribute crucially to the performance of our system.
3. We identify the overhead of labeling data as by far our biggest impediment to using the DBN. We explore ways to mitigate labeling overhead, including the impact of labeling different fractions of the training data available to us and using a simple semi-automatic labeling system.
4. We present a comparison between a reasoning system based on simple Bayesian reasoning and that based on simple rule-based reasoning. To our knowledge a direct comparison of these two approaches is rare, and perhaps unsurprisingly our insights support claims from supporters of both approaches. We reflect on the pros and cons of the two approaches in the context of our real-world deployment setting.
5. We identify unexpected challenges including miscalibration of sensors over time and faulty data collection procedures, and describe how we countered them.

The reasoning system described was part of a larger project called Context Aware Medication Prompting (CAMP). The CAMP project was not intended to showcase advanced reasoning techniques. The engineering goal in building CAMP was to provide conservatively designed sensing, communication, data management, reasoning, interaction and logistic support to validate medication adherence hypotheses on a tight schedule. In particular, at every stage of design of the reasoning system, we took pains to simplify requirements, design and implementation to maximize chances of success and minimize resource (time and staffing) requirements while providing performance adequate to the task. In some cases, these pragmatics make for a reasoning system that is less intricate than one designed to illustrate novel reasoning capabilities: the reasoning problem itself is deliberately simple, and the tools we used are deliberately over- or under-provisioned. The focus of this paper is therefore on presenting conservative engineering that proved effective in practice rather than presenting novel or intricate design.

2 Related Work

There are few examples of longitudinally deployed ubiquitous computing applications that reason about user context. One outstanding exception is the Independent LifeStyle Assistant (ILSA) from Honeywell [6,5], which deployed a variety of sensors in 11 elder homes over 6 months. ILSA delivered alerts to both elders and caregivers in an attempt to improve elders' medication adherence and mobility. It is unclear whether ILSA succeeded in this primary goal. No detailed description or quantitative analyses have been presented on the design space or efficacy of various parts of the ILSA reasoning system. On the other hand, ILSA involved sophisticated AI machinery, including agents, plan trackers and a variety of machine learning schemes. One of the primary post-mortem recommendations was to avoid most of these complexities. Our work, which presents a simple design that yielded a successful outcome, is a beneficiary of some of these insights. Further, we believe that the detailed quantitative evaluation we present should be of substantial additional value to the practitioner.

An extensive literature exists on sensors and reasoning techniques for inferring user context including location [7,17], activities [13,18,12,20], interruptibility [8,4] and affect [11]. These efforts focus on developing (often sophisticated) techniques to handle limitations in existing systems. Common themes include the use of machine learning techniques to learn models and the use of a few representations such as Bayesian Networks, Support Vector Machines and boosted ensembles. To our knowledge, none of these techniques were deployed as part of longitudinal applications. Our work may be regarded as an early application of simple versions of these techniques in a realistic setting. We focus on how to produce adequate models using these techniques, and how to minimize the overhead of using them.

Labeling has long been recognized as a bottleneck to scaling machine learning. Our work provides empirical support for the importance of reducing the overhead of labeling; it is in fact not practical for us to label sufficient data by hand. Proposed solutions include semi-supervised learning [21] (which utilizes unlabeled data in addition to hopefully small quantities of labeled data), active learning (where users are queried for profitable labels) [2], the use of prior information [16] and clustering data automatically before labeling aggregate clusters instead of individual data points. We adapt the latter idea because of its simplicity: we present a simple interactive approach to labeling that groups similar data before presenting it for labeling.

The question of how and when to prompt subjects most effectively has been examined extensively both in the attention sensitivity [9,4] and the interaction planning [8,3,19] communities. One focus of the former work is identifying when users are most receptive to prompts and how to identify this with sensors. The latter considers how to jointly perform state estimation and identify optimal sequences of actions under uncertainty of observation and effect. In our work, we focus on identifying (using sensors) simple cues that subjects are receptive. However, based on ethnographic work we discuss below, we restrict ourselves to providing point (i.e., not multi step) reminders to users without explicit cost/benefit reasoning.

3   Context-Aware Prompting Requirements

Our reasoning system was built to support a project called Context Aware Medication Prompting (CAMP). One of the two hypotheses that CAMP was designed to test is that *automated contextual prompting can significantly improve medication adherence* (compared to state-of-the art techniques). The state of the art in medication prompting are medication dispensers that beep loudly at fixed times, dispense medication and in some cases, verbally prompt the elder to take medication. Although these devices do improve adherence significantly, there is still a residual lack of adherence. Based on extensive formative work, CAMP ethnographers and domain experts noted a variety of reasons limiting these devices. Based on an iterative process between ethnographers and engineers on the team, two particular failure modes were chosen to be addressed using context aware techniques. When time-based prompts go off, the elder:

1. May not be at home. Prompting the elder to take their medication before leaving the home (if appropriate) could be useful.
2. May be sleeping, on the phone, or engaged in activity away from the medication dispenser. It could be useful to deliver the prompt when the elder is close to the dispenser and neither sleeping or on the phone.

Our reasoning system is therefore designed to track two pieces of context about the user: whether they are about to leave the house, and which room of the house they are in. Use of phone, whether the elder is sleeping and whether the elder took their medication was inferred deterministically with custom sensors and we will not discuss these much further. Below, we go into these requirements in more detail.

3.1   Rules for Prompting

CAMP researchers distilled the functionality of the prompting system into a set of rules. These rules were executed within the pill taking window, in our case, 90 minutes before and after the recommended time to take the medication.

1. Never prompt outside the window.
2. Don't prompt if pill is already taken within the current window.
3. Don't prompt if the participant is not home. Prompting will resume if the participant returns home before the window expires.

4. Don't prompt if participant is in bed.
5. Don't prompt if participant is on the phone.
6. Prompt at level 2 if participant is leaving (this is the only time we prompt before the usual pill taking time).
7. Wait till the time the user *usually* takes the pill. If it is earlier than the recommended pill taking time, start checking for level 1 prompting opportunities at the usual pill time.
8. If only less than 20 minutes left till the window expires, start prompting at level 1 disregarding all other rules (except 1-3).

The system supported two kinds of prompting:

- Level 1: Prompt using the nearest device every minute. The chime is played 10 seconds each time and lights stay on till location changes. Stop if pill is taken. Escalate to level 2 after 10 minutes.
- Level 2: Prompt using all prompting devices in the house every minute. Lights on devices stay on and chime is played for 10 seconds every minute.

The team briefly considered a planning-based approach to the reasoning and prompting engine, where relevant states of the world (elder, home and prompting system), possible actions and their costs, and the likely results of actions would be encoded in a representation like a (Partially Observable) Markov Decision Process (POMDP)[10]. However, we decided on a deterministic rule-based implementation of the prompter for two reasons:

- It was much simpler for engineers and ethnographers to agree on the rules than on costs, and to implement the tens of lines of dispatch code. This was especially so because we decided against sophisticated sequences of prompts.
- Although we initially thought that minimizing user annoyance would be a crucial and subtle aspect of prompting (and therefore worthwhile for a sophisticated technique to maximize the value of actions), formative work found that elders' tolerance threshold to medication reminders was surprisingly high. In fact, with time-based devices, they were comfortable with, and to some extent preferred, loud and persistent reminders.

3.2   Subjects and Infrastructure

To test CAMP hypotheses, we recruited elders who were known to be at risk for medication non-adherence from a prior study from two apartment complexes. Twelve subjects over the age of 70, 10 women and 2 men agreed to participate in the study. No subjects were currently receiving formal long-term care, so they are not completely (or mostly) devoid of cognitive and physical abilities. All subjects lived on their own. Figure 1 shows the typical layout of an apartment, along with the sensor deployment.

Sensors installed were mostly stock devices. They included 4 to 6 wireless infra-red motion sensors (roughly one per room or major area in the home), a pressure mat on the bed, contact sensors on apartment doors and refrigerator

 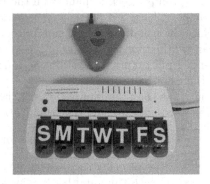

Fig. 1. Typical Floorplan (left); Activity Beacon (top) and MedTracker (bottom)

doors, and sensor for reporting phone use. Figure 1 shows two devices built specifically for the study.

The MedTracker is a pill box that allows pills to be allocated into individual compartments for a whole week. Sensors on the lid for each day of the week can detect if the lid is opened and wirelessly communicate this information to the computing device in the house. In our study, we assumed that the MedTracker provided direct evidence on whether a pill is taken: if the lid for the current day is opened during a period when a medication is supposed to be taken, we assume that the subject successfully took the pill. This indirect notion of adherence is in line with existing practice in such studies. Although there are many documented cases of subjects misplacing pills taken out of a bottle, an informal check revealed that this was rare in our case, perhaps because we ensured that the subjects had reasonable cognitive abilities. The MedTracker is also capable of beeping, flashing and delivering a text message on an LED.

The activity beacon is a wireless, battery backed-up device the size of a saucer that can be placed easily at points around the space being monitored. It is capable of flashing a light, beeping and delivering an audio message. Both the MedTracker and the activity beacon serve as prompting devices.

3.3   The Experiment

Subjects were required to take a vitamin C pill three times a day, morning, midday and evening at a fixed time with a 90 minute window allowed on either side of the prescribed time.

We installed sensors, reasoning system and actuators in the apartments for a period of 28 weeks on average. Our original intention was to have a 6-week baseline period where infrastructure would be installed but no prompts would be delivered, followed by two 4-week stretches where subjects would get prompts either from a time-based prompting system or from the context-aware system.

The baseline period would be used to evaluate adherence level with no intervention as well as to construct an appropriate model for the user, which could be used during the subsequent context-based prompting period. In practice, because of initial problems with the infrastructure, we spent 7-16 weeks in baseline followed by 12-15 weeks of intervention.

The original group of 12 subjects dwindled to 6 during the baseline period, so that we were able to perform prompting only on the latter smaller group. We will refer to these subjects by the labels HP05, HP52, M26, M32, M44 and M45. Most of the drop-offs were due to personal reasons (e.g. sickness, marriage).

3.4 Modeling Choices

Our final inference tasks (inferring location and whether leaving home) were carefully selected so that they were likely to provide useful reminders to users while still being fairly directly inferable from our sensors. For instance, we expected that motion sensor readings would tell us subject location most of the time, and that a location next to the front door of a home coupled with the opening of the door would indicate whether the user is leaving home. However, we also expected a number complications:

- Motion sensors readings are often only indirect indicators of subject location. In particular sensor lockout periods, thresholds for activity levels before triggering and detection of events in adjacent areas through open doors all result in sensors firing or failing to fire unexpectedly (relative to subject motion). Techniques that reason about uncertainty and noise have therefore proved valuable in inferring location from motion sensors [14].
- Contact sensors, such as those for the front door and refrigerator are prone to missing events especially when installed imperfectly or when misaligned due to common use. It is important therefore to make inferences with incomplete information.
- Given noise in sensor data, it is possible to get contradictory information from multiple sensors. For instance, the bed sensor may indicate that the subject is on the bed while the kitchen sensor fires in the same time slice or the refrigerator door sensor triggers (due to vibrations). It is important therefore to weigh evidence from different sensors when inferring the final result.
- In some cases, the duration of stay in a particular state is important. For instance, a subject in the passage way next to the door may be much more likely to leave if they spend more than a few seconds there.
- In all cases, we expect considerable variability in layout of homes and behavior of subjects. We therefore expected some level of customization to each subject to be important.

The choice of reasoning technique needed to be made months before actual data from elderly subjects was available in order to allow for implementation, testing and integration with CAMP infrastructure. The above concerns about noise and variability in the sensor data led us to select a statistical (Bayesian) approach as opposed to a deterministic rule-based one. The decision came with a risk: much of the design exploration work and all implementation work for the CAMP reasoning system was to be done with an engineer with little prior experience with statistical reasoning. The engineer worked with two experienced users of Bayesian techniques as occasional advisers, based on a two-week crash course in Bayesian Networks. The learning curve for a "heavyweight" technique such as Bayesian network was a serious concern. We were pleasantly surprised to find that as long as we limited ourselves to simple structures, the Bayesian approach corresponded closely to intuitive rules.

Before the deployment, and based partially on data from a trial with a friendly subject, we defined the structures for a family of models for the elders' behavior. During the baseline period, we trained these models on roughly 100 hours of data per subject spread over a week using leave-one-week-out cross validation (with 5 folds) and picked the best performing one for each subject. The model that performed best for each subject at baseline was used during their intervention period. Training originally involved substantial labeling overhead, of the order of 1 day for each day labeled. Section 4 below details the process of finding good models, and section 5 describes how we addressed the cost of labeling.

4   Selecting Models

Table 1 lists the inputs and outputs for our context model. The outputs (termed *hidden variables*) are the location of the user and a boolean variable indicating whether they are about to leave their home. The inputs, or *observed variables*, correspond to information pooled from differently sized time windows preceding the current moment. The time windows and the information represented by the observables were selected based on experience. We track the last motion sensor fired because there are runs of time slices with no motion sensor information. In these cases, we found that the last motion sensor fired is a good indicator of current location. In our initial design, we instead tracked the motion sensor that fires in the current time slice (and allowed a NoSensor value). The two other MS variables track the "level of activity" in the home because we believed that high levels of activity may correlate with intent to leave the home.

4.1   A Dynamic Bayesian Model

Model 1 of Figure 2 shows our basic model, a Dynamic Bayesian Network (DBN) [15]. Nodes in the graph correspond to hidden and observation variables in a 5-second time slice. We choose to infer at this granularity because we have a narrow window of 10 or more seconds when a subject is leaving the home. Each node n has a *conditional probability table* (CPT, not shown), which represents the probability distribution $\Pr(n|\mathrm{Pa}(n))$, where $\mathrm{Pa}(n)$ are the parent nodes of n. The dotted line separates values of variables in two adjacent time slices, with the left side representing the current time slice and the right representing the next

Table 1. Model Variables and Their Possible Values

Variable	Values	Comment
Location	NotHome, Bedroom, Kitchen,	Hidden variable
	Livingroom, Bathroom, Frontdoor	Hidden variable
Leaving	True, False	Hidden variable
LastMSFiring	MS1, MS2, ..., MSN	Which motion sensor
		(MS) got fired last?
MSFiringsFreq	None, L(1-2), M(3-5),	Num. MS firings
	H (more than 5)	in last 1 minute
MSTransitions	None, L(1-5), M(6-10),	Num. MS transitions
	High(more than 10)	in last 5 minutes
Bed	In, Out	
DoorEvent	OpenEvent, CloseEvent, NoEvent	
Refrigerator	OpenEvent, CloseEvent, NoEvent	
Time	EM (6-9am), MM (9-11am),	
	Noon (11-2pm), A (2-5pm),	
	E (5-9pm), Night (9pm-6am)	

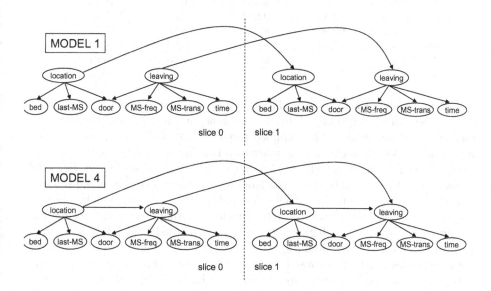

Fig. 2. The Baseline (Model1) and Best (Model4) DBNs

time slice. Arrows across the boxes represent temporal conditional dependences between variables.

Regardless of the values in the CPT, this model encodes the following assumptions:

1. The Bed, LastMSFiring and Refrigerator variables depend just on Location. Once the Location is known, the subject's Leaving status has no effect on

these. Similarly for MSFiringFreq, MSTransitions and Time with respect to Leaving.

2. DoorEvent depends in the same sense on both Location and Leaving, since if you are located close to the door and not leaving, you will likely not open the door, and if you are leaving but your current location is not next to the door, you will again not open the door.

3. Location and Leaving in a given time slice are independent of all other variables in the previous time slices given their values in the previous time slice.

This model is one of the simplest dynamical models using our variables: it is very close to one Naive Bayesian model for each hidden variable with a temporal constraint on hidden variables thrown in to smooth their values over time.

Table 2. Best Classifiers for Leaving (% Correct Averaged Over Folds)

House	Model	Leaving=true	Leaving=false	Loc=AtHome	Loc=NotHome
HP05	Model3	0	95.66	96.87	18.73
HP52	Model4	86.89	92.69	98.06	95.67
M26	Model4	92.00	88.33	90.96	77.72
M32	Model4	77.29	97.60	96.99	98.42
M45	Model4	90.73	90.76	97.86	95.01

We experimented with a few variants on this basic structure encoding slightly different sets of assumptions. Model 4, also shown in Figure 2, was the best performing of all our models when applied to subject data during the test period. It encodes an additional dependency between Leaving and Location. This dependency was crucial in the detection of leaving, because in its absence (e.g., in model 1), leaving has no access to either the hidden location or its determining sensors. Since leaving is a combination of being located near the door followed by opening the door, it is essentially impossible to determine without location information. For one of our subjects, a slightly different model (named Model 3) was the best performing. Exploring the design space of these DBNs by adding dependence arcs between random variables proved to be surprisingly powerful. However, we should note that we stopped reasoning about every conditional independence encoded in the DBN (in particular verifying whether various V-structures were sensible) early in our explorations. We simply drew an arrow between a hidden node and an observed node when the latter depended on the former. We expect that more sophisticated DBNs where encoding correct conditional independence structure is key would be much more resource-intensive to develop.

We used the above analysis to select, for each subject, the appropriate model (of five possibilities) for use intervention phase of CAMP. Table 2 shows the true positive and true negative rates of the model that performed best on classifying

Table 3. Results from Non-Temporal Classifiers (% Correct)

House	Model	Leaving=true	Leaving=false	Loc=AtHome	Loc=NotHome
HP05	Model3 (Fold0)	0	95.66	96.87	18.73
HP05 NT	Model3 (Fold0)	0	95.26	99.53	0
HP52	Model4 (Fold1)	96.97	93.51	99.64	99.23
HP52 NT	Model4 (Fold1)	0	92.77	99.82	99.29
M26	Model2 (Fold3)	100.00	89.86	93.74	80.28
M26 NT	Model2 (Fold3)	0	87.37	94.64	79.86
M32	Model4 (Fold1)	100.00	98.67	98.00	98.58
M32 NT	Model4 (Fold1)	0	98.46	97.78	98.66
M44	Model4 (Fold3)	100.00	93.32	99.55	98.14
M44 NT	Model4 (Fold3)	0	83.44	96.97	98.82
M45	Model4 (Fold2)	100.00	92.31	98.99	99.70
M45 NT	Model4 (Fold2)	0	91.36	98.99	91.37

Leaving (all models did quite well on Location) for each subject. Although for compactness we show Location results as an AtHome/NotHome classifier, we actually performed an N-way classification over the rooms in the house, and the numbers reported ar the results of the N-way classification. HP05 turns out to be an anomalous case: it had very few (4) leaving examples and less data overall than the others because the subject spent much her time at her friend's home.

4.2 Dropping Temporal Information

Although our intuition was that temporal reasoning (i.e., incorporating reasoning from past time slices in the present) would contribute strongly to performance, we tested a model that omitted the temporal arrows in the DBN so that we had a conventional Bayesian Network to classify each time slice. Table 3 shows the results of applying this model on a single folds (we did not validate over all folds due to time; we picked the fold with the best Leaving result for the temporal model). For instance HP52 data is analyzed with Model 4 on Fold1 of the data; the "NT" line gives results without temporal dependences. Location is classified quite well even without temporal dependences. This primarily because LastMSFired is an excellent indicator of current location. Although it may seem surprising that the Bayes Net uniformly resulted in zero detection of labeling (for instance, one would expect at least an occasional guess for leaving when door opens), an examination of the learned networks reveals that that this was because of the prior bias towards not leaving the house; leaving is a rare event.

5   Using the Model

5.1   Implementation

We implemented our model in C++ using the Probabilistic Network Library (PNL) [1] toolkit for graphical modeling. We perform inference by filtering with a junction tree algorithm and stick to fully supervised parameter learning. The models were easy to implement and reason with, involving under a hundred lines of code. However, the toolkit itself was not mature and required debugging.

5.2   Labeling

The biggest bottleneck in using our models was to label data so that parameters of the DBNs could be learned on the basis of observed data. Purely manual labeling of all 5 folds of data in each case was unsustainable because labeling an hour of data often took roughly an hour. In what follows, we examine a simple semi-automated labeling technique, the impact of labeling (and learning with) less data. We also considered (but do not report here) the potential for transferring models across homes.

Interactive Labeling. After labeling manually for a few days, we noticed that the labels remained unchanged for long stretches. In particular, in the absence of observations or if observation values were unchanged, labels did not change. Alternately, segmenting the time series data by missing or identical observations resulted in segments with unique labels. We therefore decided to segment the data before presenting to the user for labeling.

Algorithm 1 specifies the rules for labeling location. We assume that location remains fixed over time unless an observation is detected from a sensor in a different room. If such an observation is detected, we give the user to provide a new label. Note that in some cases because of noise in the sensors, it is incorrect to simply label with the location of the sensor that generated the new observation. We have a similar scheme for labeling Leaving.

Table 4 shows the degree to which the tool can cut labeling overhead. For each house, the table lists the number N of events to be labeled, the number M of events for which the tool requests manual help, and ratio of M to N. The tool reduced labeling requirements by 1 to 2 orders of magnitude, and in practical terms made the difference between being able to train our DBNs and not.

The reduction brings up the question of whether labeling could have been done away with completely using further heuristics. Note however, that the success of the above segmentation algorithm depends wholly on having the correct label at the points where a new label is introduced. The key question therefore is whether the "challenging" events that were manually labeled by the human can be automatically labeled using (simple) rules. To understand this better, we implemented a simple set of rules that sets the location of a time slice to the location of the last bed, refrigerator or motion sensor (tried in that order) fired in that time slice. We declare that the subject is leaving if their location is

---

Algorithm 1. INTERACTIVELABEL(s)

Require: A list s of sensor events.
1: set l to **unknown**
2: **for all** events e_i in s **do**
3:    **if** room in which sensor for e_i is located is l **then**
4:       label e_i with l
5:    **else**
6:       display $e_i \ldots e_{i+10}$
7:       **if** user labels e_j with location $l' \neq l$ **then**
8:          label $e_i \ldots e_{j-1}$ with l
9:          set l to l'
10:          continue loop at event e_j
11:       **else**
12:          label e_i with l
13:       **end if**
14:    **end if**
15: **end for**

Table 4. Reduction in Manual Labeling Using Labeling Tool

House	#events labeled (N)	#hand(M)	$\frac{M}{2*N}$(%)
HP05	45105	1871	2.07
HP52	34333	839	1.22
M26	66237	2365	1.79
M44	63979	941	0.74
M45	54909	6031	5.49

Frontdoor and we see an OpenEvent. If no sensor readings are seen for $n = 30$ seconds, then the user's location is set to their last computed location; if the last location was Frontdoor, then we set the location to NotHome. Table 5 shows the results.

Overall, the rule-based system does quite well; in fact it often has higher true negative and true positive rates for Leaving and Location = AtHome than the Bayesian system does. However, it has a few failure modes, which result in significantly lower true positives and true negatives on Leaving and Location respectively. Note that missing instances of Leaving is especially debilitating because it results in missed opportunities to prompt the user. The failures occur for the following reasons, all having to do with sensor noise. First, because of anomalous motion sensor firings away from the front door while the door is being opened (e.g., in M26 the kitchen sensor near the front door fired after the front door OpenEvent) the rule-based system concludes that the subject is not leaving after all. This results in missing Leaving = true cases. Second, after the user actually leaves in this case, since the last observed sensor is not Frontdoor, the location is set to the last sensor seen (e.g., Kitchen for M26) as opposed to NotHome. This results in missed cases of Location=NotHome.

Table 5. Results of Stochastic vs. Rule-Based (RB) Systems (% Correct)

House	Model	Leaving=true	Leaving=false	Loc=AtHome	Loc=NotHome
HP05	Model3	0	95.66	96.87	18.73
HP05 RB	Model3	50	99.54	99.59	25.81
HP52	Model4	96.97	93.51	99.64	99.23
HP52 RB	Model4	78.79	98.66	99.9	99.7
M26	Model2	100.00	89.86	93.74	80.28
M26 RB	Model2	71.43	98.78	99.6	9.18
M32	Model4	100.00	98.67	98.00	98.58
M32 RB	Model4	20	98.93	99.8	13.64
M44	Model4	100.00	93.32	99.55	98.14
M44 RB	Model4	77.78	98.8	99.88	26.08
M45	Model4	100.00	92.31	98.99	99.70
M45 RB	Model4	12.5	99.14	99.17	31.95

Finally, the DoorOpen sensor message is occasionally missed (e.g., in M44); the rules therefore do not detect Leaving = true; interestingly the Bayesian Network was able to infer just from the fact that the Location=FrontDoor that Leaving=True was likely for the user.

This brief analysis shows that the requirement of dealing with noise can complicate rule-based systems. We do not make any claims about the superiority of the statistical approach to the deterministic one, since it is possible that a few simple extensions to the existing rules may suffice to substantially improve performance. However, we also note that the overhead of using the simple Naive-Bayes type Bayesian network was low enough (after the initial 2-week crash course and with the interactive labeling tool) that we think it unlikely that a good set of rules would be substantially easier to develop.

Labeling Data Partially. Another option to reduce labeling overhead is to label only as much data as is useful. Excess labeled data can lead to over-fitting. Table 6 shows the result of learning models using only a fraction of the data from each fold. Due to time constraints, these numbers are from a single fold. We trained model 4 on first 10, 35, 60 and 100% of the data from the fold. It seems that we could have gotten away with labeling roughly half of the data we did label. The savings are, however, small relative to interactive labeling. It is possible, that if we had used the unlabeled data for learning (using unsupervised learning techniques), we could have gotten acceptable performance with below 35% of the labels. An order of magnitude reduction seems unlikely, though.

Table 6. Inference Results for M32 and M45 With Partial Labeling (% Correct)

% Training Data	Leaving=true	Leaving=false	Loc=athome	Loc=nothome
10	0	79.72	77.67	98.42
35	0	99.26	98.36	97.95
60	100	98.89	98.06	98.66
100	100	98.67	98.00	98.58

% Training Data	Leaving=true	Leaving=false	Loc=athome	Loc=nothome
10	0	73.23	69.34	98.48
35	100	91.66	99.07	99.74
60	100	92.73	99.12	99.81
100	100	92.31	98.99	99.70

5.3 Other Challenges

The deployment posed a variety of unexpected challenges beyond the expected ones of model selection and labeling. Two particularly worth mentioning are drift in sensors and anomalous data due to infrastructure errors. Figure 3 shows data from one of our bed sensors. Note that the value of the sensor when no one is on the bed (e.g., between 0800 and 1400 hours) drifts downwards substantially even during the course of one day. This was a common occurrence with our bed sensors. Since we convert the bed sensor into a binary sensor (In, Out, as per Table 1) by thresholding, it is important for us to recompute thresholds if the baseline drifts too far downwards. We opted to take low-tech approach to the problem: an engineer monitored the baseline signal relative to threshold for each house every day and reset the threshold manually if needed. We had to perform this operation just once over all houses during the deployment. Of course, engineers performing manual thresholding does not scale and some unsupervised thresholding scheme is in order here.

A second challenge that recurred was the occasional corruption of data due to sensor and connectivity problems, and also because in some cases our maintenance staff entered homes without logging that they did so. We handled this problem manually by scanning through visualizations of the data looking for telltale signs such as an excess of reset messages and evidence of multiple people in the house. Reliable computer readable documentation of these sources of anomaly would have noticeably reduced the burden of training.

6   End-to-End Results

The end goal of the reasoning system was to produce context-aware prompts that enhanced the subjects' medication adherence. We counted a subject as having taken their pill if they opened the appropriate compartment of the MedTracker

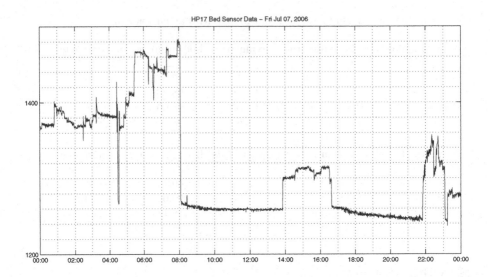

Fig. 3. Drift in Bed Sensor Calibration

Table 7. Change in Adherence Rates

Participant	Baseline%	Time-Based%	Context-Aware%
HP05	33.3	69.1	54.2
HP52	75.8	70.2	84.9
M26	65.8	71.3	81.6
M32	47.7	77.0	93.1
M44	N/A	45.7	48.0
M45	58.3	46.1	81.8
avg.	56.2	63.2	73.9

pillbox during the 3-hour period. We measured adherence in this manner during the baseline, conventional (time-based) prompting period and the context-based prompting periods. Table 7 shows the results. In every case except HP05, context-based prompting improved over no prompting and time-based prompting, often substantially. It is not surprising that HP05 decreased in adherence, since she took to spending long periods outside her home (caring for a friend) after the baseline period. Baseline data for M44 is not available because we discovered at the end of the baseline that the MedTracker had been malfunctioning.

7   Conclusions

We have described the specification, design, implementation and use of a reasoning system for prompting subjects to take their medication in a context-sensitive manner. The system was deployed longitudinally with 6 elderly subjects and resulted in significant increase in adherence rates among most of these subjects. We provide a detailed account of the pragmatics of using conventional statistical reasoning techniques in the real world, starting with utilizing domain constraints to simplify the problem as far as possible, using sensors that are strongly correlated with hidden variables, performing an exploration of the space of possible models, using simple but effective techniques to minimize labeling and handling a variety of other problems related to real-world deployment. Although the description of a system sufficient for producing significant results in an important application is itself of potential interest to Ubicomp practitioners, our detailed analysis of design choices may be of especially strong interest.

Acknowledgements

This paper would not have been possible without the work of the CAMP team: Stephen Agritelley, Kofi Cobbinah, Terry Dishongh, Farzin Guilak, Tamara Hayes, Jeffrey Kaye, Janna Kimel, Michael Labhard, Jay Lundell, Brad Needham, Kevin Rhodes and Umut Ozertem.

References

1. Open Source Probabilistic Networks Library,
   https://sourceforge.net/projects/openpnl/
2. Anderson, B., Moore, A.: Active learning for hidden markov models: objective functions and algorithms. In: ICML, pp. 9–16 (2005)
3. Boger, J., Hoey, J., Poupart, P., Boutilier, C., Fernie, G., Mihailidis, A.: A planning system based on markov decision processes to guide people with dementia through activities of daily living. IEEE Transactions on Information Technology in Biomedicine 10(2), 323–333 (2006)
4. Fogarty, J., Hudson, S.E., Atkeson, C.G., Avrahami, D., Forlizzi, J., Kiesler, S.B., Lee, J.C., Yang, J.: Predicting human interruptibility with sensors. ACM Trans. Comput.-Hum. Interact. 12(1), 119–146 (2005)
5. Haigh, K.Z., Kiff, L.M., Ho, G.: The Independent LifeStyle Assistant^{TM} (I.L.S.A.): Lessons Learned. Assistive Technology (2006)
6. Haigh, K.Z., Kiff, L.M., Myers, J., Guralnik, V., Geib, C.W., Phelps, J., Wagner, T.: The Independent LifeStyle Assistant^{TM} (I.L.S.A.): AI Lessons Learned. In: AAAI, pp. 852–857 (2004)
7. Hightower, J., Borriello, G.: Particle filters for location estimation in ubiquitous computing: A case study. In: Davies, N., Mynatt, E.D., Siio, I. (eds.) UbiComp 2004. LNCS, vol. 3205, pp. 88–106. Springer, Heidelberg (2004)
8. Horvitz, E., Jacobs, A., Hovel, D.: Attention-sensitive alerting. In: UAI, pp. 305–313 (1999)
9. Horvitz, E., Apacible, J.: Learning and reasoning about interruption. In: ICMI, pp. 20–27 (2003)
10. Kaelbling, L.P., Littman, M.L., Cassandra, A.R.: Planning and acting in partially observable stochastic domains. Artificial Intelligence 101, 99–134 (1998)

11. Kapoor, A., Picard, R.W.: Multimodal affect recognition in learning environments. In: ACM Multimedia, pp. 677–682. ACM Press, New York (2005)
12. Lester, J., Choudhury, T., Kern, N., Borriello, G., Hannaford, B.: A hybrid discriminative/generative approach for modeling human activities. In: IJCAI, pp. 766–772 (2005)
13. Liao, L., Fox, D., Kautz, H.: Location-based activity recognition using relational markov networks. In: IJCAI (2005)
14. Adami, A.G., Jimison, H.B., Kaye, J., Pavel, M., Hayes, T.L.: Unobtrusive assessment of mobility. In: EMBS (2006)
15. Murphy, K.P.: Dynamic Bayesian Networks: Representation, Inference and Learning (2002)
16. Oliver, N., Rosario, B., Pentland, A.: Graphical models for recognizing human interactions. In: NIPS, pp. 924–930 (1998)
17. Otsason, V., Varshavsky, A., LaMarca, A., de Lara, E.: Accurate gsm indoor localization. In: Ubicomp, pp. 141–158 (2005)
18. Philipose, M., Fishkin, K.P., Perkowitz, M., Patterson, D.J., Kautz, H., Hahnel, D.: Inferring activities from interactions with objects. IEEE Pervasive Computing Magazine 3(4), 50–57 (2004)
19. Pollack, M.E., Brown, L.E., Colbry, D., McCarthy, C.E., Orosz, C., Peintner, B., Ramakrishnan, S., Tsamardinos, I.: Autominder: an intelligent cognitive orthotic system for people with memory impairment. Robotics and Autonomous Systems 44(3-4), 273–282 (2003)
20. Tapia, E.M., Intille, S.S., Larson, K.: Activity recognition in the home using simple and ubiquitous sensors. In: Ferscha, A., Mattern, F. (eds.) PERVASIVE 2004. LNCS, vol. 3001, pp. 158–175. Springer, Heidelberg (2004)
21. Zhu, X.: Semi-supervised learning literature survey. Computer Sciences TR 1530, University of Wisconsin, Madison (2005)

Tracking Free-Weight Exercises

Keng-hao Chang[1], Mike Y. Chen[2], and John Canny[1]

[1] Berkeley Institute of Design, Computer Science Division
University of California, Berkeley, CA 94720 USA
{kenghao,jfc}@cs.berkeley.edu
[2] Ludic Labs, USA
mike@ludic-labs.com

Abstract. Weight training, in addition to aerobic exercises, is an important component of a balanced exercise program. However, mechanisms for tracking free weight exercises have not yet been explored. In this paper, we study methods that automatically recognize what type of exercise you are doing and how many repetitions you have done so far. We incorporated a three-axis accelerometer into a workout glove to track hand movements and put another accelerometer on a user's waist to track body posture. To recognize types of exercises, we tried two methods: a Naïve Bayes Classifier and Hidden Markov Models. To count repetitions developed and tested two algorithms: a peak counting algorithm and a method using the Viterbi algorithm with a Hidden Markov Model. Our experimental results showed overall recognition accuracy of around 90% over nine different exercises, and overall miscount rate of around 5%. We believe that the promising results will potentially contribute to the vision of a digital personal trainer, create a new experience for exercising, and enable physical and psychological well-being.

1 Introduction

Exercise is an important contributor to physical and psychological well-being. Regular exercise reduces many chronic diseases, such as heart/cardiovascular diseases, diabetes, hypertension, obesity, etc [1][2][3]. A recent Surgeon General report indicated that approximately 300,000 U.S. deaths are associated with obesity and overweight each year. Proper exercises and related interventions are effective in ameliorating symptoms and improving health [4].

To help people exercise effectively, several recent works focus on tracking and user feedback via exercise management systems. For example, in the category of aerobic exercises such as bicycling, swimming, and running, there are accelerometer and GPS-based pedometers to track running pace and distance, ECG monitors to track exertion [5], and electronic exercise machines such as treadmills, elliptical trainers, stair climbers and stationary bikes. Weight training, in addition to aerobic exercises, is an important component of a balanced exercise program [6]. However, mechanisms for tracking free weight exercises have not yet been explored. Weight training involves combinations of different types of exercises, varying weight amount to lift, number of repetitions and sets to be done, and so on. Managing a diverse training

J. Krumm et al. (Eds.): UbiComp 2007, LNCS 4717, pp. 19–37, 2007.

sequence should be well supported on site. During the process of working out, people may forget their progress, skip steps, or miscount a sequence. Even though people may try to organize by keeping notes on their progress, this is tedious and easily turns the workout into a chore.

We are exploring several applications in weight exercise management. The first is an *exercise tracker*: a system which automatically keeps track of your progress of free weight exercises. You only have to focus on doing the exercises without worrying about remembering your progress. It can be *accessed anytime, anywhere*: this system is embedded in the mobile device that you normally bring with you when you walk into a gym, illustrated in Fig. 1. You can check it before, during, or after your training process. The second application is an *exercise planner*: you can review your exercise history from the mobile device and this system can help you design a proper exercise plan. Eventually we would like to build a *digital personal trainer*: it warns you if you exercise too hard or in incorrect form.

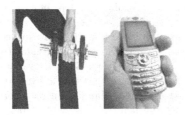

Fig. 1. Scenario of an exercise tracker

This paper focuses on exercise tracking: it explores methods that automatically recognize what type of exercise you are doing and how many repetitions you have done so far. In fact, recognizing exercise types belongs to the area of activity recognition, which has been extensively explored in the past few years. In this work, we applied some well-studied methods and found that these methods can also achieve good results in our application. We first incorporated a three-axis accelerometer into a workout glove to track hand movements, and put another accelerometer on a user's waist to track body posture. We investigated the effectiveness of two methods to recognize exercise type: Naïve Bayes Classifiers and Hidden Markov Models. In addition, since the number of repetitions is another important factor of weight training, merely recognizing types of exercises is insufficient for an exercise tracker. So, we developed and tested two methods to count repetitions: a peak counting algorithm and a method using the state sequence predicted by Hidden Markov Models.

Experimental results proved that the methods can be applied to a variety of exercises, users, and conditions. For the *exercise recognition goal*, it achieved 95% accuracy based on single user data, and the accuracy was around 85% when we cross-validated training results with new user data. For the *counting goal*, both proposed methods achieved around 5% miscount rate in general, which means if a user performs 100 repetitions, the system may miscount by less than 5 repetitions. The experimental results were based on exercise data we collected by asking ten subjects to perform nine different exercises, with different weight settings. The total length of the data was 9740 seconds (162.5 minutes), with a total of 4925 repetitions.

The remainder of this paper is organized as follows. Section 1 describes the related work. Section 2 describes a taxonomy of exercises and the rationale for using accelerometers to approach free weight exercises. Section 3 presents the development and evaluation of the algorithms. Finally, Section 4 states our future work and conclusions.

2 Related Work

The related work is categorized into the following two categories: exercise-specific work and studies of activity recognition. In the first category, FitLinxx [7] used sensors to track the usage of weight machines and showed training progress on a built-in display. Nonetheless, their sensors and tracking methods cannot be directly applied to free weight exercises, since FitLinxx only tracks predefined exercise routines on specific machines, and cannot perform the initial identification of type. In addition, iPod + Nike [8] tracked jogging and used music feedbacks to promote a new exercise experience. In fact, both products promote the idea of a digital personal trainer to coach exercise. As for research projects, House_n [9] is building a system to recognize gym- and exercise-related activities with accelerometers. They also intend to better estimate calorie expenditure in real time, which is different from our goal of tracking and eventually creating a digital personal trainer for free weight exercises.

In the category of activity recognition, there have been a large number of studies using different sensors, including accelerometers, gyroscopes, microphones, barometers, RFID readers, and GPS units, to recognize a variety of activities, and those studies use a variety of different machine learning techniques. Rather than developing brand new techniques, we applied and extended existing work to test the applicability within this new domain. For example, Mithil [10] and House_n [11] have shown great success using accelerometers to recognize activities such as walking, running, bicycling, etc, so we adopted their methods in which a Naïve Bayes Classifier was used to classify features extracted from sliding windows. We further leverage the characteristics of free weight exercise. For example, we only used accelerometers, rather than using both accelerometers and gyroscopes as in Minnen's work [12]. The design choice was based on the observation that sensors attached and constrained to gloves should be rotated with less degree of freedom in compare to being rotated freely in the air with no constraint (i.e. fixed on hands) and using only accelerometers is sufficient. The gravity effect on accelerometers was therefore emphasized and extracted as an extra feature. In fact, both their and our approaches achieved comparable 80~90% recognition accuracy. Hidden Markov Models have been widely applied. For example, Ward [13] and Georgia Tech Gesture Toolkit [14] applied HMMs to acceleration data. Moreover, Benbasat [15] identified a forward/backward (or a combination of both) hand movement as an atom, and they regarded a gesture as a composition of gesture atoms. Similarly, we identified "atoms" in acceleration data to count repetitions with two different approaches.

More techniques were proposed to contribute to the area of activity recognition. Minnen [12] made an unsupervised learning technique to avoid labeling effort. They first used information theory to identify best motifs, and then, they applied HMM to learn motif sets, which is exactly what we applied to our work. Wynatt [16] and Hamid [17] also proposed similar methods. In addition, Lester [18] applied the AdaBoost technique to let algorithms selecting best set of features, which is different from traditional approaches and what we did in this work to tune features manually. As for the settings in evaluation, we applied methods to recognize sets in isolation, rather than to recognize the entire exercise session. In future work, we would address this harder setup, as those by Lester[16], Ward[13], and Subramanya [19].

3   Approaching Free Weight Exercises with Accelerometers

This paper addresses two goals. The first *recognition goal* is to detect what type of exercise a user is doing. The second *counting goal* is to count how many repetitions she has been performing so far. To approach them, we provide a taxonomy of free weight exercises, discuss the accelerometer-based approach, and provide rationale and deployment details.

3.1   The Taxonomy of Free Weight Exercises

To fulfill the goals, we have identified the most common, representative free weight exercises in the gym environment in Table 1. Each exercise listed here is common and representative in a sense that people frequently use those exercises to train each individual muscle group in the human body [20]. Exercises are listed based on the muscle groups they are designed to train. For example, to train the arms, people often perform *bicep curls* for biceps and *tricep curls* for triceps. To train the upper body, users perform *bench press* and *flye* to work on their chest muscles. They also perform *bent-over row* to strengthen their upper backs, and use *lateral raise* to train shoulder muscles. Finally, in the lower body category, people use *deadlift* to train quadriceps and *standing calf raise* to train calves. Table 1 also lists the posture required to perform each exercise. The details of how to perform each free weight exercise can be found in reference [21], and some of the exercises will be explained in section 2.2 and section 2.3. We regard these exercises as the targets of our paper and we want to

Table 1. Representaive and commonly performed exercises for each muscle group

	Exercise	Muscle groups	Body part	Posture
1	Biceps curl	Biceps	Arms	Standing/Sitting
2	Tricep curl	Triceps		Standing/Sitting
3	Bench press	Chest		Lying
4	Flye			Lying
5	Bent-over row	Upper back	Upper Body	Standing
6	Lateral raise	Shoulders		Standing
7	Overhead dumbbell press			Standing/Sitting
8	Deadlift	Quadriceps	Lower Body	Standing
9	Standing calf raises	Calves		Standing

figure out whether it is possible to track them well. Throughout this paper, these commonly performed exercises are used as examples to explain our work and as baselines to test our system, in order to prove that our system is applicable to real world gym environments.

3.2 The Accelerometer Glove and the Posture Clip

To track the various free weight exercises listed in Table 1, we use accelerometers and incorporated acceleration data with machine learning techniques. Since in free weight exercises people hold and move weights, shown in Fig. 3, we instrumented a three-axis accelerometer onto a workout glove on the right hand, shown in Fig. 2-(a). We say this setting is applicable because people usually wear workout gloves when they perform free weight exercises. We call it the *accelerometer glove* throughout this paper. The three-axis accelerometer used is an off-the-shelf product, called WiTilt v2.5 by Spark Fun Electronics [22]. WiTilt v2.5 employs a FreeScale MMA7260Q triple-axis accelerometer. The accelerometer samples acceleration at a frequency of 80 Hz and in the range of +/- 1.5g. In addition, WiTilt v2.5 has Bluetooth wireless connectivity.

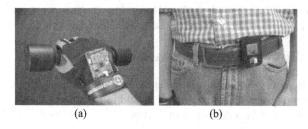

(a)   (b)

Fig. 2. (a) The *accelerometer glove* and the directions of three axes on the accelerometer. The z-axis is vertical to the palm. (b) The *posture clip*.

In addition to hand movements, it is also important to differentiate whether people are standing or lying on a bench. For example in Fig.3, the hand movement of the *overhead dumbbell press* is quite similar with the hand movements of *bench press*, in that people push free weights straight up to the air in both cases. But these two exercises are essentially different because the posture of lying down makes chest muscles to be trained in *bench press*, while standing/sitting helps training shoulder muscles in the *overhead dumbbell press*. Therefore, we use a complementary posture clip to detect postures during exercises, shown in Fig. 2-(b). The posture clip is also made of a WiTilt v2.5 three-axis accelerometer.

Considering the trade-off between accuracy, cost, and the nature of exercises themselves, we claim that it is sufficient to use only accelerometers to track free weight exercises. Although accelerometers are much less expensive and much smaller than Inertia Measurement Systems [23], three-axis accelerometers cannot track the six degrees of freedom that Inertia Measurement Systems can. However, because human motions are relatively restricted, the inherently lower variation of acceleration patterns sensed by accelerometers fixed on gloves should be sufficient for tracking

Fig. 3. Illustrations of (a) overhead dumbbell press, (b) bench press, (c) bent-over row, (d) lateral raise, (e) bicep curls, and (f) deadlift

free weight exercises well. In fact, results of this paper do justify that using accelerometers are sufficient to track free weight exercises. In addition, we have once considered putting accelerometers on free weights and use free weights themselves to track exercises. However, as we have just mentioned, the incapability of sensing six degrees of freedom keeps us from going in this direction.

The other important focus of tracking free weight exercise is to know how much weight a user is lifting. This can be enabled by simply attaching RFIDs on free weights, instrumenting a glove with an RFID reader, and keeping RFID-weight mappings. As the RFID-related work [24] is pretty mature, we are not focusing on this in our paper and consider it as future work when we are building a real system.

3.3   Acceleration Responses for Free Weight Exercises

In this subsection we discuss how different exercises result in different acceleration patterns and how repetitions of exercises respond in acceleration data, which serve as a basis to design algorithms described in Section 3.

Recognition Goal (how exercises differ from each other in acceleration data)
With the *accelerometer glove* and the *posture clip*, let's take a look at the acceleration data resulting from the nine exercises in Fig. 4. We only plot the data from the *accelerometer glove* to maintain legibility. Some of them are quite distinct from each other, which is due to both the characteristics of exercises and the characteristics of accelerometers themselves. For exercise characteristics, movements from different exercises impose acceleration in different axes, which we called the *major axis*. As for accelerometer characteristics, since different exercise postures make different axes vertical to the ground, gravity affects acceleration readings in the corresponding axes, which we called the *gravity effect*. For example, although both the *overhead dumbbell press* and the *bent-over row* cause acceleration in the same y-axis[1] (see references in Fig. 2 and Fig. 3), the average acceleration magnitudes are different. It's the gravity effect making the difference: in the *overhead dumbbell press*, hands are raised up such that the positive direction of y-axis faces down to the ground, so gravity makes the acceleration value larger. On the contrary, gravity[2] pulls the acceleration value of

---

[1] Since there are three axes in both the *acceleration glove* and the *posture clip*, for cases where we don't explicitly state where the axis is from, by default we mean the axis from the glove.
[2] When an axis directs to the ground and the accelerometer is stable, the accelerometer returns value around 800 (+1g). When the axis faces to the air, it returns value around 200 (-1g).

bent-over row and makes it smaller. The similar idea can also be applied to the comparison of *deadlift, standing calf raise,* and *bent-over row*. They are similar because they all impose acceleration in *y*-axis, and they all have the same gravity effect because all *y*-axes face up. However, *deadlift* and *standing calf raise* are different from *bent-over row* because the body movements in *deadlift* and *standing calf raise* make the *posture clip* move up and down in the *y*-axis on the clip whereas bodies stand still in *bent-over row*.

Take another example, the *bicep curl* shown in Fig. 3. It's an exercise in which users bend their arms to curl the weights toward their shoulders, and lower their arms to the starting position. The arm-bending movement not only induces acceleration in the *z*-axis, but gravity also affects the acceleration readings of the *y* and *z* axes alternately: while the arms are bent at the closest position to the shoulders, the *y*-axis is affected the most by the gravity. In contrast, the *z*-axis has the largest gravity effect while arms are in the horizontal position during the bending movement. Other exercises such as *tricep curls, lateral raise,* and *flye* all lie in the same family. They are similar because they all create acceleration change in more than one axis, but they are different in the combination of axes and in the directions facing ground, i.e. different gravity effect.

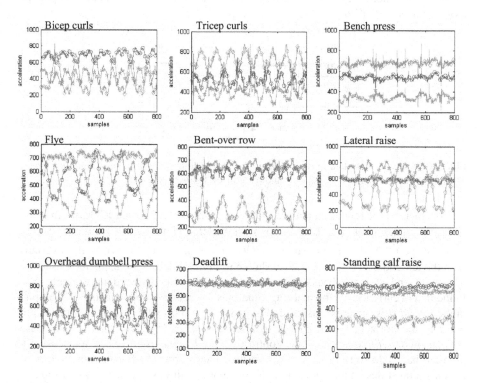

Fig. 4. Acceleration data from the *acceleration glove* in each of the nine exercises. *X*-axis is shown with blue circles. *Y*-axis is shown with green diamonds. *Z*-axis is shown with red stars.

Counting Goal (how repetitions of exercises show up in acceleration data)

Here we take the *overhead dumbbell press* as an example to explain how repetitions of free weight exercise show up in acceleration data. In general, people start this exercise by keeping the dumbbells to the sides of the shoulders (*starting position*). Then, they smoothly lift the dumbbells overhead until the arms are straight (*forward* movement). They slowly lower the dumbbells back to the starting position (it's called a *backward* movement), and repeat. In general, repetition pattern of all free weight exercises includes a starting position, a forward movement, and a backward movement. Fig. 5 shows the pattern of repetitions for the *overhead dumbbell press*. As we can see from Fig. 5, there exists a repetition pattern in acceleration and we give the reason for such pattern in the following. During the *overhead dumbbell press*, since the user's hand goes in the "negative" direction of y-axis in the glove during the forward movement (Fig. 2), muscles should induce "negative" acceleration to turn the velocity of the hand to "negative" and make it move. Around the end of the movement, she has to slow down her hand and stop her hand in the air, so "positive" acceleration occurs to turn the negative velocity of her hand to zero. As a result, the acceleration starting as negative and turning to be positive makes the pattern look like a "right $\mathcal{X}$" ($\sqrt{}$: because the shape of the forward movement is similar to the second stroke of the letter $\mathcal{X}$) . On the other hand, the backward movement makes the pattern look like a "left $\mathcal{X}$" ($\diagdown$).

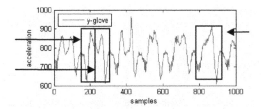

Fig. 5. The acceleration data in the y-axis of the glove while doing *overhead dumbbell press*. The rectangles mark repetition patterns and patterns of "left/right $\mathcal{X}$".

Nonetheless, the repetition pattern may vary from the "left / right $\mathcal{X}$" form. In some cases, the right end of "left $\mathcal{X}$" overlaps with the left end of "right $\mathcal{X}$" and merges into a "$\mathcal{V}$" shape ($\mathcal{N}$) (or into the shape of $\sqrt{}$ if the right end of the "right $\mathcal{X}$" overlaps with the left end of the "left $\mathcal{X}$"), also shown in Fig. 5. Such a case happens if users do not pause and start the backward movements right after forward movements. We found that occurrences of the merging situations are exercise-dependent. For example, in the *lateral raise* exercise, users tend to pause for a short while when their hands are lifted to the horizon, which causes the "left $\mathcal{X}$ " plus "right $\mathcal{X}$" pattern. The case happens in *deadlift* as well. On the contrary, in the *bicep curl* exercises, users usually put their hands down right after they curl their hands up to the highest position. As a result, we must design an algorithm able to count repetitions whether a waveform has "left $\mathcal{X}$" plus "right $\mathcal{X}$" shapes, or the overlapped version "$\mathcal{V}$". In other words, we must be able to consider whether users pause between forward and backward movements.

4 Algorithms and Experimental Results

This section presents several algorithms we have used to achieve the *recognition goal* and *counting goal*, along with experimental results. In summary, these algorithms follow the diagram shown in Fig. 6. Acceleration data is first streamed from an *accelerometer glove* and a *posture clip*. Data is then fed into the *type recognizer* which serves the *recognition goal*. After the recognizer recognizes what type of exercise a given segment of a data stream belongs to, it labels the acceleration data streams with a type and feeds them into the *repetition counter*. Then, because different exercises cause acceleration in different axes, the *repetition counter*, serving the *counting goal*, counts the number of repetitions from the acceleration data in the corresponding axis based on the *type* labeled. Finally, the *repetition counter* reports the type of exercise and how many repetitions a user performed. Such reports can be used by many possible weight exercise management applications in the future.

For the *recognition goal*, we present a set of features we selected and we show how we applied them to Naïve Bayes Classifier (NBC) and Hidden Markov Model (HMM), which are chosen based on past success [10][11][13]. We do not mean to constrain to these two methods. These methods are used to verify the selected features and hardware settings. For the *counting goal*, we developed algorithms that detect peaks in acceleration data and detect repetitions in the state sequence predicted from Hidden Markov Model. In addition, this paper compares the pros and cons of the algorithms in the experimental results subsections.

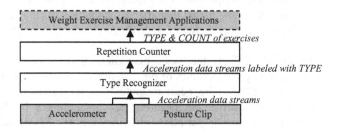

Fig. 6. Flow diagram

4.1 Algorithms of Recognition Goal

Naïve Bayes Classifier and Hidden Markov Model
Here we briefly introduce how to use Naïve Bayes Classifier and Hidden Markov Model. For the NBC, first features are extracted from sliding windows on acceleration data streams, each sliding window overlaps 50% with its adjacent windows. Then, the feature vector of each sliding window is fed into a NBC, which has been trained with other feature vectors into a Gaussian mixture. The NBC classifies each sliding window as a certain type of exercise based on the highest likelihood. Finally, the algorithm collects and reports a continuous sequence of windows with the same classified type. For HMM, we have to train a separate HMM for each individual exercise. Given any sequence of interest, the algorithm first extracts and transforms data as a stream of features. Then, it calculates likelihoods from each trained HMM.

Finally, it classifies the sequence to a specific type based on the HMM with the largest likelihood.

The Feature Space

Based on the discussion in section 2.3, we selected a set of features to identify the major axes, the gravity effect, and the correlation feature. The major axes are the axis in which users impose acceleration (for the particular exercise). The correlation feature is used to capture whether an exercise imposes acceleration in multiple axes at the same time. In particular, we customized the feature calculation while applying them to NBC and HMM: in NBC we calculated a feature vector for each sliding window while in HMM we transformed the stream of acceleration to a stream of features.

To identify the major axes, we found that it didn't achieve good accuracy if we directly applied raw acceleration data. Therefore, we integrate it to some extent to achieve good results. In NBC, an energy feature was chosen; we first applied Fast Fourier Transform to a sliding window and calculated the summation of the results. In other words, it summed up the squared magnitudes of waves. It is also divided by the window size to make the result independent of window size. In HMM, the velocity feature was chosen. It not only presents lower order than acceleration data, it also allows HMM to model temporal relationships, since velocity of a time point depends on the velocity of the previous time point. Velocity is the integral of acceleration and is approximated by cumulatively summing over acceleration and adding an adjustment factor that keeps the velocity over time from diverging. The adjustment factor works as the constant component in the integration equation. Doing this can make sure the calculated obeys the nature that after a long period of time, the velocity of human hands should still change between positive, zero and negative values, rather than diverging.

To capture the gravity effect, the peak magnitude feature is captured. It's calculated as the average magnitude values of positive and negative peaks in a sliding window. In particular in HMM, the peak magnitude of a sample in time t are calculated as the average positive and negative peak magnitudes in the sliding window centered in t (e.g. the sliding window of $[t\text{-}win/2, t\text{+}win/2]$). In fact, before we finalized the feature set for HMM, we didn't choose peak magnitudes as features. Instead, we used only raw acceleration data and tried to model peaks with more states. For the case between *flye* and *bench press*, it turned out raw acceleration feature didn't work well. There reason is the following. Since the acceleration in y-axis of *bench press* vibrates in the "sub-range" where the acceleration of *flye* vibrates (see Fig. 4), the acceleration of *bench press* falls exactly in the Gaussian mixture in the Hidden Markov Model of *flye,* which was trained to model acceleration of *flye* falling in the sub-range. As a result, it produced an ambiguous likelihood. The feature of peak magnitudes, instead, can avoid this problem by only providing information that acceleration of *flye* vibrates "larger" than *bench press*.

Finally, the correlation feature is calculated in the same way as first major-axis feature (i.e. the energy for NBC and the velocity for HMM), but it's calculated from the acceleration difference between each pair of axes. There are a total of four pairs of axes we consider, including every pair of axes from the *accelerometer glove*, (e.g. *x-y, y-z* and *x-z* in the glove), and the pair of the *y*-axis from the *acceleration glove* and from *y*-axis in the *posture clip* (e.g. *y_glove-y_posture*). The reason we choose the pair of *y_glove* and *y_posture* is to capture that the posture clip is moved up and down in y-axis in *deadlift* and *standing calf raise*, described in section 2.3. In addition, both the first and second features are calculated for each of the three axes from the *accelerometer glove* and the three axes from the *posture clip*. As a result, there are 22 features in a feature vector. Features are globally standardized so as to avoid numerical complications with the model learning algorithm.

4.2 Evaluation of Recognition Goal

To figure out whether the algorithms can be applied to a variety of users, say users with different gender, height, weight, level of experience with free weight exercises, etc., we collected data by asking *ten subjects* to perform the nine exercises listed in Table 1. There were eight male and two female subjects. To figure out whether the algorithms work well in different situations, we designed a data collection process in which we asked subjects to perform exercises with dumbbells of *different weights*. Weight difference is assumed to affect users' exercise performance. For example, light weights make users perform faster. Heavier weights cause users to move slower and may affect users' form.

Before collecting data, we showed subjects (or helped them review) how to perform each of the nine exercises. Then we asked subjects to do each exercise in three sets. Subjects performed 15 repetitions of each set and we manually started and stopped the recording process around each set. In addition, each set was designed with a different weight setting. We asked subjects to do the first set with normal weights, the second set with heavy weights, and finally the third set with light weights. Since the term of heaviness varies from subject to subject, depending on experience of free weight exercises, gender, height, etc., we asked subjects to decide the suitable heavy/light weights. Subjects stopped exercising if they felt tired. On the other hands, we let subjects do more than 15 repetitions if they could. In summary, we have collected data for 9740 seconds (162.5 minutes), with a total of 4925 repetitions. We applied methods to sets in isolation, rather than to the entire exercise session. In future work, we will address this harder setup.

Here we give details of the implementation of the algorithms. The implementation is based on the Bayes Net Toolbox in Matlab [25] and HMM Toolbox in Matlab [26]. The acceleration data streams are filtered with a low-pass filter before feature calculation. For NBC, each sliding window 256 samples long, approximated as a duration of 3 seconds at the sampling rate of 80Hz. The duration is selected to be large enough to capture dynamics in exercises. For HMM, each Hidden Markov Model was trained with parameters of one mixture and optimal number of states, which was around 3.

Two Cross-validation Protocols and Results
We tested both algorithms with two cross-validation protocols. The first *user-specific* protocol checks the algorithmic robustness for each single user, under different weight situations. Classifiers were trained on two out of three weight settings for each subject and tested on the remaining weight setting. This user-specific protocol was repeated for all ten subjects. The second *leave-one-subject-out* protocol aims to understand the robustness under user variety. Classifiers were trained on all the data from all subjects except one. The classifiers were then tested on the data from the

only subject left out of the training set. This leave-one-subject-out validation process was repeated for all ten subjects.

Table 2 lists the confusion matrices and recognition accuracy of the NBC using two cross-validation protocols. The user-specific protocol results in an overall 95% accuracy listed in Table 2-(a). The leave-one-subject-out protocol shows an overall accuracy of 85% in Table 2-(b). Table 3 lists the confusion matrices and recognition accuracy of Hidden Markov Models using the leave-one-subject-out protocol. As Hidden Markov Models can recognize the exercise type of a long sequence of data, Table 3-(b) lists the accuracy of each set. Nonetheless, to compare with NBC, we

Table 2. Confusion matrices and recognition accuracy of Naïve Bayes Classifier by (a) the user-specific protocol and (b) the leave-one-subject-out protocol: number in *(i, j)* of the matrix means number of sliding windows in exercise *i* recognized as exercise *j*

(a) User-specific protocol

	Bicep	Tricep	Bench	Flye	Bent.	Later.	Overh.	Dead.	Stand.	
Bicep	649	0	0	0	0	1	1	0	0	0.99
Tricep	0	663	0	0	0	0	0	0	0	1.00
Bench.	0	0	791	1	0	0	0	0	0	0.99
Flye	0	0	14	775	0	0	0	0	0	0.98
Bent.	0	0	0	0	520	0	0	2	0	0.99
Later.	0	0	0	0	1	599	0	1	2	0.99
Over.	0	0	0	0	0	0	522	0	0	1.00
Deadl.	0	0	0	0	6	3	0	612	43	0.92
Stand.	0	0	0	0	0	0	0	15	551	0.97

(b) Leave-one-subject-out protocol

	Bicep	Tricep	Bench	Flye	Bent.	Later.	Overh.	Dead.	Stand.	
Bicep	651	0	0	0	0	0	0	0	0	1.00
Tricep	0	663	0	0	0	0	0	0	0	1.00
Bench	0	0	675	117	0	0	0	0	0	0.85
Flye	0	0	20	769	0	0	0	0	0	0.97
Bent.	0	0	0	0	439	20	0	55	1	0.84
Later.	0	0	0	0	4	595	0	0	4	0.98
Over.	9	3	0	0	0	0	510	0	0	0.97
Deadl.	0	0	0	0	14	0	9	393	257	0.59
Stand.	0	0	0	0	0	0	0	58	508	0.89

Table 3. Confusion matrices and recognition accuracy of Hidden Markov Model by the leave-one-subject-out protocol. (a) The number in *(i, j)* of the matrix means number of sliding windows in exercise *i* recognized as exercise *j*. (b) The number in *(i, j)* of the matrix means number of sets in exercise *i* recognized as exercise *j*.

(a) Window-based

	Bicep	Tricep	Bench	Flye	Bent.	Later.	Overh.	Dead.	Stand.	
Bicep	640	1	0	0	0	9	0	0	0	0.98
Tricep	0	651	0	0	0	0	10	0	0	0.99
Bench	0	0	692	100	0	0	0	0	0	0.87
Flye	0	0	8	767	0	0	0	0	0	0.93
Bent.	14	0	0	0	497	10	0	1	0	0.93
Later.	0	0	0	0	15	586	0	0	0	0.97
Over.	52	21	0	0	0	0	447	0	0	0.86
Deadl.	0	0	0	0	0	0	0	569	94	0.86
Stand.	0	0	0	0	6	3	0	184	372	0.67

(b) Sequence-based

	Bicep	Tricep	Bench	Flye	Bent.	Later.	Overh.	Dead.	Stand.	
Bicep	36	0	0	0	0	0	0	0	0	1.00
Tricep	0	34	0	0	0	0	0	0	0	1.00
Bench	0	0	32	5	0	0	0	0	0	0.86
Flye	0	0	2	31	0	0	0	0	0	0.94
Bent.	1	0	0	0	29	2	0	0	0	0.91
Later.	0	0	0	0	1	31	0	0	0	0.97
Over.	3	0	0	0	0	0	29	0	0	0.90
Deadl.	0	0	0	0	0	0	0	29	4	0.87
Stand.	0	0	0	0	0	0	0	11	20	0.64

explicitly segmented data into sliding windows and used HMM to recognize data in each window. This worked by feeding the stream of features of each window to HMM. Table 3-(a) lists the results. As we can see, both methods achieved similar results.

Nonetheless, when we tried to test HMM using the user-specific protocol, it turned out the results were not acceptable. We do not list the results here. We believed that the data was not sufficient to train HMM well in the user-specific protocol, since we could only use data from two out of three sets to train the model, which was too few for HMM. In addition, because of the fact that there are multiple state settings and therefore multiple Gaussian mixtures to be trained in HMM, in comparison with only one Gaussian Mixture in the NBC, the same amount of data that is sufficient is for NBC may be too little for the HMM. Nonetheless, since we used the same feature set in both HMM and NBC, we believe if we collect enough data from each individual user in the future, HMMs may achieve comparable results.

In general, the NBC performs well in the user-specific protocol, so we conclude that the algorithm is robust for every single user, even with different weight settings. The reasons are the following. Sometimes heavier weights made subjects perform exercises slower, but the NBC is still able to capture the acceleration dynamics since we chose big sliding windows. Sometimes their hands shook, but resulting signal noise was filtered out by a low-pass filter. More importantly, there is a factor favoring such results: we found individuals tended to perform exercises in consistent patterns.

However, consistent patterns by individuals don't imply different users would perform exercises with the same pattern. As a result, it shows worse performance in the leave-one-subject-out protocol. For example, it is ambiguous between *deadlift* and *standing calf raise*. The reason is that some subjects tended to do *deadlift* slowly and caused smaller acceleration in y-axis, whereas some others performed *standing calf raise* more abruptly and caused larger acceleration in y-axis. The two cases make *deadlift* (with decreased acceleration) and *standing calf raise* (with increased acceleration) alike; making it harder to differentiate them. Others including *bent-over row* versus *deadlift*, *bench press* versus *flye*, and *bent-over row* versus *lateral* also present a similar ambiguity. However, there was an important implication. Although it showed that it's less robust under a variety of users, the robustness of tracking individuals leads us to an opportunity: calibration. Calibration done for each individual user can boost the recognition performance, and such recognizers would become persistent throughout the use of that user.

Discussion
In fact, the ambiguity problem comes from free weight exercises themselves: some exercises would impose similar acceleration responses, on the hardware setting we currently have. For *deadlift* and *standing calf raise*, situations would happen that just can't tell from the acceleration by the glove and clip. The acceleration only shows people up and down in y-axis. Nonetheless, if we add extra accelerometers on thighs, it's easier to differentiate them, since people would have to bend their knees in *deadlift*. Similarly, it could also help in differentiating *bench press* and *flye* if we add another accelerometer on the upper arm. In other words, it's a tradeoff between

minimalist design and more clues for better accuracy. Actually, we have already made the promise by adding an accelerometer clip, since posture is an important factor to be captured.

Another solution is to try dynamic time warping (DTW) [27]. In particular, we found that *standing calf raise* usually responses like a sharp peak and *deadlift* usually performs like a rather flatter one. DTW may identify the shape difference better and could give us more hints. As this could only be applied to *deadlift* and *standing calf raise* at this point, I would say it's only a partial solution.

In addition, based on the evaluation results, it turned out that the feature of simple peak magnitudes was better than raw acceleration. This also led to another conclusion that the dynamics of gravity effect should be well-captured to track free weight exercises. Peak magnitudes achieved good results. However, dropping raw acceleration from the feature space is actually not the best idea for the long term goal of detecting whether users do exercise in a proper form, since raw acceleration data contains the most details.

4.3   Algorithms of Counting Goal

Peak Detection

To count how many repetitions a user has done so far, we have to look at the acceleration data, find the pattern that repeats itself, and count how many repetitions there are. As we just mentioned, each exercise causes acceleration in certain axis (or a combination of axes), which we have called the *major axis*. Experiments show that we can avoid the noise that exists in the other axes and get better results if we find patterns only in the major axis can. The major axis is chosen based on the exercise type labeled on the acceleration data by the type recognizer. In Table 4, we list the major axis that we chose for each of the nine exercises. For those exercises associated with acceleration changes in two axes, such as *bicep curl*, we picked one of them as the major axis.

In section 2.3, we mentioned that a pair of forward/backward movements causes acceleration with a shape similar to the shape "left/right $\mathcal{X}$" or shape "$\mathcal{V}$". From those observations, we developed an algorithm that applies a strong low-pass filter with high order to the acceleration data in the major axis. As an example shown in Fig. 7, this can filter a pair of "left $\mathcal{X}$" and "right $\mathcal{X}$" waveforms into an overlapped shape "$\mathcal{V}$", making the acceleration data follow "$\mathcal{V}$" patterns. Then, the algorithm simply counts the number of peaks in the resulting data. A peak is identified by checking whether in data there is a decrease followed by an increase, and vice versa. We have evaluated the algorithm with different parameters and will discuss the results next.

Table 4. The major axes chosen for free weight exercises

Major axis	Free Weight Exercises
x-axis	Tricep curl
y-axis	Biceps curl, bench press, flye, bent-over row, shoulder press, deadlift, standing calf raises
z-axis	Lateral raise

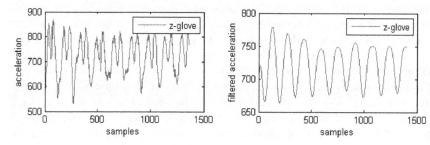

Fig. 7. (a) The raw acceleration data in the major axis *(z-axis)* of *lateral raise* and (b) the acceleration data being applied with a strong low-pass filter

State Sequence in Hidden Markov Models

The peak detection algorithm is expected to depend strongly on the selection of a good filter: it is necessary to find a low-pass filter with exact strength to correctly filter data into "$\mathcal{V}$" patterns. So, we decided to leverage the modeling power of Hidden Markov Models for this problem. The Hidden Markov Model should be able to model and tolerate the coexistence of the pattern of "left/right $\mathcal{X}$" and "$\mathcal{V}$", and predict corresponding state sequences. We reduced the problem of counting repetitions in acceleration data (with continuous values) into a problem of counting repetitions in the predicted state sequence (with finite states). The algorithm worked by first calling the Viterbi algorithm [28] to predict the state sequence from acceleration data. Then, it counted the repeating patterns in the state sequence.

We trained a *counting version* of Hidden Markov Models for each exercise, using the features extracted from the acceleration data in the major axis, listed in Table 5. The features included acceleration and velocity, in which the calculation of velocity has been described in section 3.1. In addition, features were normalized to make sure it predicts a good state sequence: feature values were shifted to let its waveform vibrate around the zero point and are scaled to be bounded by a specific range ($\pm d$). The reason is to model the pattern of "left/right $\mathcal{X}$" and "$\mathcal{V}$", because it's more important to model the change of the waveforms rather than absolute magnitudes.

4.4   Evaluation of Counting Goal

Peak Detection

To obtain the best filter, we tried a number of low-pass filters with different strengths on acceleration data, and fed the filtered data into the peak detection algorithm. The counting results are listed in Table 5, with filters of order n = 64, 96, and 128 samples. The filter coefficients were generated by the *fir1* [3]function by MATLAB, with order n and with low-pass frequency of *1/n of the Nyquist frequency*. As the sampling frequency of the accelerometers is 80Hz, the filters are on the order of 0.8, 1.2, and 1.6 seconds. As we can see, this simple algorithm achieves acceptable counting results, which is less than five percent error rate. In other words, if a user performs

---

[3] The *fir1* function implements the classical windowed linear-phase FIR digital filter design [29].

100 repetitions of an exercise, the algorithm miscounts five reps. Nonetheless, the *bench press* had a 16% of miscount rate. We found that since subjects lay on a bench to do a *bench press*, some tended to have tiny preparation motion (by lowering arms a little), before they pressed the dumbbells up, and caused more peaks to be counted.

The algorithm is simple, easy to implement, and achieves good performance, but there are problems. Since the key is to successfully filter "left/right $\mathcal{X}$" patterns into an overlapped version of "$\mathcal{V}$", the choice of filter parameters thus becomes tricky. If we choose a filter not strong enough, i.e. with smaller order, it may not be able to merge into "$\mathcal{V}$". However, if we choose a filter too strong, it may instead merge two adjacent "$\mathcal{V}$" together and increase the miscount rate. For example, the order of 64 gives *bicep curl* the best count accuracy, whereas *deadlift* must be applied with a filter of order higher than 94 to achieve acceptable accuracy. Therefore, we can find in Table 5 that there is not a filter setting that achieves the global best accuracy.

In addition, we can expect that the filter strength depends on how long a user pauses between forward/backward movements. If a user pauses longer, for example the user is using heavier weights, the order of a filter should be large enough to merge the "left X" and "right X" together, which makes a fixed filter setting more infeasible.

Table 5. Counting accuracy of the peak detection algorithm. The table lists results using low pass filters of different strengths, each with order 64, order 96, and order 128. The miss count, miss count rate, and the base actual count for each exercise are listed. [4]

Exercise		Bicep curl	Tricep curl	Bench press	Flye	Bent. row	Later. raise	Over. press	Deadl.	Stand. calf r.
Actual Count		596	566	640	561	535	507	523	570	541
Order 64	Miss Count	3	22	137	28	5	143	31	130	80
	Error Rate	.0050	.0389	.2141	.0499	.0093	.2821	.0593	.2281	.1479
Order 96	Miss Count	8	18	105	19	17	41	61	25	36
	Error Rate	.0134	.0318	.1641	.0339	.0318	.0809	.1166	.0439	.0665
Order 128	Miss Count	25	36	127	43	58	85	161	49	108
	Error Rate	.0419	.0636	.1984	.0766	.1084	.1677	.3078	.0860	.1996

State Sequence Prediction with Hidden Markov Models

Table 6 shows that this method can achieve overall good accuracy. Here was the process of the experiment. We first applied a low-pass filter of order $n=32$ to the acceleration data, and extracted features to train each Hidden Markov Model. It turned out that trained Hidden Markov Models can map hidden states to different parts of a repetition: the starting position, the forward/backward movements, the ending position of forward movements, and the pause between forward/backward movements. Then, we selected one of the states as an anchor state, say the state of forward movement, to serve as the evidence that the pattern repeats. In other words,

---

[4] Actual count is the number of repetitions subjects actually performed, which was manually counted during data collection. Miss count is the absolute value of the difference between the actual count and the count from the repetition counter. Error rate is calculated as miss count over actual count.

we count how many segments are predicted to be the anchor state. The error, as expected, came from the incorrect prediction of the state sequence, which might results from noise or different user patterns. The errors can be categorized as insertion, deletion or substitution errors, which could be solved using sequence reconstruction [30] or autocorrelation. We leave this as our future work. Similar to the peak counting algorithm, *bench press* cannot be counted well because of the preparation motions some subjects did.

Table 6. Counting accuracy of state sequence in Hidden Markvo Model. The miss count, miss count rate, and the base actual count for each exercise are listed.

Exercise	Bicep curl	Tricep curl	Bench press	Flye	Bent. row	Later. raise	Over. press	Deadl.	Stand. calf r.
Actual Count	596	566	640	561	535	507	523	570	541
Miss Count	8	19	90	44	18	4	47	26	41
Error Rate	.0134	.0336	.1719	.0784	.0336	.0073	.0899	.0456	.0758

Discussion

For counting algorithms, although the filtering and peak counting approach can count pretty well, without really looking into data patterns, it is less adaptive. One way to improve it could be using FFT to approximate the length of repetition first and then applying an adaptive filter to the data. The approach of the state sequence and Hidden Markov Model is of course more adaptive, but it requires more work to train. Another outcome of the peak detection algorithm is to help detect improper form. It's important to maintain constant and reasonable speed doing free weight exercise, and measuring the duration between peaks can help achieve the goal.

5   Conclusion and Future Work

The paper proposes a new application domain with free weight exercises: an exercise tracker, an exercises planner, and a digital personal trainer. It describes a feature space and the evaluation of methods to track free weight exercises. We incorporated a three-axis accelerometer into a workout glove to track hand movements and put another accelerometer on a user's waist to track body posture. With the accelerometer settings, both approaches of Naïve Bayes Classifier and Hidden Markov Models resulted in around 90% accuracy to recognize the types of exercise. We also developed a peak counting algorithm and used state sequence with Hidden Markov Model to count how many repetitions you have done so far, which achieved around a 5% miscount rate. We also discuss the implications in the evaluation sections.

One of our future works would be developing a real-time system in mobile devices. To achieve that, we have to first train a garbage model for movements that do not belong to any of the target exercises to avoid false positives. In addition, we are planning to model exercises in detail in order to detect improper form, which would be able to serve as the basis of a *digital personal trainer.*

References

1. Ades, P.A.: Cardiac rehabilitation and secondary prevention of coronary heart disease. The New England journal of medicine 111, 369–376 (2001)
2. Shephard, R.J., Balady, G.J.: Exercise as Cardiovascular Therapy. Circulation, New York 99, 963–972 (1999)
3. Sothern, M.S., Loftin, M., Suskind, R.M., Udall, J.N., Blecker, U.: The health benefits of physical activity in children and adolescents: implications for chronic disease prevention. European Journal of Pediatrics 158(4), 271–274 (1999)
4. Dishman, E.: Inventing wellness systems for aging in place. IEEE Computer 37, 34–41 (2004)
5. Healey, J., Logan, B.: Wearable Wellness Monitoring Using ECG and Accelerometer Data. HP Laboratory Tech Report, HPL-2005-134 (July 2005)
6. The President's Council on Physical Fitness and Sports. Fitness fundamentals guidelines for personal exercise programs. online council publications (2003), http://www. fitness. gov/fitness.htm
7. FitLinxx, http://www.fitlinxx.com/brand.htm
8. Apple – Nike + iPod, http://www.apple.com/ipod/nike/
9. Intille, S.S.: Designing a home of the future. IEEE Pervasive Computing 1(2), 76–82 (2002)
10. DeVaul, R., Sung, M., Gips, J., Pentland, A.S.: MIThril 2003: Applications and Architecture. In: Proceedings of the 7th IEEE International Symposium on Wearable Computers, October 2005, pp. 4–11. IEEE Computer Society Press, Los Alamitos (2005)
11. Bao, L., Intille, S.S.: Activity recognition from user-annotated acceleration data. In: Ferscha, A., Mattern, F. (eds.) PERVASIVE 2004. LNCS, vol. 3001, pp. 1–17. Springer, Heidelberg (2004)
12. Minnen, D., Starner, T., Essa, I., Isbel, C.: Discovering Characteristics Actions from On-Body Sensor Data. In: Int. Symp. On Wearable Computing (ISWC), Montreux, CH, October 2006, pp. 11–18 (2006)
13. Ward, J.A., Lukowicz, P., Tröster, G.: Gesture spotting using wrist worn microphone and 3-axis accelerometer. In: Proceedings of the 2005 joint conference on Smart objects and ambient intelligence: innovative context-aware services: usages and technologies, vol. 121, pp. 99–104 (2005)
14. Westeyn, T., Brashear, H., Atrash, A., Starner, T.: Georgia Tech Gesture Toolkit: Supporting Experiments in Gesture Recognition. In: Proceedings of International Conference on Perceptive and Multimodal User Interfaces 2003, pp. 85–92 (2003)
15. Benbasat, A.Y., Paradiso, J.A.: An Inertial Measurement Framework for Gesture Recognition and Applications. In: Wachsmuth, I., Sowa, T. (eds.) GW 2001. LNCS (LNAI), vol. 2298, pp. 9–20. Springer, Heidelberg (2002)
16. Wyatt, D., Philipose, M., Chouhury, T.: Unsupervised Activity Recognition using Automatically Mined Common Sense. In: proceeding of the Twentieth National Conference on Artificial Intelligience, AAAI2005, Pittsburg, PA, July 2005, pp. 21–27 (2005)
17. Hamid, R., Maddi, S., Johnson, A., Bobick, A., Essa, I., Isbell, C.: Discovery and Characterization of Activities from Event-Streams. In: Proceedings of UAI 2005, Edinburgh, Scotland, pp. 71–78 (2006)
18. Lester, J., Choudhury, T., Kern, N., Borriello, G., Hannaford., B.: A Hybrid Discriminative –Generative Approach for Modeling Human Activities. In: Proceedings of International Joint Conference on Artificial Intelligence, IJCAI 2005, July 2005, pp. 766–772 (2005)

19. Subramanya, A., Raj, A., Blimes, J., Fox, D.: Recognizing Activities and Spatial Context Using Wearable Sensors. In: Proceedings of the 22nd Annual Conference on Uncertainty in Artificial Intelligence (2006)
20. Delavier, F.: Strength Training Anatomy, 2nd edn. Human Kinetics Publishers (2005)
21. Cane, J., Glickman, J., Johnson-Cane, D.: Complete Idiot's Guide to Weight Training. Alpha Books (1999)
22. Spark Fun Electronics, http://www.sparkfun.com/
23. Benbasat, A.Y.: An Inertial Measurement Unit for User Interfaces, Master Thesis, MIT Media Lab (September 2000)
24. Philipose, M., Fishkin, K.P., Perkowitz, M., Patterson, D.J., Fox, D., Kautz, H., Hähnel, D.: Inferring Activities from Interactions with Objects. IEEE Pervasive Computing 3(4), 50–57 (2004)
25. Murphy, K.P.: The Bayes net toolbox for MATLAB. Technical report 94720-1776, Dept. Comp. Sci., University of California at Berkeley, Berkeley, CA (2001)
26. Murphy, K.P.: Hidden Markov Model (HMM) Toolbox for Matlab, http://www.cs.ubc.ca/murphyk/Softwared/HMM/hmm.html
27. Hartmann, B., Abdulla, L., Mittal, M., Klemmer, S.R.: Authoring sensor-based interactions by demonstration with direct manipulation and pattern recognition. In: Proceedings of ACM CHI 2007 Conference on Human Factors in Computing Systems, CHI2007, pp. 145–154. ACM Press, New York (2007)
28. Forney, G.D.: The Viterbi algorithm. Proceedings of IEEE 61(3), 268–278 (1973)
29. Programs for Digital Signal Processing. Algorithm 5.2. IEEE Press, New York (1979)
30. Lenenshtein, V.I.: Efficient reconstruction of sequences from their subsequences or super sequences. J. Comb. Theory Ser. A 93(2), 310–332 (2001)

Playful Tray: Adopting Ubicomp and Persuasive Techniques into Play-Based Occupational Therapy for Reducing Poor Eating Behavior in Young Children

Jin-Ling Lo[1,2], Tung-yun Lin[3], Hao-hua Chu[3,4], Hsi-Chin Chou[1], Jen-hao Chen[4], Jane Yung-jen Hsu[3,4], and Polly Huang[3,5]

[1] School of Occupational Therapy
College of Medicine
[2] Department of Physical Medicine and Rehabilitation
National Taiwan University Hospital
[3] Graduate Institute of Networking and Multimedia
[4] Department of Computer Science and Information Engineering
[5] Department of Electrical Engineering
National Taiwan University
hchu@csie.ntu.edu.tw

Abstract. This study has created the Playful Tray that adopts Ubicomp and persuasive techniques into play-based occupational therapy for reducing poor eating behavior in young children after they reached their self-feeding age. The design of the Playful Tray reinforces active participation of children in the activity of eating by integrating digital play with eating. Results of a pilot user study suggest that the Playful Tray may improve child meal completion time and reduce negative power play interactions between parents and children, resulting in an improved family mealtime experience.

1 Introduction

Recently, many Ubicomp researchers have been working on applying digital technology to modify human behavior [1] [2] [3]. This area is known as *persuasive computing* [4]. From a computing perspective, persuasive computing involves designing and developing digital technology that not only can automatically sense and track behavior, but can also engage people via *intelligent interaction* to motivate or influence their behavior. From an occupational therapist perspective, persuasive computing involves extending the reach of occupational therapists from their treatment clinic into the actual living environment of a client, enabling the therapists to utilize Ubicomp technology to implement an effective behavior intervention program at the place where the client's target behavior occurs and when the treatment is most effective.

This work targets *mealtime behavior*, one of the most frequently cited problems by parents of young children [5]. Despite nutritional concerns, spending excessive time to eat a meal affects the participation of children in daily school and family routines, and often contributes to negative parent-child interaction during mealtime [6]. For example, poor eating habits at home by children can cause stressful confrontations

J. Krumm et al. (Eds.): UbiComp 2007, LNCS 4717, pp. 38–55, 2007.

with parents, often taking the form of a *power play* involving mental persistence and pitting parental persuasion against unrelenting refusal from the children. At school, children who eat lunch slowly are likely to experience frustration resulting from the disapproving looks of teachers or the scorn of their peers. Delayed meal completion may also reduce the time available to children to engage in after-lunch activities. To address this eating behavior issue, this study has designed and implemented the Playful Tray as a tool to assist occupational therapists and parents in reducing poor eating behavior in young children. This tool can be used either at home or in school. A pilot user study where autistic and non-autistic children with mealtime problems participated suggested that the Playful Tray may improve child meal completion time when compared to traditional parental verbal persuasion. Results also suggest that the Playful Tray may reduce negative power play interactions between parents and children.

Fig. 1. On the left, a young child is performing her imitation skit and not paying attention to eating her food. By the time her parents are done with their meals, her meal is hardly touched. By then, her parent will become angry with her. Her parent's angry voice will also wipe out her appetite. On the right, this young child is actively eating to interact with the Playful Tray.

The Playful Tray is embedded with an interactive game played over a weight-sensitive tray surface, which can recognize and track the natural eating actions of children in real time. Child eating actions are then used as game inputs. As shown in Fig. 1, engaging children in this fun interactive game motivates the children to change their eating behavior. This design connects and integrates the fun part (coming from the digital game activity) with the activity of eating. We believe that this is the main reason why the Playful Tray may be effective in reducing poor eating behavior in young children.

The tray design is based on learning theories and the key components of *playfulness* [7] [8], including intrinsic motivation, internal control, and suspension of reality described in more detail in Section 2. The design reinforces active participation of children in the activity of eating by integrating digital play with eating, thus making mealtimes more enjoyable for both parents and children. Additionally, the flexibility of the digital game control enables occupational therapists to easily grade the challenge to match the ability of the child. For example, changing the weight sensibility of the tray affects the size of the bites required to trigger a game response.

Traditional eating behavior interventions depend heavily on parents actively modifying their behaviors and interactions with children during mealtimes [9]. For example, therapists seek to modify parent behaviors by teaching mealtime related parenting skills via didactic instruction, modeling, role playing, and behavioral rehearsal and structured home programs. We would like to clarify the intention of the Playful Tray is not to replace occupational therapists and the training they provide to parents on how to interact with young children, but to be used as an assistive tool that supplements the skills taught by occupational therapists. This work hypothesizes that by using the Playful Tray, it can assist parents to enhance children's motivation to eat. Results of a pilot user study involving the use of the tray by young children with eating problems suggested that the Playful Tray may address these hypotheses.

The remainder of this paper is organized as follows. Section 2 provides an overview of play-based feeding behavior intervention. Section 3 then states the design considerations for the playful tray. Next, Section 4 presents the design and implementation. Section 5 then describes the user studies and results. Subsequently, Section 6 discusses related work. Finally, Section 7 presents our conclusions and future work.

2 Play-Based Feeding Behavior Intervention

"Play is a child's way of learning and an outlet for his innate need of activity" [10]. For a child, any activity can be turned into a game. Children often engage actively and fully in an activity only if that activity includes the critical ingredients of play. Therefore, traditionally, pediatric occupational therapists (OTs) frequently leverage the desire of children to play as an effective means to cultivate the general skills and abilities needed to perform their functional activities. This is an indirect approach of training children in general skills via play activities, rather than directly targeting specific functional activities. For example, by feeding dolls or scooping play dough from one container to the other, children can improve their fine motor skills and the eye-hand coordination required for eating. However, this indirect approach suffers from the problem that improvements in perceptual-motor skills do not guarantee improved performance in the target functional activity, i.e., self-feeding. A more direct approach is to make the target functional activity playful to engage the child into active participation.

According to the model of human occupation (MOHO) [11], an occupational behavior such as eating is the result of the organization of three subsystems of a person: volition, mind-brain-body performance and habituation. To develop children's functional ability and become a part of their daily routines, they first need to have motivation to participate in the target behavior and sufficient physical and mental functions to meet the need of performing the target activity. Based on MOHO, this work developed a play-based occupational therapy model for designing the playful tray shown in Fig. 2. In this model, the three subsystems are facilitated by applying theories of playfulness and reinforcement into the design. According to theories of play and playfulness [8], play comprises three primary elements: *intrinsic motivation, internal control*, and *suspension of reality*. Intrinsic motivation means that the individual pays more attention to the process than to the product or outcome. It is the activity itself rather than its consequences that attracts the individual to active participation. Moreover, internal control is defined as individuals being in charge of *their* actions and at least some aspects of the activity outcome. Suspension of reality refers to the pretend quality of play. The three elements of play comprise the foundation of activity design. To successfully induce active child participation in an activity, activity designs should provide a strategy to elevate the degree of intrinsic motivation (less extrinsic motivation), internal control (less external control), and suspension of reality. Mind-brain-body performance refers to an individual's physical and cognitive capability to perform a target activity. Introducing digital play into an activity design should avoid increasing the physical and cognitive difficulty levels beyond those in the target activity. For example, the digital play in our Playful Tray adopts the strategy of using natural eating actions, which all children know how to do, to play a game.

On the other hand, acquisitional theory views behavior as a response to an environment [12]. The environment thus either reinforces behavior or fails to provide positive reinforcement by instead giving no reinforcement at all. Positive reinforcement strengthens behavior by rewarding the desired behavioral response. Previous studies [7] have shown that partial reinforcement is the strongest form of reinforcement in shaping behavior. Partial reinforcement is defined as reinforcement only given on some occasions when the behavior occurs, meaning there is no discernible pattern regarding when the reinforcement will take place. To strengthen desirable behavior, the design should employ the principle of partial reinforcement embedded in an activity. Through partial reinforcement, the desired behavior can be internalized and become a habit.

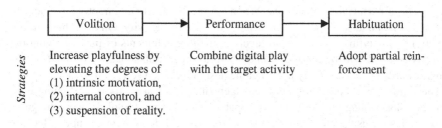

Fig. 2. Our play-based occupational therapy model

Feeding problems can occur in children with normal development and those with developmental problems. For children with significant developmental problems, feeding problems are treated seriously because the treatment outcome significantly affects child development [13]. However, for children with normal development or mild developmental problems, such as those with Asperger's Syndrome or High Function Autism, feeding problems are generally ignored or underscored. The most common complaint regarding mealtime behavior for these children is eating too slowly. Such problems create stress for caregivers, often the children's parents, negatively impacting the parent-child relationship. Therefore, this study targeted the second group of children and applied the play-based occupational therapy model to design a playful tray for them with the goal of improving their eating pace and reducing their maladaptive behavior.

3 Playful Tray Design Considerations

Based on the play-based occupational therapy model described above, this work has identified the following four main design considerations for the proposed playful tray: (1) *attention* split between game playing and eating activities, (2) *enjoyment* to encourage intrinsic motivation of children, (3) *engagement* to connect digital playfulness to active participation in the target activity of eating, and (4) *control* to give children choices in determining game outcome.

The first design consideration is the degree to which a child pays attention to the digital interaction. Since children need to focus their attention on feeding activity during mealtimes, introducing a digital game will inevitably divert some of their attention away from the eating activity. Because the use of the digital game is intended to motivate active child participation in the eating activity, the digital game design should not draw too much attention away from the eating activity and thus lead to the undesirable result of digital playing overtaking or distracting eating. That is, a game design should bring in just enough digital interactivity to maintain the interest of children in the eating activity. The game thus should avoid fast-moving, excessively fancy animation or frequent input and output.

The second design consideration is enjoyment. The digital game activity must bring sufficient enjoyment and pleasure to children to attract their active participation in eating. Motivation to perform an activity usually comes from two sources: external rewards and enjoyment of the activity itself. External rewards mean the accompanying benefit of performing an activity. When the rewards seem unattractive to a person, he/she will feel a lack of motivation to participate in the activity. On the other hand, if an activity is playful, i.e., with high levels of the three elements of play, carrying out the activity itself will be enjoyable and self-reinforced rather than reinforced by external rewards [14]. This study used a game design based on self-reinforcement.

The third design consideration is engagement. Since target users are young children and most young children are not capable of operating digital devices, the game design relies on using the *natural* eating actions of children as game input. Because eating is the target activity, once children are attracted to the game, they find that they have to eat to continue playing. Through this engagement design, this work links fun (from the digital game) with eating.

The fourth design consideration is control. Control refers to the opportunities for children to make choices and decisions during a game. The game design allows children to choose from a selection of characters and determine their eating pace.

Two further design considerations are presented below:

- It is important to minimize the change on the lunch tableware accustomed to young children during their normal eating routines at home or in schools. Hiding digital components beneath a tray surface prevented the installed digital hardware from adversely affecting the normal eating of the children.
- Given the limited cognitive level of young children, the design of the interactive game must be simple enough for them to understand and attractive enough to maintain their attention.

4 Playful Tray Design and Implementation

Two prototypes of playful trays were created. Fig. 3 shows the initial prototype, called the Coloring Game Tray. The design of this tray incorporates a dining surface of 30x45 cm^2, divided into a matrix of 2x3 cells. Besides the middle top cell onto which the game is projected, each of the other five cells contains a weighing sensor underneath the cell plate to detect eating events. The eating events are then fed as inputs to a coloring game played on the middle top cell. Each food item corresponds to a specific crayon color. When a child eats a specific food item, the corresponding color is drawn on a cartoon character selected by the child. To make the selected cartoon character colorful, the child thus should be motivated to eat and finish all food items on the table, including disliked items.

Fig. 3. Initial playful tray prototype called the Coloring Game Tray

A preliminary pilot user study of the Coloring Game Tray reported in [15] identified four problems with the initial design. (1) Some children felt extreme frustration when the cartoon character did not look colorful and happy at the end of the game, and refused to play again. (2) Although some children were attracted to the coloring game the first few times they played with it, they quickly became bored because the color mappings never changed. (3) Some children paid so much attention to playing the digital game that they became distracted from eating properly. (4) Some children ate too quickly as they became impatient to see their favorite cartoon characters fully colored.

Based on the problems of the initial prototype, a second, simpler prototype was created, called the Racing Game Tray. Although the revised design and implementation are simpler than the initial prototype, results of a pilot user study (discussed below in Section 5) suggest that the Racing Game Tray is more effective than the Coloring Game Tray.

4.1 Single-Cell Tray

The Racing Game Tray prototype is shown in Fig. 4. The dimensions of the tray are 33 cm x 31cm x 3.5cm. The top of the tray is embedded with a small palm-top PC containing a touch-screen LCD showing the racing game. The tray uses only one weighing sensor to detect child eating behavior. This weighing sensor is placed below the slightly lower rectangular area on the tray, and has a bowl positioned directly above it. The weighing sensor can detect and recognize child eating actions and the weight of food consumed from the bowl during each eating action. Since children are likely to touch all areas of the tray, the weight sensing area was just large enough to fit a bowl, minimizing the chance of touching of the tray interfering with the weight readings on the weight sensing area.

Palm-top PC with touch screen

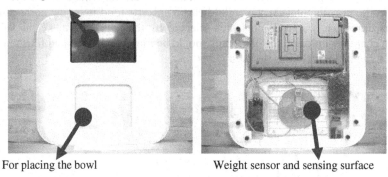

For placing the bowl   Weight sensor and sensing surface

Fig. 4. The revised playful tray prototype, called the Racing Game Tray

The system architecture is shown in Fig. 5. Child eating activity was first sensed by the weight sensing surface, then recognized via the *Weight Change Detector*. The weight change detector performs one task: reporting *Weight-Change* events involving the food container by filtering out noises from the stream of weight samples. These weight change events include the amount (weight) of food consumed. A weight decrease event is generated each time the weight of the bowl decreases.

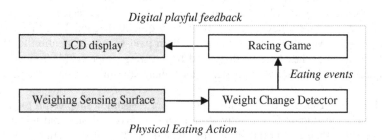

Fig. 5. System architecture

Through observations of young children taking meals in our clinic and interviews with their parents, we have realized that young children can exhibit a wide variety of eating and non-eating behaviors during meal times. As a result, not all weight decrease events will in fact be eating actions. For example, children may play with their food by hitting the bowl with their hands or utensils, scoop up some food and then put it back without eating it or after taking only a tiny bite, they may press their hands into the bowl, they may knock hard or push the tray, and so on. Since these non-eating actions affect the weight readings, they can confuse the system in recognizing some of these non-eating actions as valid eating actions. As a result, some *non-eating actions* may receive the same positive reinforcement and encouragement from the digital game as valid eating actions. To give an example, children may first press their hands into the bowl, creating a weight increase reading, and then lift their hands away from the bowl, creating a weight decrease reading. Because of the potential for these and other similar behaviors, simply using relative weight decrease over time will not accurately identify poor eating behaviors.

To address this issue, eating actions are recognized by calculating the *absolute weight decrease over time* value (Δw_t^{abs}), defined as follows:

$$\Delta w_t^{abs} = w_t - min\ (w_{1..t-1})\ . \tag{1}$$

w_t denotes the current weight reading, and *min* ($w_{1..t-1}$) represents the accumulative minimum weight reading from the start of the meal to the last reading. All relative weight decreases or increases are ignored. This method was found to be effective in filtering out most non-eating actions, though at the cost of missing some good eating actions. However, this tradeoff is acceptable given that encouraging bad eating actions is worse than missing feedback to some valid eating actions. Notably, this method can fail in one case, namely when a child picks up the entire bowl from the tray, causing the minimum weight reading to reach zero and creating a situation in which good eating actions can no longer be detected. To address this problem, the bowl is taped and fixed to the tray, preventing a child from easily lifting it up. Another situation can involve a child scooping up food and then putting it back without eating it. Although our system would incorrectly recognize this non-eating action as a valid eating event the first time it occurred, repeating the action would have no effect. When applied to young children in the pilot study discussed below, analyzing the logged eating events and the taped videos shows that this method can achieve accuracy of 70~80 % in recognizing valid eating actions, and only very rarely incorrectly recognizes bad eating actions as good ones. These eating actions are then used as inputs to the *racing game* described below.

4.2 The Racing Game

Screenshots for the racing game are shown in Fig. 6. Upon detecting each eating action, one of the characters would race one step forward to the right. The character is selected based on a random probability similar to a slot machine. The rationale for applying this randomness in this game is to adopt the partial reinforcement described in Section 2, which is the strongest form of reinforcement in shaping behavior. The distance traveled is fixed regardless of the size of the weight change from each eating action. The right screenshot in Fig. 6 shows the state of a race after a number of eating actions. When starting a meal, a child selects a favorite cartoon character, marked under the red arrow in the screenshot of Fig. 6. When the child finishes all of the food in the bowl, the game ends and the character that has traveled the furthest distance to the right wins. When a child eats too quickly (that is, the time interval between subsequent eating actions is smaller than a pre-defined *eating-too-quick* value), a

Fig. 6. Screen shots for the Racing Game Tray

notification is sent to the child to slow down his/her eating since eating will temporarily no longer be rewarded. This system prevents excessively aggressive eating.

The racing game design strategies follow the play-based occupational therapy model described in Section 2. It adopts partial reinforcement strategy by randomly selecting a character to race one step forward after each eating action. Due to the effect of partial reinforcement, children are motivated to continue eating to try and help their character win the game. The game motivation and enjoyment confirm to the self-reinforced strategy. This game also provides internal control to children, allowing them to choose a favorite cartoon character to compete in the race. The pace of the game is also controlled by children's eating behavior. Using the *natural* eating actions of children as inputs to the game is *critical* because eating is the target activity. Once children become attracted to the playful digital game, they find that they must eat to continue playing. Compared to video games, the racing game diverts only a moderate portion of the child's attention away from eating. This design connects and integrates the fun part (coming from the digital game activity) with the activity of eating.

5 Pilot User Studies and Results

In this section, we describe the details of a pilot study.

Participants. The participants comprised four child-parent pairs: three were recruited from the occupational therapy clinic of a teaching hospital; one was recruited by an office colleague. The four children were 4 to 7 years old. All participants are Taiwanese living in Taiwan. These four child-parent pairs are referred to here as *A, B, C,* and *D*. Children *A* and *B* were diagnosed with Asperger's syndrome, child *C* had high function autism, and child *D* had no specific diagnosis. The common complaint regarding mealtime for all parent participants was long meals, ranging from near 30 minutes to over one hour, after the children reached the age of self-feeding.

Procedure and measures. This study was conducted in Taipei, Taiwan. An occupational therapist first administered a semi-structured interview. A parent-report, Children's Mealtime Behavior Checklist (shown in Appendix A), was filled out and followed by an interview to clarify behavioral details. This checklist, including 19 types of child behaviors and nine types of parent behaviors, was modified from the Behavioral Pediatrics Feeding Assessment Scale [16] and the Children's Eating

Behavior Questionnaire [17]. After receiving informed consent from parents, the child/parent pair were: (1) invited to take their meals at our clinic or an investigator was dispatched to the home of the pair during their mealtime to record their eating activities before using the Racing Game Tray, then (2) another mealtime appointment was made within one week to record their eating activities using the Racing Game Tray. As for the locations of the studies, the Child D's study was conducted at her home, and other studies were conducted in the clinic. The served meals were familiar, traditional Chinese food prepared by the children's parents, consisting of mostly rice mixed with vegetables and meat. The mealtime episodes were videotaped via a video camera set in the same room. After setting up the video camera and/or Racing Game Tray, the parent and the child were left in the room by themselves until the meal was finished. To perform a fair comparison on child eating behavior, approximately the same amount of food was served during the meals with and without the Racing Game Tray.

An eating behavior coding system, as listed in Appendix B, was modified from the system created by Moore *et al.* [18]. The coding system consists of three behavioral categories: *active feeding*, *interaction*, and *social behaviors*. Active feeding refers to child active eating behavior or any related behavior. Furthermore, interaction refers to actively initiated behavior and the synchronous responsive behavior of the feeding partner. Finally, social behavior only refers to the behavior toward the feeding partner but not that directly related to feeding. In the active feeding and interaction categories, behavior was classified as either positive or negative: positive behavior describes behavior associated with promotion of self-feeding, whereas negative behavior describes behavior associated with aversion, intrusion, or interruption of self-feeding. The codes are mutually exclusive. Appendix B lists the details of the codes together with behavioral examples.

The mealtime videos of each child/parent pair were coded based on the eating behavior coding system listed in Appendix B, according to which unit of behavior was the smallest meaningful action or utterance. The coding was done by an occupational therapist trained in identifying the behaviors of interest. A pilot coding was conducted on two different child/parent mealtime videos twice to check for the reliability of the coding. Each parent and child received scores of three behavioral categories reflecting the frequencies at which they exhibited behaviors in these categories.

Results. Table 1 lists the age and diagnosis of individual participants. All children had average or above-average intelligence. Regarding the Children's Mealtime Behavior Checklist, all of the children had at least 10 of the 19 eating behavioral problems, and their parents had at least six of the nine types of maladaptive behavior. We caution that since the results presented here are from a small, pilot user study, they do not provide conclusive evidence of the Racing Game Tray reducing poor eating behavior in young children. A much longer study with more subjects would be needed to show its effectiveness. However, we provide these results as they suggest that the Racing Game Tray affects eating behavior. Fig. 7 shows the mealtime duration of the four child/parent pairs both with and without the Racing Game Tray. Mealtime duration was measured by rounding up the time taken to complete the meal to the nearest minute. Before using the Racing Game Tray, the mealtimes for the four children (A, B, C, D) were (23, 40, 41, 25) minutes. Meanwhile, with the Racing Game Tray, their mealtimes were reduced to (23, 25, 29, 9) minutes. Except for child *A* whose meal time duration remained the same with the Racing Game Tray, children *B*, *C*, and *D* all exhibited improvements, reducing mealtime duration from 29% to 64%, suggesting that the Racing Game Tray may improve meal completion time. The lack of improvement in child *A* might be that her mealtime duration in our observation session was fine under 30 minutes without the Racing Game Tray, despite a complaint from her parent regarding long mealtime behavior.

Table 1. Results from the Children's Mealtime Behavior Checklist completed by parents

	Child			Parent	
	Gender	Age (Year)	Diagnosis	Relation	Age (Year)
A	Girl	7	Asperger's Syndrome	Mother	33
B	Boy	5	High function autism	Mother	43
C	Boy	5	Asperger's Syndrome	Mother	45
D	Boy	4	No specific diagnosis	Father	36

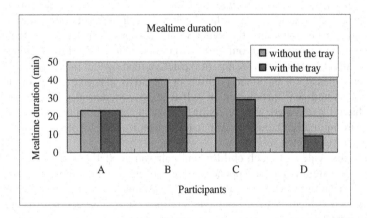

Fig. 7. Mealtime duration with and without the Racing Game Tray for the four children

Table 2 shows the results of mealtime interaction behavior between the four children and their parents with and without the use of the Racing Game Tray. By manually analyzing the recorded mealtime videos with and without the Racing Game Tray, this study identified positive, negative, and social behaviors of the parent and the child according to the definitions listed in Appendix B. For all parents and three children, the frequency of negative behavior decreased after using the Racing Game Tray; the frequency of negative behavior for child *D* was modest and showed only a slight increase from 3 to 8. The frequency of positive behavior for children either increased or didn't change much. However, for the parent's positive behavior in mealtime, the changes varied. Since the children were actively engaged in the eating activity when using the Racing Game Tray, their negative behaviors decreased. As a result, the necessity for the parents to promote self-feeding to their children might actually decrease. Regarding social behavior frequency, such behavior decreased for three of the

Table 2. The mealtime behavior with and without the Racing Game Tray

Pair	Location	Positive behavior		Negative behavior		Social behavior	
		Without tray	With tray	Without tray	With tray	Without tray	With tray
		Child's behavior					
A	Lab	52	88	18	6	19	9
B	Lab	80	76	37	4	19	12
C	Lab	40	79	50	5	6	28
D	Home	40	39	3	8	21	6
		Parent's behavior					
A	Lab	22	43	14	10	19	9
B	Lab	43	30	20	1	19	12
C	Lab	27	25	34	3	6	28
D	Home	8	10	2	0	14	6

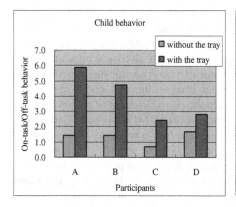 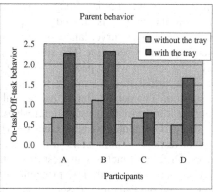

Fig. 8. On the left shows the child's on-task/off-task behavior ratio with and without the Racing Game Tray. On the right shows the parent's on-task/off-task behavior ratio with and without the Racing Game Tray. Positive behavior is on-task behavior, whereas both negative and social behaviors are off-task behavior. A high ratio of the on-task/off-task behavior is considered desirable, because it suggests greater frequency of on-task behavior versus off-task behavior.

child-parent pairs, and increased for one of the pairs. Since social behavior in this study is defined as behavior directed toward the feeding partner only but not directly related to feeding, such behavior can be a cause and/or effect of poor eating behavior.

Since the target task of this study is self-feeding, according to the definition listed in Appendix B, positive behavior is on-task behavior, while both negative and social behaviors is off-task behavior. A high ratio of the on-task/off-task behavior suggests greater frequency of on-task behavior versus off-task behavior. Results from Fig. 8 show that the ratios of on-task/off-task behavior improve for all children and parents. Without using the Racing Game Tray, child C had more off-task behavior than on-task behavior. For the other three children, about 40% of behavior is off-task. By using the Racing Game Tray, only 14~29% of behavior is off-task. These results suggest that by using the Racing Game Tray, children were more focused on self-feeding than without using the Racing Game Tray. In other words, the Racing Game Tray did not appear to distract them from self-feeding. In addition, Fig. 8 suggests that the parents also became more focused on the feeding task.

In summary, the preliminary results of using the Racing Game Tray designed based on the play-based occupational therapy model are encouraging. Due to the time constraint, we adopted a single-subject research design with four subjects. Each subject child used the Racing Game Tray only once. Continuing research is needed to investigate whether the effects of this study will be maintained when a child uses this Racing Game Tray repetitively until good eating behavior becomes a habit.

6 Related Work

King *et al.* [19] describe five persuasive strategies of adopting digital technology to change people's attitudes and behaviors. Specifically, these five strategies are simulated experiences, surveillance, environments of discovery, virtual groups, and personalizing. In the simulated experiences strategy, a simulated environment or object similar to its real part is created for a person to experience results of choosing different behavior. The surveillance strategy works by using monitoring and tracking to affect a person's behavior. The strategy of environments of discovery presents a fantasy environment where people's positive rewards can be given for their good behavior. The virtual group strategy leverages social competition and collaboration for persuasion. The personalizing strategy enhances the persuasiveness of information by tailoring it to individual users' interests or concerns. Fogg [4] introduces Captology, the study of computer-based persuasion. He presents a functional triad on how people view or respond to computers in three general ways, as tools, as media, and as social actors. Different functions suggest different types or designs for persuasive influence. He also maps out a total of 42 principles to design persuasive technologies. An example is called the Principle of Social Learning, which states that observing other people being rewarded for performing a certain behavior can serve as a good motivation. Some of these persuasive strategies and principles from King *et al.* [19] and Fogg [4] are adapted in the design presented here, including using digital media feedback as positive reinforcement for behavioral intervention. Additionally, this study emphasizes the playful aspect of the persuasive technology to maintain the interest of the children during the persuasion process.

There have been several case studies of persuasive technologies that target different behaviors with varying physical manifestations. We group these case studies under two general categories. The first category is focused on promoting physical activity in people's everyday life. Fish'n'Steps [2] is an interactive computer game to encourage physical activity. This game is based on a metaphor in which the act of growing a virtual fish in a tank symbolizes a similar act of caring for one's own body by walking a high step count. That is, the more players walk, the bigger their fishes grow in a virtual fish tank. By showing fishes from different players in the same virtual fish tank, this game adds the elements of social cooperation and competition among players. Houston [3] is a mobile phone application that encourages physical activity by sharing step counts and supportive comments among friends. Sharing of step counts and supportive comments provide social influence to persuade users to increase their daily step counts. The UbiFit Garden system [20] also wants to encourage physical activities. By using wearable sensors to detect and track people's physical activities, UbiFit displays their levels of exercises on a flower garden shown a cell phone. ViTo (as opposed to TiVo) [1] is a persuasive TV remote controller. This technology targets excessive TV watchers. By suggesting alternatives to TV watching, such as playing the Non-Exercise Activity Thermogenesis (NEAT) games (i.e., simple puzzles that use physical activity as their input), ViTo promotes reduced television viewing time.

The second category includes demonstrations of persuasive technology manifested into various everyday objects at home or in cars to motivate different behavioral change. These everyday objects are ideal for embedding persuasive technology because everyday activities naturally involve their use. The persuasive mirror [21] aims to motivate a lifestyle change by showing individuals what they may become in the future. If a person has poor lifestyle habits such as excessive eating, smoking, lack of exercise, *etc.*, the mirror will conjecture an unpleasant future-face to persuade lifestyle change. Tooth Tunes [22] is a smart toothbrush designed to encourage better teeth-brushing in young children. The toothbrush is embedded with small pressure sensors to recognize brushing activity when the toothbrush is pressed against teeth. Upon the sensors being activated, a two-minute piece of music is played to reinforce children in continuing brushing for at least two minutes. Waterbot [23] is a persuasive device installed at a bathroom sink to track the amount of water usage in each wash. The system contains flow sensors to detect the amount of water usage. By showing the current water usage in comparison to the average household water usage, the system encourages behavioral change toward water conservation. Out [24] designed a high-tech doll that resembles a human baby to simulate the difficulty of caring for a baby. The target users are teenagers with the goal being to prevent teen pregnancy. The doll contains an embedded computer that triggers a crying sound at random intervals. To stop the crying, a caregiver must pay immediate attention to the doll by inserting a key into the back of the baby for a specific length of time to simulate a care session. CarCoach [25] is an educational car system that can utilize sensors in a car to detect good or bad driving habits, such as excessive braking, sudden acceleration, the use of signals when turning, *etc.* Subsequently, CarCoach aims to provide *polite*, proactive, and considerate feedback to drivers by factoring into their mental state and current road conditions.

Compared to the related work described above, the work presented here adopts a similar approach of embedding behavioral intervention into everyday objects. However, the approach proposed in this study also differs from that above. Most significantly, the proposed approach takes a play-based occupational therapy approach that uses persuasive technology to target young children, in which play-based persuasion provides the most effective means of solving child behavioral problems. In this work, we have found that persuasive, ubicomp technology is a good match for occupational therapy because occupational therapy emphasizes functional behavioral improvements that are often observable and measurable. Ubicomp technology can be deployed in patients' environments to detect their functional behaviors and provide just-in-time behavior modification intervention.

7 Conclusion and Future Work

In this paper, we have presented the Racing Game Tray, a playful tray that adopts Ubicomp and persuasive techniques into play-based occupational therapy for reducing poor eating behavior in young children after they reach their self-feeding age. Utilizing Ubicomp and persuasive technology extends the reach of occupational therapists from their treatment clinic into the actual living environment of a patient, enabling therapists to implement a direct intervention approach at the place where young children's eating behavior occurs and when the treatment is most effective. The design of the playful tray connects physical eating to digital playing activities to reinforce active participation of children in the activity of eating. Results of a pilot user study suggest that the Racing Game Tray may improve child meal completion time and reduce negative power play interactions between parents and children, resulting in an improved family mealtime experience.

An essential part of learning at home or in school for young children is about developing good habits, from brushing teeth properly in the morning to going to sleep on time at night. As shown in this study, children love to play and persuading behavior through games is effective for children. This study opens up many potential applications for adopting Ubicomp and persuasive techniques in play-based occupational therapy of young children.

Acknowledgement

We gratefully thank Sunny Consolvo for her tremendous effort on shepherding this paper.

References

1. Nawyn, J., Intille, S.S., Larson, K.: Embedding behavior modification strategies into a consumer electronic device: a case study. In: Proceedings of the 8th International Conference on Ubiquitous Computing, pp. 297–314 (2006)
2. Lin, J., Mamykina, L., Lindtner, S., Delajoux, G., Strub, H.: Fish'n'Steps: encouraging physical activity with an interactive computer game. In: Proceedings of the 8th International Conference on Ubiquitous Computing, pp. 261–278 (2006)
3. Consolvo, S., Everitt, K., Smith, I., Landay, J.A.: Design requirements for technologies that encourage physical activity. In: Proceedings of the SIGCHI Conference on Human Factors and Computing Systems, pp. 457–466 (2006)
4. Fogg, B.J.: Persuasive Technology: Using Computers to Change What We Think and Do. Morgan Kaufmann (2002)
5. Manikam, R., Perman, J.: Pediatric feeding disorders. Journal of Clinical Gastroenterology 30, 34–46 (2000)
6. Ha, P.B., Bentley, M.E., Pachon, H., Sripaipan, T., Caulfield, L.E., Marsh, D.R., Schroeder, D.G.: Caregiver styles of feeding and child acceptance of food in rural Viet Nam. Food and Nutrition Bulletin 23(4 Supplement), 95–100 (2002)
7. Hergenhahn, B.R.: An Introduction to Theories of Learning, 3rd edn. Prentice Hall, Englewood Cliffs, NJ (1988)

8. Bundy, A.C.: Play and playfulness: What to look for. In: Parham, L.D., Fazio, L.S. (eds.) Play in Occupational Therapy for Children, L, Mosby, MO (1997)
9. McMahon, R.J., Forehand, R.L.: Helping the noncompliant child—Family-based treatment for oppositional behavior, Guilford, NY, pp. 20–27 (2003)
10. Alessandrini, N.A.: Play—A child's world. Am. J. Occup. Ther. 3, 9–12 (1949)
11. Kielhofner, G.: A model of human occupational: Theory and application. Lippincott Williams & Wilkins, MD (2002)
12. Royeen, C.B., Duncan, M.: Acquisition frame of reference. In: Kramer, P., Hinojosa, J. (eds.) Frames of Reference for Pediatric Occupational Therapy, 2nd edn., pp. 377–400. Lippincott Williams & Wilkins, Wolters Kluwer Health (1999)
13. O'Brien, S., Repp, A.C., Williams, G.E., Christophersen, E.R.: Pediatric feeding disorders. Behavior Modification 15(3), 394–418 (1991)
14. Parham, L.D., Primeau, L.A.: Play and occupational therapy. In: Parham, L.D., Fazio, L.S. (eds.) Play in Occupational Therapy for Children, Mosby, MO (1997)
15. Lin, T.-Y., Chang, K.-H., Liu, S.-Y., Chu, H.-H.: A Persuasive Game to Encourage Healthy Dietary Behaviors of Young Children. In: Adjunct Proceedings of the 8th International Conference on Ubiquitous Computing (2006)
16. Crist, W., McDonnell, P., Beck, M., Gillespie, C., Barrett, P., Mathews, J.: Behavior at mealtimes and the young child with cystic fibrosis. Journal of Developmental and Behavioral Pediatrics 15(3), 157–161 (1994)
17. Wardle, J., Guthrie, C.A., Sanderson, S., Rapoport, L.: Development of the children's eating behaviour questionnaire. Journal of Child Psychology and Psychiatry and Allied Disciplines 42(7), 963–970 (2001)
18. Moore, A.C., Akhter, S., Aboud, F.E.: Responsive complementary feeding in rural Bangladesh. Social Science & Medicine 62(8), 1917–1930 (2006)
19. King, P., Tester, J.: The landscape of persuasive technologies. Communications of ACM 42(5), 31–38 (1999)
20. Consolvo, S., Paulos, E., Smith, I.: Mobile persuasion for everyday behavior change. In: Fogg, Eckles (ed.) Mobile Persuasion 20 Perspective on the Future of Behavior Change, Stanford Captology Media (2007)
21. Andrés del Valle, A.C., Opalach, A.: The persuasive mirror: computerized persuasion for healthy living. In: Proceedings of the 11th International Conference on Human-Computer Interaction (2005)
22. Hasbro, Inc., TOOTH TUNES, http://www.hasbro.com/toothtunes/
23. Arroyo, E., Bonanni, L., Selker, T.: Waterbot: exploring feedback and persuasive techniques at the sink. In: Proceedings of Conference on Human Factors in Computing Systems, pp. 631–639 (2005)
24. Out, J.W.: Baby Think It Over: Using role-play to prevent teen pregnancy. Adolescence 36(143), 571–582 (2001)
25. Arroyo, E., Sullivan, S., Selker, T.: CarCoach: a polite and effective driving coach. In: Proceedings of the SIGCHI Conference on Human Factors in Computing Systems, pp. 357–362 (2006)

Appendix A: Children's Mealtime Behavior Checklist

Child's Name:	Date:	
Filled by:	Relation to the child:	
Child Behavior		**Descriptions**
My child eats `less` `more` `the same` when s/he is upset.		
My child eats `less` `more` `the same` when s/he is angry.		
My child eats `less` `more` `the same` when s/he is tired.		
My child eats `less` `more` `the same` when s/he is happy.		
My child eats `less` `more` `the same` when s/he is anxious.		
My child eats `less` `more` `the same` when s/he is annoyed.		
My child eats `less` `more` `the same` when s/he is worried.		
My child eats `less` `more` `the same` when s/he has nothing to do.		

Please check all boxes that apply	**Descriptions**
☐ My child chokes at mealtime.	
☐ My child eats only ground or soft food.	
☐ My child refuses to eat meals but requests food immediately after meal.	
☐ My child has trouble tasting new foods.	
☐ My child gags or vomits at mealtime.	When? How often?
☐ My child is a picky eater.	Likes or dislikes what?
☐ My child gets up from table during a meal.	
☐ My child keeps food in his/her mouth without swallowing it.	
☐ My child Spits out food during a meal.	
☐ My child plays with food, such as eating rice one grain at a time, or noodles one string at a time.	
☐ My child stops eating by talking or singing during a meal.	
☐ My child stops eating or chewing while doing nothing.	
☐ My child attempts to negotiate what he/she will and will not eat.	
☐ My child always leaves leftover or requires other people to feed him/her.	
☐ My child would rather drink milk than eat meals.	
☐ My child likes to eat snack foods.	Type? Time? Frequency?
☐ My child always asks for a drink.	
☐ My child eats slowly.	
☐ My child eats more and more slowly during the course of a meal.	

Parent Behavior	**Descriptions**
☐ I get anxious and/or frustrated when feeding my child.	
☐ I coax my child to get him/her to take a bite.	
☐ I use threats to get my child to eat.	
☐ I feel worried my child doesn't get enough to eat.	
☐ If child doesn't like what is served, I make something else.	
☐ I feel that there is no way for me to get my child to eat in a well-behaved manner.	
☐ When my child refuses food, I force food into his/her mouth.	
☐ Getting my child to eat often makes me very angry.	
☐ I will feed my child if he/she doesn't eat himself/herself.	

Appendix B: Behavioral Feeding Codes for Children

(1) Self-feeding: a child place food into his/her own mouth	
Parent	**Child**
Positive: A parent allows or promotes self-feeding, such as verbal encouragement, praises, etc.	**Positive**: A child attempts self-feeding, such as holding utensils, putting food into mouth, etc.
Negative: A parent discourages, disallows, or interrupts self-feeding, such as pushing the child's hands away, telling the child that she will feed the child, etc.	**Negative**: A child rejects self-feeding, such as saying "no" or pushing away given food.

(2) Interaction: Actively initiated behavior and the synchronous responsive behavior of the feeding partner	
Parent as the actor	**Child's responsive behavior**
Positive: A parent attempts to arouse a child's interest, such as talking about food, models, food games, etc. A parent refocuses the child's attention on food when the child is distracted.	**Positive**: A child accepts food when it is offered, or self-feeds food.
	Negative: A child ignores the parent's cue, refuses, or walks away from the parent's cue.
Negative: A parent intrusively attempts to direct feeding, such as force-feeding the child, holding a child's head, body, or hand, and threatening the child.	**Positive**: A child responds by self-feeding.
	Negative: A child ignores the parent's attempts, refuses, or walks away from the parent's attempts.
Parent's responsive behavior	**Child as the actor**
Positive: A parent synchronously responds to promote continuous feeding, such as interpreting a child feeding cues, responding to a child's needs, etc.	**Positive**: A child initiates an attempt to eat, such as looking at food, talking about food, requesting food/drink, or touching food.
Negative: A parent synchronously responds to interrupt the child's feeding.	
Positive: A parent synchronously responds to promote continuous feeding, such as interpreting the child feeding cues, responding to the child's needs, etc.	**Negative**: A child shows disinterest, discouragement, or stops eating or chewing.
Negative: A parent synchronously responds to interrupt the child's feeding.	

(3) Social behavior: Toward feeding partner only but not directly related to feeding	
Behavior such as talking, touching, smiling, looking, laughing, etc.	Behavior such as talking, touching, smiling, looking, laughing, whining, or crying.

(4) Others	
The parent feeds the child directly without any special responsive or encouraging strategy.	A child stops or refuses to eat without any evidence of environmental distracters.

Privacy Enhancing Technologies for RFID in Retail-
An Empirical Investigation

Sarah Spiekermann

Institute of Information Systems, Humboldt University Berlin,
Spandauer Strasse 1, 10178 Berlin, Germany
sspiek@wiwi.hu-berlin.de

Abstract. This article investigates the conflicting area of user benefits arising through item level RFID tagging and a desire for privacy. It distinguishes between three approaches feasible to address consumer privacy concerns. One is to kill RFID tags at store exits. The second is to lock tags and have user unlock them if they want to initiate reader communication (user scheme). The third is to let the network access users' RFID tags while adhering to a privacy protocol (agent scheme). The perception and reactions of future users to these three privacy enhancing technologies (PETs) are compared in the present article and an attempt is made to understand the reasoning behind their preferences. The main conclusion is that users don't trust complex PETs as they are envisioned today. Instead they prefer to kill RFID chips at store exits even if they appreciate after sales services. Enhancing trust through security and privacy 'visibility' as well as PET simplicity may be the road to take for PET engineers in UbiComp.

Keywords: RFID, privacy, security, privacy enhancing technology, RFID kill-function, authentication, identification, user behavior.

1 Introduction

Radio Frequency Identification (short RFID) is considered to be an important technological building block of Ubiquitous Computing. Provided that RFID tags are embedded in everyday objects and accessed by a networked reader infrastructure, it will be possible to create myriad new information, tracking and access services across industries. A relatively new and promising application domain for RFID is the retail sector. Retailer logistics, shop-floor management, marketing and after-sales services are all in the verge of being optimized with the help of RFID. As a result, retailers and their product suppliers are now starting to deploy RFID tags as the next generation bar code on individual products.

However, the introduction of RFID on products has met criticism in the press and through privacy rights organisations to an extent that – despite all expected benefits – retailers hesitate about whether and how to fully launch the technology in areas where it interfaces with consumers [1]. On the shopfloor, recognizing customers individually and automatically upon arrival, tracking them through the store, observing their interactions with products and offering them personalized advertisements and

J. Krumm et al. (Eds.): UbiComp 2007, LNCS 4717, pp. 56–72, 2007.

information services are all activities which can be realized through RFID, but have the potential to be viewed as privacy intrusive [2-4]. More important, privacy advocates point to retailers' responsibility to not let RFID enabled products leave their stores. They fear that accessible RFID tags on most objects in the public domain will lead to ubiquitous surveillance of people [5]. And indeed, their concerns are reflected in qualitative research studies with consumers on the technology. In 2004 four focus groups were organized in Berlin with 30 participants discussing RFID in a retail context. They were shown 2 films (a positive and a critical one) about the technology to inform about RFID, its service vision, benefits and potential ethical drawbacks. Focus group participants were recruited by a research agency to represent a spectrum of consumers similar to the German population in terms of age, sex and education. Based on these recorded sessions and transcribed discussions six major privacy concerns could be discerned (free translation of citations) [4]:

(1) **Fear of losing control over one's belongings:** "...but if I don't know where this thing is?", "The product I have bought is my property and I want to do with it what I want. This is of nobody else's business."
(2) **Tracking of objects and people:** "If chip services are only offered inside stores ...then that's fine. But I would have a problem with further tracking outside stores", "I would start to constantly fear being tracked."
(3) **Responsibility for objects** (due to the individual attribution of unique products to people): "...but what is important to me is that I am not linked as a person to the product that I have bought", "Then I am as a buyer responsible for the yoghurt can? That's crazy!"
(4) **Technology paternalism** – the idea that objects recognize and punish misbehaviour: "The question is whether it starts beeping when I leave the yoghurt besides the cashier, and then there is a signal, and then everybody knows...", "I imagine myself taking a nice caviar box and then my computer tells me 'no, this is not for you'."
(5) **Information collection and personalization** (due to recognizing individual product IDs): "...then they classify me as 'low budget' and then my neighbour sees that I am only offered the cheap stuff", "They know all about me and I know nothing about them."
(6) **Abuse** (attacks on one's privacy by hackers or other unauthorized parties): "I also find this technology horrible and believe that it could quickly be abused in negative situations", "I think that it could quickly be abused in negative situations, such as for spying."

One major conclusion drawn by the observers of the focus groups was that participants seemed to unanimously call for RFID tags to be killed at retailer exits. Emotional levels seemed to rise considerably when people learned that they would carry multiple functioning chips with them out of the store. And it seemed as if they were drawing a line of legitimacy for RFID use by retailers in their own proper facilities, but not beyond: "They can use this technology in their business environment, their production units, their sales domain, but that's it! Then they have to leave me alone. I leave the store and I don't want to be tracked". Results equally critical of RFID technology were also obtained in focus groups conducted by the Auto-ID centre in the US, UK, France and Japan [6].

Given these qualitative research results, a question confronted by retailers today is how to treat RFID chips at store exits. Should they make use of the kill-function foreseen in the generation 2 specification for mass-market class 1 RFID chips [7] and permanently deactivate tags' functionality to transmit data when their buyers leave the store? Or should they ignore consumer and privacy rights calls and leave the chips' functionality intact? Might it be a viable option for them to demand the inclusion of privacy enhancing technologies (PETs) in the RFID infrastructure so that RFID tags are not killed at store exits, but only accessible by authorized entities? And if so, which PETs should retailers support? To answer these questions, retailers need to understand how vital the privacy issue really is for their customers and how willing they are to trade their concerns with the technology's benefits; in particular, in the after-sales domain where permanent deactivation of RFID tags would impede any further service potential.

Against the background of these questions two quantitative consumer studies were conducted in co-operation with the Metro Group from 2004 to 2006. The Metro Group is Europe's largest retail company. The goal was to assess peoples' perception of different technological scenarios to treat RFID at store exits and to understand the role of peoples' RFID usefulness perceptions in this conflicting area. Furthermore, individual attitudes towards privacy, group pressure and general technical affinity were included as independent variables to potentially explain preferences for different exit solutions. In the following sections, this paper will present the hypotheses and technological proposals which have driven this research effort (section 2), the experimental set-up used (section 3) and results obtained (section 4). In a final section implications will be deducted for those who build and deploy RFID to create intelligent infrastructures (section 5).

2   Privacy Enhancing Technologies for RFID and User Perceptions

RFID technology comes in many different forms. Tag classes ranging from 0 to 4 can be discerned depending on the tags' memory, power source and features [8]. Furthermore, tags operate at different frequencies and as a result employ very different transmission mechanisms with distinct read-ranges, bandwidths and capabilities to penetrate line-of-sight barriers. Much of the technology to date has been built to serve the needs of closed proprietary systems with specific use cases. Depending on the RFID system chosen for a specific purpose privacy problems can more or less arise. For example, RFID chips which transmit data over an UHF band (typically at 865 – 928 MHz) currently have reliable read ranges of around six to eight meters. In contrast, tags which transmit their data at 13,56 MHz only achieve reliable read ranges of around 1 ½ metres. As this comparison makes plain, privacy implications of RFID technology vary: the probability that an attacker can read out a person's belongings unnoticed is much more likely in an UHF scenario than it is in a 13,56 MHz environment. For this reason, the research presented hereafter needed to be grounded in a specific type of RFID deployment scenario. More precisely, the author built her research on the assumption that EPCglobal's class 1 generation 2

RFID tags and infrastructure vision would be deployed on an item level [7, 9, 10]. EPCglobal is today's main private international standardization body for both future numbering standards as well as the technical infrastructure for number processing (based on RFID). The organisation envisions all items to carry a passive UHF tag with one unique identifier, the electronic product code (EPC) [11]. The EPC is supposed to be used as a key to find information about the item it is attached to. This information is maintained within a backend network consisting of myriad EPC-Information Services (EPC-IS) [12]. These services can be accessed via an Object Name Service (ONS) and are ubiquitously accessible provided that the retriever holds respective access rights [13].

2.1 PETs for RFID – A Classification for Empirical Investigation

From a bird's eye three major blocks of PETs for RFID can be discerned for the after-sales area. First, the most straight forward approach is to simply kill the tags' ability to transmit its electronic product code (EPC). This solution is embedded in EPCglobal's generation 2 specification for mass market class 1 tags [7]. It would entail retailers to integrate a kill-command into their electronic check-out processes. From a technological standpoint it is the most radical privacy solution, but from a market perspective it implies the disadvantage that after sales scenarios for using RFID would equally be killed.

A second set of PETs builds on the vision that users exert immediate control over their RFID tags at the client side. These solutions are proposing that tags are 'locked' before leaving stores, but can be unlocked with the help of user controlled authentication mechanisms. As a result, object tags do not a priori respond to network requests. Instead the user self-initiates the use of intelligent services if they are available and useful in the respective context. The context decision when and how the use of tags is appropriate in a situation is thus taken by the object owner [4, 14-17]. If the owner of an object has some benefit from reviving an object's RFID tag and transmitting its information she can do so by authenticating herself vis-à-vis the tag and then give the tag explicit and situation specific permission to release its data. The authentication process would typically be handled via a password scheme where one or multiple passwords are either remembered by users or stored in a separate mediating device which maintains some type of password management system. However, regardless of the concrete authentication process and mechanism chosen (i.e. with separate user device or without separate user device; via passwords or via biometrics) the architectural vision puts the user in the role of the *initiator* of communication with the intelligent infrastructure. Hereafter, we want to refer to PETs in this domain as "User PETs". An underlying hypothesis to the current work was that User PETs should lead to a high level of perceived control with users since the intelligent infrastructure does not act in a pro-active manner. Figure 1a illustrates this interaction paradigm by visualizing it as a password protection scheme.

In contrast to User PETs, "Agent PETs" are based on the idea that RFID tags are unlocked by default and that the network takes the initiative to communicate with a user's tags. Access control to user tags in this scenario is provided (automatically) via some "watchdog" device carried by the user (i.e. a PDA) [18-20]. This device may - in the long run - determine whether the reader infrastructure has the right to access a person's tag(s) by transferring "mother" rights to a network once the network reader has proven its identity and adherence to a user's privacy preferences [21]. It could run a protocol similar to the one specified by the Platform for Privacy Preferences Project (P3P) in the context of E-Commerce transactions. P3P enables websites to express their privacy practices in a standard format that can be retrieved automatically and interpreted easily by user agents [22]. Metadata included in this protocol comprise, for example, the type of information collected, the purpose of information collection and URIs to the data collector(s). In the RFID context first efforts have been made to integrate this metadata information into the generation 2 reader - tag exchange protocol [18, 20]. So far, however, watchdog devices are only able to display that communication has happened. In the context of the empirical studies presented hereafter it has been assumed that network requests to access RFID chips would be negotiated by a user's device. Figure 1b illustrates this interaction paradigm visualizing a mobile phone as the network interface and shield to users' RFID tags.

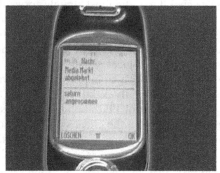

Fig. 1a. The User Scheme: Users personally initiate the communication of their tags and take the context decision to start exchange

Fig. 2b. The Agent Scheme: Users delegates tag – network communication to phone agent and network takes context decision to start exchange

Of course, it must be acknowledged that more PET technologies are in the verge of creation or have already been proposed such as blocker tags [23] or mechanisms to physically destroy tag antennas [24]. Not all of these technologies may strictly adhere to one of the two paradigms of interaction. However, the author of this paper does believe that also in the long run one key question is whether a user initiates a data exchange selectively and upon taking the context decision to interact or whether the network will take care of this decision pro-actively. In the following sections the two distinct interaction paradigms are being compared empirically and it is being investigated how they are perceived by users relative to the most radical PET solution which is to kill RFID tags altogether. We will refer to the User and Agent scheme as "complex PETs" as opposed to the kill approach.

2.2 Hypotheses

Qualitative user studies and media attention to RFID drive retailers to seriously consider PETs at store exits. But which of the three schemes should they prefer? An important factor for answering this question is the degree to which buyers will want to take advantage of after-sales services available through RFID. It seems rational to expect that consumers who appreciate after-sales RFID services would prefer to know that threats to their privacy are being avoided while valued services are still available to them. We therefore hypothesize that for those consumers who appreciate after sales RFID services any PET scheme, whether that be the user scheme or the agent scheme is superior to chips being killed:

H1: The user scheme is considered superior to the kill option if people appreciate after-sales RFID services.

H2: The agent scheme is considered superior to the kill option if people appreciate after sales RFID services.

As was argued above, users are in the driver's seat if they initiate the communication between their tags and the network. It therefore seems sensible to expect that users will perceive more control over their RFID tags' communication when being confronted with a User Scheme than when delegating privacy decisions to an agent. And they will rather want to kill tags in an agent scheme scenario than in a user scheme scenario. We therefore hypothesize:

H3: When confronted with an Agent PET users will want to kill RFID tags more readily than when confronted with a User PET.

H4: The User PET is perceived by users to provide more control to them over the reader infrastructure than the Agent PET.

Finally, retailers need to understand the dynamics behind buyers' appreciation of more complex PETs versus the killing of tags. What would drive buyers to rather kill a tag or use a complex PET? An immediate answer could be that the ease of use of a complex PET drives this decision. But equally, the degree to which one feels informed as well as (intuitively) protected through the PET is important. These three factors, ease-of-use of the PET, information and reduction of helplessness through the PET (vis-à-vis an intelligent infrastructure) have been identified in earlier work of the author as constructs to measure the perceived effectiveness of PETs [25]. They were therefore included in the current work as independent dimensions driving the judgement of complex PETs.

In addition to this control perception of complex PETs, the theory of reasoned action [26] suggests that other attitude elements as well as peer opinions (subjective norm) play a role when humans determine their intentions to act (or use a technology). In the current context, theory of reasoned action was used as an underlying framework to identify constructs potentially influencing the use of complex PETs. For example, it could be argued that the perception of RFID services as useful will drive peoples' intention to adopt complex RFID PETs, because only these PETS will allow for maintaining the technology's valued services. Equally, ease of use anticipated for the technology could play a role for attitude formation. Finally, the influence of valued peers may be important [27, 28]. If RFID services are going to be appreciated by one's peer group, the likelihood to equally embrace the technology's service spectrum and not kill it will probably increase. Against this background the following hypothesis was formulated:

H5: A common set of technology acceptance factors, namely the perceived usefulness and ease of use of RFID, perceived control through the PET and the opinion of others on RFID will drive users' preference to prefer complex PETs for RFID over a kill approach.

Personal factors may equally play a role in how people judge PETs. Innovation diffusion theory has found that peoples' openness towards new technologies and technical affinity are an important characteristic of 'innovators' who are typically the first ones to try a new technology [29]. If people have these characteristics they may want to take advantage of RFID after sales services. Furthermore, they may be less afraid to embrace more complex PETs.

Finally, compatibility of a new technology with existing social and ethical standards as well as practices is important for adoption [29]. Therefore, the personal awareness for one's privacy maintenance could play a role for PET choice: If people are highly privacy sensitive they may have a tendency to prefer the more radical solution to kill RFID chips rather than to use a complex PET. Based on this reasoning we formulated hypothesis 6:

H6: Personal characteristics, in particular technical affinity, privacy attitudes and general attitudes towards new technologies have an impact on the preference for complex PETs over killing chips.

3 Method

3.1 Participants and Procedure

Two empirical studies were conducted following the same experimental procedure. 234 participants were recruited for study ① by a market research agency in the city of Berlin. They were selected to reflect average German demographics in terms of age, sex, education and income. One year later, the same study was replicated with an extended questionnaire including 306 participants. Participants for this study were recruited according to the same demographic parameters but included urban citizens from four different German regions.

Participants were briefed to participate in a study conducted by Humboldt University on the future of shopping and invited to a hotel in the respective region. Upon arrival, they received an initial questionnaire addressing their satisfaction with current retail environments and investigating their current knowledge about RFID (both studies). Study ② additionally included the measurement of attitude towards new technologies, technical affinity and privacy attitudes. Participants then watched a film informing them about RFID technology and future services on the shopfloor and after sales. Before seeing the film 86% had never heard about RFID in study ① and 81% in study ②.

Table 1. Experimental groups and demographics

		Study ①				Study ②	
		Chips ON	Chips Killed	User PET	Agent PET	Chips ON	User PET
Stimulus used		Film 1	Film 2	Film 3	Film 4	Film 1	Film 3
Film evaluation						6,9/11	7,7/11
Sex	Male	26	28	34	27	47	103
	Female	27	23	40	28	50	104
Age	< = 29	21	15	28	19	35	67
	30-49	23	26	34	26	56	134
	> = 50	9	10	12	10	6	6
Education	No high-school	25	21	31	20	42	81
	High-school	28	29	41	35	55	122
Income pre tax	< € 10 k	21	20	26	24	33	66
	€ 10 - 30 k	22	15	33	17	25	62
	> € 30 k	8	14	10	14	29	64
TOTAL		54	51	74	55	98	208
		234				306	

The film material used in these two quantitative studies was a different material than the ready-made RFID documentations used in earlier focus groups. It was exclusively produced to inform people in a neutral manner about RFID services as well as different potential PET solutions envisioned by engineers. The four different PET options (kill, chips left on, user or agent scheme) were not presented as alternatives in the film. Instead we used a between-subject experimental design varying the film's ending and informing each group participating in a study on a different PET deployed at store exits (see appendix 1). Following the respective film stimulus they received a second questionnaire asking them to evaluate the benefits of the RFID services they had just seen as well as the respective PET displayed to them. In particular, they had to decide on an 11-point differential scale whether they would want to use a complex PET (if they had seen one) or rather kill RFID chips at store exits. The judgements participants made on this scale have been taken as the dependent variable to test hypotheses 1 through 5. Study ① embedded the four PET variations mentioned above. Study ② only differentiated between the User Scheme and leaving chips unprotected. Table 1 gives an overview of the two studies conducted.

The independent variables investigated in study ① included the perceived usefulness of RFID after sales services, the anticipated ease of use of RFID, peer opinion and perceived control through the PET (in terms of information control through the PET, ease of use of the PET and helplessness despite the PET). In study ② the same constructs were measured (except for peer opinion) and in addition personal variables were controlled for, including personal attitudes towards new technologies, technical affinity and general privacy awareness. Appendix 2 details the items used to measure these constructs.

3.2 Materials and Apparatus

The film stimulus was developed with the goal to inform participants in a neutral way about RFID technology, its benefits and drawbacks. It started out by showing a future retail outlet with RFID based services and then proceeded to introduce some retail related after-sales benefits of the technology. The film material used was taken from several existing television documentaries on RFID and combined with a professionally synchronized audio track. The audio track's text was carefully developed and tailored to contain an equal number of positive and negative messages about the technology. It was spoken with a view to maintain maximum neutrality. Equally, the film stimulus contained no background music or any other emotionally biasing signals.

In study ①, the film stimulus presented the retailer's check-out and after-sales scenarios in four different versions. Film 1 suggested that RFID chips would be left fully functional when checking out of the supermarket allowing for seamless RFID services after sales, but also potential attacks on one's privacy. The use of UHF chips was presumed for this scenario informing participants of read ranges between five and eight metres. Film 2 suggested that RFID chips would be killed by the retailer's cashpoint and no after sales services were presented to the participants. The appreciation of RFID after sales services was tested in a hypothetical way in this set-up before the film was shown and without mentioning the technology. Film 3 showed and explained the User Scheme, visualized as a password protection scheme. Participants were briefed to believe that all chips would be simultaneously deactivated and thus be privacy preserving unless the owner of an object would switch RFID chips back on with his or her personal password. Film 4 showed a user specifying his privacy preferences with a mobile operator. The reader network would then exchange privacy preferences with the mobile phone agent. The phone serves as a kind of watchdog service in this scenario. The two films 3 and 4 contained an equal number of positive and negative messages about the technology. They varied only in the description of the functioning of the technology which was described in a highly neutral way. Appendix 1 contains images and the exact wording used in films 3 and 4.

The focus in study ② was to better understand the dynamics behind using a User Scheme PET. For this purpose, only films 1 and 3 were used. Neutrality towards RFID technology and it was evaluated and confirmed in this study for films 1 and 3 with a median judgement of 7 on an 11 point scale (with 1 = film is negative about RFID and 11 = film is positive about RFID technology).

4 Results

4.1 Quantitative Evaluation of PET Solutions

A first analysis of the usefulness perceptions of RFID after sales services shows that participants feel neutral to positive about them regardless of the PET employed (table 2). There is no significant difference in service evaluation between the user and the agent scheme. However, not knowing about RFID technology as an enabler of smart services yielded a significantly higher appreciation of them.

Respondents to films 3 and 4 were split into two groups depending on whether their usefulness ratings were above or below mean group average. It was then tested whether those with usefulness ratings above average would value the use of a respective PET more in comparison to the kill alternative than those with low usefulness ratings.

In accordance with hypotheses 1 and 2 participants with above average usefulness perceptions of RFID valued both the User and the Agent PET significantly higher than those with low average usefulness ratings. On the 11-point scale anchoring the opposing preference for rather killing (1) or rather using a complex PET (11) people appreciating RFID after sales services in the User Scheme scenario rated the PET on average at 5,61. Those expecting less benefits from RFID rated the User PET at 2,49 (p=.000). In the group where participants saw the Agent Scheme appreciators of RFID valued the complex PET at 4,44 while non-appreciators valued it at 2,26 (p=.002). These results suggest that the perception of usefulness of RFID after sales services is an important driver for preferring complex PETs over the kill solution. Yet, absolute judgements show that all participants clearly prefer to kill RFID tags at store exits rather than adopting any of the two complex PET solutions presented to them.

Table 2. Mean (m) usefulness ratings of RFID after sales services in study ① *

Usefulness of RFID based after-sales services	User Scheme (m)	Agent Scheme (m)	kill Chips (m)	sig. (User vs. Agent)	sig. (User vs. kill Chips)	sig. (Agent vs. kill Chips)
Replace goods without receipt	3,84	3,85	4,44	.909	.002	.002
Warranty access without receipts	3,89	4,05	4,63	.621	.000	.000
Outdoor product recommendations	2,61	2,84	3,1	.290	.021	.252
Add. product information access at home	3,64	3,80	4,37	.494	.000	.000
Durability display of goods by fridge	3,45	3,67	4,00	.353	.009	.032
Washing machine warning	3,61	3,5	4,20	.347	.002	.000
Recipe recommendations	3,49	3,46	3,82	.803	.145	.101
Medical cabinet alerts	3,99	4,02	4,20	.966	.110	.088
Medical cabinet reminders	3,73	3,69	4,27	.630	.006	.001
Average Service Appreciation	**3,58**	**3,65**	**4,11**			

*) usefulness was measured on a 5 point scale (1 = very unsavoury, 5 = very welcome).

Average preferences among the appreciators of RFID services suggest that the User Scheme is slightly more valued than the Agent Scheme. To investigate this tendency reflected in hypothesis 3 the author compared participants' average tendency to kill in the User Scheme with the one in the Agent Scheme. And indeed the kill approach is preferred more often when the Agent PET is the alternative (m=3.31) than when the User PET is the alternative (m=4.03). However, this difference is not significant (p=.273). Therefore, hypothesis 3 that Agent Scheme users will want to kill RFID tags more readily than those confronted with the User Scheme must be rejected.

This finding of indifference between the two complex PET solutions is also reflected in a more thorough analysis of control perceptions raised through the two PETs. The author hypothesized that the User Scheme would lead to higher perceptions of control than the Agent Scheme (hypothesis 4). The reasoning behind this hypothesis as outlined above was that in the User Scheme users initiate communication with the reader infrastructure and need to confirm individual transactions before they take place. In the Agent Scheme they delegate these initiation decisions to an agent. As table 3 shows none of the three aspects of PET control significantly varies between the two PET solutions. Hypothesis 4 therefore needs to be rejected. In absolute terms users feel helpless vis-à-vis the reader infrastructure regardless of the type of PET employed. And this is the case even though they anticipate both PETs to be quite easy to use (which was suggested by the two films). Furthermore, they perceive information control on a medium level.

Table 3. Mean (m) control ratings in the experimental groups (study ①)

CONTROL MEASURES	Average Evaluation of the PET (m)		
	User PET	Agent PET	sig.
Ease of Use of PET	4,09	3,78	.052
Information through PET	3,28	3,40	.480
Helplessness despite PET	4,07	4,35	.112

Finally, we wanted to understand the relative importance of control, usefulness, ease of use as well as personal variables for preferring one ore the other PET scheme. For this purpose multiple regression analysis was conducted. Table 4 gives an overview of the results obtained.

All three regression models summarized in table 4 displayed significant F-Values proving that for each model the observed constructs have some systematic relationship with the decision to use a complex PET rather than kill the chip. The adjusted R^2 values (coefficients of determination) indicate that 40% to 48% of the variance in opting for a complex PET can be explained by the constructs included in the analyses. This level of variance explanation is quite satisfactory seen that there are potentially many factors for which the experimenters could not control. For example, participants' prior experience with remembering passwords or using mobile phone functionality, identity theft incidents, retailer trust, etc. could all influence the judgement in favour or against a complex PET. Since it is impossible to control for all of these factors explaining between 40 and 48% of the variance seems a satisfying result.

A revealing result of the regression models is that the reasons to opt for one or the other complex PET are not identical. When participants opt in favour of the User PET what counts for them most is the perception of usefulness of RFID after sales services. In contrast, participants who saw the Agent Scheme scenario seem to follow a different rationale. They opt for the complex Agent PET if their peers are in favour of using RFID. In both groups a perception of helplessness despite PET existence leads to a general tendency to reject both complex PETs. The more helpless users feel despite the User or Agent PET, the more they want to kill RFID tags. Mixed evidence was found on information properties of PETs and their effects on PET adoption. For the User PET information control seems to play a role, yet the direction of influence is unclear from the current analysis. For the Agent PET, in contrast, information control does not seem to play a role for adoption. It may be speculated that this is the case, because Agent PETs do not regularly inform users about read-outs. However, for this construct, as well as for peer opinion internal factor consistency (see α values) was mediocre and therefore do not allow making a very final judgement on the reliable influence of these constructs.

When personal variables were added to explain the preference for the kill function or the User PET in study ② it turned out that neither attitudes towards new technologies or technical affinity nor privacy concerns play a significant role for explaining peoples' judgement for PET usage or kill. Equally trust in the retailer was controlled for an yielded no impact on the adoption of PETs.

Table 4. Regression analyses: Divers for preferring the kill-function over a complex PET*

	Study ①								Study ②			
PET scenario	**User PET**				**Agent PET**				**User PET**			
Dependent Variable	Rather kill or rather use a PET scheme? (11-point scale: 1=kill, 11=PET)											
			Mean	**SD**			**Mean**	**SD**			**Mean**	**SD**
			4,03	3,15			3,31	2,55			4	3,13
Adjusted R² →			.476				.396				.411	
Independent Variables ↓	no of items	α	ß	Sig.	no of items	α	ß	Sig.	no of items	α	ß	Sig.
Constant			3,963				3,285				3.991	
Peer Opinion	2	.740	.145	.194	2	.468	**.438**	**.003**	2	-	-	-
Ease of use of RFID	3	.880	.238	.068	3	.785	.220	.255	3	.816	(-).010	.902
Usefulness of RFID	9	.929	**.323**	**.005**	9	.878	.036	.824	9	.886	**.413**	**.000**
Ease of use of PET	3	.881	(-).176	.164	3	.915	(-).082	.647	3	.809	.036	.629
Information PET	3	.837	(-)**.335**	**.004**	3	.836	.144	.224	4	.773	**.146**	**.027**
Helplessness PET	2	.650	(-)**.218**	**.019**	2	.579	(-)**.347**	**.007**	4	.729	(-)**.210**	**.003**
Attitude new technologies	-	-	-	-	-	-	-	-	4	.569	.001	.990
Technical Affinity	-	-	-	-	-	-	-	-	3	.798	.076	.220
Privacy Profile Aware	-	-	-	-	-	-	-	-	6	.877	.038	.513
Privacy Identity Aware	-	-	-	-	-	-	-	-	4	.821	.049	.384

The results suggest that in contrast to hypothesis 5 the two RFID PETs are not judged upon by a common set of acceptance factors. Depending on the PETs' interaction design different adoption parameters are determinative for preferring it over the kill option. Equally, hypothesis 6 can only be partially confirmed. Privacy awareness and general attitudes toward technology do not seem to be determinative for preferring one or another PET.

4.2 Qualitative Evaluation of PET Solutions

A final step in the analysis of PET perception was an attempt to understand why the large majority of participants generally prefer to kill RFID chips at store exits and what drives a smaller portion of users to instead opt for a more complex PET. In order to investigate this issue, participants in study ② were asked to explain their judgment for or against the User PET vis-à-vis the kill option. Explanations were given in a free text format (open question) by 175 out of the 208 participants in the User PET study. The author analyzed the reasoning for preferring a complex PET or rather killing tags with the help of a content analysis [30]. Each answer typically had one main *theme* (reason) for why a participant would judge for the User PET or rather favour the killing of RFID tags. These reasons are summarized in table 5.

Table 5. Main themes for participants when opting for a User PET or instead kill tags

Reasons given for Preferring Kill Function over User PET (or vice versa)	Kill (1-4)	Neutral (7-5)	User PET (11-8)
	108	32	35
	62%	18%	20%
mistrust "security" of password scheme	27	6	1
feeling to still be "recognized" somehow	17	0	0
unspecified "misuse"	15	0	0
maximum protection through kill	9	0	0
desire to not be controlled/feel in "control"	8	1	0
uncertainty towards any privacy solution	0	9	1
TRUST related reasons against User PET	*76 (70%)*		
consequences for society	23	2	0
other	6	0	1
transaction cost of the password scheme	3	1	0
lost RFID benefit	0	11	16
appreciation of the PET	0	1	8
transaction cost to kill	0	1	5
unconcerned	0	0	1
passive resignation	0	0	2

175 out of the 208 participants who viewed the User PET scenario in study 2 (84%) gave a reason for why they rather preferred the kill function over the User PET or vice versa. Out of the 108 (62%) participants who were in favour of killing RFID tags 70% described some feeling of mistrust in the password PET. They expressed their belief that passwords could be "hacked" or that "security" is generally weak. They also feared some unspecified "misuse" or that they would still be recognized or scanned somehow. These findings clearly hint to the importance of security visibility when engineering RFID PETs. The second largest group of those who want to rather kill RFID tags (21%) are people who seem to base their judgements on the consequences of RFID they fear for themselves and for society at large. They mention "privacy" and "data protection", but also express rejection of marketing practices, surveillance ("Big Brother") and the course of a "chipped" society.

Subjects which were in favour of using the User PET mostly based their decision on the fact that they appreciated RFID benefits and liked the idea to have a "choice". Some participants (18%) finally were stuck in the middle in seeing RFID benefits on one side, but equally mistrusting the PET solution.

5   Discussion, Conclusions and Limitations

The main finding of the presented research is that complex PETs as they are envisioned today by many UbiComp privacy researchers are highly likely to run into acceptance problems with users. The majority of consumers seem to want to kill RFID chips at store exits rather than using any of the complex technical solutions presented to them. This is the case even though the films suggested high ease of use and seamless privacy management. The desire to kill RFID tags is *not* due to the fact that consumers do not comprehend or value the benefits of RFID services (as is often argued by industry today). In contrast, consumers do value the service spectrum which can be realized through RFID. But they are willing to forgo these benefits in order to protect their privacy. This highlights the importance of the topic of privacy for the UbiComp research community.

Content analysis suggests that what users are looking for are highly trustworthy and straight forward solutions to privacy. Solutions that leave no room for speculation about security levels as passwords may be hacked or network protocols may be intransparent. Instead signalling security and trust to users through respective interface design may be very relevant for privacy engineering in UbiComp.

A further finding of the study is that the User Scheme does not seem to be superior to the Agent Scheme. Despite user initiation of network communication the PET does not induce higher levels of perceived control. However, the results from regression analyses suggest that User Scheme appreciation can be improved by working on the PET itself: Information control provided through the User PET seems to directly influence its appreciation. Thus, if users have the impression that they have a direct choice in a context to activate chips on an informed basis then they are also more likely to prefer the User PET over the kill option. Content analysis furthermore revealed that information provided here should include reassuring messages about the security level achieved by the PET. Therefore, research in security visibility as currently driven by the W3C may be of high interest in the UbiComp community [31].

In contrast, Agent PETs do not seem to be based on the same dynamics. If network agents organize users' privacy in a largely autonomous way, then people seem to rely more on the recommendations of peers when deciding not to kill. If peers say that RFID is fine to use, then trust which is placed in the Agent PET seems to increase.

A limitation of the present research is that it only showed one type of User PET which was based on passwords. People often attribute problems to passwords, both in handling them and in terms of security [32]. Different results may have been obtained if the User Scheme film had shown, for example, biometrics as the authentication mechanism. Thus, the empirical investigation presented here is really only viable for the concrete technological scenarios shown to the participants and not sufficient to deduct conclusions about user initiated communications in general. More research is needed for generalize the findings.

Furthermore, film scenarios may bear the methodological risk of bias. We made an effort to minimize bias and controlled for the neutrality of the film material. Yet, we can hardly measure how strongly people were impacted by the sole mentioning of privacy issues. Privacy is a subject of prime importance to Germans and it may be that this cultural background has led to stronger results in favour of killing RFID chips than may be the result if the study was replicated in other cultures. Furthermore, it is well known that behavioural intentions as expressed in such surveys, even though being strong indicators for actions taken cannot be equalized with actual behavior [28, 33, 34] (mean correlations are around .53 according to [35]).

An advantage of using film scenarios is the wide spectrum of services that can be shown as well as the visualization of service and protection alternatives. Drawbacks of usability studies with real prototypes can be avoided in this way. For example, malfunctioning of prototypes, difficulties of use, very small sample sizes, etc. The methodological approach taken in the studies presented here therefore is new. Yet, it may be interesting for UbiComp researchers in general, because they have to envision what exactly their applications will look like to future users and test alternatives in advance. In this way potential acceptance problems may be detected and corrected early in the development cycle.

References

1. Fusaro, R.: None of Our Business. Harvard Business Review, 33–44 (2004)
2. Smith, J.H., Milberg, J., Burke, S.: Information Privacy: Measuring Individuals' Concerns About Organizational Practices. MIS Quarterly 20(2), 167–196 (1996)
3. Jannasch, U., Spiekermann, S.: RFID: Technologie im Einzelhandel der Zukunft: Datenentstehung, Marketing Potentiale und Auswirkungen auf die Privatheit des Kunden, Lehrstuhl für Wirtschaftsinformatik, Humboldt Universität zu Berlin: Berlin (2004)
4. Berthold, O., Guenther, Spiekermann, S.: RFID Verbraucherängste und Verbraucherschutz. Wirtschaftsinformatik, Heft 6 (2005)
5. FoeBuD e.V. (ed.): Positionspapier über den Gebrauch von RFID auf und in Konsumgütern, FoeBuD e.V.: Bielefeld (2003)
6. Duce, H.: Public Policy: Understanding Public Opinion, A.-I. Center, Massachusetts Institute of Technology. MIT, Cambridge, USA (2003)
7. Auto-ID Center (ed.): 860 MHz – 930 MHz Class 1 Radio Frequency (RF) Identification Tag Radio Frequency & Logical Communication Interface Specification, EPCGlobal, Cambridge, Massachusetts, USA (2004)

8. Sarma, S., Weis, S., Engels, D.: RFID Systems, Security & Privacy Implications, A.-I. Center. Massachusetts Institute of Technology. MIT, Cambridge, USA (2002)
9. Auto-ID Center, (ed.): Technology Guide. Massachusetts Institute of Technology, MIT, Cambridge, USA (2002)
10. GCI (ed.): Global Commerce Initiative EPC Roadmap, G.C. Initiative and IBM (2003)
11. Auto-ID Center, (ed.): EPC-256: The 256-bit Electronic Product Code Representation. Massachusetts Institute of Technology, MIT, Cambridge, USA (2003)
12. Auto-ID Center, (ed.): EPC Information Service - Data Model and Queries. Massachusetts Institute of Technology, MIT, Cambridge, USA (2003)
13. Auto-ID Center, (ed.): Auto-ID Object Name Service (ONS) 1.0. Massachusetts Institute of Technology, MIT, Cambridge, USA (2003)
14. Engels, D.: Security and Privacy Aspects of Low-Cost Radio Frequency Identification Systems. In: Hutter, D., Müller, G., Stephan, W., Ullmann, M. (eds.) Security in Pervasive Computing. LNCS, vol. 2802, Springer, Heidelberg (2004)
15. Engberg, S., Harning, M., Damsgaard, C.: Zero-knowledge Device Authentication: Privacy & Security Enhanced RFID preserving Business Value and Consumer Convenience. In: Proceedings of the Second Annual Conference on Privacy, Security and Trust, New Brunswick, Canada (2004)
16. Spiekermann, S., Berthold, O.: Maintaining privacy in RFID enabled environments - Proposal for a disable-model. In: Robinson, P., Vogt, H. (eds.) Privacy, Security and Trust within the Context of Pervasive Computing, Springer Verlag, Vienna, Austria (2004)
17. Inoue, Y.: RFID Privacy Using User-controllable Uniqueness. In: Proceedings of the RFID Privacy Workshop, Massachusetts Institute of Technology, MIT, Cambridge, MA, USA (2004)
18. Floerkemeier, C., Schneider, R., Langheinrich, M.: Scanning with a Purpose - Supporting the Fair Information Principles in RFID Protocols. In: Murakami, H., Nakashima, H., Tokuda, H., Yasumura, M. (eds.) UCS 2004. LNCS, vol. 3598, Springer, Heidelberg (2005)
19. Langheinrich, M.: A Privacy Awareness System for Ubiquitous Computing Environments. In: Borriello, G., Holmquist, L.E. (eds.) UbiComp 2002. LNCS, vol. 2498, Springer, Heidelberg (2002)
20. Christian, M., Floerkemeier, C.: Making Radio Frequency Identification Visible – A Watchdog Tag. In: Proceedings of the 5th Annual IEEE International Conference on Pervasive Computing and Communications, New York (2007)
21. Stajano, F.: Security for Ubiquitous Computing. John Wiley & Sons, Chichester, UK (2002)
22. Platform for Privacy Preferences (P3P) Project, W3C (2006)
23. Juels, A., Rivest, R., Szydlo, M.: The Blocker Tag: Selective Blocking of RFID Tags for Consumer Privacy. In: Proceedings of the 10th Annual ACM CCS, ACM Press, New York (2003)
24. Karjoth, G., Moskowitz, P.A.: Disabling RFID Tags with Visible Confirmation: Clipped Tags are Silenced. In: Proceedings of the ACM Workshop on Privacy in the Electronic Society, ACM Press, Alexandria, VA, USA (2005)
25. Spiekermann, S.: Perceived Control: Scales for Privacy in Ubiquitous Computing. In: Acquisti, A., De Capitani di Vimercati, S., Gritzalis, S., Lambrinoudakis, C. (eds.) Digital Privacy: Theory, Technologies and Practices, Taylor and Francis, New York (2007)
26. Fishbein, M., Ajzen, I.: Belief, Attitude, Intention and Behavior: An Introduction to Theory and Research. Addison-Wesley, Reading, MA, USA (1975)

27. Ajzen, I.: From intentions to actions: A theory of planne behavior. In: Kuhi, J., Beckmann, J. (eds.) Action - control: From cognition to behavior, pp. 11–39. Springer, Heidelberg (1985)

28. Ajzen, I., Fishbein, M.: The Influence of Attitudes on Behavir. In: Albarracin, D., Johnson, B.T., Zanna, M.P. (eds.) The Handbook of Attitudes on Behavior, pp. 173–221. Erlbaum, Mahwah, New York (2005)

29. Rogers, E.: Diffusion of Innovations. The Free Press, New York (1995)

30. Kassarjian, H.H.: Content Analysis in Consumer Research. Journal of Consumer Research 4(1), 8–18 (1977)

31. W3C, (ed.): Web Security Experience, Indicators and Trust: Scope and Use Cases, W3C Working Draft (25 May 2007)

32. Adams, A., Sasse, A.: Users are not the enemy - Why users compromise computer security mechanisms and how to take remedial measures. Communications of the ACM 42(12), 40–46 (1999)

33. Berendt, B., Guenther, O., Spiekermann, S.: Privacy in E-Commerce: Stated Preferences vs. Actual Behavior. Communications of the ACM 48(4) (2005)

34. Sheeran, P.: Intention-behavior relations: A conceptual and empirical review. In: Stroebe, W., Hewstone, M. (eds.) European Review of Social Psychology, pp. 1–36. Wiley, Chichester, UK (2002)

35. Trafimow, D.: Evidence that perceived behavioural control is a multidimensional construct: Perceived control and perceived difficulty. British Journal of Social Psychology 41, 101–121 (2002)

Ninja: Non Identity Based, Privacy Preserving Authentication for Ubiquitous Environments

Adrian Leung* and Chris J. Mitchell

Information Security Group
Royal Holloway, University of London
Egham, Surrey, TW20 0EX, UK
{A.Leung,C.Mitchell}@rhul.ac.uk

Abstract. Most of today's authentication schemes involve verifying the identity of a principal in some way. This process is commonly known as entity authentication. In emerging ubiquitous computing paradigms which are highly dynamic and mobile in nature, entity authentication may not be sufficient or even appropriate, especially if a principal's privacy is to be protected. In order to preserve privacy, other attributes (e.g. location or trustworthiness) of the principal may need to be authenticated to a verifier. In this paper we propose Ninja: a non-identity-based authentication scheme for a mobile ubiquitous environment, in which the trustworthiness of a user's device is authenticated anonymously to a remote Service Provider (verifier), during the service discovery process. We show how this can be achieved using Trusted Computing functionality.

Keywords: Security, Privacy, Ubiquitous, Trusted Computing.

1 Introduction

In the Mobile VCE[1] Core 4 research programme on Ubiquitous Services, it is envisaged that in a mobile ubiquitous environment (as shown in figure 1), users (through one of their mobile devices and via some network access technologies) will be able to seamlessly discover, select, and access a rich offering of services and content from a range of service providers. To realise this vision, security and privacy issues must be addressed from the outset, alongside other technological innovations. Only if users are confident that their security and privacy will not be compromised, will we see the widespread adoption of ubiquitous services.

As shown in figure 1, one of the primary aims for a user is to access the various services that are offered. But, before any services can be accessed and consumed, they must first be located via a process known as service discovery. Many service discovery schemes [1,2,3] have recently been proposed for ubiquitous environments, but few [4,5] have addressed security and privacy issues,

---

* This author is supported by the British Chevening/Royal Holloway Scholarship, and in part by the European Commission under contract IST-2002-507932 (ECRYPT).

[1] http://www.mobilevce.com/

J. Krumm et al. (Eds.): UbiComp 2007, LNCS 4717, pp. 73–90, 2007.

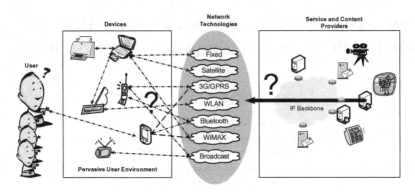

Fig. 1. A Ubiquitous Computing Environment

despite their fundamental importance. It is imperative that the process of service discovery is conducted in a secure and private way, in order to protect the security and privacy of both users and service providers. One fundamental security requirement is mutual authentication between a user and service provider.

Authentication is important for several reasons. Firstly, it is a basic security service upon which a range of other security services (e.g. authorisation) can be built. Secondly, it gives users and service providers assurance that they are indeed interacting with the intended parties, and not some malicious entities. Unfortunately, conventional entity authentication [6] may not be adequate for a ubiquitous environment [7], because an identity may be meaningless in such a setting. Instead, other user attributes [7] may need to be authenticated to a service provider. Furthermore, consumers are becoming increasingly concerned about their privacy [8,9], and the potential risks (such as identity theft) of leaving any form of digital trail when making electronic transactions. Given a choice, users may prefer to interact with service providers anonymously (or pseudonymously). Under these circumstances, it may in fact be undesirable to authenticate the identity of a user. Preserving user privacy can be particularly challenging in a ubiquitous environment [10,11], and if privacy is preserved (through user anonymity), how can we then convince a service provider that an anonymous user is trustworthy? This is the challenge addressed in this paper.

We thus propose Ninja: a non-identity based, privacy preserving, mutual authentication scheme designed to address the service discovery security and privacy challenges in a mobile ubiquitous environment. During service discovery, a service user and service provider are mutually authenticated, whilst preserving the privacy of a user. Instead of authenticating the user identity to a service provider, the user's trustworthiness is authenticated. Our scheme employs two key functionalities of Trusted Computing (TC) technology [12,13], namely, the Integrity Measurement, Storage and Reporting Mechanism, and the Direct Anonymous Attestation Protocol. We therefore implicitly assume that a user device is equipped with TC functionality; current trends suggest that this is a reasonable assumption for the near future. Ninja is an application layer solution, and possesses many desirable security and privacy properties, such as: user anonymity, service information confidentiality, unlinkability, and rogue blacklisting.

The remainder of the paper is organised as follows. In section 2, we discuss various service discovery security and privacy issues. Section 3 describes the relevant Trusted Computing functionality. In section 4, we present the Ninja authentication scheme, and in section 5 analyse its security. In the penultimate section, we discuss related work, and finally, conclusions are drawn in section 7.

2   Service Discovery Security and Privacy Issues

In this section, we focus on the security and privacy issues arising from the service discovery process in a ubiquitous computing environment.

2.1   Adversary Model

Service discovery typically involves interactions between a user, the user's device, a service provider, and at times, a trusted third party. Unfortunately, these entities may be malicious, and pose a variety of threats to the service discovery process and to the participating entities. Against this backdrop, we identify eight adversary settings, covering both active and passive adversaries. They are:

1. **Innocent User with Malicious Device (IUMD).** Unbeknownst to a user, his/her device is compromised (e.g. with malware, keystroke-logger, etc).
2. **Malicious User with Trustworthy Device (MUTD).** A malicious user who has taken physical control of (e.g. stolen) another entity's device.
3. **Malicious User with Malicious Device (MUMD).** The combination of IUMD and MUTD.
4. **Malicious Service Provider(s) (MSP).** A MSP's main motive is to masquerade to a user as a legitimate service provider.
5. **Curious Service Provider(s) (CSP).** A CSP is not malicious, but seeks only to learn more about the behaviour of its users.
6. **Malicious Man-in-the-Middle (MitM).** A MitM's actions are intended to disrupt the proper operation of the service discovery process.
7. **Curious Trusted Third Party (CTTP).** A CTTP performs its role correctly, but also seeks to learn about the activities and habits of a user.
8. **Passive Eavesdropper (PE).** A PE does not disrupt the communication, but monitors it to learn the content and the entities involved.

2.2   Security and Privacy Threat Model

We now consider possible service discovery threats. We also consider what threats are posed by each of the above adversarial settings, and present them in a Threats versus Adversary Matrix (in Table 1). The service discovery threats are:

1. **Spoofing.** A malicious entity may masquerade as a legitimate service provider or service user either by sending false service advertisements/requests, through replay, or by man-in-the-middle attacks.

2. **Information Disclosure**
   (a) **User's Personally Identifiable Information (PII).** During the process of service discovery, a user's PII, such as his/her identity (e.g. in the form of a long lived key) or physical location, may be revealed (either willingly or unwillingly) to a service provider or passive eavesdropper.
   (b) **Service Information (SI).** By observing the service information exchanged by a user and service provider (e.g. the service request types), a passive adversary may build up a profile of the user. This information may later be used to predict future patterns and habits of the user. The privacy of the user is potentially compromised as a result.
3. **Profile Linking.** Colluding service providers may buy, sell or exchange information about their users or customers. This could not only provide service providers with monetary benefits, but also enhance their business intelligence and gain competitive advantage, e.g. if they are able to build more comprehensive user profiles (with or without their permission). Finally, the consequences for user privacy could be even more serious if a trusted third party colludes with service providers.
4. **Encouragement of Rogue Behaviour.** With the knowledge that privacy enhancing technologies are employed to protect their identities, users may be tempted to "misbehave" or act maliciously, since it may be difficult or even impossible for service providers to determine who is misbehaving.

Table 1. Threats and Adversary Matrix

Threats vs Adversary	IUMD	MUTD	MUMD	MSP	CSP	MitM	CTTP	PE
Spoofing	✓	✓	✓	✓		✓		
User Identity Disclosure	✓	✓	✓	✓	✓	✓	✓	✓
SI Disclosure	✓		✓		✓	✓		✓
User Profile Linking					✓	✓	✓	
Rogue Behaviour Denial	✓		✓					

2.3 Specific Security and Privacy Requirements

From the above threat analysis, we derive the corresponding security and privacy requirements:

- **Mutual Authentication.** This is one of the most important requirements, as it can prevent spoofing (by malicious users or service providers). The mutual authentication scheme should also be designed to prevent replay and man-in-the-middle attacks. To protect privacy, a user may want to remain anonymous to a service provider. So, instead of authenticating his identity to a service provider, the user may want to somehow prove or authenticate his "trustworthiness" to the service provider.
- **User Anonymity.** Unique user identifying information (e.g. an identifier or a long lived key) should not be divulged to a service provider during service discovery. A user may interact with service providers using a pseudonym.

- **Service Information Confidentiality.** To further preserve the privacy of the user, service information originating from the user may be encrypted.
- **Unlinkability.** Colluding service providers should not be able to link the activities of a user. Similarly, when a trusted third party colludes with a service provider, they should not be able to correlate the actions of a particular user. In other words, it should be impossible for colluding service providers to tell if two sets of prior service transactions (made with different providers) involved the same or different user(s).
- **Transaction Linkability/History.** For billing or other purposes, it may be necessary for a service provider to maintain the transaction histories of its users. A service provider may thus need to be able to determine whether a particular user is a repeat user (and, if so, which one) or a first time user, whilst still being unable to determine the unique identity of the user. This is not always a requirement, and providing it may require user consent.
- **Rogue Blacklisting.** Service providers should be able to identify and blacklist malicious and untrustworthy hosts.

2.4 Challenges

We therefore need to devise a mutual authentication scheme that meets all these requirements. This is particularly challenging for several reasons. Conventional mutual authentication schemes normally require the user identity to be authenticated to a verifier. But here, user privacy is a priority, and so user anonymity is required during authentication. How then can we convince a service provider that an anonymous user is trustworthy? Also, if user anonymity is provided, can we detect malicious or illegitimate users? We are, in fact, trying to achieve security and privacy concurrently, whilst protecting the interests of both users and service providers. This is the challenge addressed here.

Our scheme, Ninja, allows a user to authenticate the service provider, whilst simultaneously allowing a service provider to anonymously authenticate a user's trustworthiness. The scheme is so called because the process is to some extent analogous to the process of a ninja assassinating a person in Japanese folklore[2].

3   Trusted Computing Overview

Trusted Computing, as developed by the Trusted Computing Group[3] (TCG), is a technology designed to enhance the security of computing platforms. It involves incorporating trusted hardware functionality, or so called "roots of trust", into platforms. Users can thereby gain greater assurance that a platform is behaving in the expected manner [12,13,14]. The trusted hardware, in the form of

---

[2] A ninja is asked to assassinate someone (Bob) whom he has never met; he is only given Bob's photograph. When they meet, the ninja authenticates Bob physically. Bob, on seeing a ninja with a sword, knows (trusts) that the ninja wishes to kill him, but does not need to know the ninja's real identity, whose anonymity is preserved.

[3] http://www.trustedcomputinggroup.org/

a hardware component called the Trusted Platform Module (TPM), is built into a host platform. The TPM provides the platform with a foundation of trust, as well as the basis on which a suite of Trusted Computing security functionalities is built. The TPM and its host are collectively referred to as a *Trusted Platform*.

We next introduce the keys used by a TPM, as well as the Trusted Computing functionality used in our scheme, i.e. the Integrity Measurement, Storage and Reporting Mechanisms, and the Direct Anonymous Attestation (DAA) Protocol. The descriptions below are based upon v1.2 of the TCG TPM specifications [14].

3.1   TPM Keys and Identities

Each TPM has a unique 2048-bit RSA key pair called the *Endorsement Key* (EK). The EK is likely to be generated by the TPM manufacturer, and the EK private key, together with a certificate for the corresponding public key, can be used to prove that a genuine TPM is contained in a platform. However, since a TPM only has one such key pair, a TPM can be uniquely identified by its EK.

The EK is therefore only used in special circumstances. A TPM can, however, generate an arbitrary number of 2048-bit RSA *Attestation Identity Key* (AIK) key pairs, which are used for interacting with other entities. AIKs function as pseudonyms for a trusted platform, and platform privacy can be achieved by using a different AIK to interact with different entities. In order to prove that a particular AIK originates from a genuine TPM, a platform has to prove that the AIK public key is associated with a genuine trusted platform; this involves using the EK with a trusted third party in such a way that the AIK cannot be linked to a particular EK, even by the trusted third party that sees the EK public key. The DAA protocol (discussed in Section 3.3) is used to support this process.

3.2   Integrity Measurement, Storage and Reporting

Integrity Measurement, Storage and Reporting (IMSR) is a key feature of Trusted Computing that builds on the three Roots of Trust in a trusted platform: a *root of trust for measurement* (RTM), a *root of trust for storage* (RTS), and a *root of trust for reporting* (RTR). Together, they allow a verifier to learn the operational state of a platform, and hence obtain evidence of a platform's behaviour. This functionality is extremely important, as a platform may potentially enter a wide range of operational states, including insecure and undesirable states.

Integrity Measurement. Integrity measurement involves the RTM, a computing engine in the TPM, measuring a platform's operational state and characteristics. The measured values, known as integrity metrics, convey information about the platform's current state (and hence trustworthiness).

Integrity Storage. Details of exactly what measurements have been performed are stored in a file called the *Stored Measurement Log* (SML). Using the RTS, a digest (i.e. a cryptographic hash computed using Secure Hash Algorithm 1 (SHA-1) [15]) of the integrity metrics is saved in one of the TPM's internal registers, called *Platform Configuration Registers* (PCRs). The SML contains the sequence of all measured events, and each sequence shares a common measurement digest. Since an SML may become fairly large, it does not reside in the TPM. Integrity protection for the SML is not necessary, since it functions as a means to interpret the integrity measurements in the PCRs, and any modifications to the SML will cause subsequent PCR verifications to fail.

There are only a limited number of PCRs in the TPM. So, in order to ensure that previous and related measured values are not ignored/discarded, and the order of operations is preserved, new measurements are appended to a previous measurement digest, re-hashed, and then put back into the relevant PCR. This technique is known as *extending* the digest, and operates as follows:

$$PCR_i[n] \leftarrow SHA\text{-}1(PCR_{i-1}[n] \,||\, \text{New integrity metric}),$$

where $PCR_i[n]$ denotes the content of the nth PCR after i extension operations, and $||$ denotes the concatenation of two messages.

Integrity Reporting. The final phase of the IMSR process is Integrity Reporting. The RTR has two main responsibilities during Integrity Reporting:

1. to retrieve and provide a challenger with the requested integrity metrics (i.e. the relevant part of the SML, and the corresponding PCR values); and
2. to *attest to* (prove) the authenticity of the integrity metrics to a challenger by signing the PCR values using one of the TPM's AIK private keys.

To verify the integrity measurements, the verifier computes the measurement digest (using the relevant portion of the SML), compares it with the corresponding PCR values, and checks the signature on the PCR values. The process of integrity reporting is also often referred to as *Attestation*.

3.3   Direct Anonymous Attestation

Direct Anonymous Attestation (DAA) [16,13] is a special type of signature scheme that can be used to anonymously authenticate a TCG v1.2 compliant platform to a remote verifier. The key feature that DAA provides is the capability for a TPM (a prover) to convince a remote verifier that:

- it is indeed a genuine TPM (and hence it will behave in a trustworthy manner) without revealing any unique identifiers;
- an AIK public key is held by a TPM, without allowing colluding verifiers to link transactions involving different AIKs from the same platform.

The above-mentioned features help to protect the privacy of a TPM user. Another important feature of DAA is that the powers of the supporting Trusted Third Party (DAA Issuer) are minimised, as it cannot link the actions of users (even when it colludes with a verifier), and hence compromise the user's privacy.

DAA allows a prover to anonymously convince a remote verifier that it has obtained an anonymous attestation credential, or DAA Certificate (a Camenisch-Lysyanskaya (CL) signature [17]), from a specific DAA Issuer (Attester). The

DAA Certificate also serves to provide the implicit "link" between an EK and an AIK. The DAA scheme is made up of two sub-protocols: *DAA Join* and *DAA Sign*. We now provide a simplified description of these two sub-protocols [16].

DAA Join Protocol. The Join protocol enables the TPM to obtain a DAA Certificate (also known as an anonymous attestation credential) from the DAA Issuer. The Join protocol is based on the CL signature scheme [17].

Let (n, S, Z, R) be the DAA Issuer public key, where n is an RSA modulus, and S, Z, and R are integers modulo n. We assume that the platform (TPM) is already authenticated to the DAA Issuer via its Endorsement Key, EK.

The platform (TPM) first generates a DAA secret value f, and makes a commitment to f by computing $U = R^f S^{v'} \bmod n$, where v' is a value chosen randomly to "blind" f. The platform (TPM) also computes $N_I = \zeta_I^f \bmod \Gamma$, where ζ_I is derived from the DAA Issuer's name, and Γ is a large prime. The platform (TPM) then sends (U, N_I) to the DAA Issuer, and convinces the DAA Issuer that U and N_I are correctly formed (using a zero knowledge proof [18,19]). If the DAA Issuer accepts the proof, it will sign the hidden message U, by computing $A = (\frac{Z}{US^{v''}})^{1/e} \bmod n$, where v'' is a random integer, and e is a random prime. The DAA Issuer then sends the platform (i.e. the TPM) the triple (A, e, v''), and proves that A was computed correctly. The DAA Certificate is then $(A, e, v = v' + v'')$.

DAA Sign Protocol. The Sign protocol allows a platform to prove to a verifier that it is in possession of a DAA Certificate, and at the same time, to sign and authenticate a message. The platform signs a message m using its DAA Secret f, its DAA Certificate, and the public parameters of the system. The message m may be an Attestation Identity Key (AIK) generated by the TPM, or an arbitrary message. The platform also computes $N_V = \zeta^f \bmod \Gamma$ as part of the signature computation (the selection of ζ will be discussed in the next section). The output of the Sign protocol is known as the DAA Signature, σ.

The verifier verifies the DAA Signature σ, and on successful verification of σ, is convinced that:

1. the platform has a DAA Certificate (A, e, v) from a specific DAA Issuer, and hence it is a genuine TPM containing a legitimate EK; this is accomplished by a zero-knowledge proof of knowledge of a set of values f, A, e, and v such that $A^e R^f S^v \equiv Z \pmod{n}$;
2. a message m was signed by the TPM using its DAA secret f, where f is the same as the value in the DAA Certificate (used in step 1); if m includes an AIK public key, then the AIK originates from a genuine TPM.

In summary, once a platform (TPM) has obtained a DAA Certificate (which only needs to be done once), it is able to subsequently DAA-Sign as many AIKs as its wishes, without involving the DAA Issuer.

Variable Anonymity. Anonymity and unlinkability are provided to a user by using two parameters: ζ, also referred to as the *Base*, and the AIK. The choice of the base directly affects the degree of anonymity afforded to a TPM user. If perfect anonymity is desired, then a different, random, base value should be used for every interaction with a verifier. Conversely, if the same base value is used for every interaction with a verifier, then the verifier can identify that this is the same TPM. In addition, if the same base value is used to interact with different verifiers, then they are able to correlate the activities of a particular TPM. (A more detailed discussion of the effects of choices of base values is given in [20]).

As discussed in Section 3.1, a TPM is capable of generating multiple platform identities, simply by generating different AIK key pairs. Different AIKs may therefore be used to interact with different verifiers so as to remain unlinkable (provided the base is different).

4   The Ninja Authentication Scheme

In this section, we present the Ninja authentication scheme, designed to mutually authenticate a user (via his platform) and a service provider, whilst preserving the privacy of the user. The Ninja scheme is intended to be used during the service discovery process, immediately prior to service provisioning. It is designed to meet all the security and privacy requirements set out in Section 2.3.

First, we introduce the entities participating in the protocol. Next, we state the assumptions upon which the scheme is based. Finally, we describe the operation of the scheme.

4.1   The Entities

The entities involved in the protocol are as follows.

- The **Service User**, often a human, is the end consumer of a service.
- The trusted platform, or **Platform** in short, is the device which a service user will use to interact with other entities.
- The **DAA Issuer** issues DAA Certificates to legitimate platforms.
- The **Service Provider** is an entity that provides service(s) or content (e.g. music, videos, podcasts) to service users (via the platform). A service provider also acts as the verifier of a platform's DAA Signatures.

4.2   Assumptions

The correct working of the scheme relies on a number of assumptions.

- The service user is already authenticated to the platform.
- The platform running the Ninja protocol is equipped with TC functionality conforming to v1.2 of the TCG specifications [14].
- Service users only obtain DAA Certificates from trustworthy DAA Issuers (i.e. those that use the same public key for a very large set of users) [21].

- Each service provider possesses one or more X.509 v3 [22] public key certificates, issued by trustworthy Certification Authorities (CAs). The platform is equipped with the root certificates of these trusted CAs, and is capable of periodically receiving Certificate Revocation List (CRL) updates.
- Service users and service providers have loosely synchronised clocks (e.g. within an hour of each other). This enables service users and service providers to check that a service advertisement message or a service reply message is fresh (or recent enough).
- Service providers have set up system parameters, p and g, for the Diffie–Hellman (DH) key agreement protocol [23], prior to the protocol run. The (large) prime p is chosen such that $p-1$ has a large prime factor q (e.g. $p = 2q+1$), and g is chosen to have multiplicative order q, so that it generates a multiplicative subgroup of $\mathbb{Z}_p^*$ of prime order q.

Finally note that the scheme is independent of the underlying transport and network layer protocols, as it is purely an application layer solution.

4.3   The Scheme

Before describing the scheme, we first introduce some notation (see Table 2).

The Ninja scheme involves three distinct phases, the *Join Phase*, the *Mutual Authentication Phase*, and the *Verification Phase*, described below.

Join Phase. The *Join Phase* enables a platform to obtain a *DAA Certificate* from a *DAA Issuer*. The platform later uses this DAA Certificate, in the mutual

Table 2. Notation

Notation	Description
P	The Platform
SP	The Service Provider
I	The DAA Issuer
f	A non-migratable DAA secret value generated by the TPM
v', v'', e	DAA parameters (described in Section 3.2)
p, g	System parameters for DH–key agreement
$SrvAdv$	Service Advertisement Message
$SrvRep$	Service Reply Message
$SrvInfo$	Service Information
$AdvID$	An Advertisement ID number
t_A	A Timestamp generated by a principal, A
N	A Nonce (a random value)
ID_A	The identity of a principal, A
(EK_{pk}, EK_{sk})	The pair of Public and Private Endorsement Keys
(AIK_{pk}, AIK_{sk})	A pair of Public and Private Attestation Identity Keys
(PK_A, SK_A)	The Public and Private Key pair of a principal, A
$Cert_A$	An X.509 v3 Public Key Certificate for a principal, A
H	A cryptographic hash-function
$Enc_K(M)$	The encryption of a message, M, using the key K
$Dec_K(M)$	The decryption of a message, M, using the key K
$MAC_K(M)$	The message authentication code (MAC) of a message, M, computed using the key K
$Sig_K(M)$	A signature on a message, M, signed using the key K

authentication phase, to anonymously authenticate itself to a service provider. The entities involved are the *Platform*, *P*, and the *DAA Issuer*, *I*. Note that the Join Phase is identical to the DAA Join Protocol specified in [16]; it may have taken place before a device is shipped to the user. The sequence of events is as follows (see also figure 2).

1. The platform (TPM) generates its DAA Secret value f, and a random value v'. It computes U and N_I (as described in Section 3.3), and then sends U, N_I, and its Endorsement Public Key, EK_{pk} to the DAA Issuer.
2. To verify that U originates from the TPM in the platform that owns EK_{pk}, the DAA Issuer engages in a simple *Challenge-Response* protocol with the platform. It generates a random message m, and encrypts m using EK_{pk}. It sends the challenge, $Chl = Enc_{EK_{pk}}(m)$ to the platform.
3. If the platform owns EK_{pk}, it should have the corresponding EK_{sk}, and hence be able to decrypt $Enc_{EK_{pk}}(m)$, to retrieve m. The platform (TPM) then computes and sends the response $r = H(U||m)$ to the DAA Issuer.
4. The DAA Issuer computes $H(U||m)$ using the value of m it sent in step 2, and compares the result with the value of r received from the platform. If the two values agree, then the DAA Issuer is convinced that U originated from the TPM that owns EK_{pk}.
5. Finally, the DAA Issuer generates v'' and e, and then computes A (as described in Section 3.3). The DAA Issuer then sends (A, e, v'') to the platform.
6. The DAA Certificate is (A, e, v), where $v = v' + v''$. The DAA Issuer does not have full knowledge of the DAA Certificate, since the certificate was jointly created by the platform and the DAA Issuer. This property helps preserve the anonymity of the user/platform.

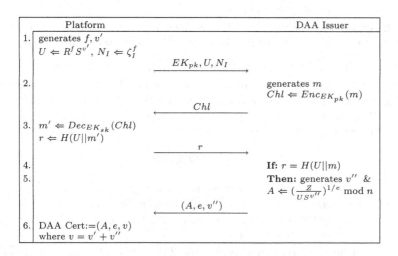

Fig. 2. Join Phase

Mutual Authentication Phase. Service discovery typically involves the exchange of service advertisement and service reply messages between the user and service provider. To avoid increasing the communication overheads, we incorporate the authentication mechanisms into these messages. In other words, service discovery and mutual authentication take place concurrently. We now examine how the messages are constructed to achieve our aim of mutual authentication.

The service provider, SP, initiates the service discovery and mutual authentication processes by constructing and sending an authenticated service advertisement message, as follows (also shown in figure 3).

1. SP generates a random number b and computes g^b mod p. These values are used later as part of a Diffie-Hellman key agreement protocol to establish a shared key with the user.
2. SP constructs the service advertisement message,

$$SrvAdv = (ID_{SP}, SrvInfo, AdvID, N, t_{sp}, g, p, g^b \bmod p).$$

3. SP signs $SrvAdv$, using its private key, SK_{SP}, and obtains the signature, $Sig_{SK_{SP}}(SrvAdv)$. SP then broadcasts $SrvAdv$, $Sig_{SK_{SP}}(SrvAdv)$, and $Cert_{SP}$ to the platforms of prospective service users:

$$SP \rightarrow \text{platforms} : SrvAdv, Sig_{SK_{SP}}(SrvAdv), Cert_{SP}.$$

Suppose that a prospective user receives the above service advertisement (via his platform), and is interested in the advertised service. The user's platform then authenticates the service provider by retrieving PK_{SP} from $Cert_{SP}$, and then using it to verify $Sig_{SK_{SP}}(SrvAdv)$, and checking to see if the timestamp is valid. If the verification outcome is satisfactory, then, at this point, the service provider is authenticated to the user.

Using the platform, the user now anonymously authenticates itself (i.e. its trustworthiness) to the service provider, as follows (see also Protocol 3).

1. The platform generates an AIK key pair (AIK_{pk}, AIK_{sk}).
2. The platform sends its SML and the corresponding PCR values to the service provider for validation. To further prove that the PCR values originate from the TPM, the TPM signs the PCR values (from $SrvAdv$), using AIK_{sk} (from step 1), to create:

$$Sig_{AIK_{sk}}(PCR\|N).$$

The Nonce N is included to prevent replay attacks.
3. The platform computes $\zeta = H(ID_{SP})$. It then creates a pseudonym, $N_v = \zeta^f$ (where f is the DAA Secret generated during the join phase) for use when interacting with the service provider.
4. To prove that the AIK (from steps 1 and 2) originates from a genuine TPM, the platform DAA-Signs AIK_{pk} using f, *DAA Certificate*, and the other public parameters of the system. The output is the DAA Signature σ (which also includes ζ and N_v).

5. To complete the Diffie-Hellman key agreement protocol, the platform generates a random number a, and computes:

$$g^a \bmod p \quad \text{and} \quad K = (g^b)^a \bmod p.$$

6. The platform constructs the Service Reply message as:

$$SrvRep = (AdvId, SrvInfo, AIK_{pk}, SML, Sig_{AIK_{sk}}(PCR\|N), \sigma, t_p).$$

7. The platform encrypts $SrvRep$ using the key K_1, and then computes a MAC of the encrypted $SrvRep$ using the key K_2, where $K = K_1\|K_2$, to give:

$$Enc_{K_1}(SrvRep) \quad \text{and} \quad MAC_{K_2}(Enc_{K_1}(SrvRep)).$$

8. The user sends $Enc_{K_1}(SrvRep)$, $MAC_{K_2}(Enc_{K_1}(SrvRep))$, and $g^a \bmod p$ to the service provider.

$$P \rightarrow SP : Enc_{K_1}(SrvRep), MAC_{K_2}(Enc_{K_1}(SrvRep)), g^a \bmod p.$$

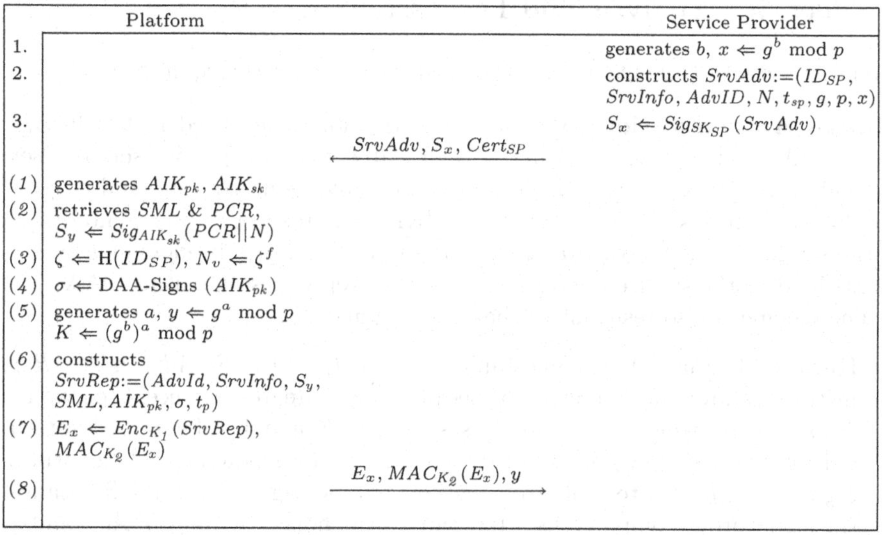

Platform	Service Provider
1.	generates b, $x \Leftarrow g^b \bmod p$
2.	constructs $SrvAdv:=(ID_{SP},$ $SrvInfo, AdvID, N, t_{sp}, g, p, x)$
3.	$S_x \Leftarrow Sig_{SK_{SP}}(SrvAdv)$
$\xleftarrow{\quad SrvAdv, S_x, Cert_{SP} \quad}$	
(1) generates AIK_{pk}, AIK_{sk}	
(2) retrieves SML & PCR, $S_y \Leftarrow Sig_{AIK_{sk}}(PCR\|N)$	
(3) $\zeta \Leftarrow H(ID_{SP})$, $N_v \Leftarrow \zeta^f$	
(4) $\sigma \Leftarrow$ DAA-Signs (AIK_{pk})	
(5) generates a, $y \Leftarrow g^a \bmod p$ $K \Leftarrow (g^b)^a \bmod p$	
(6) constructs $SrvRep:=(AdvId, SrvInfo, S_y,$ $SML, AIK_{pk}, \sigma, t_p)$	
(7) $E_x \Leftarrow Enc_{K_1}(SrvRep),$ $MAC_{K_2}(E_x)$	
(8) $\xrightarrow{\quad E_x, MAC_{K_2}(E_x), y \quad}$	

Fig. 3. Mutual Authentication Phase

Verification Phase. On receiving a service reply message from a platform, the service provider SP performs the following steps to verify its trustworthiness.

1. SP computes $K = (g^a)^b \bmod p$ and hence obtains K_1 and K_2 (where $K = K_1\|K_2$). SP then checks the integrity of the received value of $Enc_{K_1}(SrvRep)$ by recomputing the MAC using K_2 and comparing it with the received value.
2. SP extracts $SrvRep$ by decrypting $Enc_{K_1}(SrvRep)$ using K_1. SP also checks that the timestamp t_p extracted from $SrvRep$, is valid.

3. SP verifies the DAA Signature σ, and is thus convinced that the platform is in possession of a legitimate DAA Certificate from a specific DAA Issuer, which implies that a genuine TPM is contained in the platform.
4. SP is also convinced that AIK_{pk} was signed using the platform's DAA Secret f. Even though the value of f is never revealed to SP, SP knows that the value is related to a genuine DAA Certificate.
5. SP checks that the nonce N is the same as that sent in $SrvAdv$.
6. SP verifies the trustworthiness of the platform by examining the platform integrity measurements. This involves recursively hashing the values contained in the SML, and comparing them with the corresponding PCR values.
7. If SP is satisfied with the integrity measurements, then the platform (and hence the user) is authenticated to SP.

To authenticate to another service provider, the user platform should generate a new AIK key pair, but only needs to repeat the mutual authentication phase, i.e. it does not need to perform the join phase again. The user platform should also use a different N_v value.

5   Security Analysis and Discussion

We now assess the scheme against our security and privacy requirements.

Mutual Authentication. Mutual authentication is achieved in the following way. A service provider is first authenticated to a prospective service user through a service advertisement message, protected using conventional cryptographic mechanisms (e.g. as enabled by a PKI). If a prospective user is interested in the service, then the trustworthiness of the user platform is anonymously authenticated to the service provider via a service reply message, using DAA.

The scheme is also resistant to the following attacks.

- **Replay:** The use of the timestamps t_{sp} and t_p in the $SrvAdv$ and $SrvRep$ messages allows the recipients to check that they are fresh or recent (enough). An adversary which knows an old session key K may be able to decrypt an old $SrvRep$ message, and could try to use the corresponding old signature, $Sig_{AIK_{sk}}(PCR\|N)$, to reply to a new $SrvAdv$ message. This will fail because the signature is computed as a function of the nonce N from $SrvAdv$, and a replayed signature will have been computed using a different value of N.
- **Man-in-the-Middle (MitM):** Since $SrvAdv$ is authenticated, a MitM cannot masquerade as an SP to a user. A MitM can make a response on its own behalf (as can anyone receiving $SrvAdv$). However, a MitM cannot masquerade as a legitimate user by manipulating the $SrvRep$ message. If it tries to generate a $SrvRep$ with a different Diffie-Hellman parameter y, then it can only generate a completely new response, since it cannot decrypt a $SrvRep$ generated by another user. If it leaves y unchanged, then any modifications to $SrvRep$ will be detected by the service provider, since it is integrity protected using a MAC computed as a function of the Diffie-Hellman key.

User Anonymity. The public part of the Endorsement Key, EK_{pk}, is never disclosed to a service provider, since it would function as a permanent identifier for the platform. Users instead interact with service providers using AIKs, which act as pseudonyms. Since it is computationally infeasible for service providers, or even the DAA Issuer, to link two AIK public keys from the same platform (see Section 3.3), users will remain anonymous to service providers (e.g. CSPs), as well as curious DAA Issuers (i.e. CTTPs) and passive eavesdroppers.

Service Information (SI) Confidentiality. A *SrvRep* message contains service information which, if disclosed, could reveal a user's service preferences and habits, thereby compromising user privacy. To prevent such a disclosure (e.g. to eavesdroppers or a MitM), *SrvRep* is encrypted using a secret key known only to the service user and the service provider. Whilst there is nothing to prevent a MSP from divulging the SI of an anonymous user, the user's SI confidentiality is still preserved, as the MSP is unable to determine which SI corresponds to which user.

Unlinkability/Collusion Resistance. User platforms should interact with different SPs using different AIK public keys and N_v values. It is computationally infeasible for colluding service providers to link these keys (see Section 3.3), i.e. a user's service activities with different service providers are unlinkable. This remains true even in the case of a colluding DAA Issuer (i.e. a CTTP), again as discussed in Section 3.3. Our scheme is therefore resistant to two or more colluding SPs (the CSP case), as well as a DAA Issuer colluding with one or more SPs (the CTTP case).

Transaction History. For business reasons (e.g. to support customer loyalty rewards or discounts), it may be necessary for service providers to link a repeat service user. This can be achieved without compromising a user's privacy or anonymity if a service user always uses the same value of N_v to interact with a particular service provider. A service user will not need to store N_v, as it will be recovered during re-computation (since ζ and f should remain unchanged).

Blacklisting Malicious Parties. A detected rogue service provider can be added to the appropriate CRL, enabling users to avoid known fraudulent SPs. Similarly, an SP may want to blacklist a misbehaving or malicious user, to bar this user from future service interactions. This requires a means for the SP to recognise a malicious platform, whilst it remains anonymous. This can be achieved by blacklisting platform pseudonyms, i.e. the N_v values of such platforms. Blacklisting the AIK will not work, as a rogue user can simply generate a new AIK, DAA-Sign it, and then interact with the service provider again.

A rogue user could only avoid detection by obtaining a new pseudonym, N_v. This would involve using a new value for f (the DAA secret). Although a TPM could generate a new f value, it is unlikely that it will be able to obtain a DAA Certificate for it. DAA certificate issue is expected to be subject to careful checks, and a platform is not expected to possess more than one DAA Certificate from a DAA Issuer. Also, if a DAA Certificate (i.e. a triple of values A, e, v) and the value f are found in the public domain (e.g. on the Internet), then they should be sent to all potential service providers for blacklisting. The service providers can then add them to privately maintained lists of rogue keys.

6   Related Work

Apart from being unsuitable for ubiquitous computing environments [3], existing service discovery approaches (such as Java Jini [24], UPnP [25], SLP [26], DEAPspace [27] and Salutation [28]) do not address the privacy issues raised here. Zhu et al. describe a privacy preserving service discovery protocol [29,4], where users and service providers progressively reveal Personally Identifiable Information (PII) to each other. A user's PII is eventually divulged to a service provider, and so service providers could still collude and link user activities. Abadi and Fournet proposed a private authentication scheme [30], which protects two communicating principals' privacy (identity and location) from third parties. This only protects a user's PII against eavesdropping third parties, and not from the service providers. Ren et al.'s privacy preserving authentication scheme [31] uses blind signatures and hash chains to protect the privacy of service users. This scheme requires a mobile user and service to authenticate each other via some out of band mechanisms, prior to a privacy-preserving service interaction. This may not be a realistic approach for a mobile ubiquitous environment.

In the k-Times Anonymous Authentication scheme [32], a user can anonymously access a service a predetermined number of times (as decided by the service provider). This approach is extremely inflexible for a ubiquitous environment. For instance, a service provider cannot prevent a malicious user from having future service interactions. In the Chowdhury et al. Anonymous Authentication scheme [33], users interact with different service providers using different surrogates (one-time values) every time, to preserve user anonymity. However, the trusted 'Issuing Authority', can still link user activities. Similarly, in v1.1 of the TCG specifications [12,34], a user's activities are unlinkable by different service providers, but if the trusted 'Privacy CA' colludes with the service providers, then the activities of a user are linkable, and his/her privacy will hence be compromised. In the Ninja scheme, the trusted third party, i.e. the DAA Issuer, is unable to collude with service providers and link the activities of a user.

7   Conclusions

We identified security and privacy threats that may arise during service discovery in a ubiquitous computing environment; we also derived corresponding security and privacy requirements. We presented the Ninja mutual authentication scheme, using Trusted Computing functionality, which preserves user privacy. Apart from being communications-efficient (only two messages are required), the scheme also satisfies all the identified security requirements. To a service user and service provider, security and privacy are both desirable. However, they are potentially conflicting requirements, and it is challenging to achieve them both. However, this is achieved by the Ninja mutual authentication scheme presented here, enabling services to be discovered securely and privately.

In future work we plan to integrate anonymous payment mechanisms into the scheme, and to explore ways to secure the process of service provisioning between a user and a service provider, whilst (again) protecting user privacy. A formal security analysis of the scheme is also being performed.

Acknowledgements. We would like to thank Liqun Chen, Marc Langheinrich, Rene Mayrhofer, Kenny Paterson, and the anonymous reviewers for their valuable comments.

References

1. Chakraborty, D., Joshi, A., Yesha, Y., Finin, T.: Toward distributed service discovery in pervasive computing environments. IEEE Transactions on Mobile Computing 5(2), 97–112 (2006)
2. Friday, A., Davies, N., Wallbank, N., Catterall, E., Pink, S.: Supporting service discovery, querying and interaction in ubiquitous computing environments. Wireless Networks 10(6), 631–641 (2004)
3. Zhu, F., Mutka, M., Li, L.: Service discovery in pervasive computing environements. IEEE Pervasive Computing 4(4), 81–90 (2005)
4. Zhu, F., Mutka, M., Ni, L.: A private, secure and user-centric information exposure model for service discovery protocols. IEEE Transactions on Mobile Computing 5(4), 418–429 (2006)
5. Zhu, F., Zhu, W., Mutka, M.W., Ni, L.: Expose or not? A progressive exposure approach for service discovery in pervasive computing environments. In: 3rd IEEE Conf. on Pervasive Computing & Communications, pp. 225–234. IEEE Computer Society Press, Los Alamitos (2005)
6. Gollmann, D.: What do we mean by entity authentication? In: IEEE Symposium on Security and Privacy, pp. 46–54. IEEE Computer Society Press, Los Alamitos (1996)
7. Creese, S., Goldsmith, M., Roscoe, B., Zakiuddin, I.: Authentication for pervasive computing. In: Hutter, D., Müller, G., Stephan, W., Ullmann, M. (eds.) Security in Pervasive Computing. LNCS, vol. 2802, pp. 116–129. Springer, Heidelberg (2004)
8. Bao, F., Deng, R.H.: Privacy protection for transactions of digital goods. In: Qing, S., Okamoto, T., Zhou, J. (eds.) ICICS 2001. LNCS, vol. 2229, pp. 202–213. Springer, Heidelberg (2001)
9. Berendt, B., Günther, O., Spiekermann, S.: Privacy in e-commerce: Stated preferences vs. actual behavior. Communications of the ACM 48(4), 101–106 (2005)
10. Campbell, R., Al-Muhtadi, J., Naldurg, P., Sampemane, G., Mickunas, M.D.: Towards security and privacy for pervasive computing. In: Int'l Symposium on Software Security, pp. 1–15 (2002)
11. Wu, M., Friday, A.: Integrating privacy enhancing services in ubiquitous computing environments. In: Borriello, G., Holmquist, L.E. (eds.) UbiComp 2002. LNCS, vol. 2498, p. 71. Springer, Heidelberg (2002)
12. Balacheff, B., Chen, L., Pearson, S., Plaquin, D., Proudler, G.: Trusted Computing Platforms: TCPA Technology in Context. In: PH PTR, Upper Saddle River, NJ (2003)

13. Mitchell, C.J. (ed.): Trusted Computing. IEE Press, London (2005)
14. Trusted Computing Group (TCG): TCG Specification Architecture Overview. Version 1.2, The Trusted Computing Group, Portland, Oregon, USA (2004)
15. National Institute of Standards and Technology (NIST): Secure Hash Standard. Federal information processing standards publication (FIPS), pp. 180–182 (2002)
16. Brickell, E., Camenisch, J., Chen, L.: Direct anonymous attestation. In: 11th ACM Conf. on Computer & Communications Security, pp. 132–145. ACM Press, New York (2004)
17. Camenisch, J., Lysyanskaya, A.: A signature scheme with efficient protocols. In: Cimato, S., Galdi, C., Persiano, G. (eds.) SCN 2002. LNCS, vol. 2576, pp. 268–289. Springer, Heidelberg (2003)
18. Goldreich, O., Micali, S., Wigderson, A.: Proofs that yield nothing but their validity or all languages in NP have zero-knowledge proof systems. Journal of the ACM 38(3), 690–728 (1991)
19. Goldwasser, S., Micali, S., Rackoff, C.: The knowledge complexity of interactive proof systems. SIAM Journal on Computing 18(1), 186–208 (1989)
20. Trusted Computing Group (TCG): TPM v1.2 Specification Changes. A summary of changes, Trusted Computing Group, Portland, Oregon, USA (2003)
21. Rudolph, C.: Covert identity information in direct anonymous attestation (DAA). In: 22nd IFIP Int'l. Information Security Conf (SEC2007) (2007)
22. Housley, R., Polk, W., Ford, W., Solo, D.: Internet X.509 Public Key Infrastructure. RFC 3280, The Internet Engineering Task Force (IETF) (2002)
23. Diffie, W., Hellman, M.E.: New directions in cryptography. IEEE Transactions on Information Theory 22(6), 644–654 (1976)
24. Sun Microsystems: Jini Architecture Specification. Version 1.2, Sun Microsystems, Palo Alto, CA, USA (2001), http://www.sun.com/software/jini/specs/
25. Universal Plug and Play (UPnP) Forum: UPnP Device Architecture. version 1.0 (2003), http://www.upnp.org/
26. Guttman, E., Perkins, C., Veizades, J., Day, M.: Service Location Protocol, Version 2., RFC 2608, The Internet Engineering Task Force (IETF) (1999)
27. Nidd, M.: Service discovery in DEAPspace. IEEE Personal Communications 8(4), 39–45 (2001)
28. Salutation Consortium: Salutation Architecture Specification (1999), http://www.salutation.org/
29. Zhu, F., Mutka, M., Ni, L.: Prudent Exposure: A private and user-centric service discovery protocol. In: 2nd IEEE Conf. on Pervasive Computing & Communications, pp. 329–328. IEEE Computer Society Press, Los Alamitos (2004)
30. Abadi, M., Fournet, C.: Private authentication. Theoretical Computer Science 322(3), 427–476 (2004)
31. Ren, K., Luo, W., Kim, K., Deng, R.: A novel privacy preserving authentication and access control scheme for pervasive computing environments. IEEE Transactions on Vehicular Technology 55(4), 1373–1384 (2006)
32. Teranishi, I., Furukawa, J., Sako, K.: k-times anonymous authentication. In: Lee, P.J. (ed.) ASIACRYPT 2004. LNCS, vol. 3329, pp. 308–322. Springer, Heidelberg (2004)
33. Chowdhury, P.D., Christianson, B., Malcolm, J.: Anonymous authentication. In: Christianson, B., Crispo, B., Malcolm, J.A., Roe, M. (eds.) Security Protocols. LNCS, vol. 3957, pp. 299–305. Springer, Heidelberg (2006)
34. Trusted Computing Platform Alliance (TCPA): TCPA Main Specification. Version 1.1b, Trusted Computing Group, Portland, Oregon, USA (2002)

Field Deployment of *IMBuddy*: A Study of Privacy Control and Feedback Mechanisms for Contextual IM

Gary Hsieh, Karen P. Tang, Wai Yong Low, and Jason I. Hong

Human-Computer Interaction Institute
Carnegie Mellon University
5000 Forbes Ave, Pittsburgh, PA 15213
{garyh,kptang,wlow,jasonh}@cs.cmu.edu

Abstract. We describe the design of privacy controls and feedback mechanisms for contextual IM, an instant messaging service for disclosing contextual information. We tested our designs on *IMBuddy*, a contextual IM service we developed that discloses contextual information, including interruptibility, location, and the current window in focus (a proxy for the current task). We deployed our initial design of *IMBuddy*'s privacy mechanisms for two weeks with ten IM users. We then evaluated a redesigned version for four weeks with fifteen users. Our evaluation indicated that users found our group-level rule-based privacy control intuitive and easy to use. Furthermore, the set of feedback mechanisms provided users with a good awareness of what was disclosed.

Keywords: Contextual instant messaging, context-aware, IM, privacy.

1 Introduction

Instant messaging (IM) is a growing communication medium that is useful for both social and work purposes [1, 2]. While it functions as a multi-purpose communication medium, current commercial designs of IM provide minimal support for disclosing contextual information (such as location and work status) to other users. To address this concern, prior research have explored augmenting IM to include contextual information disclosure so that IM users can have better awareness of where other users are and what they are up to, and to improve IM as a communication media for collaboration, coordination and social interaction [3-6].

However, for contextual IM to flourish in everyday use, significant privacy concerns need to be addressed for supporting contextual information sharing. Previous work has highlighted two principles in designing for privacy: control and feedback [7, 8]. Without enough control, sensitive and private information could be disclosed to others. Without sufficient feedback, users would not know what has been disclosed, and that may prevent them from taking necessary precautions to protect their privacy. One design for privacy controls is to manage information disclosure on a case-by-case basis. The problem with this design is that users are always required to make the disclosure decision, which incurs interruption costs and prevents useful disclosures when they are busy or away. Another design of privacy control is a customizable rule-based control. A previous lab study has suggested that group-level

J. Krumm et al. (Eds.): UbiComp 2007, LNCS 4717, pp. 91–108, 2007.
© Springer-Verlag Berlin Heidelberg 2007

rule-based controls are sufficient for contextual IM [9]; however, without actual field use, it is not clear what needs to be included in privacy controls and how much feedback is necessary to make contextual IM acceptable for general everyday use.

To explore this design space, we designed privacy controls and feedback mechanisms for *IMBuddy*, a contextual IM service that we developed. *IMBuddy* allows any AIM user to query an AOL Instant Messaging Robot (AIMBot) about three types of information: interruptibility, location, and current window in focus (a proxy for current task). Currently, users can only ask about selected AIM users who run our client software which collects and reports their contextual information.

We iterated our privacy designs based on actual field use. For the first deployment, ten participants used *IMBuddy* for two weeks. Although users felt comfortable using the first iteration of privacy controls and feedback mechanisms, they suggested additional feedbacks and improvements to the system. We then redesigned the system and deployed it to fifteen other students over the span of four weeks. We evaluated our designs focusing on the effectiveness of our control and feedback mechanisms.

This work offers two main contributions. First, we introduce a design for privacy control and feedback mechanisms for contextual IM. Our user study suggests that our feedback mechanisms provided ample information allowing our users to notice when their information was disclosed. Specifically, most users were aware when someone asked for their information in a suspicious way. During the study, our participants were comfortable with their privacy settings and discussed various scenarios where the information disclosed was both appropriate and useful. Components of our design can be easily reused for other contextual IM and can even be extended to information disclosure through other devices. Second, our design offers evidence that a rule-based group-level privacy control for contextual IM can work well in practice.

2   Related Work

With ubiquitous computing pushing to embed technologies in our everyday devices, it is becoming easier to sense and share user information (e.g. location). For example, prior work has demonstrated the benefits of contextual information disclosures for Media Space [10]. Similarly, the idea of contextual information sharing in instant messengers has also been explored, showing that these clients are helpful for sharing locale and activity information [3, 4, 6] and project related information [5].

As ubiquitous computing strives to make technology more invisible and integrated in our everyday lives, it becomes imperative to consider and design privacy mechanisms to properly managing information disclosures. Work by Belotti and Sellen has highlighted this issue, and they propose a design framework that focuses on feedback and control in ubicomp environments [7]. Drawing on prior research in Media Spaces [8], they define two important principles in designing for privacy: **control**, empowering people to stipulate what information they project and who can get hold of it, and **feedback**, informing people when and what information about them is being captured and to whom the information is being made available.

To inform our initial privacy designs for *IMBuddy*, we also drew upon several other guidelines. Previous work indicates the need for coarse-grained control as "users are accustomed to turning a thing off when they want its operation to stop" [11,

12]. Other work has demonstrated the importance of having abstract views of information [13], allowing for flexible and personalized replies [11, 14], and having mechanisms for controlling the quantity and fidelity of information disclosure [15].

An open question related to privacy is the usefulness of rule-based mechanisms. On one hand, work by Patil and Lai suggests that controlling privacy at a group level is sufficient for contextual IM [9]. On the other hand, Palen and Dourish argue that privacy is more than authoring rules [16], but rather an ongoing "boundary definition process" in which boundaries of disclosure, identity, and time are fluidly negotiated. In *IMBuddy*, we provide control and feedback mechanisms that utilize both of these philosophies. For example, we provide a rule-authoring interface as well as a history disclosure mechanism. We felt that since attention remains a scarce resource, using a rule-based approach can minimize interruptions and allow for useful disclosures when the user is busy or away. We also provide social translucency mechanisms to help users be more aware of what others know about them. Most importantly, we provide an evaluation of these different mechanisms, showing that they work well in practice.

The importance of feedback has been discussed extensively in prior work. Feedback is important because if users are not aware that their information is being disclosed, then they will be unable to react appropriately to potentially harmful requests. As Langheinrich points out, "in most legal systems today, no single data collection...can go unnoticed of the subject that is being monitored" [17]. Feedback can be further broken down into providing adequate history and immediate feedback as discussed in Nguyen and Mynatt's work on Privacy Mirrors [18]. Our work here presents the design and evaluation of several different feedback mechanisms.

3 Designs of Privacy Control and Feedback

We used *IMBuddy*, a contextual IM service that uses an AOL Instant Messaging Robot (AIMBot), to provide a framework for evaluating privacy control and feedback. IMBuddy answer queries about three types of contextual information: interruptibility, location, and active window. Our initial designs were based on formative evaluations with paper and interactive prototypes tested with five IM users.

3.1 Control

In this section, we discuss three aspects of *IMBuddy*'s privacy controls, namely its multiple information granularity levels, group-based controls, and convenient access.

Information Granularity. *IMBuddy* can disclose three types of information: interruptibility, location, and active window. To support multiple information abstractions levels, we created different levels of disclosure (see Table 1). The lowest disclosure level for all three information types is "none", which results in disclosing "no information available". Our design goal was to keep the controls simple and straightforward while still providing meaningful and appropriate information disclosures for our users; therefore, we focused on the simplest types of granularity controls and did not explore more complex controls based on time or location, etc.

For interruptibility, the highest disclosure level provides a percentage accuracy of busyness, while the lowest level provides a simple abstraction (e.g. <33% is interpreted as the "user may not be busy"). We provide users a buffer for interpreting busyness by phrasing the disclosed information in terms of possibilities ("may not be busy") rather than absolute terms ("is not busy"). For location, the highest disclosure level uses the user's self-specified location tags while the lowest level indicates if the user is on or off campus. For active window, the highest disclosure level reports the name of the window in focus (e.g. "Mozilla Firefox – YouTube.com"), while the lowest level only reports the name of the application in focus (e.g. "firefox.exe").

Table 1. Example of the different information abstractions based on the level of disclosure

Type	Level	Sample disclosure
	none	no information available for screenname
Interruptibility	low	screenname is somewhat busy 10 mins ago
	high	screenname is 60% available 10 mins ago
	none	no information available for screenname
Location	low	screenname last seen off-campus 10 mins ago
	high	screenname last seen at home 10 mins ago
	none	no information available for screenname
Active Window	low	screenname last used firefox.exe 10 mins ago
	high	screenname focused on Blackboard Academic Suite - Mozilla Firefox 10 mins ago

Groups-Based Privacy Policy Controls. We adapted a group-based approach based on prior work by Patil and Lai [9]. Users can specify privacy settings at any time via a web browser (see Figure 1a). Initially, a user's IM buddies are put in a 'default' privacy group, which uses the minimum information disclosure levels for all three information types. Users can create new privacy groups and populate them by moving buddies from the default group to any of their other newly created groups. If an unknown AIM user (a screenname who is not on the user's buddylist) requests information from *IMBuddy*, then he will automatically be added to the default group so that users can also adjust settings for strangers.

Through formative user tests, we found that people preferred using a vertically-oriented view for listing a group's privacy information, mostly because of its similarity to existing IM buddylist views. Within each group's container, drop-down controls let users set the disclosure level for each information type. As users change the disclosure level, dynamic "privacy transparency" feedback shows how their changes would affect the information disclosed to AIM buddies in that group.

Convenient Controls. While running the *IMBuddy* service, users have easy access to the privacy controls via a context menu (see Figure 1b). From this menu, users can: 1) suppress immediate notifications (as described in the next section), 2) turning on invisibility to prevent disclosing information (allowing for coarse-grained on/off control as suggested by [19]), and 3) quickly access their group privacy settings.

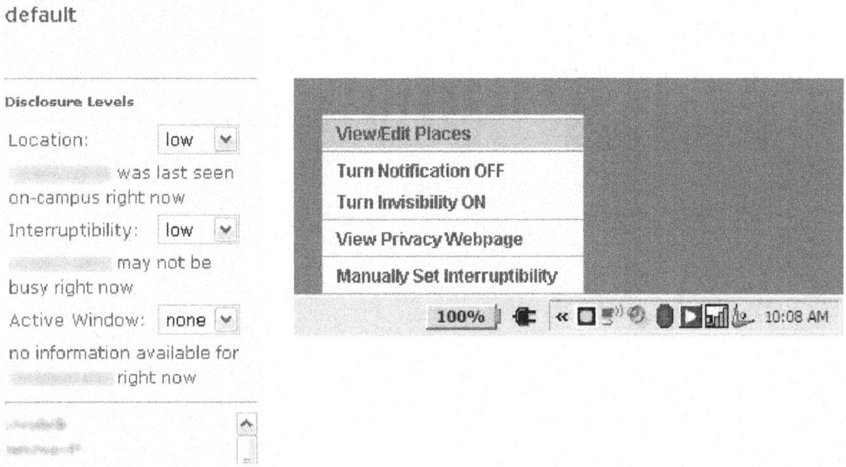

default

| (a) | (b) |

Fig. 1. (a) Group-oriented view with group name, disclosure levels, and buddies for privacy control; (b) System tray icon allowing coarse-grained control and access to privacy settings

3.2 Feedback

IMBuddy supports three types of feedback: 1) informing users what information was disclosed to the requestor (disclosure history), 2) informing users when their information is being disclosed (notification), and 3) facilitating conversational grounding by informing users what others know about them (social translucency).

Disclosure History. The disclosure history is part of the privacy settings webpage, and provides a quick view of who has requested a user's information and what was disclosed (see Figure 2). From formative user tests, we found that people preferred viewing their disclosure history by date and buddy name as opposed to by information type or group. Our participants also rated the need to quickly view anomalies (based on the number of information requests) as an important privacy feedback feature. Moreover, our users found the relative amount of queries was more interesting than the absolute number. To visualize this, an at-a-glance feature using color highlights to indicate the number of requests was preferred over using the number of requests, with one participant saying that it "makes it easy to see who the stalkers are." As such, we see the disclosure history as an important feature for users to gauge if there are any problems in their privacy control settings. We note that our design used static thresholds for color highlighting, but more dynamic coloring schemes could be used.

Notifications. When someone requests a user's information, a bubble popup notification provides real-time feedback showing what was disclosed (see Figure 3a). These notifications remain on-screen if the user is not interacting with the computer (e.g. they are away from their computer at the time of disclosure). By not having an automatic notification dismissal, users have a chance to notice that a disclosure occurred while they were away and can readjust their privacy settings, if needed.

September

Sun	Mon	Tue	Wed	Thu	Fri	Sat
					1	2
3	4	5	6	7	8	9
10	11	12	13	14	15	16
17	18	19	20	21	22	23
24	25	26	27	28	29	30

The following buddies have requested information abou

Date time	Sender	Information type	Last active	Devi
Wed Sep 27 02:31:41 Eastern Daylight Time 2006		location	Sun Sep 24 22:15:34 Eastern Daylight Time 2006	data
Wed Sep 27 00:10:02 Eastern Daylight Time 2006		activewindow	Sun Sep 24 22:15:20 Eastern Daylight Time 2006	data

Buddies Who Queried

Fig. 2. The Disclosure History Page lets users see who has seen what, and when

We have also incorporated a non-distracting peripheral notification. When a disclosure occurs, our system tray icon changes from a white dot to a red dot, mimicking the red light used to indicate active recording status in recording equipments. This icon change alerts the user that their information is being recorded, accessed, and can be potentially sent to their buddies (depending on their privacy control settings). Moreover, this peripheral notification becomes the primary notification mechanism for users, if they choose to turn off bubble notifications.

(a)   (b)

Fig. 3. (a) Bubble notifications provide immediate feedback on requests; (b) A popup is also displayed when a conversation occurs after a buddy has made an inquiry

Social Translucency. We also provide a notification reminding users what their buddies know about them when a conversation starts (see Figure 3b). This feedback mechanism provides conversational grounding [20] as well as social translucency of what information buddies have been requesting [3]. Using this information, users are less likely to be confused by their buddies' understanding (or lack thereof) of their current communication context. Furthermore, if people wish to provide a white lie while chatting, they will know the boundaries of which they can plausibly lie. For example, a person would not lie and say they were on campus if the notification said that the other person saw that they were at home. During our field deployments, we provided these IM-based notifications by having our participants install a plugin we developed for Trillian Pro, a commercial IM client [21].

4 System Implementation

The *IMBuddy* system consists of three parts: an *IMBuddy* AIM Bot ("*imbuddy411*"), an *IMBuddy* server, and an *IMBuddy* client running on each participant's machine.

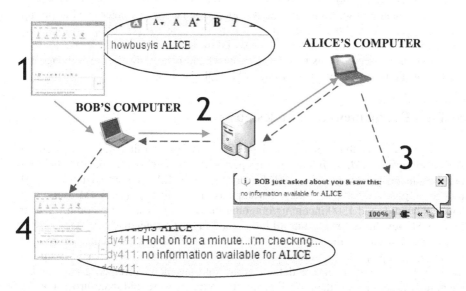

Fig. 4. (1) Bob queries on the busyness of Alice by typing "howbusyis ALICE" to *imbuddy411*; (2) *imbuddy41* passes the request to the *IMBuddy* server, which forwards it to the appropriate *IMBuddy* client to process the request; (3) Alice's client responds to the request and alerts Alice of the information that is being disclosed to Bob; and (4) *imbuddy411* then displays the privacy-filtered response from the client or database to Bob's chat window

Any AIM user can request a user's information by typing a command in a chat window to *imbuddy411* (implemented using JAIMBot, an open-source Java-based AIM library [22]) (see Figure 4). For example, he can type "*howbusyis* X" to get X's interruptibility, where X is the screenname (step 1). *imbuddy411* passes this request to the *IMBuddy* server, which then communicates with the appropriate *IMBuddy* client to retrieve the appropriate context information (step 2). The *IMBuddy* client notifies the user of the disclosure and relays the information back to the *IMBuddy* server (step 3). Based on the user's privacy settings, the *IMBuddy* server reports the privacy-filtered response back to the requester in the original chat window (via *imbuddy411*). Information requests are also stored in a MySQL database on the *IMBuddy* server, which lets the server share the most recent disclosure information if a user is offline.

The *IMBuddy* client software runs as a background process that collects interruptibility, location, and active window information. We use Subtle [23], a toolkit which uses sensor-based statistical models, to collect active window data and to estimate a user's interruptibility. When tested with a group of 10 office workers, Subtle is capable of reaching 80% accuracy in predicting interruptibility. The model we used is built with data from human resource personnel and two graduate students [24]. Location estimates are done using a two-pronged approach. Because our participants are college students, the first level of location abstraction checks to see if users are on or off campus by determining if their IP address is within the university's subnet. To provide more precise location information, we rely on Place Lab [25] to sense nearby wireless access points. When our software sees a new set of wireless access points, we prompt users to provide a location tag. Later, we use Place Lab to recognize when the user returns to that location, so that we no longer need to prompt the user again. The *IMBuddy* client is also responsible for providing notifications, along with locally storing data to provide social translucency for IM conversations.

The *IMBuddy* server hosts the privacy control and history disclosure webpage and is implemented using Ruby on Rails and a MySQL database.

5 First Deployment and Redesign

To evaluate our feedback and control mechanisms, we recruited ten undergraduate students to use the *IMBuddy* system for a period of two weeks. We specifically chose undergraduates who were active AIM users that used IM for both social and work related purposes. On average, these participants are medium to heavy IM users; they have 90 buddies and 1300 incoming/outgoing messages a week. Based on the Westin Privacy Survey, these participants all fall in the Pragmatic category.

On the first day of the study, we installed the *IMBuddy* client software on each participant's laptop. They were also asked to set up their initial privacy groups by moving their buddies from the default group into any newly created groups and/or changing the settings for the default group. Participants were told that, throughout the study, they can change their settings by creating/deleting groups and moving buddies around anyway they like. For the purposes of our study, we wanted to have an initial set up so we could see how the initial groups change over the course of the study.

To introduce our *IMBuddy* service to our participants' buddies, we included a short description about the service in each participant's IM profile. However, because our participants said their buddies do not often check profiles, we modified our Trillian plugin to also advertise the *IMBuddy* service whenever an IM conversation is started.

There were a total of 242 individual queries made to *IMBuddy*. The breakdown of the different information types that were requested include: 66 for interruptibility, 104 for location, and 72 for active window. Since information requesters can ask for multiple types of information (for a given subject) in one session, we grouped such queries as a single instance. In all, there were 117 instances of use and on average two types of information were queried per use. 43 of those instances were times when *IMBuddy* disclosed information stored in the database (i.e. when users were not online or running our client). There were 53 distinct screen names who queried *IMBuddy* and 13 of those were repeat users.

A total of 43 groups were created. On average, there were 4.3 groups ($\sigma = 2.5$) per participant. One participant had only one group (default) and said that besides his active window, he was fine with anyone seeing his information. Other participants had group names that contain keywords relating to class, major, clubs, gender, work, location, ethnicity, and blood relations. 6 of the 43 groups disclosed no information, while 7 of them disclosed all three information types at the highest level.

5.1 Findings

During a mid-deployment interview, we reviewed the disclosure history with each of the participants. At the end of the study, each participant completed a Likert-style questionnaire, where they were asked to rate 15 statements (where 1=strongly disagree and 5=strongly agree).

Our participants agreed that the three information types being disclosed were all potentially sensitive information that they would not carelessly disclose (interruptibility: 3.6/σ=1.3, location: 4.1/σ=1.1, active window: 4.9/σ=0.3). However, despite the potential sensitivity of this information, our participants said they were comfortable with their privacy settings for *IMBuddy* (4.1/ σ=0.9).

We found that our group-based control was intuitive to our users because they were used to similar levels of control from other sites and applications (*e.g* LiveJournal). They agreed that our privacy controls were easy to understand (4.4/σ=0.5) and easy to modify (4.2/σ=1.0). Users did, however, express a desire to be able to self-set interruptibility level, in the same way that they could self-tag location.

In terms of feedback, most users felt that they had a good sense of who had seen their information (3.9/ σ=1.2), and all of them had reviewed their disclosure history at least twice in the two weeks. They reviewed their disclosure log usually after noticing a query, which prompted them to find out what other information was disclosed since they last checked the disclosure history. The participants who gave low scores for this question indicated a need for a fourth type of feedback (that we later implemented), informing them about disclosures that occurred while their computers were off.

Our users did not feel that the notifications were problematic. For example, one user said, "[the notification was] at a good spot to ignore it if I wanted to." One participant did express concerns if the frequency of use increased: "if it were to happen all the time, then it might get annoying." One solution for this is to summarize disclosure histories. One participant suggested that "it would be cool if it was like summarized, like your location has been checked like 5 times, like something like that. I wouldn't want like it all to be listed. It would be too much." In specific cases where malicious users query the AIMBot and bombard users with unwanted notifications, one solution could be to have a blacklist where no information is disclosed and no notification is shown for blacklisted users; this is similar to the blocking option that current IM clients already have.

5.2 Redesign

The survey results indicated that users were mostly satisfied with the privacy controls. They felt the controls were easy to use and understand. Most importantly, they were comfortable with their privacy control settings. Therefore, in our redesign, we only added minor changes to the control mechanisms, such as allowing users to correct the interruptibility information being disclosed. Instead, our redesign focused on the reported need for different types of privacy feedback mechanisms.

System and Control Modifications. One concern with our first deployment was the inability to correct the information being disclosed. While our system would ideally only disclose accurate contextual information, we found that interruptibility was often not accurate enough for our users. Hence, participants from our first deployment requested the ability to self-tag their interruptibility, much in the same way that we allow for location self-tagging. Thus, we modified our *IMBuddy* client to allow users to manually set their interruptibility though the client's context menu. All manual interruptibility settings would only last for one hour, after which the user's interruptibility would revert back to the system-inferred value.

We also found that the highest level of interruptibility disclosure (a percentage) is generally not as useful as an abstract text description of the user's interruptibility (e.g. "not busy"). To address this, we modified interruptibility's highest disclosure level to include both the percentage and a brief text description.

Lastly, we modified the client to auto-update the user's contextual information to the server every five minutes, as opposed to only when a query is sent. This way, the latest information in the server will remain reasonably up-to-date, so that information requestors can still get useful information when the user's computer is offline.

Additional Feedback. We added two new feedback mechanisms. The first provides feedback to the users when they logon to the system, showing them the number of information requests that occurred while they were offline in a bubble notification (see Figure 5a). The purpose for this feedback is to provide the users a better sense of how their privacy was handled while they were offline.

The second feedback mechanism appears when a user mouses over the client's system tray icon (see Figure 5b). A small tool-tip popup window appears, showing the number of requests for each information type within the past 6 hours. We designed this mechanism to provide a lightweight summary of disclosure history. This is especially useful if the users have not been actively keeping track of the disclosures (e.g. because they were away from their computer for an extended period of time).

(a)   (b)

Fig. 5. (a) Feedback after logging-on; (b) a mouse-over notification providing a summary

6 Second Deployment

To evaluate our modified redesign, we conducted a second field study and deployed our contextual IM system to 15 students for four weeks. These are different participants than the ones from our first deployment. These participants, on average, are medium to heavy IM users; they have 120 buddies and 1580 incoming/outgoing messages a week. These users were also all Pragmatic according to the Westin scale. We used the same advertising techniques as in the first deployment.

In all, there were 140 instances of use. 74 of those instances disclosed information stored in the database (i.e. when users were not online or running our client). The breakdown of the requested information types were: 67 for interruptibility, 175 for location, and 79 for active window (for a total of 321 individual queries). There were 61 distinct screennames who queried *IMBuddy*. As expected, some users queried the system due to novelty, but there were 15 repeat users who continually used the system throughout the duration of the study.

A total of 56 groups were created. On average, 3.3 groups ($\sigma = 1.3$) were created per user. Groups were again separated by an array of factors: class, major, clubs, gender, location, ethnicity, and blood relations. When asked, users often described a sense of closeness as the underlying separating factor between the groups. 6 of the 56 groups disclosed no information, while 10 of them set all three information types at the highest disclosure level. All but 2 default groups disclosed no information, while others allowed for at least a medium disclosure level for interruptibility.

For this deployment, we again focused our evaluation on the privacy control and feedback mechanisms provided in *IMBuddy*. Our metrics of evaluation include awareness (how successful our system was in keeping our users informed), convenience and ease of use (how easy it was to understand and use the controls), and appropriateness (how the users felt about the disclosed information).

We solicited participants' thoughts using multiple evaluation techniques. We conducted interviews and used surveys/questionnaires[1]. We also created a "stalker-bot" (*jasonkats722*), to test the effectiveness of our feedback and notification systems and to observe how our participants would react to an unknown and potentially malicious user. The stalker-bot was implemented as another AIMbot which would query *IMBuddy* for different users and about different information types at random times. The stalker-bot was deployed near the end of the study, when our participants were already familiar with how *IMBuddy* works and had enough time to settle into a "comfortable" privacy setting. On average, the stalker-bot made 2 sets of queries a day, asking for two or three types of information per session.

6.1 Evaluation of Control

To evaluate our control mechanism, we asked our participants to comment on three things: 1) the general usability of the controls (e.g. do users know how to modify the settings and is the design easy to use), 2) their comfort level in regards to the stalker-bot, and 3) their perception of the information disclosed.

Usability. Similar to our first study's results, the participants in our second deployment again felt the privacy controls were intuitive, easy to use, and allowed for easy and quick corrections to any errors. The extended length of the second study combined with the increased number of participants, strengthened our findings from the first-iteration. Our survey questions regarding the understandability of our privacy controls and the ease of changing privacy policies are both highly rated ($4.5/\sigma=0.7$).

---

[1] The means reported here use the same 5-point Likert scale as in our first field deployment, unless otherwise noted.

During our interviews, participants repeatedly made statements such as "I really liked the privacy settings the way they are. I thought they were easy to use, especially changing between privacy settings." Ability to access the control easily was also mentioned: "I felt pretty comfortable with using it because you can just easily modify the privacy settings." Another participant concurs, saying: "it's flexible; you can create as many groups as you want. Moving people around is relatively easy. Since it's on a website, it's not like you have to open up an application."

However, a couple of participants did comment that setting up their initial privacy groups was a bit tedious. "It's time consuming, if you have a long buddylist, to set up for each person." Such comments suggest a need to reduce initial costs that may occur with using group-level control. There were also desires by certain participants to allow for more levels of disclosure granularity. Specifically, a few participants wanted one more disclosure levels for location information, where users could say that they were around a certain place (versus at a specific place).

Comfort. Our participants said they were comfortable with their privacy settings for *IMBuddy* ($4/\sigma=0.9$). Moreover, users' comfort levels were not changed after introducing the stalker-bot. Participants who did not notice the stalker-bot, reacted no differently than hearing about any other user querying for their information. They reasoned that *jasonkats722* was perhaps one of their buddies, or that he was an old friend that was no longer on their buddy list. Most important is that they were not concerned. They were confident in their privacy control settings and it did not matter to them that a potential stranger had been checking their information multiple times: "I know they won't get any information, because I set the default so they won't be able to see anything."

Appropriateness of Disclosures. For our mid-deployment interview, we asked our participants to describe scenarios where they felt that: 1) the information disclosed was inappropriate (either too much or not enough information was provided), and 2) the information disclosed was just right and/or extremely useful.

Overall, the participants were not able to state any particular incidences where they felt the information disclosed was inappropriate. This is partly because the overall number of queries was not that high, but it also reflects that users felt comfortable with the information their buddies would potentially see. One user mentioned that he experimented with the system and realized that active-window queries could lead to potentially embarrassing information disclosures (e.g. someone could find out if he happened to be visiting a porn site). While he had initially allowed his friends to see the most detailed information regarding his active window, after this discovery, he went back and changed the settings to prevent potential embarrassing incidents from occurring. Another participant discussed how she lowered her privacy settings for a particular classmate who frequently asked for her information because she felt he did not need such detailed information as she was originally disclosing.

While the amount of use has not been extremely high, we were still able to witness incidents where participants found contextual IM to be very useful. We describe one such scenario below, where the participant's buddy used the service to coordinate with our participant, without bothering them directly.

Quote 3 <participant L> *"Someone asked where I was [using IMBuddy], did not IM me and then showed up there... there is a room that I hang out in a lot and she comes there a lot. But you need a key to get in, and I have a key but she doesn't. She's not going to show up if there is no one there that has the key. So she'll check if I'm there and then come...and I knew [that she had asked for my information] because it shows me in that little thing [notification bubble]...she would complain when it is not accurate and stuff, like I'll leave my computer on with my IM up and go and get food or something, and she'll be in the room when I get back, and she'll be like 'it told me you're here and you're not.'"*

As indicated by the quote above, one complaint was actually the inaccuracy of some information disclosures as opposed to its inappropriateness. Inaccuracies of information existed in two forms: the system-inferred interruptibility is not always 100% accurate, and the location accuracy is limited by the extent to which the user takes their laptop with them.

According to our participants, the most useful information type is location. Location was preferred over availability in terms of utility because most IM users are accustomed to sending an IM message (e.g. "are you free") to determine availability, which is an interruption in of itself. One participant said "I don't really get the point for how busy I was, because people would IM me regardless." Location is also more useful than active window because our participants did not use IM often in group-work scenarios, where awareness of each other's task might be more helpful.

During the study, *IMBuddy* would also randomly survey information requestors to get a sense of the appropriateness of the disclosed information using a 5-point Likert scale, where 1 is "wanted more information", 3 is "obtained just the right amount of information", and 5 is "got a lot more than asked". Based on 61 logged entries, the mean was 2.47 ($\sigma = 0.91$). Since we did not specifically indicate to these people the range of responses they could have gotten, one might question if most have selected the 3 simply because of a lack of comparison point. However, the average rating does suggest the right level of information was disclosed.

6.2 Evaluation of Feedback

We evaluated the awareness of disclosure both in terms of user feedback (using our survey results), and by our users' reactions to our stalker-bot, *jasonkats722*.

General Awareness of Disclosures. From our first field deployment, users reported having a fairly good sense of who had seen what ($3.9/\sigma=1.2$). It was, however, apparent from our interviews that some participants desired different types of feedback from what we had designed. Mainly, participants desired feedback to support their awareness of disclosures when they are not able to monitor the disclosure bubble notifications. With the two newly added feedback mechanism, the mean agreement rating to the question "while using the system, I always have a good sense of who has seen what" increased to 4.1 ($\sigma=0.8$).

We speculated that if asked, participants would claim that they had found all of the feedback mechanisms to be helpful. Therefore, to gain a better understanding for which feedback was more essential, we asked our participants to rank the 6 different types of feedback mechanisms that we had designed (with 1 being most useful). The average rankings from most useful to least useful were: bubble notification, 1.6 (σ=0.6); disclosure log, 1.8 (σ=1.3); mouse-over notification, 3.7 (σ=1.0); offline statistic notification, 4 (σ=1.4); social translucency Trillian tooltip popup, 4.8 (σ=1.1); and peripheral red-dot notification, 5.4 (σ=0.7).

Awareness of Stalker-Bot. One of the main purposes for using awareness as a metric for evaluating privacy control and feedback is to ensure the users are able to detect if there are any cases of misuse. By doing so, users can take the necessary actions to protect themselves in a timely fashion. We tested user awareness by deploying a stalker-bot named *jasonkats722* 2-5 days before the end of the study[2]. During the post-study interview, we asked our participants to describe their relationship with a list of screennames who had previously queried for their information. As we proceeded down the list, we focused on *jasonkats722* and asked follow-up questions to better understand how our participants' reaction to his stalker behavior.

There were 12 participants who noticed *jasonkats722* (1 participant was out of town and did not use the system during that period). Of these, only a couple of them did not think too much about it, since they only noticed 1 or 2 queries made by *jasonkats722* and assumed it was some random person or another participant's buddy testing out the system: "It does bother me that someone I don't know has looked at it, but the fact that I've gone in and set my settings appropriately, minimizes that." Other participants, however, did go back to the disclosure log in an attempt to figure out what *jasonkats722*'s motivation may have been. One user even went as far as attempting to message *jasonkats722* whenever he went online.

Quote 1 <participant A> *"I think yesterday was the first time that I'd noticed him and I think yesterday was the first time that happened. I then went to my privacy settings to check, cuz I'd forgot what his screenname was. I went and checked his screenname. Added to my buddylist and asked who he was but I never got a reply. He would sign on and off...it was the popup bubble [that first notified me]...first time I thought it was unusual, but I didn't do anything. But then I saw it the second time like 10 minutes later, so I was intrigued, wanted to know why this person who I don't know is asking about me."*

We asked our users about the potential use of a blacklist, an idea that we got from our first iteration, where a particular screenname would not get any information and participants would also not be bothered by disclosure requests from that screenname. While participants liked the idea of screening certain users from accessing any information, they still wanted to know who was asking for their information.

Quote 2 <participant A> *I wouldn't like in real life if someone randomly asked where I was, but I would like to know who these people are. Like my friends would tell me someone was asking about me, and tell me who that person was. But over the internet I can't do that, so I have to find out myself."*

---

[2] Some participants ended slightly earlier than others.

7 Discussion

The goal of this work is to provide a better understanding about the types of control and feedback mechanisms that would be valuable and necessary for privacy-sensitive contextual information disclosure through instant messaging. While it is unfortunate that *IMBuddy*'s use was not as high as we had hoped for, we were still able to draw informative findings using our qualitative data collected from people's perception of our control and feedback mechanisms. Two groups of student users interacted with our service and design for a period of 2-4 weeks, in everyday social and work settings, and were exposed to potential misuse by strangers. Our first iteration indicated the need for more feedback to provide disclosure awareness while the user is away or offline. Our second iteration explored use of controls and feedback in more depth, through more users and longer use.

7.1 Controls

Users from both deployments thought our controls were easy to understand and use. They were able to disclose their information at a level they were comfortable with, while still getting value from using the system. Even though we cannot make any strong claims stating that our control mechanisms offered the best balance between usefulness and appropriateness and will generalize to more complicated information types, we do believe from our deployments that it provides a set of baseline mechanisms for future work to be compared against. The coarse-grained invisible control was useful for providing users some "alone time" and the notification-off control was useful for preventing distractions.

Although no previous research has clearly demonstrated that group-based privacy control is sufficient for contextual information disclosure, our work does providing promising evidence that it works well in practice. One of the primary reasons is that it is easy to understand. People have been using groups to organize IM buddylists, as well as other social application (e.g. flickr and LiveJournal).

One key issue about using group-based privacy controls is how to decrease the initial set-up costs. Given that our participants had on average 90+ buddies, creating groups and placing their buddies into groups took some time. One idea is to bootstrap the system using existing IM buddy groups and screennames. However, from our deployments, we found that IM buddy groups are quite different from the privacy groups created in *IMBuddy*. Groups created in *IMBuddy* tend to be separated by levels of closeness. On the other hand, IM buddy groups are typically separated by where and how the user knows the buddy. This distinction prevents users from leveraging their current IM buddy groups to simplify the process of creating their privacy groups.

Our evaluation also indicates that when preloading the system with an initial group of buddies, those preloaded buddies should be automatically placed in a group separate from the "default" group. This would differentiate between actual strangers and buddies. In addition, based on our interviews, there is evidence that suggests the need for a blacklisted group. Disclosure requesters from that group could potentially receive false information both to maintain plausible deniability and to prevent requesters from realizing they are in the blacklisted group. Such a design would fulfill the recommended design guideline of supporting deception [11]. But such mechanisms need to be carefully designed.

Another concept worth exploring is allowing buddies to have multiple memberships. That was suggested by participants in both deployments. It makes sense why this particular use of groups would be intuitive. We can have more than one type of relationship with a buddy. Depending on the context, we might want to give certain groups that a buddy belongs to more control than others. Thus, by allowing for multiple memberships, we can increase the flexibility of group-based privacy controls. However, we would also need to then address how to resolve potential privacy policy conflicts. Nevertheless, this idea deserves further exploration as it has not been explore in prior work on group-based privacy configuration designs.

7.2 Feedback Mechanisms

In both deployments, our surveys indicated that participants thought they had a good sense of who had seen their information. In our first iteration, there were four types of feedback: disclosure history, bubble notification, peripheral notification (the red dot) and Trillian tooltip popup supporting social translucency. Our first deployment led to two additional feedback designs, an offline statistics notification and a mouse-over notification. While the second deployment's survey response to the same question was slightly higher, it was not statistically significant. The rankings of the 6 different types of feedback indicated that the bubble notification, as expected, is the most important notification for our users. It allows for immediate feedback regarding who has seen what, giving users an opportunity to react to the disclosure if necessary. This suggests that future contextual IM services should minimally include this type of feedback mechanism for their users.

Our exploration with the stalker-bot *jasonkats722* suggests a good start for modeling when to alert users regarding potential misuse, namely to provide alerts based on if the information queries has occurred more than once and how much time has elapsed since the last query. Queries by strangers should also result in more immediate alarms than by someone who is on the user's buddylist. One participant mentioned this potential design of stalker alert:

Quote 3 <participant M> I think it would be good like if a strangers asks and if they don't find anything, or that you would ignore it, maybe there's some kind of threshold so if they keep asking, like I don't know how many times...the same guy keeps asking, and I don't know him then it would let me know like hey there's this guy, you might want to check into this see if someone you know is trying to get a hold of you or if it's someone you don't know that is trying to stalk you.

8 Conclusions

In this work, we present the design of privacy controls and feedback mechanisms using a contextual IM service called *IMBuddy*. We conducted an initial two week field study of our systems and re-iterated our system design based on our initial findings. We then deployed our system in a second field study, lasting 4-weeks with 15 users. Our findings suggest that *IMBuddy* successfully provided effective awareness for our users (e.g. participants were aware of when and to whom their information was disclosed to) in addition to intuitive, easy-to-use privacy controls that enabled them to configure their privacy settings to a comfortable level. Furthermore, *IMBuddy* provides positive evidence that group-based privacy configuration is intuitive and sufficient for our contextual IM framework. We believe results from this study can and should be extended to future designs of contextual IM and contextual telephony applications.

9 Future Work

We plan to explore how to encourage more *IMBuddy* use to further validate our findings. It is not clear if the problem lies with a lack of critical mass, or if using an AIM Bot to disclose contextual information is an inappropriate design metaphor. Greater use will also facilitate longer and larger field trials that will help us more fully understand the intricacies of privacy, privacy controls, and social perceptions.

Acknowledgments. This work is funded in part by NSF grants CNS-0627513, IIS-0534406, and ITR-032535. We also thank the contributors to Place Lab, JAIMBot, and the jdic project, as well as James Fogarty, Joe Tullio, Ian Li, Scott Hudson, Robert Kraut, and our Common Meeting group members.

References

1. Isaacs, E., Walendowski, A., Whittaker, S., Schiano, D.J., Kamm, C.: The character, functions, and styles of instant messaging in the workplace. In: ACM conference on Computer Supported Cooperative Work (CSCW), pp. 11–20. ACM Press, New York (2002)
2. Nardi, B., Whittaker, S., Bradner, E.: Interaction and Outeraction: Instant Messaging in Action. In: ACM Conference on Computer Supported Cooperative Work (CSCW), pp. 79–88. ACM Press, New York (2000)
3. Erickson, T., Kellogg, W.A.: Social translucence: an approach to designing systems that support social processes. In: TOCHI, vol. 7, pp. 59–83 (2000)
4. Isaacs, E., Walendowski, A., Ranganathan, D.: Hubbub: A Sound-Enhanced Mobile Instant Messenger that Supports Awareness and Opportunistic Interactions. In: ACM Conference on Human Factors in Computing Systems (CHI), pp. 179–186. ACM Press, New York (2002)
5. Scupelli, P., Kiesler, S., Fussell, S.R., Chen, C.: Project view IM: a tool for juggling multiple projects and teams. In: Extended Abstracts of ACM Conference on Human Factors in Computing Systems (CHI), ACM Press, New York (2005)
6. Tang, J.C., Yankelovich, N., Begole, J., Kleek, M.V., Li, F., Bhalodia, J.: ConNexus to awarenex: extending awareness to mobile users. In: ACM Conference on Human Factors in Computing Systems (CHI), pp. 221–228. ACM Press, New York (2001)
7. Bellotti, V., Sellen, A.: Design for Privacy in Ubiquitous Computing Environments. In: Third European Conference on Computer Supported Cooperative Work (ECSCW), pp. 77–92 (1993)
8. Gaver, W., Moran, T., MacLean, A., Lovstrand, L., Dourish, P., Carter, K., Buxton, W.: Realizing a video environment: EuroPARC's RAVE system. In: ACM Conference on Human Factors in Computing Systems (CHI), pp. 27–35. ACM Press, New York (1992)

9. Patil, S., Lai, J.: Who gets to know what when: configuring privacy permissions in an awareness application. In: ACM Conference on Human Factors in Computing Systems (CHI), pp. 101–110. ACM Press, New York (2005)

10. Bly, S.A., Harrison, S.R., Irwin, S.: Media spaces: bringing people together in a video, audio, and computing environment. ACM Communications 36, 28–46 (1993)

11. Iachello, G., Smith, I., Consolvo, S., Chen, M., Abowd, G.D.: Developing privacy guidelines for social location disclosure applications and services. In: Symposium on Usable Privacy and Security (SOUPS), pp. 65–76. ACM Press, New York (2005)

12. Lederer, S., Hong, J.I., Dey, A., Landay, J.A.: Personal Privacy through Understanding and Action: Five Pitfalls for Designers. Personal and Ubiquitous Computing 8, 440–454 (2004)

13. Begole, J.B., Tang, J.C., Smith, R.B., Yankelovich, N.: Work rhythms: analyzing visualizations of awareness histories of distributed groups. In: ACM Conference on Computer Supported Cooperative Work (CSCW), pp. 334–343. ACM Press, New York (2002)

14. Terveen, L., Akolkar, R., Ludford, P., Zhou, C., Murphy, J., Konstan, J., Riedl, J.: Location-Aware Community Applications: Privacy Issues and User Interfaces. In: Location-Privacy Workshop (2004)

15. Hong, J.I., Landay, J.A.: An Architecture for Privacy-Sensitive Ubiquitous Computing. In: Second International Conference on Mobile Systems, Applications, & Services (MobiSys), pp. 177–189 (2004)

16. Palen, L., Dourish, P.: Unpacking "Privacy" for a Networked World. In: ACM Conference on Human Factors in Computing Systems (CHI), pp. 129–136. ACM Press, New York (2003)

17. Langheinrich, M.: Privacy by Design: Principles of Privacy-Aware Ubiquitous Systems. In: Abowd, G.D., Brumitt, B., Shafer, S. (eds.) Ubicomp 2001. LNCS, vol. 2201, pp. 273–291. Springer, Heidelberg (2001)

18. Nguyen, D.H., Mynatt, E.D.: Privacy Mirrors: Making Ubicomp Visible. In: ACM Conference on Human Factors in Computing Systems (CHI), Workshop on Building the User Experience in Ubiquitous Computing (2001)

19. Lederer, S., Hong, J.I., Dey, A.K., Landay, J.A.: Personal privacy through understanding and action: five pitfalls for designers. Personal and Ubiquitous Computing 8, 440–454 (2004)

20. Clark, H.H., Brennan, S.E.: Grounding in communication. In: Resnick, L., Levine, J., Teasley, S. (eds.) Perspectives on Socially Shared Cognition, pp. 127–149. American Psychological Society, Washington, DC (1991)

21. Cerulean Studios - Trillian Pro, http://www.trillian.cc

22. Java AIMBot, http://sourceforge.net/projects/jaimbot

23. Fogarty, J., Hudson, S.E.: Toolkit support for developing and deploying sensor-based statistical models of human situations. In: ACM Conference on Human Factors in Computing Systems (CHI), pp. 135–144. ACM Press, New York (2007)

24. Tullio, J., Dey, A.K., Chalecki, J., Fogarty, J.: How it works: a field study of non-technical users interacting with an intelligent system. In: ACM Conference on Human Factors in Computing Systems (CHI), pp. 31–40. ACM Press, New York (2007)

25. LaMarca, A., Chawathe, Y., Consolvo, S., Hightower, J., Smith, I.E., Scott, J., Sohn, T., Howard, J., Hughes, J., Potter, F., Tabert, J., Powledge, P., Borriello, G., Schilit, B.N.: Place Lab: Device Positioning Using Radio Beacons in the Wild. In: Third International Conference on Pervasive Computing (Pervasive), pp. 116–133 (2005)

Yours, Mine and Ours? Sharing and Use of Technology in Domestic Environments

A.J. Bernheim Brush[1] and Kori M. Inkpen[1,2]

[1] Microsoft Research, Redmond, WA, 98052, U.S.A.
ajbrush@microsoft.com
[2] Dalhousie University, Halifax, NS, B3H 1W5, Canada
inkpen@cs.dal.ca

Abstract. Domestic technologies have been a popular area of study for ubiquitous computing researchers, however there is relatively little recent data on how families currently use and share technologies in domestic environments. This paper presents results from an empirical study of 15 families in the U.S in early 2007. We examined the types of technologies families own, including TVs, music players, phones and computers; where they were situated within the home; and the degree of shared ownership and use. Our results call attention to the prevalence of shared usage of technology in domestic environments and also suggest opportunistic spaces for ubiquitous computing technology. While not all ubiquitous computing technologies for domestic environments will be shared, the diverse ways families chose to share their computers suggest that future devices might better match how families wish to use shared technology by supporting both the shared usage model of appliances and the ability to access a personal profile.

Keywords: domestic technology, home, sharing, empirical studies, login.

1 Introduction

Domestic environments have long been a place of interest for ubiquitous computing research. In Weiser's original vision of the disappearing computer [20], Sal starts her coffee machine by talking to her alarm clock, wipes her intelligent pen over her physical newspaper to send quotes to her office, and tells her lost garage door manual to find itself. Regardless of whether one prefers Weiser's vision of the disappearing computer or ubiquitous technology that seeks to engage the user [16], homes will be involved. Research on ubiquitous technology in domestic environments has a long history including the smart home movement [1] and recent advocacy for homes that make us smart [18]. Rodden and Benford [17] outlined three key approaches to technology in domestic environments: information appliances, interactive household objects, and augmented furniture.

In this research we focus on existing usage and sharing of technology in domestic environments. A fundamental characteristic of many homes is that they have multiple inhabitants. As we begin to think about the realities of using ubiquitous computing devices in a domestic environment, we are immediately confronted with questions

J. Krumm et al. (Eds.): UbiComp 2007, LNCS 4717, pp. 109–126, 2007.

about whether these devices should support sharing and personalization. For example, would Sal's alarm clock only allow her to start the coffee machine or can Sal's spouse use it as well? Does her pen only work for her or require some type of identification in order to send the scanned information to her?

We have identified two sharing models typically used by technology devices in domestic environments: an *appliance model* and a *profile model*. Technology devices that use the appliance model (e.g., TVs, refrigerators, and landline phones) allow anyone in the home to use the technology and rely on social protocols to mediate sharing of these items. In contrast, technology devices that use the profile model support multiple users on the device by asking users to identify themselves. These devices may also require the user to authenticate themselves. The profile model is typically used in workplace settings and because of this, many computers used in domestic environments, including computers running the Windows and Macintosh operating systems, support profiles. Regardless of whether a particular technology device supports the profile model or not, some households choose to purchase one device for each person, be it a music player, mobile phone, or computer. Using *individual ownership* instead of *shared ownership* attempts to avoid issues of sharing and eliminate any potential for contention by giving each person their own device.

It is perhaps tempting to think that many ubiquitous technology devices and systems could avoid issues of sharing in household settings by adopting the appliance model. Past research does suggest that families do not make use of profile options on their computers [9]. However, Grinter et al. [7] point to problems caused by the use of the appliance model by TiVos, a brand of Personal Video Recorder. TiVos have a single viewer model that does not distinguish between multiple viewers, and thus has no way to differentiate viewing data or generate personalized recommendations. The appliance model also assumes that very little personalization or privacy is needed. It seems naïve to assume that individual family members might not have some desire to customize or have information they would like to keep separate from others. Another way for ubiquitous technology solutions to avoid issues regarding sharing would be to require individual ownership. However, this approach assumes that devices are never shared which is unlikely for a variety of reasons. First, many households do not have the financial means to purchase several devices. Second, the form factor and functionality of some devices make them inappropriate for individual ownership (e.g. most families do not have individually owned toasters). While individual ownership may be appropriate for some ubiquitous devices, certainly, some will be shared.

To better understand how families currently use and share some of their technology and gain insights into sharing models that might be appropriate for future ubiquitous computing devices, we interviewed 15 families in the northwest United States (50 people total). We visited families in their homes and inquired about their current use of several different technologies including computers, TVs, phones, music devices, and game consoles. In particular, we looked at where families located these devices in their homes, how families handled ownership of the devices, and how they managed sharing of computers through use or non-use of logins and passwords.

Whether a family shares one computer or has five computers available can have a significant impact on how they manage share usage. Therefore, we interviewed families in three different groups based on level of computer ownership: families with a single computer, families with fewer computers than people, and families with an equal or greater number of computers than members of the household. Due to our focus on sharing, we recruited households where at least one computer was used by two or more people on a weekly basis. Based on the findings of Kraut et al. [11] about the role teenagers played in motivating Internet use at home, we also selected families at different life stages to explore issues of family dynamics.

Results from our field study showed that families often shared ownership of technology placed in public living spaces, including desktop computers. The differences we observed between where computers were located compared to the other technologies we studied point to semi-private and private spaces as potentially opportunistic locations to focus on for deploying ubiquitous computing devices. Of the families we visited, eight had multiple profiles enabled on some or all of their computers, but whether or not these multiple profiles were used varied widely across the families. Families that did use multiple profiles emphasized a desire to provide family members with the ability to personalize their computing environment and organize their information, rather than a need for privacy. The willingness of several participants to use the computer logged in as other family members, particularly for quick activities, suggests that shared devices might better meet the needs of families by supporting aspects of both the appliance and profile model.

2 Related Work

Our study follows in the tradition of several studies conducted in the late 1990s that explored the use and sharing of technology in domestic environments, typically with a focus on personal computers [10,11,12,13]. More recently, Woodruff et al. [22] looked specifically at the locations and use of wireless laptops in the home and Grinter et al. [7] studied household networks. In our study, in addition to studying computers we also collected information for other technology devices including TVs, phones, and music players. We now motivate and provide context for our study by reviewing findings from previous work on the location of technology in domestic environments, sharing and contention, and the use of profiles.

2.1 Location of Technology

Previous studies of technology in domestic environments have often examined the location of technology as an important aspect that helps characterizes its use. Venkatesh [19] refers to this as the *technological space* in his theoretical framework for understanding the role technology plays in social life and the diffusion of technology. One of the three models Mateas et al. [12] developed based on an ethnographic study of 10 homes in 1996 was a spatial one. They found the PC in every home they visited was located in what they termed the *work space*, rather than the *hang-out* space. Our study allows us to explore whether or not this model still holds ten years later when there are more computers in homes.

Frohlich and Kraut [9] motivate the significance of studying the position of computers in the home by observing the relationship between computer location and sharing. They note that putting computers in private spaces gives special privileges to the owner of the space and discourages sharing, while placing computers in a more public space encourages sharing. In [9] which brings together data from 35 families drawn from their two earlier studies [10,11], Frohlich and Kraut found that 50% of computers were in public spaces like dining rooms, kitchens, and family rooms, while 26% were in semi-private spaces like a study and 24% were in private spaces such as a parent or child's bedroom. Families with more than one computer in their sample placed them in a variety of locations. In their study of 10 English households, O'Brien and Rodden [13] also found the physical configuration of the domestic environment had an influential role in how the technology was used, particularly with regards to ownership. In a 2003 study, Crabtree et al. [4] identified ecological habitats (places where communication media live), activity centres (places where media are produced), and coordinate displays (places where media is displayed) as prime sites for ubiquitous computing in domestic environments. From their study of laptop use by 34 people in 12 households, Woodruff et al. [22] developed a framework of favored places based on whether the location was open or closed and ergonomic or comfortable. They found that laptops were used in a small set of favored places (2 or 3) rather than throughout the home. The data we have collected on technology in the homes of 15 families allows us to see how the locations of computers may have changed after the passage of 10 years from many of the earlier studies [11, 12, 13] and also compare the use of laptops we saw with the findings of Woodruff et al. [22].

2.2 Sharing and Contention

In our study we focus on how households share technology. Most of the U.S. households studied in the 1995 HomeNet study [11] had a single computer (Kraut, personal communication). In the U.S. households in Boston that Frohlich et al. studied in 1997 [10], roughly three quarters of the families had second computers, mostly cast-offs for kids (Frohlich, personal communication). Due to the relatively limited number of computers, it is perhaps not surprising that Frohlich and Kraut [9] reported that "contention for computer time is a heated issue in many of the families we visited," describing fights and arbitration by parents to manage the scarce resource of computer time. In fact, the relationship between parents and children was an important theme of their research, with parents opting to regulate computer usage and internet access.

While technology adoption has greatly increased in the last ten years,[1] the challenges between individuality and collective action observed by Grinter et al. [7] suggest that sharing and contention remain interesting issues to study. In Grinter et al.'s study, iPods and TiVos were identified as causing particular challenges. iPods must be associated with a specific computer and music library which causes problems in shared usage scenarios. TiVo's appliance model does not allow personalization, which led to a competition between members in some households. With different levels of computer ownership in the families we studied, we can gauge whether contention on computers remains an issue for them. By also gathering data for other types of technologies, we can understand how the sharing methods used by families

---

[1] For reference, the UN's MDG Indicator of Personal computers per 100 population estimate for the United States in 1997 was 39.98 computers per 100 population and 76.22 computers for 2004, while for the United Kingdom it was 23.89 computers in 1997 and 60.02 in 2004 (http://mdgs.un.org/unsd/mdg/SeriesDetail.aspx?srid=607&crid=).

for those technologies are similar or different from how they manage sharing of computers.

2.3 Profiles and Personalization

When technologies support the profile model, users have the option to create separate profiles. As Badram [2] has pointed out, logins on computers involve multiple concepts, the *identification* of the user, *verification* of the user's identity and determining whether the user has *authorization* to use the computer. While computer use in a workplace setting typically requires identification, verification and authorization, this may not be necessary in a domestic environment. Frohlich and Kraut [9] reported that most of the systems encountered in their study were not managed using multiple profiles. However, this was not without challenges, as users of the shared computer could find changes made by one user (e.g. software installed, bookmarks) to be disruptive. One reason families might choose to adopt profiles is for personalization; having separate profiles allows users of a shared computer to have their own background and easily separate their bookmarks.

In discussing a study of forced login use in hospitals, where multiple people shared several computers, Badram [2] discussed a number of problems that logins caused. These problems included disrupting the ability of the staff to work collaboratively and share computer related materials, and the ways that people circumvented the logins by having a universal login or annoyed colleagues by locking a computer so it could not be accessed by anyone else. While domestic environments are not hospitals, studies by Crabtree et al. [4, 5] and others [6, 17] highlight the stark difference between domestic environments and the office environment from which the profile model has been transplanted. One of our goals was to understand whether or not families have chosen to make use of multiple profiles, and their reasons for doing so. More generally with respect to personalizing technology in domestic environments, Randall's case study of life in a smart home [14] discusses a continuum between *personalization* of technology which may make it most useful for a particular individual, but difficult for others and *integration* where all functionalities could be used by all family members. Our investigation looks at whether families were using *personalization by profile* [14] on their home computers. By looking specifically at the use or non-use of multiple profiles we gain insight into whether the profile model fits families' needs for sharing.

3 Study Method

To gather data from families about how they use and share technology, two researchers visited each family at their home and conducted a semi-structured interview that typically lasted about 2 hours. The visits were conducted in January and February of 2007. The home visit was modeled on the method used in Grinter et al. [7] and had four components: a demographic questionnaire, sketching exercise, tour around the house, and wrap-up discussion. We visited 15 different families for a total of 50 people. We asked families to have all members present for the interview and achieved that for 12 of the 15 families. Because of scheduling challenges, one person was missing from the three other families, in which case the family members present described the technology owned by the missing participant and their usage patterns. The families all resided in the Seattle metropolitan area in the northwest United States. Families received two pieces of software as a gratuity.

We recruited families that use computers frequently and had at least one computer that was shared. We were also interested in whether the number of computers in the home impacted shared usage so we recruited 5 families in each of three different groups: single computer families (C=1), multiple computer families (C<P), and computer per person families (C≥P). The C=1 families had one shared computer, the C<P families had more than one computer, but not one for each person, and the C≥P families had at least one computer for each family member (old enough to use a computer). For each of the three categories we aimed for a diversity of families. Eight of our fifteen families had teenagers (aged 13 or older) and five had adolescents (7-12 years old). The remaining two families had toddlers (0-3 years old), but data from these children were not included in our analyses since they rarely used the computer. Our families ranged from those living in large private homes to smaller apartments and included single parents, blended families with step children, and families with two working parents. While not intentional, all families primarily used personal computers running the Windows operating system, although one family had recently purchased a Macintosh.

To start our visit, similar to previous studies [e.g. 10, 12], we brought a pizza dinner to each family which served as an ice breaker. We first gathered demographic information, and then asked each member of the family to sketch a floor plan of their house. Participants then used red circular stickers to indicate the location of the computers they used. For laptops, participants indicated all locations of use. To help determine whether the computers were viewed as belonging to a particular member of the family (e.g. Mom's computer) or were associated with a particular space (e.g. living room computer) we asked participants to label the computers using the name they would use when referring to the computer when talking with others. We then gathered additional data for each computer including how long the family had owned it and the percentage of time each family member used that particular computer. Next, we had participants add TVs using yellow stickers, game systems (yellow sticker with black dot), music players including portable ones such as iPods (green stickers), and phones including mobile phones (blue stickers). Participants denoted technology they carried with them around the house, such as a mobile phone or iPod, by putting a stick figure on the diagram. If a mobile device typically stayed in a specific place while in the house (e.g., mobile phone charger), the sticker for the device was put in that location. For each TV, game system, music player, and phone, we collected additional details on who used the technology. Figure 1 shows two example sketches. While we had each participant complete their own sketch, we allowed them to interact while doing the sketches which often led to interesting discussions.

Next we took a home tour, visiting each computer indicated on the sketches. For shared computers, we asked how family members managed the sharing, including whether or not they used multiple profiles. If families made use of profiles, we

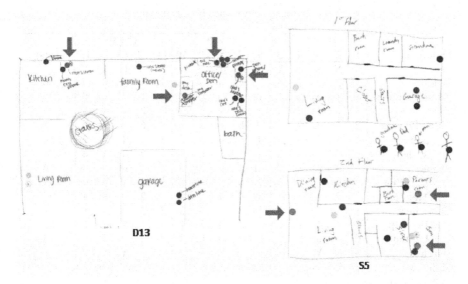

Fig. 1. Participants' sketches of their house's floor plans annotated with dots indicating different pieces of technology. The red dots (representing computers) are marked with arrows.

discussed which profiles were used, whether people might use the computer logged in as someone else, how documents were managed, and how features such as Internet bookmarks and email accounts were handled. We also inquired about the extent to which people personalized their computers. If the computer was a laptop used in multiple locations, we visited all of the locations where the computer was used, and discussed how the person chose the location to use the computer. We also took a digital picture of each computer in its primary location within the home.

We concluded our home visits with a wrap-up interview where we asked participants to describe positive aspects of their current setup and what they were planning to change. We also asked specific questions related to privacy and comfort with home guests and others using their computer(s) and additional questions about personalization of mobile phones and other devices. We analyzed our data by counting the technology present in each household and coding its location. We collected over 650 observations and quotes from participants during the interviews and used the affinity diagramming technique from [3] to derive themes.

4   Results

The interviews and sketches gave us a fascinating picture of the number and type of technology devices owned by the families. We first describe the types of technologies families owned (4.1) and where the technology was located (4.2). Section 4.3 discusses how families shared their technology, looking in particular at the use or non-use of computer profiles. Section 4.4 describes the family dynamics we observed.

Table 1. Technology owned by each family

Family Id.	C = 1					C < P					C ≥ P					Total
	1	2	3	4	5	6	7	8	9	10	11	12	13	14	15	
Teens	N	N	N	N	Y	Y	Y	Y	N	Y	N	N	N	Y	Y	
People	2	2	2	3	4	3	4	4	4	6	2	3	3	4	4	50
Game Consoles	1	1	1	0	1	1	1	0	0	2	4	1	1	0	0	14
TVs	1	2	1	2	4	3	4	4	2	2	3	2	5	5	3	43
Music Players	2	2	4	7	7	11	8	6	3	6	4	6	8	5	6	85
Stereo*	1	2	3	4	5	9	6	4	3	5	3	4	1	4	2	56
Mobile	1	0	1	3	2	2	2	2	0	1	1	2	7	1	4	29
Phones	3	3	4	4	7	10	8	9	4	6	4	4	11	9	13	99
Landline	2	1	3	2	3	7	4	5	2	2	3	2	7	5	9	57
Mobile	1	2	1	2	4	3	4	4	2	4	1	2	4	4	4	42
Computers	1	1	1	1	1	2	3	3	3	3	3	3	4	4	8	41
Desktop	1	1	1	1	1	2	1	3	3	1	1	1	2	2	2	23
Laptop	0	0	0	0	0	0	2	0	0	2	2	2	2	2	6	18
Wireless	N	N	Y	N	N	Y	Y	N	Y	Y	N	Y	Y	Y	Y	9

* different families had different perceptions about what was considered to be a stereo (i.e. alarm clocks).

4.1 Technology in Homes

Table 1 shows the technology owned by each family, with families grouped based on their level of computer ownership. All of the families had a high-speed Internet connection and 9 families had a wireless network running in their house[2], which included 6 of the 7 families with laptops. Four of the 6 families who did not have wireless were single computer families.

Most families with game consoles (PS2, Xbox, etc.) clearly adopted a *shared ownership* approach for them. Eight families each had 1 console, while Family 11 had four consoles for two people. In Family 10, one of the sons also had a Nintendo DS used only by him, but all family members that played games shared their Xbox. For TVs, the raw numbers begin to suggest a move toward *individual ownership,* with 8 of the 15 families having the same number or more TVs than family members. However, families reported considerable shared use, telling us that 37 of the 43 TVs were at least occasionally watched by everyone. Mobile music players and phones are where we truly observed *individual ownership.* Mobile music players were always attributed to a particular individual when described to us (e.g. "Matt's iPod", "my iPod"), similarly each mobile phone was owned by an individual and was referred to using the person's name. Mobile phones were quite popular, 40 participants had a mobile phone and two of the fathers (F4[3], F13) had two mobile phones. The 10 people

---

[2] For reference, the PEW Internet & American Live survey in 2006 reported that 42% of American homes had a broadband connection (http://www.pewinternet.org/pdfs/ PIP_Wireless.Use.pdf) and 19% of internet users had wireless networks at home (http://www.pewinternet.org/pdfs/ PIP_Wireless.Use.pdf).

[3] Using the convention of [11], individuals are identified using their family role and id. For example, F4 is the father in Family 4 and D9b is the second daughter of Family 9.

without mobile phones included M3, who refused to carry a phone saying "[I] just don't want people to be able to reach me," and the 9 children under twelve.

Since we sampled specifically for different levels of computer ownership and some shared usage, we saw families with both completely shared ownership of computers and more individualized ownership, which we discuss further in Section 4.3. One interesting type of usage we observed was *specialized individual ownership* in Family 15 (8 computers for 4 people) and Family 13 (7 iPods for 3 people). For example, F15 uses each of his three laptops for different things, one is for daily work, another for presentations (called "the Beast"), and the third for international travel, while D13 keeps her three iPods in different locations including her bathroom and gym bag.

We found the number of laptops present in the different groups interesting. The C=1 families had no laptops, while 4 of the 14 computers (29%) in the C < P families were laptops, and 14 of the 22 computers (64%) in the C ≥ P families were laptops. Certainly families with more computers had a higher percentage of laptops, but this did not mean that all recently purchased computers were laptops. Both Families 6 and 13 had purchased desktop computers within the month before our visit. M6 told us she bought a desktop because she had never had a laptop and her perception was that they were not as powerful and not as good. She liked the solidness of the desktop.

4.2 Locations of Technology

Examining the participant's sketches, it is clear that technology was pervasive throughout the homes we visited. For each computer we coded its primary location of use as being either public or private (proposed in [9]) based on whether the space was accessible and used by all household members. Mobile devices (e.g. laptops, ipods, mobile phones) were coded according to their primary location of use. If the device was carried around with the person, it was coded as being in a private space. Table 2 gives a detailed breakdown of the locations of technology within the home.

Technology in Public Spaces. Public spaces were defined as areas in the home that were accessible to everyone in the family such as living rooms, dining rooms, kitchens, and home offices. TVs, game consoles, music players, phones, and computers were all common in public spaces within the home. In total, 50% of the technologies we examined were located in a public space. We also examined whether the public locations were completely public (i.e. accessible to everyone in the family) or were semi-private (i.e. controlled by certain people in the family but available to everyone such as a home office) and compared this to previous results [9]. In our study, 20% of the computers were located in completely public spaces (compared to 50% in [9]) while 39% were located in semi-private areas (compared to 26% in [9]). Computer locations differed slightly from locations of other technology with very few families reporting any computer use in the kitchen, and no one reporting use in a garage or bathroom. In contrast, seven families (1,5,6,7,13,14,15) indicated using other technology such as TVs, phones, and stereos in the garage or bathroom.

While music players and phones were common in public spaces, it partially depended on whether the technology was stationary or mobile. Landline phones and stereos were primarily found in public locations (67% and 57% respectively). In contrast, while mobile phones and music players were used occasionally in public

Table 2. Where technology was located in the home: public (e.g., living room, family room, study) or private (e.g., bedrooms, carried with the person)

		Public	Private	Total
TV		26 (60%)	17 (40%)	43
Games		6 (43%)	8 (57%)	14
Music	Stereo	32 (57%)	24 (43%)	56
	Mobile	7 (24%)	22 (76%)	29
Phones	Landline	38 (67%)	19 (34%)	57
	Mobile	7 (17%)	35 (83%)	42
Computer	Desktop	17 (74%)	6 (26%)	23
	Laptop	7 (39%)	11 (61%)	18
TOTAL		140 (50%)	142 (50%)	282

spaces, they were primarily carried around with the person or kept in a bedroom (phones 83%, mobile music players 76%). For computers, 59% were located in a public space with the majority of those being desktop computers (17/24). Overall, desktop computers were significantly more likely to be located in public spaces (74%) than private spaces (t_{14}=2.22, p=.044). Similar to what Mateas et al. [12] observed, these computers were often placed in sections of the public space designated as *work spaces,* typically on a desk (termed an *ergonomic* place by Woodruff et al. [22]). For example, M3 commented she "likes that it [the desktop computer] is in that case [a large furniture cabinet] so we can close it off and it doesn't look like a junky office and keeps kids out of it."

Many of our participants expressed positive comments about having the computers in a public living area. People liked the *togetherness* of the public space, e.g. "Even when we are both doing separate things, we are together" (M2), "I like the fact that the computer is in the open because it encourages conversation" (M5). Also, many parents indicated that they liked having the computers in a public space to keep an eye on the children's activities, e.g. "we decided to put the computer in the living room so we know what everyone is doing on it" (M5). Similar to [9], several parents clearly stated that they would not have computers and Internet in the children's bedrooms: "the kids want the computers upstairs but it's not going to happen!" (M8). Although many of our families liked having the computer in a public space, some family members indicated problems resulting from this approach. In particular, noises from the fan, alerts, or others' usage, as well as light and motion from screensavers can be distracting to other activities in the room.

Of the 24 computers located in public spaces, 16 were kept on the majority of time (11 on all the time, 5 turned off at night) making them available for walk-up use. Desktops were more likely to be left on compared to laptops (14 and 2 respectively). The remaining 8 computers were off unless being used (3 desktops, 5 laptops).

Technology in Private Spaces. We considered spaces to be private when individuals or a group such as parents had primary control over the space (i.e. bedroom). Technologies that people always carried with them throughout the house were also considered to be in a private space. This does not include mobile devices that had a primary location within the home (e.g. a mobile phone that typically stayed in the kitchen instead of with its owner). TVs, game consoles, music players, phones, and computers were common in private spaces within the home. As mentioned previously, 50% of all the technologies discussed in our study were located in private spaces. For computers, 41% were in private spaces (6/23 desktop computers and 11/18 laptops) which is higher than the 24% reported in earlier work [9]. The computers found in private spaces were more likely to be laptops with 11 of the 17 computers being laptops.

We found a roughly even split between technology in adults' versus children's bedrooms (of the technology identified as being in bedrooms, 50% of non-computer technologies and 57% of computers were located in adults' bedrooms). However, laptops were more common in parents' bedrooms (7) as compared to children's bedrooms (1), while desktop computers were more common in children's bedrooms (5) as compared to parents' bedrooms (1). Many of the desktop computers found in children's bedrooms were hand-me-down computers. Not surprisingly, mobile phones and music players were the most common technologies that people carried around and used throughout the home. In our discussions about these devices, it was clear that these were very personal devices and were rarely shared with others in the family. This is different from many of the other technologies in the home, which were much more likely to be shared.

Computers found in private spaces were often turned off when not in use (11/17). Whether or not these computers were laptops was also a factor, 10/11 laptops were turned off when not in use (or put in sleep mode) compared to 1/6 desktop computers.

Laptop Usage. As Woodruff et al. [22] noted, laptops are particularly interesting because they can be moved to different places in domestic environments. Eighteen families in our study had laptops (none from the C=1 group, 3/5 from the C<P group, and all families in the C≥P group). In our study, nine of the 18 laptops (5 from Family 15, and one from each of Families 7,11,12,13) were used primarily in a single location (home office or bedroom), while the other 9 laptops were used in multiple locations throughout the home. Three laptops were considered highly mobile because their owners, three daughters (ages 11, 12, 21) used the laptops extensively, taking them wherever they went in the home (D14a, D14b, D15b). One mother stated, "if it was waterproof, she'd be in the shower with it!" (M14). This exceedingly mobile use seems to be different than usage of laptops in a few favored places observed in Woodruff et al. [22], which we did observe for our adult participants and one 17-year old male (S7), all of whom had individualized ownership of a laptop[4]. The reasons our participants moved between their favored places are similar to those discussed in Woodruff et al. [22] and included where others were in the house; other activities going on; and affordances of the environment.

4.3 Sharing

We observed a large amount of sharing across the technologies we examined. Technology located in public areas was generally shared. All TVs, stereos, and

---

[4] When coding the locations of technology, laptops with a few favored places were coded according to their primary location of use (which was between 70-100% of the time).

landline phones in public spaces were shared by everyone in the family and "place based" names were primarily used when describing the technology (e.g. the one in the garage; the TV in Mom and Dad's bedroom). Computers in public spaces were also generally shared, with the exception of those owned by Family 15 (who had 8 computers) who had *specialized individual ownership*. For the remaining 14 families, 16 of the 18 computers in public areas were shared by multiple members of the family. While Family 15 did not have any computers that family members took turns using, M15's desktop computer was referred to as "the computer" and left on so that everyone in the family could look at and add to the main family calendar which was kept in Outlook (M15 was typically the only person who added calendar events).

Technologies located in private areas, had a lower amount of shared usage. The TVs, stereos, and landline phones found in bedrooms were primarily used by the owner(s) of the bedroom with the exception of TVs in parents' bedrooms, which were often used by several members of the family. As mentioned previously, mobile music players and mobile phones had very little sharing. Computers in private spaces also had much less shared usage, with only 6/17 computers being shared. In three of these cases, it was younger children using the computer in their parent's bedroom (D1, S11 (2 computers)). In one case Family 4 had the family computer in one of the daughter's bedrooms (D4) and the remaining two cases involved family members (D13, M14) borrowing a laptop and taking it out into a public space to use it.

Profiles. One focus for our study was investigating the use (or non-use) of profiles on computers. Windows and Macintosh operating systems support multiple profiles with a feature called 'user accounts.' In both systems, multiple user accounts can be created and each account has its own context including a separate default document structure. Both systems support fast user switching, which allows switching between different accounts without logging off and keeps the other accounts active in the background. We observed three different types of profile use on the computers in the families we studied: having a single profile (7 Families, 4 with teens), having multiple profiles configured, but using only one (4 families, 1 with teens) and regularly using multiple profiles (5 families, 4 with teens). Note that family 8 fell into two categories, all of their computers had multiple profiles, but on two of the computers they only used a single profile. No usage differences were found between the groups representing level of computer adoption, however, the existence of teens in the family seemed to increase the likelihood that separate profiles would be configured and used, unless the teenagers had a computer of their own they could use.

Single Profile. Seven families chose to share a single profile (4,9,10,11,13,14,15) on their computer(s). Convenience and ease of use were common reasons expressed by families. Comments included: "It's more convenient, I'm all about easy" (D10), "You can start using it right away" (M12[5]), "It's a hassle to log in and log off all the time" (M14). Related to the possible use of profiles for privacy and security, some families suggested there was no reason, for example, F11 said "Nothing on there. No need for security". Others felt that they could control and monitor what their children were

---

[5] Family 12 had multiple logins enabled, but choose to share one account. This comment is related to the use of a single profile.

doing more easily when they shared one profile. One mother (M10) explained that they used to have multiple profiles (a year ago), but when the kids started using passwords, she was not happy about it and the family switched to share a single profile.

While participants viewed shared profiles as being simpler, it was not without its disadvantages. First, individual customization was not possible, so everyone would have to be comfortable with choices made by members of the group, such as the background someone chooses to put on. Second, many computer applications have convenience features which save default data to facilitate usage, however, with multiple users, the correct data may not be loaded (i.e., default login information). This was particularly problematic for web browsers which have many convenience features. Family 12 had an interesting work-around to resolve this issue. Although they shared a profile, the desktop had icons for two different instances of their browser (Opera). Each instance was personalized for one of the parents, allowing them to have quick access to their favorites without cluttering up their spouse's list.

Have Multiple / Use One. Four families had multiple profiles enabled, but chose to share a single profile (1,3,8,12). Several families commented that this was because someone else set up their computer or that they had initially envisioned that they would use multiple profiles, but ended up using just one. Some families had a separate administrator profile set up, but it was rarely used. Other families commented that they shifted to sharing a single profile because of specific things set up on one profile (e.g. Internet access) or problems with other profiles. D8a explained that she and her sister used the same login because it gets Internet and IM. Family 5 (who had shifted to use multiple profiles) commented, "When it was dialup, mom's setup was used because it was the easiest (and remembered the password)" (F5).

Four families (10,11,13,15) indicated that they used to have multiple profiles set up on their computer(s), but they switched to only have one profile. Some commented that multiple profiles were "a pain" (D10) or "drove [them] nuts" (M15) so they removed them. In other cases, as new computers were brought into the home, their usage patterns changed. D13 commented that as they gravitated towards individual computers, the need for multiple profiles was less critical. Similarly, D15a explained that they used to have multiple profiles, but took them off now that everyone has their own computer. She said: "It's one less hassle to not have to login."

Multiple Profiles. Five families chose to use multiple profiles (2,5,6,7,8). Interestingly, none of the $C \geq P$ families used multiple profiles. Personalization and organization were common reasons expressed for utilizing multiple profiles. Families explained that profiles enabled them to personalize their environment, including backgrounds, screensavers, and favorites. For example, "Carol can do her own thing, I can do my own thing. We can set up our screens differently and have different backgrounds" (M6). Personalizing backgrounds was popular in our study, with 29 of the 41 computers having custom backgrounds. Families in our study also indicated that individual profiles enabled each person in the family to have their own things on their own profile which some felt was more organized and made it easier to find information. Comments included: "I have all my stuff" (F2), and "His stuff doesn't get in the way" (M2). Some of our participants also commented that individual profiles can provide a sense of identity, "Feels like it's yours" (M5).

Families also indicated disadvantages of having multiple profiles. Six families, who either currently or previously used multiple profiles, expressed confusion about the file structure when using multiple profiles (3,5,6,12,13,15). They had trouble finding shared documents such as digital pictures and remembering which profile certain files were stored under. Additionally, there was some frustration expressed that logging on and off was slow. When asked whether they utilized fast user switching, several families commented that they did utilize it sometimes, but that it often caused the computer to run slow, or were frustrated by notifications (e.g. AIM instant messenger and other pop-ups) that were still received from other profiles.

We asked families using multiple profiles how they handled logging off. Only Family 8 indicated that they logged off after using the computer. In Family 5, most of the family members did not bother logging off, so the typical log-in procedure required logging off the previous person first. In families 6 & 7, both mothers did not tend to log off while other family members did. S7 referred to this as "bad computer etiquette." S7 indicated that one of the reasons why he and his sister try to log off is because their mom has been known to talk to their friends on IM. Family 2 explained that the computer is always logged into the mother's account and if her spouse wants to access his account, he has to first log her out (he always logs himself off when he is done). Family members also told us that they would sometimes use the computer in someone else's profile. This was particularly common if the participant had something quick to do, they would just go ahead and use the active profile.

Contention. Although we recruited families that had least one shared computer, our participants reported very little contention over computers. This is in sharp contrast to previous research which indicated heavy contention over family computers [9]. Two families (6,13) mentioned that there used to be contention over the computer, but now that there are more computers available (one family bought a new computer and the other's daughters moved away to college), this no longer seems to be a problem. The few comments we did receive from families regarding contention indicated only mild concern ("sometimes I have to get off the computer for mom" (D10)) or pointed out a priority or sharing scheme for the computers ("Vanessa gets first crack at the desktop because she doesn't have a laptop" (S7)). Families that had multiple computers often indicated that they would use one of the other computers if the main one was tied up.

4.4 Family Dynamics

The high degree of trust that existed within the families was clear during our study. Several families indicated that they share many technologies in their homes (e.g., M5 said "we pretty much share everything"). In our study, only four families (3,6,8,9) were using passwords on shared machines. Three of these families (6,8,9) indicated that the passwords were a mechanism to limit the children's access to the computer while Family 3 explained that the password was used in case outsiders hacked into their system (both people in the family knew the password). None of the families in our study discussed using passwords to maintain their personal privacy nor did anyone indicate that this was a concern, e.g. "Never tried a password. I don't see a reason unless you want different backgrounds" (D13). In terms of multiple profiles, none of our families expressed privacy as a reason for why they would want or need multiple profiles. While talking with us as a group might have limited their candor, the file organization used by families and the fact that people in families with multiple profiles did not always log off supports our observation that privacy was not a large concern for family members.

While families did not feel a need to protect their privacy from others in the family, similar to [9], many parents did express concern over controlling or monitoring their children's computer and Internet activities. This included limiting the amount of time children were allowed to be on the computer or on the Internet, limiting what web sites they could visit and what information they were allowed to download, determining which computer they were allowed to use, and limiting or preventing certain activities such as IM or chat. For some families, this control or supervision was a way to protect their children from inappropriate activities. For others, the concern was related to a fear that the children would inadvertently download a virus.

While computer administration and technical support issues were not the focus of our study, similar to [7] and [15] we also saw that families typically had a 'technology czar' (proposed by [15]) who managed the family's technology. While our sample of 15 families is not broadly representative, and skews toward upper middle class families comfortable with technology, we found a roughly equal division across gender for which family member was the technology czar. This was surprising given previous research [e.g. 21] on gendered use of computers.

5 Discussion

The results we have presented offer a picture of technology use and sharing in domestic environments in the U.S. which designers of ubiquitous technology can use to inform their decisions on what types of spaces and sharing models may be most appropriate for the technology they are building. In this section, we describe some of the themes that emerged from our investigation that we found most compelling.

Opportunistic Places for Ubiquitous Computing in Domestic Environments. Ubiquitous computing devices proposed for domestic environments are frequently designed to be used in public spaces such as kitchens or living rooms, often in what Mateas et al. [12] termed the *hang-out* spaces. For example, the devices cited by Rodden and Benford [17] include Internet fridges, augmented household notice boards, cups, and garden furniture. Taylor et al. [18] describe augmented magnets, message boards, and clocks. While we do not disagree with the appeal of public spaces as locations of interest for ubiquitous devices, we feel that our study suggests other spaces within domestic environments that may also be appropriate and opportunistic to focus on.

The amount of technology in private and semi-private spaces, suggests to us that these spaces may be a more receptive environment for additional technology than public spaces. One reason for this might be that more private spaces may have fewer aesthetic concerns than public spaces, for example around power cords, noise levels, or furniture style. While certainly we do not advocate creating ugly prototypes, pragmatically during the development and field testing of novel ubiquitous devices, deployment in a private space with less rigid aesthetic concerns might mean the difference between use and feedback on a prototype or it being stuffed in a closet when visitors arrive. Semi-private spaces, such as offices, already include the coordinate displays, ecological habitats and activity centres that Crabtree et al. [4] identified as prime site for ubiquitous computing, and many also contain considerable amounts of computer and non-computer technology. Other public spaces that might be of interest include bathrooms and garages where we were surprised that many of our participants reported having phones and music players. Our intent is not to say that kitchen and living room spaces are uninteresting, merely to point out that since these other environments are conducive to having technology, they might be opportunistic locations to consider for ubiquitous computing devices.

Yours, Mine, and Ours. In the beginning of the paper we identified two sharing models, appliance and profile. We found it interesting that for quick activities like checking a web page, participants would often go ahead and use the active profile even if it was not theirs. While this opportunistic use may be related to time delays when switching users (and future research could explore this further), the treatment of the computer as an information appliance (e.g. for looking at the family calendar or getting directions) and use of the active profile without switching suggests to us the potential for technology devices that support a mixed profile model.

A mixed profile model would incorporate aspects of the appliance model, essentially a single profile shared by everyone, and the profile model that requires a particular profile be active. For example, imagine Sal's alarm clock generally runs in appliance mode allowing anyone to use it to start the coffee maker. But Sal can activate her personal profile, perhaps by saying her name or touching a particular button to identify herself, at which point asking for traffic information would give information about the route to her office rather than her spouse's commute. After a period of inaction, the alarm clock would revert to the shared alarm clock appliance. Given that we saw that many of the computers in public spaces were relegated to a 'work space', a mixed sharing profile, which would better support awareness and quick interactions, might help computers earn a place in the family 'hang-out' space. For example, one can imagine a computer that functioned by default as an awareness appliance, showing information customized for the household, but allowed people to easily transition to longer interactions in their own profile.

Personalization not Privacy. During the study we focused on how families manage sharing of their technology, particularly their computers. We saw more families utilizing multiple profiles than we expected (5 of 15 families), especially given previous research [e.g., 9], although we still observed that many family members were relatively unconcerned about privacy within the family. The password use we did observe was typically used to control access to resources such as the Internet, rather than to keep information private.

So, rather than using profiles to ensure privacy, the primary motivation we heard from our participants was personalization. Participants were not concerned that other family members might have access to their documents and in fact wanted easy visibility of each others' documents since people reported forgetting which profiles they had been in when they saved a document. The depth to which the environment changed when participants switched profiles led to considerable confusion among our participants. We instead propose treating the desire for multiple profiles more like providing different *skins* for the computer, much like one might buy a decorative face plate for a mobile phone or an attractive case for a music player. This approach would change the physical appearance as well as some of the preferences and history for different profiles, but would not require a complete context switch of the entire environment, and would more closely match the experience our participants desired.

6 Concluding Remarks

In this study we have examined the locations and sharing of technologies in 15 homes in the northwestern United States. Clearly the results we have presented must be interpreted with regard to the culture in which they were collected, and our results are most applicable for those developing ubiquitous technologies for domestic environments in the United States or countries with similar cultures and levels of technology adoption.

By examining how families share technology, including their use of profiles on shared computers, our aim is to call attention to the prevalence of shared technology in domestic environments and raise awareness of the importance of considering shared usage. While not all ubiquitous computing technologies will necessarily be shared, developers need to consider whether or not the technology they are developing should support sharing or if it would be more appropriate to require individual ownership. While we have proposed some possible ways that technologies might mix features of the appliance and profile models to better match the ways in which we observed participants using their technology, we see this research as one part of a continuing conversation about how technology functions with respect to sharing in domestic environments. Certainly there are many interesting scenarios left to explore. For example, how devices might support multiple active profiles to record collaborative use of computers or recognize that two people are watching a television program and would both like it added to their personal history. We look forward to continued experimentation with technologies in domestic environments, and hope that in 2017 researchers are not observing that ubiquitous technologies in the home need to better match the ways families share them.

Acknowledgments. We thank the families that participated in our study. We also thank Louise Barkhuus, David Frohlich, Bob Kraut, and our anonymous reviewers.

References

1. Aldrich, F.: Smart Homes: Past, Present and Future. In: Harper, R. (ed.) Inside the Smart Home, pp. 17–39. Springer, Heidelberg (2003)
2. Bardram, J.: The trouble with login: on usability and computer security in ubiquitous computing. In: Personal Ubiquitous Computing, vol. 9, pp. 357–367. Springer, London (2005)
3. Beyer, H., Holzblatt, K.: Contextual Design. Morgan Kaufman (1998)

4. Crabtree, A., Rodden, T., Hemmings, T., Benford, S.: Finding a Place for UbiComp in the Home. In: Dey, A.K., Schmidt, A., McCarthy, J.F. (eds.) UbiComp 2003. LNCS, vol. 2864, pp. 208–226. Springer, Heidelberg (2003)
5. Crabtree, A., Rodden, T.: Domestic Routines and Design for the Home. JCSCW 13(2), 191–220 (2004)
6. Davidoff, S., Lee, M., Yiu, C., Zimmerman, J., Dey, A.: Principles of Smart Home Control. In: Dourish, P., Friday, A. (eds.) UbiComp 2006. LNCS, vol. 4206, pp. 19–34. Springer, Heidelberg (2006)
7. Grinter, R., Edwards, W., Newman, M., Ducheneaut, N.: The Work to Make a Home Network Work. In: Proc. ECSCW 2005, pp. 469–488. Springer, Heidelberg (2005)
8. Hamill, L.: Time as a Rare Commodity in Home Life. In: Harper, R. (ed.) Inside the Smart Home, pp. 63–78. Springer, Heidelberg (2003)
9. Frohlich, D., Kraut, R.: The Social Context of Home Computing. In: Harper, R. (ed.) Inside the Smart Home, pp. 127–162. Springer, Heidelberg (2003)
10. Frohlich, D., Dray, S., Silverman, A.: Breaking Up is Hard to Do: Family Perspectives on the Future of the Home PC. Int. J. Human-Computer Studies 54, 701–724 (2001)
11. Kraut, R., Scherlis, W., Mukhopadhyay, T., Manning, J., Kiesler, S.: HomeNet: A Field Trial of Residential Internet Services. In: Proc. CHI 1996, pp. 284–291. ACM Press, New York (1996)
12. Mateas, M., Salvador, T., Scholtz, J., Sorensen, D.: Engineering Ethnography in the Home. In: Companion Proc. CHI 1996, pp. 283–284. ACM Press, New York (1996)
13. O'Brien, J., Rodden, T.: Interactive Systems in Domestic Environments. In: Proc. DIS 1997, pp. 247–259. ACM Press, New York (1997)
14. Randall, D.: Living Inside a Smart Home: A Case Study. In: Harper, R. (ed.) Inside the Smart Home, pp. 227–246. Springer, Heidelberg (2003)
15. Rode, J., Toye, E., Blackwell, A.: The Domestic Economy: a Broader Unit of Analysis for End User Programming. In: Proc. CHI 2005, pp. 1757–1760. ACM Press, New York (2005)
16. Rogers, Y.: Moving on from Weiser's Vision of Calm Computing: Engaging UbiComp Experiences. In: Dourish, P., Friday, A. (eds.) UbiComp 2006. LNCS, vol. 4206, pp. 404–421. Springer, Heidelberg (2006)
17. Rodden, T., Benford, S.: The evolution of buildings and implications for the design of ubiquitous domestic environments. In: Proc. CHI 2003, pp. 9–16. ACM Press, New York (2003)
18. Taylor, A., Harper, R., Swan, L., Izadi, S., Sellen, A., Perry, M.: Homes that make us smart. In: Personal Ubiquitous Computing, Springer, Heidelberg (2006)
19. Venkatesh, A.: Computers and other Interactive Technologies for the Home. Communications of the ACM 29(12), 7–54 (1996)
20. Weiser, M.: The computer for the 21st century. Scientific American, 94–104 (1991)
21. Wheelock, J.: Personal computers, gender and an institutional model of the household. In: Silverstone, R., Hirsch, E. (eds.) Consuming Technologies Media and Information in Domestic Spaces, Routledge, London, pp. 97–112 (1992)
22. Woodruff, A., Anderson, K., Mainwaring, S., Aipperspach, R.: Portable, But Not Mobile: A Study of Wireless in the Home. In: LaMarca, A., Langheinrich, M., Truong, K.N. (eds.) Pervasive 2007, vol. 4480, pp. 216–233. Springer, Heidelberg (2006)

How Smart Homes Learn: The Evolution of the Networked Home and Household

Marshini Chetty, Ja-Young Sung, and Rebecca E. Grinter

GVU Center & School of Interactive Computing
College of Computing, Georgia Institute of Technology
Atlanta, GA, USA 30308
{marshini,jsung,beki}@cc.gatech.edu

Abstract. Despite a growing desire to create smart homes, we know little about how networked technologies interact with a house's infrastructure. In this paper, we begin to close this gap by presenting findings from a study that examined the relationship between home networking and the house itself—and the work that results for householders as a consequence of this interaction. We discuss four themes that emerged: an ambiguity in understanding the virtual boundaries created by wireless networks, the home network control paradox, a new home network access paradox, and the relationship between increased responsibilities and the possibilities of wireless networking.

Keywords: home networking, smart home, infrastructure.

1   Introduction

As computing has migrated into the home, research exploring the implications of domestic technology has grown [2,5,6,8,14,29]. To date most research focuses on individual devices, although recently a few studies on networked systems have emerged [13,17,27]. However, home networking remains under-explored, and in particular, the question of how these networks interact with the home's infrastructure has not been addressed.

This omission seems problematic, given that domestic ubiquitous computing research typically relies on home networking. This home network is oft assumed to be seamlessly integrated into the home's infrastructure—the physical structure and services (*e.g.*, cable and electricity) and all those involved in their establishment and maintenance. In this paper, we report on empirical research that sought to determine whether these assumptions held true. We found that householders' home infrastructures do not readily enable home networking and we identify some of the challenges that the Ubicomp community will need to overcome if domestic ubiquitous computing applications are going to become widespread in people's homes.

We begin by reviewing domestic technology research. Then we describe our methods and participants and present the framework (based on [23]) used to organize our results. We conclude by discussing four themes that emerged: an ambiguity in understanding the virtual boundaries created by wireless networks, the home network control paradox, a new home network access paradox, and the relationship between increased responsibilities and the possibilities of wireless networking.

J. Krumm et al. (Eds.): UbiComp 2007, LNCS 4717, pp. 127–144, 2007.

2   Background: Domestic Technologies and Home Networking

In the last decade, empirical studies of domestic technologies have surfaced a variety of themes. One set of studies has opened up the idea of "home" for investigation, and shows how householder's routines structure domestic life [2,6,29]. These studies have also shown that rooms—part of the home infrastructure—play a role in establishing and maintaining routines.

Other studies have explored the use of technologies such as set-top boxes [20] and VCRs [26]. These studies illustrate how users' adoption is a product of the interaction with the device. They also highlight how adoption is situated within broader contexts of the home (*e.g.,* routines and divisions of labor) [3]. Further, these studies comment on space use in the home, but also pick up on some of the complexities associated with the technical infrastructure required to manage devices.

Another category of studies has focused on the Internet, and its influence on domestic activities. Early studies, dominated by telecommuting, focused on the blurring of boundaries between employment and leisure, showing that work at home was negotiated as spaces changed to support the creation of home offices [30]. As Internet applications have evolved, studies have continued to report the evolving domestic uses of the network at home [7].

Finally, some studies of domestic technologies have deployed systems in the home. For example, systems such as CareNet, an ambient display for elderly health care, involved making a technological intervention within the home [5]. In these studies, home infrastructure comes up in the context of how and where the technologies are used, and also in deployment challenges.

While studies of domestic technologies have surfaced questions of home infrastructure—of which networking is a part—this has not been a primary focus. Smart home research, by contrast, has solved the problems associated with infrastructure through controlling the building of physical and computational infrastructure [14-16]. Yet, these living laboratories—often held up as a solution— also serve as testaments to the complexity of home networking because of the significant commitment required to make the problems "go away" [10]. Further, these smart homes exhibit an interesting duality, in that many of them serve as "offices" where researchers explore the possibilities of their technologies, and where the infrastructure itself might share some advantages of its office counterpart—the presence of administrative support. Yet, even in the office, reports of difficulties in encounters with infrastructure exist, particularly when it breaks [28].

More obviously, smart homes serve as a means by which to compare most housing stock. While smart homes have built in networks, most householders find themselves needing to retrofit their existing homes to accommodate new technologies (or decide whether or not to do this [19]). Relatively little research reports on the challenges associated with using the home's existing infrastructure for networked applications, but what does exist suggests difficulties [13,17,27].

Kiesler *et al.* [17] found that householders relied on family and friends, as well as service providers, to make their home infrastructure accommodate a networked device. More recently, Grinter *et al.* [13] identified problems with home networking including learning that householders relied on 3-7 companies to provide infrastructure support (*e.g.*: Internet Service Providers, cable, phone) on top of the work they did themselves. Although Grinter *et al.* comment on home infrastructure, their findings focused on the networks themselves, with limited attention to the infrastructure required to support it, and we sought to extend their results. We also expanded on Grinter *et al.'s* work, which was limited to dual-income couple households, by focusing on families with children and other household types—allowing us to explore the role of children in infrastructure work.   Critically, we focused on home infrastructure centrally—grounding the troubles with networking in a broader context of technologies and services, and those who administer and support them.

Shehan and Edwards [27] propose a variety of futures for home networking. Many, if not all, of their models for the future rely on infrastructure agreements—for example, the outsource model which suggests professional home network provisioning (affordable for all).   Inspired, in part, by their models, our research complements theirs by offering empirical evidence about the relationship between home infrastructure—the physical structure and services, and all of those involved in their establishment and maintenance—and home networking.

To analyze our data, we used Rodden and Benford's framework [23], which, although it speaks to Ubicomp broadly (and has been applied at the applications level [24]), emphasizes the relationship between infrastructure and technology. Specifically, Rodden and Benford applied Brand's [4] "layers" theory of home evolution showing how technologies fit in.   They suggest that previous domestic research has largely focused on layers that change the most, and argued that little was known about the more stable layers—those focused on utilities.   By doing that, Rodden and Benford made home infrastructure visible, highlighting interactions between the technical and physical, and the diversity of people responsible for systems administration.   We will return to a discussion of their framework in Section 4.   Next, we describe participants and methods.

3 Participants and Methods

Our study consists of 11 households (drawn from the metro-Atlanta area in the United States) with a total of 28 participants, including 5 teenagers who provided their perspectives on engaging with infrastructure (see Table 1).   We recruited participants by word of mouth, email, and by visiting a high school parent-teachers association meeting, and we did not offer compensation.   Given that our participants come from Atlanta, we recognize that our findings are physically, socially, technically and culturally grounded in household norms, that may not exist in other regions or countries (as others have observed [2, 25]) however, some of our findings echo and build on previously reported encounters with home infrastructure.

For our study, we defined a home network as having one or more computers connected to the Internet and to each other and/or a wireless network.   Additionally, we included Audio/Visual (AV) equipment, at minimum a TV and a receiver.   We included AV networks for two reasons.   First, AV networks have been in homes for a longer time, and we wondered whether experience with them influenced computer networking.   Second, and more importantly, AV and computer networks are converging, and we wondered about those challenges.

Table 1. Participants' demographics (house codes, occupants—occupation and children's ages if relevant—number of computers, wireless or wired computer network—check indicates presence, cross absence—type of Internet connection, and primary caretaker—network administrator—for AV and computer networks)

Home	Occupants	No. of PCs	Wired	Wireless	DSL/Cable	Primary Caretaker AV	Primary Caretaker Computer
P1	Boyfriend [Networking Administrator], Girlfriend [Grad. student, technical field]	4	✓	✓	Cable	Both	Both
P2	Husband [Marketing/Sales], Wife [Grad student, technical field]	3	✓	✓	DSL	Husband	Both
P3	Husband [Builder], Wife [Usability Engineer] (Children not living at home)	2	✓	✓	DSL	Husband	Wife
P4	Husband [Prof., technical field], Wife [Homemaker], Son (8), Son (6), Daughter (3)	2	✓	✗	DSL	Husband	Husband
P5	Boyfriend [Office Manager in firm], Girlfriend [Grad. student, non-technical field] (engaged)	3	✓	✓	DSL	Boyfriend	Both
P6	Husband [Network Engineer], Wife [Usability Engineer], Son (4), Son (1)	7	✓	✓	DSL	Husband	Husband
P7	Husband [Office worker in business], Wife [Homemaker], Daughter [User Interface Designer] (24)	4	✓	✓	Cable	Daughter	Daughter
P8	BrotherA [Grad. student, technical field], BrotherB [Undergrad. student, technical field], Roommate	5	✓	✓	Cable	Brother A	Brother A
P9	Husband [Prof., technical field], Wife [Instructor, technical field], Son (14), Daughter (11), Daughter (<11), Daughter (<11)	5	✓	✓	DSL	Husband	Husband
P10	Husband [Prof., technical field], Wife [Grad. student, technical field], Son (15), Son (9)	7	✓	✓	Cable	Husband	Husband
P11	Husband [Businessman], Wife [Homemaker], Son (>11), Daughter (<11)	5	✓	✓	Cable	Husband	Wife

Clearly, these choices skewed our sample—typically one householder had considerable formal or self-taught knowledge of the technologies (which in and of itself speaks to the usability difficulties associated with home networking), but the other householders varied widely as to their backgrounds and knowledge of networking. We chose these people, despite their high-degree of technical knowledge that existed in most households, because these people were those who were attempting to set up, configure, maintain and evolve their home networks—and relying on household infrastructure to do so. We wanted to understand what real problems these people faced—with particular attention to those ones encountered by the less technical members of each household who might be more typical of the broader middle and upper classes (those who could potentially afford the services and technologies required to create a home network today).

Like Grinter *et al.* [13] we used a two-step data gathering process. First, we asked each household to complete an inventory listing all the computing and AV devices in their homes—allowing us to screen potential participants and customize the protocol for each home. Second, we arranged a home visit (which typically lasted 1-2 hours), which began with each householder sketching the computing, AV, and ideal networks. We noticed that some householders sketches used the physical form of the house to explain their networks (also observed in some of the sketches in [13]). After sketching, participants took us on a tour of their home showing us their networked devices. Proximity to particular parts of the network elicited explanations about the relation between the network and the infrastructure. We audio-recorded the interviews and tours, took photographs of devices, and asked questions. Finally, we finished the visit by asking any outstanding questions. Analysis consisted of transcribing the interviews and examining the resulting data (the interviews combined with pictures, drawings, and inventories) with reference to Rodden and Benford's framework. We report on our results in the next section—grouped around the layers of home infrastructure evolution.

4   Findings: Networking in the Evolving Home

Our findings are organized by the layers of Brand [4] as used by Rodden and Benford [23]. Brand [4] proposed that buildings are composed of six *layers* from the outside in: *Site*, *Structure*, *Skin*, *Services*, *Space Plan* and *Stuff*. *Site* is the fixed geographic location and boundaries of a building. *Structure* is the foundation and load bearing elements of the building. *Skin* refers to the external surfaces of the home. Embedded in Structure is the *Services* layer—the "working guts' of the building including all the wiring and plumbing. Interior layout is determined by the *Space Plan* layer, which includes walls, ceilings, floors and doors. All other things filling up the interior including furniture, appliances and decorative artifacts are called *Stuff*. Brand [4], differentiates each layer by how often it changes and the people who interact and manage it. For example, Structure changes infrequently because of expense and skill, whereas Stuff moves frequently. Responsibility for making changes tends to shift from professionals at Site to householders for Stuff.

Using these layers, we describe how householders interact with these layers as they setup, maintain and troubleshoot their home networks. Our data did not yield any significant interactions between Skin, the external surface of the building and home networking—it came up for one participant in a discussion of the aesthetics of the satellite dish on P3's roof. Consequently, we omit a section on Skin.

4.1   Site: Shaping Services and Managing Boundaries

For our participants, Site—the permanent restricted geographical setting—affected the types of Services available, and in so doing influenced the home network. Numerous participants described a Service, such as the inability to get a choice of Internet connectivity, *e.g.*, lack of Digital Subscriber Line, as limiting how they connected their home to a broader network.   Additionally, Site affected what equipment (Stuff) our participants installed or required.   For instance, one of our households, P6, said there were frequent power outages in their area, and consequently they installed Uninterrupted Power Supplies (UPS), a battery backup, to ensure that they could safely power down devices in an outage.

Reciprocally, home networking affected how householders' perceived their Site. Markedly, most of our participants did not know how far their wireless networks reached.   Nor did they have a strong sense of the degree of mismatch between that and Site boundaries.   And yet, participants realized the potential for mismatch because they saw the networks of other houses bleeding into their own Site.

Households differed in whether and how they managed this mismatch between their physical and wireless Sites.   Several participants used Wireless Encryption Protocol (WEP) keys and Media Access Control (MAC) filtering to restrict wireless access to approved people on their own Site—a type of "digital Site boundary". Others expressed less concern about erecting these boundaries, because for example, they used their computer over a secure Virtual Private Network (VPN) to access work data (P1), and more generally they did not view other people as a threat.   A more extreme example emerged in one interview where a household (P6) relied on the physical Site to contain and secure the wireless Site.   As he put it:

"The only security is like we are 700 feet from the road."

A final reason for leaving the boundaries down emerged during the interviews—some households did not have the knowledge to secure their networks.

Ironically, while some participants expressed concern and took steps to erect digital Site boundaries, those same participants largely saw and used their neighbor's less protected networks.   For example, when P9's Internet Service Provider (ISP) connection went down, the administrator used his neighbors open wireless network to contact his ISP and report the problem.   In another case, P1 described how whenever their ISP went down, their laptop automatically connected to the neighbor's network, the next strongest signal on their Site.   P1's householders reported feeling guilty about being able to see private files on this network but when asked about informing their neighbors about their lack of security one participant spoke of the convenience and utility of having another on-Site connection when their own went down.

In summary, Site affected householder's Services options and influenced Stuff purchases. The interaction between Site and wireless networks showed the most interesting problems (and while we recognize wireless networking is also tied to layers like Services for access to electricity and Stuff since a router is Stuff, we do not focus on these relationships in this paper).   The mismatch between physical and virtual Site boundaries led some to find digital means to reassert the type of control that people desire over their physical property (even if that is not always possible either).   Others' inability or lack of interest in erecting digital fences, allowed some of our participants to cross into their neighbors' virtual Sites and use their network.

4.2 Structure: Modification and Work Arounds

Households varied on whether, and how, they modified the Structure—load-bearing elements—of their home for networking. For example, P10 installed Ethernet in their home, when it was undergoing remodeling, to get a reliable high-speed network. They also built a basement office with a patch panel to centrally control sharing of cable, telephone and Internet connections throughout the house.

Other participants described more problematic encounters with Structure. For example, P11 explained that they wanted to install Ethernet around the house because of the reliability of connectivity (in comparison with wireless). The primary network administrator, the wife in this household, successfully crawled underneath flooring and drilled holes through wooden panels to connect most of the computers in the home. However, the Structure, and in particular a large wall *en route* to her son's bedroom was a sufficient obstacle, that she abandoned that part of the wired plan, opting for wireless to connect that particular machine.

P1 who also installed Ethernet to distribute Internet access around the house, explained that he preferred wired connections because of the security vulnerabilities associated with wireless security, also described difficulties working with Structure. He found drilling holes in the walls for cables time-consuming and in some cases, the holes did not lead to places where cables could be run. In this case, he persevered out of a strong desire to hide the wires. Indeed, our participants often spoke of aesthetics as a reason to engage with the Structure, to remove ugly wires that did not "belong" in sight or if not possible to consider the purchase of wireless technologies.

However, embedding the home network into the Structure of the home could and did cause householders' problems. For example, a participant in P4 laid Ethernet throughout his home while it was being built. After the home was completed, he discovered that he had a dead socket in his office. But, unwilling to tear apart the wall, he was unable to fix the broken connection.

A final unusual example of Structure challenges involves a household, P3, who sought to connect multiple buildings on their property—in this case a guesthouse to the main property. In this case, the household chose wireless, but perhaps more unusually, this decision was made by a regular guest to that home—as they explained:

"He works from StateX...then he comes to [sic] in to CompanyX ... so he stays in the room above the garage and he's the one that set up the router so that he could have wireless access."

Despite these exceptions, most of our participants did not modify Structure for home networking, citing expense and complexity as deterrents. However, we were surprised by the number of participants who saw advantages in wired network infrastructure, reliability and speed, as compelling reasons to engage in complex home modification or take advantage of remodeling opportunities. And of course, for some, wireless networking was a means for working within or around Structure.

4.3 Services: Making and Designing the Network

Households used a number of Service layer technologies—the cabling and wiring that comes into the home from outside (*e.g.*, electricity) as well as the wiring inside the house. Participants described using Ethernet (a dedicated Service), and PowerLine and X10 technologies that both leverage existing Services in the home, the power network and telephone cables. Interestingly, while both Brand [4] and Rodden and Benford [23] suggest that third parties own the responsibility for this layer, our participants spoke of sharing the responsibility when it came to home networking.

This was most clear in the case of laying Ethernet. While two households contracted outside services to wire their homes—four households wired their own homes. Of all six households, four installed a patch panel to allow them to centrally control a variety of infrastructures implicated in converged home networking, the Internet, cable, and phone lines. All six households described Herculean efforts—working together, spread across the house, to determine which outlet matched which connection on the patch panel or where to drill holes for cables to wire their homes. When asked why some chose to lay their own cable, householders cited cost, specific needs such as high grade cabling, sockets in appropriate places, and to ensure a correspondence between the network and physical layout of the house in addition to not trusting third parties to do a good job.

Before commencing these, or even smaller Service projects, households frequently reported having design problems. Participants told us they found the process of designing how Services would support home networking time-consuming and requiring significant forethought (particularly if they wanted to design for continued growth and evolution of the applications and devices supported by the home networking). Perhaps unsurprisingly then, the most complex "home-grown" Service infrastructures came from people who had graduate degrees in computing.

One consequence of the complexities of planning Service infrastructures was on-line representations of the home networks. The system administrator for P8's network used Microsoft Visio to plan out Services-level changes to their home network. In this household, this diagram then subsequently served as a reference which he used whenever considering an update to the network.

One householder in P11 refined our understanding of what "home-grown" complexity meant. She self-described herself as having a lack of technical training, but yet was able to wire her house with Ethernet. She described the effort as hard physical labor, but not mentally complex. Indeed, what participants seemed to find complex as they took on responsibilities at the Service layer—not to underplay the physical labor—was managing all the constraints imposed by networking technologies. Systems needed to be proximate to multiple Services, such as power or data, and had to share a variety of resources, including in some cases limited outlets. Accommodating home networks' multiple and competing Service needs appeared to be at the heart of the complexity.

Our participants varied in their degree of engagement with Services. However, it was clear that by comparison with other accounts, particularly Brand's [4], householders in our study often needed to increase their engagement with this layer by taking increased responsibility. Specifically, they designed and planned how the home network could most appropriately interact with and leverage the Services.

4.4 Space Plan: Controlling Access and Aesthetics

Space Plan refers to a home's room layout including décor. Rodden and Benford [23] argue that previous domestic technologies studies have surfaced relationships between Space Plan and computing. Consequently, we focus on findings that speak to the less examined relationship between householders' use of Space Plan and the home network (as opposed to individual devices). Critically, home networks supported householders in bringing content into spaces of the house, and consequently we found that rooms played a central role in structuring access and engagement with both the computing and AV networks.

Four households in our study used permanent or portable computers in their kitchens. For example, a P8 participant used a computer in the kitchen to access other machines on both his home and work networks, but also to get recipes and check the commute times. He also described the kitchen computer as a convenient means for checking email and for continuing tasks he had originally begun on the computer in the bedroom upstairs. A P7 householder described why he decided to place his computer, which also serves as a TV, in the kitchen.

"I want it closer to the activities at the house. I didn't want to set it up upstairs. The kitchen is kind of a gathering place for us."

The ability to access new types of content in new places presented some of our participants with another challenge, focused on controlling access. Specifically, householders, particularly those with children, described using the Space Plan to create public and private spaces for computing and AV. Parents purposely placed the computers that their children used in rooms—such as kitchens and dining rooms—where the adults could supervise and monitor usage [18]. Simultaneously, other rooms were designed to be "off-grid" for children. For instance, the mother in P11 allowed her children to use their computers in their bedrooms but without an Internet connection (*e.g.,* by physically removing a wireless card from her son's laptop). This house had an Internet-enabled computer in the kitchen where the mother could monitor her children's online activities.

Householders also used their Space Plan to create more private places for some home network uses. We observed this phenomenon with AV networks, perhaps because the primary family equipment was usually placed in public space—such as the living room—[2,13]. Consequently, parents described watching "unsuitable" programming (for their children), *e.g.,* violent films, on AV networks in their bedrooms, which they characterized as a private part of their Space Plan.

Our participants used the Space Plan to create aesthetic and noise-free places. To mitigate the ubiquity of unsightly wiring, participants designated certain rooms as appropriate for highly networked technologies. For example, in P10 the mother moved her son's gaming systems (wires connecting gaming consoles to controllers, the AV network through the TV, and the Internet) to the basement to make her living room more aesthetically appealing. This move also had the effect of reducing noise levels in the shared and central parts of the house.

Participants also described using wireless networks to create a visually pleasing environment that still supported access to the home network. We see this type of aesthetic concern as speaking to householders' desire to work the home network into the décor of their homes. However, the interactions between wireless technologies and home infrastructure sometimes created problems. Households expressed frustration with poor wireless signals leading to loss of Service that they thought— correctly—were caused by thick walls and possible interference from other electronic equipment nearby (most notably the kitchen, a room full of appliances).

Participants described an interesting relationship between Space Plan and home networking. On the one hand, home networking changed the possible activities that could take place within the Space Plan, and was used to hide some activities in new places. Simultaneously, the Space Plan was used to constrain that same range of activities for some home network users, notably children. Finally, Space Plan was used to make some technologies disappear from certain rooms by designating other places as more appropriate or using technologies that would render the artifacts of home networking perceptually invisible. The latter was not without issue.

4.5 Stuff: Complex and Potentially Isolated

Devices—computing and AV related equipment—are the Stuff of the home network and householders add, move, and disconnect equipment. Householders moved equipment for various reasons. New equipment purchases often triggered the movement of an older equivalent to a different network (in the case of AV) or part of the Space Plan (in the case of the computer network). Inhabitants engaged in device migration for other reasons as well. For example, the P4 household moved their TV and purchased new audio speakers because they felt that the old position was sub-optimal for watching and listening. They reported leaving the old, unused speakers mounted on the wall because removing them was a complicated process.

Participants reported that the Service layer constrained their movement of equipment. For example, power and Ethernet wall plugs determined the position of some home network devices. Additionally, the placement of Service plugs, often determined and shaped the place of non-networking Stuff, used to enhance aesthetics. Participants told us about using carpets, rugs, cupboards and couches to hide the Stuff of home networking. We also observed examples of using Stuff of the home network to obscure other home networking Stuff, such as hiding cables behind TVs.

Complexity of device configuration and interoperability emerged as a theme when we examined the relationship between Stuff and home networking. In a study of AV networks, Petersen *et al.* [21] described how onerous participants found configuring their devices to work together, for example to make surround sound work. We observed similar difficulties emerging with computer network Stuff in this study.

These problems stood in stark and almost ironic contrast to the aspirations of all the participants in our study. Most householders in our study described wanting a fully networked home, one where they could share media between the Stuff of both computing and AV networks. Another surprisingly common theme in our study was the desire of our participants to be able to access, manipulate, and consume media stored on devices in one part of the house on devices in other areas of the home. For example, in household P11, participants connected and distributed speakers throughout the house so that they could listen to sports on the deck without having to place the radio there. Other participants indicated a desire to be able to listen to and watch the TV, located in their living room, from their kitchen while muting the sound in the living room, so as not to awaken their children.

Sadly, despite the desire to connect the Stuff of computing and AV together and across these networks, most of our participants had not attempted to do this in practice. Citing complexity, some households had simply not tried. Other households admitted that they lacked the in-home skill to connect Stuff. Following Brand, and Rodden and Benford's analysis, responsibility for Stuff falls to the householders, and this was certainly true in the case of home networking devices. And yet, participants spoke of a complexity that made this responsibility particularly challenging, a lack of detailed technical knowledge and the difficulties of connecting an eclectic mix of devices. The latter also appeared to exacerbate the former—eclectic Stuff included legacy devices that might be older than some householders themselves (hand-me-downs, or purchases made prior to the arrival of children)—consequently requiring knowledge of the history of the evolution of connection standards, and an awareness of whether and how these older devices could be "made to work" with newer ones.

The lack of device or Stuff interconnection had implications for the degree of "online" data interconnection. Most participants described transferring data among devices as being a process that involved USB flash drives, CDs or emailing the document to people with accounts on the target device. In other words, even though participants desired a networked home, they still used physical means or the internet to transfer information between devices, sometimes even in cases when these devices were connected together.

Only two households had connected their AV and computer networks, which they used to stream media from a server to a television. Both households had occupants who were technology aficionados and had created customized Linux solutions that turned machines into media centers. These individuals had also set up a complex system of switches to configure different input and output devices (*e.g.,* switching from DVD input to input from a computer server).

Given the complexity of connecting Stuff (within computer and AV networks, let alone crossing them), households resorted to a number of mechanisms for explaining the state of the network. For example, the P6 participants used notes and post-its on each wire going into various AV devices to remind them how their Stuff network was connected together. Other households, aware of the complexity of operating, let alone administrating or troubleshooting their networks, produced instructions. Participants told us that instructions were given to guests, babysitters, and children, to help them orchestrate the operation of the Stuff in the network. Our participants seemed to accept this work and responsibility, albeit grudgingly, to reap the benefits of home networking. In other words, participants produced instructions and reminders so that they themselves as well as their guests could understand and operate the Stuff that comprised their home networks.

Although Stuff has been a focus of previous research of computing in the home [23], home networking brings a new perspective on how householders' connections shape devices. Movement, while desired by householders, is constrained by Services, and the Space Plan. Additionally, the work of connecting devices is outside the reach of some households and creates a new burden—remembering and explaining the combined functionality to potential users. For our participants, the home network as a whole was more than the sum of its parts—an equation that pitted complexity of dealing with the whole against their own visions of a future with networked services.

5 Discussion: Reconsidering the Layered Smart Home

This paper used Rodden and Benford's framework [23] (based on Brand [4]) to examine the relationship between home networking and home infrastructure. Throughout the analysis we were struck by the need to consider aesthetics in the design not just of Ubicomp technologies, but in the infrastructure required to support them. Aesthetics caused our participants to take up challenging projects, notably hiding things because of their lack of appeal, even if that meant opening up walls. As a community clearly we need to consider the role that aesthetics can play in the easy adoption of the solutions we seek to provide. In this section, we turn to a discussion of four other themes that emerged as householders engaged with infrastructure. First, we discuss an ambiguity in understanding the virtual boundaries created by wireless networks and the need to design systems that help users manage these boundaries more easily. Next, we revisit the home network control paradox, particularly for avid network tinkerers, which suggests that householders may need to be supported through appropriate metaphor and network visualization. We also present a new home network access paradox arising when children are present in the home that affects the types of network management systems we design. Finally, we discuss the relationship between increased householder responsibilities for home networking and how wireless networking and external service providers may help ease the burden of networking the home.

5.1 Re-placing Site Space: Exploring Physical and Virtual Boundaries

Focusing on Site highlighted a mismatch between physical and virtual boundaries. Physical Site boundaries are, according to Brand [4], the most immutable of outlines, being the least likely to evolve over time because change requires working with governmental agencies to have lines redrawn.   By contrast, wireless networks presented our participants with new ways of considering their and other households' Sites by being able to bleed over physical boundaries.

Our participants had mixed responses to what it meant to have a virtual Site to manage. Some did little to prevent others "trespassing" onto their virtual Site, taking advantage of the resources on offer in that other Site but others sought a variety of technical solutions. One was to share their virtual Site, but protect their own access by using technologies such as VPN. Another was to attempt to erect boundaries, akin to virtual fences, using WEP and MAC controls. Finally, we found people who seemed unaware of the implications of this potential mismatch, or that they were creating a new Site, one that was accessible in ways that their physical Site typically is not.

One interpretation of this observation concerns security.   Clearly, the difficulties that some of our participants had in using security to establish and manipulate virtual Site boundaries—not to mention the fact that even if they did use WEP, they had not technically secured their network [1]—speaks to the need for usable systems. Ubiquitous computing for the masses presses particularly on this because the types of applications proposed often contain potentially sensitive data; for example, household rhythms tracked by sensor networks could reveal appropriate times to rob a home, or health data transmitted to the doctors office could expose illnesses—exposure being particularly serious if it reveals that a householder has a socially stigmatized disease.

However, another argument suggests that designs that treat virtual and physical Sites as equal exclude other possibilities. Another interpretation of our findings is that Site concerns speak to another debate, the re-placing of space [9]. Physical Site, grounded in a set of practices about land management seemed natural to our participants—taken for granted as a consequence of a long-ago institutionalized set of governmental arrangements—thus lending themselves to an interpretation of space as a "fact". By contrast, Sites created by wireless networks did not have this property.

Instead they produced mixed responses, some seeking to erect walls and some not minding if others used their networks, suggesting that the virtual Site has not become as solidified in people's and practices. Indeed, we would argue that the ambiguity in interpretation of "appropriate behavior" in a virtual Site was even more pronounced among those participants who created their own fences while simultaneously exploiting the lack of boundaries around other's wireless networks.

Like others who have explored occasions where multiple interpretations exist [11], this ambiguity presents an opportunity for Ubicomp designers and we should perhaps not rush to constrain the virtual to the physical. As Dourish [9] argues, technologies present an opportunity to reconsider our spatial experiences and—for ubiquitous computing—this offers a possibility to explore how we might leverage wireless technologies to help people reconsider what their virtual Site contains. But, solutions that allow people to manage security, while not binding the virtual to the physical, will likely involve creating applications that give end-users a degree of choice in whether to, and if so, how, secure and bind their wireless networks. This calls for further work to understand what types of choices ought to be provided, and how to offer them to end-users in meaningful ways. In addition to partnering with usable security researchers, as a first step, we suggest considering questions of Site and spatiality, something that Rodden and Benford's [23] framework supports.

5.2 Managing Networked Stuff: Revisiting the Control Paradox

In a seminal study of family life in a smart home, Randall [22] identified a control paradox (also suggested by [8]). Simply put, the smart home's systems for controlling the lived experience were so complex that some, if not all, of the householders experienced a lack of control along with an intense frustration. Even the simple functions such as turning lights on and off required complex manipulation of menu-based systems with householders being irritated and uncertain whether they could in fact complete their task.

In our participants' homes, we observed phenomena that suggested a similar type of control paradox, in this case a control of network paradox. On home tours, and in the spaces where we interviewed people—although sometimes they had been tidied away prior to our arrival—we observed evidence of multiple remotes. We also learned about and noticed maps and instructions to support the manipulation of systems. These mechanisms suggest that the control paradox exists in "normal" homes, and as we learned, people respond through persistence in use and by creating a number of representations that explained the network to them.

We also saw a difference between Randall's control paradox and some of the ones that we encountered. In particular, some of our participants' networks seemed to be in a continual on-going project state. Attempts to upgrade and refine the network often seemed to lead to further projects. Intriguingly though, when we asked about these projects, we were sometimes left with an impression that some householders saw the home network as a Do-It-Yourself project. The lack of control that resulted when the project was on-going (sometimes spanning weeks, while the householder did not have leisure time to continue working on the project) led to a certain lack of control that appeared self-inflicted, and based on a desire to explore home networking recreationally. We suggest that these projects constitute part of the nascent

Digital-Do-It-Yourself (DDIY) culture that will likely exist for the network infrastructure as it already does for the physical infrastructure [12]. And although DDIY-ers do not represent all potential consumers of Ubiquitous computing technologies, they raise questions. For example, what does it mean that the systems that we design will be potentially altered, upgraded, and implicated in projects that restructure the home network and its services? Ubiquitous computing systems are typically designed from end-to-end, as whole solutions implemented to solve a particular problem. But, when they enter certain environments, they may be disassembled, rearranged, and partially upgraded. How do we account for this in our design process?

Irrespective of whether our participants engaged in DDIY, we saw people coping with control by generating representations—notably maps and instructions. But these representations were woefully inadequate for dealing with many aspects of the "seeing" that participants desired in order to make their home network work. They did not have representations that allowed them to see obstacles inside the Structure, or the ability to see the Services offered to their home, let alone the ability to map between their virtual and physical Sites. We see opportunities for reconsidering representations, and in particularly designing new types of network visualization that are householder-centric rather than technologically-centric. Today's network visualizations target network administrators, as opposed to home users, resulting in systems that focus on specialized network-technical details [27]. Taking a household-centered approach, we would argue that exploration of the control paradox through the perspective of layers suggests a variety of complementary visualizations that could support home networking. Visualizing the physical Structure of the home, creating maps that show the range of wireless devices (based on signal type) and representations that support roll-back to previous network states would all increase householders' sense of control. But, we also see the need to understand what types of metaphors would make the most sense to householders, and suggest a need for further research to understand what metaphors could be leveraged.

Beyond representations, control speaks to what it means for the network to work or not. Specifically, networked Stuff adds a dimension of complexity, transforming the network into something that spans the Services and Stuff layers, because it requires devices to provide service to the applications on it. So, unlike Service level failures—electricity and water outages—the network itself, not the applications on it, could partially fail if one device ceased to work. These partial failures, of Stuff in the service of Service, were particularly troubling for participants to diagnose and repair, but all speak to what it means to control the network.

5.3 Space Plan: Introducing the Access Paradox

Our study suggests another paradox related to access to the network. Our examination of Space Plan showed that in homes with children the Space Plan and home network interacted to simultaneously increase and decrease access to content.

Adult participants in our study described how their network allowed them to reconfigure their use of space increasing their opportunities for networked-based activities from a variety of rooms within the home, such as the kitchen. Simultaneously, these same adults described two types of restricted access that turned on manipulating the Space Plan—and the behaviors appropriate or possible within that—in conjunction with the home network. First, they described carving out a private space for the consumption of sensitive media, such as films deemed too violent for children. In this case, the home network again supported a redirection of activities, out of public spaces and into more private ones. Second, they described using the Space Plan to restrict their children's access to and use of the very content that the home network provided. By disconnecting machines from the network that were in isolated parts of the Space Plan, and by placing connected computers in public settings such as the kitchen, adults described how that provided them a sense of control over the access that their children had to the Internet in particular.

Contrast this with some visions of Ubiquitous computing, and the networks that support it, that tend to emphasize increased access. In homes with children, increased access is not always desirable, instead the ability to control and manipulate access is desired. In some cases, this might be possible by simply disconnecting devices, but when that is not the case, we need to be open to the design of systems that can be virtually disconnected (which again speaks to a relationship between Ubiquitous computing and the usable security community).

Beyond access controls, Space Plan highlights the relationship between technical and social infrastructures. This has been commented on before with a focus on particular devices in rooms (*e.g.*, [2,6,20]). Our study suggests that the home network is also implicated in this relationship and must be deeply considered to both provide and facilitate content provision while simultaneously restricting access. In particular, the home network is technically neutral, providing the possibility of access throughout the Structure and Site, but it is the Space Plan that seemed to highlight and shape the access paradox. In particular, the householders' manipulation of the Space Plan framed their decisions about access. We suggest that this insight offers an opportunity for reflection by the Ubicomp community. How will Space Plan shape the ways in which householders seek to adopt and use, or restrict and deny, access to systems based on their presence in various rooms of the home? Minimally, we argue that considering these questions in the deployment of systems in homes, particularly those with children, may yield implications for the results of these experiments.

5.4 Service and Responsibility, Structure and Wireless

The Service and Structure layers also spoke to issues that we wish to revisit. The Service layer revealed a changing shift in responsibility. In comparison with Brand's description of this layer—one where external parties made changes, and thus guided its evolution—we observed a greater degree of household responsibility for designing and delivering the Service of the home network.

One reason why participants took up the work of designing the Service was that they told us that they did not trust external parties. External service providers had not, in the eyes of our participants, yet reached the stage where they were able to design a home network that met our householders' needs. One explanation of this situation relies on a temporal argument that some people, our participants, at least in this region, at this time, have such "cutting edge" expectations of what a home network should be that they cannot find an appropriate contractor. This suggests that in time the situation could change and eventually outside sources will be sufficiently sophisticated to make modifications to the Service layer—retrofitting houses for Ethernet and so forth with the technical ability required to produce home networks for complex and varied needs (although, as Shehan and Edwards observe there are downsides to this particular approach [27]). But, if this is the case, then the Ubicomp community might take heed of, and potentially encourage the emergence of these outside service providers, to ensure that they enable ubiquitous computing services. Further, the evolutionary properties of home networking suggest that the external service providers will also have to evolve their services to meet the demands of the changing home network or supply enough access that householders can do this work.

Another potential explanation is that responsibility is permanently shifting for this layer. Outsiders will not emerge to provide Service, and householders will either develop their own knowledge and skill, or be unable to have home networks. This latter argument poses significant challenges for the Ubicomp community—if a class of people cannot or choose not to accept this responsibility for Service, and if external providers do not fill the need, or if their services are not largely affordable—we have a situation where our user base is the manifestation of the next digital divide. This divide would be based on financial and technical literacy needed for home networking Service and all the applications it makes possible.

Into this mix comes the hope of wireless technologies. Within this study, we observed participants using wireless technologies to work around the constraints and complexities imposed by interactions between wires and virtually every layer of the home. Yet, we were surprised to find, despite wireless, there was an enthusiasm and need for wired solutions. Participants spoke of reliability, speed and security as reasons for wanting wires. Further, participants showed us legacy equipment that was not ready for (or ever would be) for wireless solutions. Old computers, and favored AV equipment such as receivers and amps, ranged in ages by as much as decades.

Again, we can view this as a temporal anomaly and assume that with time, the oldest of machines will be out of the house, and the new so-called "old" machines will be running 802.11b wireless technologies. One problem with this argument is that by the time this occurs, there is a distinct possibility that the newest of technologies will no longer support that wireless standard. More generally, wireless hints at a problem that the age range of technologies, that are not as uniformly new as those found in the workplace, presents challenges for the types of systems that the Ubicomp community seeks to design.

6   Conclusions

We used Rodden and Benford's framework [23] to explore the relationship between home networking and home infrastructure. We discussed four themes: an ambiguity in understanding the virtual boundaries created by wireless networks, the home network control paradox, a new home network access paradox, and the relationship between increased responsibilities and the possibilities of wireless. More generally, we offer this research as a starting point for discussions within the Ubicomp community about for whom and how the home network will be designed.

Acknowledgments

We thank our participants, reviewers, and shepherd. This work was supported by NSF CNS #0626281.

References

1. Balfanz, D., Durfee, G., Grinter, R.E., Smetters, D.K., Stewart, P.: Network-in-a-Box: How to Set Up a Secure Wireless Network in Under a Minute. In: Proc. USENIX Security Symposium, pp. 207–222 (2004)
2. Bell, G., Blythe, M., Sengers, P.: Making by making strange: Defamiliarization and the design of domestic technologies. ACM Trans. Comput-Hum. Interact. 12(2), 149–173 (2005)
3. Bly, S., Schilit, B., McDonald, D., Rosario, B., Saint-Hilaire, Y.: Broken expectations in the digital home. In: Extended Abstracts of Conference on Human Factors in Computing Systems (CHI 06), pp. 568–569 (2006)
4. Brand, S.: How Buildings Learn: What Happens After They're Built. Penguin, New York (1994)
5. Consolvo, S., Roessler, P., Shelton, B.E.: The CareNet Display: Lessons Learned from an In Home Evaluation of an Ambient Display. In: Davies, N., Mynatt, E.D., Siio, I. (eds.) UbiComp 2004. LNCS, vol. 3205, p. 17. Springer, Heidelberg (2004)
6. Crabtree, A., Rodden, T., Hemmings, T., Benford, S.: Finding a place for UbiComp in the home. In: Dey, A.K., Schmidt, A., McCarthy, J.F. (eds.) UbiComp 2003. LNCS, vol. 2864, p. 126. Springer, Heidelberg (2003)
7. Cummings, J.N., Kraut, R.E.: Domesticating Computers and the Internet. Inf. Soc. 18(3), 1–18 (2002)
8. Davidoff, S., Lee, M.K., Yiu, C., Zimmerman, J., Dey, A.K.: Principles of smart home control. In: Proc. UbiComp 2006, pp. 19–34 (2006)
9. Dourish, P.: Re-Spacing Place: Place and Space Ten Years On. In: Proc. Computer Supported Cooperative Work (CSCW 06), pp. 299–308 (2006)
10. Edwards, W.K., Grinter, R.E.: At Home with Ubiquitous Computing: Seven Challenges. In: Abowd, G.D., Brumitt, B., Shafer, S. (eds.) Ubicomp 2001: Ubiquitous Computing. LNCS, vol. 2201, p. 108. Springer, Heidelberg (2001)
11. Gaver, B., Dunne, T., Pacenti, E.: Design: Cultural probes. Interactions 6(1), 21–29 (1999)
12. Gelber, S.M.: Do-It-Yourself: Constructing, Repairing, and Maintaining Domestic Masculinity. American Quarterly 49(1), 66–112 (1997)
13. Grinter, R.E., Ducheneaut, N., Edwards, W.K., Newman, M.: The Work To Make The Home Network Work. In: Proc. Ninth European Conference on Computer-Supported Cooperative Work (ECSCW 05), pp. 469–488 (2005)
14. Harper, R. (ed.): Inside the Smart Home. Springer, London (2003)
15. Intille, S.: Designing a home of the future. IEEE Pervasive Computing 1(2), 76–82 (2002)
16. Kidd, C.D., Orr, R., Abowd, G.D., Atkeson, C.G., Essa, I.A., MacIntyre, B., Mynatt, E.D., Starner, T., Newstetter, W.: The Aware Home: A Living Laboratory for Ubiquitous Computing Research. In: Proc. Second International Workshop on Cooperative Buildings, Integrating Information, Organization, and Architecture, pp. 191–198 (1999)
17. Kiesler, S., Lundmark, V., Zdaniuk, B., Kraut, R.E.: Troubles with the Internet: The dynamics of help at home. Human Computer Interaction 15(4), 323–351 (2000)

18. Livingstone, S.: Young People and New Media: Childhood and the Changing Media Environment. Sage Press, London (2002)
19. Mainwaring, S.D., Chang, M.F., Anderson, K.: Infrastructures and Their Discontents: Implications for Ubicomp. In: Davies, N., Mynatt, E.D., Siio, I. (eds.) UbiComp 2004. LNCS, vol. 3205, p. 17. Springer, Heidelberg (2004)
20. O'Brien, J., Rodden, T., Rouncefield, M., Hughes, J.: At home with the technology: an ethnographic study of a set-top-box trial. ACM Trans. Comput.-Hum. Interact. 6(3), 282–308 (1999)
21. Petersen, M.G., Madsen, K.H., Kjær, A.: The Usability of Everyday Technology—Emerging and Fading Opportunities. ACM Trans. Comput.-Hum Interact. 9(2), 74–105 (2002)
22. Randall, D.: Living Inside a Smart Home: A Case Study. In: Harper, R. (ed.) Inside the Smart Home, Springer, London (2003)
23. Rodden, T., Benford, S.: The evolution of buildings and implications for the design of ubiquitous domestic environments. In: Proceedings of Conference on Human Factors in Computing Systems (CHI 03), pp. 9–16 (2003)
24. Rodden, T., Crabtree, A., Hemmings, T., Koleva, B., Humble, J., Åkesson, K., Hansson, P.: Between the dazzle of a new building and its eventual corpse: assembling the ubiquitous home. In: Proc. Designing interactive systems: processes, practices, methods, and techniques, pp. 71–80 (2004)
25. Rode, J.: Appliances for whom? Considering place. Personal Ubiquitous Comput. 10(2), 90–94 (2006)
26. Rode, J., Toye, E., Blackwell, A.: The domestic economy: a broader unit of analysis for end user programming. In: Extended Abstracts of Conference on Human Factors in Computing (CHI 05) Systems, pp. 1757–1760 (2005)
27. Shehan, E., Edwards, W.K.: Home Networking and HCI: What Hath God Wrought? In: Proceedings of Conference on Human Factors in Computing Systems (CHI 07), pp. 547–556 (2007)
28. Star, L.: The Ethnography of Infrastructure. American Behavioral Scientist 43(3), 377–391 (1999)
29. Taylor, A.S., Swan, L.: Artful systems in the home. In: Proceedings of Conference on Human Factors in Computing (CHI 05) Systems, pp. 641–650 (2005)
30. Vitalari, N.P., Venkatesh, A., Gronhaug, K.: Computing in the Home: Shifts in the Time Allocation Patterns of Households. Communications of the ACM 28(5), 512–522 (1985)

"My Roomba Is Rambo": Intimate Home Appliances

Ja-Young Sung, Lan Guo, Rebecca E. Grinter, and Henrik I. Christensen

GVU Center & School of Interactive Computing
College of Computing, Georgia Institute of Technology
Atlanta, GA, USA 30308
{jsung,languo,beki,hic}@ cc.gatech.edu

Abstract. Robots have entered our domestic lives, but yet, little is known about their impact on the home. This paper takes steps towards addressing this omission, by reporting results from an empirical study of iRobot's Roomba™, a vacuuming robot. Our findings suggest that, by developing intimacy to the robot, our participants were able to derive increased pleasure from cleaning, and expended effort to fit Roomba into their homes, and shared it with others. These findings lead us to propose four design implications that we argue could increase people's enthusiasm for smart home technologies.

Keywords: Empirical study, home, robot, intimacy.

1 Introduction

As robots enter the domestic sphere in the form of pets, caretakers, and vacuum cleaners, a growing body of research argues the need to make robots fit into people's lives [5,7,12,22,31]. Yet, far fewer studies have sought to empirically understand (with the exception of [11]) whether robots change domesticity as people adopt them. In this paper, we address this omission by reporting the results of our study of one type of robot (iRobot's Roomba™ shown in Fig. 1) to learn whether, and if so, how, householders responded to their presence. What we learned suggests that people do form strong intimate attachments to these technologies.

Studying domestic robots is timely, given globally rising adoption [38], and the increasing popularity of Roomba itself as evidenced by the media[1][2][3]. Beyond rising numbers though, media reports also suggest that people engage in a variety of practices with robots. For example, an online video recently posted was called "Caroling Roombas" and featured three Roombas with Christmas hats programmed to sing and dance[4]. This story and others like it, reminded us of narratives (in books, films and comics) that have long existed that portray robots as partners in our lives. As robots enter homes, now is the right time to understand how householders adopt them and form intimate relationships. Further, we see robots playing a role in what some have described as intimate ubiquitous computing [2].

---

[1] http://www.wired.com/news/technology/0,59249-1.html?tw=wn_story_page_next1
[2] http://www.usatoday.com/tech/news/robotics/2004-08-31-robotics_x.htm
[3] http://www.mercurynews.com/mld/mercurynews/news/16190006.htm
[4] http://www.gizmodo.com/gadgets/robots/caroling-roombas-sing-dance-223938.php

J. Krumm et al. (Eds.): UbiComp 2007, LNCS 4717, pp. 145–162, 2007.

This paper is organized as follows. We begin by reviewing literature about intimacy and emotion within computing, robotics and psychology disciplines. After describing our methods and participants, we present three themes that spoke to the nature of the intimate relationships people formed with their Roombas. First, we learned about participants' happiness with Roomba because it helped them be cleaner and tidier. Second, people used anthropomorphic and zoomorphic qualities to engage with Roomba. Third, people demonstrated their Roomba to others, and went great lengths to change the home to accommodate it better. We conclude by discussing how intimacy can inform device adoption and help people to manage unreliability, and by presenting four implications from this study, concerning the role of form, ambiguity, accountability and support in the design of domestic ubiquitous computing systems.

Fig. 1. Photos of Roomba Discovery™: with and without custom-made covers

2 Related Work: Intimate Relationships with Technology

Various terms have been used to describe close personal relationships with technology including intimacy, affective quality, and emotional attachment. According to Bell et al. [2], *intimate ubiquitous computing* consists of at least one of three types of intimacy existing: a cognitive or physical closeness to technology, and feelings of intimacy between people mediated by technology. Others have argued that objects have an affective quality if they cause changes in a persons mood, emotions, and/or feelings—definitions typically used to assess intelligent agents [40]. Norman [26] uses the term *emotional attachment* to describe how some technologies change people's first impressions of, engagement with, and behavior. Finally, Bill Gaver's concept of *ludic engagement* speaks to the playful and unanticipated consequences of people's interactions with technology [14].

What all these perspectives on intimacy suggest are strong human-technology engagements. For our study, Norman's [26] definition was most useful because of its particularly detailed description of humans' relationships with non-human artifacts. That said, we decided to replace the term emotion with intimacy, because we felt that the former represented a more limited range of human responses: subjective feelings, physiological activation, and motor expressions (evidenced by [18]). Our study hypotheses, based on media accounts of Roomba usage, suggested people's responses were inter-personal and social, relying on behavior, intention, as well as emotion. This realization led us to review the social psychology literature which emphasizes relationships with families, partners, society and so forth [17,34]. As one social psychologist notes, intimacy is "warmth, closeness, and sharing in a relationship" [33]. Thus, in this research we broadened Norman [26] to include inter-personal and social, while retaining and using his detailed descriptions of engagement with technology to examine relationships people form with their Roombas.

Reeves and Nass [24,28] did early work on intimacy in computing, finding that people ascribe human qualities to machines such as gender, ethnicity and politeness. Other research has explored intimacy in web sites, games, and intelligent agents [1,21,35,40]. Despite differences in technologies, these studies have a common theme: intimacy leads to greater acceptance of technology and perceived usability. Further, Venkatesh [39], found that intimacy plays a crucial role in the acceptance of domestic computational technology. Others showed that if software or intelligent agents were designed with anthropomorphic/zoomorphic qualities, it increased system acceptance [16,35]. These results convinced us of the need to understand intimacy— to facilitate the experience of domestic ubiquitous computing.

In robotics research we also found accounts of the potential for intimacy to exist between people and robots. Dauntenhahn's [7] survey of the social roles people would like robots to take, found that 70% of the participants wanted them as companions. Building on this study, others have designed companion robots for entertainment, assistance to the elderly and handicapped, education and everyday tasks [6,8]. Studies have shown that Sony's entertainment AIBO—with its dog-like form and AI-based software—did encourage intimacy, particularly among children who treated the robotic dog like a pet (more so than traditional stuffed toys) [12,19,23]. A study of PARO, a robotic baby seal found that it enhanced elders' quality of life in nursing homes and enhanced children's rehabilitation [20,32].

While entertainment and nursing robots are known to encourage intimate relationships, less is known about whether that's possible with service robots like Roomba. This omission is surprising given the range of service robots that exist to support vacuuming, mopping, guarding, lawn mowing and ironing. However, Forlizzi and DiSalvo's [11] seminal ethnographic study of Roomba suggests that it is possible. In addition to learning that Roombas change families' cleaning patterns and physical home arrangements, they saw people developing relationships with Roomba by naming and ascribing personality traits to the device. We built on this work in two ways. First, by focusing on intimacy exclusively, we sought to deepen the knowledge of naming and personality practices associated with Roombas, as well as to look for other signs of intimacy. Second, rather than giving Roombas to our participants, we recruited "natural" owners, to see whether these traits held for people who had adopted them outside a study setting.

In conclusion, related work suggests that people can and do form intimate relationships with technologies, including Roomba. In the remainder of this paper we report the results from our study that sought to examine how intimacy manifests itself in the case of a service robot—Roomba. In the next section, we describe our methods and participants, before turning to the results, and the design implications that arise from our findings.

3 Study Design

Our study consisted of two empirical research steps: collecting written discourse from an online Roomba forum and interviewing current Roomba users who we recruited from the forum. We used the forum postings to identify Roomba enthusiasts who we followed up with for interviews. By focusing on a forum, we recognize that our data may not hold true for all Roomba owners—but we were most interested in the enthusiastic owners, the ones who had established intimate relationships with their robot. We suggest that studying this group provides unique insights into the properties and features that a robot might need to help people connect with it.

3.1 Methods

We began by collecting postings from a publicly accessible Roomba forum—roombareview.com. We collected postings from 137 message threads, which came to a total of 760 discrete messages. Analyzing those 760 messages, we found 188 that contained at least one description of an intimacy towards Roomba (based on our revision of Norman's [26] theory of emotional attachment). In addition to confirming our hypothesis that Roomba owners (at least those on roombareview.com) had strong bonds with their robots, the postings helped us understand the types and range of practices that we thought constituted intimacy, which guided our interview design.

We also used these postings for screening participants to find those who self-expressed (without us asking) strong ties to their Roomba. The online posts helped us customize our interview questions to fit the circumstances of each user (e.g., multiple vacuums, type of Roomba and so forth). Also, we used these online posts to confirm the data that we collected from the interviews.

After a pilot phase to refine our interview protocol, we conducted interviews with 30 people in the United States, United Kingdom, Finland, and Austria. We conducted 18 interviews via the telephone and sent 12 participants the guide via email, which they filled out and returned. Although we preferred phone interviews, we used email because some participants preferred not to use the phone citing privacy and security reasons (in the US) and being too busy (Austria). While we recognize the richness of face-to-face interviews, roombareview.com participants did not live locally to us, and we saw advantages to having international participants who allowed us to reach beyond regional and cultural differences. In each interview, we focused on three main themes. First, we asked about Roomba demographics: model types, number owned, and where and how often each robot was used. Second, we asked people whether, and if so, what they named their Roomba, whether they ascribed gender and a personality to it. Third, we asked participants to describe the advantages and disadvantages of owning and using Roomba and their opinions on potential improvements. We closed the interview by asking participants for some demographic information.

Two researchers coded the data looking for themes related to intimacy by following Friedman's et al.'s [12] description of their analysis of online AIBO forums—which was focused on understanding people's relationships with robots. Friedman et al. [12] offer five categories which emerged in people's descriptions of AIBO: technological essence, life-like essence, mental states, social rapport, and moral standing. Beginning with these categories, we conducted a top-down analysis of the roombareview.com postings. First, we tried to list all relevant postings under the five categories. To accommodate differences between AIBO and Roomba we extended categories to create more coherent groupings of postings. We iterated on this process when analyzing the interview data. The categories from the online posting analysis guided our top-down analysis and led to the final set of themes. Our analysis of the interviews relied on the phone interviews, because the email replies did not contain as much overall detail. However, the emails did provide supplementary data when counting frequencies (e.g. how many people named their Roomba). Hence, the quotes and observations described in this paper mainly come from the phone interviews.

We present our results organized around three themes that spoke to the nature of the intimate relationships people formed with their Roombas. First, people spoke of happiness with Roomba because it positively changed their attitude toward cleaning. Second, people used anthropomorphic and zoomorphic qualities to engage with Roomba. Third, people valued their Roombas and consequently took pleasure in demonstrating it to others and by changing the home to accommodate it better.

3.2 Participants

Among our 30 participants, all owned at least one Roomba: 18 owned just one, nine owned two, and the remaining three owned three, five, and nine (with two more being shipped) respectively. The average length of ownership among our participants was 10 months, varying from one week to five years.

Our sample, to the best of our knowledge, was fairly gender balanced with 16 men and 14 women who ranged in age from 27 to 76 years. Six participants were in their 20's and seven were in their 30's, while 12 participants were in their 40's. We had one participant in their 50's and 2 participants each in their 60's and 70's. Eight of our participants were single, and four of those people owned pets. The remaining 22 participants came from households where they lived with a spouse or a partner. In these households, 8 families did not have children or pets, 5 families had children but no pets, 5 families had both children and pets, and 4 had pets but no children.

Our participants had a wide range of technical expertise based on the self-reports of their education, professional backgrounds, and their experience with technologies (we asked about latter to see if any of our participants were self-taught technology enthusiasts). Twenty-six of the 30 participants had college degrees, while 13 had majored in science and engineering related degrees, such as mechanical engineering, computer science and electrical engineering. Our participants had diverse professions including lawyers, full-time homemakers, software engineers, a nurse and a hair salon owner. Finally, 13 households owned robots other than Roomba, such as Scooba, AIBO, Lawn Mower and humanoid robot toys (i.e., Robosapience).

What all of our participants shared in common was an enthusiasm for their Roombas. We recognize that this may not hold true of all Roomba users although the thriving businesses surrounding Roomba such as the production of costumes suggest a bigger market than the self-identified enthusiasts of the Roombareview.com could sustain. That said, we were intrigued by this sample of people who had managed to develop a strong bond with their Roombas. In particular, we wanted to learn what it took to achieve the bond and what it possibly means for ubiquitous computing.

4 Manifestations of Intimacy

In this section, we describe findings that show how our participants established and maintained intimate relationships with their Roombas. Specifically, we present themes focused on changing attitudes towards cleaning, using life-like associations to engage with Roomba, and valuing the robot enough to demonstrate it to others and change the home to accommodate it better.

4.1 Feeling Happiness Towards Roomba

Some social psychologists [17,34] argue that intimacy increases happiness and satisfaction with life. We found this type of intimacy for some of our participants. They were elated that house cleaning no longer required manual labor, and even described vacuuming as changing "from a drudgery to a happy thought". We sought to understand what might have caused this change in perspective towards cleaning, and turned to sociological literatures on housework [29,30]. These literatures argue that as house size has increased and maid/servant labor declined, the women responsible for cleaning (increasingly engaged in paid-labor themselves) found themselves in a dilemma. Either they took more time to clean, or they simply cleaned less—leading to negative feelings associated with vacuuming including guilt [30].

By contrast, and possibly one reason for happiness, our participants described a noticeable increase in their standard of cleanliness since adopting Roomba. Participants told us that they could see that there was less pet hair and dust, which made them feel confident and comfortable inviting guests into their house. In addition to simply being motivated to run Roomba more frequently than to vacuum, our participants also spoke of a desire to keep Roomba running smoothly which itself involved being tidy. For instance, three of our participants told that they tended to pick objects up off the floor because small items could harm Roomba. Another householder expressed happiness because his children now picked their toys up off the floor voluntarily before going to sleep, knowing that Roomba would clean the floor early in the morning. Further, he described that Roomba helped the whole family become neater. In his words:

> When we know the Roomba is going to be cleaning the next day, we don't want that stuff to get in the way so we tend to put things away more. I think its kind of forcing us to be neater people.

The happiness generated by Roomba also seemed to compensate for the extra work required from the robot. Like other domestic technologies [6,7], Roomba did not save householders' time and labor because it both took time, and also created monitoring and maintenance tasks. Participants described that cleaning with a Roomba took longer than with a traditional vacuum cleaner—albeit in smaller chunks—because of the need to move the machine around the rooms of the house. They also described new cleaning tasks: monitoring and rescue. For example, participants told us about their Roombas getting stuck underneath chairs or trapped in the bathroom. Indeed some householders described monitoring the robot in order to "rescue" it from danger.

This monitoring and rescue work also generated surprising responses among our participants. For example, instead of complaining about the extra work, they often told us how they "worried" and "felt sorry for" the robot when it was in danger or had gotten stuck. They also characterized the monitoring process as a form of entertainment, watching and wondering whether Roomba would avoid obstacles. Cleaning almost sounded like a spectator sport.

Another new task was to clean the robot itself. Participants described how brushes, bins and motors needed cleaning to remove the fine dust that might corrupt the sensors and affect Roomba's function. The majority of our participants performed this (approximately 15 minute) task most times they used the robot. This task was the only one that our participants complained about having to do, but unilaterally they preferred this task to that of manual cleaning.

For some, the happiness and joy of using Roomba changed their entire outlook on cleaning. Some preferred and even insisted that what they did with the Roomba should not be described as vacuuming. For example, a male participant explicitly told his friends that he was playing with a robot rather than saying, "I am vacuuming my house". Another participant shared his experience of getting upset when he saw Roomba being advertised as a vacuum cleaner in a store. His argument was that the label "vacuum cleaner" does not provide an appropriate description of Roomba. Interestingly we note that it was men who were more likely to characterize experiences with the Roomba as being something unlike vacuuming, an activity typically associated with women. However, we do not have sufficient evidence to fully explore the gendered implications of these comments.

Roomba seemed to make our participants very happy. They recounted experiences monitoring, rescuing and watching Roombas. Also, they talked about the positive benefits of a cleaner house and described how they enjoyed seeing other and new householders participating in the cleaning activities. As one participant put it, Roomba seems to sit "somewhere between a pet and a home appliance" which we turn to in the next section.

4.2 Lifelike Associations and Engagement with Roombas

Breazeal [4] argues that one form of affection that people can show to robots involves ascribing anthropomorphic/zoomorphic characteristics. We saw ample examples of this in our study. We conjecture that people's ability to anthropomorphize and zoomorphize helps them value Roomba high enough to treat the robot as a trusted and dear object. For example, one of our interview questions asked, 'what does Roomba mean to you?' Responding to that question, we found that people expect the domestic robots to become companions (also observed in [7]). The majority of our participants described Roomba as some form of household companion with lifelike properties, such as "a helpful assistant", "a pet-like being" and "a valuable family member". Perhaps somewhat extremely, three participants actually listed their Roombas (including their names and ages) as family members when we asked them to provide demographic information about members of their household.

Another prevalent anthropomorphism was the description of personality. Eighteen participants felt that Roomba had intentions, feelings, and unique characteristics. One participant who owns two Roombas and one Scooba felt that each unit had a unique personality although he was well aware that technology had not advanced that far:

*Mine, I feel they are different... For me how they look, each one has
certain different behavior. And I know definitely they have a same
firmware or a similar firmware so the difference should not be much but
ah, for example, my discovery, he's more crazy. He runs into things and
sometimes and goes into different places he should not be going to. And
the scheduler he's more like refined. He knows what he's doing.*

Like this participant, Norman [27] argues that movement helps people perceive
robotic objects as lifelike. Most of our participants latched onto the randomness of
Roomba's movement—generated by an algorithm designed to promote Roomba's
passage across all sections of the space being cleaned—as being something that
triggered an expression of personality. Some people told us that behavior such as
getting stuck on particular furniture, constantly missing a certain spot, or bumping
into the same wall was part of their Roomba's personality. Our participants saw these
behaviors as different from the routine movements of machines, and consequently it
seemed akin to the unforeseen actions of humans. Participants also used sound as
another signifier of personality, using descriptions including "energetic and spirited".
In actuality, Roombas make a series of sounds to communicate the start and end of
their cleaning cycles, as well as communicating success, failure and repairs required.
None of these sounds are human (taking the form of beeps instead).

Breakdown and repair were other occasions for people to anthropomorphize about
their Roombas. After sending Roomba to be repaired, some participants expressed
surprise at their own grief, describing Roomba being "dead, sick, or hospitalized". For
example:

*We did a non-warranty exchange and it was emotionally...it's interesting
that 'Spot' was not actually just a robot; it was a....we had some real
reservation knowing that we are going to send this one back to the
company and we are going to get a different one back.*

Scherer [15] argues that intimate feelings determine whether people will engage in
social interaction. In our study, we learned that people communited with their
Roombas by greeting, praising and reprimanding them. For example, one participant
described how he reprimanded his Roomba and Scooba when they nearly collided in
the kitchen, and how much he was surprised by his own reaction that he treated robots
as somehow alive and able to respond to and absorb his admonishment. This echoes
other research that shows that people apply social norms and rules to intelligent
technology [24,28,31]. In our study, the social norms that most frequently arose for
our participants who viewed Roomba as life-like were giving names, a gender, and a
status within the family to the robot.

Surprisingly to us, 21 out of 30 householders told us that they gave names and
nicknames to Roombas. Although many of our participants could not explain their
motivation behind this action, they reported that it seemed natural, and that Roomba
"deserved" a name particularly considering the benefits the robot provided. Some
people also explained that they need a name to call Roomba since it was a frequent
topic of conversation among family members, or as a way to distinguish a particular
unit among multiple robots.

In all cases, naming involved much thought and consideration, and often resulted
in explicit decoration or engraving onto the firmware itself. In one household, the

family members put their favorite names into a hat and selected a winner as a way of deciding between competing entries. Other householders decided on a name before the Roomba arrived. Many people draw on their favorite sci-fi or other movie characters. We also learned that people changed the names of their Roombas over time. For instance, one household changed the name of their Roomba from Robocop to Aarnold (not "Arnold") after the Terminator because the latter seemed to be a better fit to the personality of their robot. This shows that the householders evolve intimate relationship with their Roomba. In another house where they could not find a name that everyone liked, Dad had called it Fred and the children had called it R2D2 (after Star Wars character) while Mother used both names, calling it by the preferred name of the person that she was talking with.

However, naming was not always a barometer of intimacy. One of our participants told us she did not name her Roomba because she felt the name "Roomba" already expressed the nature and personality of the robot well enough. Instead—and in a sign of what we would suggest is intimacy—she typically referred to it in more sentimental forms. For example, in her words:

> *I can't imagine not having him any longer. He's my BABY!!...When I write emails about him which I've done that as well, I just like him, I call him Roomba baby...He's a sweetie.*

Also, reflected in the quote above was an ascription of gender to the Roomba. In fact, 16 participants told us that they talked about Roomba in gendered terms. While we saw both genders being used in online discourse, all of our interviewees described Roomba as male. While some participants were very careful not to address Roomba as "it" because of their sense that Roomba was more than just a machine, most of the people who used "he" interchanged that pronoun with "it".

Our participants also explained how they had decided Roomba's gender. They described its masculinity as coming from its shape, color and a preconception of male-dominance in the realms of technology and machinery. The last reason, that of ascribing gender based on a sense that men have dominated the history of technology—and perhaps especially in the area of robotics—speaks to what we might term the "genealogy of technology." By technological genealogy we mean that people seem to make sense of new technologies by drawing on their historical knowledge of similar objects. We also found some more unusual reasons. The gender of one Roomba in this study came from the person previously in charge of the manual vacuuming, a man. By contrast, two female participants explicitly told us that they referred to Roomba as "he" because they liked the idea of having a man do the cleaning for them.

In conclusion, our participants engaged their Roomba by ascribing it life-like and social characteristics. Many saw their Roombas as somehow cognitive and physical as well as having a personality, name and gender. This in turn helped them engage sufficiently so that they could talk and write about it, through which we argue, they formed a relationship with their robots.

4.3 Valuing Roomba: Promoting and Protecting It

In this section, we discuss another dimension of the intimate relationship that people formed with Roomba—one associated with feeling that it was of such value that they wanted to promote to their friends and colleagues, and also protect it by making it welcome in their homes. Our participants demonstrated how valuable they felt Roomba was by telling us how they recommended it to other people. All of our participants have shown Roombas to visitors in their homes, irrespective of whether their guests are adults or children, which extensively implicates whether or not they have the purchasing power. Also, they have extolled the virtues of the Roomba to close friends and their extended family. For example, one participant told us about writing email and talking about Roomba on the telephone to friends and family, and many have even purchased Roombas as gifts.

In addition to encouraging others to purchase Roombas, some of our participants had made their own acquisition after seeing it in someone else's house. For example, two female participants purchased their Roombas after they saw the quality of its performance in their neighbor's home. Another participant said that she received the robot as a gift from her adult son. Our participants lead us to believe that Roomba adoption by word of mouth is how a healthy percentage of people come to own these technologies. One participant described his own promotional work:

> (I have taken the Roomba to my parents' house to show how well it
> works) Anyway, my parents ended up buying 2..., their next-door
> neighbor bought one, and my aunt bought one. Now my brother is looking
> to buy one.

Beyond local promotion, particularly within families, we also encountered owners who had taken their Roomba to work and to their vacation homes. In addition to potentially using it, particularly in the latter setting, these participants described showing it to their colleagues and holiday neighbors. Our Finnish participant worried about sales in Finland, and made a video of her Roomba, and sent to her local distributor to help them promote the technology. Another participant offered Roombas as prizes in a business-based competition she ran, for which she received a number of entries.

The strength of the relationship that our participants felt with their Roombas not only encouraged them to promote Roomba to others, but also motivated them to modify their living environment to accommodate the floor vacuum. Twenty-seven of the 30 households we spoke with had made changes to their houses to accommodate Roomba. This is known more widely as "Roombarization".

Roombarization consists of a variety of activities. For example, participants described raising the wires off the floor in order to prevent Roomba from "choking" on them. Others talked about moving furniture around so that Roomba could navigate through their house without getting stuck. Some of our participants learned Roombarization techniques through trial and error after watching Roomba navigate and get caught, such as raising the height of chairs to let Roomba pass underneath. But, surprisingly, some people configured their homes prior to Roomba's arrival.

In a few cases, we learned that Roombarization could bring drastic changes to the home. One of our participants told us that she threw away her rug in the living room because her Roomba kept "getting frustrated" with the length of the shag, getting it caught in its brushes. Another participant taped down the entire tassel on the carpet every time he ran the robot. Also, we had a participant who replaced the old refrigerator with a new one that had enough space underneath for Roomba.

Although these last descriptions may seem somewhat extreme, the majority of our participants had done something to accommodate Roomba. Roombarization appears to be a vital part of the adoption process, and our participants all tried hard to make their Roombas fit into their domestic environment. Many reported spending time following Roomba during its initial uses to understand how and where they could make changes that would better suit the robot. The intimacy that was built during this process became apparent when a participant raised his concern about taking Roomba to un-Roombarized environment.

> *I brought mine ... when I visited my parents soon after I bought it so they could see if they wanted one. I ended up being very protective of it since there were a lot of things in their house that it could get choked on or stuck on.*

In this, and the last two sections, we have argued that the Roomba owners in our study had developed an intimate attachment to their Roombas. These attachments manifested themselves in a variety of ways. People were willing to take on extra cleaning and maintenance work in order to make Roomba function effectively—replacing one form of cleaning for another. Also, our participants saw Roomba as more than an appliance, and consequently were motivated to ascribe personality, name, and give their robot a gender. Finally, they wanted to share their experience with Roomba with others, allowing other people to benefit and share the joys of ownership.

5   Discussion: The Role of Intimacy in Domestic Appliances

Scholars argue that in human-human relationships intimacy helps people to be happier and healthier [17]. Our study suggests, as others have found for other types of computing and robots outside of the service domain, that people seem to be able to form intimate relationships. In this section, we discuss how those relationships may inform device adoption and help people to manage unreliability—potentially useful attributes for ubiquitous computing technologies more generally.

5.1 Visibility and Device Adoption

Within ubiquitous computing and related communities, researchers have begun discussing what it means for technology to disappear into household routines. Some researchers [37] question whether perceptual disappearance is the only criteria for success integration, but others [10] suggest that visibility of a technology's location can help adoption. Our study also speaks to questions of visibility and its relationship to domestic routines and device acceptance.

Our participants described the highly visible presence of Roomba in their homes. They spoke of loud operational noises generated by its movement, and of light and sound patterns generated when Roomba had information to communicate. Additionally, as an autonomous moving device, Roomba was inclined to appear in the field of view of our participants, their family and pets, as it moved around the home cleaning. Indeed, one participant who lived alone told us how he felt a stronger connection to his Roomba than his Scooba—iRobot's mopping robot—precisely because they tended to share the same space. By contrast, his Scooba tended to work in parts of the house that he didn't spend much time in, such as the kitchen and bathroom. In other words, high visibility of Roomba brought comfort to our householders, which led to easier adoption of the robot.

The adoption of Roomba also changed domestic routines (also seen by [11]). In addition to the cleaning routines, other activities took place, such as making time to name, ascribing gender and personality traits to the device, and talking about it within the family (as well as outside). This was in contrast with other studies of adoption, particularly those associated with adoption of white-goods (refrigerators, cookers, non-robotic vacuum cleaners) where we generally saw an emphasis on how *much* time and how *frequently* people engaged in activities associated with these devices. More broadly, they were coupled to assessments of the ongoing labor associated with housework. By comparison, our study of Roomba yielded much more information about social routines with the device rather than tasks performed with the device. Instead of counting the hours of housework, people talked to us about the complexities of naming their vacuum cleaner. Further, we would argue that this suggests an adoption process that is not only different from that associated with conventional technologies (even potentially computational ones) but also perhaps more enjoyable and rewarding.

Clearly, future research remains to explore the possibilities for adoption when people form an intimate relationship to an object. However, our study suggests that the presence of intimacy opens up new possibilities for how people will incorporate this technology into their home routines. We also suggest that intimacy might be a means to explore artful systems [36]—those that couple their support to household projects in artful rather than strictly functional—as facilitators of device adoption.

Finally, while routines have received considerable attention within the ubiquitous computing community, the nature of intra-family relationships and their affect on technology adoption has been less discussed. Family relationships came up throughout our study; with participants describing how some people adopted Roomba before others. For example, some participants told us that they were initially skeptical when their spouses and sons brought Roomba home. Indeed, one participant described it as an "expensive toy" for her husband. However, after the husband ran the robot a few times, she told us that on seeing the amount of dust that it picked up, she decided that it was actually a useful appliance. Further, within a year, that household added two more robots—another Roomba and a Scooba.

An interesting possibility that we raise here is that while accounts of vacuuming suggest that it is an activity that belongs to someone, the arrival of Roomba creates opportunities for a reallocation of responsibility. More generally, many of our participants articulated a sense of value that the robot created for them in their cleaning routines. Even though it required Roombarization, the use of Roomba changed how and what was involved in vacuuming, and people spoke of it in positive terms. Adoption of the device was not just functional, but also included being a helpful assistant, entertainment, a pet-like being, and a valuable member of the house.

5.2 Reconsidering Reliability

In their paper on challenges for domestic ubiquitous computing, Edwards and Grinter [9] introduce reliability as an issue for this community. Specifically, they argue that ubiquitous computing systems will likely need to be highly reliable in order to meet householders' expectations about the systems they have in their home. Our study showed that while Roomba users hoped that their robot would be reliable, they did not expect it to work flawlessly. Further, they took on extra work to increase Roomba's odds of working well. For example, almost all the people we interviewed and surveyed opened up Roomba and cleaned its motors and brushes frequently—in some cases each time they ran it. They explained to us that they did this work to avoid the "Circle Dance"—Roomba going around and around in the same spot—which happens when the sensors are clogged by dust.

Day-to-day then, our participants tolerated Roomba's potential for flaws, although they tried to mitigate the possibility of failure through preventative measures. In addition to taking care of Roomba, we saw lots of other examples of day-to-day measures designed to keep the robot working. People picked up small items up off the floor to protect Roomba when it was out on its next "mission"[5]. We heard that this was not just associated with the person in charge of running Roomba, but in many cases an activity that other householders participated in. Indeed, people reconfigured their homes—Roombarization—also to increase the odds that Roomba would complete its mission successfully.

So, we asked our participants whether this work of picking things up was a burden. Surprisingly, we heard from people that this work of tidying was a token of their appreciation for the hard cleaning work that their Roomba did. Some people even termed this feeling as being the least that they could do given how hard they worked their Roomba. This raises an interesting question—and something we would like to explore further—about the relationship between Roomba owners and their vacuum cleaner. Specifically, the almost guilt-like quality to this relationship makes us wonder whether it turns on a master-servant dynamic, something that might make many people today feel uncomfortable. More generally, we think that intimacy—that sense of a relationship—helps engage people in doing work to change their routines to accommodate technology. Further, this stands in marked contrast with previous research that has argued that technology succeeds when it is absorbed into existing patterns of activity.

We also learned about a different type of reliability—that this happens over the long-term. For instance, we had a female participant who bought her first Roomba when iRobot launched its initial product (about 5 years ago). Early Roombas, she explained, did not last long due to some technical problems. Yet, she told us that she kept purchasing replacements—instead of being frustrated and ceasing to use this product. Other participants shed some insight into why this might be the case. For example, two other women (although we are not sure whether this particular type of relationship is gendered) explained that "I can never not have one" and more extremely perhaps "I will always have one until I die". Our data suggests that forming

---

[5] Another example of a technology's genealogy, iRobot describes Roombas cleaning cycle as a "mission" speaking to the origin of this robot: the military.

a strong bond with the technology is possible even in the face of technical issues, and further might lead people to persist in adoption despite problems.

6 Design Implications

Throughout this paper, we have suggested that there are advantages when people can develop intimate relationships with technology by which we mean deep ties that inspire and engage people to interact with and accommodate a system. In addition to describing the dimensions of this intimacy that we observed in our research, we discussed how intimacy and adoption and reliability interact. In this section, we wish to explicitly raise some of the design implications that intimacy raises.

6.1 Form Follows Function?

In the last decade, a considerable amount of research has been undertaken to explore the possibilities presented by intelligent agents. Whether built in hardware or software, this research has typically assumed that mimicking lifelike objects such as humans and animals offers advantages. This assumption has been reinforced through confirmatory empirical research. For example, the laboratory study of Kismet, a robot that can express human emotions, found that the lifelike form yielded stronger emotional responses [4].

However, other research (e.g. [35]) raises an important concern that using a lifelike form carelessly can decrease people's intimate responses to the technology. In our study, we complement but extend this research by showing that a non-lifelike form can also engender strong attachment. Despite being designed with cleaning in mind— a low round object that travels underneath furniture to maximize the vacuuming— Roombas generated strong responses among our participants.

Further, we even found evidence that lifelike forms might be inappropriate for domestic technologies. For example, one of our participants told us that while he wanted to buy a Sony AIBO, his wife refused to have a "fake dog" in their home. He told us that she felt much more comfortable with non-lifelike robotic forms. Many more participants spoke enthusiastically about Roombas shape; because of its perceived appropriateness for the job it was designed to do—clean. And, of course, people were always able to dress and name their robots to "add" lifelike properties. Minimally, we suggest that a humanoid or animalistic form may not be required to generate strong responses—which in turn opens the design space of possibilities.

6.2 Intimacy Through Ambiguity

One interpretation of ambiguity for ubiquitous computing is a degree of confusion that could lead to error [9]. The arguments for simplicity, ensuring that householders can control their smart homes—and through their lives—abound. By contrast, Gaver voices different vision of ambiguity as a powerful resource that can promote close personal relationships fueled by curiosity and engagement [13].

This study supports Gaver's argument. Our participants described delight in following Roomba, trying to figure out its algorithm and examining it to learn more about how the robot worked. Also, like Forlizzi and DiSalvo [11], our participants told us that they experimented with Roomba, particularly when they first owned it. For example, one man put dust in front of his new Roomba to see whether it really vacuumed. Others put multiple Roombas together to see how they would interact— although Roomba does not do collision detection. And, we even heard people describing how they let their children and pets ride on their Roomba! We suggest that ambiguity has the potential to inform the design of engaging smart home appliances, perhaps even increasing their sense of smartness, by giving them characteristics that are hard for owners to understand. Further, it puts an interesting spin on the question raised by Edwards and Grinter [9]: how smart does smart home technology have to be, if people enjoy ambiguity and through that develop a commitment to a particular technology? In conclusion, we suggest that exploring ambiguity further, and potentially adding elements of the ambiguous have much to offer in the design of ubiquitous systems for the home.

6.3 Intimacy Through Accountability

Researchers like Bell [3], Norman [25], and others argue that technologies should make their actions accountable. In other words, people should be able to see into a technology's process to understand how a system got from start to finish. Our participants told us that they liked being able to see how Roomba worked. For example, householders ran Roomba multiple times per day to check how much dust Roomba picked up. Many admitted astonishment that Roomba picked up lots of dirt (possibly from areas difficult to get at with a traditional vacuum cleaner) when first used. This astonishment has evolved, over time and with regular use, to a sense of comfort and relief that the amount of dust decreased. Most spoke explicitly about how seeing the dust made them aware of the fact that Roomba was really cleaning their homes, and they spoke of valuing the robot's performance.

The exploration of state as a mechanism for accountability, we suggest, has much to offer in the design of domestic appliances. In addition to showing the current state of the system, Roomba's ability to "show" how the dirt situation was changing over time, provides an example of how people enjoyed being able to see *change over time*. We recognize however, that achieving these trades off against the potential for ambiguity is a topic open for further exploration.

6.4 Intimacy Through Support

Scholars have had a long-standing interest in the social implications of domestic technology, studying among other things such as privacy, gender, ownership patterns and societal expectations of usage [9,36,39]. Our study suggests that for some, Roomba changed cleaning from an individual act to a household activity with people participating in aspects of using, maintaining and caring for Roomba. Further, it was clear that cleaning was a topic of conversation by using the names in discussion and showing Roomba to people outside the home.

One significantly change, we heard, was the increase of support. For example, a woman told us that she felt comfortable to invite her friend with an infant over because the floor was hygienic enough for the baby to crawl on. Roomba supported her by helping her have a house that was hygienic. Other people told us that Roomba helped them by doing work that they couldn't easily do, which was pronounced among people whose physical injuries made cleaning difficult. Finally, one participant described support that comes through independence. In this case, he was disabled, and by using Roomba he no longer needed to ask his mother to clean for him. We suggest that ubiquitous computing in its agenda of providing technologies to support treatment and care, should consider the implications of support not just on the individuals that are affected, but also on the ways that they will in turn influence the relationships between technology and people.

7 Conclusions

In this paper, we built on and extended the seminal research conducted by Forlizzi and DiSalvo [11]—who reported engagement between people and service robots—by exploring the nature of these intimate human-robot relationships. Our goal, in exploring these relationships by people who have formed them "in the wild", was to understand what the strength of those bonds had to offer ubiquitous computing researchers interested in providing householders with rich, meaningful, engaging, and long-term relationships with the systems.

We found three themes that spoke to the nature of the intimate relationships people formed with their Roombas. First we learned about how householders feel happiness toward Roombas for helping them become neater. Second, people used life-like associations to engage with Roomba. Third, people valued Roomba enough to promote to others and to change the home for better accomodation. We conclude by discussing how intimacy can inform device adoption and help people to manage unreliability, and by presenting four implications from this study concerning the role of form, ambiguity, accountability and support in the design of domestic ubiquitous computing systems.

We offer our findings as the beginning of what we hope will be a much longer discussion within this and other communities that focus on understanding the depth and richness of the ubiquitous computing experience. Further, as the service robot industry continues to grow, and people increasingly adopt robots to help them manage aspects of their housework, we see the need to consider robots as a feature of the smart home of the future, and therefore a part of the ubiquitous computing agenda.

Acknowledgements. We thank Roombareview.com users and Nikolai Telsa for sharing rich and valuable experiences. Also, we thank work2play lab, Kris Nagel, Ken Anderson, and the anonymous reviewers for their constructive guidance and enthusiasm for this topic. This work is supported by the NSF CNS #0626281.

References

1. Axelrod, L., Hone, K.: E-motional Advantage: Performance and Satisfaction Gains with Affective Computing. In: CHI '05 extended abstracts on Human factors in computing systems, ACM Press, Portland, OR, USA (2005)
2. Bell, G.: Intimate Ubiquitous Computing. In: Proceedings of Ubicomp 2003, ACM Press, New York (2003)

3. Bell, G., Kaye, J.: Designing Technology for Domestic Spaces: A Kitchen Manifesto. Gastronomica 2(2) (2001)
4. Breazeal, C.: Affective Interaction between Humans and Robots. In: Kelemen, J., Sosík, P. (eds.) ECAL 2001. LNCS (LNAI), vol. 2159, Springer, Heidelberg (2001)
5. Breazeal, C.: Robots in Society: Friend or Appliance? In: Agents99 Workshop on Emotion-based Agent Architecture, Seattle, WA, USA (1999)
6. Christensen, H.I.: Intelligent Home Appliances. Springer Tracts in Advanced Robotics (STAR) 2003(6), 319–330
7. Dautenhahn, K., et al.: What is a Robot Companion - Friend, Assistant or Butler? (2005)
8. Decuir, J.D., et al.: A Friendly Face in Robotics: Sony's AIBO Entertainment Robot as an Educational Tool. Comput. Entertain. 2(2), 14–14 (2004)
9. Edwards, W.K., Grinter, R.E.: At Home with Ubiquitous Computing: Seven Challenges. In: Abowd, G.D., Brumitt, B., Shafer, S. (eds.) Ubicomp 2001. LNCS, vol. 2201, p. 143. Springer, Heidelberg (2001)
10. Elliot, K., Neustaedter, C., Greenberg, S.: Time, Ownership and Awareness: The Value of Contextual Locations in the Home. In: Beigl, M., Intille, S.S., Rekimoto, J., Tokuda, H. (eds.) UbiComp 2005. LNCS, vol. 3660, Springer, Heidelberg (2005)
11. Forlizzi, J., DiSalvo, C.: Service Robots in the Domestic Environment: a Study of the Roomba Vacuum in the Home. In: Proceeding of the 1st ACM SIGCHI/SIGART conference on Human-robot interaction, ACM Press, Salt Lake City, Utah, USA (2006)
12. Friedman, B., Kahn Jr., P.H., Hagman, J.: Hardware Companions?: What Online AIBO Discussion Forums Reveal About the Human-Robotic Relationship. In: Proceedings of the SIGCHI conference on Human factors in computing systems, ACM Press, Ft. Lauderdale, Florida, USA (2003)
13. Gaver, W.W., Beaver, J., Benford, S.: Ambiguity as a Resource for Design. In: Proceedings of the SIGCHI conference on Human factors in computing systems, ACM Press, Ft. Lauderdale, Florida, USA (2003)
14. Gaver, W.W., et al.: The Drift Table: Designing for Ludic Engagement. In: CHI '04 extended abstracts on Human factors in computing systems, ACM Press, Vienna, Austria (2004)
15. Hadden, J., Shupe, A.: Televangelism in America. Social Compass 34(1), 61–75 (1987)
16. Herbsleb, J.D.: Metaphorical representation in collaborative software engineering. In: Proceedings of the international joint conference on Work activities coordination and collaboration, ACM Press, San Francisco, California, United States (1999)
17. Higgins, E.T., Kruglanski, A.W.: Social Psychology: Handbook of Basic Principles, pp. 523–557. Guilford Press, New York (1996)
18. Izard, C.E.: Human Emotions. Plenum Press, New York (1977)
19. Kahn, P.H., et al.: Robotic Pets in the Lives of Preschool Children. In: CHI '04 extended abstracts on Human factors in computing systems, ACM Press, Vienna, Austria (2004)
20. Kidd, C.D., Taggart, W., Turkle, S.: A Sociable Robot to Encourage Social Interaction Among the Elderly (2006)
21. Mahlke, S., Minge, M., Thring, M.: Measuring Multiple Components of Emotions in Interactive Contexts. In: CHI '06 extended abstracts on Human factors in computing systems, ACM Press, Montreal, Qubec, Canada (2006)
22. Marti, P., et al.: Engaging with Artificial Pets. In: Proceedings of the 2005 annual conference on European association of cognitive ergonomics, University of Athens, Chania, Greece (2005)
23. Melson, G.F., et al.: Robots as Dogs?: Children's Interactions with the Robotic Dog AIBO and a Live Australian Shepherd. In: CHI '05 extended abstracts on Human factors in computing systems, ACM Press, Portland, OR, USA (2005)

24. Nass, C., Moon, Y.: Machines and Mindlessness: Social Responses to Computers. Journal of social issues 25(1), 81–103 (2000)
25. Norman, D.A.: Design of Everyday Things, Currency Doubleday (1989)
26. Norman, D.A.: Emotional Design: Why We Love (or Hate) Everyday Things. Basic Books, New York, USA (2004)
27. Norman, D.A.: Robots in the Home: What Might They Do? Interactions 12(2), 65 (2005)
28. Reeves, B., Nass, C.: The Media Equation. Cambridge University Press, New York, USA (1996)
29. Robinson, J.P., Milkie, M.: Dances with Dust Bunnies: Housecleaning. In: America. American Demographics 19(1) (1997)
30. Robinson, J.P., Milkie, M.A.: Back to the Basics: Trends in and Role Determinants of Women's Attitudes toward Housework. Journal of Marriage and the Family 60(1), 205–218 (1998)
31. Scopelliti, M., Giuliani, M.V., Fornara, F.: Robots in a Domestic Setting: a Psychological Approach. Journal Universal Access in the Information Society 4(2) (2005)
32. Shibata, T., et al.: Human Interactive Robot for Pscyhological Enrichment and Therapy. In: AISB'05 Social Intellignece and Interaction in Anismals, Robots, and Agents, Hatfield, UK (2005)
33. Sternberg, R.J.: A Triangular Theory of Love. Psychological Review 93, 119–135 (1986)
34. Sternberg, R.J., Grajek, S.: The Nature of Love. Journal of Personality and Social Psychology 47, 233–464 (1984)
35. Suganuma, T., et al.: Bridging the E-gaps: Towards Post-Ubiquitous Computing. In: 20th International Conference on Advanced Information Networking and Applications (AINA) (2006)
36. Taylor, A.S., Swan, L.: Artful Systems in the Home. In: Proceedings of the SIGCHI conference on Human factors in computing systems, ACM Press, Portland, Oregon, USA (2005)
37. Tolmie, P., et al.: Unremarkable Computing. In: Proceedings of the SIGCHI conference on Human factors in computing systems: Changing our world, changing ourselves, ACM Press, Minneapolis, Minnesota, USA (2002)
38. U.N., World Robotics, 2005, United Nations Economic Commissions for Europe and International Federation of Robotics, Frankfurt, Germany (2005)
39. Venkatesh, V.: Determinants of Perceived Ease of Use: Integrating Control, Intrinsic Motivation, and Emotion into the Technology Acceptance Model. Info. Sys. Research 11(4), 342–365 (2000)
40. Zhang, P., Li, N.: The Importance of Affective Quality. Commun. ACM 48(9), 105–108 (2005)

Symbolic Object Localization Through Active Sampling of Acceleration and Sound Signatures
(Nominated for the Best Paper Award)

Kai Kunze and Paul Lukowicz

Embedded Systems Lab, University of Passau,
Insstr 43, 94032 Passau, Germany
{kai.kunze|paul.lukowicz}@uni-passau.de
www.wearable-computing.org

Abstract. We describe a novel method for symbolic location discovery of simple objects. The method requires no infrastructure and relies on simple sensors routinely used in sensor nodes and smart objects (acceleration, sound). It uses vibration and short, narrow frequency 'beeps' to sample the response of the environment to mechanical stimuli. The method works for specific locations such as 'on the couch', 'in the desk drawer' as well as for location classes such as 'closed wood compartment' or 'open iron surface'. In the latter case, it is capable of generalizing the classification to locations the object has not seen during training. We present the results of an experimental study with a total of over 1200 measurements from 35 specific locations (taken from 3 different rooms) and 12 abstract location classes. It includes such similar locations as the inner and outer pocket of a jacket and a table and shelf made of the same wood. Nonetheless on locations from a single room (16 in the largest one) we achieve a recognition rate of up to 96 %. It goes down to 81 % if all 35 locations are taken together, however the correct location is in the 3 top picks of the system 94 % of the times.

1 Introduction

The location of an object can be interesting for a variety of reasons. Most obvious is the 'where did I put my x' scenario. An example where this scenario is relevant are so called assisted living systems. Such systems use on body devices for behavioral monitoring and assistance for elderly and/or cognitively impaired persons. In such a scenario, an important concern is to make sure that the user has the device with him all the time. This implies checking if the user carries the device and, if not, using for example the TV, the radio or the phone to remind him to pick it up. In particular for cognitively impaired users, it is important to be also able to tell the user where the device is located, in case it was lost.

Another well known example is a mobile phone that knows whether it is in a pocket, on the table, or in the user's hand and adjust the volume accordingly. Generally, we can use the location of 'smart objects' as an indication of the user needs and intentions. Thus if a device is put in the drawer where it is usually stored, it is reasonable to assume that it will not be used in the near future and

J. Krumm et al. (Eds.): UbiComp 2007, LNCS 4717, pp. 163–180, 2007.
© Springer-Verlag Berlin Heidelberg 2007

it can go into power saving mode. Going even further the location of a set of objects can be an indication of more general user activity and intentions.

Clearly understanding how object location can be used in different applications is a complex topic that needs further research. Nonetheless, the type of considerations sketched above indicates that object location is a useful piece of information. From this motivation we present and systematically evaluate a novel method for object localization. The method provides so called symbolic (sometimes also called semantic) location (e.g. [1]) rather then absolute coordinates. Thus the output of the system is of the type 'on the couch' or 'in the drawer'. The key contribution of our work is to present a method that requires no infrastructure, relies on simple, cheap sensors and still produces useful results.

The method is derived from the observation that the a ringing mobile phone sounds differently depending on where it is located. Whereas a phone in a jacket pocket sounds 'dumped', a phone on a metal cabinet can make the entire cabinet resonate. This is true for a ringing as well as for merely vibrating phone. We thus propose to use sound from a built in speaker and vibration from a built vibro-motor to create a mechanical 'excitation' of the environment and analyze the response with an accelerometer and a microphone. In an extensive experimental study (47 locations with total of 1200 data points) we demonstrate that two types of information can be derived from this analysis. First, the system can be trained to recognize specific locations such as the 'kitchen table', or the 'dining room table'. Second, it can recognize more abstract locations based on materials such as a 'wood table', 'a closed metal cabinet', or a 'jacket pocket'. While this leads to less specific positioning, it has the advantage that the system does not need to be trained for each single location. Instead, after being trained on, for example, several wood tables, it will recognize others it has not seen before.

1.1   State of the Art and Related Work

Indoor location is known to be a hard problem (see [2] for an overview). As described above our work aims at the localization of simple objects in environments with no, or only minimal augmentation. This means that many of the more reliable, standard methods are not applicable. This includes ultrasonic location such as the BAT [3] or the MIT cricket systems [4] which both require extensive instrumentation of the environment with ultrasonic transceivers. In addition ultrasonic system require free line of sight and will fail to locate objects in closed compartments. This means that infrastructure free, relative positioning methods based on ultrasonics (see ([5]) are also unsuitable. Cost and effort also make the use of complex time of flight based radio frequency (RF) methods such as the commercial UBISENSE ultra wide band system (www.ubisense.net) infeasible. Similar can be said about RFID (radio frequency identification), which require a reader to be put on every location which needs to be recognized.

Simple Beacon Based Systems. Much work has been put into localization based on simple RF beacons, often based on standard communication systems such as Bluetooth, Zigbee and of course WLAN ([6], [7] and [8]). This includes a wide body of work on positioning in wireless sensor networks [9]. In particular work based on, low power radio systems is clearly relevant to object localization. However it must be seen as complementary rather then a competing approach. Such systems are virtually all based on signal strength, which is inherently unreliable in complex, indoor environments. As a consequence, they are predominantly used for room level location (determining which room or large room segment a sensor node is in). This is not sufficient for the type of symbolic location targeted by this paper. However knowing approximate physical location can be used to constrain the search space for our symbolic location method.

Indirect Localization with Sensor Signatures. Both sound and acceleration have been previously used in location related research. In [10], the authors present a technique for performing accurate 3D location sensing using off-the-shelf audio hardware. Van Kleek et al. has also done some work in this direction, using sound fingerprints to detect collocation in [11].

The general concept of using acceleration signatures to extract location related information can be traced to the 'Smart-Its Friends' paper, [12]. Building on this idea [13] have demonstrated how to determine if a set of devices is being carried by the same person by correlating their acceleration signatures. Kunze et al. has taken this concept even further to show how the acceleration signature of walking can be used to determine where a user is carrying a device [14].

The most direct relation to the work presented in this paper is a patent by Griffin [15] titled: User hand detection for wireless devices. It proposes to use vibration detected by an acceleration signal to determine if a mobile phone is in the user hand, in a holster or in a holder.

1.2 Paper Contributions and Organization

From the above discussion it can be seen that symbolic localization of objects with no external infrastructure and simple sensors suitable for small, cheap nodes is an open problem. This paper proposes a solution for this problem. In terms of hardware the solution requires only a microphone, an accelerometer, a small speaker capable of emitting 'beeps' and a miniature vibration motor. An important feature of our method is the fact that it can be used on both specific locations (e.g. my 'kitchen table'), and abstract location types.

We discuss the physical principle, key issues, and limitations behind our approach (section 2). We then provide a detailed description of the recognition algorithm, including, feature computation,classification, and classifier fusion (section 3). Finally, we validate our method on an extensive, realistic data set (section 4). The data set contains a total of over 1200 measurements from 35 specific locations (taken from 3 different rooms) and 12 abstract location classes. The location were chosen to include examples that demonstrate the limits of the method such as an attempt to distinguish between the inner and the out pocket of the same jacket and between table and a book shelve both made of identical material. The data points at each symbolic location area taken at a number of randomized spots to ensure representativity.

Despite such challenging evaluation our method produces promising results. On room bases (16, 9 and 10 locations) we arrive at an accuracy of between 89 % and 93 % with the correct answer being in the to 2 first picks of the classifier between 97 % and 99 % of the time. With all 35 locations from the 3 rooms in one data set the recognition goes down to 81 %. However we still get the correct answer in the top 2 picks of the classifier 91 % and in the top 3 94 % times.

2   Approach Overview

2.1   The Method

Procedure Description. The proposed method consists of two parts, each of which can be used alone or in combination with the other.

The first part is based on vibrating the device using a vibration-motor of the type commonly found in mobile phones. During the vibration, which last a couple of seconds, motion data is recorded with an accelerometer and sound with a microphone. The motion and sound signals are used separately for an initial location classification using standard feature extraction and pattern recognition methods. The final classification is obtained through appropriate fusion of the two classification results.

The second part is based on sound sampling. The device emits a series of beeps, each in a different, narrow frequency spectrum. The microphone is positioned is such a way that it receives only little energy directly from the speaker. Instead a significant part of the energy comes from reflections from the immediate environment (see section 2.2 for a more detailed discussion). For location recognition the sound received from the different beeps is compared.

When the two parts are used together, the corresponding results are fused using an appropriate classifier fusion method.

General Principles Behind the Recognition. In abstract terms the above method is about analyzing the response of the environment to a mechanical 'excitation' with different frequencies. By vibrating the device we provide a low frequency (a few Hz) relatively high intensity (as compared to sound) source of excitation. By emitting fixed frequency 'beeps' we generate different, low intensity high frequency stimuli. The accelerometer detects the low frequency response (in our case up to 15Hz due to sampling frequency of the used device limited at 30Hz), the microphone the high frequency part.

The response to the above stimuli falls into several categories. First we get a low frequency response that directly mechanically couples to the vibrating object and is detected by the accelerometer. This response can range from a more or less complete absorption of the vibration energy (e.g. when the object is lying on pillow) to a resonant response where the surface, on which or device is lying, joins in the vibration. This fact contains information on two things. For one, it can reveal if, and how the device is fixed (in the hand, in a tight pocket, lying freely). In addition it reveals how hard and elastic is the surface on which the device is placed. This information can be expected to reliably distinguish between soft surfaces such as a sofa and hard ones like a table. Distinction between several similarly hard surfaces (e.g. metal and stone) is difficult.

Second, we get a high frequency response to the vibration, which is essentially a sound from the device hitting the surface. Assuming that placement of the device does lead to this kind of response (it will not, if the device is in a soft pocket or say hanging), it is quite location specific. The sound depends not only on the surface material but also on the overall structure. Thus a small, solid cube will produce a different sound then a large thin surface, even if both are made of the same material. Finally, objects light and close enough to the device to be influenced by the vibration (e.g. a key chain) might also contribute to the sound. In general, this is a source of noise rather then usable information. Figures 1 show two different vibration spectra.

Third, we get a high frequency response from the beeps which is given by the absorption spectrum of the environment. [1] Clearly this response is only useful if it comes from the immediate vicinity of the device. This can either be the surfaces on which the device is lying or, if the semantic location is a closed compartment, the walls of this compartment (see next section for a discussion of microphone placement issues). It is well known that the acoustic absorption spectrum is a distinct material property. The topic has been extensively studied in the context of musical instruments and sound isolation in construction ([16]). Typically the absorption is given at discrete frequencies as a fraction of the perfect absorption at an open window (lack of any reflecting surface) of equal area. As an example we consider the following coefficients from [16]

frequency	128 Hz	256 Hz	512 Hz	1,024 Hz	2,048 Hz	4,096 Hz
concrete unpainted	0.010	0.012	0.016	0.019	0.023	0.035
brick wall painted	0.012	0.013	0.017	0.020	0.023	0.025
carpet on concrete (0.4inch)	0.09	0.08	0.21	0.26	0.27	0.37

The above clearly demonstrates that, in principle, even seemingly similar materials can be separated with a small number of discrete frequencies.

Applying the Method: Specific Locations vs. Location Classes. The above description shows that our method provides information on abstract properties such as surfaces material as well as information on properties characteristic of a single specific location (e.g. a solid cube vs. large surface with several legs). As a consequence this paper investigates two different usage modes of our method:

1. 'Specific Location Mode'. In this mode we train the system on concrete locations such as a specific table or a specific chair. The advantage of this approach is that the user is provided with exact location information. The main disadvantage is the effort involved in training each individual location. In addition, there is the question being able to distinguish a large enough number of locations to satisfy relevant applications.
2. 'Abstract Location Class'. In this mode we divide locations into abstract classes. The two main criteria are the surface material and being open (e.g.

---

[1] Note that the absorption also influences the sound caused by the device vibration.

tabletop) or closed (e.g. inside a cupboard). In this mode the system is trained on several instances of each class. It is then able to recognize arbitrary other instances of this class. Thus the training problem is avoided, as the system can pre-trained at 'production time' and given to users without the need for further training. The disadvantage lies in the less exact location information, which has to be further interpreted and/or combined with additional information to find out where the object is actually located.

2.2   Issues to Consider

Microphone and Speaker Placement. As described above for the analysis of the absorption spectrum we must ensure that the sound emitted by the loudspeaker is reflected from the surface on which the device is lying and/or, in case of the symbolic location being a closed enclosure, from the enclosure walls. The second part is trivial. The first implies an appropriate placement of the microphone and the speaker. Optimally the speaker and the microphone should be located close to each other on the side of the device, preferably (but not necessarily) facing downwards with a sound proof barrier blocking the direct sound path between them. The main problem in implementing this type of setup is the definition of 'on the side' and 'downwards'. In the worst case we could be dealing with a cubic or round object with no preferred 'down' or 'side'. For such object two loudspeakers located at a 90 degree angle would have to be used to ensure that there is always a sidewards facing one. Our experiments (see section 4) indicate that the position of the microphone is less critically and we achieved good results despite the microphone facing upwards, so that one microphone might suffice.

Variations within Symbolic Locations. Many symbolic locations such as 'table' or 'desk' have considerable physical dimensions. This means that the response to the mechanical stimuli may be subject to spatial variations. Thus for example the low frequency response to vibration (acceleration data) may be different over the leg then in the middle of a large table. Similarly, on a table adjacent to the wall, the response to the 'beeps' will vary depending on how close to the wall the device has been placed. As a consequence both for training and testing a sufficient number of random physical locations must be sampled for each symbolic location (as has been done in experiments described in section 4).

Number of Relevant Locations. Clearly there are limits to how many locations can be reliably recognized. At the same time, in every day environments such as home or office, there are many places where objects can be put. The question is, whether the number of locations that can be distinguished is sufficient to be useful in relevant applications. An authoritative answer to this question can only be found through an analysis of specific applications. As stated in the introduction this is a technology, not an application paper and we make no claim to such an answer. Instead, exploring the technology side, we demonstrate and argue the following:

1. Our system shows reasonable recognition performance even using the combined data set of 35 locations. In our experiments these are collected from 3 rooms. It seems unlikely that this would not be sufficient to cover all relevant symbolic locations in a single room. At the same time , as has been discussed in the introduction, room level location of RF enabled sensor nodes is a manageable problem.

2. Provided that a adequate number of sufficiently abstract classes is chosen, the number of locations issue is avoided by the 'abstract location classes' usage mode. In the experiments we demonstrate near perfect recognition for 7 and reasonable results for 12 classes. The type of classes used in the experiments '(open wood surface', 'closed wood cabinet' etc.) is clearly abstract enough to describe a large number of locations.

Sensor Requirements. In the introduction we have stated our aim of developing a method suitable for smart objects. Accelerometers and a microphones are among the most widely used components in small sensor nodes. Small loudspeakers capable of emitting beeps are also commonly integrated in sensor nodes. As will be described in section 3 we work with frequencies between 500 and 4000 Hz, which can be handled by small, cheap speakers and microphones. Finally, although vibration motors have so far not been used in sensor nodes, they are available in sizes around 1cm and smaller (see figure 3a) and cost a few dollars.

In summary it can be said that the proposed sensor configuration is compatible with the target domain of small, cheap smart objects.

Complexity. Any method that is to be deployed on low end sensor nodes and smart objects needs to be resource conscious. However, when considering the method proposed in this paper it is important to remember, that it is not meant for continuous tracking of a moving device. Instead we assume that the method would be run once after the acceleration sensor has detected that the device has been moved and then let to rest. Thus there is no need to deal with speed and consider the power efficiency of the algorithm. We just need to show that with typical resources available in such nodes it is feasible to either perform the required computation or transmit the data to a remote server for processing. For the sake of simplicity we restrict ourselves to the communication requirements of the raw data. With 16 bit resolution and the sampling rates given in section 3 we have a data rate of about 130Kbps for the sound and a about 05Kbps for the acceleration. These have to be sustained for total of 13 seconds.

With respect to online execution we merely point to related work by our group in which we have studied implementations of sound and acceleration based activity recognition (e.g. [17]). With sampling rates, features and classifiers similar to the ones proposed in this paper we were able to demonstrate power efficient execution on nodes using the TI MSP 430 microcontroller with less then 100K of RAM. This leads us to believe that executing the proposed method, or at least computing most of the features (in particular FFT) to avoid transmitting the raw sound data on a low power sensor node would also be feasible.

3   Recognition Method

As described in section 2, our approach can be divided into two distinct methods, mechanical vibration and sound sampling.

Table 1. Selected features used for frame-by-frame classifications

Feature Name	Description
Standard, simple Features	Zero Crossing Rate, median, variance, 75% percentile, inter quartile range
Frequency Range Power	computes the power of the discrete FFT components for a given frequency band.
Sums Power Wavelet Determinant Coefficient	describes the power of the detail signals at given levels that are derived from the discrete wavelet transformation of the windowed time-domain signal. This feature has successfully been used by [18].
Root Mean Square (RMS)	$\sqrt{\frac{1}{N} * \sum_i x_i^2}$, with N the number of samples in a sliding window, and x_i the i'th sample of the window.
Number of Peaks	The number of peaks in the window with different thresholds, low medium and high.
Median Peak Hight	The median of the peak hight.

3.1   Vibration

During the vibration phase the device itself records the sound and the acceleration. Classification is performed separately on each signal and the information of the two modalities is combined on classifier level (see 3.3).

Vibration Sound Processing. For the vibration sound some 30 individual features were calculated over a 500 msec. sliding window (250 msec. overlap). From those we picked 5 based on initial tests and plots of the data: the zero crossing rate, the frequency range power, 75%Percentile, sums power wavelet determinant coefficient and the median. On these features we trained common machine learning algorithms, e.g. K-NN, Naive Bayes, C 4.5. We found C 4.5 to be the most robust and best (however only by a narrow margin). The frame-by-frame output provided by the C 4.5 classifier is smoothed using a majority decision over the entire length of a single vibration phase. We have also performed experiments using Hidden Markov Models either on the features calculated in the 500ms windows or on the classifier output of the frame by frame classifier. Since none of the above produced significant improvement, we have opted for the less computationally intensive majority decision.

Vibration Acceleration. The process described above for the vibration sound, is essentially repeated for the acceleration. The only differences are the length of the window (1 sec with 0.5 sec. overlapping) and the final feature set (variance, the RMS, number of peaks, median peak hight, the 75%Percentile, inter quartile range). Again C 4.5 has proven to be the best classifier and HMM has showed no advantage over the majority decision.

3.2 Sound Sampling

The active sound sampling procedure differs from the vibration method in several ways. We know from literature (see section 2) that few discrete frequencies between a few hundred and a few thousand Hz are enough to separate a large range of material in terms of their absorption coefficients. Therefore, we have selected 8 discrete, equidistant frequencies between 500 and 4000. The frequency range choice was dictated by the performance of small, cheap speakers (not capable of very low frequency tones) and the need for a reasonable sampling rate. From the recorded beeps we first isolate 8 frequency prints using a variable threshold. As features we have empirically selected RMS, frequency range power and the sums power wavelet determinant coefficient. These are calculated again 30 features in 200 msec. sliding windows (150 msec. overlapping).

The features of all 8 frequency prints are combined into one feature set. This means that a feature instance contains the calculated RMS etc. of each frequency band. The rest of the procedure is identical with the vibration recognition (frame by frame classification using C 4.5 and majority decision).

3.3 Fusion

The two main approaches to fusion are signal/feature level and classifier level fusion. Feature level fusion works best for features that are computed at the same sampling rate (sliding window size). This is not the case for the three recognition modalities described above. As the different window sizes were determined heuristically to produce best results for each modality, dropping them for the sake of fusion make little sense. As a consequence no direct feature level fusion was investigated. However we have investigated a fusion approach based on the results of the frame by frame classification. This can be viewed as kind of feature level fusion, since this result is input to the majority decision. Thus we have computed the majority decision for an event over the frame by frame results from all three modalities put together, instead of computing it for each modality separately.

In terms of classifier fusion we have opted for a Bayesian Belief Integration method (see. [19] for an overview of classifier fusion methods). The method uses the confusion matrix obtained from testing the classifiers on the training data set to determine class probabilities as for different combinations of classifier outputs. This allows the system to take into account the peculiarities of each classifier. With just 3 classifiers and a constrained number of classes it is also computationally tractable. If the number of classes and/or is increased the method would could be replaced by for example logistic regression.

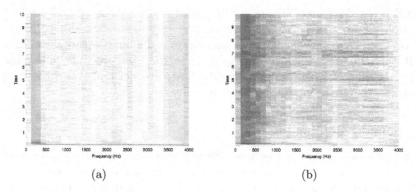

(a)   (b)

Fig. 1. The vibration sound spectrum for: (a) carpet. (b) desk.

4   Experimental Validation

4.1   Validation Scenarios

Specific Location Mode. As basis for our study we have picked three scenarios: an office, a living room, and a one room student apartment. In each scenario a set of obvious locations for placing objects was selected. These included the furniture present in this room (both open such as table or sofa and closed such as cupboards), the floor, the window ledges and additional things such as the stereo. In the office scenario we have also included three pockets (two different pockets from a jacket and a jeans pocket), the inside of a backpack and a suitcase as well as a the trashcan. A full listing of the investigated location is given in table 2 and illustrated in Figure 2. There are 16 locations in the office, 9 in the living room and 10 in the apartment (total of 35).

We recorded 30 experimental runs on each specific location (a total of over 1000 events), each time randomly varying the exact position of the recording. The object was placed according to positions drawn randomly from a uniform distribution. From the 30 runs, 10 are randomly picked to train the classifiers, the remaining 20 are used as test set. Evaluation is performed first on each individual scenario (under the assumption that room level location could be obtained from other means). To see how our method behaves as the number of location increases we have also done an evaluation on a data set containing all the locations from the three scenarios.

Abstract Location Type Mode. The abstract location types were defined according to the surface material and the location being open (e.g. a table) or closed (e.g a cabinet or a drawer). As shown in table 2 this has lead us to 12 classes that include most typical surfaces (wood, glass metal stone, poster). To get a sufficient number of different instances of each class we have recorded the data in a furniture store. For every abstract class we have picked 6 different furniture. Two recordings were done on each specific piece of furniture leading to 12 data points per abstract class and a total of 144 events. For the evaluation

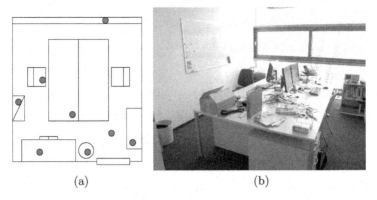

(a)   (b)

Fig. 2. The semantic locations we try to detect are marked in red for the office in (a). In (b) you can see the actual office we conducted the experiments in.

Table 2. Chosen symbolic locations and abstract location classes. The letter in front is the identification for the individual confusion matrix plots presented later in the paper. The letter in brackets behind the 3 scenarios concerned with the symbolic location, is the identifier for the confusion matrix plot over all 35 locations. In j. , o. j. and tr. pocket stand for inside jacket, outside jacket and trousers pocket.

Office		Living room	Appartment	Surfaces
a. backpack(a)	k. in j. pocket(C)	a. desk(h)	a. bath carpet(f)	a. polster open
b. cupboard(z)	l. tr. pocket (e)	b. floor(u)	b. bed(p)	b. glass open
c. suitcase(w)	m. cartbox (F)	c. sofa(n)	c. chair(b)	c. iron open
d. drawer(t)	n. ledge (H)	d. table(A)	d. desk (wood) (l)	d. stone closed
e. desk(D)	o. chair (v)	e. chair(c)	e. radiator(d)	e. wood closed
f. top drawer(E)	f. drawer (m)	f. ledge(k)	f. glass closed	
g. cabinet (x)	p. shelf (i)	g. ledge (G)	g. carpet floor(B)	g. iron closed
h. o j. pocket(j)		h. stereo (s)	h. cupboard(g)	h. metal open
i. trashcan(I)		i. tv (j)	i. drawer(q)	i. polster closed
j. carpetfloor(r)			j. wardrobe (o)	j. stone open

two pieces of furniture from each class (four events per class) were picked for training and 4 (8 events per class) were retained for testing. This is consistent with the envisioned application mode where the user would be given a device 'factory pre-trained' for each class and use it to recognize instance of the class not seen by the system before.

4.2   Experimental Procedure

Setup. For the experiments, we use the Nokia 5500 Sport. It is a mobile of Nokia's third S60 series, equipped with an accelerometer and an extra loudspeaker. The mobile is able to run C++, Java and python code. For the first experiments, we coded a C++ application to record the sensor values. Yet, we soon swapped to Python, as it is much faster for prototyping, less error-prone

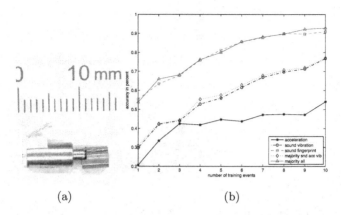

(a)   (b)

Fig. 3. A common vibration motor (Figure (a), picture from Ulf Seifert under the licence GNU FDL). On the right (b) is the Classification accuracy depending on the number of training events for the office scenario depicted.

debugging using an interactive bluetooth shell and still not lacking low level sensor access, through easy extensibility using C extensions. The evaluation is done in batch processing using a mixture of Python, Matlab scripts and Java code, mainly the Weka machine learning package.

Data Acquisition. An experimental run consists of the following steps. First the mobile is placed on a random spot on a particular location. A python script is used to determine this spot. Then the measurement is started. While the mobile vibrates for 5 sec. lying face up on the surface, a python script running on the mobile records the sound and acceleration simultaneously. The sound is sampled with 8000 Hz, the acceleration with 30 Hz. After the vibration measurement is done the mobile plays the sound sample consisting of 8 tunes in distinct frequencies from 500 to 4000 Hz in 500 Hz steps. Each tune is 1 sec. long. While the mobile plays this using the extra loud-speaker, the python script records the sound with 8000 Hz over the inbuilt mobile microphone. The loud speaker faces the surface, as depicted in Figure 3. We get around a problem of accessing full-duplex mode in python on the Nokia phone by using the music player and the extra speaker.

4.3   Experimental Results

The recognition performance for different scenarios experiments and recognition modalities are summarized in figures 4a (for the three individual scenarios of the specific location mode and the abstract location class) and in 4b (combining all 3 locations and second/third best voting). In addition examples of confusion matrices are visualized for the office, scenario, the combination of all three specific location mode scenarios and the abstract location type mode in figures 6a, 6c, and 7 respectively.

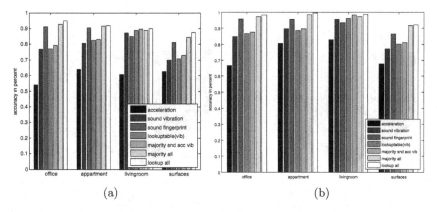

Fig. 4. Barcharts for living room, office, apartment, and abstract classes using just the first result of the classification (a) and allowing the 2nd best vote (b)

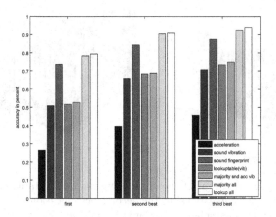

Fig. 5. Barchart for office living room, apartment and all combined including 1st 2nd 3rd best

In the more detailed discussion of the results given below and the some of the figures we at times discuss '2nd best evaluation' or '3rd best evaluation'. This refers to the percentage of cases where the correct class is among the 2 (3) first picks of the classification system.

Office. In the office scenario, 14 of the 16 locations can be classified near perfect accuracy. The single biggest confusion is between the pocket on the inside of the jacket with the one on the outside of the jacket. This is plausible and was expected. An unexpected result is the poor recognition of the metal window ledge. It is confused with the cartbox top the shelf and the chair.

The classification accuracy is 54% using the event-based acceleration classifier, 77% for vibration sound, 91% for the sound sampling, 77% and 79% for the vibration fusion cases, up to 93-94% for the majority decision and lookup-table

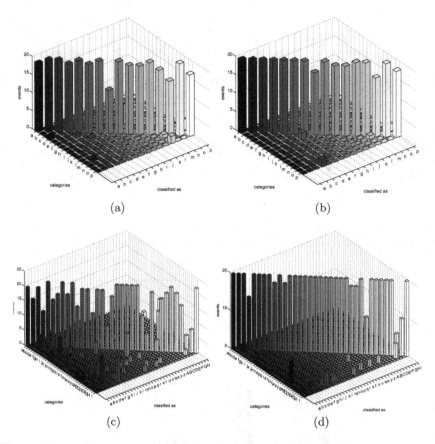

Fig. 6. The confusion matrix (a) of the office using the lookup-table fusion compared with the confusion matrix in (b) using the second best locations in addition to the lookup-table. The same is depicted, below only for all the 35 different semantic locations. Figure (c) shows the classification of the lookup-table fusion, whereas Figure (d) shows the lookup-table fusion considering up to the 3rd best.

fusion using all modalities. The sound sampling is the best non-fusion method with 91%. The '2nd best evaluation' pushes the correct classified up to 96%.

Living room. In the living room scenario, most of the samples from 7 of the 9 locations can be classified correctly. A lot of the sofa instances are confused with the chair, as the chair is also padded. This is the worst confusion. Again the classifiers perform poorly for window ledge category. The living room classification accuracy starts with 60% for acceleration alone, and goes up to 87% for the vibration sound. In this scenario, the sound sampling is worse than the vibration methods at 85%. This explains also why the fusion methods on top of the vibration work so well and are nearly as good as the fusion over all methods, at 88 and 89% respectively. The fusions over all methods just 0.5 % better. Only one/two events are corrected by this fusion. In the '2nd best evaluation' the accuracy ranges from 66% for acceleration alone, up to 97% for the lookup-table fusion over all methods. Here also the acceleration and sound vibration fusion do extremely well with 93% and 96%.

Appartment. In the appartment case, the worst miss classification happens in the cupboard category, which is confused with the desk. Both are made out of the same wood. The radiator class is also confused with several other classes. Here the acceleration accuracy is at 65%, the vibration sound at 81%, sound sampling 90%. The fusion using just the vibration method is at 82 and 84% respectively, as with all the fusion examples the lookup-table is slightly better. Finally, the fusion techniques on all 3 modalities are all over 90%. Taking a look at the '2nd best evaluation', there the accuracy ranges from 80 % for acceleration to up to 99% for the look-up table over all three classifiers.

Combined over all rooms (35 classes). As already seen in the single scenarios, the ledge classes perform poorly; even in the 2nd and 3rd best evaluation. Also one of the table classes does badly and is confused with several other classes. The classification accuracy over all 35 semantic locations is expectably lower that those of the single scenarios, ranging from 26% for acceleration, 51% for vibration sound, 74% for sound sampling, over 52% for the vibration fusion, up to 78% for the fusion of all methods. The 2nd and 3rd best evaluations look considerably better. Second best is up to 90%. Third best reaches 94%.

Abstract Location Classes. For the abstract classes, the iron and wood classes are easily confused, as well as the stone and glass. Acceleration classification alone performs reasonably well compared to the other scenarios with 63%. Sound vibration is better with 69%. As nearly always, sound sampling performs better compared to the vibration method, with 81% accuracy. For the fusion techniques, also nothing surprising. The vibration fusion majority decision is at 70%, the vibration lookup-table around 71% accuracy. The two fusions based on all methods are on 83% for the simple majority decision case and 86% for the lookup-table. Allowing the second best classification method, one can stem up the performance to 92% for the lookup-table fusion method.

4.4 Lessons Learned and Implications

Overall Performance. The performance of the system is extremely inhomogeneous with respect to the classes. There is a large proportion of classes for which the classification is perfect or near perfect, and a small one with very poor performance (see confusion matrices in figures (6a, 6b, 6c and 6d)). As a consequence the overall recognition accuracy figures are strongly influenced by few classes that the system has problems with. This is best exemplified by the abstract location type confusion matrix and 3rd best evaluation of the combined specific location classes. As can be seen in the plots the former has 8 perfect or near perfect classes, 1 reasonably good ad 3 very poor. The latter has 31 perfect to very good (27 perfect), 1 mediocre and 3 very poor classes.

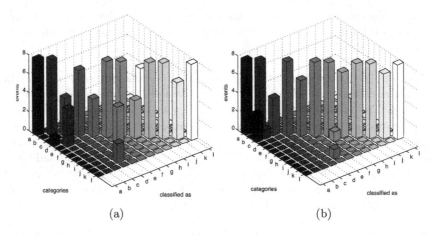

Fig. 7. Confusion matrix (a) of the abstract classes compared with the corresponding 2nd best confusion matrix in (b)

Class by Class Performance. For some of the classes such as the inside and outside pocket poor performance was expected, as they were included to test the limits of the system. In fact the recognition for this locations is better then expected. Better then expected recognition has also been achieved in a number of locations that were included as 'hard cases' such as the backpack and the trousers pocket. Surprising is the poor performance of the window ledge and the radiator. At this stage we have no verified explanation. On possibility is a spatial inhomogeneity of those symbolic locations. On the ledge the sound sampling is certainly different depending when the speaker faces the window and when it faces away from the window.

Value of the 2nd and 3rd Best Evaluation. The performance of the system is particularly appealing for applications that can live with choice of two or three most probable locations as system output. This has already been mentioned for the case of 3rd best evaluation of the 35 combined symbolic locations. For the other data sets even the 2nd best produces close to perfect recognition for the vast majority of classes.

Value of Different Classification Modalities. While from the discussion in 2 it was to be expected that sound sampling will produce the best results and acceleration the poorest, the difference between the two is larger then we expected. In particular the fact that in most cases little is gained by adding acceleration and vibration sound to the sound fingerprint is surprising. On the other hand combining vibration sound and acceleration is often produces significant gains.

Significance of Training set Size. For the specific location mode the user needs to train the system for every single relevant location. Thus the training effort is a significant issue. As shown on the example of the office scenario in figure 3b the system starts to display significant recognition performance from around 5 training examples and stagnates at about 10. We have found this behavior to be typical for all the specific location mode scenarios.

5 Conclusion and Future Work

Summarizing the discussion from section 2.2 and the experimental results from section 4.3 we conclude the following

1. The proposed method is well suited for low end, simple sensor nodes and smart objects and requires no additional positioning infrastructure.
2. The key source of information is sound sampling. Thus if size is critical the vibration motor can be left out.
3. The system can reliably (90% and more accuracy) resolve a sufficient number of specific locations to cover one room a or a small flat. It is advisable to combine our system with room level positioning
4. The performance of the system is extremely inhomogeneous with respect to the classes, with most classes being recognized with high accuracy and few 'rogue' lasses showing very poor performance.
5. Settling for the two or three best picks instead of a crisp single classification greatly increase the number of locations that are reliably recognised and the tolerance towards 'rogue' classes.
6. If training by the user is an issue the abstract location class mode offers a possibility to provide 'pre trained' systems at the price of a more 'fuzzy' location information.

Key points to investigate in the future are improved vibration sampling (using different amplitudes and frequencies to improve acceleration based performance), an investigation of the sources of errors on the problematic classes, more elaborate fusion methods, and a combination with radio signal strength based location methods. In addition in specific application projects, in particular in the area of assisted living, we will work towards real life applications of our method.

References

1. Becker, C., Dörr, F.: On location models for ubiquitous computing. Personal Ubiquitous Comput. 9, 20–31 (2005)
2. Hightower, J., Borriello, G.: Location systems for ubiquitous computing. Computer 34, 57–66 (2001)
3. Want, R., Hopper, A., Falcö, V., Gibbons, J.: The active badge location system. ACM Trans. Inf. Syst. 10, 91–102 (1992)
4. Priyantha, N., Chakraborty, A., Balakrishnan, H.: The Cricket location-support system. In: Proceedings of the 6th annual international conference on Mobile computing and networking, pp. 32–43 (2000)
5. Hazas, M., Kray, C., Gellersen, H., Agbota, H., Kortuem, G., Krohn, A.: A relative positioning system for co-located mobile devices. In: MobiSys '05: Proceedings of the 3rd international conference on Mobile systems, applications, and services, pp. 177–190. ACM Press, New York (2005)

6. Bahl, P., Padmanabhan, V.N.: RADAR: An in-building RF-based user location and tracking system. In: INFOCOM, (2), pp. 775–784 (2000)
7. LaMarca, A., Chawathe, Y., Consolvo, S., Borriello, G., et al.: Place lab: Device positioning using radio beacons in the wild. In: Gellersen, H.-W., Want, R., Schmidt, A. (eds.) PERVASIVE 2005. LNCS, vol. 3468, Springer, Heidelberg (2005)
8. Krumm, J., Cermak, G., Horvitz, E.: Rightspot: A novel sense of location for a smart personal object. In: Dey, A.K., Schmidt, A., McCarthy, J.F. (eds.) UbiComp 2003. LNCS, vol. 2864, Springer, Heidelberg (2003)
9. Doherty, L., Pister, K.S.J., Ghaoui, L.E.: Convex position estimation in wireless sensor networks. In: INFOCOM, IEEE, Los Alamitos (2001)
10. Scott, J., Dragovic, B.: Audio location: Accurate low-cost location sensing. In: Gellersen, H.-W., Want, R., Schmidt, A. (eds.) PERVASIVE 2005. LNCS, vol. 3468, Springer, Heidelberg (2005)
11. Van Kleek, M., Kunze, K., Partridge, K., Bo Begole, J.: Opf: A distributed context-sensing framework for ubiquitous computing environments. In: Youn, H.Y., Kim, M., Morikawa, H. (eds.) UCS 2006. LNCS, vol. 4239, Springer, Heidelberg (2006)
12. Holmquist, L.E., Mattern, F., Schiele, B., Alahuhta, P., Beigl, M., Gellersen, H.W.: Smart-its friends: A technique for users to easily establish connections between smart artefacts. In: UbiComp '01: Proceedings of the 3rd international conference on Ubiquitous Computing, pp. 116–122. Springer, London, UK (2001)
13. Lester, J., Hannaford, B., Borriello, G.: "are you with me?" - using accelerometers to determine if two devi ces are carried by the same person. In: Ferscha, A., Mattern, F. (eds.) Pervasive Computing (2004)
14. Kunze, K., Lukowicz, P., Junker, H., Tröster, G.: Where am i: Recognizing on-body positions of wearable sensors. In: LOCA'04: International Workshop on Location-and Context-Awareness, Springer, London, UK (2005)
15. Griffin, J., Fyke, S.: User hand detection for wireless devices U.S.Patent 20,060,172,706 (August 3, 2006)
16. Olson, H.: Music, Physics and Engineering. Courier Dover Publications (1967)
17. Stager, M., Lukowicz, P., Troster, G.: Implementation and evaluation of a low-power sound-based user activity recognition system. In: McIlraith, S.A., Plexousakis, D., van Harmelen, F. (eds.) ISWC 2004. LNCS, vol. 3298, pp. 138–141. Springer, Heidelberg (2004)
18. Sekine, M., Tamura, T., Fujimoto, T., Fukui, Y.: Classification of walking pattern using acceleration waveform in elderly people. Engineering in Medicine and Biology Society 2, 1356–1359 (2000)
19. Ruta, D., Gabrys, B.: An overview of classifier fusion methods. Computing and Information Systems 7, 146–153 (2000)

An Exploration of Location Error Estimation

David Dearman, Alex Varshavsky, Eyal de Lara, and Khai N. Truong

Department of Computer Science
University of Toronto
Toronto, Ontario M5S 3G4 Canada
{dearman,walex,delara,khai}@cs.toronto.edu

Abstract. Many existing localization systems generate location predictions, but fail to report how accurate the predictions are. This paper explores the effect of revealing the error of location predictions to the end-user in a location finding field study. We report findings obtained under four different error visualization conditions and show significant benefit in revealing the error of location predictions to the user in location finding tasks. We report the observed influences of error on participants' strategies for location finding. Additionally, given the observed benefit of a dynamic estimate of error, we design practical algorithms for estimating the error of a location prediction. Analysis of the algorithms shows a median estimation inaccuracy of up to $50m$ from the predicted location's true error.

1 Introduction

Developers of location-aware applications have a variety of localization systems [1,2,3,4,5,6,7,8] available to them. However, the accuracy and infrastructure requirements of each localization system constrains its applicability and the way in which application designers and end-users use them. For example, Wi-Fi [6] and GSM [7] localization are applicable for wide spectrum of applications, but their accuracy has shown to be highly variable. That is, the distance between the *actual location* and the *predicted location* fluctuates. We define this distance as the *true error* (see Figure 1) of the localization system. Unfortunately, many localization systems provide no information about the accuracy of their location predictions. As a result, the end-user of a location-aware application is entrusted to make sense of the location prediction presented to them without an awareness of the possible positioning error.

In this paper, we argue that presenting the error for a location prediction improves the usability of a location-aware application from the end-user's perspective. We present our examination of how users cope with an existing localization system and how they benefit from the presentation of the positioning error. We study user navigation strategies toward four predicted locations under four different error visualization conditions, where the user is presented with:

- only the predicted location and no additional information
- a region defined by a ring of fixed size, inside which the localization system is 95% confident that the actual location is contained

J. Krumm et al. (Eds.): UbiComp 2007, LNCS 4717, pp. 181–198, 2007.

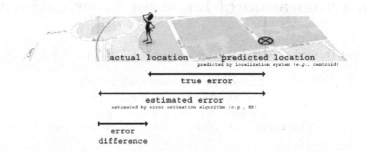

Fig. 1. Explanation of the positioning terminology used in this paper

- a region defined by a ring of variable size, inside which the localization system is N% confident that the actual location is contained; where N is defined by the user
- a region defined by a ring of variable size, inside which the localization system is optimally confident that the actual location is contained

In addition to understanding how users perform given the various error visualization conditions, we identify the effect of revealing the positioning error on users' navigation strategies for location finding. The results show that while a fixed estimate of positioning error provides little advantage to the user, a dynamic estimate of positioning error provides a significant benefit. A dynamic error estimate provides users with a better understanding of the true error at the time of prediction, whereas with a fixed error estimate, users are unable to differentiate between a high or low error location prediction until the actual location is found.

Finally, we describe two practical algorithms for dynamically estimating the error of a localization system and evaluate their performance. We show that our algorithms perform well, reaching a median difference of up to $50m$ between a location prediction's true error and the error as estimated by our algorithms.

2   Related Work

In this section, we introduce the most prevalent technologies used for location sensing. We discuss the importance of presenting their error for the usability of location-aware applications.

2.1   Location Sensing Technologies and Error

Many localization systems are available: Ultra-wideband[9], ultrasonic [1,2], infrared [3] , GSM [7], Wi-Fi [5,6], power lines [8] and GPS. The application of each system typically depends on its accuracy [10], infrastructure requirements and operating environment. Each of these systems has been experimentally tested [5,4,1,6,2] such that their error can be quantified for a particular environment. This measure is appropriate for validating the error of the localization system, but for end-users, it does not help them understand the true error of their *current* location's prediction. This issue is the focus of our research.

2.2 Expressing Uncertainty

Rather than refining the localization systems, our approach improves the usability of location-aware application from the end-user perspective. A location-aware application typically presents predicted locations to a user in such a way that it may require her to rationalize with the information [11]. Uncertainty in a context-aware application is inevitable [12], but the onus of identifying the true error of a predicted location should not be placed solely on the user. Rather, as Greenberg suggests, the context-aware application should not hide ambiguity and uncertainty from its users [13], but present the information truthfully in such a way that users can trust the information and react appropriately [14,15]. Chalmers and Galani advocate "seamful design", in which systems designers reveal the finite nature or "seams" of their technology [16]. In doing so users and designers can leverage the system's finite nature (in our case positioning error) to provide a benefit. Antifaskos *et al.* [17] have shown in their memory aid study that user performance can be improved by expressing the system's uncertainty. Uncertainty is not always something that should be avoided. Depending on the context of use, uncertainty can be beneficial and used as a strategic element as seen in the mobile game 'Can You See Me Now' [15]. Participants were able to identify situations where GPS performed poorly and leverage the situations as part of their game play strategy. We believe that location-aware applications should truthfully present their location predictions as a measure of their *estimated error*, not simply the predicted location (see Figure 1).

Probabilistic localization systems that incorporate Kalman filtering or particle filters, typically have an internal representation of a confidence value in their location estimates that should be accessible by a system designed. GPS provides an easily accessible estimate of its uncertainty that is derived from the geometric dilution of precision (DOP). Of particular importance is the horizontal dilution of precision (HDOP). The HDOP does not provide a measure of error (*i.e.*, meters), but provides a scaling factor for the GPS receiver's accuracy based on the geometry of the visible satellites. A HDOP value of three or less indicates good satellite geometry and an accurate location estimate. Given the DOP, some GPS providers have implemented additional feedback that equates the DOP to an actual error measure.

3   Field Study Examining the Effects of Revealing Error of a Localization System

We conducted a between subjects field study that explores the effects of providing an estimate of the true error for a predicted location to users within the context of a location-aware map application. Specifically, we were interested in gauging the impact error has on users navigation strategies. To accomplish this issue, we conducted a location finding field study. Participants, aided by a location-aware mobile device, were required to find four posters positioned around the University of Toronto campus, while spending no more than 15 minutes to find each poster. We limited the time to find each poster to 15 minutes because it provided sufficient time to travel between poster locations (approximately three to five minutes) and search for the poster. Additionally, it limited the participant's exposure to the cold. We conducted the study during January and February of 2007 when the temperature around campus varied between -21°C and 1°C, while the weather varied from sunny to light snow.

3.1 Experimental Setup and Hardware

For the field study, we used Intel's POLS [4] GSM-based centroid algorithm as the underlying localization system for our location-aware map application. Our application and POLS were both installed on a Pocket PC T-Mobile MDA device. Prior to the study, we war-walked every street of the University of Toronto campus, carrying the T-Mobile MDA to train the centroid algorithm.

With the trained POLS system, we were able to analyze the true error of the centroid algorithm for our environment by identifying its cumulative distribution function. At the 95th percentile, we determined the estimated error to be $467m$. Knowing the error levels associated with the positioning associated with our campus, we then chose four easily accessible locations that people frequently travel on campus such that the system would predict locations 1 and 3 with low error, and locations 2 and 4 with high error (see Table 1).

We physically marked the four locations with a unique poster (see Figure 2(a)). The posters came in two different dimensions: $61cm$(w) x $46cm$(h) and $40cm$(w) x $60cm$(h). Each poster was pressed against an equally sized piece of plywood and posted into the ground (see Figure 2(b)). None of the posters were placed inside a building, nor in an area that participants would have to walk through a building to find. The intent was to make each poster easily visible if the participants navigated within the poster's proximity. To motivate the participants to find each poster as fast as possible regardless of their previous failures or successes, for each poster, $25 was promised to the participant who found that location the fastest.

After installing a poster at each of the four locations, we used a T-Mobile MDA to collect 15 minutes of GSM measurements for each location and used the trained centroid algorithm to generate location predictions for each measurement. The location predictions for each poster were recorded in separate log files. The purpose of the logs was to ensure the consistency of the location predictions for all the posters across participants during the study. We then installed our map application on the same T-Mobile MDA. The application displayed a map of campus, annotated with the centroid algorithm's (live) prediction of the participants location and the predicted location of the poster (as read from the poster log file). Both locations were updated every two seconds. The map application provided three different zoom levels, where zooming in and out is achieved by pressing the respective up and down direction on the hardware directional pad.

Table 1. For each poster, the median, min, max and standard deviation of the centroid algorithms true error

	Median	Minimum	Maximum	St.Dev
Poster 1	$111m$	$13m$	$161m$	$40m$
Poster 2	$228m$	$211m$	$237m$	$50m$
Poster 3	$43m$	$19m$	$63m$	$11m$
Poster 4	$248m$	212	$451m$	$39m$

(a) Poster   (b) Poster in context (poster circled)

Fig. 2. One of the four posters (a) placed around campus (b). Each poster displays a different image. The five digit code in the bottom right of the poster (a) is used by the application to validate the correct poster was found.

It is also possible to pan the map in any direction by applying pressure to the screen and dragging the map in the desired direction.

3.2   Participants

Thirty-two paid volunteers (27 male, 5 female) were recruited through the University of Toronto. Participants included both students and staff members from a variety of faculties. The age of participants was between 18 and 45, with most (27) between 20 and 35 years old. All participants are frequent computer users, interacting with a desktop and/or laptop computer on a daily basis. Most are mobile phone owners, but have varying experience with mobile computing beyond telecommunication (*i.e.*, text messaging or mobile WWW browsing): 14 are frequent (weekly) users, four are infrequent (monthly) users and 19 have no or little experience. Only three participants indicated previous experience with location-aware a technology (*e.g.*, GPS). Participants were drawn from the active university community to ensure they would be familiar with campus.

3.3   Experimental Conditions: Visualizing Error

We explored four technique of visualizing the error of the predicted locations: *predicted location, 95% confidence, customizable confidence* and *optimal error*.

Table 2. The mapping between the confidence level and the prediction error

Confidence (%)	5	10	15	20	25	30	35	...	65	70	75	80	85	90	95
Positioning error (m)	57	82	103	123	139	153	164	...	262	281	307	343	378	413	467

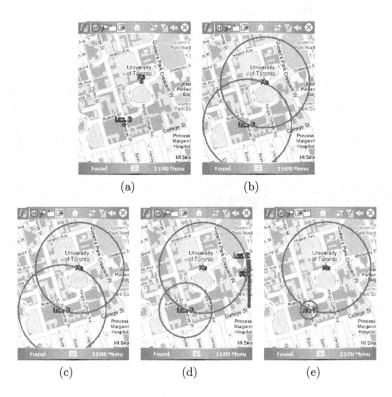

(a)   (b)

(c)   (d)   (e)

Fig. 3. The experimental four conditions: predicted location (a); 95% confidence (b); customizable confidence by default (c) and after the confidence value has been manipulated (d); and optimal error (e)

Given our between subjects study design, each participant was exposed to only one visualization, not multiple.

Predicted Location. In the predicted location condition, we provided participant with the predicted location of herself and the poster (see Figure 3(a)) as generated by POLS. This condition served as our base case to compare the other conditions against. The map is annotated with two dots representing the predicted locations of the participant and the poster. Participants were instructed that the error for the predicted locations could vary within the range of 467m.

95% Confidence. In the 95% confidence condition, we provided participants with a region defined by a confidence ring (see Figure 3(b)), in which the application is 95% confident that the actual location is contained within the ring.

The ring was drawn using our localization systems prediction of each location as the origin. The radius of the confidence ring was set to 467m; the 95th percentile training error determined for our environment. The size of the confidence ring remained constant (in meters) throughout the experiment, but scaled (in pixels) to match the map's zoom level. The participants were not instructed that the confidence ring was drawn around an origin defined by the location prediction, but simply what the visualization represented.

Customizable Confidence. In the customizable confidence condition, we provided participants (by default) with the same visualization as the 95% confidence condition (see Figure 3(c)); however, they could manipulate the confidence level of the ring. By default the confidence is set to 95%, but by using the directional pad they could increase or decrease the confidence value respectively; the confidence is customizable in increments of five percent, from 5% to 95%. In changing the confidence value, the radius of the confidence ring would similarly change. A smaller confidence value would provide an smaller confidence ring; for example, Figure 3(d) shows the confidence ring set to 70%. If participants want a smaller area to search, they can decrease the confidence value, but in doing so they are decreasing the confidence the location is contained within the new confidence ring. Table 2 shows the relationship between the confidence levels and the ring size. Again, participants were not instructed that the confidence ring was drawn around an origin defined by the location prediction.

Optimal Error. In the optimal error condition, we provided participants with a ring for each location (see Figure 3(e)) where the ring's radius is defined by the true error of the location prediction. We could calculate the true error for each prediction because our software knew the actual location of both the participant (via GPS) and the posters. This means that the size of each ring is variable, but it provides optimal confidence because the rings always contain the actual location they represent. Again, participants were not instructed that the confidence ring was drawn around an origin defined by the location prediction. In actual practice, obtaining the true error of a location prediction given current technology is difficult at best. We attempt to address this issue in Section 4.

3.4   Procedure

The study began with participants filling out a background questionnaire to provide us with demographics information. Next, we introduced the participants to the experimental condition they would be using, explained the software and allowed them explore the interface. The explanation of the condition was repeated until the participants expressed an understanding of the condition. This ensured that the participants understood what the application was showing them. Each participant took part in only one experimental condition.

After the participants had sufficient time to explore the interface and were familiar with their condition, they began the actual experiment. We outfitted each participant with a voice recorder to record verbal comments made during the experiment and a Bluetooth GPS synchronized with the Pocket PC to record where participants walked. We escorted participants outside to the same initial location and instructed them to press the start button displayed on the handheld to begin. All participants were required to find the same posters, in the same order. No attempt was made to counter balance the poster ordering. Participants were instructed regarding a 15 minute time limit to find each poster. If after 15 minutes they were unsuccessful in finding the poster, the application indicated 15 minute time limit had elapsed and annotated the map the poster's actual location, to which the participant still must proceed. Once a participant had found a poster they entered the five digit code in the bottom right corner of the poster (see Figure 2(a)) to validate that they had indeed found the correct poster. If the poster code was valid, the application presented the participant with a Likert Scale questionnaire on the handheld inquiring about their perceived difficulty of the scenario. After completing the questionnaire, the application presented the participant with the map and the location for the next scenario. This process repeated for all four posters.

After finding the final poster and completing the questionnaire, the participants completed a semi-structured interview concerning their experience. Additionally, we asked them to rank the four posters according to difficulty.

4   Results of Field Study

In this section, we present the findings of our study. In particular, we focus on the participants' completion times and perceived difficulty for each poster. We highlight participants' navigation strategies and discuss the influence of the experimental conditions on their location finding strategies.

4.1   Time to Find a Poster

In Figure 4, we observe a significant dichotomy in the time to find a poster because of the magnitude of the estimated error; only 6 of 32 participants found poster 2 and only 10 found poster 4. Prior to our analysis, we applied the *Rankit*[1] procedure to normalize the timing data to make it more appropriate for variance analysis. The estimated error for a poster's location prediction and the condition had a significant affect on the time it took a participant to find a poster. A four (Condition) by four (Poster) analysis of variance (ANOVA) with the time to find a poster as the dependent variable, yielded a significant main effect for condition [$F(3,112) = 1.27$, $p<0.05$] and poster [$F(3,112) = 33.52$, $p<0.005$], but no significant interaction [$F(9,112) = 1.51$, $p>0.10$].

Post hoc comparisons were made using Tukeys HSD test. Results revealed that participants in the optimal error condition performed their poster finding task significantly faster ($p<0.05$) than those in the customizable condition. Additionally, those in the optimal error condition showed a trend towards performing the

---

[1] Timing data was normalized using the *Rankit* procedure as defined in SPSS v14.0.

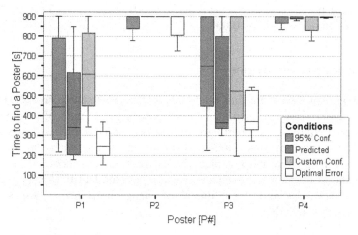

Fig. 4. Box plot of the time to find each poster for each condition. The box of the plot displays the median value and the interquartile range. The whiskers display the minimum and maximum time. All participants in the predicted and customizable confidence conditions could not find poster 2 in the 15 minute (900s) time limit.

poster finding tasks faster (p=0.06) than those in the 95% confidence condition. As expected, participants were able to find posters 1 and 3 significantly faster (p<0.001) than posters 2 and 4.

4.2   Perceived Difficulty of the Poster

The difficulty of each poster was assessed by two techniques. Upon finding a poster, participants rated the posters difficulty on a 5-point Likert scale (1-Very Easy, 2-Easy, 3-Neutral, 4-Difficult, 5-Very Difficult). After completing all posters, participants ranked the four posters in order according to their difficulty; 1 being the easiest and 4 the most difficult. The rank and Likert data is analyzed using Friedmans Two-Way Analysis of Variance. Post hoc analysis of the Likert and rank data is conducted using the Wilcoxon Signed-Ranks Test with a Bonferroni adjustment of $\alpha = 0.008$.

The Friedman analysis demonstrated a significant difference for the perceived difficulty between posters [χ^2 (3, N = 32) = 35.58, p<0.001], a significant difference for the perceived difficulty between conditions [χ^2 (3, N = 32) = 13.45, p<0.005] and a significant ordering of the posters perceived difficulty rankings [χ^2 (3, N = 32) = 36.34, p<0.001].

Post hoc analysis of the conditions revealed participants perceived the optimal error condition to be significantly less difficult that the customizable confidence (Likert: z=-2.93, p<0.005) condition. Additionally, as expected given the estimated error, participants perceived poster 1 to be significantly less difficult than poster 2 (Likert: z=-411, p<0.001; rank: z=-4.72, p<0.001) and poster 4 (Likert: z=-3.40, p<0.005; rank: z=-3.72, p<0.001) and poster 3 significantly less difficult than poster 2 (Likert: $z=-3.74$, $p<0.001$; rank: $z=-3.55$, $p<0.001$) and poster 4 (Likert: $z=-3.37$, $p<0.005$).

4.3   Navigation Strategies

Each participant, upon finding all four posters created a retrospective route map by tracing their route from memory onto a paper map of campus. Using the map, participants could highlight unique occurrences during the experiment and easily convey locations alluded to during discussion with the interviewer. Using the retrospective map, a plot of each participants recorded position via GPS and their interview transcript, it was possible to identify typical and unique navigation strategies and the influence of each condition on these strategies. These strategies include:

- **Navigate to the middle.** In 99 of the 128 completed scenarios, participants either navigate to the predicted location and search the vicinity, or in the case of a ring, they navigate and search the region alluded to by the ring's centre. In the case of location predictions with low true error, this strategy was advantageous because it brought participants close to the posters; as such the majority of participants successfully find posters 1 (28/32) and 3 (24/32). However, for location predictions with high true error, navigating to the ring's centre region was detrimental in that it focused the participants search on an incorrect region; as such we observed only a small number of participants finding posters 2 (6/32) and 4 (10/32).
- **Confine the area to search.** In the predicted location condition, the application presented each poster as a single dot. Despite participants' understanding that error existed in the localization system (as described by the experimenter), participants' comments suggest that they struggled to translate the range of potential error into a meaningful search area. For location predictions with high true error, without an awareness of the error magnitude, participants typically searched one street (poster 4) or intersection (poster 2) exhaustively, without success (see Figure 4). For the most part, participants confined their search to too small an area and as such were unsuccessful in finding posters 2 and 4. In the three conditions in which participants were presented a region defined by the estimated error, the region helped to confine the participant's search. As mentioned, participants would typically start by searching the rings center region, but then expand their search to additional regions bounded by the estimated error ring.
- **Identify a path that provides the largest coverage of the surrounding area.** Rather than initially heading toward the error ring's centre region, some participants leveraged their understanding of the ring and their familiarity with campus to identify a path that would allow for maximum coverage of the suggested search area. This strategy included finding a sequence of streets and paths that would allow them to navigate the ring, encompassing as much area as possible, without backtracking.

- **Associate the target with a landmark.** Rather than initially going to the error ring's centre region, some participants relied on their knowledge of campus within the ring to specifically identify a unique location, or locations to search. They often associated a specific landmark or a well known location on campus as a probable location to find a poster. The justification for choosing the location(s) was based more on prior knowledge of the environment rather than the map. They made educated decisions as to where the poster could be based on their knowledge of the area within the ring.

- **Ignore the 'Me' location.** The majority of participants (27/32) explicitly expressed in their interviews that they ignored the application's prediction of their location for the majority of the study; they commented that their location prediction was not very accurate. However, 17 of the 32 participants indicated in their interviews that they did attempt to use their location's prediction on one or more occasions to help guide them. They tried to: 1) apply the error observed in the prediction of their location (given they knew where they were) to the predicted location of the poster, 2) align the 'Me' location with the poster location, and 3) infer greater accuracy when their predicted location and poster location overlapped. It was typical to see participants use these techniques with the first poster as their initial strategy (while they were inexperienced) or for the remaining three posters when they were unsuccessful in locating the poster where they expected. Most participants who relied on the 'Me' location at one point or another described their usage as a "last ditch" attempt to find the poster. Very few participants (3/32) repeated the same technique a second time for a subsequent poster. These strategies, although well conceived and seemingly plausible, were based on a nave understanding of the localization system; the perceived relationship between the two location predictions did not exist because the systems accuracy is variable depending on environmental features.

In addition to the strategies described above, we also identified important findings that highlight the need for presenting the estimated error of a localization system to users dynamically. In the customizable confidence condition, participants reduced the confidence ring, commenting in their interview, that is made the size of the prediction area more manageable. The application logs support this observation. This was appropriate for location predictions with low true error, however, it was detrimental in the case of high true error. A ring that dynamically shrinks and grows, such as the one in our optimal condition provides a more accurate awareness of the true error. Without this awareness, users are unable to differentiate between low and high true error.

- **Experience could not allude to the level of error.** The first two scenarios introduced participants to the fact that the error for a location predictions is variable. However, participants in the predicted location, 95th percent confidence and customizable confidence condition did not show a significant change in their navigation strategies for posters 3 and 4. Participants commented that they searched regions closer to the rings edge (if they were presented with a ring), but overall most maintained the same strategy of searching the middle. Analysis of the GPS logs and the retrospective map supported their comments. Participant comments reveal that their strategy did not change because, 1) they had no awareness of the error level for the predicted location until they found the actual location of the poster and 2) they could not conceive a more beneficial strategy based on the information that they had:

> (P24-95th) *"In one [the first scenario] it [the poster] was in the centre, in two [the second scenario] it [the poster] wasn't. I didnt know what to choose! I chose the centre route [referring to scenario three] and I was lucky it was there."*

- **Desired reduction of the search area to a manageable size.** No participant in the customizable confidence condition maintained the 95% confidence level while trying to find the posters. All participants in this condition felt that the area defined by 95% confidence was too great to search within 15 minutes. At the default level of 95% confidence, the posters' actual location was always contained within the confidence ring. After participants reduced the confidence ring, the actual location was contained within the confidence ring 86% of the time for poster 1, 64% for poster 2, 99% for poster 3 and 43% for poster 4. For posters 2 and 4, given the high true error in the location prediction, reducing the confidence level resulted in the poster not being contained with the ring a substantial amount of the time.
- **Required awareness of true error.** Participants in the optimal condition were given a ring that provided them with an awareness of the true error for a location prediction. The size of the ring was proportional to the predicted locations true error: small error resulted in a small ring, large error resulted in a large ring. For posters 1 (M = $107m$) and 3 (M = $43m$) the size of the ring was significantly smaller than the ring for posters 2 (M = $228m$) and 4 (M = $266m$). For predictions with low true error, as in the case of posters 1 and 3, the participants had a much smaller region to search than the 95% confidence and customizable confidence conditions, but had the same confidence in the region. As such, we observed all participants in the optimal error condition found posters 1 and 3. However, only 12/16 found poster 1, and 10/16 found poster 3 for the 95% confidence and customizable confidence conditions. Additionally, the dynamic changes in the ring size afforded participants an awareness of the true error level for the current location prediction. As such, they could perceive the difficulty of each poster based on the size of the ring. In all the other conditions, participants did not have this awareness. They were ignorant of the true error for a prediction until they found the actual poster location.

> (P37-Optimal) *"[Referring to poster 2] I expected it to be more work, the circle was much larger than the first one."*

4.4 Summary

We observed a significant benefit of presenting the estimated error on participants ability to find the poster locations. The predicted location gave participants only one point to reference, as such they had difficulty defining an area to search when the predicted location was inaccurate. The 95% confidence, customizable confidence and optimal error conditions provided participants with a defined area to search. However, participants in the 95% confidence and customizable confidence condition could not identify the true error of the estimated error, as such they could not differentiate between an accurate and inaccurate location prediction. For the customizable confidence, participants found the default 95% presented them with an unmanageable search area. As a result, they reduced the confidence value which in the case of the low true error was beneficial, but in the case of high true error, it often resulted in the posters actual location being outside the confidence ring. Participants in the optimal condition had the benefit of a smaller ring provided the true error was low, but always had a consistently high level of confidence in their error estimates. We believe given our results that, not only is providing the localization error important, but that the presentation should present the true error as accurately as possible. In the next section, we address the issue of appropriately estimating the true error.

5 Dynamic Error Estimation

In the previous section, we showed that revealing the error of a localization system is beneficial to the end-user. In this section, we describe and evaluate two algorithms for dynamically estimating the true error of a location prediction as generated by a radio-based localization system such as centroid [10] or fingerprinting [7]. The algorithms are not tested in a similar field study as presented in the previous sections. We have left this exploration for future work.

5.1 Multiple Regression Error Estimation

The Multiple Regression (MR) error estimation algorithm takes as input a radio measurement (a list of beacons and their associated signal strength values), as fed into a localization system, and returns an error estimate of the location prediction in meters. To create a mapping from radio measurements to error estimations, MR uses the multiple regression method [18] to build a linear function from features of the radio measurements to error estimations. We experimented with a variety of features, eventually building a function that incorporates: the strongest signal strength value; the average of the three strongest signal strength values; the average of the five strongest signal strength values; the average of all signal strength values; the standard deviation of all signal strength values; the weakest signal strength value; the number of beacons observed; the number of strong signal strength values; the number of medium signal strength values; and the number of weak signal strength values. The strong, medium and weak signal strength values are device specific and need to be normalized across different devices. Once the linear function has been generated based on a set of training data, the error estimation can be generated in real time by extracting features from the current radio measurements and evaluating the linear function.

5.2   Zone Based Error Estimation

The Zone Based (ZB) error estimation algorithm takes as input a location prediction from a localization system (lat/lon coordinate) and returns an error estimate in meters. The main assumption behind the ZB algorithm is that localization systems are more or less stable. That is, if today a localization system predicts that the user is at coordinate B when she is actually at coordinate A, then tomorrow the localization system will still predict that the user is somewhere close to B, when she is at A.

ZB maintains a database of locations and errors associated with every location. Such a database is built off-line by running a given localization system on a set of measurements for which actual locations are known and recording the predicted locations and their associated error in the database. For example, predicted locations that fall around coordinate A may have a true error in the range of $100m$ to $120m$. This fact is recorded in the database.

Given the predicted location from a localization system, the estimated error is generated at real time by searching for known errors near the predicted location. Since a number of errors may have been recorded around the predicted location, ZB algorithm first sorts the errors and then chooses one of the errors based on an additional parameter given to the algorithm. For example, ZB50 uses the 50th percentile (a median) value, while ZB75 uses the 75th percentile value.

5.3   Evaluation

To evaluate the accuracy of the MR and ZB algorithms, we collected three sets of GPS-stamped GSM measurements using Intel's POLS software [4]. The data was collected by war-walking major streets of the University of Toronto campus. For each trace, we walked a distance of about $4.5km$, covering approximate area of $590,000m^2$. We evaluated MR and ZB on two localization systems: centroid and fingerprinting. We used the first set of collected data to train each localization system, and then tested their accuracy by feeding the two additional sets into each localization system to generate traces of GPS-stamped GSM measurements and corresponding location predictions.

Figures 5 and 6 show our algorithms performance for the centroid and fingerprinting localization systems, respectively. The figures show the 25th, 50th, 75th and 95th percentiles of the absolute difference between the true error and the estimated error for six error estimation algorithms. The Stat95 algorithm always predicts the same error, equal to the 95th percentile of the error in the training data, while Random picks a random error estimation from the training data. Stat95 and Random are the straw man approaches and are presented for comparison. The numbers in parentheses represent the percentage of predictions

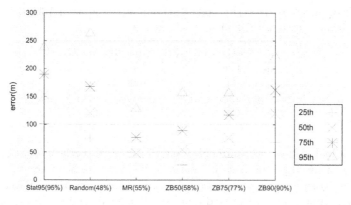

Fig. 5. The absolute difference between the true error and the estimated error for the centroid localization system using the Stat95, Random, MR and ZB algorithms

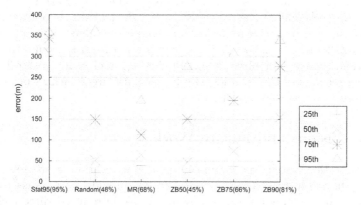

Fig. 6. The absolute difference between the true error and the estimated error for the fingerprinting localization system using the Stat95, Random, MR and ZB algorithms

for the respective algorithm that are greater than the true error. The percentage can be thought of as the confidence value for predictions generated by the algorithm. For example, an error estimate generated by ZB75 is approximately 77% more likely to be greater than the true error than lower.

Both MR and ZB perform better than the straw man approaches, with MR typically being more accurate. MR achieves 95th percentile error of $128m$ for centroid and $194m$ for fingerprinting, with Stat95 (the best performing straw man) trailing behind with $238m$ for centroid and $357m$ for fingerprinting. ZB75 appears to have a good balance between accuracy and achieved confidence, but performs slightly worse in terms of accuracy than MR. Interestingly, there appears to be a high correlation between the parameters passed to the ZB algorithm and the achieved confidence level. This suggests that ZB may be used in systems where the confidence level may need to be adapted to the user's requirements.

Table 3. Median of the true error and estimation error (in meters) for the ZB75 and ZB90 algorithm at each of the four poster locations

	Poster 1	Poster 2	Poster 3	Poster 4
True	111	228	43	248
MR	196	208	142	124
ZB75	122	196	266	298
ZB90	148	243	519	364

As described in Section 3, we collected 15 minutes worth of location predictions at each for the four poster locations. To test the accuracy of our error estimation algorithms, we supplied these locations into our MR, ZB75 and ZB90 algorithms. Table 3 shows the median of the true error and estimation error for each poster. MR performs well for posters 1 and 2, but over estimates the error for poster 3 and under estimates for poster 4. Both ZB75 and ZB90 perform well for posters 1, 2 and 4, but they estimate a much larger error for poster 3. Looking more carefully at the data reveals that the training data around poster three contains a varied mixture of low and high error values. The nature of the ZB75 and ZB90 is to pick the 75th and 90th percentile error around the area of a prediction, therefore we observe high predictions of error for poster 3. We are developing techniques that can identify problematic areas such as poster 3 and reveal these inconsistencies to the user.

6   Conclusions and Future Work

Many localization systems exist and can be used in location-aware applications. However, the majority of these systems do not provide easy access to an estimation of the prediction error, if any at all. We introduced three techniques for presenting the estimated error to address this problem; *95% confidence, customizable confidence* and *optimal error*. We conducted a field study to explore the benefits and influences of presenting the estimated error on location finding, by comparing our three visualization techniques against simply presenting the predicted location. Our results show that presenting an estimate of the positioning error provides a significant benefit. Fixed estimates of error (*e.g.,* 95% confidence and customizable confidence) provided little additional benefit, but they do help confine the search area. The optimal error condition strongly and positively influenced participants' search strategies. Participants found all posters where the true error was small. When the true error was large, participants experienced the same problems for finding the posters as the participants in the other conditions. However, participants in the optimal condition could identify that the true error was large and differentiate between high and low true error, where as participants in all other conditions could not.

Based on the result of our field study, we designed two practical algorithms for estimating the error of a localization system. The Multiple Regression algorithm estimates the error based of the raw GSM measurements, by extracting features from the measurement and evaluating a linear function learned on the training data. The Zone Based algorithm generates an error estimate based on the predicted locations supplied by the localization system using a mapping of the predicted locations to errors. We evaluated the performance of our algorithms on the centroid and fingerprinting localization systems. Our algorithms perform well, showing a median estimation inaccuracy of up to $50m$ from the predicted location's true error.

In future work, we plan to continue with the refinement of our error estimation algorithms. The success of our algorithms and the simplicity of their design provide encouragement for the exploration of more robust methods. Additionally, we will explore alternate presentation of the estimated error beyond a simplistic ring. We believe that a different presentation may significantly improve the perception and understanding of the estimated error.

Acknowledgments

The authors would like that thank all the participants for their time and willingness to brave the cold weather. This research is supported in part by the Natural Science and Engineering Research Council of Canada (NSERC) and the Walter C. Sumner Foundation.

References

1. Harter, A., Hopper, A., Steggles, P., Ward, A., Webster, P.: The anatomy of a context-aware application. In: MobiCom '99: Proceedings of the 5th annual ACM/IEEE international conference on Mobile computing and networking, pp. 59–68. ACM Press, New York (1999)
2. Priyantha, N.B., Chakraborty, A., Balakrishnan, H.: The cricket location-support system. In: MobiCom '00: Proceedings of the 6th annual international conference on Mobile computing and networking, pp. 32–43. ACM Press, New York (2000)
3. Want, R., Hopper, A., Falcao, V., Gibbons, J.: The active badge location system. ACM Trans. Inf. Syst. 10(1), 91–102 (1992)
4. Chen, M.Y., Sohn, T., Chmelev, D., Hähnel, D., Hightower, J., Hughes, J., LaMarca, A., Potter, F., Smith, I.E., Varshavsky, A.: Practical metropolitan-scale positioning for gsm phones. In: Dourish, P., Friday, A. (eds.) UbiComp 2006. LNCS, vol. 4206, p. 126. Springer, Heidelberg (2006)
5. Bahl, P., Padmanabhan, V.N.: Radar: an in-building rf-based user location and tracking system. In: INFOCOM '00: The 19th annual joint conference of the IEEE Computer and Communication Societies, pp. 775–784. IEEE Computer Society Press, Los Alamitos (2000)
6. Lamarca, A., Chawathe, Y., Consolvo, S., Hightower, J., Smith, I., Scott, J., Sohn, T., Howard, J., Hughes, J., Potter, F., Tabert, J., Powledge, P., Borriello, G., Schilit, B.: Place lab: Device positioning using radio beacons in the wild. In: Gellersen, H.-W., Want, R., Schmidt, A. (eds.) PERVASIVE 2005. LNCS, vol. 3468, pp. 116–133. Springer, Heidelberg (2005)
7. Otsason, V., Varshavsky, A., LaMarca, A., de Lara, E.: Accurate gsm indoor localization. In: UbiComp 2005, pp. 141–158. Springer, Heidelberg (2005)

8. Patel, S.N., Truong, K.N., Abowd, G.D.: Powerline positioning: A practical sub-room-level indoor location system for domestic use. In: Dourish, P., Friday, A. (eds.) UbiComp 2006. LNCS, vol. 4206, p. 126. Springer, Heidelberg (2006)
9. Ubisense, www.ubisense.net
10. Varshavsky, A., Chen, M., de Lara, E., Froehlich, J., Haehnel, D., Hightower, J., LaMarca, A., Potter, F., Sohn, T., Tang, K., Smith, a.I.: Are GSM phones THE solution for localization? In: IEEE Workshop on Mobile Computing Systems and Applications, April 2006, IEEE Computer Society Press, Los Alamitos (2006)
11. Smith, I., Consolvo, S., LaMarca, A., Hightower, J., Scott, J., Sohn, T., Hughes, J., Iachello, G., Abowd, G.D.: Social disclosure of place: From location technology to communication practices. In: Gellersen, H.-W., Want, R., Schmidt, A. (eds.) PERVASIVE 2005. LNCS, vol. 3468, p. 197. Springer, Heidelberg (2005)
12. Dey, A., Mankoff, J., Abowd, G., Carter, S.: Distributed mediation of ambiguous context in aware environments. In: UIST '02: Proceedings of the 15th annual ACM symposium on User interface software and technology, pp. 121–130. ACM Press, New York (2002)
13. Greenberg, S.: Context as a dynamic construct. Human-Computer Interaction 16, 257–268 (2001)
14. Edwards, W.K., Grinter, R.E.: At home with ubiquitous computing: Seven challenges. In: Abowd, G.D., Brumitt, B., Shafer, S. (eds.) Ubicomp 2001. LNCS, vol. 2201, p. 143. Springer, Heidelberg (2001)
15. Benford, S., Anastasi, R., Flintham, M., Drozd, A., Crabtree, A., Greenhalgh, C., Tandavanitj, N., Adams, M., Row-Farr, J.: Coping with uncertainty in a location-based game. IEEE Pervasive Computing 02(3), 34–41 (2003)
16. Chalmers, M., Galani, A.: Seamful interweaving: heterogeneity in the theory and design of interactive systems. In: DIS '04: Proceedings of the 2004 conference on Designing interactive systems, pp. 243–252. ACM Press, New York (2004)
17. Antifakos, S., Schwaninger, A., Schiele, B.: Evaluating the effects of displaying uncertainty in context-aware applications. In: Davies, N., Mynatt, E.D., Siio, I. (eds.) UbiComp 2004. LNCS, vol. 3205, p. 17. Springer, Heidelberg (2004)
18. Krumm, J., Hinckley, K.: The nearme wireless proximity server. In: Davies, N., Mynatt, E.D., Siio, I. (eds.) UbiComp 2004. LNCS, vol. 3205, p. 17. Springer, Heidelberg (2004)

Security by Spatial Reference: Using Relative Positioning to Authenticate Devices for Spontaneous Interaction

Rene Mayrhofer, Hans Gellersen, and Mike Hazas

Lancaster University, Computing Department, South Drive, Lancaster LA1 4WA, UK
{rene,hwg,hazas}@comp.lancs.ac.uk

Abstract. Spontaneous interaction is a desirable characteristic associated with mobile and ubiquitous computing. The aim is to enable users to connect their personal devices with devices encountered in their environment in order to take advantage of interaction opportunities in accordance with their situation. However, it is difficult to secure spontaneous interaction as this requires authentication of the encountered device, in the absence of any prior knowledge of the device. In this paper we present a method for establishing and securing spontaneous interactions on the basis of *spatial references* that capture the spatial relationship of the involved devices. Spatial references are obtained by accurate sensing of relative device positions, presented to the user for initiation of interactions, and used in a peer authentication protocol that exploits a novel mechanism for message transfer over ultrasound to ensures spatial authenticity of the sender.

1 Introduction

Spontaneous networking is of potentially great value to mobile users as it can enable them to associate their personal devices with devices encountered in their environment, and thereby to take advantage of serendipitous interaction opportunities. Spontaneous interaction in ubiquitous computing has for example been studied for applications such as social interaction and game-playing in mobile user communities. However, the potential of such interactions extends into areas that may involve more sensitive data and transactions, such as use of a vending machine over a wireless link, or direct payment transactions between two mobile devices. For such applications to be acceptable in a spontaneous network setting, a user must be able to authenticate the interaction of their personal device with the intended target device. They must be able to ascertain that the network entity their device connects to is identical with the physical device 'in front of them'. Furthermore, given the inherent vulnerability of a wireless communication channel, they must be able to rule out the presence of a third party established as 'man-in-the-middle' between their device and the target.

In a managed network environment, device-to-device authentication would be based on prior knowledge of each other or access to a trusted third party, but

J. Krumm et al. (Eds.): UbiComp 2007, LNCS 4717, pp. 199–216, 2007.

in spontaneous networks neither can be assumed to be available. Instead it is necessary to provide an out-of-band mechanism alongside the wireless channel, for secure key exchange or verification of keys that have been 'speculatively' exchanged over the wireless channel. A wide range of mechanisms have been discussed in the literature, from user entry of PIN codes [1] and direct electrical contact [2] to use of communication channels with inherent physical limitations, such as infrared, audio and ultrasound [3,4].

In this paper we present a novel approach for device-to-device authentication in spontaneous networks. The main contribution is a method that uses *spatial references* to establish and authenticate interaction between a pair of devices. Spatial references capture the spatial relationship with a target device in terms of bearing and distance, and are used in an authentication protocol that couples key verification with verification of the relative position of the sender. The method and protocol are a general contribution in the sense that they can be implemented with any peer-to-peer sensing approach capable of providing accurate relative bearing and distance. However, we also contribute a concrete implementation, using a combination of radio frequency (RF) and ultrasonic (US) communication for measurement of spatial relationships.

As ultrasonic ranging is susceptible to certain attack scenarios (as we will explain in the course of the paper), we further contribute a novel coding technique for spatially-dependent message transfer over an ultrasonic channel. This technique allows a sender to transmit a message such that it can only be successfully decoded if it is received at a particular range. The technique is a key component in the protocol implementation we present, but can have wider application in ultrasonic systems independent of the particular problem we consider here.

In the subsequent section we will position our research with respect to related work, and then proceed to a description of the overall design of our method, the underlying sensing approach and the proposed user interface. This will be followed by a threat analysis, the description of a peer device authentication protocol as our core contribution, and an analysis of security and performance.

2   Related Work

Peer device authentication was first highlighted as a distinct security challenge emerging in ubiquitous computing by Stajano and Anderson, who proposed the 'Resurrecting Duckling' model for secure transient device association, bootstrapped from direct electrical contact [2]. Others have proposed channels for authentication that do not require direct contact but are 'location-limited' [3] or 'physically constrained' [4], including infrared beams [3], laser beams [5], and ultrasound [6]. Our method of spatial references effectively expands on the idea of location-limitation, using spatial measurements in addition to channel limitations, in order to further limit the position from which a device can successfully authenticate.

A variety of methods rely more on the user for device authentication, for instance for manual key entry [1], scanning of visual tags on the target and comparison with wirelessly received material [7] and verification of spoken messages generated by devices [8]. Our approach also has the user in the loop, however does not involve any user interaction *solely* targeted at security. Instead, we provide the user with a spatial technique for initiating interaction with another device; the spatial relationship is captured in this process and is then used for securing the interaction without need for further intervention of the user.

Our concrete implementation is based on the use of US as out-of-band channel. Kindberg et al. have before us proposed the use of US alongside an RF wireless channel in a protocol for validation and securing of spontaneous interaction [6]. The idea of the protocol is for devices to first exchange keys, and then to verify that the intended device is in possession of the correct key, by having the device send a nonce in plaintext over ultrasound and over RF. However, the protocol design does not consider potential attacks on the ultrasonic channel. A specific problem is the reliance on ultrasonic time-of-flight measurements for verification of device authenticity, as these involve synchronisation over the RF channel and are open to attack scenarios in which an attacker may appear nearer or further than they are [9]. As the protocol has not been implemented it is also not clear how precisely the nonce would be transmitted and what the security implications of this would be. In its general design, our protocol is similar to that of Kindberg et al., but we attend specifically to the issue of trustworthiness of ultrasonic ranging, and provide a complete implementation with security and performance analysis.

Other related work includes spatial interaction techniques. Hazas et al. [10], while not considering security, have presented an approach that uses ultrasonic peer-to-peer sensing for spatial discovery of other devices within interaction range, and work expanding on this has considered visualisation of the devices' positions in the user interface in order to ease interaction across devices (e.g. enabling transfer of a document to another device by a simple drag-and-drop operation) [11,12]. We employ the same principle in our method to let users initiate spontaneous interactions by means of spatial discovery and selection of the target device, but extend the approach by adding security in a seamless manner.

3   Security by Spatial Reference

Central to our method is the concept of *Spatial References*. A spatial reference captures the spatial relationship of a client device with a target device. A key aspect of spatial references is that they can be obtained independently by a user (seeing devices in front of them) and by their device (using sensors), and that a user can match what their device senses with what they see. Spatial references thus serve to establish shared context between a user and their device: a device can report a discovered network entity in a manner that the user can match with encountered devices, and a user can identify a target device in a way that their device can match with network entities.

3.1 Design of the Method

In our method for establishing and securing spontaneous interactions, spatial references are used for discovery of devices, for selection of a target devices, and for verification that interaction is secured between the 'right' devices. This involves the following steps:

1. The user's device uses a combination of network discovery and spatial sensing for *spatially-bounded discovery* of devices.
2. The spatially discovered devices perform spatial measurements to compute their relative positions.
3. Users are provided with a visualisation of available devices, integrated in the user interface of their personal device and laid out in correspondence with computed positions relative to the user's device.
4. Users initiate interaction and communication with a device by selection of the corresponding visual object, using direct manipulation techniques available in their user interface.
5. Selection of a device for spontaneous interaction triggers a protocol for key exchange with the target device and verification that no other devices can be present as 'man-in-the-middle' between the user's device and the target.
6. Once it has been asserted that exchanged keys are authentic, they are used for securing the communication channel between user device and target, and the initiated interaction can take place.

3.2 Spatial Discovery and Sensing

For a concrete implementation of spatial discovery and sensing we base our method on the *Relate* system for relative positioning introduced by Hazas et al. [10]. The Relate system provides wireless sensors implemented as USB dongles that can be readily used to extend host devices (such as laptops or PDAs) with spatial sensing. The Relate sensors contain three ultrasonic transducers (to cover space in front, left and right of the device) and they operate their own ad hoc network over combined radio frequency (RF) and ultrasound (US) channels (note this sensor network is separate from the wireless network that connects their host devices). Protocol functions implemented over the sensor network include network discovery and management, collaborative ultrasonic sensing, collection of measurements, and exchange of host information. The Relate sensors specifically support spatial discovery of their host devices by exchanging the hosts' network addresses over the sensor network.

The Relate sensors use RF messages to co-ordinate ultrasonic sensing. Sensing is performed by one node emitting ultrasound on its transducers, while all other nodes listen for a pulse on their transducers. The receiving sensors measure the peak signal values and the times-of-flight of the ultrasonic pulse with their three transducers. The smallest time-of-flight is used to calculate a distance estimate, and an angle-of-arrival estimate is derived from the relative spread of peak signal values measured across the transducers. The Relate sensors use

Fig. 1. Integration of spatial references to near-by devices in the mobile user interface; left: extension of Guinard et al.'s Gateways [12]; right: Kortuem et al.'s map view [11]

RF to share and collect sensor data, and each sensor provides the collected data to its host device. This then enables the host devices to compute their relative positions very accurately. Hazas et al. report a 90% precision around 8 cm in position and 25° in orientation [10]: these figures and our practical experience suggest sufficient accuracy for reliable disambiguation of devices. By collaboratively sharing US measurements over RF, partial obstruction can be dealt with in principle. However, for spatial authentication we rely on direct line of sight between the authenticating devices.

3.3   User Interface Design

Spatial discovery and sensing happen automatically and unobtrusively. Users are then provided with a visualisation of the computed relative positions of devices in the interface on their own personal device. The visualisation has to be such that a user can associate a visual screen object with a device in their environment. Figure 1 shows two possible implementation. The one on the left is based on Guinard et al.'s *Gateways* [12]: these are screen objects arranged around the edge of the user interface, representing devices in the indicated direction relative to the user's device, and here extended to also show distance information. The one on the right is adapted from [11] and shows a map view with icons spatially arranged in correspondence with the actual layout of devices discovered around the user's device. Key to our concept is that the visualisation reflects the 'real' spatial layout, so that users can make a connection between what they see and what their device sees (and visualises). This allows users to invoke interactions by spatial reference, for example simply by dragging an object onto a Gateway or icon representing a remote device. A device thus selected as targeted is associated with a particular bearing and distance as measured with on-board sensors.

4   Threat Analysis

The key idea underlying our method is to use spatial references for verification of device authenticity. In this section we consider threats in the context of the ultrasonic sensing approach we introduced above, as well as threat scenarios that arise on application level.

4.1 Attacker Capabilities

There are three channels of concern: the communication network between devices, e.g. wireless LAN with a TCP/IP stack, the radio frequency channel used for communication between spatial sensing devices (RF), and the ultrasound channel used for sending and receiving ultrasonic pulses (US). We assume an attacker ('Eve') to be capable of gaining complete control over the wireless communication channels. This allows Eve to perform a 'man-in-the-middle' (MITM) attack on the wireless channels. Assuming to devices A and B, the attacker E can pretend to A that it is B, and to B that it is A, and thus agree to a cryptographic key with A and separately with B. A and B will be unaware of this and believe to communicate securely with each other when in fact they are communicating via E (who might be partially or completely relaying their messages).

The aim of our method is to prevent that a man-in-the-middle can succeed. To this end, spatial references are used during the authentication process, and are therefore subject to potential attack. We can distinguish between three different attacker capabilities with regards to tampering with spatial references, in order of increasing complexity:

1. *RF-only*: Attacks on any of the wireless channels (RF) are the most dangerous, because they can be carried out inconspicuously (see e.g. [13]). With directed antennas, the possible range of an attacker can significantly exceed the normal range of the RF channel, as has been demonstrated by an attack on mobile phones via Bluetooth over a distance of over 1.7 km.
2. *US in room*: Control over the US channel, on the other hand, is assumed to be limited. First, for attacks on this channel, an attacker needs to be physically present in the same room (US is effectively blocked by solid materials such as walls, doors, and windows). Second, although eavesdropping is easily possible, injecting US pulses is more difficult. We assume an attacker to be capable of injecting US pulses at any time with arbitrary strength. Injection in this sense means to insert completely new messages into the US channel, while modifying, replacing, or removing other messages is not possible without detection.
3. *US in line*: An attacker in the same room can inject US pulses, but receiving devices will be able to detect the different angle of arrival. The reason is that – in contrast to distance measurements – angle of arrival is inferred from relative measurements, i.e. differences in time of arrival or signal strength. We assume it impossible to fake the angle of arrival of a US pulse, bar the capability of sound forming for US (which has not yet been shown to be possible). However, an attacker could be placed in line with A and B, and thus not be required to fake the angle.

4.2   Sensing-Level Threats

Attacking the RF channels creates three threats specific to our spatial sensing system:

(a) by removing all RF messages sent from or to a single device, an attacker Eve can prevent the device from entering the sensor network, and thus *make a specific device disappear* for all other devices – however, this can be detected by the device in question.

(b) by changing RF messages, Eve can *tamper with shared measurements*, i.e. those that are taken by remote sensors and exchanged between Relate sensors. Additionally, US ranging depends on trigger packets sent via RF.

(c) by controlling these trigger packets, Eve can *manipulate distance measurements*.

If Eve is spatially aligned line with A and B, she could also send US messages delayed or ahead of schedule to the effect that her position, from Alice's point of view, appears to be where Bob is. This creates a fourth specific threat, namely (d) to *fake the perceived distance*.

Note that, in contrast to ranging measurements, angle of arrival measurements are trustworthy in our sensing system, as they are derived from signal peak values measured on with sensors oriented in different directions, and not from time-of-flight as proposed in [6].

4.3   Application-Level Threats

The possibility to tamper with spatial references leads to three specific attack scenarios on the application level.

1. *Replacement*: The first possibility for attack is to virtually replace another device. This requires two steps: First, the original communication partner, in this case B, needs to be 'silenced' so that it will no longer be visible in terms of wireless communication and measurements. Second, Eve needs to fake her position to appear at the same place where the user ('Alice') expects B to be. In this attack, interaction happens only between Alice and Eve, and no interaction happens with B. Scenarios for this threat are thus limited to asymmetric settings where B is an infrastructure device not monitored by users.

2. *Asynchronous MITM*: When the scenario includes application-level feedback from B to Alice, there is the possibility for an asynchronous MITM attack. An example for such expected feedback is printing: Alice, when sending a document to B, expects her document to print shortly afterwards. In this case, Eve first replaces B as in the first threat, but only temporarily. After finishing authentication with Alice, she authenticates with B and forwards the intercepted messages that were originally intended for it. Eve could therefore try to avoid detection by forwarding to B and thus completing the high-level interaction. This scenario requires that B does not verify the origin of the messages, i.e. that only Alice authenticates B, but not the other way around.

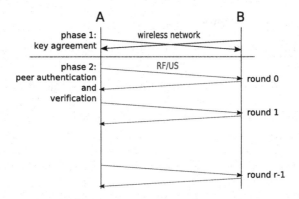

Fig. 2. Devices A and B secure their interaction by key agreement over a wireless network channel, followed by peer authentication over the RF and US channels of their spatial sensors

3. *Synchronous MITM*: For live interaction, like a chat or voice communication between two users (Alice and Bob) over the secure channel, even the slight delay of an asynchronous MITM attack would be noticeable. The most dangerous threat, because it is hard to detect when the attack is being performed, is that of a synchronous MITM. For a synchronous MITM, Eve first attacks the wireless channel as in the previous threat scenarios. But then she remains passive during spatial discovery and mutual positioning of Alice and Bob. Only during spatial authentication she tampers with the spatial measurements. Thus, she remains virtually undetectable for both Alice and Bob, while still having full access to their communication. This requires Eve to be physically between Alice and Bob, because both verify angle of arrival of spatial relationships.

5   Key Agreement and Peer Authentication

We secure spontaneous interaction between two devices A and B in two phases, *key agreement* and *peer authentication*, as shown in Fig. 2. In the first phase, we let A and B establish a shared key using a standard, unauthenticated key agreement protocol, such as Diffie-Hellman (DH) [14]. If this is successful, then A and B can use the agreed key to protect their communication against eavesdropping and tampering, with E being unable to gain sufficient knowledge of that shared key. To protect A and B against MITM attacks, we use a second phase for peer authentication (A establishing that it is really talking to B, and vice versa), and for verification that A and B are in possession of the same key (which would rule out the presence of a MITM due to the unique-key property of a protocol such as DH).

5.1   Peer Authentication

The peer authentication process is designed to be symmetric, which means that the two devices A and B authenticate each other. Even though the interaction is initiated by A in response to Alice's selection of B as target, it will often be appropriate that B can also verify the sending device and its relative position, for example to provide its user Bob with a verified visual indication in his user interface of *where* a received document has been sent from (and thus prevent replacement or asynchronous MITM attacks). As a starting point for authentication, A has a spatial reference to B as derived from the user's selection of B as her target, and B can base authentication on a corresponding spatial reference to A.

Devices A and B use the RF and US channels of their sensor nodes for peer authentication in order to tightly couple this process with spatial sensing. The devices engage in a protocol designed to establish that (i) they have agreed to the same key, and (ii) they are A and B as mutually verifiable by spatial reference. The devices approach this by generating a nonce (a random number used only once) and by transmitting the nonce encrypted over the RF channel. They also transmit the plaintext nonce over the US channel in a series of smaller parts that are coded within the actual distance measurements. When the devices receive these transmissions, they decrypt the RF message, verify that the content matches the nonce received via US, and thus establish whether their keys match. For this approach to be secure, the encoding and the transmission of these nonces need to be coordinated. In the following, we discuss these two issues and how they interact with each other.

5.2   A Spatial Coding Technique for Trustworthy Ultrasonic Ranging

When a device receives an ultrasonic pulse, it computes a distance measurement based on the time-of-flight. As explained above in section 4.2, these distances can be tampered with. We therefore introduce a method to embed information in ultrasound pulses, which (i) allows to use US as an out-of-band channel for message exchange, and (ii) makes the distances trustworthy.

During authentication, the sender delays the sending of pulses to the effect of adding a certain perceived distance to the measurement, where the added distance represents information (in our protocol, a substring of the nonce). When for instance A receives a pulse and computes a distance, this distance is the actual distance from the sender plus a distance representing the message. A proceeds with subtracting the reference distance it has of B (note the reference distance is captured when the user selects a device for interaction). This will let A retrieve the information (represented as added distance) correctly only if the received pulse has been sent from a range that corresponds with the relative position of B. That is, a correct reconstruction of the message implies that the distance is equal to the reference measurement, and therefore constitutes and implicit check of spatial integrity. Figure 3 illustrates this mechanism for message transmission over ultrasound with implicit verification of sending range. In addition to this implicit distance check, A can verify that the pulse was received from a direction corresponding with the reference held for B, thus effectively eliminating the possibility that the US transmission originates from another device but B.

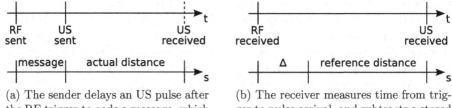

(a) The sender delays an US pulse after the RF trigger to code a message, which corresponds to a distance in the spatial domain.

(b) The receiver measures time from trigger to pulse arrival, and subtracts a stored reference from the corresponding distance to retrieve the message.

Fig. 3. Message transmission embedded with ultrasonic ranging: The receiver will only be able to retrieve the message if the sender's distance matches the stored reference

5.3   Preventing MITM Relaying

A and B can thus verify that ultrasound pulses are received from the intended partner device but it is still possible that E is present as MITM on the RF channel. E would be able to infer the nonces exchanged between A and B by taking its own US measurements (note that this only requires eavesdropping on US pulses, which is simple to do as long as E is in the same room), and it could then use its keys (maliciously agreed with A and B in the key agreement phase) to re-encrypt the nonces in order to pass the key verification checks of A and B. To rule this possibility out we use an interlock protocol, which in essence commits the sender of a message to the message content before it has been transferred completely [15]. For this purpose, A and B split the encrypted nonces into multiple parts and take turns in transmitting their parts. The nonces are encrypted with a block cipher, which means that all message parts need to be reassembled before the message can be decrypted to retrieve the nonce. If E now receives a message part from A intended for B, it can not retrieve any part of the nonce. E will also not receive more message parts from A unless it passes the current one on to B, as A and B strictly adhere to turn-taking. E's only choices are then to guess the content for all message parts that will 'pass through' (before they are even transmitted by A and B, let alone decrypted by them) in order to re-encrypt these successfully (this is practically impossible), or to relay message parts unchanged in which case A and B will discover that their keys do not match (thereby detecting the presence of a MITM and aborting authentication). The interlock protocol thus rules out that a MITM attack on the RF channel can succeed during peer authentication.

5.4   Protocol Specification

An overview of the protocol phases is shown in Fig. 2. Key agreement takes place over a wireless network channel, and subsequent key verification and peer authentication over the RF/US channels of their spatial sensors. The second phase involves turn-taking of the parties in an interlock protocol over a number of rounds r. This number will be agreed between devices, in consideration of the security level, protocol duration, and US channel capacity. The US channel capacity b_u is the number of bits that can be reliably transmitted as distance offset in each round, and will depend on the characteristics of the sensors used and sensing protocol details. Assuming a nonce of 128 bits, we would need $\lceil 128/b_u \rceil$ rounds for transmission of the nonce over US. However, a smaller number of rounds may be agreed to complete the protocol faster, compromising on how many bits of the nonce are eventually compared for key verification. With r agreed, we then set the number of bits that will transmitted over the RF channel in each round to $b_m := \lceil 128/r \rceil$, splitting the encrypted nonce into equal message parts.

We will now describe our protocol more formally using the following notation: $c := E(K, m)$ describes the encryption of plaintext m under key K with a symmetric block cipher, $m := D(K, c)$ the corresponding decryption, $H(m)$ describes the hashing of the message m with a secure hash algorithm, and $m||n$ describes the concatenation of strings m and n. Additionally, the notation $M[a : b]$ is used to describe the substring of a message M starting at bit a and ending at bit b. Messages that are transmitted to the other party are printed in bold.

1. *Key agreement*, using the Diffie-Hellman key establishment protocol:
   (a) A chooses a random number $a \in \{1, ..., q - 1\}$ and transmits $\mathbf{X} := g^a$,
       B chooses a random number $b \in \{1, ..., q - 1\}$ and transmits $\mathbf{Y} := g^b$
   (b) A computes $K_a^{Sess} := H(\mathbf{Y}^a)$ and $K_a^{Auth} := H(\mathbf{Y}^a || PAD)$ with some secure hash algorithm,
       B generates K_b^{Sess} and K_b^{Auth} correspondingly from $\mathbf{X}^b$
   The numbers g, q and the string PAD are assumed to be publicly known. Although we envisage the use of ephemeral keys, i.e. new values for a and b for each protocol run, it might be advantageous to use long-term values for performance reasons. We use K^{Auth} ($= K_a^{Auth} = K_b^{Auth}$) for key verification in the peer authentication phase, and K^{Sess} ($= K_a^{Sess} = K_b^{Sess}$) for subsequent channel security if the verification succeeds. The additional hashing to compute two different shared keys provides forward secrecy in the case of leaked authentication key material (cf. [16, section 15.8.4]), for example by a known plaintext attack on $E(K_x^{Auth}, N_x)$ after the respective N_x is revealed in the following steps.
2. *Peer authentication*:
   (a) A chooses a nonce $N_a \in \{1, ..., 2^{128} - 1\}$ and computes $M_a := E(K_a^{Auth}, N_a)$,
       B chooses N_b and computes M_b correspondingly with K_b^{Auth}
   (b) *For each round $i := 0 \ldots r - 1$:*
       - A transmits a RF packet $\mathbf{M_a^i} := M_a[i \cdot b_m : (i + 1) \cdot b_m - 1]$ and an US pulse $\mathbf{USP_a^i}$ delayed by $N_a[i \cdot b_u : (i + 1) \cdot b_u - 1]$ units,
       - B receives message part $\mathbf{M_a^i}$ and US pulse $\mathbf{USP_a^i}$, derives a distance measurement $d_{b,a}^i$, and uses the stored reference measurement $d_{b,a}$ to reconstruct the distance-coded message $\Delta_a^i := d_{b,a}^i - d_{b,a}$. B also verifies the angle of arrival $\alpha_{b,a}^i$ and compares it with the stored reference

measurement $\alpha_{b,a}$. If the difference exceeds the typical measurement error, B aborts the authentication protocol with an error message.

- B transmits $\mathbf{M_b^i} := M_b[i \cdot b_m : (i+1) \cdot b_m - 1]$ and $\mathbf{USP_b^i}$ delayed by $N_b[i \cdot b_u : (i+1) \cdot b_u - 1]$ units, and acknowledges receipt of A's RF and US messages for round i,
- A receives $\mathbf{M_b^i}$ and $\mathbf{USP_b^i}$, verifies angle of arrival, computes $d_{a,b}^i$, uses the reference measurement $d_{a,b}$ to reconstruct $\Delta_b^i := d_{a,b}^i - d_{a,b}$, and acknowledges B's messages for round i

(c) A reassembles all received RF packets $M_b' := \mathbf{M_b^0}||\ldots||\mathbf{M_b^{r-1}}$, decrypts the message $N_b' := D(K_a^{Auth}, M_b')$, reassembles the nonce from the distance offsets $N_b'' := \Delta_b^0||\ldots||\Delta_b^{r-1}$, verifies that $N_b'' = N_b'[0 : r \cdot b_u - 1]$, and sets $K := K_a^{Sess}$ on match or $K := null$ otherwise,
B reassembles $M_a' := M_a^0||\ldots||M_a^{r-1}$, decrypts $N_a' := D(K_b^{Auth}, M_a')$, reassembles $N_a'' := \Delta_a^0||\ldots||\Delta_a^{r-1}$, verifies that $N_a'' = N_a'[0 : r \cdot b_u - 1]$, and sets $K := K_b^{Sess}$ on match or $K := null$ otherwise

Note, if $b_u < b_m$ (i.e. if fewer bits are transmitted via US than via RF) then step 2c) only compares $r \cdot b_u$ bits of the nonce.

If key agreement and peer authentication are completed successfully, then A and B can use the session key K to establish a secure channel. The key can be used as a shared secret for one of the standard protocols such as IPSec with PSK authentication, or one of the recently specified TLS-PSK cipher suites [17]. Other options are WPA2-PSK or EAP-FAST. K can be used directly as key material, rendering additional asymmetric cryptographical operations in the secure channel implementation unnecessary and thus speeding up channel establishment.

5.5   Implementation

We have implemented the key agreement phase of our protocol over TCP/IP. As a secure hash we use SHA$_{DBL}$-256, which is a double execution of the standard SHA-256 message digest to safeguard against length extension and partial-message collision attacks [16]: SHA$_{DBL}$-256 = SHA-256 $((\text{SHA-256}\,(m))\,|m)$.

The peer authentication phase of the protocol has been implemented over the RF/US channel of the Relate sensors, using AES (Rijndael) with a key size of 256 bits as secure block cipher for the interlock protocol. The protocol is tightly integrated with the Relate spatial sensing protocol. RF packets transmitted for authentication serve simultaneously as trigger packets for ultrasonic time-of-flight measurement. Pulses emitted on the US channel serve simultaneously for ranging and for transmission of nonce message parts.

Derived from the characteristics of the Relate sensors, we have set the number of bits transmitted in each round over US to $b_u := 3$. In each round, the 3 bit number is coded as multiples of 25.6 cm which the sender adds as offset to the receiver-perceived distance by delaying the US pulse. At the receiver end, this allows for +/-12.8 cm of measurement inaccuracy to retrieve the 3 bits correctly (note the reported precision of Relate sensors for this level of accuracy is over 95%). The duration of a round is about 200 ms (longer if other devices present are allowed to 'interrupt' the authenticating peers for spatial sensing and exchange of measurements). Transmission of the complete nonce would require 43 rounds but the number of rounds has been kept variable in our implementation to allow users to define their required level of security.

6   Security Analysis

6.1   Message Channels

In our case, information is transmitted both via RF and via US. To safeguard against *eavesdropping* all RF packets are encrypted with an authentication key, but over US the nonce will become gradually revealed as the protocol proceeds. The interlock protocol ensures that this will be of no use to an attacker, as the protocol forces commitment of encrypted nonce message parts over RF before the entire nonce can be intercepted on the US channel. The nonce is also strictly used only once which rules out *replay* attacks. Complete or selective *denial-of-service* attacks can not be protected against under our assumption of completely insecure RF channels.

As described above, the main motivation for using the interlock protocol is to protect against man-in-the-middle attacks *during* authentication. An RF-only MITM attack would be noticed, and we therefore need to analyse the possibilities for a concurrent attack on the US channel.

6.2   Ultrasonic Sensing and Message Transmission

Our approach to coding random nonces (section 5.2) and transmitting them via interlock (section 5.3) prevents all the threats outlined in section 4.2: Threat (a) constitutes a selective denial-of-service attack that can be detected by time-outs (when the selected device does not respond at all) or authentication failures (when the attacking devices responds from a different spatial position). Threat (b) does not apply to our protocol, because shared measurements are not used during authentication. Threats (c) and (d) are prevented by the random delays. As E can not know in advance when a US pulse will be sent by A or B (the delays are derived from the random nonce part that is kept secret until sending the pulse), it can not construct the encrypted RF packets to match these delays. If E injected own US pulses, A and B would also receive the original ones and thus detect that an attack is happening. E's only chance would be to cancel US pulses in-transit by generating appropriate anti-US pulses, but this is considered prohibitively difficult. Furthermore, E would need to be positioned precisely in the line-of-sight between authenticating devices in order to attempt interception and manipulation of US pulses but this presence literally in the middle between devices would be obvious to the user. Note that this MITM device can not be arbitrarily small due to a physical limits on the minimum size of ultrasound transducers.

One remaining risk is that E is positioned in line with A and B, but farther away instead of in between. If E performs a selective denial-of-service attack on B and forges distance measurements before authentication is started, it will be able to fake its perceived and subsequently visualised position as seen by A. Although for security purposes one does usually not trust other devices's measurements (they might be collaborating for an attack), we note that these measurements, shared by benign devices over the Relate RF network, may serve to reveal ongoing attacks such as this one. The shared measurements are not used for increasing trust in an authentication protocol run or providing proof of authentication, but they may still be used for decreasing trust in a protocol run, when shared measurements do not match local ones. Attacking networks of multiple Relate devices should therefore be considered significantly harder than attacking just two devices.

We should also note that attacks on the sensing level become harder in scenarios involving mobility of devices. Positioning an attacker unsuspiciously and directly in line between A and B is not trivial even in static settings. When at least one of the interacting devices is mobile, an attacker would need to be constantly re-positioned (or virtualized by sound forming, which is considered infeasible with the current state of the art in ultrasonic systems).

6.3 Applications

The application-level threats described in section 4.3 are specific to our method. With the protections of the sensing level described above, the remaining threat is the misrepresentation of E at the position of B as seen by A. *Replacement* of infrastructure devices is hard to detect, and therefore difficult to protect against. One possibility is to create an explicit application-level feedback from B that can be verified by Alice, for example to lighting an LED for a few seconds whenever authentication has succeeded. If Eve replaces B, then B will not light its LED and Alice can subsequently abort the interaction. The same protection can be used against *asynchronous MITM*, which effectively transforms these two scenarios into a *synchronous MITM* setting. However, this adds an additional step in the interaction process that may not be desirable for many applications. A more pragmatic protection against these remaining replacement and asynchronous MITM threats is to protect against E being in line with A and B by physical means, e.g. simply placing B directly in front of a wall and thus making it impossible for E to be hiding 'behind' it.

Synchronous MITM seems prohibitively difficult to perform under the above analysis of the sensing level protection, because of the necessary in-transit attacks on US pulses.

6.4 User Interaction

The overall security of our method depends on the correct selection of the target device, and the correct association of the target with a spatial reference. We need to consider two possible sources of error or incorrect association. One is that the network communication in the initial steps of our method is not secure. A user can trust the relative position information it has of other devices as this is measured with on-board sensors but any additional information exchanged may be interfered with by an attacker. For example, the Gateway interface shown in Fig. 1 is based on locally measured spatial information but in addition visualises type of discovered device based on information received over the wireless network. An attacker might tamper with this to the effect that a different device type is indicated, which might mislead the user.

The second risk at the level of user interaction is that the user selects the 'wrong' device in their user interface, in the worst case an attacker positioned near the actual target. i.e. E instead of B, in their user interface. The visual design of the UI and the accuracy of the spatial layout in correspondence with the 'real world' arrangement of devices will be key factors in reducing the risk of faulty selection, which of course will also be dependent on number and arrangement of devices discovered and visualised.

7   Performance Evaluation

The authentication protocol involves evaluation of sensor data with inherent limitations in accuracy and precision. It is therefore critical to assess impact of sensor limitations on practical performance.

7.1   Robustness Against 'False Negatives'

Sensors are inherently imprecise. Our authentication protocol is designed to account for the resulting variance in sensor readings, but only within limits that are consistent with secure authentication of devices by spatial reference (i.e. there must be no possibility that devices become confused due to allowances made for sensor error). As a consequence, the protocol can fail to authenticate legitimate peers when sensor errors occur that exceed built-in tolerance.

Figure 4 shows the success rate of authenticating legitimate peers dependent on the number of rounds of the interlock protocol and the distance between the devices. For this experiment, two devices were positioned facing each other in direct line of sight at distances of 50cm and 100cm. For each number of rounds, 250 protocol runs were performed. As shown in Fig. 4, success rates are at least 85% and typically above 95%.

Authentication only succeeds if every single US measurement taken during the protocol rounds is sufficiently accurate. In our experiment, the success rate did not decrease significantly with the number of rounds. However under less controlled conditions (e.g. slight movement of devices during the protocol run) a more notable decrease might be expected, as the probability of an erroneous measurement increases with the number of rounds. Note that the impact of distance on success rate is not very pronounced and appears to be within error of measurement (success rates for the larger distance are on average lower, but not consistently).

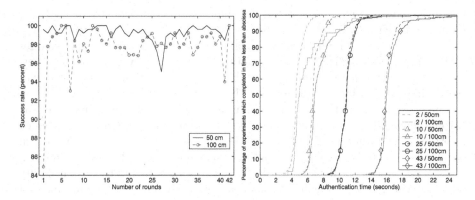

Fig. 4. Authentication success rate depending on the security level and distance (left); Authentication speed depending on the security level and distance (right)

7.2 Speed Versus Security

There is an inherent trade-off in our protocol between speed and security. The resistance against attacks increases with the number of rounds used for the interlock protocol, because each round transmits 3 bits of entropy for verifying the nonce. Therefore, an attacker's chance of guessing a nonce equals $1/2^{3r}$. To put this into perspective, after only 5 rounds a nonce would already be harder to guess than a randomly generated 4-digit PIN number. Also note that our protocol is symmetric, which means that an attacker would need to guess two nonces correctly in order to deceive the authenticating devices as MITM.

Figure 4 (right) shows this trade-off with measurements taken for 2, 10, 25, and 43 rounds, obtained with the same experimental setup of devices as described above. The variations in the time necessary for authentication over a certain number of rounds stem from the specifics of the underlying RF/US sensing protocol which can require message retransmits. The dependency on the distance between the devices is again marginal. As can be seen, a complete authentication takes around 12 s for 25 rounds.

It is important to understand that a compromise on the number of rounds in our protocol only impacts on an attacker's one-off chance to guess the correct nonce to stage an undetected MITM attack. It does not impact on the security level of 128 bits that will be provided after successful authentication. This difference is even more pronounced than in the usual online vs. offline attack discussion, because of the tight coupling with interaction at the user level. An attacker can not repeatedly attack the authentication protocol with an online attack, because it is only triggered by an explicit user action. Therefore, there is only a one-off chance for an attack, and any computational attacks are therefore matched with a security level of 128 bits. Nonetheless, our protocol allows the user or application to choose the best compromise between speed and security and scales up to a 128 bit level even for the single attack possibility.

8   Conclusion

We have contributed and discussed a method for establishing secure spontaneous interaction on the basis of spatial references. Spatial references are a type of context that allows users to match what they see with what their device sees. At the core of our method is a peer authentication protocol that uses relative bearing and distance between devices. We have presented an implementation using ultrasound for spatial measurements; however, the method can also be realised with other sensors. For example, one could consider use of cameras (which are becoming ubiquitous in mobile phones and handhelds) and vision techniques to obtain spatial references between devices.

The concrete implementation we have presented uses ultrasound, for peer-to-peer spatial sensing, and for out-of-band message transfer as part of a key verification protocol. We have provided a comprehensive threat analysis for ultrasonic ranging and contributed a novel coding technique that allows a sender to guarantee that a message was sent from a particular range. This technique can thus be used to to construct a spatially-authentic channel from sender to receiver.

Our protocol implementation is embedded in a spatial sensing scheme that more generally provides devices with accurate relative positions of peers discovered within interaction range. The method further involves a user interaction model based on visualisation of relative device positions, integrated in the user interface for direct manipulation. The method as presented relies on spatial sensors, however, the sensors are not specific to the purpose of providing security but have broader use for support of spatial interaction and services. Cameras and various other sensors are already ubiquitous in mobile devices, and given the general utility of ultrasonic transducers for ranging tasks it is easily perceivable that these will become commonplace as well.

As a final note it has to be stressed that the presented approach fundamentally differs from proximity-based methods such as near-field communication (NFC). Any proximity-based method that relies on a *quantitative* property of the out-of-band channel such as radio signal strength is open to attack from further afield — for example to attack NFC by increasing communication range with more powerful senders and/or more sensitive receivers. In contrast, our method exploits the *qualitative* out-of-band properties of ultrasound: that it is blocked by solid materials and that angle of arrival can not be faked.

The complete source code is available under an open source license at `http://ubicomp.lancs.ac.uk/relate/`.

Acknowledgements

We acknowledge support for the presented research by the Commission of the European Union under contracts 013790 "RELATE" and the FP6 Marie Curie Intra-European Fellowship program contract MEIF-CT-2006-042194 "CAPER", and by the Engineering and Physical Sciences Research Council in the UK under grant GR/S77097/01.

References

1. Gehrmann, C., Mitchell, C.J., Nyberg, K.: Manual authentication for wireless devices. RSA Cryptobytes 7(1), 29–37 (2004)
2. Stajano, F., Anderson, R.: The resurrecting duckling: Security issues for ad-hoc wireless networks. In: Proc. 7th Int. Workshop on Security Protocols, pp. 172–194. Springer, Heidelberg (1999)
3. Balfanz, D., Smetters, D.K., Stewart, P., Wong, H.C.: Talking to strangers: Authentication in ad-hoc wireless networks. In: Proc. NDSS'02, The Internet Society (2002)
4. Kindberg, T., Zhang, K., Shankar, N.: Context authentication using constrained channels. In: Proc. WMCSA 2002, pp. 14–21. IEEE Computer Society Press, Los Alamitos (2002)
5. Kindberg, T., Zhang, K.: Secure spontaneous devices association. In: Dey, A.K., Schmidt, A., McCarthy, J.F. (eds.) UbiComp 2003. LNCS, vol. 2864, p. 126. Springer, Heidelberg (2003)
6. Kindberg, T., Zhang, K.: Validating and securing spontaneous associations between wireless devices. In: Boyd, C., Mao, W. (eds.) ISC 2003. LNCS, vol. 2851, pp. 44–53. Springer, Heidelberg (2003)
7. McCune, J.M., Perrig, A., Reiter, M.K.: Seeing-is-believing: Using camera phones for human-verifiable authentication. In: Proc. IEEE Symp. on Security and Privacy, pp. 110–124. IEEE Computer Society Press, Los Alamitos (2005)
8. Goodrich, M.T., Sirivianos, M., Solis, J., Tsudik, G., Uzun, E.: Loud and clear: Human verifiable authentication based on audio. In: Proc. ICDCS 2006, p. 10. IEEE Computer Society Press, Los Alamitos (2006)
9. Clulow, J., Hancke, G.P., Kuhn, M.G., Moore, T.: So near and yet so far: Distance-bounding attacks in wireless networks. In: Buttyán, L., Gligor, V., Westhoff, D. (eds.) ESAS 2006. LNCS, vol. 4357, pp. 83–97. Springer, Heidelberg (2006)
10. Hazas, M., Kray, C., Gellersen, H., Agbota, H., Kortuem, G., Krohn, A.: A relative positioning system for co-located mobile devices. In: Proc. MobiSys 2005, pp. 177–190. ACM Press, New York (2005)
11. Kortuem, G., Kray, C., Gellersen, H.: Sensing and visualizing spatial relations of mobile devices. In: Proc. UIST 2005, pp. 93–102. ACM Press, New York (2005)
12. Guinard, D., Streng, S., Gellersen, H.: Relategateways: A user interface for spontaneous mobile interaction with pervasive services. In: CHI 2007 Workshop on Mobile Spatial Interaction (2007)
13. Shaked, Y., Wool, A.: Cracking the Bluetooth PIN. In: Proc. MobiSys 2005, pp. 39–50. ACM Press, New York (2005)
14. Diffie, W., Hellman, M.E.: New directions in cryptography. IEEE Trans. on Information Theory IT-22(6), 644–654 (1976)
15. Rivest, R.L., Shamir, A.: How to expose an eavesdropper. Commununications of ACM 27(4), 393–394 (1984)
16. Ferguson, N., Schneier, B.: Practical Cryptography. Wiley Publishing, Chichester (2003)
17. Eronen, P., Tschofenig, H.: RFC4279: Pre-shared key ciphersuites for transport layer security (TLS) (December 2005)

Users and Batteries: Interactions and Adaptive Energy Management in Mobile Systems

Nilanjan Banerjee[1], Ahmad Rahmati[2], Mark D. Corner[1],
Sami Rollins[3], and Lin Zhong[2]

[1,3] Dept. of Computer Science, [2] Dept. of Electrical and Computer Engineering
[1] Univ. of Massachusetts, Amherst, [2] Rice University, [3] Univ. of San Francisco

Abstract. Battery lifetime has become one of the top usability concerns of mobile systems. While many endeavors have been devoted to improving battery lifetime, they have fallen short in understanding how users interact with batteries. In response, we have conducted a systematic user study on battery use and recharge behavior, an important aspect of user-battery interaction, on both laptop computers and mobile phones. Based on this study, we present three important findings: 1) most recharges happen when the battery has substantial energy left, 2) a considerable portion of the recharges are driven by context (location and time), and those driven by battery levels usually occur when the battery level is high, and 3) there is great variation among users and systems. These findings indicate that there is substantial opportunity to enhance existing energy management policies, which solely focus on extending battery lifetime and often lead to excess battery energy upon recharge, by adapting the aggressiveness of the policy to match the usage and recharge patterns of the device. We have designed, deployed, and evaluated a user- and statistics-driven energy management system, Llama, to exploit the battery energy in a user-adaptive and user-friendly fashion to better serve the user. We also conducted a user study after the deployment that shows Llama effectively harvests excess battery energy for a better user experience (brighter display) or higher quality of service (more application data) without a noticeable change in battery lifetime.

1   Introduction

It is clear to any mobile user that the reliance on a battery and charging cord has a significant impact on usability, affecting when, where, and how people use mobile systems. Despite its importance, we understand little about how users replenish the energy on their devices. As a result, systems employ ad-hoc solutions for controlling power consumption, regardless of when users charge their devices or the lifetime they hope to achieve. Further, solutions are typically static, ignoring variance in the usage patterns exhibited by different users as well as differences in usage patterns across different devices. We believe that a better understanding of user-battery interaction will help us to ensure that systems

J. Krumm et al. (Eds.): UbiComp 2007, LNCS 4717, pp. 217–234, 2007.

are not overly conservative or aggressive, and adequately adapt to changing user behavior and device modalities.

To address this deficiency, we present the results of a systematic study of how users manage batteries. The goal of our efforts is to identify patterns in user behavior that can be leveraged to build systems that adaptively balance the quality of the user experience with longevity. We have collected battery traces using automatic logging tools, conducted a series of user interviews on battery management, and collected results from an *in situ* survey that asks about charging context. We have collected data from users of 56 laptops and 10 mobile phones. To our knowledge, this is the largest public study of battery use and recharge behavior in mobile systems.

This study has yielded three notable results. The first is that the test subjects *frequently* recharged their devices with a large percentage of their battery remaining. The second is that the test subjects' charging behavior was driven by one of two factors: context, such as location and time, or battery levels that are much higher than an empty battery. This can be contrasted with the fact that they are only occasionally driven by a truly low battery level. The third is that there are significant variations in patterns exhibited by users and particular mobile systems. For instance, laptop users typically use either very little of the battery capacity or almost all of it, whereas the mobile phone users generally use a greater portion of their battery, but rarely run completely out. These results highlight the problem of existing energy management policies, which are designed to extend battery lifetime without considering user-battery interaction.

Based on these observations, we have designed, implemented, and deployed an experimental adaptive system, named Llama, to help manage energy consumption in mobile systems. Because users frequently have excess energy remaining in their batteries at recharge, we hypothesize that existing energy management policies are often too conservative as they are designed to simply extend the battery lifetime. For instance, a laptop may reduce the brightness of its screen when unplugged even though the user will charge the device in the near future. In contrast, Llama estimates, for a particular user and device, how much battery is likely to go unused and adaptively adjusts the quality of service to meet the predicted requirement. In a deployment of Llama, we employed display brightness and data synchronization (health monitoring and web browsing data) as the example services for which Llama will use excess battery energy.

Based on a test deployment of Llama using 10 laptop and 10 mobile phone users, we present three results. First, Llama rarely caused the system to run out of energy causing a loss of working time. Second, as intended, users did recharge their laptops at a lower battery level, although it did cause some users to recharge their devices more often. This is because many users charge based on context, and others based on battery levels. Third, Llama provided improved quality of service, i.e., brighter displays and more health and web data. More importantly, the users were qualitatively pleased with the system, with only one user in twenty noting a change in charging behavior.

	Laptop		Phone	
	Users	Data	Users	Data
Trace Collection	56	15–150 days	10	42–77 days
User Interviews	10	N/A	10	N/A
In Situ Survey	10	30 days 415 responses	10	10–45 days 91 responses

Fig. 1. The number of participants and the amount of data for each research method of the user study

2   User Study of Mobile Battery Use

In this study of user-battery interaction, we primarily wanted to examine where, when, and why people charge mobile systems. To this end, we have employed three complementary methods. The first method is an automatic trace collection tool that samples and records battery related information. This yields quantitative data on recharging behavior, but does not reveal information about why users do what they do. Thus, we also conducted user interviews to collect qualitative experiences with mobile battery use. Finally, as interviews rely on users' imperfect memories, we developed and deployed an *in situ* survey tool that delivers a questionnaire to participants at the moment they plug in their devices.

In this section we describe each of the three data collection methods, then present a summary of our findings with regard to aggregate and individual user behavior. All of our studies were conducted in parallel on laptop computers and mobile phones. The total number of participants and amount of data is shown in Table 1.

2.1   Methodology

Trace Collection: Our first method was a passive logging tool that periodically recorded the battery level and charging status. The laptop implementation is Java-based, runs on both Microsoft Windows and Apple OS X, and is downloadable and installable by the users themselves [1]. It samples the state of the machine every five minutes and the results are reported to our server once per day. Given the latency, high energy cost, and fragility of suspension and hibernation, we have made the tool completely passive: it records measurements only when the system is in an active or idle state and does not wake it. This leaves some gaps in the traces, such as plugging then unplugging the device while suspended, but we believe these cases are uncommon.

The phone logging tool is written in C++ and runs on Microsoft Windows Mobile, recording information every minute. We collected the results manually as not all users had data plans. Due to the well-known difficulties in producing software portable for mobile phones—especially when using low-level APIs—we chose to distribute the logging tool pre-installed on T-Mobile MDA phones [12]. In the case of phones, transition to suspension and other low-power modes is much more reliable, so the logging tool is more aggressive; it wakes the phone every 1 minute to record the battery and charging status of the system. The logging

---

[1] http://prisms.cs.umass.edu/llama.html

tool reduces the phone battery lifetime to approximately two days. Given that participants had little or no prior experience with this particular phone, they had no preconceived expectations of its battery lifetime.

For the laptop study, we have made every effort to gather a large pool of participants. We recruited participants from a large number of academic departments, friends and relatives, as well as community mailing lists and forums. For the mobile phone study, we recruited ten engineering undergraduate and graduate students. All but one were males with ages between 20 and 26. There was no overlap in participants for the laptop and phone studies. Given the method by which participants were recruited for each study, we make no claims about the randomness or represented demographics of the selection process, something we hope to improve in future work.

To gather information about the type of users in the laptop study, we asked them to fill out a short survey when downloading the tool. Of the respondents, 75% claimed to use their laptop as their primary machine at home and 52% said it was their primary machine at work. Only 3% of the participants said that they used multiple batteries in their laptops.

The total amount of data and number of participants are shown in Table 1. The laptop users have contributed between 15 and 150 days of data with an average of 68 days. The phone users have contributed 42 to 77 days of data with an average of 59 days. Our analysis and experiments are independent of the amount of data collected per-user, although the results for users with more data can be used with greater confidence.

User Interviews: Our second method was to interview users for qualitative data regarding their battery usage. Our goal in the interviews was to obtain more information about the context of battery usage and the subjective experience. 10 of the 56 laptop users and all 10 phone users participated in the interviews. The 10 laptop users consisted of 3 female and 7 male participants with age ranging between 20 and 30.

In the interviews, we provided some sample scenarios to think about and asked the participants about the last time they were in each scenario, what they were doing with the system, why it happened, how it impacted their future behavior. We encouraged the interviewees to tell their stories and anecdotes.

***In Situ* Survey:** Our third method was to ask users *in situ* why they recharge their system. All 10 phone users and the 10 laptop users that participated in the interviews were asked to install a tool that displays a pop-up survey, as illustrated in Figure 2. The window appears each time the system is plugged in. To minimize the intrusion and encourage users to supply only honest answers, the window can be easily dismissed and will disappear if there is no response in 60 seconds. We filtered out any intervals between charges that were less than 5 minutes to account for times when users accidentally unplugged the system and plugged it in again. We collected 415 responses from the 10 laptop users and 91 responses from the 10 mobile phone users over an average period of 30 and 28 days, respectively.

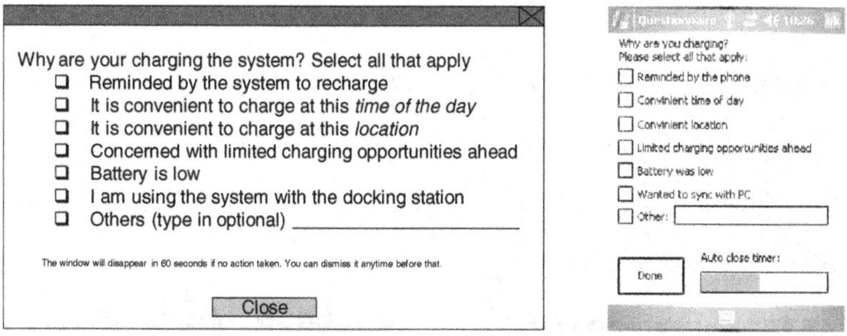

(a) Laptop   (b) Phone

Fig. 2. *In situ* survey design for (a) laptops and (b) mobile phones

2.2 Findings Regarding Battery Use and Recharge Behavior

Battery use and recharge behavior is an important aspect of user-battery interaction. Using a combination of data from the trace study, survey, and *in situ* questionnaire, we have reached several conclusions about the recharging behavior of the participants in the study. When attempting to correlate a combination of interviews, trace collection, and *in situ* questionnaires, we were often faced with difficulties in correlating large amounts of imperfect data, resolving discrepancies between collected and quoted information, and a seemingly unlimited number of questions and conclusions. In each instance, we have attempted to distill the highest confidence conclusions and those with the greatest implications for building systems.

The conclusions are as follows: First, when users plug in their devices to charge them, there is typically a significant amount of energy left in the battery. Second, charging of both laptops and phones was mostly and equivalently driven by context and battery levels significantly greater than empty, rather than low battery alarms. Third, there is significant variation among users and between devices. For instance, laptop users typically use very little of the battery capacity or almost all of it, whereas the mobile phone users generally use a greater portion of their battery but rarely run completely out.

The majority of recharges occur with a significant portion of the battery remaining: Figure 3, drawn from the automatic traces, shows the histogram and cumulative distribution of the battery remaining at recharge for both laptops and mobile phones. For each type of device, more than 50% of recharges occur when the battery is more than 50% full. Further, nearly 70% of laptop recharges and nearly 80% of phone recharges occur when the battery is more than 20% full.

Charging is mostly and equally driven by context and battery levels rather than low battery alarms: The automatic traces cannot explain why users charge their devices, so we must draw results from the *in situ* questionnaire and user interviews. The results from our questionnaires are shown in Figure 4.

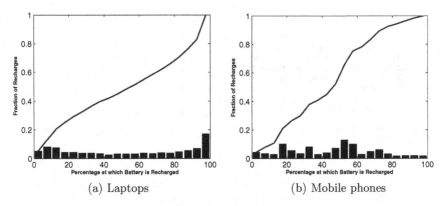

(a) Laptops   (b) Mobile phones

Fig. 3. Histograms and cumulative distribution of remaining battery upon recharge in the collected traces

The results indicate that *around half* of all recharges are triggered by context, including location, time of day, and for the case of phones, to synchronize with a PC. This was corroborated by our interviews; most laptop interviewees stated they usually recharge at the office, at home, and/or at night, driven by context, or based on the battery reaching a certain level. From the phone interviews, four out of ten participants claimed they charge the phone once or twice per day, without even looking at the battery level indicator. This is unsurprising, as many mobile phone users do not typically carry the phone charger thus only charge in a single location. For instance, mobile phone users said:

"I always recharge every night."
"I recharge every night, unless I forget."
"I usually recharge every night, or the other night if I have forgotten."
"I always keep my phone connected [to the USB/charge cable] when I'm working behind my computer."

Conversely, 28% of the laptop and phone responses indicated the reason for charging was a "low battery". At first this seems incongruent with the trace data shown in Figures 3(a) and 3(b). However, a cross examination of the responses and battery traces shows that when users select "low battery" as their reason for recharging, the average remaining battery level was actually 40%. This indicates that although users indicated that they weren't concerned with limited recharge opportunities ahead (7% and 5% of responses for laptops and phones), they were still acting in a very conservative manner. Six of the ten phone users indicated similar behavior, such as:

"I usually charge in the office, when the indicator shows 1 [of 2] bars."
"I check the extra battery information screen and recharge around 40%, or when I want to sync"
"I recharge when I get the low battery warning, [since] I still have plenty of time left after that."

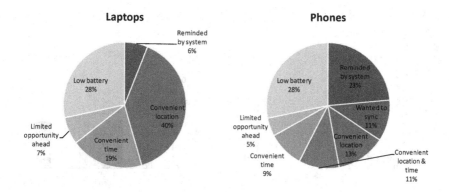

Fig. 4. *In situ* survey results

In contrast, it is less common for laptop users to charge triggered by low battery alarms. Figure 5 illustrates, for each user, the number of times the device was recharged when the battery was below 5%. These scenarios are likely the result of a low battery warning or automatic system hibernation. Users reported that such scenarios occurred only during elongated trips without recharge opportunities. In these scenarios, the users took all measures to elongate the battery lifetime to focus on accomplishing key tasks, for example minimizing display brightness and turning off the network interface. Most users indicated that they usually mitigated the effects of these situations by fully charging their device beforehand.

Users and devices demonstrate significant variation in battery use and recharge behavior: Figure 6 is a box-and-whiskers plot of the remaining battery upon recharge for each participant. The graph shows the median, 25th & 75th percentiles, max-min values within 1.5x of the interquartile range, and outliers. We observe that not only is there significant variation across users, each user demonstrates variation in her own recharge pattern as well. We also note that there are significant differences between laptop and mobile phone charging patterns, as Figures 6 and 3 clearly show. Laptop users tend to use a larger portion of their energy and, as shown in Figure 5, they encounter low battery scenarios more commonly than mobile phone users. We suspect this is due to the fact that mobile phones often have a longer battery lifetime offering more physical opportunities for charging.

2.3   Summary and Motivation for Adaptive Energy Management

The findings from our traces, interviews and questionnaire indicate several opportunities to provide an adaptive energy management system for mobile systems. The most compelling conclusion is the first one: users frequently charge their systems with a significant amount of energy remaining. If the system can perfectly predict how much energy the user will leave in the battery at recharge, it can

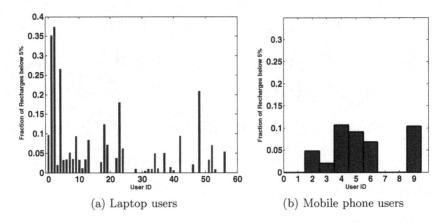

(a) Laptop users   (b) Mobile phone users

Fig. 5. The fraction of the time the battery falls below 5% for our participants

proactively use the remaining energy to improve the quality of service given to the user. Such a system must be adaptive across users and systems, a necessity dictated by the third set of conclusions that such variations are common. By increasing the quality of service, fueled by so-called "excess energy", systems can deliver better usability such as increased screen brightness or lower latency responses.

However, such a system forms an implicit feedback loop with the user: if it uses extra energy, the user may recharge earlier. Even worse, it may cause the system to run out of energy prematurely, frustrating the user with an unexpectedly short battery lifetime. From the second set of conclusions, we see that there are primarily three kinds of behavior: charging based on context, charging based on conservative battery levels, and charging based on true low-battery conditions. Before designing an adaptive system, one can speculate that for context charging, an adaptive system will have little or no effect on the users—they will charge at the same times regardless of the adaptive system. In the case of charging based on battery levels, the system may have more of an effect, causing the user to charge the device more frequently. However, the adaptive system must carefully avoid the third case, true low-battery conditions, as they will be the most frustrating to the user.

Along the same lines, one should *not* interpret our findings as showing that longer battery lifetime is not desirable. Instead, longer battery lifetime will help users better deal with the current true low-battery conditions. More importantly, users will adapt to it with different battery use and recharge behavior, as our user study showed that they deal with laptops and mobile phones in very different ways. Most recharges happen with substantial battery because mobile users have developed realistic expectations and learn to effectively deal with the limited battery lifetime. The goal of an energy adaptive system is to find how long the user *needs* the device to last, and conform to that expectation. We certainly do not consider this a closed subject, and our work is a step along a new direction of research in *user-centric* power management.

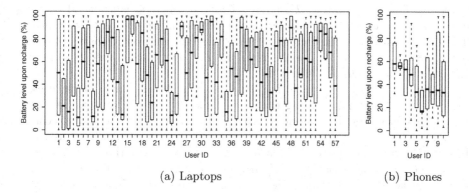

(a) Laptops   (b) Phones

Fig. 6. Boxplot of remaining battery upon recharge for each participant. The middle dark line shows the median value, the boxes show the 25 & 75th percentiles, while the whiskers show the max and min values within 1.5x of the interquartile range. The circles show outliers.

In the next section we describe the design of a novel adaptive energy management system, named Llama, that addresses all of these requirements.

3 Llama: User-Driven Energy Management

Based on the results of our user-study, we have designed a system, named Llama, to manage battery energy on mobile computing systems. Llama tracks how much of the battery is typically used on a system, and uses it to predict the *excess battery energy* of the system, or how much energy will be left in the battery when the system begins its next recharge cycle. One other system has attempted to use this excess energy, SMERT [15], an energy-efficient multimedia messaging system on mobile phones. However, unlike Llama, it is based on pre-set knowledge of expected battery lifetime without automatically tuning to a user's patterns.

Llama, in its current incarnation, assumes that the default system power management decides the minimum acceptable level of power consumption. Llama then devotes the predicted excess battery energy to extra, non-critical services or applications. Such a Llama application can be anything that has a fidelity-power tradeoff. Examples include increased screen brightness, periodic synchronization with a distributed file server, periodic collection and transfer of sensor readings, providing services to peers in a cooperative system, and web prefetching. Llama applications can either be continuous in their use of energy, such as screen brightness, or discrete, such as periodic sensor readings.

3.1 Energy-Adaptive Algorithm

First, we formally define the optimization problem that the Llama algorithm solves. If E_b and E_f are the energy consumed by the Llama application and all other applications between two consecutive recharges, the algorithm tries to maximize E_b—subject to $Pr[E_b + E_f > C] \leq p$—where C is the total battery capacity and p is the confidence of Llama not exceeding the battery capacity. Though we have used the number of times the user runs out of battery as the optimization constraint on Llama, other criteria could also be used to quantify the effect of Llama on user behavior.

There are two key features in the Llama system design. First, Llama uses a *probabilistic* algorithm, ensuring that the Llama application impacts the user-perceived lifetime of the system only a small percentage of the time. Second, Llama is *adaptive*; it responds to short-term and long-term changes in user behavior. The main component of Llama is a *predictor* that estimates the excess battery energy using a histogram of previous battery usage and the current battery capacity. The histogram is measured using the same technique used in the user-study—when the system is awake, Llama periodically records the battery level and tracks when a recharge begins. Using the predicted excess battery energy, the predictor can decide how much energy to devote to the Llama application. The process is adaptive: it recalculates the energy to devote to Llama tasks periodically, as the battery drains.

As an example of how the Llama algorithm operates, suppose a user wants to assure with a confidence of 95% that their battery will not run out before the next expected recharge. Llama determines the current battery capacity to be 30%. It consults the histogram of recharges and determines that 95% of the time that the battery drains below 30% the user recharges at or above 10%. It then allows the Llama application to use up to 10% of the battery.

Algorithm 1. Energy-Adaptive Algorithm

Confidence of not exceeding battery capacity $= p$
Histogram for CDF of recharges given present battery remaining $C_p = H$
Size of Histogram bin $= \Delta H$
Find x such that $H(x) \leq (1 - p) \leq H(x + \Delta H)$
Excess energy for Llama tasks $= x$
Energy for foreground tasks $E_f = 100 - x$

The algorithm, shown as Algorithm 1, tracks the probability distribution of when the user recharges to determine the amount of energy that can be spent on the Llama application. For a continuous application, such as screen brightness, the application spreads this energy usage over the remaining time before the next recharge, and uses energy at the rate $\frac{E_b}{T_d}$, where T_d is the expected time before the next recharge. Llama currently uses the mean time between past recharges as the measure for T_d.

3.2   Supporting Discrete Background Tasks

Llama also enables a new kind of functionality not typically used in laptops, PDAs, and portable music players: *adaptive, self-initiated wake-up*. Generally, once a system places itself in a low-power state, such as suspension, hibernation, or off, it requires user intervention to start again. However, Llama can schedule wake-sleep cycling to proactively run background tasks while the user is not actively using the system. Note that at a hardware level this is already well-supported, but concerns over using excess energy has kept it from being widely adopted. Thus, Llama can execute a background task, such as taking sensor readings, or checking for new email, on a periodic basis by waking up the system and executing the task.

As the transition cost from sleeping to awake can be significant in any platform, Llama must take this cost into account when deciding how often to initiate a wake-up. In such cases, the interval after which a background operation should occur is calculated as $\frac{T_d}{E_b} \cdot (e_b + E_t)$, where e_b is the energy for one background task, and E_t is the cost to transition the system to the active state to complete the task. The system has a predetermined set of time intervals after which a task can be executed. These intervals determine how aggressive the task is. For example, the intervals could determine how often a perfecting occurs. T_d is mapped to the closest time interval. However, E_t will vary depending on the beginning state of the system; it costs more to transition a system from suspended to active than from idle to active. Since we do not know what state the system will be in when we execute a task, we predict it will be in the same state as the last time a task was executed. If the the last time Llama initiated a background operation the system was active, then $E_t = 0$. Otherwise we use the energy needed to resume and then suspend the system, which can be measured online using information provided by the operating system.

3.3   Measuring Energy Usage

Llama's calculation relies upon knowledge of the power consumption of the Llama application and the rest of the system, as well as the measured histogram of recharges collected by the logging tool. Llama measures the power consumption of the system and the Llama application by observing the power or energy of the system as it executes the Llama application at different rates. For example, if the screen brightness level of the system is mapped to an interval $[0, 1]$, where 0 is totally dark and 1 is fully bright, Llama measures the power consumption at 0, 0.25, 0.5, 0.75 and 1.0. It can then set the brightness according to its estimate of excess battery energy and T_d. If the task is periodic it must measure the energy to execute the task once, and use that to estimate the power at different intervals.

Recall that Llama may create a feedback loop with the user, causing them to recharge their device earlier, rather than accepting the excess energy use. However, due to the obvious complexities and ambiguities introduced by trying to factor the user into the algorithm, we have designed the algorithm based on an idealized system that does not contain such feedback. Only through deployment and experimentation, the subject of the next section, can one discover how this relationship bears out.

4   Llama Evaluation

To evaluate the efficacy of the Llama system, we built a working implementation and deployed it on 10 laptops and 10 mobile phones for approximately one month. Before the addition of Llama, mobile systems are already set with a default energy management policy, or one previously tuned by the user. For the purposes of this evaluation we take this policy as the minimum acceptable quality of service and Llama will only use more energy than this policy, not less.

4.1   Llama Deployment

To test the Llama algorithm, we tried a variety of applications, some noticeable to the user and some invisible.

Laptop Screen Brightness application: For Mac laptops we employed a screen brightness adjustment application. We chose screen brightness levels in discrete intervals of 0.25, 0.5, 0.75, 1.0 where 0.25 is the least amount of backlight and 1 is full brightness. After installation, the application trains itself to learn the amount of power consumed by the laptop at each level. From then on, the predictor wakes up every 5 minutes to estimate the amount of battery capacity that will remain in the battery when the next recharge takes place. The predictor does so through the history of recharges stored on the machine from the readings taken by our tracing tool. The scheduler then calculates what the screen brightness level should be such that the laptop does not run out of battery with a probability p = 0.9. Consequently, the scheduler sets the screen brightness to the level using a script.

Laptop Web Prefetching application: For Windows laptops, we used a web prefetching application that downloads a random webpage from a set of 10 preconfigured choices. The application only runs when the device is active or idle and does not wake it from a suspended state. In this case, the user did not interact with the application and we did not serve prefetched pages to the user. The downloading interval determines the aggressiveness of the application, chosen as once every 30, 60, 120, or 180 seconds. Similar to the screen brightness application the predictor determines the battery capacity at the next recharge. It then uses the excess energy to determine how often the web prefetching application should run given the excess energy.

Mobile Phone background task: For the mobile phones, we employed a remote health monitoring application used in a previous projectthe original application periodically uploaded data from a wireless electrocardiogram (ECG) sensor.We have replaced the sensor with preprogrammed data, and adapted it to report at variable intervals from once every 5 minutes to once every 60 minutes. This leads to an average extra phone power consumption of 3.3 to 40mW. These intervals reduce the two-day idle battery lifetime of the phone by 1.5 to 14 hours respectively.

4.2   User Studies After Llama Deployment

We deployed Llama for both laptop and phone users, and collected battery usage and Llama operation traces for approximately 30 days. We interviewed participants to gather additional subjective experience regarding Llama. The interviews were semi-structured and were conducted in very casual fashion, focusing on eliciting stories from our participants to gauge the effectiveness and user-friendliness of Llama. We first asked the same set of questions regarding different charging scenarios, as described in Section 2.1. For the laptop participants, we then asked whether the interviewee was comfortable with automatic adjustment of brightness and whether they were concerned with its battery impact. At the end, we asked both laptop and phone participants whether Llama had impacted their battery lifetime, charging behavior, and their work.

Effectiveness of Llama in Using Excess Energy: Figure 7 shows the energy use of Llama per recharge for the laptop and mobile phone applications. Figure 8 shows the cumulative distribution of the recharges for approximately 30 days before and 30 days after installation of Llama software.

For laptops, users 2 through 9 correspond to the web prefetching application while users 0 and 1 had the screen brightness application installed on their Mac laptops. Llama used variable amounts of energy, varying from 2depding on the amount of battery remaining at recharge.

From Figure 8(a) we find that the percentage at which users recharge their laptop goes down after installation of Llama. For example, for more than 50of the recharges, users recharge their laptops at 5installation of Llama. Beneficially, the use of Llama led to an average of 629 webpages of average size 90 KB prefetched each day for the Windows laptop participants and a 3 times brighter display for 16the two MAC participants. Though we do not directly evaluate improved user experience as a result of Llama, these results strongly indicate that Llama can provide significant benefit to the user.

For mobile phones, Figure 7(b) shows that Llama effectively employed excessive battery energy and enabled the reporting of an average 23 MB of data per recharge for each participant. The average Llama transfer interval for different participants was between 13 and 59 minutes. The average among all phone participants was 26 minutes, corresponding to a power consumption of 7.6mW or about 5% of the battery capacity per day.

User-perceived effect: During the interviews, we found that none of the laptop users had noticed a change in battery life after Llama deployment. After we suggested that Llama may induce extra battery usage, we noted two comments:

> "It must have been small, since I didnt notice it." "Even though I didn't notice it, I would definitely care in situations where I require maximum battery life."

These and other similar comments confirm that Llama has been successful in only employing excessive battery energy, although in the second case the user expressed some concern over using the system.

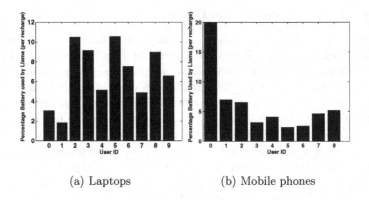

(a) Laptops   (b) Mobile phones

Fig. 7. The figure shows the amount of energy used by Llama for the web-prefetching and screen brightness applications for the laptop, and the health monitoring application for the phones

The mobile phone users also expressed similar satisfaction. Only one mobile phone participant noticed a shorter battery lifetime. He also indicated in the user interview that he always checks the extra battery information screen and charges at around 40%. He offered the only negative comment about the system:

> "The battery lifetime was better last month. I have to recharge it every day now, but it used to be every day and a half."

It is important to note that no participants noticed increase in the time taken to fully recharge the battery, although the average remaining battery level is lower after Llama deployment. One reason is that the difference in remaining battery level often leads to much smaller difference in the time required to fully recharge. For example, 10% lower battery level may only need 3% longer charge time. The second reason is that participants typically keep their devices plugged in for more than 3-4 hours, enough time to recharge any battery, as we observed from the field-collected battery traces.

Recharge behavior change: Table 9 shows the average number of recharges per week, pre- and post-Llama. As Llama employed considerable battery energy, we did observe an increase in the recharge frequencies in laptops, but not so in mobile phones. Further, the pre-Llama traces show that show 1% of recharges for laptops and 4% for mobile phones occur with the battery below 5%. In contrast, after Llama was installed the battery ran below 5%, in 1% of recharges for laptops and 7% for mobile phones. We have more confidence in the laptop results, but in both cases the number of instances of an empty battery is small.

We believe that this increase in charging activity is due to users charging their laptops driven by the battery indicator. This is an example of the feedback loop we speculated at the end of Section 2.2. For users that are primarily driven by context such an effect does not occur, and for those primarily driven by the battery indicator, it will cause an increase in charging activity, but not an

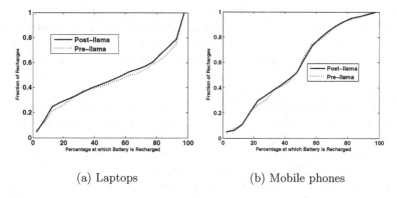

(a) Laptops   (b) Mobile phones

Fig. 8. The figure shows the cumulative distribution of all recharges before and after installation of Llama

	Before Llama	After Llama
All Laptop Users	6.5	7.8
All phones	10.1	8.9

Fig. 9. Average charge attempts per week on phones and laptops before and after Llama

increase in dead batteries. It is our view that users have learned over time to be quite conservative with their batteries because the default, static policies of mobile systems have trained them to be so. We feel that users will adapt to Llama to charge their systems at lower levels over a long term. The results also motivate the need for further study to determine if Llama can be more aggressive without the increased recharging rate frustrating the users, or if there are ways to improve the prediction capabilities of Llama to use battery power without increasing recharges. Our interview results also suggested the need of a "maximum battery mode" for a user to override Llama when they anticipate a scenario like air travel.

5   Related Work

Extensive research has been devoted to energy-efficient design of mobile systems; however, little is known about why and when users recharge their batteries. Froehlich and Chen presented a small-scale battery study on four participants for two weeks as a case study of their *in situ* survey tool MyExperience [6]. While limited in scope and scale, they also found there was still significant battery upon recharge and less than 30% of the recharges were driven by "low battery". With a focus on understanding mobile battery use and recharge behavior, we present a systematic study at a much larger scale with multiple research methods, including trace logging, interviews as well as *in situ* surveys for both laptops and mobile phones. We reported a complementary study of user-battery interaction on mobile phones with a focus on revealing mobile phone design problems that lead to ineffective user-battery interaction [10]. In this work, however, our focus is on understanding how mobile users decide to recharge and on applying the new knowledge to user-adaptive system energy management, for both mobile phones and laptops.

Related to our strategy of considering human factors in energy management, HP Labs researchers selectively darkened part of organic light-emitting diode (OLED) displays for energy reduction [9] and evaluated the user acceptance for this technology [7,1]. Cheng *et al.* [2] exploited limitations in human visual perception to reduce the power consumption of traditional LCDs and Vallerio *et al.* studied the effect of user-interface design on energy efficiency [13]. All of these projects focus on improving the battery lifetime of mobile systems. In contrast, our work focuses on understanding mobile battery use and how to make better use of the available battery energy.

Similar research methodologies have been developed as studies on tools for studying mobile users in their natural settings [3,4,8,6]. In particular, Demumieux and Losquin presented a mobile phone logging tool for studying human-computer interaction on mobile phones [4]. We have employed similar logging to specifically to capture battery use and recharge behavior. MyExperience described an *in situ* survey tool, similar to the one employed in our work. *In situ* survey tools make event-based user experience assessment possible by delivering inquiries at the time of interest [3] . While each of these have contributed to the development of tools, our focus is on the use of these tools for studying mobile battery use. More importantly, we employ a triangulation of research methods, including logging, interviews, and *in situ* surveys, to provide a combined strength in studying how mobile users deal with the limited battery lifetime. Our work presents an example of leveraging the complementary strengths of both quantitative measurements and qualitative inquiries as well as both monitoring and self-reporting.

We note that many projects, including Odyssey [5], ECOSystem [14], and work by Simunic *et al.* [11], attempt to balance performance and system-wide energy usage. The general problem of how to allocate energy, or power, to competing system components and applications, is orthogonal to our work. Ultimately, we envision the integration of Llama with such systems to provide a power management solution that adapts to individual user behavior and can appropriately allocate energy based on competing needs.

6   Future Work

We wish to expand our work in several ways: (i) a larger number of test subjects, particularly mobile phone users, (ii) a less biased subject selection method, or perhaps one that is demographically weighted, (iii) more types of mobile systems including portable music players, (iv) linking user behavior, thus adaptive energy management, with other contextual clues, such as location, mobility, and work patterns, and (v) longer-term studies of Llama to see if users can be retrained to use adaptive systems more effectively. We also hope that researchers will use the results of our study in building new systems and designing new user studies.

7 Conclusions

In this paper we have presented the results of an extensive trace collection and user study that provides a first glimpse into the battery use and recharge behavior of mobile systems, in particular laptops and mobile phones. We have made three key observations in three comprehensive user studies: (i) many users frequently leave excess energy in the battery when recharging devices, (ii) charging behavior is more often than not driven by opportunity, context, and conservative behavior, rather than low battery conditions, and (iii) significant variations occur across mobile users and systems. Based on these three observations, we have created an adaptive energy management system, named Llama that can scale energy usage to user behavior, probabilistically matching energy consumption with the expected recharge time. We have deployed this tool on a number of laptops and mobile phones and received generally positive feedback.

We fully realize that the concept of "excess energy" in a mobile device is not without controversy. After extensive casual conversations with many users on the pros and cons it is clear that, prima facie, such a system may work well for some, but perhaps not all users. However, we believe that our research on user behavior and the Llama system is a first step in discovering better adaptive energy policies in mobile systems.

Acknowledgements

We would like to thank our shepherd Adrian Friday and the anonymous reviewers for their valuable comments. We would like to thank all the test subjects who participated in the user study. We would also like to thank Denitsa Tilkidjieva, Maria Kazandjieva and Nitin Ramamurthy who helped with the development of the llama software and an earlier version of the paper. This research was supported by NSF grants CNS-0519881, CNS-0520729, CNS-0447877, and CNS-0509095. A. Rahmati and L. Zhong were supported in part by Enhancing Rice through Information Technology program, a seed grant funded by Sheafer/Lindsay from the Computer and Information Technology Institute at Rice University and the TI Leadership University Innovation Fund.

References

1. Bloom, L., Eardley, R., Geelhoed, E., Manahan, M., Ranganathan, P.: Investigating the relationship between battery life and user acceptance of dynamic, energy-aware interfaces on handhelds. In: Proc. Int. Conf. Human Computer Interaction with Mobile Devices & Services (MobileHCI), September 2004, pp. 13–24 (2004)

2. Cheng, W.-C., Chao, C.-F.: Perception-guided power minimization for color sequential displays. In: Proc. Great Lake Symp. VLSI, pp. 290–295 (2006)
3. Consolvo, S., Walker, M.: Using the experience sampling method to evaluate ubicomp applications. IEEE Pervasive Computing 2(2), 24–31 (2003)
4. Demumieux, R., Losquin, P.: Gather customer's real usage on mobile phones. In: Proc. Int. Conf. Human Computer Interaction with Mobile Devices & Services (MobileHCI), pp. 267–270 (2005)
5. Flinn, J., Satyanarayanan, M.: Energy-aware adaptation for mobile applications. In: SOSP 99, Kiawah Island, SC, USA, December 1999, pp. 48–63 (1999)
6. Froehlich, J., Chen, M., Consolvo, S., Harrison, B., Landay, J.: MyExperience: A system for in situ tracing and capturing of user feedback on mobile phones. In: Proc. Int. Conf. Mobile Systems, Applications, and Services (MobiSys) (June 2007)
7. Harter, T., Vroegindeweij, S., Geelhoed, E., Manahan, M., Ranganathan, P.: Energy-aware user interfaces: An evaluation of user acceptance. In: Proc. Conf. Human Factors in Computing Systems, April 2004, pp. 199–206 (2004)
8. Intille, S., Tapia, E., Rondoni, J., Beaudin, J., Kukla, C., Agarwal, S., Bao, L., Larson, K.: Tools for studying behavior and technology in natural settings. In: Dey, A.K., Schmidt, A., McCarthy, J.F. (eds.) UbiComp 2003. LNCS, vol. 2864, pp. 157–174. Springer, Heidelberg (2003)
9. Iyer, S., Luo, L., Mayo, R., Ranganathan, P.: Energy-adaptive display system designs for future mobile environments. In: Proc. Int. Conf. Mobile Systems, Applications, and Services (MobiSys), May 2003, pp. 245–258 (2003)
10. Rahmati, A., Qian, A.C., Zhong, L.: Understanding human-battery interaction on mobile phones. In: Proc. Int. Conf. Human Computer Interaction with Mobile Devices & Services (MobileHCI) (September 2007)
11. Simunic, T., Benini, L., Glynn, P., DeMicheli, G.: Dynamic power management for portable systems. In: MobiCom, August 2000, Boston, MA, USA (2000)
12. T-Mobile MDA, (2006) http://www.t-mobile.com/
13. Vallerio, K.S., Zhong, L., Jha, N.K.: Energy-efficient graphical user interface design. IEEE Trans. Mobile Computing 7(5), 846–859 (2006)
14. Zeng, H., Ellis, C., Lebeck, A., Vahdat, A.: ECOSystem: managing energy as a first class operating system resource. In: ASPLOS, October 2002, San Jose, CA, USA (2002)
15. Zhong, L., Wei, B., Sinclair, M.J.: SMERT: energy-efficient design of a multimedia messaging system for mobile devices. In: Proc. ACM/IEEE Conf. Design Automation (DAC), San Francisco, CA, pp. 586–591 (2006)

An Empirical Study of the Potential for Context-Aware Power Management

Colin Harris and Vinny Cahill

Distributed Systems Group, Department of Computer Science,
Trinity College, Dublin 2, Ireland
{colin.harris,vinny.cahill}@cs.tcd.ie
http://www.dsg.cs.tcd.ie

Abstract. Context-aware power management (CAPM) uses context (e.g., user location) likely to be available in future ubiquitous computing environments, to effectively power manage a building's energy consuming devices. The objective of CAPM is to minimise overall energy consumption while maintaining user-perceived device performance.

The principal context required by CAPM is when the user is NOT USING and when the user is ABOUT TO USE a device. Accurately inferring this user context is challenging and there is a balance between how much energy additional context can save and how much it will cost energy wise. This paper presents results from a detailed user study that investigated the potential of such CAPM.

The results show that CAPM is a hard problem. It is possible to get within 6% of the optimal policy, but policy performance is very dependent on user behaviour. Furthermore, adding more sensors to improve context inference can actually increase overall energy consumption.

1 Introduction

With more and more computing devices being deployed in buildings there has been a steady rise in buildings' electricity consumption. These devices not only consume electricity but also produce heat, which increases loading on ventilation systems, further increasing electricity consumption. At the same time there is a pressing need to reduce overall building energy consumption. For example, the European Union's strategy for security of energy supply [1] highlights energy saving in buildings as a key target area[1]. One approach to reducing energy consumption of devices in buildings is to improve the effectiveness of their power management.

Context-aware ubiquitous computing describes a vision of computing everywhere that seamlessly assists us in our daily tasks, i.e., many functions are intelligently automated. Information display, computing, sensing and communication will be embedded in everyday objects and within the environment's infrastructure. Seamless interaction with these devices will enable a person to focus on

---

[1] About 40% of total energy is used within the building sector.

J. Krumm et al. (Eds.): UbiComp 2007, LNCS 4717, pp. 235–252, 2007.

their task at hand while the devices themselves vanish into the background. Realisation of this vision could exacerbate the building energy problem as more stationary computing devices are deployed but it could also provide a solution. Context information (e.g., user location information) likely to be available in such ubiquitous computing environments could enable highly effective power management for many of a building's energy consuming devices. We term such power management techniques as context-aware power management (CAPM), their principal objective being to minimise overall energy consumption while maintaining user-perceived device performance.

The *oracle* power management policy is a theoretical optimal policy that switches a device down to its low-power standby state the instant it is not being used and switches it back on just before the user requests its service again. Coming close to this oracle policy is a hard problem as it requires accurate prediction of the user's future intent. For example, the user has just left the room but will she be gone long enough to justify powering down the fluorescent lighting. The longer the policy waits to make the power down decision the more energy is being wasted. Then the user re-enters the room but is she going to use the desktop PC or is she just popping in to pick up some lecture notes. To develop effective CAPM policies that approach this ideal we need to obtain useful context from the user of the device.

We have identified several key requirements and designed a framework for CAPM. The principal context required for effective CAPM is (i) when the user is NOT USING for a sufficiently long period (see Section 2.1) and (ii) when the user is ABOUT TO USE a device. Accurately inferring this user context is the most challenging part of CAPM. However, there is also a balance between how much energy additional context can save and how much it will cost energy wise. To date there has been some research in the area of CAPM but to our knowledge there has been no detailed study as to what granularity of context is appropriate and what are the potential energy savings.

We have conducted an extensive user study to empirically answer these questions for CAPM of desktop PCs in an office environment. The sensors used are idle time based on keyboard/mouse input, user presence based on Bluetooth beaconing, near presence based on ultrasonic range detection, face detection, and voice detection. Results from the study show that coming close to the oracle is a hard problem and that performance is very dependent on user behaviour. For those who are HeavyUse users (i.e., use their PC greater than 85% of the time when they are in its vicinity) it is possible to get within 6-9% of the oracle policy and maintain user-perceived performance with a simple policy based on idle time and user presence. For LightUse users the median performance is 22-31% from the oracle and the standard deviation is large (21-28%). For these users a policy based on idle time, user presence, and near presence does better but incurs some user-perceived performance degradation. Beyond this face detection and voice detection consumed more than they saved.

The remainder of this paper is structured as follows. The following section briefly describes the background, requirements for CAPM and related work.

Section 3 describes our CAPM framework design and Section 4 describes the user study. Section 5 presents the results and evaluation. Finally, Section 6 concludes.

2 Background

CAPM is a dynamic power management technique. This section gives an overview of dynamic power management, the requirements for CAPM of stationary (i.e., plugged in) devices and a brief overview of related work.

2.1 Dynamic Power Management

Dynamic power management [2] is the term usually used to categorise techniques that dynamically power manage a device during its runtime operation. It is an effective technique that simply powers down a device (or some of its sub-components) during idle periods that occur during its operation. The two fundamental assumptions are that (i) idle periods will occur during the device's operation and (ii) these periods can be predicted with a degree of certainty. There is also a trade-off in powering down to save energy as, typically, making a power state transition has a significant cost. Possible costs are (i) extra energy is consumed in the power state transition, (ii) device performance is degraded as it becomes slower to respond, and (iii) device lifetime is reduced due to extra wear in powering down and up. Therefore a break-even time is defined as the minimum time a device must spend in a lower power state to justify the cost of transitioning down to that state and back again. For example, break-even time due to energy transition costs for a hard-disk may be around 10 seconds [3], break-even time due to lifetime for fluorescent lighting is around 5 minutes [4]. The resume time is the time taken for the device to resume to the operating state.

The current state of the art in dynamic power management is predominantly focused on developing policies for mobile computing devices. The key trade-off for these policies is increased battery life versus device performance. For example, a hard disk may be aggressively power managed to extend battery life (i.e., minimise energy consumption) but its performance will deteriorate as it will be slower to respond to user requests. Policies for mobile devices typically use low-level information such as the current idle time of the device. They can only predict short idle periods and are not able to predict the time of the next user request. Therefore, they are only suitable for managing devices or sub-components which have relatively short break-even and resume times (order 10 and 1 seconds respectively [3]). An example commonly used policy is the *threshold* policy which simply powers down the device when the idle time for the device is greater than a given threshold limit (e.g., after 10 seconds of inactivity, power down the hard-disk).

A number of issues relating to power management are already dealt with in most operating systems. Background processes can deny a power down request if they are performing a critical task such as file backup. Also, a process can set a wake-up timer to resume the device at a given time to perform its task. Finally, Wake-on-LAN enables a device to be resumed via the network by another device which requests its service.

2.2 Requirements for CAPM of Stationary Devices

Requirements for power management of stationary devices are different to mobile device requirements. Typically, the most significant power savings for stationary devices are achieved by switching the entire device to standby. For example a typical desktop PC may consume 60 Watts (W) when on-idle and as low as 1W in standby. However, switching to a deep standby state has two implications as the device break-even and resume times are significantly longer. Firstly, since break-even times are longer, policies need to accurately predict longer idle periods (order 1 to 10 minutes). Second, switching to low-power standby states can cause significant user annoyance as resume times are longer (order 10 seconds) and there is the possibility of false power downs (i.e., powering down when the user is actually still using the device). Furthermore, stationary computing devices do not have battery limitations so users expect little or no performance degradation. Therefore, policies need to be near certain before powering down and they need to predict the time of the next user request to avoid resume-time delays. In order to predict longer idle periods and the time of next user request, policies need to use high-level user context.

We define context-aware power management as a dynamic power management technique that employs high-level user context to effectively power manage users' devices while maintaining user-perceived device performance. CAPM requires the accurate prediction of the context NOT USING for at least the given break-even period and ABOUT TO USE at least the resume time beforehand. However, achieving this accurate context has a cost energy wise.

For example, coarse-grained location/presence information can be a good cue for a person ABOUT TO USE their PC, if for example, their behaviour is that they always check their email when they re-enter the office. For other users it may not be a good cue, they may often pop in and out of their office without checking their email and without using the PC[2]. Adding additional sensors to the scene may help us do better. For example, knowing the time of day could help in determining whether they are about to use their PC (e.g., they always check their email first thing in the morning, after lunch and at the end of the day). Time of day is cheap to obtain but does depend on the user being very regular in their behaviour. Adding other physical sensors could improve the situation, for example, to detect whether the user is alone or with others, where the user is in the space, or whether the user is moving towards the PC. These observations could possibly be made with additional sensors such as acoustic, video, object ranging, and more accurate location, to try to establish finer-grained context.

As the primary objective of CAPM is to minimise overall energy consumption, there is a bound on the granularity of context that is appropriate. Overstepping

---

[2] These users may check their email with a hand-held device.

this bound and the system will start consuming more sensor energy than the device energy it is saving due to the additional context. The additional consideration is that user-perceived device performance must also be maintained. To date there has been some research in the area of CAPM but to our knowledge there has been no detailed study as to what granularity of context is appropriate and what are the potential energy savings.

2.3   Related Work

Our previous work [5] evaluates the use of location as a key piece of context for CAPM of desktop PCs in an office environment. A simple location-aware policy was implemented that uses location context derived from detecting the user's Bluetooth-enabled mobile phone. This standby/wakeup on Bluetooth (SWOB) policy runs on the users PC. When the PC is on the policy polls for the user's phone via the Bluetooth discovery mechanism. If the phone is not found (after 5 discovery attempts) the PC powers down to standby. The PC is powered up again the next time the phone is found in range. Six user trials were performed, each over a period of a week.

The results from the user trials highlight that user behaviour significantly affects the performance of the policy. The results show two clear user types, HeavyUse users who use the PC a lot when in its 10-metre Bluetooth vicinity and LightUse users who use the PC occasionally when in its vicinity. The policy performs very well energy-wise for HeavyUse users (8% from oracle), whereas for LightUse users the performance deteriorates (>50% from oracle), consuming energy when the user is in the vicinity but not using the device. The user-perceived performance is good for both HeavyUse and LightUse users as the PC remains on while the user is in its vicinity. The threshold-5[3] policy's user-perceived performance deteriorates significantly for LightUse users as the PC goes into standby many times while in the vicinity. The results demonstrate that coarse-grained location alone is not sufficient to determine the detailed user behaviour necessary for effective CAPM for all users.

Finer-grained context is needed to predict (i) the user in the vicinity but NOT USING the device and (ii) the user in the vicinity and ABOUT TO USE the device. The second scenario is difficult to achieve, as one key advantage of coarse-grained location is that it is a distant sensing device, i.e., it senses the user at a distance thereby enabling time for the device to resume before the user requests its use. Saving energy by switching off devices in the near vicinity of the user is difficult to achieve transparently. In this paper we examine in a detailed user study, how much better can be done than the SWOB policy with the use of finer-grained context.

Mozer's Adaptive House project [6] employs a sophisticated framework, ACHE, that has been developed over eight years of actual implementation and experimentation, to power manage devices in a house. ACHE is the most advanced CAPM application that we know of, employing in total 75 sensors monitoring

---

[3] The threshold-5 policy initiates a power down after 5 minutes of idleness.

temperature, light, motion, sound, door and window positions, and weather. The techniques used are a neural network for mobility prediction, and a reinforcement learning technique for the decision making policy. The book chapter [7] concentrates on the issue of lighting control, the objective being to automate the setting of lighting levels within the house to maximise inhabitant comfort and minimise energy consumption.

The real-life experience from this project highlights the subtle requirements for effective power management. The two main discomforts the author experienced were the slow response of the system (due mainly to X10 communication delay) and the occasional false anticipation of zone entry. This caused switching of lights on in unoccupied zones. Results from the project show the cost of lighting and user discomfort values dropping over time as the system learns the user behaviour. However, the control of lighting level is based on user activity prediction, which currently is only inferred from the motion sensors. For example, the user being still for 5 minutes equating to the user READING and frequent zone change equating to CLEANING HOUSE. There is no evaluation as to how well the current activity classification works, but Mozer states that it is an area for future research.

Being able to infer these finer-grained user activities could increase the performance of the control decisions but it will also require the use of additional sensing and thereby increase energy cost.

Oliver et al. [8] present a system, SEER, that infers user activity from real-time streams of video, acoustic, and computer interactions in an office environment. The system is based on a set of layered hidden Markov models (LHMMs) that combine the readings from binaural microphones, a USB web camera, and a keyboard and mouse, to infer the activities, PHONE CONVERSATION, FACE TO FACE CONVERSATION, ONGOING PRESENTATION, DISTANT CONVERSATION, NOBODY IN THE OFFICE, and USER PRESENT ENGAGED IN SOME OTHER ACTIVITY. The results claim a prediction accuracy of 99% for the system.

A further paper [9] presents an extension to SEER, S-SEER, which attempts to address the significant CPU usage of the feature processing algorithms. They say that, although the methods have performed well, a great deal of video and acoustic feature processing has been required by the system, consuming most of the resources available in a PC. They have developed an approach, expected value of information (EVI), which uses the principle of maximum expected utility to determine dynamically which are the most useful features to extract from the sensors in different contexts.

This is possibly the closest work to our research in the sense it uses similar sensors (video, audio, keyboard/mouse) in a similar office environment. They appear to achieve very good results for activity recognition but at a very high computational cost. Even with their EVI sensor selection policy the activity recognition algorithm consumes 33.4% of CPU time (on average). A typical desktop PC power consumes 60W when on and the CPU is idle. Running the activity recognition algorithm will increase the power consumption to about 80W. Increasing the power consumption of the PC by one-third is clearly too costly energy wise. For CAPM it is necessary to find much more energy-efficient ways of accurately determining the context NOT USING and ABOUT TO USE.

3   CAPM Framework Design

The CAPM framework is composed of three main components: data capture and feature extraction, context inference, and decision making. The data capture and feature extraction layer captures the raw sensor events and in most cases preprocesses the data to obtain relevant features. For example, a video signal could be preprocessed to obtain features such as density of foreground pixels, density of motion, density of face pixels and density of skin colour [8]. A Bluetooth detection event could be preprocessed using a counter to count the number of times a Bluetooth tag has not been detected. This gives a history of when the tag was last seen, for example, a count of 10 means the tag has not been detected in the last ten polls. Sensors can include any physical sensing devices, power state changes of other devices, and "software sensors", such as time of day, or day of week.

The context inference layer is responsible for inferring more certain, higher-level context from the low-level sensor and feature data. The inference can involve combining redundant data to achieve more certainty and multi-modal data to infer context based on a combination of the multiple sensor modes. This is the most challenging part of the data processing as it is trying to infer high-level notions from low-level, noisy, and incomplete sensor data and/or their features. Bayesian networks are used to deal with this uncertainty in the data. This gives a level of confidence/probability in the proposition of a certain context being true. Furthermore, the Bayesian network can be trained to the specific user's usage pattern. The probabilistic inference of the contexts NOT USING and ABOUT TO USE is made available for use by the decision layer.

The decision layer is responsible for taking the power-management actions. For the initial version of the framework the decision layer was designed as a simple threshold rule. If the probability of NOT USING exceeded the given threshold (80%) then the action to power down was taken. Likewise, if the probability of ABOUT TO USE exceeded the given threshold (60%) the action to power up was taken.

3.1   Choice of Sensors

The CAPM framework was implemented for the power management of desktop PCs in an office environment. Users were given dedicated Bluetooth tags to attach to their key ring in order to achieve coarse-grained user location. The choice of additional sensors was motivated by the preference to use sensors that we believe will be part of future ubiquitous computing environments.

It is likely that a web camera and microphone will become integrated in the PC display as the popularity of video communication applications increases. Therefore we chose to use both of these sensors to capture finer-grained context.

For our system we chose a standard face detection algorithm [10] as the single feature to extract from the video stream and a basic voice activity detection algorithm [11] for the acoustic stream. The face detection only detects a face that is looking straight at the camera and the voice activity gives a measure from 0% to 100% of the level of voice activity detected in the environment.

The final sensor chosen was an ultra-sonic object range sensor in order to detect near presence of the user. We do not envisage this sensor as being part of a standard ubiquitous computing environment and so it would need to be installed as part of a CAPM solution. The motivation for choosing it was that it could possibly give good information at low energy cost, as there is no need for expensive feature processing.

3.2   Bayesian Network Design

We divided the problem into designing a distinct type of BN for each inference task, i.e., NOT USING for at least the break-even period and ABOUT TO USE at least the resume time beforehand. The structure of both types of BN is similar but they use different sensors and different sensor models. Development of the two types of BN was an iterative approach, starting with simple models and evolving the models to cope with issues that occurred. Fig. 1 details the final BN for the NOT USING (NU) context. The IsNotUsing node is the query node, we are asking what is the probability (P) that the user is not using the device for at least the given break-even time. This node has causal connections to each of the sensor nodes. This represents the fact that the user using (U) or not using the device is causing the observed sensor readings. The conditionality probability tables (CPTs) are initially set to default values and are subsequently learnt using supervised training data for each of the users. Given the full set of CPTs the model can reason diagnostically from the sensor values to give the probability of the user NOT USING the device. The actual value for each of the sensors is input into the BN and the probability of the context NOT USING is calculated. The power-down decision threshold was set at a probability of NOT USING greater than or equal to 0.8 (80%). This threshold figure was derived from trial and error experimentation with the model.

We also experimented with using a dynamic Bayesian network to capture possible temporal patterns but we found no significant improvement in performance.

4   User Study

The user study focuses on power management of desktop PCs in an office environment. We defined the population of the study to be all workers in an office environment that use a desktop PC. Our previous work [5] shows that the performance of the location-aware SWOB policy depends primarily on whether the user is LightUse or HeavyUse. A random sample of twenty users from the academic, administrative, technical and postgraduate staff and also office users from outside the college were selected for the trial. This ensured a wide range of different users and office types and layout. The trial length was set to run for 5

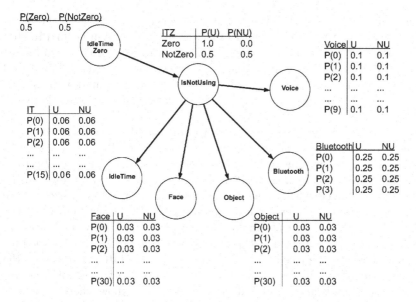

Fig. 1. Bayesian network for NOT USING context

working days. Based on initial results, we believed this would give enough data for training and simulation of the CAPM policies.

In order to compare the range of sensors and policies for each user's usage trace it was necessary to collect all sensor data simultaneously as the user was using the PC during the trial and subsequently run policy simulations on the real usage data. Hence, the trial is broken into a data collection and processing phase, and a subsequent simulation phase. The simulation enables comparison of a range of CAPM policies, the SWOB policy, the optimal oracle policy, threshold policies and an always-on policy.

4.1   Data Collection and Processing

A set of Windows services were implemented to collect data for each of the sensors every 5 seconds; each value was date stamped and stored to file. Furthermore, all idle periods (i.e., periods when there is no mouse/keyboard events) of 30 seconds or more and all power events were logged to the Windows event log. The most difficult data to collect was the actual usage of the display and PC, i.e., when the user was actually USING or NOT USING these devices. To measure the actual usage, the NOT USING service attempts to power off the user's display if the PC has been idle for greater than 60 seconds. The 60-second period of time attempts to balance accuracy against the experiment causing excessive user disruption. A message box appears asking the user if they are still using the PC; if they are the message box disappears by simply moving the mouse. This short mouse input is removed in the data processing as it would not have happened during normal device usage.

We imagined the effect that the NOT USING service may have on the users' behaviour was that they would tend to make more inputs than normal to stop the monitor being powered off. This would lead to a higher frequency of short idle periods than usual occurring in the usage trace. For this reason, idle period data was collected for several weeks after each trial and compared with the idle periods that occurred during the trial. This evaluation suggests that there was no significant effect from the trial.

The event logs are processed to create the measured device-usage trace, of when the user was USING and NOT USING the display or PC. Such a trace is graphed in Fig. 2 where the top-level line represents USING and the bottom-level line represents NOT USING the PC. The level below USING represents IDLE PERIODS that occurred when using the PC. There are periods in every trace where we don't know whether the user was using the PC or not. These are the idle periods before the service attempts to power down the display. The user may or may not be using the device at this time. These idle periods are scanned for face detection events. If a face is detected, we assume the state is USING (i.e., the user was looking at the display during this idle period). If a face is not detected, a DON'T KNOW state is inserted to indicate that we don't know whether the user was using the PC or not at this time. This DON'T KNOW state is represented by the line below the IDLE PERIODS state.

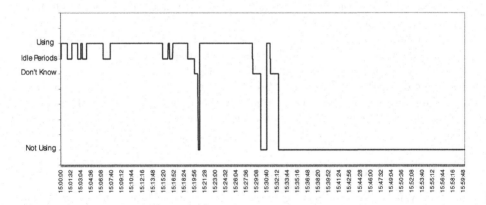

Fig. 2. Measured device-usage trace

4.2   Simulation of Policy Traces

All of the policy traces are generated from the measured usage trace. We assume the behaviour of all the users is good in that they power down their PC when leaving the office for the evening. So, for all traces the device is switched to off for the night time period. For all policies, the policy is allowed to power down in the DON'T KNOW and NOT USING states; attempting to power down when the user is still USING represents a false power down.

From the measured trace, it is straightforward to generate the estimated oracle policy trace and the always-on trace. The oracle policy trace is generated by placing the device in its standby state for all NOT USING periods that are greater than the device break-even time. The always-on trace is generated by leaving the device on for the duration of the day.

The SWOB policy was generated by running through the measured trace at a 5 second time step. The policy attempts to power down if the Bluetooth tag is not detected more than 5 times and the current idle time is greater than 60 seconds. If the measured usage is still in the USING state a false power down is reported, otherwise the policy powers down the device. The policy powers up when it detects the Bluetooth tag.

The range of threshold policy traces were generated by running through the measured trace at a 5 second time step. If the current idle time was greater than the given threshold, then the policy initiates a power down. There is no automated power up for the threshold policies.

The Bayesian CAPM policies required a learning stage and a simulation stage. To be rigorous, we employed a five-fold cross-validation strategy to the learning and simulation of the policies [12]. This involved training the model on one day of data and simulating for the other four days, and repeating this five times, training on each of the days. The resulting values were then estimated as the average of the five simulation results, giving a more robust analysis of the policies.

The Bayesian policies we chose to compare, were idle time (IT), IT-Bluetooth (IT-BT), IT-object range (IT-OR), IT-BT-OR, IT-BT-face detect (IT-BT-FD), IT-BT-OR-FD and IT-BT-OR-FD-voice activity (IT-BT-OR-FD-VA). This selection of models gives an increasing order of sensor granularity to enable comparison of each sensor's affect on the CAPM policy (see Table 1). Idle time was included in every model as it is also used in the SWOB and threshold policies, and Bluetooth was included in all but one model as it gives the coarse-grained user presence, which is the basis of the SWOB policy. We selected IT-OR as a special case to investigate the affect of only having the near presence information. Parameter learning of the models was carried out using the standard Spiegelhalter Lauritzen algorithm [13].

The set of BN policy traces were generated by running through the measured usage at a 5-second time step in both the power-down cycle and the power-up cycle. The power-down cycle operates when the device is on waiting to be powered down and the power-up cycle operates when the device is in standby. At each time step sensor values from the sensor records are applied to the BN power-down or power-up model and the model is updated to give the new probability of NOT USING or ABOUT TO USE. If the probability exceeds the threshold the policy initiates a power down or power up of the device. Fig. 3 shows the IT-BT BN policy powering down soon after the idle period begins.

The 7 Bayesian models plus the oracle, SWOB, six threshold policies and always-on policy resulted in 16 different policies to compare in total for each of the devices.

Table 1. Bayesian CAPM policies

IT	Idle time
IT-BT	Idle time, Bluetooth
IT-OR	Idle time, Object range
IT-BT-OR	Idle time, Bluetooth, Object range
IT-BT-FD	Idle time, Bluetooth, Face detection
IT-BT-OR-FD	Idle time, Bluetooth, Object range, Face detection
IT-BT-OR-FD-VA	Idle time, Bluetooth, Object range, Face detection, Voice activity

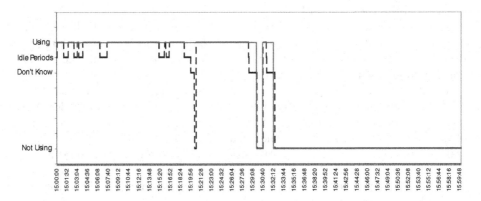

Fig. 3. IT-BT BN policy versus Measured device-usage trace

5   Results

Of the 18 user studies selected for analysis, 7 users were HeavyUse ($<=$ 15% NotUsing when in the vicinity) and the remaining 11 were LightUse users. The policies were run for both the display unit and the desktop PC. The energy consumption of the display unit is 45.8W when on and 1.8W in standby. The transition energy is assumed to be negligible. Its estimated break-even period is 1 minute and its resume time is 2 seconds. The PC's break-even and resume times are significantly longer at 5 minutes and 7 seconds respectively. The energy consumption is 60.0W on and 2.8W in standby. The transition energy was measured to be 0.19Wh per transition.

The results first highlight the potential extra energy that can be saved for both the display unit and PC if we can do better than the simple location-aware SWOB policy. Results are given in terms of the actual Watt hours (Wh) of energy consumed per day and the percentage from the oracle policy.

5.1   Potential Extra Energy from SWOB

Fig. 4 shows the potential extra energy per day that could be saved for both LightUse and HeavyUse users of the display and PC. The potential extra energy is

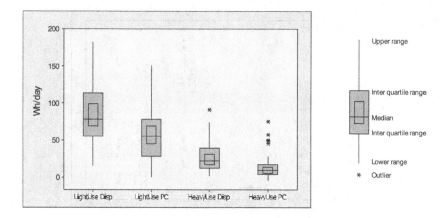

Fig. 4. Potential extra energy per day from SWOB

calculated as the difference in energy consumption of the SWOB policy and the oracle policy for each of the users. The box plots show the range, interquartile range, median and 95% confidence interval around the median for each of the groups.

The results show there is significantly more energy to be saved for LightUse users and also there is a larger variance in their energy consumption. For LightUse of the display, the median percentage from oracle is 31.1% (median 78Wh, range 20Wh to 185Wh). Similarly, for LightUse of the PC, the median percentage from oracle is 22.1% (median 59Wh, range 5Wh to 150Wh).

For HeavyUse of the display, the median percentage from oracle is 9.0% (median 22Wh, range 5Wh to 80Wh). For HeavyUse of the PC, the median percentage from oracle is 5.7% (median 13Wh, range 0 to 30Wh). Trying to do better than the SWOB policy for HeavyUse users is therefore difficult.

We next estimate the energy consumption of the sensors used by the CAPM policies.

5.2   Energy Consumption of Sensors

The power of each sensor was inferred by measuring the difference in the average power of the PC with and without each of the sensors running. The average power of the Bluetooth detection is 0.41W. This is based on the Bluetooth attempting to make a connection every 5 seconds and includes the energy cost of recharging the Bluetooth tag. The face detection's average power is significantly higher at 2.47W[4]. Again the sample rate is every 5 seconds and the high power consumption is due to the large amount of processing needed to perform the face detection algorithm. The voice activity detection's average power is 0.78W as its algorithm is less CPU intensive. Finally the object range detection's average power is based on the average power of the sensor hardware, which was measured at 0.07W.

---

[4] This is significantly less than the estimated 20W used by the feature processing in Oliver (see Section 2.3).

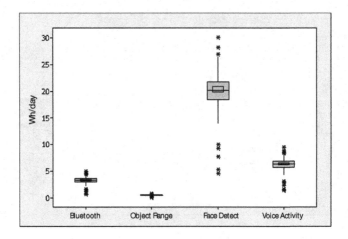

Fig. 5. Estimated sensor energy consumption per day

Fig. 5 shows the estimated energy consumption per day for each of the sensors. This is calculated as the average power of the sensor (at the sample rate) times the number of hours for each of the user's days. The median energy consumption per day for the sensors is BT 3.4Wh, OR 0.6Wh, FD 20.2Wh and VA 6.4Wh.

FD and VA consume a significant amount compared to the potential savings from the SWOB policy for the PC and display (LightUse - 59Wh and 78Wh, HeavyUse - 13Wh and 22Wh). It may be possible to decrease the sensor energy consumption by employing some form of power management for the sensors, but this is not explored here.

We next examine if using additional sensors and more sophisticated Bayesian CAPM policies can improve on the SWOB policy for both LightUse and HeavyUse users.

5.3   Comparison of Additional Sensors

The comparison is based on energy consumption and user-perceived performance, which is evaluated in terms of the number of false power downs (FPDs) that occurred in a day and the number of manual power ups (MPUs) that the user had to invoke per day.

Energy Consumption. Fig. 6 shows the extra energy consumed per day for each of the policies from the oracle for both LightUse and HeavyUse of the display unit. The plots highlight the SWOB policy performing well (close to the oracle) for HeavyUse users and significantly worse for LightUse users.

The policies closest to the oracle for LightUse are IT-OR 40Wh, IT-BT-OR 46Wh and threshold-5 46Wh (median 17.3% to 19.5% from oracle). For HeavyUse the lowest consuming policies are IT-OR 21Wh, IT-BT-OR 21Wh, SWOB 25Wh, IT-BT 25Wh and threshold-5 30Wh (median 8.9% to 13.1% from oracle).

User-Perceived Performance. Table 2 details the user-perceived performance of the CAPM policies in terms of median FPDs per day and median MPUs per day for all LightUse and HeavyUse users. The policies are ordered in ascending order of MPUs.

Table 2. User-perceived performance of policies in terms of median FPDs and MPUs per day for LightUse and HeavyUse users

Policies	LightUse		HeavyUse	
	FPDs	MPUs	FPDs	MPUs
SWOB	0	0	0	0
IT-BT	0.5	2	0	0.25
IT-BT-OR	0.75	4.75	0.5	1
IT-BT-FD	1.25	6.75	0.5	2
IT-BT-OR-FD	0.75	7	0.75	2.75
IT-BT-OR-FD-VA	0.75	7	0.75	2.75
IT-OR	0.25	8	0.25	7

The best CAPM policy in terms of manual power ups for LightUse users is SWOB with median 0, then IT-BT (median 2) and IT-BT-OR (median 4.75) next. Since the power-up policy for all BN policies was limited to only powering up on BT, the more times the device was powered down when the user was in the vicinity, the more MPUs were incurred. The MPUs are less for HeavyUse users. This intuitively makes sense as HeavyUse users do not allow the device to power down as often, therefore requiring less power ups (SWOB median 0, IT-BT median 0.25, IT-BT-OR median 1).

The SWOB policy also performs best in terms of false power downs with no FPDs for both LightUse and HeavyUse users. The BN policies for LightUse are similar with median of 0.5 to 1.25 per day and range of 0 to 3 FPDs per day. There is no significant difference for HeavyUse users with median 0.25 to 0.75 and range of 0 to 5.

5.4   Summary

From these results for the display, it is clear that the best policy for HeavyUse users is the SWOB policy performing well both energy wise and user-perceived performance wise. On average the energy consumption is 9.0% from the oracle per day, there are median 0 FPDs and median 0 MPUs, resulting in very good user-perceived performance. The BN CAPM policies did not save significantly more energy and caused additional FPDs and MPUs.

For LightUse users the SWOB energy consumption is not as good and varies considerably across the users. It is equivalent to the threshold 15 to 20 policies and is on average within 31.1% of oracle. To do better energy wise, it seems we must accept some performance penalties in terms of false power downs and

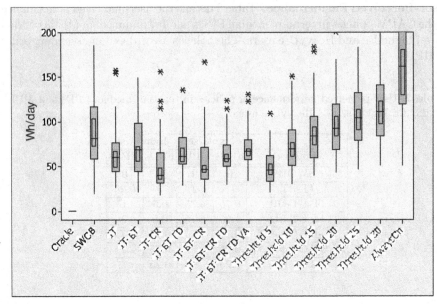

(a) Light Use

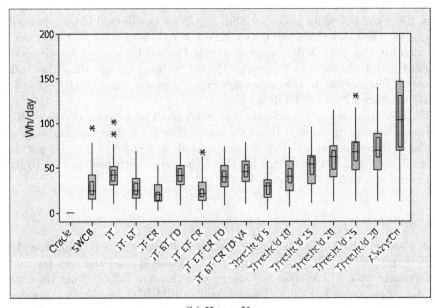

(b) Heavy Use

Fig. 6. Extra energy consumption per day from the oracle (including sensor energy)

manual power ups. Of the BN policies, the IT-BT-OR policy is one of the lowest energy policies with the least MPUs and FPDs.

The overall pattern of results for power management of the PC are similar to that of the display. For HeavyUse the SWOB policy is again the clear choice with both low delta energy consumption 13Wh (5.7% from oracle) and no FPDs and few MPUs. The fact that the break-even time is longer means the policies achieve percentages closer to the oracle policy. The number of standby periods that were less than the break-even time were median 4 per day. This would be a concern for the lifetime decay of this PC.

For LightUse of the PC the IT-BT-OR policy has one of the lowest delta energy consumptions 30Wh (12% from oracle) with the least FPDs and MPUs (FPDs median 0.5, MPUs median 3.75 per day). The number of MPUs is significant as the resume time of 7 seconds will cause significant user annoyance. The SWOB policy delta energy consumption for LightUse is 59Wh (22.1% from oracle). This appears to be the best overall policy due to it having no false power downs and very few manual power ups (median 0).

In all cases the face detection sensor consumes significantly more energy than the object range detection sensor and does not provide significantly better information. The voice activity sensor information does not improve the IT-BT-OR-FD policy at all as the quality of its information for determining the context NOT USING is very weak.

6   Conclusions

Development of effective context-aware power management has an essential part to play in reducing overall building energy consumption. Achieving close to optimal performance is a hard problem as it requires accurate prediction of the user's future intent. Furthermore, performance varies significantly with user behaviour and there is a balance whereby adding more sensors to improve context inference can increase overall energy consumption.

The user study of desktop PCs shows that for HeavyUse users, a policy based on idle time and user presence (Bluetooth tag) performs well both energy and user-perceived performance wise. For LightUse users, a policy based on idle time, user presence and near presence (object range detection) performs well for the display, but may incur too many manual power ups for the PC, which has a long resume time. Therefore, for LightUse users of devices with long resume times it may be necessary to accept increased energy consumption to maintain user-perceived performance. To improve on this case, better sensor information is needed which has a low energy cost.

Finally, there is a concern of reducing device lifetime due to the policies not being able to predict long enough idle periods. Future work will look at including time-of-day information to reduce the number of short standby periods that are less than the break-even time (e.g., 5 minutes for the PC). If this is not sufficient, remote sensing may be necessary to detect user location throughout the building in order to predict these longer idle periods.

References

1. E.U.: Towards a european strategy for the security of energy supply (2000), http://europa.eu.int/comm/energy_transport/en/lpi_lv_en1.html
2. Benini, L., Bogliolo, A., Micheli, G.D.: A survey of design techniques for system-level dynamic power management. IEEE Transactions on Very Large Scale Integration (VLSI) Systems 8(3), 299–316 (2000)
3. Douglis, F., Krishnan, P., Marsh, B.: Thwarting the power-hungry disk. In: USENIX Winter, pp. 292–306 (1994)
4. Tetri, E.: Profitability of switching off fluorescent lamps: Take-a-break. In: RIGHT LIGHT 4, vol. 1, pp. 113–116 (1997)
5. Harris, C., Cahill, V.: Exploiting user behaviour for context-aware power management. In: International Conference On Wireless and Mobile Computing, Networking and Communications, pp. 122–130. IEEE Computer Society Press, Los Alamitos (2005)
6. Mozer, M.: Adaptive house project, http://www.cs.colorado.edu/~mozer/nnh/
7. Mozer, M.: 12. In: Smart environments: Technologies, protocols, and applications, pp. 273–294. J. Wiley and Sons, Chichester (2004)
8. Oliver, N., Horvitz, E., Garg, A.: Layered representations for human activity recognition. In: Fourth IEEE Int. Conf. on Multimodal Interfaces, pp. 3–8. IEEE Computer Society Press, Los Alamitos (2002)
9. Oliver, N., Horvitz, E.: S-seer: Selective perception in a multimodal office activity recognition system. In: Multimodal Interaction and Related Machine Learning Algorithms, pp. 122–135 (2004)
10. Viola, P., Jones, M.: Rapid object detection using a boosted cascade of simple features. In: Computer Vision and Pattern Recognition (2001)
11. Rabiner, L., Juang, B.H.: Fundamentals of speech recognition. Prentice-Hall, Inc., Upper Saddle River, NJ, USA (1993)
12. Dietterich, T.: Statistical tests for comparing supervised classification learning algorithms. Technical report, Department of Computer Science, Oregon State University (1996)
13. Spiegelhalter, D.J., Lauritzen, S.L.: Sequential updating of conditional probabilities on directed graphical structures. Networks 20, 579–605 (1990)

Amigo: Proximity-Based Authentication of Mobile Devices

Alex Varshavsky[1], Adin Scannell[1], Anthony LaMarca[2], and Eyal de Lara[1]

[1] Department of Computer Science, University of Toronto
{walex,amscanne,delara}@cs.toronto.edu
[2] Intel Research Seattle
anthony.lamarca@intel.com

Abstract. Securing interactions between devices that do not know each other a priori is an important and challenging task. We present Amigo, a technique to authenticate co-located devices using knowledge of their shared radio environment as proof of physical proximity. We present evaluation results that show that our technique is robust against a range of passive and active attacks. The key advantages of our technique are that it does not require any additional hardware to be present on the devices beyond the radios that are already used for communication, it does not require user involvement to verify the validity of the authentication process, and it is not vulnerable to eavesdropping.

1 Introduction

We envision that with the increased adoption of mobile devices, spontaneous communication between wireless devices that come within proximity of each other but lack a pre-existing trust relationship will become common. For example, patrons at a bar, guests at a party or conference participants may use their mobile phones to exchange private contact information over Bluetooth or WiFi. Consumers may use their mobile devices as electronic wallets to pay for tickets at the train station or groceries at the store. A user may take advantage of resources available in the environment by pairing their mobile phone to a public full-sized display and keyboard [3], or share music by pairing their phone to a friend's home entertainment system.

An important precondition for the widespread proliferation of spontaneous communication among wireless devices is securing these interactions against eavesdropping, impostors, and man-in-the-middle attacks, in which an attacker reads and inserts messages between two parties without either party knowing that the channel between them has been compromised. Obviously, users would not want their private contact or banking information to be overheard or tampered with by a malicious third party.

We refer to the problem of securing the communication between devices in proximity as *secure pairing*. Unfortunately, traditional cryptographic techniques, such as the Diffie-Hellman protocol [6], by themselves are not sufficient for securely pairing devices that spontaneously come into wireless contact. Whereas

J. Krumm et al. (Eds.): UbiComp 2007, LNCS 4717, pp. 253–270, 2007.
© Springer-Verlag Berlin Heidelberg 2007

they provide a secure binding of keys to electronic identifiers, such as network addresses or device names, these techniques cannot guarantee that the two devices that the user holds in their hands are in fact the ones that are paired – an attacker hundreds of meters away with a directional antenna could be impersonating the device name or network address. What is required is a natural way to authenticate that the keys obtained through the cryptographic exchange belong indeed to devices that are within physical proximity.

This paper shows that it is possible to securely pair devices that come within close proximity by deriving a shared secret from dynamic characteristics of their common radio environment. This approach takes advantage of three observations. First, many mobile devices come equipped with radios that can sense their immediate radio environment. Second, devices in close proximity that simultaneously monitor a common set of ambient radio sources, e.g., WiFi access points or cell phone base stations, perceive a similar radio environment. For high frequency radio technologies, receivers only a few centimeters away may perceive different radio environments due to multi-path effects; however, these differences are generally small compared to differences perceived by receivers at larger distances. Third, due to environmental factors the radio channel varies in unpredictable ways over short time scales. For example, at a single location, signal strength from a cell phone base station fluctuates from one moment to the next, but devices in close proximity perceive similar fluctuations.

Together, these observations imply that it is possible for devices in close proximity to derive a common radio profile that is specific to a particular location and time. This paper shows that this profile can be used to securely pair devices in close proximity by using knowledge of their common radio environment as proof of physical proximity.

We describe Amigo, a technique that extends the Diffie-Hellman key exchange with verification of device co-location. Initially, the two devices perform a Diffie-Hellman key exchange in order to derive a shared-secret. After this exchange alone, it is not possible for either device to be sure whether it shares a secret with the other co-located device or with some potentially malicious third party. Next, both devices monitor their radio environment for a short period of time and exchange a signature of that environment with the other device. Finally, each device independently verifies that the received signature and its own signature are similar enough to conclude that the two devices are in proximity. The verification takes into consideration both transmissions received by the devices and perceived signal strength fluctuations.

An evaluation conducted using WiFi-enabled laptops shows that without requiring user interaction, Amigo can recognize an attacker located as close as 3 meters away. However, if the user is willing to create some localized entropy in the radio environment by, for example, walking or waving their hand in front of the antennas of the two co-located devices, Amigo can detect an attacker located as close as 1 meter away, and can defeat a powerful attacker that has surveyed the environment and has control over ambient radio sources.

Amigo has three advantages over existing solutions: (a) it requires no additional hardware to be present on the devices besides the standard wireless radio already available on most devices; (b) in most cases, it requires no user involvement (beyond specifying that the devices are to be paired); and (c) because devices determine co-location by listening to their radio environment, as opposed to transmitting, Amigo is immune to eavesdropping attacks.

2   Problem Definition and Threat Model

We define the problem of secure pairing of devices in close proximity as follows. Two devices that are located nearby (within 1 meter) to each other but do not know each other a priori need to establish a channel between them that is both secure and authentic. A secure channel implies that no eavesdropper may intercept and decrypt messages between the endpoints, while authenticity requires that both endpoints are able to confirm the identify of each other. We assume that the devices can communicate over compatible wireless radios (e.g., WiFi) and that neither additional out-of-band communication channels are required (e.g., ultrasound) nor is additional hardware present on the devices (e.g., accelerometers).

We assume the presence of an attacker that will try to pair with one or both of the legitimate devices. We assume that the attacker is located beyond the distance that separates the two legitimate devices, and can sense the wireless environment, inject new traffic, and replay packets. Moreover, we assume that the attacker could have surveyed the location where the two legitimate devices are attempting to pair. The attacker can use this knowledge to convince the legitimate devices that they are co-located by predicting the perceived signal strength of ambient radio sources at the location and time of pairing. In the most extreme case, we assume that the attacker both knows what packets were heard by the legitimate device and has access to distributions of signal strengths for each radio source as received by the legitimate device at the time and location of pairing. This is a best-case scenario for the attacker who, even with full control over ambient radio sources, would at best be able to transmit packets at known power levels and predict which packets were received by the legitimate device and at what signal strengths.

We consider two kinds of possible attacks: An *impostor attack* where the attacker succeeds in disabling one of the co-located devices and attempts to impersonate it; and a *man-in-the-middle attack* where the attacker attempts to pair with the two co-located devices simultaneously, and hides its presence by relaying authentication traffic between them.

3   Secure Pairing of Devices in Physical Proximity

In this section, we describe our algorithm to authenticate co-located devices using measurements of their shared radio environment as proof of physical proximity. Our solution is based on the observation that due to environmental effects it is very hard to predict fluctuations in the radio environment at a specific location and at a specific time without being physically present at that location at that time. On the other hand, devices that are positioned in proximity not only tend to successfully decode radio transmissions from the same sources, but also perceive similar fluctuations in signal strength. We will show how this common radio environment can be used as a basis of an authentication scheme for co-located devices.

The Diffie-Hellman protocol allows two parties to create a shared secret key that can be used to secure future communications. While the protocol cannot be compromised by eavesdropping, it is susceptible to man-in-the-middle attacks by a third party. The protocol also does not provide any assurances as to the identity or the proximity of the devices that end up pairing. To both protect the protocol against man-in-the-middle attacks and to ensure that the pairing actually happens with a device in close proximity (as opposed to a far away attacker with a sensitive antenna), we extended the Diffie-Hellman key exchange with a *co-location verification* stage.

In our scheme, after the two devices perform a Diffie-Hellman key exchange, each device monitors the radio environment for a short period of time and generates a signature, which includes a sequence of packet identifiers[1] and the signal strength at which the packets were received. This signature is then transmitted to the other device over the secure channel via a commitment scheme intended to secure the pairing against a man-in-the-middle attack. Finally, each node independently verifies that the received signature and its own signature are similar enough to conclude that the two devices are co-located. At the end of the verification, each device either accepts the signature or rejects it. Because the signatures are used only to validate the keys being exchanged, but not as the basis for encryption, the signatures do not have to remain secret once the authentication takes place. The only requirement on the signatures is that they have to be hard to guess during the authentication phase.

Next, we present our co-location verification algorithm and describe our commitment scheme which is designed to prevent a man-in-the-middle attack.

3.1   Co-location Verification Algorithm

The problem of co-location verification can be described as follows. Given a signature captured locally by a device A, and a signature received from a device B, A needs to reach a binary decision as to whether B is co-located or not. For A to conclude that B is co-located, the signature received from B should be sufficiently similar to the signature captured locally. The verification algorithm has four stages: temporal alignment, slicing, feature extraction and classification. This process is shown in Figure 1.

Since the two devices capture packets locally, they may have started capturing packets at slightly different moments. To meaningfully compare sequences of packet identifiers and signal strength measurements, they need to be temporally

---

[1] We use hashes of packet headers as packet identifiers.

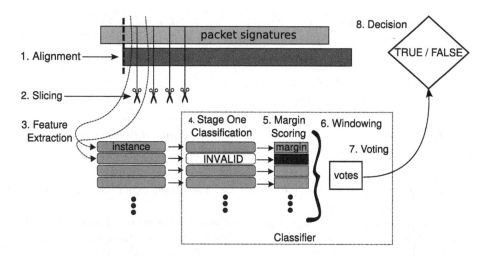

Fig. 1. The complete co-location verification process

aligned. The verification algorithm begins by aligning the packet sequences using the first common packet identifier and discarding all preceding elements in each sequence.

Once the signatures are temporally aligned, we slice them into smaller consecutive subsequences of a fixed timespan, known as *segments*. Slicing allows the verification algorithm to first give a similarity score to each pair of aligned segments and then combine these scores into a final classification decision. Using segments of one second in length typically allows enough packets to be observed for good performance while still keeping the protocol responsive.

The verification algorithm then extracts a set of features from each of the resulting aligned segment pairs. Each feature captures a particular relationship between the two segments to be used by the classification algorithm. For example, percentage of packets that are common to both segments is a useful feature because a higher percentage is associated with a higher likelihood that the two devices are co-located. We describe the set of features used by our classifier in Section 4.2. We further refer to a set of features extracted from a pair of segments as an *instance*.

Finally, we feed the set of instances (one for each segment) into a classifier, which gives a decision as to whether the two signatures have been captured by co-located devices.

The Classifier. We distinguish instances generated by co-located devices from instances generated by non co-located devices using a two stage boosted binary stump classifier. The first stage was added in order to filter noisy data before the more complex binary stump classifier, allowing effective training with less data. During the first stage, instances that have less than a minimum percentage of packets in common are marked as invalid; these are treated in a special way at the end of the second stage. Instances with a low percentage of packets in common (which occur much more commonly with non co-located pairs) were

$$Margin(i) = 2.64 \times x_1(i) + 1.79 \times x_2(i) + \ldots + 1.16 \times x_9(i) + 2.61 \times x_{10}(i)$$

$$x_1(i) = \begin{cases} 1 & \text{if } i.feature_A \leq 4.31625 \\ -1 & \text{otherwise} \end{cases}$$

$$\ldots$$

$$x_{10}(i) = \begin{cases} 1 & \text{if } i.feature_B \leq 5.297 \\ -1 & \text{otherwise} \end{cases}$$

Fig. 2. A sample margin calculation for an instance i during the second stage of classification. The same feature may appear within multiple x_i definitions.

found to have very high classification error. We found experimentally that a threshold of 75% works well.

In the second stage, valid instances are assigned a score, referred to as a *margin*. A margin is derived by evaluating a set of simple functions on an instance and combining the results in a weighted-sum. A sample margin calculation is shown in Figure 2. A larger positive margin indicates more confidence that the devices are co-located. A lower negative margin indicates more confidence that the devices are not co-located. A margin near zero indicates a lack of confidence about the decision.

Finally, the classification algorithm aggregates a window of margins and makes a prediction. Windowing allows the classifier to tolerate a lower degree of accuracy with each individual instance classification. The decision for each window is made with a simple voting scheme. We convert margins into votes based on an adjustable margin threshold; margins that are higher than the threshold are converted to TRUE votes and margins that are below the threshold are converted to FALSE votes. Instances that are marked as invalid do not contribute any vote. At the end, if the window contains a majority of TRUE votes, the devices are classified as co-located. Excessive invalid instances or a majority of FALSE votes will cause the classified to be classified as not co-located. In Section 4.4, we show that the margin threshold of 4 works well in practice and, in Section 4.3, we evaluate the effect of the window size on the classification accuracy.

In order to train the classifier, appropriate features, constants and weights for the margin calculation must be selected. This process is discussed in Section 4.2.

3.2   Dealing with a Man-in-the-Middle Attack

In order to deal with a man-in-the-middle attack, our algorithm employs a simple commitment scheme. The trace collection is broken into short periods of a fixed duration during which a device captures one block of data. The devices are required to exchange the blocks at the end of each time period, otherwise the pairing is rejected. Before sending a block, a device concatenates the block with a hash of its Diffie-Hellman session key and its device identifier, encrypts the result using a nonce value and sends this encrypted block to the other device. Concatenation of the session key is required to prevent the attacker from simply forwarding blocks back and forth between the co-located devices as explained below, and concatenation of the device identifier prevents the attacker from simply "mirroring" the messages. After all blocks have been transferred, both devices exchange the set of nonces required to decrypt the sequence of encrypted blocks and verify the hashes of the session keys and device identifiers.

At the end of each time period, the attacker is required to supply a block. Since the attacker cannot decrypt received blocks until the end of the collection process, he has only two choices. The attacker can either pass on the encrypted block received from a co-located device or can generate a new block with its own session key. Since the session keys between the attacker and each co-located device are different, simply passing the encrypted blocks between devices will not allow the attacker to pair with either of the devices. In Section 4, we show that trying to forge new packets based on the radio environment is also likely to be fruitless, unless the attacker is very close to the co-located devices.

This scheme is equivalent to a fixed-delay interlock protocol [15]. The nonce used to decrypt the blocks can be sent one collection period after the encrypted blocks. However, unlike the fixed-delay interlock protocol, it is not necessary to use the delays to simply detect a man-in-the-middle; after the relevant time period has passed, each block becomes useless, as they are strictly time-dependent. The attacker can not extract useful information from any block in order to pass it to a target when it is required. The nature of the secrets implicitly detects a man-in-the-middle by forcing him to generate fake traces.

4   Evaluation

In this section, we first discuss our data collection and training procedures, then we proceed to evaluate the performance of Amigo under various conditions. First, we test the basic configuration, similar in nature to our training configuration, but using data collected at a different time and place. We then test the effect of obstacles between the attackers and the co-located devices. Subsequently, we experiment with more sophisticated attacker scenarios, and explore having the user generate localized entropy in order to improve accuracy. Finally, we briefly discuss current limitations of this evaluation.

4.1   Data Collection

We collected WiFi traces using a testbed consisting of 6 laptop computers (3 ThinkPad, 2 Dell and 1 Toshiba), all equipped with Orinoco Gold WiFi cards. WiFi is a practical technology for evaluating Amigo, since it is increasingly prevalent. At 2.4GHz, a few centimeters can make a difference in a multi-path channel, but in our experience the differences in the radio environment observed by nodes separated by greater distances tend to dominate these smaller dissimilarities.

Two laptops that were playing the role of the co-located devices were positioned 5 centimeters apart in an opposite orientation, so that their WiFi cards would be located as close as possible. Four additional laptops positioned 1 meter, 3 meters, 5 meters and 10 meters away from the co-located laptops

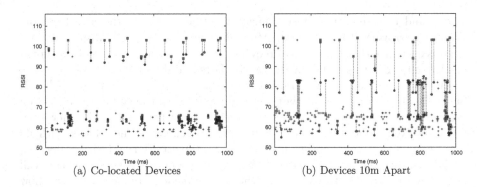

(a) Co-located Devices   (b) Devices 10m Apart

Fig. 3. The received signal strength for packets heard by two devices in a 1 second period. Packets marked as "+" were received by only one laptop. Lines connect packets heard by both devices.

were playing the roles of malicious devices. We felt that these distances would provide a good indication of the ability of the algorithm to differentiate adversaries at various distances. Whereas most of our experiments only consider the devices positioned 5 centimeters apart to be co-located, we explore stretching this distance to 1 meter in Section 4.6.

We wrote a script that simultaneously switches the WiFi cards on all laptops into a monitor mode and captures packets overheard by the cards. The WiFi drivers on all laptops were modified not to discard corrupted packets, but simply mark the packets as corrupted.

An active scan for WiFi access points in the lab environment where data collection took place reveals 11 access points on average. With a 10 minute trace taken in the afternoon, each laptop captured between 30 thousand and 50 thousand packets (including all WiFi beacons, etc.) and heard between 45 and 58 unique transmitters. The majority of transmitters heard in this environment were not loquacious - each laptop captured less than 100 packets from most sources.

Figure 3 shows the packets received by two co-located devices and non colocated devices over a period of 1 second . The y axis represents the Received Signal Strength Indicator (RSSI) value associated with each packet. The packets marked by "+" were received by only one of the two laptops, while packets connected by lines were received by both laptops. For the co-located pair, during this time period approximately 85% of the packets received were common to both. For the distant pair, only 40% of the packets were common. Comparing the figures also immediately makes apparent the similarity of RSSI values for the co-located pair.

4.2   Training the Classifier

As discussed in Section 3.1, the classifier must be trained. For this purpose, we used a MultiBoost [24] algorithm with decision stumps (single node decision trees) as its base learner. The MultiBoost algorithm is a decision committee

Table 1. A relevant subset of features extracted from aligned segments. The sequences of RSSI values for the N common packets in each instance are represented by a_i and b_i, $0 \leq i \leq N$.

Feature Name	Feature Definition	Description
signal:abs	$\frac{\sum_1^N |a_i - b_i|}{N}$	The mean absolute difference between received signal strength measurements.
signal:eucl	$\sqrt{\sum_1^N (a_i - b_i)^2}$	The euclidean difference between received signal strength vectors.
signal:exp	$\frac{\sum_1^N e^{|a_i - b_i|}}{N}$	The mean exponential of the difference between signal strength measurements.
signalexp:diff:eucl	$\sqrt{\sum_2^N \left(e^{(a_i - a_{i-1})} - e^{(b_i - b_{i-1})} \right)^2}$	The euclidean difference between exponential signal strength deltas.

technique that combines AdaBoost [7] with wagging. This approach has been shown to be more effective in reducing error than either of its constituent techniques [24]. The MultiBoost algorithm selects the appropriate set of weighted linear classifiers that are used for the margin calculation for each valid instance.

For training, we captured 10 minutes worth of packets on all 6 laptops. We aligned and sliced all packet sequences captured by each pair of laptops in our testbed, and then extracted features from all pairs of sequences that included the first co-located laptop. We trained our classifier using 596 instances from co-located devices and 2279 instances from non co-located devices.

To evaluate the effectiveness of the classifier, we investigate its performance in terms of false positive and false negative rates. False positives occur when the algorithm predicts that the devices are co-located when they are in fact not, and the *false positive rate* is the number of false positives divided by the total number of non co-located instances. False negatives occur when the algorithm predicts that the devices are not co-located when they in fact are, and *false negative rate* is the number of false negatives divided by the total number of co-located instances. Note that in general, reducing false positives is ultimately more important that reducing false negatives because confusing a malicious device for a co-located device is a more serious flaw than not admitting the co-located device and requiring the user to wait for a longer period before the devices get paired together.

Training the classifier with all available features achieves 23 false negatives out of 596 true instances and 50 false positives out of 2279 instances. Although we constructed dozens of features, only four were selected by the MultiBoost algorithm during training: the mean absolute difference in signal strength (*signal:abs*), the mean exponential difference in signal strength (*signal:exp*), the euclidean difference between signal strength vectors (*signal:eucl*) and the euclidean difference between exponential signal strength deltas (*signalexp:diff:eucl*). These are the features shown in Table 1.

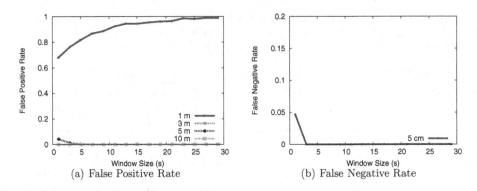

Fig. 4. Co-located devices are 5cm apart. The attackers are 1m, 3m, 5m and 10m away.

4.3   The Base Case

After training the classifier, we collected a second set of data for testing our technique. To allow time for the radio environment to evolve, the testing data set was collected two months after the training data set was collected. To prevent the classifier from recognizing any anomalies with the particular physical arrangement of devices, the collection setup was moved from one end of our lab to the other (approximately 10 meters). Besides changing the location and time of collecting the testing data, the experimental setup was left unchanged – two co-located laptops were positioned 5 centimeters apart and 4 other laptops were positioned 1 meter, 3 meters, 5 meters and 10 meters away from the co-located laptops. All laptops were positioned at the same height and the attackers had a line of sight to the co-located devices, a likely best-case scenario for the attackers.

We tested the ability of our classifier to authenticate co-located devices and reject non co-located device as a function of the classifier's window size. Since we are using 1 second segments, the window size represents the amount of time, in seconds, that a user needs to wait to authenticate the devices. Figure 4(a) plots the false positive rates of attackers trying to authenticate while located 1 meter, 3 meters, 5 meters and 10 meters away, while Figure 4(b) plots the false negative rate of not authenticating a co-located device located 5 centimeters away. The results show that in 5 seconds both the false negative rate falls to 0, meaning that all attempts of the co-located device to authenticate are successful. In the same 5 seconds, the false positive rate falls to 0 for the attackers located 3 meters, 5 meters and 10 meters away, meaning that the attacks initiated from at least 3 meters away were all unable to fool the system. Unfortunately, the attacker device that is located 1 meter away is able to convince the other device that it is co-located. Since more than 60% of instances from the attacker 1 meter away are incorrectly classified as co-located, increasing the window size results in aggregation of a larger proportion of these instances in every window and consequentially a more consistent misclassification of the attacker.

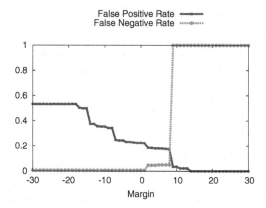

Fig. 5. The false positive and false negative rates for different margin thresholds

To prevent attackers as close as 1 meter from succeeding, we explored a technique as we proposed [23] to generate localized entropy in the radio environment. The user that suspects that a possible attacker may be nearby simply needs to wave their hand in front of the antennas of the two mobile devices during the pairing. This motion will generate unique fluctuations in the radio environment perceived only by the co-located devices. We tested the effect of hand waving on the ability of the 1 meter away attacker to authenticate with a device. In this case, the false positive rate of the attacker falls to 0 within 5 seconds. Hand waving is a natural and non-burdensome action for users to perform in order to pair devices. To provide a more secure pairing, users can be encouraged to move around and use their preferred hand motions as if invoking some form of personal sorcery by casting a pairing spell.

4.4 The Effect of Margin Threshold

Recall that the classifier assigns a margin to each valid instance which is compared to a threshold in order to determine a vote. Increasing this threshold makes the classifier less likely to accept the devices as co-located, increasing the chance of a false negative but also decreasing the chance of a false positive. Reducing the threshold has the opposite effect. Figure 5 plots the false negative and false positive rates for all individual segments as a function of this margin threshold. As the margin threshold grows, fewer segments belonging to impostors are authenticated and as a consequence the rate of false positives falls. The jumps in the false positive and false negative rates result from the finite number of values that the margin can take, since it is the sum of a finite number of constants. Setting the margin threshold to a value beyond 8 results in no attackers being authenticated, but also in no co-located devices being authenticated, in which case the false negative rate rises to 1. The plateau between the margin threshold of 2 to 8 seems to consistently strike a good balance between false positives and false negatives. We used margin threshold of 4 for all our experiments.

Table 2. The effect of different materials on the ability of the attacker to authenticate with a device

Obstruction	False Positive Rate
None (1m)	0.81
Drywall (10cm)	1.00
Human (1m)	0.12
Concrete Wall (30cm)	0.00

4.5   The Effect of Obstacles

In all the experiments described above, the attacker had a clear line of sight to the co-located devices. In reality, that might not be the case as different kinds of materials may block or obstruct the path between the attacker and the target. We looked at the effect of three common materials blocking the line of sight between the attacker and co-located devices, including drywall, concrete and a human body. Table 2 summarizes our findings in terms of false positives.

For the attacker 1 meter away and with a 5 second window, the false positive rate is about 80% as was shown in Figure 4(a). In contract, when the attacker is separated from the co-located devices by two sheets of gypsum drywall, a wall about 10 centimeters thick, the false positive rate climbs to 1. This has the implication that drywall does not protect users from an attacker who is immediately behind the wall. This is in line with other signal propagation studies that have shown that dry wall does not have a profound effect on radio signal propagation in the 2.4GHz range [20]. When a human being is standing between the the attacker and the two co-located laptops located 1 meter away, the false positive rate falls to just above 10%. This is encouraging, as it means that humans, being basically bags of water, by just the sheer blocking of the authentication with their buddies, may make it significantly more secure. Finally, when a 30 centimeter-thick concrete wall separates the attacker from the co-located devices, the false positive rate is 0. When passing through a concrete wall, radio signals attenuate strongly enough to make it extremely hard for the simple attacker to authenticate without more sophisticated attacks.

4.6   Stretching Co-location

Up until now, we used a classifier trained with data that indicated that two devices were co-located if they were 5 centimeters apart. In this section, we study the effects of extending the notion of co-location to include devices located up to 1 meter away. We retrained our classifier on the same training data, but this time we marked the segments belonging to the device located 1 meter away as also co-located. Figures 6(a) and 6(b) plot the false positive and false negative rates as a function of time the user needs to wait to authenticate the devices. The results show that after 5 seconds the false positive rate falls to 0 for all attackers located 3 meters or more away, while the false negative rate falls to 0.05. This means that in 5% of cases a user will not succeed to pair co-located devices in

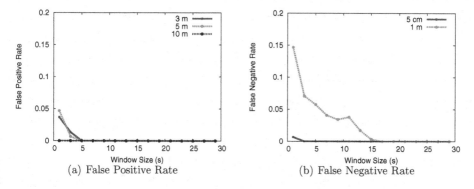

(a) False Positive Rate   (b) False Negative Rate

Fig. 6. Co-located devices are up to 1m apart. The attackers are 3m, 5m and 10m away.

5 seconds from the first attempt, and will need to retry again. However, waiting for 20 seconds always results in a correct pairing.

4.7   Sophisticated Attacks

A powerful attacker could have surveyed the location where the two legitimate devices are attempting to pair, and could attempt to use this knowledge to convince the legitimate devices that he is currently present at that particular location. We implemented a simulated powerful attacker for the purpose of evaluating the robustness of our system under such a threat.

We conducted an experiment where the attacker had access to a distribution of received signal strength measurements for each radio source, sampled by the target device itself at the pairing location only a few hours prior to the current authentication. During the authentication, when the attacker receives a packet from a radio source that he has observed before, he substitutes the signal strength value in this packet with a sample from the recorded distribution of packets previously observed at the pairing location from that transmitter. Whenever the attacker receives a packet from a source that he has no distribution for, the attacker has a choice of either pretending he never received the packet in the first place, thereby potentially decreasing the percent of common packets if the target device did get this packet, or simply leaving the signal strength in the packet as is. Experiments showed that not discarding these packets is beneficial to the attacker.

Figure 7 shows that attackers located 1 meter and 5 meters away can successfully authenticate in 15% and 45% of the cases using 5 second windows, respectively. The adversary positioned 5 meters away actually performed better in our experiments than the laptop positioned 3 meters away, due to the fact that the laptop at a distance of 5 meters generally shared a slightly larger number of packets with the target. The laptops positioned 3 meters and 10 meters away were not able to authenticate because a large portion of their instances

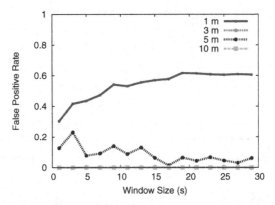

Fig. 7. False positive rate for a simulated attacker who samples from the distribution of co-located devices and then uses that signal strength to impersonate one of the devices

were rejected due to insufficient common packets before moving to the second stage of classification.

In order to defend against the attacker who has gone to the measure of rigorously surveying the environment in this way, we propose to use the hand waving enhancement discussed earlier. Even equipped with a location-specific distribution, the system has a false positive rate of 0 within all 5 second windows of the experiment for all attackers.

In a worst-case scenario, an attacker could also be powerful enough to have complete control over the radio environment. We assume that such an attacker has injected every packet into the environment, and that he knows exactly what packets the target device receives. Also, for our simulation, the attacker is equipped with an oracle, that allows the attacker to sample from the distribution of signal strength values as perceived by the target device over the duration of the experiment.

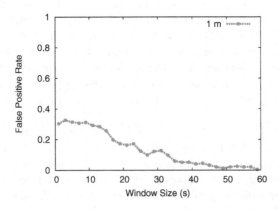

Fig. 8. Hand waving allows Amigo to prevent even the most sophisticated attack, when the attacker can predict the signal strength of the **current** distribution of packets

We tested whether hand waving will prevent this attacker from authenticating with the target device in this case. Figure 8 shows the false positive rate of authentications with the oracle attacker. The figure shows that with hand waving, after 5 seconds, the attacker is able to authenticate successfully in only 30% of the cases. If the user is willing to pair the devices for 60 seconds, the false positive rate falls to 0%! This is encouraging given the small likelihood of encountering an attacker this powerful.

4.8 Discussion

So far, we evaluated Amigo using homogeneous WiFi cards. Although using WiFi cards with different chipset designs or antenna configurations will have an effect on received signal strengths, we believe that it will be possible to generalize Amigo by normalizing the received signal strength values and make Amigo antenna and chipset agnostic. As a preliminary test of this hypothesis, we hooked an external omnidirectional antenna onto the WiFi card of one of the co-located laptops and collected a 10 minute trace. Using a simple gain-correction, wherein RSSI measurements of the antenna-equipped laptop are adjusted by a small, constant amount, Amigo was still able to achieve a low level of false negatives with zero false positives after only a few seconds using the standard classifier presented in Section 4.3.

Hardware heterogeneity is not the only factor that requires further exploration. The success of our technique may also depend on physical or network conditions. For example, the location of our experiments had moderate to heavy WiFi usage. It would be interesting to evaluate the system in quieter environments, such as at a small café. All of our experiments were also conducted on flat, stable surfaces. Experimenting with small devices held by shaky hands is a topic for our future research.

5 Related Work

SWAP-CA [21] is a specification that gives users a way to associate devices by pressing a button on two devices simultaneously, but does not provide security. In Bluetooth, users pair devices by providing each device with a secret PIN number. While the PIN provides for device authentication, it requires active user involvement and interaction with both devices. Moreover, Bluetooth pairing has been shown to be susceptible to attack by eavesdroppers equipped with sensitive directional antennas, which enable attackers to breach the security of the system from more than a mile away [5,17]. LoKey [14] uses SMS messages as an out-of-band channel to authenticate a key exchanged over the Internet. While this approach is secure, SMS delivery is slow and may incur monetary cost.

Physically shaking two devices together for authentication has recently received significant attention in the research community. Smart-It [9] used common readings from accelerometers to establish an association between devices shaken at the same time. Mayrhofer and Gellersen extended this technique to provide secure authentication between the shaken devices [12]. Both of these techniques use the accelerometer readings as the basis of the authentication. In Shake Them Up! [4], two devices establish a shared secret over an anonymous broadcast channel by taking turns transmitting parts of the key. Shaking the devices randomizes the reception power of their packets by a potential eavesdropper and makes it hard for attackers to exploit power analysis to break the channel anonymity. Unfortunately, this approach is vulnerable to attack by an eavesdropper that exploits the differences in the baseband frequencies of the two radio sources, which result from differences in their crystal clock oscillators, to differentiate between packets sent by the two transmitters. In general, shaking techniques are easy for users to understand and when accelerometers are available, provide intuitive and reliable device pairing. The obvious drawback with shaking techniques is that there are objects such as ATM machines and vending machines that are too large or too heavy to be shaken vigorously. This inspired our hand waving technique as it does not require both objects to be shaken together and only requires hands to be waved or shaken near the antennas of the two co-located devices to generate localized entropy.

Numerous research projects have suggested the use of physically constrained channels as a means of establishing secure association between devices in close proximity. Some examples include the use of a direct electric contact [19], infrared beacons [2,18], ultrasound [11], and laser beams [10]. Unfortunately, physically constrained channels often require extra hardware (e.g., an extra cable), and can be susceptible to attacks by sensitive receivers that can detect dim signal refractions and reflections [5,17].

Another technology that can be used for secure device pairing is Near Field Communication or NFC. Unlike radio-transmission based wireless communication like 802.11 and GSM, NFC transmits data via inductive loading. This limits the working range of NFC links to a few centimeters [1]. While obviously a good fit for many use cases, NFC is not without issues: like traditional radio transmissions, the range of the inductive loading can be drastically increased by eavesdropping with a large antenna – a large loop of wire in the case of NFC. It is also the case that for cultural or hygiene reasons, there are situations in which the "almost touching" nature of NFC may be inappropriate and for which the notion of proximity may be better suited by a larger distance. Lastly, NFC does add additional cost, size and weight to a mobile device in addition to the far-field communication already present.

Another solution to establishing trust between mobile devices is to use a public key infrastructure. In this case, every mobile device is uniquely named and certified by a trusted authority. Even if the effort is spent to grant every device a unique and certified name, pairing may still require significant user involvement since there may be multiple nearby devices to choose from.

Several projects proposed to delegate the verification of whether the two intended devices have been paired to the user. McCune *et al.* [13] and Saxena *et al.* [16] proposed to use the visual channel for verification, while Goodrich *et al.* [8] proposed to use the audio channel. Uzun *et al.* [22] recently performed a comparative evaluation of a number of user-driven verification methods.

In contrast, we propose to use the common radio environment as a basis to the shared secret between co-located devices – if two devices perceive a similar radio environment they are probably very close to each other. A key advantage of our approach is that it makes use of the existing radio interfaces already present on mobile devices and does not require any additional hardware. The approach is also automatic and does not require user involvement to verify the correctness of the pairing.

6   Conclusions

In this paper we showed that it is possible to securely pair devices that come within close proximity by using knowledge of dynamic characteristics of their common radio environment as proof of physical proximity. We introduced Amigo, an algorithm that extends the Diffie-Hellman key exchange with verification of device co-location. Amigo has three key advantages: it does not requirement additional hardware beyond the wireless interface used for normal communication, it does not require user involvement to verify the pairing, and it is not susceptible to eavesdropping.

We evaluated Amigo using WiFi-enabled laptops and showed that within 5 seconds it is possible to recognize attackers located as close as 3 meters away from the co-located laptops. However, if the user is willing to wave their hands in front of the antennas of the two co-located devices in order to generate some localized entropy, Amigo is resilient to an attacker located 1 meter away, even in the unlikely case of an attacker that controls all ambient radio sources and is using the signal strength values from a distribution collected at the exact location of the current pairing.

References

1. Near field communication (nfc), http://www.nfc-forum.org/resources/faqs
2. Balfanz, D., Smetters, D., Stewart, P., Wong, H.: Talking to strangers: Authentication in ad-hoc wireless networks. In: Proc. Network and Distributed Systems Security Symposium (2002)
3. Barton, J.J., Zhai, S., Cousins, S.: Mobile phones will become the primary personal computing devices. In: IEEE Workshop on Mobile Computing Systems and Applications, April 2006, IEEE, Los Alamitos (2006)
4. Castelluccia, C., Mutaf, P.: Shake them up!: a movement-based pairing protocol for cpu-constrained devices. In: Proc. of MobiSys, pp. 51–64 (2005)
5. Cheung, H.: How to: Building a bluesniper rifle - part 1 (March 2005), http://www.tomsnetworking.com/2005/03/08/how_to_bluesniper_pt1
6. Diffie, W., Hellman, M.: New directions in cryptography. IEEE Transactions on Information Theory, 644–654 (1976)
7. Freund, Y., Schapire, R.: Experiments with a new boosting algorithm. In: Proc. of International Conference on Machine Learning, pp. 148–156 (1996)

8. Goodrich, M., Sirivianos, M., Solis, J., Tsudik, G., Uzun, E.: Loud and clear: Human-verifiable authentication based on audio. In: Proc. of IEEE Internation Conference on Distributed Computing Systems, IEEE Computer Society Press, Los Alamitos (2006)

9. Holmquist, L.E., Mattern, F., Schiele, B., Alahuhta, P., Beigl, M., Gellersen, H.W.: Smart-its friends: A technique for users to easily establish connections between smart artefacts. In: Abowd, G.D., Brumitt, B., Shafer, S. (eds.) Ubicomp 2001: Ubiquitous Computing. LNCS, vol. 2201, Springer, Heidelberg (2001)

10. Kindberg, T., Zhang, K.: Secure spontaneous device association. In: Dey, A.K., Schmidt, A., McCarthy, J.F. (eds.) UbiComp 2003. LNCS, vol. 2864, Springer, Heidelberg (2003)

11. Kindberg, T., Zhang, K.: Validating and securing spontaneous associations between wireless devices. In: Boyd, C., Mao, W. (eds.) ISC 2003. LNCS, vol. 2851, Springer, Heidelberg (2003)

12. Mayrhofer, R., Gellersen, H.: Shake well before use: Authentication based on accelerometer data. In: Fifth International Conference on in Pervasive Computing (2007)

13. McCune, J., Perrig, A., Reiter, M.: Seeing-is-believing: Using camera phones for human-verifiable authentication. In: Proc. of IEEE Symposium on Security and Privacy, pp. 110–124. IEEE Computer Society Press, Los Alamitos (2005)

14. Nicholson, A.J., Smith, I.E., Hughes, J., Noble, B.D.: Lokey: Leveraging the sms network in decentralized, end-to-end trust establishment. In: Fishkin, K.P., Schiele, B., Nixon, P., Quigley, A. (eds.) PERVASIVE 2006. LNCS, vol. 3968, Springer, Heidelberg (2006)

15. Rivest, R.L., Shamir, A.: How to expose an eavesdropper. Commun. ACM 27(4), 393–394 (1984)

16. Saxena, N., Ekberg, J., Kostiainen, K., Asokan, N.: Secure device pairing based on visual channel. In: Proc. of IEEE Symposium on Security and Privacy, IEEE Computer Society Press, Los Alamitos (2006)

17. Shaked, Y., Wool, A.: Cracking the bluetooth pin. In: Proc. of Mobisys (2005)

18. Smetters, D., Balfanz, D., Durfee, G., Smith, T., Lee, K.: Instant matchmaking: Simple, secure virtual extensions to ubiquitous computing environments. In: Dourish, P., Friday, A. (eds.) UbiComp 2006. LNCS, vol. 4206, Springer, Heidelberg (2006)

19. Stajano, F., Anderson, R.J.: The resurrecting duckling: Security issues for ad-hoc wireless networks. In: Malcolm, J.A., Christianson, B., Crispo, B., Roe, M. (eds.) Security Protocols. LNCS, vol. 1796, Springer, Heidelberg (2000)

20. Stone, W.C.: NIST Construction Automation Program Report No. 3: Electromagnetic Signal Attenuation in Construction Materials (NISTIR 6055), National Technical Information Service, Washington (October 1997)

21. SWAP-CA. Shared Wireless Access Protocol (Cordless Access) Specification (SWAP-CA), Revision 1.0, The HomeRF Technical Committee (17 December 1998)

22. Uzun, E., Karvonen, K., Asokan, N.: Usability study of secure pairing methods. Technical Report 2007-02, Nokia Research Center (January 2007)

23. Varshavsky, A., LaMarca, A., de Lara, E.: Enabling secure and spontaneous communication between mobile devices using common radio environment. In: IEEE Workshop on Mobile Computing Systems and Applications (HotMobile) (February 2007)

24. Webb, G.: Multiboosting: A technique for combining boosting and wagging. Machine Learning, 159–196 (2000)

At the Flick of a Switch: Detecting and Classifying Unique Electrical Events on the Residential Power Line
(Nominated for the Best Paper Award)

Shwetak N. Patel, Thomas Robertson, Julie A. Kientz,
Matthew S. Reynolds, and Gregory D. Abowd

College of Computing, School of Interactive Computing, & GVU Center
Georgia Institute of Technology
85 5th Street NW, Atlanta GA 30332-0280 USA
{shwetak,troomb1,julie,mattr,abowd}@cc.gatech.edu

Abstract. Activity sensing in the home has a variety of important applications, including healthcare, entertainment, home automation, energy monitoring and post-occupancy research studies. Many existing systems for detecting occupant activity require large numbers of sensors, invasive vision systems, or extensive installation procedures. We present an approach that uses a single plug-in sensor to detect a variety of electrical events throughout the home. This sensor detects the electrical noise on residential power lines created by the abrupt switching of electrical devices and the noise created by certain devices while in operation. We use machine learning techniques to recognize electrically noisy events such as turning on or off a particular light switch, a television set, or an electric stove. We tested our system in one home for several weeks and in five homes for one week each to evaluate the system performance over time and in different types of houses. Results indicate that we can learn and classify various electrical events with accuracies ranging from 85-90%.

1 Introduction and Motivation

A common research interest in ubiquitous computing has been the development of inexpensive and easy-to-deploy sensing systems to support activity detection and context-aware applications in the home. For example, several researchers have explored using arrays of low-cost sensors, such as motion detectors or simple contact switches [15, 16, 18]. Although these solutions are cost-effective on an individual sensor basis, they are not without some drawbacks. For example, having to install and maintain many sensors may be a time-consuming task, and the appearance of many sensors may detract from the aesthetics of the home [3, 7]. In addition, the large number of sensors required for coverage of an entire home may increase the number of potential failure points. To address these concerns, recent work has focused on sensing through existing infrastructure in a home. For example, researchers have looked at monitoring the plumbing infrastructure in the home to infer basic activities [6] or using the residential power line to provide indoor localization [13]. Inspired by the theme of leveraging existing infrastructure to support activity detection, we present an approach that uses the home's electrical system as an information source to

J. Krumm et al. (Eds.): UbiComp 2007, LNCS 4717, pp. 271–288, 2007.

observe various electrical events. The detection and classification of these events can be used later for a variety of applications, such as healthcare, entertainment, home automation, energy monitoring, and post-occupancy research studies.

A principal advantage of the approach presented in this paper is that it requires only the installation a single, plug-in module that connects to an embedded or personal computer. The computer records and analyzes electrical noise on the power line caused by the switching of significant electrical loads. Machine learning techniques applied to these patterns identify when unique events occur. Examples include human-initiated events, such as turning on or off a specific light switch or plugging in a CD player, as well as automatic events, such as a compressor or fan of an HVAC system turning on or off under the control of a thermostat.

By observing actuation of certain electrical devices, the location and activity of people in the space can be inferred and used for applications that rely on this contextual information. For example, detecting that a light switch was turned on can be an indication that someone entered a room, and thus an application could adjust the thermostat to make that room more comfortable. We can also detect other human-initiated kitchen events, such as a light turning on inside a refrigerator or microwave when its door is opened. The combination of these events may indicate meal preparation. Our approach also has implications for providing a low-cost solution for monitoring energy usage. An application could log when particular electrical loads are active, revealing how and when electrical energy is consumed in the household, leading to suggestions on how to maintain a more energy-efficient household. In addition, because our approach is capable of differentiating between the on and off events of a particular device in real time, those events can be "linked" to other actuators for a variety of home automation scenarios. One can imagine a home automation system that maps the actuation of a stereo system to an existing light switch without having to install additional wiring.

In this paper, we first present a review of related work in event detection for indoor settings, identifying the inspiration for our work and how it complements and extends past results. We then describe the underlying theory and initial implementation details of our approach to powerline event detection. We report the results of a series of tests to determine the stability of our approach over time and its capability of sensing electrical events in different homes. These tests consisted of installing our device in a single location of a house and collecting data on a variety of electrical events within that house. Results show our support vector machine system can learn and later classify various unique electrical events with accuracies ranging from 85-90%. Finally, we discuss the results, current limitations and potential improvements for this powerline event detection approach.

2 Related Work

We can classify research in activity and behavior recognition in a home setting by examining the origin of the proposed sensing infrastructure. The first area of classification includes approaches that introduce new, independent sensors into the home that directly sense various activities of its residents. This classification includes infrastructures where a new set of sensors and an associated sensor network (wired or wireless) is deployed. A second area encompasses those approaches that take advantage of existing home infrastructure, such as the plumbing or electrical busses in a home, to sense various activities of residents. The goal of the second approach is to lower the adoption barrier by reducing the cost and/or complexity of deploying or maintaining the sensing infrastructure.

Some research approaches use high-fidelity sensing to determine activity, such as vision or audio systems that capture movements of people in spaces [2, 10]. Chen *et al.* installed microphones in a bathroom to sense activities such as showering, toileting, and hand washing [5]. While these approaches may provide rich details about a wide variety of activities, they are often very arduous to install and maintain across an entire household. Furthermore, use of these high fidelity sensors in certain spaces raise concerns about the balance between value-added services and acceptable surveillance, particularly in home settings [3, 7, 9].

Another class of approaches explores the use of a large collection of simple, low-cost sensors, such as motion detectors, pressure mats, break beam sensors, and contact switches, to determine activity and movement [15, 16, 18]. As an example of this low-cost approach, Tapia *et al.* discussed home activity recognition using many state change sensors, which were primarily contact switches [15, 16]. These sensors were affixed to surfaces in the home and logged specific events for some period of time. The advantage of this approach is being able to sense physical activities in a large number of places without the privacy concerns often raised for high-fidelity sensing (*e.g,.* bathroom activity). There are also some disadvantages to this add-on sensor approach, which include the requirements of powering the sensors, providing local storage of logged events on the sensor itself, or a wireless communication backbone for real-time applications. These requirements all complicate the design and maintenance of the sensors, and the effort to install many sensors and the potential impact on aesthetics in the living space may also negatively impact mass adoption of this solution. As an example of the often difficult balance of the value of in home sensing and the complexity of the sensing infrastructure, the Digital Family Portrait is a peace of mind application for communicating well-being information from an elderly person's home to a remote caregiver [14]. In their deployment study, movement data was gathered from a collection of strain sensors attached to the underside of the first floor of an elder's home. The installation of these sensors was difficult, time-consuming, and required direct access to the underside of the floor. Though the value of the application was proven, the complexity of the sensing limited the number of homes in which the system could be easily deployed.

Other approaches, which are similar to ours, are those that use existing home infrastructure to detect events. Fogarty *et al.* explored attaching simple microphones to a home's plumbing system, thereby leveraging an available home infrastructure [6]. The appeal of this solution is that it is low-cost, consists of only a few sensors, and is sufficient for applications, such as the Digital Family Portrait, for which the monitoring of water usage is a good proxy for activity in the house. This approach requires relatively long timescales over which events must be detected, sometimes up to ten seconds. This longer time increases the likelihood of overlapping events, which are harder to distinguish. In contrast, powerline event detection operates over timescales of approximately half a second and thus overlapping is less likely. Some water heaters constantly pump hot water through the house, complicating the detection of some on-demand activities. Detecting noise on water pipes introduced by other household infrastructure requires careful placement of the microphone sensors. Some homes may not have plumbing infrastructure that is easily accessible, particularly those with a finished basement or no basement at all. Despite these limitations, this solution is very complementary to our approach, as some events revealed by water usage, such as turning on a faucet in a sink or flushing a toilet, do not have direct electrical events that could serve as predictive antecedents. The converse also holds, as a light being turned on often does not correlate with any water-based activity. Another "piggybacking" approach is to reuse sensing infrastructure or devices in the home that may be present for other purposes. For example, ADT Security System's QuietCare [1] offers a peace of mind service that gathers activity data from the security system's motion detectors.

There are several other techniques that employ electrical power use to sense activity. For example, some researchers have monitored electrical current flow to infer the appliances or electrical equipment being used in the house as a proxy for detecting activity [12, 16]. The MITes platform supports the monitoring of current consumption of various appliances of interest. Changes in current flow indicate some change in state for the instrumented appliance, such as a change from on to off. This solution requires a current sensor to be installed inline with each appliance or around its power cord and thus only works well if it is sufficient to study the usage of a small subset of appliances and those appliances' power feeds are easy accessible. An extension to the MITes work would be to install current sensors on major branch circuits of the power lines, but this may require professional installation to provide an acceptable level of safety. Our solution can detect a larger number of appliances with less instrumentation and with a much easier deployment phase. Our approach is influenced by our previous work in PowerLine Positioning system [13], which uses existing powerline infrastructure to do practical localization within a home. The main difference between that work and the present work is that we are passively sensing electrical events using simple events, whereas our previous work senses the location of actively tagged objects.

3 Our Approach and System Details

Our prototype system consists of a single module (see Figure 1) that is plugged into any electrical outlet in the home. Although not necessarily required, we installed it in a convenient, central location in the home while experimenting with the setup. The other end of the plug-in unit is connected via USB to a computer that collects and performs the analysis on the incoming electrical noise. The system learns certain characteristics from electrical noise produced by switching an electrical device on or off and later predicts when those devices are actuated based on the learned phenomena. Note that we present an approach for countries that use 60 Hz electrical systems, but our approach can easily be extended to different frequencies used in other countries (*i.e.,* those that use 50 Hz).

3.1 Theory of Operation

Our approach relies on the fact that abruptly switched (mechanical or solid-state) electrical loads produce broadband electrical noise either in the form of a transient or

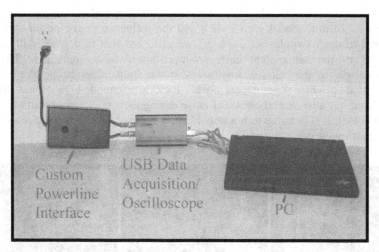

Fig. 1. Our prototype system consists of a powerline noise analyzer plugged in to an ordinary wall outlet and connected to a PC

continuous noise. This electrical noise is generated either between hot and neutral (known as normal mode noise) or between neutral and ground (known as common mode noise). Transient and continuous noise on the residential power line is typically high in energy and may often be observed with a nearby AM radio. The types of electrical noise in which we are interested are produced within the home and are created by the fast switching of relatively high currents. For example, a motor-type load, such as a fan, will create a transient noise pulse when it is first turned on and will then produce a continuous noise signal until it is turned off. In addition, the mechanical switching characteristics of a light switch itself can generate transient electrical noise [8]. Other examples of noisy events include using a garage door opener, plugging in a power adaptor for an electric device, or turning on a television. Marubayashi provides a more complete description of this electrical noise phenomenon [11].

In the case of transient noise, the impulses typically last only a few microseconds and consist of a rich spectrum of frequency components, which can range from 10 Hz to 100 kHz. Thus, it is interesting to consider both the temporal nature (duration) of the transient noise and its frequency components. Depending on the switching mechanism, the load characteristics, and length of transmission line, these impulses can be very different. For example, Figure 2a shows a sample frequency domain graph of a light switch being toggled in a house (light on followed by light off). Note the rich number of high amplitude frequency components for each pulse and their relative strengths. Also, notice that the signature of a device being turned on is different from the same device being turned off. Figure 2b shows the same switch being actuated in the same order, but taken 2 hours later, and Figure 2c shows it taken 1 week later. The amplitudes of individual frequency components and the duration of the impulse produced by each switch are similar between the three graphs, although there are a few high frequency regions that are different across the samples. Even similar light switches produce different signatures, which is likely due to the mechanical construction of each switch and the influence of the power line length connected to each switch. For example, we observed that three-way wall switches connected to the same light each produced discernable signatures. The main difference was in the relative amplitudes of the frequencies being observed. For devices that produce continuous noise, they are bounded by some transient phenomena, but also exhibit electrical noise during their powered operation. For this class of noises, it is possible to not only identify it based on its transient response but also its continuous noise signature.

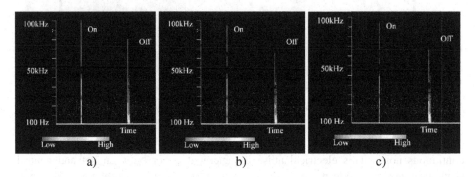

Fig. 2. Frequency spectrum of a particular light switch being toggled (on and off events). The graphs indicate amplitudes at each frequency level. Events in (b) were captured two days after (a), and events in (c) were captured one week after (a). Each sample is rich in a broad range of frequencies. On and off events are each different enough to be distinguished. In addition, the individual on and off events are similar enough over time to be recognized later.

Because we assume the noise signature of a particular device depends both on the device and the transmission line behavior of the interconnecting power line, we have attempted to capture both contributions in a single model. Figure 3 depicts a high-level overview of our simplified model of a home's electrical infrastructure and where particular noise transfer functions occur, denoted as H(s). These transfer functions reflect our expectation that both the electrical transmission lines and the data collection apparatus connected to that line all contribute to some transformation of the noise from the source to the collection apparatus. The observed noise results from the imposition of all the transfer functions against the generated noise. The influence of the transmission line's transfer function is an important contributor to the different electrical noise signatures we observed, which explains why similar device types (*e.g.*, light switches) can be distinguished and why the location of the data collection module in the house impacts the observed noise.

In our simplified model, three general classes of electrical noise sources may be found in a home (see Figure 3): resistive loads, inductive loads such as motors, and loads with solid state switching. Purely resistive loads, such as a lamp or an electric stove, do not create detectable amounts of electrical noise while in operation, although as a resistor, they can be expected to produce trace amounts of thermal noise (Johnson noise) at an undetectable level. In this particular case, only a transient

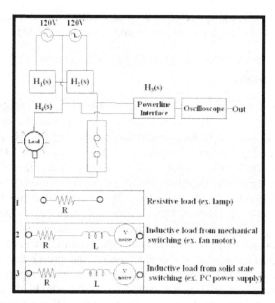

Fig. 3. Overview of the powerline infrastructure and location of particular signal/noise transfer functions, $H_n(s)$. The bottom of the figure shows three general types of loads found in a home, a purely resistive, an inductive where voltage noise is generated from a continuous mechanical switching (motors), and an inductive load where voltage noise is generated by an internal oscillator of a solid state switch.

noise is produced by minute arcing in the mechanical switch itself (wall switch) when the switch is turned on or off. A motor, such as in a fan or a blender, is modeled as both a resistive and inductive load. The continuous breaking and connecting by the motor brushes creates a voltage noise synchronous to the AC power of 60 Hz (and at 120 Hz). Solid state switching devices, such as MOSFETs found in computer power supplies or TRIACs in dimmer switches or microwave ovens, emit noise that is different between devices and is synchronous to an internal oscillator. Thus, the latter two classes contribute noise from both the external power switching mechanism (transient) and the noise generated by the internal switching mechanism (continuous).

In the United States, the Federal Communications Commission (FCC) sets guidelines on how much electrical noise AC-powered electronic devices can conduct back onto the power line (Part 15 section of the FCC regulations). Device-generated noise at frequencies between 150 kHz-30 MHz cannot exceed certain limits. Regulatory agencies in other countries set similar guidelines on electronic devices. Although this mainly applies to electronic devices, such as those that have solid state switching power supplies, this gives us some assurance about the type and amount of noise we might expect on the power line.

It is often extremely difficult to analytically predict the transient noise from the general description of a load and its switching mechanism because ordinary switches are usually not well characterized during their make-and-break times. However, it is possible to take a mapping approach by learning these observed signatures using supervised machine learning techniques. The challenge then becomes finding the important features of these transient pulses and determining how to detect the relevant ones of interest.

3.2 Hardware Details

To explore the idea of detecting and learning various electrical events in the home, we first built a custom data collector that consisted of a powerline interface with three outputs (see Figures 4 and 5). One output was the standard 60 Hz AC power signal, which we used during our initial testing and exploratory phase. The second output was an attenuated power line output that has been bandpass-filtered with a passband of 100 Hz to 100 kHz. The third output was similarly attenuated and was bandpass-filtered with a 50 kHz to 100 MHz passband. We chose these different filtered outputs to have the flexibility to experiment with different frequency ranges (see Figure 6). Both filtered outputs have a 60 Hz notch filter in front of their bandpass filters to remove the AC power frequency and enhance the dynamic range of the sampled data. We built our interface so that we could monitor the power line between hot and neutral, neutral and ground, or hot and ground. For the work reported here, we chose to observe the noise between hot and neutral (normal mode) because many loads that we would like to observe (such as table lamps and small appliances) do not have a ground connection.

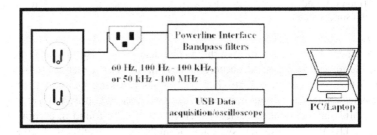

Fig. 4. Block diagram of our powerline interface system

We further chose to interface with only one 120V leg or branch of the electrical system. Most residential houses and apartments in North America and many parts of Asia have a single-phase or a split single-phase electrical system. This means there are two 120V electrical branches coming into the house to supply 240V appliances, but the two branches are still in phase. We found that the noises generated by devices of interest connected to the other electrical branch were already being coupled to the electrical branch we interfaced to, and so were detectable by our system. While this approach was practical and sufficient for our research prototype, we could also plug a coupler into a 240V outlet to ensure we have direct access to both electrical branches.

Finally, the outputs of the powerline interface are connected to a dual-input USB oscilloscope interface (EBest 2000) that has a built-in gain control. Each input has 10-bit resolution with a full scale voltage of 1V, so the least significant bit represents a

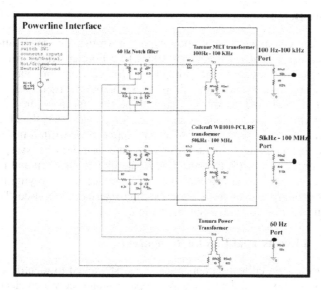

Fig. 5. The schematic of our powerline interface device

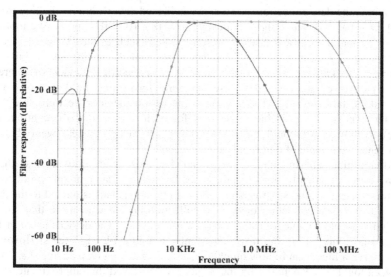

Fig. 6. A model of the frequency response curve of our powerline data collection apparatus at the 100 Hz – 100 kHz and the 50 kHz – 100 MHZ outputs. The 60 Hz dip is from the notch filter.

voltage of 4 mV. The oscilloscope interface has a real-time sampling rate of 100 million samples/sec. A C++ API is provided, resulting in a simple software interface to the sampled signal.

3.3 Software Details

For the software components of our prototype, we wrote a C++ application to sample the USB oscilloscope interface and perform a Fast Fourier Transform (FFT) on the incoming signal to separate the component frequencies for our analysis. The application also produces a waterfall plot, a commonly used frequency domain visualization in real-time used for visual inspection (such as in Figure 2). The application performs this analysis in nearly real-time, and it has the ability to record the data stream for post processing. A second application, written in Java, performs the machine learning and provides the user interface for the system. The Java application connects via a TCP connection to the FFT application and reads the data values. The Java application provides the user interface for surveying the home and remotely accessing the data from the powerline interface. We used the Weka [17] toolkit for our machine learning implementation.

3.4 Electrical Events That Can Be Recognized

Having built our data collection apparatus, we first wanted to identify the variety of electrical devices we could detect with our apparatus and see which electrical devices would produce recognizable signatures that can be used for our machine learning software. For this exploration, we installed our apparatus in a single fixed location throughout the data collection process. We collected data with both the low frequency (100 Hz – 100 KHz) and high frequency (50 kHz – 100 MHz) ports. We took care to ensure no major electrical devices were activated (such as the HVAC, fridge, water pumps, *etc.*) by turning them off for the duration of the testing so we knew which devices were causing which response. For each electrical device of interest, we visually observed and collected noise signatures for turning the device on, turning it off, and its stable on state. Table 1 shows the various devices we were able to detect and the events we were able to observe for each device (on, off, continuously on state). Although we could have observed many more devices, we only show a representative sample of commonly used devices.

After initial experimentation, we found that most loads drawing less than 0.25 amps were practically undetectable Loads above that amount produced very prominent electrical noise (transient and/or continuous). This is related to the dynamic range of our data collection device—a collection device with more than 10 bits of resolution would be able to detect lower current devices. The devices listed in Table 1 showed not only strong but also consistently reproducible signatures. However, we did observe a limitation in how quickly we could switch a given device (*i.e.*, the delay between toggles). Depending on the device, we observed that approximately 500 ms delay between subsequent toggles was required for our data collection apparatus to detect a noise impulse successfully. This is largely attributed to the sampling and processing latency from our device (*e.g.*, USB latency plus processing delays on the PC).

While most devices produced a transient pulse only a few microseconds in duration in their energized state, certain devices continuously produced electrical noise while they were powered, as expected. For example, lamp dimmers or wall-mounted dimmer switches produced noise that was very rich in harmonics while they were

Table 1. Electrical devices we tested and which events we were able detect. These devices also consistently produced detectable event signatures.

Device Class/Type	Devices Observed	On to Off Transition Noise?	Off to On Transition Noise?	Continuously On Noise?
Resistive	Incandescent lights via a wall switch	Y	Y	N
	Microwave door light	Y	Y	N
	Oven light/door	Y	Y	N
	Electric stove	Y	Y	N
	Refrigerator door	Y	Y	N
	Electric Oven	Y	Y	N
Inductive (Mechanically Switched)	Bathroom exhaust fan	Y	Y	N
	Ceiling fan	Y	Y	N
	Garage door opener	Y	Y	N
	Dryer	Y	Y	N
	Dishwasher	Y	Y	N
	Refrigerator compressor	Y	Y	N
	HVAC/Heat Pump	Y	Y	N
	Garbage disposal	Y	Y	N
Inductive (Solid State Switched)	Lights via a dimmer wall switch	Y	Y	Y
	Fluorescent lights via a wall switch	Y	Y	N
	Laptop power adapter	Y	N	N
	Microwave Oven	Y	Y	Y
	Television (CRT, plasma, or LCD)	Y	Y	N

activated. Similarly, microwave ovens also coupled broadband noise back on the power line during its use. These devices tended to produce strong continuous noise above 5 kHz and reaching up to 1 MHz. We also found that switching power supplies, such as from a laptop or PC, produced considerably higher noise in the 100 kHz – 1 MHz area than at the lower 100 Hz – 5 kHz range.

To understand devices that produced continuous noise, we tested various switching power supplies in isolation from other electrical line noise (see Figure 7). Using the higher 50 kHz – 100 MHz output on our data collection apparatus, we found that many of these devices produced more detectable continuous noise at the higher frequencies. At the lower 100 Hz – 5 kHz range, we saw fairly low amplitude, continuous noise, and a higher transient noise effect (from the flipping of the switch).

In the 100 Hz – 100 kHz range, motor-based devices, such as a ceiling or bathroom exhaust fan, exhibited slightly longer duration transient pluses when activated with a switch, but did not show continuous normal mode noise which would have been expected from the repeated electromechanical switching from the motor brushes. We attribute this difference to our 60 Hz notch filter, which blocked the 60 Hz power frequency. To confirm this hypothesis, we conducted another experiment in which we isolated various mechanically-switched devices (*e.g.*, fans) and looked at their noise output (see Figure 7). In the case of the fan, our data collection apparatus did indeed show the transient pulse, but not the continuous electrical noise.

From these observations, we are able to characterize the noise characteristics produced by different devices. We observed that transient noise produced from a single abrupt switching event (e.g., a wall switch) tended to produce signals rich in high amplitude components in the lower frequency range (100 Hz – 5 KHz). Inductive loads featuring a solid state switching mechanism generally produced continuous noise in the 5 kHz – 1 MHz range. Inductive loads with mechanically switched voltages produce noise near 60 Hz, but our data collection apparatus filtered out much of that noise. We thus observed that the analysis of the frequency spectrum may be broken up into two parts. The lower frequency space (100 Hz – 5 kHz) is effective for analysis for transient noise events, such as those produced by wall switches. The higher frequency is better for continuous noise events, such as those produced by TRIACs and switching power supplies. We even observed that dim levels can also be gathered from the continuous noise frequency generated by the TRIACs. For this particular paper, we primarily focus on exploring transient noise events. Similar analysis and learning could be applied to continuous noise events.

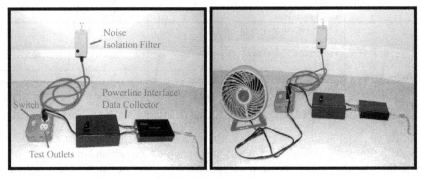

Fig. 7. The setup we constructed for isolating and testing the noise response for various electrical devices on an individual basis

3.5 Detecting and Learning the Signals

Our detection approach requires detection of the transient pulse of electrical noise followed by extraction of relevant features for learning classification.

3.5.1 Detecting Transient Pulses
The filtering hardware in the powerline interface removes most of the high frequency noise. Some broadband noise is always present, but typically at low amplitudes. To detect the transient pulses, we employ a simple sliding window algorithm to look for drastic changes in the input line noise (both beginning and end). These drastic changes, lasting only a few microseconds, are labeled as candidate signals and processed further. The sliding window acquires a 1-microsecond sample, which is averaged from the data acquired after performing the FFT on data from the data acquisition hardware. Each sample consists of frequency components and its associated amplitude values in vector form. Each vector consists of amplitude values for frequency intervals ranging between 0 and 50 kHz. We then compute the

Euclidean distance between the previous vector and the current window's vector. When the distance first exceeds a predetermined threshold value, the start of the transient is marked. The window continues to slide until there is another drastic change in the Euclidean distance (the end of the transient). Although the threshold value was determined through experimentation, we can imagine learning and adapting the thresholds over time.

After having isolated the transient, we are left with N vectors of length L, where N is the pulse width in 1 microsecond increments and L is the number of frequency components (2048 in our case). A new vector of length $L + 1$ is then constructed by averaging the corresponding N values for each frequency components. The $(L + 1)$st value is simply N, the width of the transient. This value then serves as our feature vector for that particular transient.

3.5.2 Learning the Transients

For our learning algorithm, we employed a support vector machine (SVM) [4]. SVMs perform classification by constructing an N-dimensional hyperplane that optimally separates the data into multiple categories. The separation is chosen to have the largest distance from the hyperplane to the nearest positive and negative examples. Thus, the classification is appropriate for testing data that is near, but not identical, to the training data as is the case for the feature vectors for the transients. SVMs are appealing because our feature space is fairly large compared to our potential training set. Because SVMs employ overfitting protection, which does not necessarily depend on the number of features, they have the ability to better handle large feature spaces. The feature vectors are used as the support vectors in the SVM. We used the Weka Toolkit to construct an SVM, using labeled training data to later classify the query points.

4 Feasibility and Performance Evaluation

To evaluate the feasibility and performance of our approach, we tested it in six different homes of varying styles, age, sizes, and locations. We first tested our transient isolation scheme in a single home. Next, we conducted a feasibility study in that home for a six-week period to determine the classification accuracy of various electrical events over an extended period of time. Finally, for the five other homes, we conducted a one-week study to reproduce the results from the first home.

4.1 Transient Isolation Evaluation

To evaluate the feasibility of our automatic transient detection scheme, we collected data from one home for a four-hour period and had our software continuously isolate transient signals. During that period, we actuated various electrical components and made a note of their timestamps. A total of 100 distinct events were generated during this period. For each event, we then determined if a transient was isolated successfully at the noted times. Table 2 shows the results of five different four-hour sessions. We report the percentage of successfully identified transients out of the number of event triggers. We believe the reason for the missed events was because of our static threshold algorithm. An adaptive threshold approach would mitigate this problem.

Table 2. Percentage of successfully identified transient pulses using our transient isolation scheme. Each test lasted for a four-hour period with approximately 100 possible transient events in each period.

Test 1 (% found)	Test 2 (% found)	Test 3 (% found)	Test 4 (% found)	Test 5 (% found)
98	93	91	88	96

4.2 Classifying Transient Events in Various Homes

The aim of our extended 6-week evaluation was to determine the classification accuracy of various types of electrical devices and how often we had to retrain the system (signal stability over time). The other five deployments were used to show that we could detect events similar to those of the initial home and to show that the transient noise signatures were temporally stable in other homes as well. Despite the small number of homes, we tried to test a variety of homes and sizes, including older homes with and without recently updated electrical systems (see Table 3). We also included an apartment home in a six-story building, as we expected its electrical infrastructure to be somewhat different from that of a single family home. We were interested in testing the types of electrical devices listed in Table 1, so we ensured that the homes in which we deployed had most of these devices.

For the entire testing period, we installed our data collection apparatus in the same electrical outlet. For Home 1, we collected and labeled data at least three times per week during the 6-week period. The data collection process involved running our system and toggling various predetermined electrical devices (see Table 1 for examples). For each device toggled, we manually labeled each on-to-off and off-to-on event. In addition, we captured at least two instances of each event during each session. For Home 1, we selected 41 different devices for testing (82 distinct events) and collected approximately 500 instances during each week. Thus, approximately 3000 labeled samples were collected during the 6-week period.

We collected and labeled data in a similar manner for the shorter 1-week deployments. We collected training data at the beginning of the week and collected additional test data at the end of the week. At least 4 instances of each event were gathered for the training set. Because we had control over the events, the number of distinct events were fairly equally distributed among the data and not biased towards a single device or switch for all the 6 homes.

Tables 4 and 5 show classification accuracies for the different homes we tested. For Home 1, we show the classification accuracy of test data gathered at various times during the six weeks using the training set gathered during the first week. The average overall classification accuracy in Home 1 was approximately 85% (Table 4). We also show the accuracy of the classification for varying training set sizes. Because there can potentially be many events of interest in the home, making the training process an arduous task, we wanted to find the minimum number of samples that would provide reasonable performance. The results suggest that there is only a slight decrease in classification over the 6 week period. The results also suggest that a small number of

Table 3. Descriptions of the homes in which our system was deployed. Home 1 is where we conducted the long-term 6 week deployment.

Home	Year Built	Electrical Remodel Year	Floors/ Total Size (Sq Ft)/ (Sq M)	Style	Bedrooms/ Bathrooms/ Total Rms.	Deply. Time (weeks)
1	2003	2003	3/4000/371	1 Family House	4/4/13	6
2	2001	2001	3/5000/464	1 Family House	5/5/17	1
3	1999	1999	1/700/58	1 Bed Apartment	1/1/4	1
4	2002	2002	3/2600/241	1 Family House	3/3/12	1
5	1935	1991	1/1100/102	1 Family House	2/1/7	1
6	1967	1981	1/1500/140	1 Family House	2/1/7	1

Table 4. Performance results of Home 1. The accuracies are reported based on the percentage of correctly identified events. Training happened during Week 1, and we reported the accuracies of the classifier for test data from subsequent weeks using that initial training set from week 1. Overall classification accuracy of a simple majority classifier was 4%.

Training Set Size/Instances per event	SVM accuracies during specific weeks of testing					
	Week 1 (%)	Week 2 (%)	Week 3 (%)	Week 4 (%)	Week 5 (%)	Week 6 (%)
164/2	83	82	81	79	80	79
246/3	86	84	85	84	82	83
328/4	88	91	87	85	86	86
410/5	90	92	91	87	86	87

training instances result in lower classification accuracies. In addition, the majority classifier had accuracies of only about 4% on average, because of the equal distribution of the distinct events in the training and test data,

As reported, increasing the number of training instances did increase the classification accuracy. A small number of training samples makes it very important to have accurate training data. Mislabeling of a single training sample can have major impacts on the learned model. We even caught ourselves accidentally mislabeling a few events. For example, the on and off event labels we noted were sometimes flipped for a particular electrical device. Thus, this highlights the importance of designing a training or calibration scheme that mitigates human error during the training and labeling process.

The results from the one-week deployments in the five other homes are shown in Table 5, and the test data from the end of the week showed promising results. We did not see any significant differences in accuracy between old and new homes. The lower classification accuracy for Home 5 was the result of a low frequency noise that interfered with our transient events. Although we could not find the origin of that noise, we can imagine building a smarter system that learns these erroneous noise events to avoid incorrect classifications.

Table 5. Performance results of various homes. The accuracies are reported based on the percentage of correctly identified toggled light switches or other events in the test data set. The results of a majority classifier are also shown. For each home, the training of the data occurred at the beginning of the week and the test data set was gathered at the end of that week.

Home	Distinct events	Training set (events)	Test set (events)	Accuracy (%)	Majority classif. (%)
2	82	328	100	87	4
3	48	192	96	88	6
4	76	304	103	92	3
5	64	256	94	84	3
6	38	152	80	90	8

5 Discussion of Limitations and Potential Improvements

Although we found promising results with our system, it is not without some limitations and some future considerations. In the current implementation, we purposely analyzed the lower frequency spectrum where solid-state switching devices would produce the lowest interference from potential continuous noise. However, at the same time, this choice limits our feature space. Looking at a larger frequency spectrum could provide better classification for certain transient events. In addition, a fully functional system must be able to detect and to adapt to random noise events when looking for transient pulses. In the future, we plan to improve the feature extraction step. We focused on only the amplitudes of the component frequencies. Phase difference between component frequencies, however, should be considered as part of a feature extraction scheme. In addition, the exploration of other machine learning techniques and application of more domain knowledge of the transient signals may also prove valuable in building a better classifier.

Another consideration is the scaling of our approach. Although unlikely in domestic settings, compound events, such as two lights flipped simultaneously, can produce errors in classification because their combined transient noises produce different feature vectors. This type of event is more of a concern in an extremely large home with many residents or in an apartment building that does not have individually metered units. If users regularly flip light switches nearly simultaneously, this could be trained as a separate event from the individual switches.

We have been primarily focused on domestic environments, but this type of system can also be applied to commercial settings. However, compound events and electrical noise in these settings may become a more significant issue. Another issue is that the electrical lines may be so long that the noise does not reach the analyzer. Commercial buildings typically have multiple electrical legs, and to mitigate problems with compound events and line distance, we could install multiple line noise analyzers throughout an office building to isolate the analysis to certain sections of the building. Our approach will have some difficulty differentiating between individual events among a dense collection of proximal devices that have similar switching and load characteristics. For our approach to scale to these environments, the entire frequency band may needs to be considered. Another drawback of commercial buildings is that they tend to have more noisy components, such as large HVAC systems, connected to the power line that can produce many other transients and mask the pulses of interest..

Our system is more appropriate for detecting and learning fixed electrical devices than mobile devices or portable devices. Though we could support them, portable devices require training the system on any possible outlet that they may be plugged into. In addition, plugging the device into an extension cord or power strip might produce a different fingerprint than plugging it into an electrical outlet directly. With a well-defined set of events that should be detected, a suitable training plan can be devised, but it may become time-consuming as the set grows larger.

In some respects, this system represents a tradeoff between the two categories of systems we mentioned in Section 2. Unlike the first category of prior work, our system does not require the deployment of a large number of sensing units throughout the home. A single data collection module is certainly easier to physically deploy and maintain than a large array of distributed sensors, though one could argue that a single point of failure has been introduced (*e.g.,* what if someone accidentally unplugs the data collection module?). On the other hand, this simplicity of physical installation and maintenance has its cost in terms of training the machine learning algorithm to recognize a significant number of electrical loads. The appropriateness of this tradeoff is thus expected to be application dependent.

6 Conclusion

We presented an approach for a low-cost and easy-to-install powerline event detection system that is capable of identifying certain electrical events, such as switches that are toggled. This system has implications for applications seeking simple activity detection, home automation systems, and energy usage information. We showed how our system learns and classifies unique electrical events with high accuracy using standard machine learning techniques. Additionally, a deployment of our system in several homes showed long-term stability and the ability to detect events in a variety of different types of homes. We also discussed specific events our system can detect and which events may have problems when used for specific applications. Our system has the potential to be integrated easily into existing applications that aim to provide services based on detection of various levels of activity.

Acknowledgments

This work is sponsored in part by the National Science Foundation Graduate Fellowship and the Intel Research Council. The authors would also like to thank the members of the Ubicomp Research Group and Sooraj Bhat at Georgia Tech.

References

1. ADT QuietCare, (2007) http://www.adt.com/quietcare/
2. Bian, X., Abowd, G.D., Rehg, J.M.: Using Sound Source Localization in a Home Environment. In: Proc of the International Conference on Pervasive Computing (2005)
3. Beckmann, C., Consolvo, S., LaMarca, A.: Some Assembly Required: Supporting End-User Sensor Installation in Domestic Ubiquitous Computing Environments. In: Davies, N., Mynatt, E.D., Siio, I. (eds.) UbiComp 2004. LNCS, vol. 3205, pp. 107–124. Springer, Heidelberg (2004)

4. Burges, C.J.C.: A Tutorial on Support Vector Machines for Pattern Recognition. Journal of Data Mining and Knowledge Discovery 2(2) (June 1998)
5. Chen, J., Kam, A.H., Zhang, J., Liu, N., Shue, L.: Bathroom Activity Monitoring Based on Sound. In: Gellersen, H.-W., Want, R., Schmidt, A. (eds.) PERVASIVE 2005. LNCS, vol. 3468, pp. 47–61. Springer, Heidelberg (2005)
6. Fogarty, J., Au, C., Hudson, S.E.: Sensing from the Basement: A Feasibility Study of Unobtrusive and Low-Cost Home Activity Recognition. In: The Proc of ACM Symposium on User Interface Software and Technology (UIST 2006), ACM Press, New York (2006)
7. Hirsch, T., Forlizzi, J., Hyder, E., Goetz, J., Kurtz, C., Stroback, J.: The ELDer Project: Social, Emotional, and Environmental Factors in the Design of Eldercare Technologies. In: Proc of the ACM Conference on Universal Usability, pp. 72–79 (2000)
8. Howell, E.K.: How Switches Produce Electrical Noise. IEEE Transactions on Electromagnetic Compatibility 21(3), 162–170 (1979)
9. Iachello, G., Abowd, G.D.: Privacy and Proportionality: Adapting Legal Evaluation Techniques to Inform Design In Ubiquitous Computing. In: the Proc of CHI 2005, pp. 91–100 (2005)
10. Koile, K., Tollmar, K., Demirdjian, D., Howard, S., Trevor, D.: Activity Zones for Context-Aware Computing. In: Dey, A.K., Schmidt, A., McCarthy, J.F. (eds.) UbiComp 2003. LNCS, vol. 2864, Springer, Heidelberg (2003)
11. Marubayashi, G.: Noise Measurements of the Residential Power Line. In: The Proceedings of International Symposium on Power Line Communications and Its Applications, pp. 104–108 (1997)
12. Paradiso, J.A.: Some Novel Applications for Wireless Inertial Sensors. In: Proc of NSTI Nanotech 2006, Boston, MA, May 7-11, 2006, vol. 3, pp. 431–434 (2006)
13. Patel, S.N., Truong, K.N., Abowd, G.D.: PowerLine Positioning: A Practical Sub-Room-Level Indoor Location System for Domestic Use. In: The Proceedings of Ubicomp (2006)
14. Rowan, J., Mynatt, E.D.: Digital Family Portrait Field Trial: Support for Aging in Place. In: Proc of the ACM Conference on Human Factors in Computing Systems (CHI 2005), pp. 521–530. ACM Press, New York (2005)
15. Tapia, E.M., Intille, S.S., Larson, K.: Activity recognition in the home setting using simple and ubiquitous sensors. In: Ferscha, A., Mattern, F. (eds.) PERVASIVE 2004. LNCS, vol. 3001, pp. 158–175. Springer, Heidelberg (2004)
16. Tapia, E.M., Intille, S.S., Lopez, L., Larson, K.: The design of a portable kit of wireless sensors for naturalistic data collection. In: Fishkin, K.P., Schiele, B., Nixon, P., Quigley, A. (eds.) PERVASIVE 2006. LNCS, vol. 3968, pp. 117–134. Springer, Heidelberg (2006)
17. Weka. Weka 3: Data Mining Software in Java (2007), http://www.cs.waikato.ac.nz/ml/weka/
18. Wilson, D.H., Atkeson, C.G.: Simultaneous Tracking and Activity Recognition (STAR) Using Many Anonymous, Binary Sensors. In: Gellersen, H.-W., Want, R., Schmidt, A. (eds.) PERVASIVE 2005. LNCS, vol. 3468, pp. 62–79. Springer, Heidelberg (2005)

An 'Object-Use Fingerprint': The Use of Electronic Sensors for Human Identification

Mark R. Hodges and Martha E. Pollack

Computer Science and Engineering
University of Michigan, Ann Arbor, MI, USA
{hodgesm,pollackm}@umich.edu

Abstract. We describe an experiment in using sensor-based data to identify individuals as they perform a simple activity of daily living (making coffee). The goal is to determine whether people have regular and recognizable patterns of interaction with objects as they perform such activities. We describe the use of a machine-learning algorithm to induce decision-trees that classify interaction patterns according to the subject who exhibited them; we consider which features of the sensor data have the most effect on classification accuracy; and we consider ways of reducing the computational complexity introduced by the most important feature type. Although our experiment is preliminary, the results are encouraging: we are able to do identification with an overall accuracy rate of 97%, including correctly recognizing each individual in at least 9 of 10 trials.

1 Introduction

A body of recent work has focused on the use of sensors to recognize the performance of particular human activities [1,2,3,4,5,6]. This paper describes work that also uses sensors to monitor human activity, but towards a different end: our goal is to identify individuals from their behavior. More specifically, we seek to determine whether individual people have regular and recognizable patterns of interaction with the objects they use in performing daily activities and whether these patterns create an "object-use fingerprint" that can be used for human identification.

The primary motivation for this work is a scientific one: it is interesting in its own right to know whether people interact in regular ways with objects and, if so, what these regularities are. However, there are also potential pratical implications of the work. As one example, imagine wanting to gather information about the use of various devices (a new model refridgerator or a newly designed copy machine, for instance). One way to do this would be to place the device in an open area (an office kitchen or mailroom) and gather data as multiple people interact with the device. If people indeed have "object-use fingerprints," then it should be possible to distinguish amongst different users in the collected data without having to actually identify who those users are.

J. Krumm et al. (Eds.): UbiComp 2007, LNCS 4717, pp. 289–303, 2007.

A second motivation for this work comes from our long-term goal of employing sensor-based activity monitoring to track the performance of individuals at risk for cognitive decline, so as to detect changes that may indicate a change in cognitive status. As a preliminary step, we sought to determine the degree to which people behave in regular and predictable ways while performing common activities. Of course, the existence of identifiable patterns of object use by individuals is by itself neither necessary nor sufficient for our larger goal. However, we feel that establishing that individuals have some degree of regularity in their object-use patterns makes it more likely that one can observe trends of deviation from those regularities, and in turn, learn deviations that may indicate cognitive decline.

To test our hypothesis–that individuals have "object-use fingerprints," making it possible to identify them on the basis of the way in which they interact with objects during the performance of routine daily activities–we conducted a series of experiments in a controlled laboratory setting. Specifically, we had individuals wear an RFID reader affixed to a glove while they made coffee in a kitchen in which objects were instrumented with RFID tags. We then applied machine-learning techniques to classify interaction patterns. Key research questions included determining the features of the activity that were most predictive of an individual's identity, analyzing the computational time required for the learning algorithm to process each type of feature, and developing strategies for reducing reliance on the most computationally expensive features. This was an initial investigation with a number of simplifying assumptions that we describe in section 3.4. Our results are therefore preliminary but encouraging nonetheless.

The next section briefly reviews prior work on sensor-based activity recognition. Section 3 discusses the methodology of our experiment, including the selection of the task, selection of the sensing technology, the experimental setup, and the limitations of the experiment. Section 4 describes the machine-learning techniques used to analyze the collected data. Section 5 presents the experimental results, which are then discussed in Section 6, which also presents avenues for future research.

2 Background

Automated activity recognition encompasses techniques using different types of sensors that detect activities at a wide range of granularity. One approach is to use a few extremely data-rich sensors such as video cameras or microphones. For example, Ben-Arie, et al. employ video cameras to distinguish among eight basic actions including jumping, walking, and picking an object up [7]. For many potential applications, however, data-rich sensors, and especially video cameras, may be problematic, in part because they have been shown to provoke strong privacy concerns [8].

A contrasting approach is to use a large number of very basic sensors that each capture only limited information. Accelerometers and other related sensors that are worn by individuals may be used to differentiate actions. For instance, Bao and Intille used five biaxial accelerometers, positioned at key places on subjects' bodies, to identify with high accuracy an activity from among twenty types of activities including vacuuming, reading, and watching TV. Their description of this work also provide a good overview of past work in activity recognition using accelerometers [9]. Wren and Tapia use motion detectors and hierarchical learning to recognize actions in a work environment such as walking in straight line, turning, and "joining" (coming into the same geographic region as another person) [6]. Liao et al. take an different approach and use GPS and Relational Markov Networks to recognize the locations of activities such as "home," "work," and "shop" [2,10].

The use of RFID readers as a device for recgonizing activities has also become popular. What is intersting about this approach is that it focuses on recognizing the objects with which a person interacts, rather than on monitoring the person's movements directly. Thus, Philipose and his colleagues have subjects wear a glove or bracelet with an attached RFID reader, which can sense objects in the environment that have RFID tags affixed to them [3,4,8]. Their sensing technology–an RFID reader worn on the hand–served as the inspiration for the RFID glove used in this paper. Tapia et al. also use RFID technology and naive Bayesian classifiers to perform in-home activity recognition [5].

The work just described has all addressed the question of identifying an activity, not of identifying a person. To the best of our knowledge, there has not been work done on identifying individuals based on their object-interaction patterns. However, prior work has been done on identification of individuals using other biometrics. Keystroke dynamics have been studied as a way to provide additional computer security, with a particular focus on using keystroke dynamics to harden password security. Peacock provides a good overview of the work in this area [11]. Vision-based identification techniques have also garnered significant interest to supplement the physical security of environments such as airports and banks. These efforts have focused mainly on gait recognition, which uses patterns of movement for identification [12], as well as on automatic face recognition using a photograph or a series of photographs to identify individuals [13].

3   Methodology

3.1   Selection of Task

Several criteria were used in the selection of a task for subjects to perform. Most obviously, we sought a task that was an activity of daily living, and was one that that is performed by many people on a regular basis. In addition, an ideal task would be relatively constrained in terms of the ways in which it might be performed, but would also have some natural variance in performance (not as broad as "prepare dinner," but not so narrow as "pour a glass of milk"). Finally, it should be possible to perform the task in an instrumented laboratory. The task of making a cup of coffee was chosen for this experiment since it is an excellent fit for all of these criteria.

3.2   Selection of Technology

As noted earlier, Radio Frequency Identifier (RFID) technology has been used successfully in several activity recognition projects and we thus chose to use it here as well. RFID equipment consists of tags, which can be placed throughout an environment, and readers which detect nearby tags. A key advantage of this type of sensing is that RFID has a 0% false positive rate. In addition, tags are inexpensive (less than US$0.20) and small in size (approximately the size of a postage stamp). There are two types of RFID tags, active and passive. Active tags are extremely accurate but require a power source. Passive tags, on the other hand, are not detected as reliably, but do not require a power source, instead harvesting energy from the reader to sense and communicate [14]. For this reason, they can be placed throughout an environment without a need for cords or batteries that will need to be replaced.

In earlier work done at Intel laboratories, an RFID reader placed on a glove or bracelet was used to detect detect tags that are in close proximity to the hand (within 10cm) [15,3,4,8,16]; detected objects are assumed to be ones with which the user is interacting. This form factor also has added value with regards to privacy. If a user wishes to prevent the system from observing her, she may simply remove the glove or bracelet containing the RFID reader. In addition, the short range of the reader makes it possible to observe fine-grained patterns in the way the object is held, i.e. whether an object is held from the side or from the bottom. This information is potentially valuable in identifying people from the object interactions. Because Intel's wireless iBracelet was not available in time for use in this study, a wired system was used, consisting of an off-the-shelf RFID reader and tags created by Phidgets, Inc. ®.

The sensor glove is depicted in Fig. 1 (l), while one of the tagged objects-a coffee grinder-is shown in Fig. 1 (r). Obviously, the glove as used in the experiment would not be appropriate for actual use in a home setting–and not only because of the attached wire! Nonetheless, it was satisfactory for collecting the data we needed for these experiments.

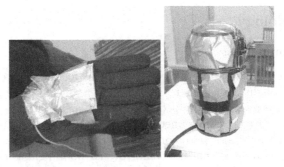

Fig. 1. (l) The glove with an RFID reader attached. (r) The coffee grinder with several RFID tags attached.

3.3   Experimental Setup

Ten subjects were recruited to participate in the experiments. For each trial, the subject was instructed to make a cup of coffee as if about to drink it, including adding sugar and creamer as preferred. Subjects wore a glove outfitted with an RFID reader on their right hand, but were told to ignore it as best they could and use both hands as they typically would. Each subject participated in ten trials, spaced out with generally at most one per day, so that the trials would reflect normal patterns of use, rather than artificial patterns created by performing trials repeatedly one after another[1].

Subjects were given a brief tour of the instrumented lab before their first trial, and those who did not know how to make coffee were given basic instructions. These instructions were as general as possible. For example, subjects were told to "put water in the reservoir at the back of the coffee-maker," rather than indicating exactly how the water should be put there, so they would choose for themselves whether to use the coffee cup or coffee carafe to transport the water from the sink. No physical demonstration of the coffee-making process was given.

The experimental set-up consisted of a coffee maker, one cup, one spoon, a coffee bean grinder, and a cabinet containing a bag of filters, a bag of coffee grounds, a bag of coffee beans, and a canister each of cream and sugar. Each item was tagged with multiple RFID tags and before each trial was put in the same place, facing the same direction. (The bag of filters did not have an obvious front and thus may have been reversed between trials).

3.4   Experimental Limitations

This study is an initial investigation and, as such, had a number of design simplifications. Possibly most significantly, the task was performed in a controlled setting–our laboratory–rather than in a naturally occurring environment. The environment was very regular, so that each time a subject began a task, all the objects he or she might use were in the same location and aligned in the same direction, without the natural variation that would occur in a real-world setting, especially in an environment shared by several users. The users performed only a single task–making coffee–and this task was not interleaved with other tasks nor was it interrupted by outside influences or distractions such as a ringing telephone. Finally, the problem of segmenting tasks was avoided by starting the trial immediately before the task began and stopping it immediately after the task was finished.

There is no question that these limitations may affect the generality of the results. Nonetheless, we believe that the results of our preliminary study, as presented below, are encouraging enough to support follow-on work that would determine their generality.

---

[1] In some cases, the availability of the subject required more than one trial per day; five subjects performed two trials on the same day at least once and one of those performed six trials on the last day of the subject's availability.

4   Machine Learning Approach

The data collected by the sensors during each subject's performance of the coffee-making task was input to a machine-learning algorithm for classification. We used a decision-tree induction algorithm for this purpose, primarily because it is the simplest form of classification algorithm and thus provided a reasonable starting point for our investigation. A decision tree is a classifier, taking a set of properties as input and outputting a "decision" by following paths on a tree, starting at the root and working to a leaf node. Internal nodes in this tree are a test of the value of a property, and the branches from that node represent the possible values of the test. The leaf node is the decision reached by the tree. In our study, we used the C4.5 decision-tree induction system, which is based on the ID3 algorithm. C4.5 particularly attempts to avoid overfitting, the condition where an overly complex tree is created that is less accurate than a simpler one would be [17].

A key question then is what features of the sensor data should be used as input to the classifier. We investigated two types of features for sensor data: observation granularity and interaction measure.

Observation granularity has to do with how abstract our observations are: do we need to provide information to the machine learning algorithm about the fact that a subject touched the coffeepot or the fact that she touched the left side of the lid (or both)? Many of the objects used in the study had multiple tags affixed to them, and we thus considered observations of interactions at three layers of abstraction:

1. Tag: Detected interaction with an individual tag affixed to an object;
2. Group: Detected interaction with any of a group of tags that are equivalent except for the orientation of the object (e.g., the tag on the left side of the coffee grounds and the tag on the right); and
3. Object: Detected interaction with an object (e.g., with any of the tags that are affixed to the coffeepot).

Table 1 shows the objects we used, and the tag groups associated with each object. Note that for some objects, like the mug, there is only one tag, so the tag, group, and object are all the same.

Independent of the level of abstraction, there are also different ways in which we can measure interactions; we explored five types of features that measure interactions, applying them to each of the levels of granularity:

1. Detected: A binary feature that is positive iff there was any interaction with a tag, group, or object.
2. Count: A scalar feature that records the number of interactions with a tag, group, or object.
3. Total Duration: A scalar feature that records the total amount of time of interaction with a tag, group, or object.

Table 1. List of Tag Groups and Objects

Objects	Groups
Coffee Maker	Lid, power switch
Carafe	Carafe
Mug	Mug
Spoon	Spoon
Coffee Grinder	Top row of tags, middle row, bottom row
Left Cabinet Door	Left cabinet door
Right Cabinet Door	Right cabinet door
Coffee Grounds	Top tags on front and back, bottom tags on front and back, tag on bottom, tags on sides
Coffee Beans	Top tags on front and back, bottom tags on front and back, tag on bottom, tags on sides
Filters	Tags on sides, tag on bottom
Creamer	Tags on top row, tags on bottom row
Sugar	Tags on top row, tags on bottom row
Faucet	Faucet

4. Average Duration: A scalar feature representing the average time of interaction with a tag, group, or object: this is a computed feature, equal to Total Duration divided by Count.
5. Order: A binary feature that is positive iff an arbitrary two- or three-tag, group, or object ordering is observed.

The order feature deserves a little more explanation. It determines whether a specific ordering of interactions is observed in a trial. This ordering may consist of two or three tags, groups, or objects, but within a specific ordering only one level of granularity is used. Because there are 70 tags, 25 groups, and 13 objects in the experiment, over 300,000 possible orderings exist. As a result, considering all possible orderings of tags comes at a significant cost in performance. This performance cost will be discussed further in Sections 5 and 6.

Although the RFID reader and tag system provides accurate and generally reliable results, an individual tag is sometimes found and lost in quick succession, either when it is near the maximum distance from the reader at which it can be sensed, or if the reader moves rapidly. In order to smooth the data, a pre-processing step can be performed on each trial prior to analysis. The pre-processing step looks for consecutive accesses of the same tag, group, or object within 0.5 seconds. When this is found, the records of the two accesses are merged into one, hopefully providing a more accurate model of the subject's actual behavior. This means that when a subject quickly draws her hand away from a tag and then puts her hand back on the tag, the action will be interpreted as one continuous interaction, and that when a subject moves her hand over several tags on the same object, the action will be interpreted as one continuous interaction at the object level (analysis on the tag feature level will not be impacted in this case). In Section 5.5 we describe the effect of this pre-processing.

We performed one additional type of pre-processing on the collected data. The task of making coffee was selected in part due to the natural variation in how people perform the task. Although more obvious indicators, such as whether people put cream or sugar in their coffee, might be considered valid differences in behavior, it is a more interesting question to ask if an individual can be determined without that information. For that reason, in most of our analyses, we removed from the data all information about cream and sugar tags. (We indicate places where this is not true.) Similarly, a subject's choice of grinding whole beans verses using grounds can be used to distinguish amongst subjects. Because removing information from the tags for the grounds, beans, and grinder from the trial would remove one-fifth of the data collected, we simply note that only one user used whole beans, and that user used whole beans in every trial. For that reason, one of the ten users can be distinguished very easily from the others.

By using ten subjects who each perform ten trials, we obtained 100 cases for analysis. We used a ten-fold cross-validation process, repeatedly using 90 of the trials as training data for C4.5 and reserving the remaining 10 trials as test data. In each iteration, the training data contained 9 trials for each subject, with the tenth reserved for testing data; however, our learning system did not use the information that there is exactly one trial per subject during the classification process.

5   Results

5.1   Full Feature Set

We begin by describing the results obtained when C4.5 is run using the full set of 15 features (5 feature types, applied to each of the three layers of abstraction) and including the cream and sugar information. In this case, the system is extremely accurate, correctly recognizing the subject in 97 of the 100 trials (again, under a 10-fold cross validation experiment). Two of the incorrectly-recognized trials were performed by the same subject, meaning that the system correctly identified at least 8 of each user's 10 trials. 8 of the 10 users were identified accurately in all 10 of their trials, with the remaining participant correctly identified in 9 of the 10 trials. Table 2 shows the confusion matrix for this feature set.

The ten decision trees produced here have an average of 10.8 internal nodes and an average maximum depth of 7.3. Well over half the internal nodes consider order features and every observation granularity appears in at least one tree, while count is the only interaction measure that does not appear in any of the trees. Figure 2 shows one of the trees produced. In this case, all but one of the ten internal nodes use order.

Perhaps surprisingly, the system has the same accuracy when using the full set of 15 features, but now ignoring the use of cream and sugar, with the subjects again being correctly identified in 97 of the 100 trials. In this case, all three of the incorrectly identified trials were from different users, meaning three users were each recognized correctly in 9 of their 10 trials, and the other seven were

Table 2. Confusion matrix of full feature set using cream and sugar

Truth	Inferred Identity									
	A	B	C	D	E	F	G	H	I	J
A	10									
B		10								
C			10							
D				10						
E				1	9					
F	1			1		8				
G							10			
H								10		
I									10	
J										10

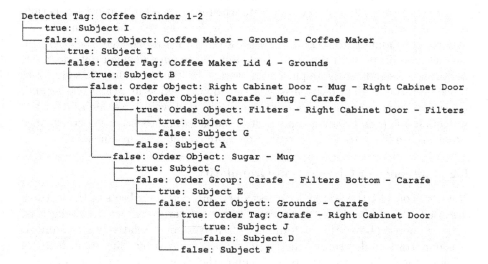

```
Detected Tag: Coffee Grinder 1-2
├── true: Subject I
└── false: Order Object: Coffee Maker - Grounds - Coffee Maker
    ├── true: Subject I
    └── false: Order Tag: Coffee Maker Lid 4 - Grounds
        ├── true: Subject B
        └── false: Order Object: Right Cabinet Door - Mug - Right Cabinet Door
            ├── true: Order Object: Carafe - Mug - Carafe
            │   ├── true: Order Object: Filters - Right Cabinet Door - Filters
            │   │   ├── true: Subject C
            │   │   └── false: Subject G
            │   └── false: Subject A
            └── false: Order Object: Sugar - Mug
                ├── true: Subject C
                └── false: Order Group: Carafe - Filters Bottom - Carafe
                    ├── true: Subject E
                    └── false: Order Object: Grounds - Carafe
                        ├── true: Order Tag: Carafe - Right Cabinet Door
                        │   ├── true: Subject J
                        │   └── false: Subject D
                        └── false: Subject F
```

Fig. 2. One of the decision trees produced with the full feature set using cream and sugar

recognized in all of their trials. The confusion matrix for this feature set is given in Table 3. We hypothesize that the sugar and cream did not improve performance because of a ceiling effect: classification was so high (97%) even without the specific information about sugar and cream that there was no room for improvement.

The ten trees produced here are slightly larger and slightly deeper than those produced when cream and sugar is considered. They have an average of 12.2 internal nodes and an average maximum depth of 7.8. Again, well over half the internal nodes consider order features, and in this case every type of interaction measure is used in at least one tree as is every observation granularity.

Table 3. Confusion matrix of full feature set without cream and sugar

	Inferred Identity									
Truth	A	B	C	D	E	F	G	H	I	J
A	10									
B		10								
C			10							
D				10						
E					9					1
F				1		9				
G							10			
H	1							9		
I									10	
J										10

Although the system is very accurate when using the full feature set, performance is not ideal. With the cream and sugar data deleted, the system takes an average of 8 minutes to compute the features and learn one tree, then perform subject identification for ten trials. Including the cream and sugar data degrades performance significantly, requiring an average of 40 minutes for the same task. Since performing identification is still very quick, taking less than one second, this performance may be considered acceptable. However, as we describe further in section 5.4, even learning time must be bounded; moreover, the performance problems are likely to be exacerbated by more complex environments.

5.2 Influence of Observation Granularity

Next, we consider the system's success when only certain subsets of the features are used in the identification process. There are three reasons for doing this. First, as noted above, the performance of the system is relatively slow, and so it is important to determine whether it can be improved by using fewer features without sacrificing accuracy. In particular, there are a huge number of order features, so it is valuable to understand their impact on performance. Second, it is useful to know if the number of tags in the environment can be reduced, both for aesthetic reasons and so that we can anticipate the effects of tags falling off during use. Third, the time spent identifying groups and objects may not be necessary if performance does not degrade when only tag-level features are used.

To begin, we consider the influence of features at different layers of abstraction; the results are shown in Table 4, which provides the accuracy of the system in performing subject identification when using only tag-level observations, group-level observations, and object-level observations. In this analysis we make use of all interaction measures, and we delete the cream and sugar data.

As can be seen, when we restrict the algorithm to object-level data, accuracy is essentially unchanged from that using the full feature set, but it degrades noticeably when using only tag or group level observations. Interestingly, this is due primarily to the inability of the system to classify a particular subject

Table 4. Comparison of feature levels

Observation Granularity	Accuracy
Tag	87%
Group	88%
Object	97%

(subject F). Using only interactions at the tag level, the system correctly identifies that subject only once, while using interaction at the group level it correctly identifies the same subject just twice. That subject's other trials at the tag and group level are all misidentified as subject D, indicating that those two may be very difficult to distinguish (although subject D is never misidentified). The accuracy of both feature sets on the other subjects remains very high at 95.6%.

5.3   Influence of Interaction Measure

We next consider the importance of each of the types of interaction measures; again, in all our analyses here, we omit the cream and sugar data. Table 5 gives the results, showing both the overall accuracy when using only a single interaction measure, and a list of subjects who were correctly identified in 5 or fewer of their 10 trials.

Table 5. Comparison of individual features

Interaction Measure	Accuracy	Subjects Correctly Identified in ≤ 5 Trials
Accuracy Detected	73%	A, C, E, J
# of Times Detected	75%	A, C, E
Total Duration	85%	F
Average Duration	72%	E, F, H
Order	93%	

Most single interaction measures result in difficulty in identifying some subjects, but no problems in identifying others. Subject F, the one consistently misidentified in the tag and group feature sets, is never identified correctly in the Total Duration feature set, and only once in the Average Duration feature set. However, the same subject is correctly identified 9 of 10 times in the # of Times Detected feature set, 8 of 10 times in the Detected feature set, and every time in the Order feature set.

5.4   "All But Order"

As described in section 5.1, the time to learn one tree and perform subject identification for ten trials can take up to forty minutes. Because the actual identification is still performed in under one second, this performance may be considered acceptable since computing the features and learning the tree would not need to happen in real time. However, even learning time must be bounded; moreover, the performance problems are likely to be exacerbated by more complex environments. Observing subjects performing larger and more complex tasks may require several times as many sensors as were used in this experiment. Additionally, allowing a user to interleave actions from multiple tasks may prevent a system from simplifying the learning process by only considering the sensors relevant to a single task.

While the number of features computed for other interaction measures grow linearly, order undergoes cubic growth since using order involves generating and considering a large number of possible two- and three-step sequences. We thus repeated the analysis, using the full feature set except for the order features. This analysis is also important to answering the question of what features are important in performing identification.

As expected, processing time decreases significantly in this case: it takes, on average, less than five seconds to learn one tree and perform identification ten times, a speed up of two orders of magnitude from the eight minutes needed when all features are considered. Unfortunately accuracy also decreases, as shown in Table 6 (which again omits the cream and sugar data). Subjects correctly identified in 5 or fewer of their 10 trials are also listed, and again we see that specific subjects are consistently misidentified while the others are identified with high accuracy.

Table 6. Comparison of 'all but order' feature sets

Observation Granularity	Accuracy	Subjects Correctly Identified in $\leq$ 5 Trials
All Levels	86%	D, E
Tag	86%	D, E
Group	80%	D, E
Object	80%	E, H

The removal of the order features results in a pattern of observation granularity that is the inverse of that seen when order features are included: now the use of only object-level observations produces the lowest, rather than the highest level of accuracy, suggesting that there is an important interaction between order and object-level observations.

5.5   The Influence of Pre-processing

A final analysis concerns the pre-processing step that we described earlier to smooth the data by combining consecutive interactions that take place with the same tag, group, or object in rapid succession. The results are shown in Table 7 (again, cream and sugar deleted).

In turns out that our pre-processing technique does not have the intended effect: in some cases it decreases accuracy slightly, and it only increases accuracy when we look just at average duration. Because consecutive usage of the

Table 7. Effects of pre-processing

Interaction Measure	Accuracy Before Pre-Processing	Accuracy After Pre-Processing
All Features	97%	95%
Detected	73%	73%
# of Times Detected	75%	76%
Total Duration	85%	81%
Average Duration	72%	81%
Order	93%	93%

same item should not affect the Detected or Order features, their accuracy, by definition, remains unchanged. The increased accuracy of average duration is expected because it is the feature most affected by the rapid finding and losing of a tag. The decreased accuracy of total duration is a surprise, however, since using pre-processing should increase how accurately duration is measured by filling gaps in detected usage that are probably not gaps in actual usage. We are uncertain at this time as to how to explain that result.

6   Discussion

The motivation for this work was to determine whether individuals have predictable object-use patterns as they carry out activities of daily living, and to determine whether these patterns could be used for identification. Although the experiment presented here is preliminary, in that it only involves 10 subjects and the performance of a single type of task in a controlled environment, it is nonetheless promising in suggesting the existence of such regularities. There are no subjects that the machine learning algorithm has trouble identifying with the best-performing feature sets. Additionally, there are no trials that are misidentified by all four of the best feature sets. However, when the computationally costly order features are omitted, the level of accuracy varies with subjects. Thus, a challenge for future research is to automatically learn which features sets are best at identifying the regularities of a given individual's behavior.

One way to address this challenge would be to reduce the number of order features required. In general, the number of possible orderings grows quickly with the number of items (tags, groups, or objects), ($O(n^3)$). However, only a small subset of these orderings are important to subject identification. Thus, rather than include all or none of the possible orderings as input to the machine-learning algorithm, the application of domain-specific knowledge to identify interesting orderings may be viable. In the trials run with every feature at every feature level and ignoring cream and sugar, order was used an average of 8.4 times per tree (84 times total). Several orderings were used multiple times, though, including one that was used 9 different times and there were only 35 unique orderings used. If one were able to identify most of these "relevant" orderings, then classification time could be significantly reduced without a penalty in accuracy.

Finally, we note that the use of object-level observations provided the highest accuracy of the three layers of abstractions, but every individual interaction measure except order performed better using tag-level observations. This suggests the added resolution of using a large number of short-range tags may be more beneficial than placing a smaller number of longer-range tags on each object. It also implies much of the benefit of using order can be gained by just considering order at the object-level, and this may also greatly reduce the computational costs of processing. In addition, the process of identifying relevant orderings may be simplified by focusing on those that occur at the object level.

A key area for future work involves replicating the experiment described here on more and different types of subjects, on a broader range of activities, and in naturalistic settings, so as to validate the generality of our preliminary results.

References

1. Barger, T., Alwan, M., Kell, S., Turner, B., Wood, S., Naidu, A.: Objective remote assessment of activities of daily living: Analysis of meal preparation patterns (poster presentation)
2. Liao, L., Fox, D., Kautz, H.: Location-based activity recognition. In: Weiss, Y., Schölkopf, B., Platt, J. (eds.) Advances in Neural Information Processing Systems 18, pp. 787–794. MIT Press, Cambridge, MA (2006)
3. Patterson, D.J., Fox, D., Kautz, H., Philipose, M.: Fine-grained activity recognition by aggregating abstract object usage. In: Gil, Y., Motta, E., Benjamins, V.R., Musen, M.A. (eds.) ISWC 2005. LNCS, vol. 3729, pp. 44–51. Springer, Heidelberg (2005)
4. Philipose, M., Fishkin, K.P., Perkowitz, M., Patterson, D.J., Fox, D., Kautz, H., Hahnel, D.: Inferring activities from interactions with objects. IEEE Pervasive Computing 3(4), 50–57 (2004)
5. Tapia, E.M., Intille, S.S., Larson, K.: Activity recognition in the home using simple and ubiquitous sensors. In: Ferscha, A., Mattern, F. (eds.) PERVASIVE 2004. LNCS, vol. 3001, pp. 158–175. Springer, Heidelberg (2004)
6. Wren, C.R., Tapia, E.M.: Toward scalable activity recognition for sensor networks. In: Hazas, M., Krumm, J., Strang, T. (eds.) LoCA 2006. LNCS, vol. 3987, pp. 168–185. Springer, Heidelberg (2006)
7. Ben-Arie, J., Wang, Z., Pandit, P., Rajaram, S.: Human activity recognition using multidimensional indexing. IEEE Trans. Pattern Anal. Mach. Intell. 24(8), 1091–1104 (2002)
8. Fishkin, K.P., Philipose, M., Rea, A.: Hands-on rfid: Wireless wearables for detecting use of objects. In: ISWC 2005, pp. 38–43. IEEE Computer Society, Los Alamitos (2005)
9. Bao, L., Intille, S.S.: Activity recognition from user-annotated acceleration data. In: Ferscha, A., Mattern, F. (eds.) PERVASIVE 2004. LNCS, vol. 3001, pp. 1–17. Springer, Heidelberg (2004)
10. Patterson, D.J., Liao, L., Gajos, K., Collier, M., Livic, N., Olson, K., Wang, S., Fox, D., Kautz, H.A.: Opportunity knocks: A system to provide cognitive assistance with transportation services. In: Davies, N., Mynatt, E.D., Siio, I. (eds.) UbiComp 2004. LNCS, vol. 3205, pp. 433–450. Springer, Heidelberg (2004)
11. Peacock, A., Ke, X., Wilkerson, M.: Typing patterns: A key to user identification. IEEE Security and Privacy 2(5), 40–47 (2004)

12. Wang, L., Tan, T., Ning, H., Hu, W.: Silhouette analysis-based gait recognition for human identification. IEEE Trans. Pattern Anal. Mach. Intell. 25(12), 1505–1518 (2003)
13. Arandjelovic, O., Shakhnarovich, G., Fisher, J., Cipolla, R., Darrell, T.: Face recognition with image sets using manifold density divergence. In: CVPR '05: Proceedings of the 2005 IEEE Computer Society Conference on Computer Vision and Pattern Recognition (CVPR'05), vol. 1, pp. 581–588. IEEE Computer Society Press, Washington (2005)
14. Finkenzeller, K.: RFID Handbook: Fundamentals and Applications in Contactless Smart Cards and Identification. John Wiley & Sons, Inc., New York, NY, USA (2003)
15. Fishkin, K.P., Jiang, B., Philipose, M., Roy, S.: I sense a disturbance in the force: Unobtrusive detection of interactions with rfid-tagged objects. In: Davies, N., Mynatt, E.D., Siio, I. (eds.) UbiComp 2004. LNCS, vol. 3205, pp. 268–282. Springer, Heidelberg (2004)
16. Smith, J.R., Fishkin, K.P., Jiang, B., Mamishev, A., Philipose, M., Rea, A.D., Roy, S., Sundara-Rajan, K.: Rfid-based techniques for human-activity detection. Commun. ACM 48(9), 39–44 (2005)
17. Quinlan, J.R.: C4.5: Programs for Machine Learning. Morgan Kaufmann, San Francisco (1993)

Key Generation Based on Acceleration Data of Shaking Processes

Daniel Bichler[1], Guido Stromberg[1], Mario Huemer[2], and Manuel Löw[1]

[1] Infineon Technologies AG, Germany
`firstname.surname@infineon.com`
[2] University of Klagenfurt, Austria
`mario.huemer@uni-klu.ac.at`

Abstract. Hard restrictions in computing power and energy consumption favour symmetric key methods to encrypt the communication in wireless body area networks which in term impose questions on effective and user-friendly unobtrusive ways for key distribution. In this paper, we present a novel approach to establish a secure connection between two devices by shaking them together. Instead of distributing or exchanging a key, the devices independently generate a key from the measured acceleration data by appropriate signal processing methods. Exhaustive practical experiments based on acceleration data gathered from real hardware prototypes have shown that in about 80% of the cases, a common key can be successfully generated. The average entropy of these generated keys exceed 13bits.

1   Introduction

Security and privacy are key issues in pervasive network environments. Despite their importance, security and privacy need to be implemented without confining the usability of the networked devices. This is particularly true, since at least conceptually, the number of devices is high, and many applications require a secure connection between dedicated devices instead of trusted zones in which many devices share a common key. However, the level of security and privacy in pervasive applications varies largely and depends highly on the application [1]. A further restriction arises because most devices in such applications are small, battery powered, and have little computational power so that complex algorithms for encryption or key exchange such as public and private key methods are infeasible [2]. Thus, we constrain our discussion to systems that rely on symmetric encryption methods. In these systems, usually one of the biggest challenges is to make sure the devices that are allowed to communicate securely have the same symmetric key. In state-of-the-art systems, this is done by key exchange methods, which are either manual (e.g. typing in the key in a keypad) or exploit key-exchange algorithms.

Let us consider creating a secure wireless communication between dedicated personal devices, for example, a mobile phone and a headset. The most popular communication technology for personal area networks is Bluetooth, which

J. Krumm et al. (Eds.): UbiComp 2007, LNCS 4717, pp. 304–317, 2007.

already provides a security mechanism to encrypt the wireless communication between dedicated devices. The security mechanism is based on a two-stepped approach. In the first step, the so-called pairing phase, the master of the local Bluetooth cell generates a random key which it transports to the slave device. In order to prevent sniffing the key, it is encrypted with the so-called personal identification number (PIN). In the subsequent second step, this transmitted key is used to encrypt and decrypt the user data. Thus, both the slave and the master Bluetooth devices operate on the same encryption key. The possible key length used in Bluetooth applications ranges from 8 bit to 128 bit depending on the security level of the participating Bluetooth devices [3,4]. Typically, the Bluetooth PIN consists of three to four digits which range from 0 to 9 [5]. This corresponds to a maximum key-strength of about 10 to 13 bits.

There are three ways in which the PIN code can be shared between devices. The first way, commonly used for devices with limited user interface (e.g. head phones), is using a fixed PIN that is factory-installed and cannot be changed. This method thus limits the level of security significantly. Alternatively, a small number of factory-default PINs can be selected using a limited user interface such as DIP switches. The third method, which is offered by cell phones, is typing in the key using a keypad. This method offers a reasonably secure way of establishing a common key, but is also the least user-friendly. In any case however, pairing Bluetooth devices is often a tedious task.

In this paper, we present and evaluate an alternative to exchanging keys using computing intensive methods or to typing the key in manually. The basic idea is to generate a key or PIN locally from exposing devices to common physical environmental conditions. In particular, we consider two devices being shaken together and to use the recorded acceleration samples to generate local keys on both devices. This is especially practical for hand held devices. As we believe that the Bluetooth application space is quite typical in respect of the required level of security for personal area networks, our goal is to develop a symmetric key or PIN which is equivalently strong as the Bluetooth PIN.

Thus, the system must be designed so the devices create exactly the same symmetric key on their own if and only if they are shaken together. To this end, a 3D acceleration sensor is used to record the motion of the devices in each direction during a shaking process. This allows us to position the sensors held in the hand arbitrarily on each device. The symmetric key is generated out of the recorded shaking process of the acceleration sensor using signal processing methods which we will disclose during the course of this paper. Shaking devices together is very user-friendly and practical, especially for small, mobile, battery powered personal devices.

Although we believe that the local generation of encryption keys from acceleration measurements without exchanging any acceleration information between the shaken devices is novel, there exist several approaches for key exchange in symmetric key encryption systems. Commonly, key distribution algorithms are time and computing power intensive because secure key distribution is based on complex mathematic algorithms. Diffie and Hellman (DH) proposed an algorithm for securely distributing a symmetric key between two parties [6]. The vulnerabilities of the so-called DH key agreement protocol are carefully described in [7]. Alternatively, the additional computational effort of complex distribution algorithms can be reduced by pre-distributing keys during an initialization phase. Afterwards, these keys can be used to encrypt and decrypt the subsequent communication or to securely exchange additional symmetric keys [8]. This method increases the initial configuration effort and complicates the usability of each device, but it ensures security and privacy.

In ubiquitous computing, accelerometers have already been used in several ways and for several applications. In context awareness applications, sensor data is jointly processed in order to estimate certain conditions of the surrounding. For example, in the case of activity recognition, people carry several sensors, such as accelerometers integrated into their clothes, which decide autonomously on particular events [9]. Finally, the acceleration information, recorded while moving, can be used to detect physical activities and to capture the local dynamics of people [10]. Additionally, acceleration sensors can be applicable to establishing connections between devices by bumping objects together [11]. Another relevant work which uses acceleration sensors is given in [12] where the sensors are used to recognize whether they are carried by the same person.

The prior work that probably has the closest relation to ours is conducted within the framework of the *Smart-Its* project, in which devices in their direct surroundings are grouped by considering their proximity [13], e.g. by measuring the acceleration while shaking the devices. The acceleration data is then broadcasted to all devices within the wireless range. If the similarity between the received acceleration data and the measured acceleration reaches a certain threshold, the devices assume that they have been moved together and hence will accept a connection. This work has been extended by using a secure transmission protocol to exchange the acceleration information between the shaken devices [14]. They use exponentially quantized FFT coefficients of the acceleration sequence [15] to derive several key parts locally on each device. Again, depending on the similarity of the received and the local key parts, the devices determine if they are shaken together or not. Finally, only the equal key parts are used to derive a cryptographic key. One drawback of this method is that both devices have to exchange their own derived key parts.

However, our prime objective is not to exchange the acceleration characteristics, but to locally generate unique keys which are kept secret on each device. In our work, both devices should work completely autonomously without exchanging any acceleration information between the dedicated devices. The methods noted above are not appropriate for our independent key generation algorithm.

This paper is organized as follows: The feasibility of our approach is generally examined in Sec. 2. In particular, we assess the similarity of the acceleration sequence between devices of the shaking processes and determine the maximum entropy of the acceleration sequences to validate that ideally, a certain randomness of the generated keys can be guaranteed. In Sec. 3, we introduce a key generation algorithm which aims at providing exactly the same key on both devices if and only if they are shaken together. The quality of the generated keys and other results are illustrated in Sec. 4. In Sec. 5, we summarize the results of our work and provide an outlook on further optimization of the key generation algorithm.

2 Signal Analysis

Let us start with considering shaking two devices in one hand. Typically, the shaking process consists of fast up and down movements in the three dimensional space, while bar-mixer type rotations seldomly occur.

In our experimental setup, we first record the shaking process as a sequence of three-dimensional vectors, each component representing the force in the x-, y-, and z-directions, respectively. We further assume that the relative orientation of the devices is not known a priori. For our subsequent calculations, we always compute and consider only the absolute values of the acceleration vectors. Firstly, this reduces the influence of the relative alignment of the acceleration sensors inside the hand. Secondly, since the shaking is usually on one fixed axis, as we have validated in some initial experiments, we lose only a small fraction of information about the shaking process. Thus, we can actually view the shaking process similar to a one-dimensional oscillation.

Since both devices are unsynchronized by default, the devices must agree on a common starting point of the shaking process. However, in order to evaluate different key generation algorithms independent of the time shift between both sequences, in this paper, we assume genie aided synchronization, for which we assume no time displacement between both sequences. In our setup, we have first completely recorded the two shaking sequences, and then off-line computed and adjusted the time displacement of the sequences by considering the peak of their cross-correlation function. In a more practical way, it would also have been possible to synchronize the start of recording the shaking process by explicit RF communication between two devices. As we will see during the course of this paper, in our current system, only the information of the starting point of the shaking process might need to be exchanged between the shaken devices.

Before we investigate how keys can be generated from shaking processes, let us first check the feasibility of our approach. There are two criteria that we consider as prerequisite for our effort: First, the devices shaken together must exhibit a much more similar sequence of the acceleration data than all other sequences, and second, the randomness of the sequence must exceed that of the desired key.

To this end, we have built prototypes with 3D acceleration sensors. The value of the acceleration sensors are 10bit A/D converted with a sampling rate of $f_s = 200Hz$ using a 16 bit micro controller. The sampled data is transmitted via serial line to a personal computer, on which we perform off-line signal processing using Matlab. All 3-D data is low-pass filtered with a first order filter with cut-off frequency of 100Hz. As discussed above, the absolute values are computed. In this paper, we consider one absolute value of the acceleration vector as one sample.

Our test data consists of 88 shaking experiments recorded from 10 individuals. All persons were asked to shake two devices together in one hand for at least 5 seconds. Our test data thus generated consists of the ensemble $\mathcal{E} = (\mathcal{A}, \mathcal{B})$ of $S = 88$ shaking experiments, where each shaking experiment consists of two sequences; $\mathcal{A}$ includes all shaking sequences from prototype device A and $\mathcal{B}$ these from prototype device B. We denote the synchronized sequences of prototype A and B by $\underline{a}_n \in \mathcal{A}$ and $\underline{b}_m \in \mathcal{B}$, where n and m are the index of our shaking experiment. We limit the duration of each shaking process to 5 seconds, which yields sequences of exactly 1000 acceleration samples. $\hat{\mathcal{E}} = (\hat{\mathcal{A}}, \hat{\mathcal{B}})$ with $\underline{\hat{a}}_n \in \hat{\mathcal{A}}$ and $\underline{\hat{b}}_m \in \hat{\mathcal{B}}$ are the zero mean and the unit energy versions of $\underline{a}_n, \underline{b}_m$, respectively.

2.1   Similarity Measure Between Shaking Processes

As we want two devices shaken together to generate exactly the same cryptographic key, the resulting sequences of the acceleration vectors shall be as similar as possible. Accordingly, two sequences of different shaking processes shall be as different as possible to avoid generating the same key when the devices are not shaken together.

The degree of similarity of two sequences is typically expressed by the cross-covariance [16]. We consider both time and frequency analyses, for which the results are summarized in Tab. 1. If devices are shaken together, the maximum value of the cross-covariance of $\underline{\hat{a}}_n, \underline{\hat{b}}_n$ is 99.8% in the time domain. The cross-covariance of the frequency spectrum is generally even higher because we ignore the time information when the respective frequency component occurs. Ideally, the maximum cross-covariance of any $\underline{\hat{a}}_n, \underline{\hat{b}}_n$ would be 1. However, the measurements are affected by tolerances of the acceleration sensors. Additionally, the spatial distance between the acceleration sensors during the shaking process has a small influence on the acceleration measurements due to receiving different centrifugal forces in case of a circular motion. These influences have an impact on the cross-covariance in both the time and the frequency domain. Furthermore, the missing timing synchronization between the ADC of the hardware prototypes results in a sub-sample displacement of the sequence in the time domain. This could be reduced by oversampling or by interpolation.

Analyzing the cross-covariance of different shaking processes, i.e. of $\underline{\hat{a}}_m, \underline{\hat{b}}_n$ for $m \neq n$, we see fundamentally different behavior of the cross-covariance measures in the time and in the frequency domain. While the maximum value of the cross-covariance is only 56.4% in the time domain, the cross-covariance of the frequency spectrum is 92.3%. Due to the high cross-covariance of the frequency spectrum, sequences from the same shaking processes are not distinguishable from others. Thus, the same key would rather likely be generated for different shaking processes if the key generation was based on a frequency-based technique. For this reason, the frequency domain is not suitable for key generation and we will continuing analyzing the sequences only in the time domain.

Table 1. Characteristics of the maxima of the cross-covariance of all shaking sequences of $\mathcal{E}$ in the time and frequency domain

	characteristics of cross-covariance			
	$cov(\hat{\underline{a}}_m, \hat{\underline{b}}_m), m = 1, \ldots, |S|$		$cov(\hat{\underline{a}}_m, \hat{\underline{b}}_n), m \neq n,$ $m, n = 1, \ldots, |S|$	
	(same shaking experiments)		(different shaking experiments)	
	time domain	frequency domain	time domain	frequency domain
minima	0.871	0.938	0.04	0.094
first 25%	0.871 to 0.973	0.938 to 0.982	0.04 to 0.128	0.094 to 0.166
50%	0.973 to 0.991	0.982 to 0.996	0.128 to 0.258	0.166 to 0.461
last 25%	0.991 to 0.998	0.996 to 0.9996	0.258 to 0.564	0.461 to 0.923
median	0.985	0.993	0.18	0.300
maxima	0.998	0.9996	0.564	0.923

2.2 Estimating the Quality of the Cryptographic Key

The quality of a cryptographic key is given by its randomness, which can be expressed by entropy [17]. In this section we will estimate the highest possible entropy of the keys we can generate by calculating the entropy of the shaking process. This is valid since the entropy of the generated keys will never exceed the entropy of the shaking process, regardless of which mathematical transformation is used to calculate the cryptographic key. The entropy of the shaking process can only be increased by extending the duration of the shaking process.

To estimate the entropy correctly, we must consider the dependencies between the samples of the sequence. To this end, the entropy must be calculated based on the conditional probability of correlated lag vectors, i.e. of segments which contain correlated samples [18]. The length of these lag vectors is indicated by the length of the autocorrelation function [19]. If the length of the autocorrelation function is one, the samples of the sequence are completely uncorrelated and the conditional probability equals the probability of each individual sample. Unfortunately, in our case the sequence is highly correlated, see Fig. 1, and the autocorrelation function is almost as long as the complete sequence. To correctly estimate the conditional probability, we would need a huge statistical basis to cover all possible lag vectors. First calculations have shown that due to the limited length of our sequences, the statistical basis is too weak to reliably estimate the conditional probabilities of the shaking sequences in this straightforward way.

Thus, we employ a different approach to calculate the entropy of the sequences by using a linear forward prediction filter. The prediction filter predicts the correlated part of the sequence according to the dependencies given by the autocorrelation function [20,21]. As we know, the entropy of a predictable sequence is zero, thus the entropy of the error of the prediction filter equals the entropy of the original sequence. The forward prediction error of the prediction filter yields a quite uncorrelated sequence, see Fig. 2. Consequently, the entropy is close to the unconditional entropy of the individual samples of the forward prediction error.

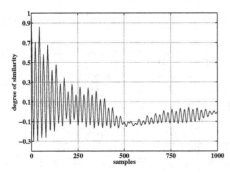

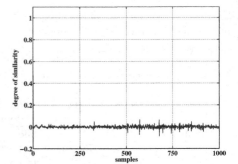

Fig. 1. Autocorrelation function of a shaking sequence

Fig. 2. Autocorrelation function of the forward prediction error

To calculate the entropy of the shaking processes, we have concatenated all shaking sequences from the prototype A of our test data, described in Sec. 2.1, to a sequence $\underline{s}^A = (\underline{a}_1, \ldots, \underline{a}_{88}), \underline{a}_n \in \mathcal{A}$. Afterwards, we have constructed a linear forward prediction filter, which exhibits the same length as the autocorrelation function of $\underline{s}^A$. Then, we have estimated the entropy of the sequence resulting from the forward prediction error of $\underline{s}^A$, which yields an average entropy of 3800bit/sequence. Note that the use of such prediction filter is infeasible for key generation and is just used for the assessment of the entropy of the shaking process.

Reflecting the presented results in this section, we assume that the cross-covariance between sequences from the same shaking processes are high enough to independently generate exactly the same key from both sequences. Additionally, the cross-covariance of sequences from different shaking processes is sufficiently small to guarantee different keys from different shaking processes. Furthermore, we have demonstrated that the shaking process of 5 seconds length exhibits a significant amount of entropy in the range of 3800 bits. This largely exceeds the entropy of the Bluetooth PIN code. Although we thus believe that the shaking process can be used for key generation, the evidence did not yield any hint on the key generation algorithm itself. The construction of such algorithm will be discussed in the following section.

3   Key Generation

Our objective is to generate exactly the same cryptographic key out of two shaking sequences obtained by two independent hardware prototypes if and only if they are shaken together and without exchanging any key parts or acceleration data. Due to the fact that both sequences are not identical, see Sec. 2.1, the key generation algorithm must have the ability to map even similar sequences to the same key and sequences with less similarity to different keys. The key generation algorithm is applied separately on both shaking sequences of the hardware prototypes without any interaction. As the algorithm is the same on both devices, let us now consider just one prototype, say device A.

In the previous section we have shown that key generation based on time domain analysis is most beneficial. To this end, our approach for generating a cryptographic key $\underline{k}_n^A$ is that we start with splitting the shaking sequence $\underline{a}_n$ into I segments

$$\underline{a}_{n,i} = (a_{n,i\cdot L}, \ldots, a_{n,(i+1)\cdot L}). \tag{1}$$

$\underline{a}_{n,i}$ indicates the ith segment $(i = 0, \ldots, I-1)$, each consisting of L subsequent samples of measured absolute samples. Note that the length of each shaking sequence is limited to 1000 acceleration samples. Thus, the number of segments $I = \lfloor 1000/L \rfloor$ only depends on the segment length L. $a_{n,i\cdot L}$ represents the $(i\cdot L)$th sample value of the shaking sequence $\underline{a}_n$. We further normalize each $\underline{a}_{n,i}$ to

$$\hat{\underline{a}}_{n,i} = \frac{\underline{a}_{n,i} - \bar{\underline{a}}_{n,i}}{|\underline{a}_{n,i}|}, \tag{2}$$

where $\bar{\underline{a}}_{n,i}$ represents the mean value of $\underline{a}_{n,i}$. Now, all segments are zero mean and have unit energy. Then, we calculate from each segment $\hat{\underline{a}}_{n,i}$ a fragment of the cryptographic key $k_{n,i}^A$. At the end, the key $\underline{k}_n^A$ consists of the concatenation of I fragments.

The calculation of the key's fragments is done in two steps as shown in Fig. 3. First, we reduce the dimensionality of the segments $\hat{\underline{a}}_{n,i}$. The objectives herein are to focus on the main attributes of all segments to the key generation algorithm, to remove outlier components of our measurement, and to reduce memory resources for the implementation of the key generation algorithm. The segments can be represented by a weighted sum of patterns which consist of common components of all segments from the test data. The weights indicate the similarity between the segment $\hat{\underline{a}}_{n,i}$ and the patterns $\underline{v}_m, m = 1, \ldots, M$ and are summarized in a weight vector

$$d_{n,i,j}^A = \sum_{j=0}^{L-1} \hat{a}_{n,i,j} v_{m,j}, \tag{3}$$

which constitute the outcome of the correlator bank as shown in Fig. 3. Thus the length of the vectors $\hat{\underline{a}}_{n,i}$ equals the length of the patterns $\underline{v}_m$. M indicates the number of patterns that are used for the representation of the segments $\hat{\underline{a}}_{n,i}$.

The patterns are computed from a separate training set $\mathcal{E}'$ using the principal component analysis (PCA) [22]. To this end, we have additionally recorded 15 shaking processes $\mathcal{E}' = (\mathcal{A}', \mathcal{B}')$ to calculate the Eigenvalues. The results of the PCA are the Eigenvectors and Eigenvalues of the covariance matrix of all segments with length L from the acceleration sequences in $\mathcal{E}'$. The Eigenvectors represent the main components and the Eigenvalues indicate how strong the respective Eigenvectors are pronounced in the segments of $\mathcal{E}'$. The segments can be completely reassembled by a linear combination of the Eigenvectors. To reduce the dimensionality of the weight vectors $\underline{d}_{n,i}^A$, obtained when correlating

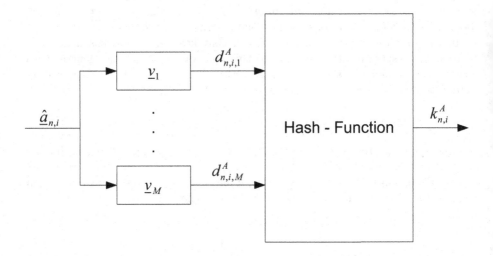

Fig. 3. Correlation of Segments with Patterns and subsequent Hash Function

the segments $\hat{\underline{a}}_{n,i}$ with the Eigenvectors, we neglect the Eigenvectors with the smallest corresponding Eigenvalues.

Fig. 4 shows the five Eigenvectors with the highest corresponding Eigenvalues of the training set $\mathcal{E}'$, where the shaking sequences are divided into I segments of $L = 40$ samples. Additionally, the graph of the Eigenvalues indicates that 5 Eigenvectors are sufficient for representing the data set $\mathcal{E}'$ to more than 95% of its signal energy. Note that the patterns $\underline{v}_m$ are only computed once and then kept fixed for all our experiments. The patterns are calculated again only if the segment length changes because both the segment length and the pattern length must be equal for the correlation.

As a second step follows a hash-function, which maps similar weight vectors $\underline{d}_{n,i}^A$ exactly to the same key segment and different $\underline{d}_{n,i}^A$ to different key segments. To this end, we establish a predefined number Q of groups. This is achieved in two phases: First, in the training phase, we use an agglomerative hierarchical clustering algorithm to find the center of Q groups. Each group is represented by a so-called representation vector $\underline{r}_{n,q}, q = 1, \ldots, Q$. To estimate the $\underline{r}_{n,q}$ we use the same method as building a dendrogram. At the beginning, all $\underline{d}_{n,i}^A$ are considered to be representation vectors. Then, iteratively, the two nearest representation vectors are replaced by their mean vector until the predefined number Q of representation vectors $\underline{r}_{n,q}^A$ is reached [22].

Second, in the quantization phase, the $\underline{d}_{n,i}^A$ are assigned to the closest $\underline{r}_{n,q}^A$, and the corresponding key fragment

$$k_{n,i}^A = \underset{q=1,\ldots,Q}{argmin} \, |\underline{d}_{n,i}^A - \underline{r}_{n,q}^A| \tag{4}$$

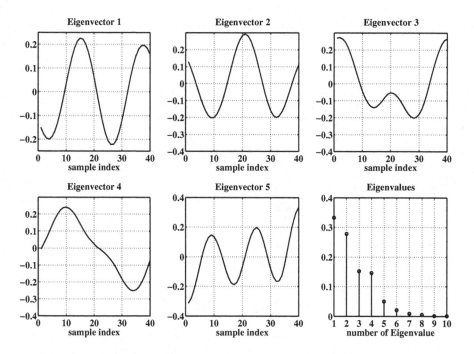

Fig. 4. The 5 most important Eigenvectors and Eigenvalues

is selected. Thus, the index q of the representation vector $\underline{r}_{n,q}^{A}$, to which $\underline{d}_{n,i}^{A}$ is closest, represents the ith fragment of the key $k_{n,i}^{A}$. Similar $\underline{d}_{n,i}^{A}$ are therefore assigned to the same representation vector and result in the same key fragment.

Therefore, the key generation is a two-step process. After the accelerometer data has been sampled and the $\underline{d}_{n,i}^{A}$ have been computed based on fixed Eigenvector patterns $\underline{v}_{m}$, first the representation vectors $\underline{r}_{n,q}^{A}$ are computed in the so-called training step. In the following classification phase, the key fragments $k_{n,i}^{A}$ are calculated using these representation vectors. The eigenvector projection as well as the classification step are therefore conducted individually for each shaking process and on each device.

As indicated above, the same procedure is applied on both prototype devices A and B. The keys for the nth shaking experiment of prototypes A and B

$$\underline{k}_{n}^{A} = (k_{n,0}^{A}, \ldots, k_{n,I-1}^{A}) \tag{5}$$

$$\underline{k}_{n}^{B} = (k_{n,0}^{B}, \ldots, k_{n,I-1}^{B}) \tag{6}$$

are composed by concatenating the key fragments $k_{n,i}^{A}$ and $k_{n,i}^{B}$, respectively.

As an example, Fig. 5 shows the result of a correct classification of the weight vectors of a shaking experiment $\underline{d}_{n,i}^{A}$ and $\underline{d}_{n,j}^{B}$ with $Q = 4$ regions and $M = 3$ patterns. The fundamental condition to generate independently the same key from $\underline{d}_{n,i}^{A}$ and $\underline{d}_{n,j}^{B}$ is that the weight vectors with the same index $i = j$ are

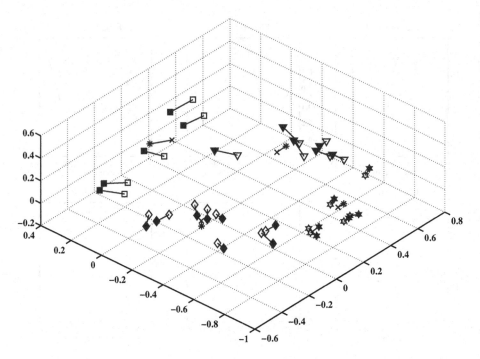

Fig. 5. Grouping of weight vectors from two shaking sequences of the first shaking experiment: The solid markers represent the $\underline{d}_{n,i}^{A}$ and the blank markers the $\underline{d}_{n,j}^{B}$. $\underline{d}_{n,i}^{A}$ and $\underline{d}_{n,j}^{B}$ with $i = j$ are connected via a line. The $\underline{d}_{n,i}^{A}$ and $\underline{d}_{n,j}^{B}$ with the same symbol are assigned to the same $\underline{r}_{n,q}^{A}$ and $\underline{r}_{n,q}^{B}$, respectively. The $*$-markers represent the $\underline{r}_{n,q}^{A}$ and x-markers the $\underline{r}_{n,q}^{B}$ of $Q = 4$ groups.

assigned to the representation vectors $\underline{r}_{n,q}^{A}$ and $\underline{r}_{n,q}^{B}$ with the same index q. Note that the representation vectors $\underline{r}_{n,q}^{A}$ and $\underline{r}_{n,q}^{B}$ are usually different.

4 Results

In this section we report on the quality of the previously explained key generation algorithm applied to the test data $\mathcal{E}$ which contains 88 shaking sequences of the prototypes A and B when shaken together. Ideally, all generated keys between prototypes A and B from the same shaking processes should be equal, thus $\underline{k}_{n}^{A} = \underline{k}_{n}^{B}$. Practically, however, we will see that it is not always possible to generate exactly the same cryptographic key on both prototypes when they are shaken together.

Especially important for estimating the quality of the key generation algorithm is the number of successful cases for which $\underline{k}_{n}^{A} = \underline{k}_{n}^{B}$ in relation to the total number of experiments. We are further interested in the average entropy of the equal keys. To this end, we calculate the entropy of the successfully

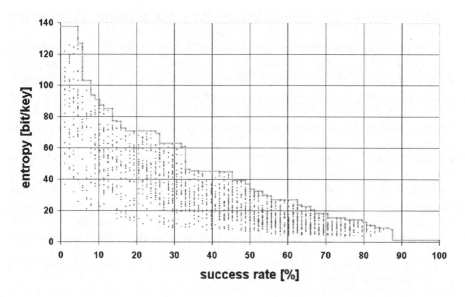

Fig. 6. Pareto chart of the results of the exhaustive search

generated keys considering the conditional probability of correlated lag vectors as explained in Sec. 2.2.

During this assessment, we assume that the duration of the shaking processes is fixed to 5 seconds which corresponds to 1000 samples. Hence, the key generation algorithm is sensitive on only three parameters:

1. **Segment length** L: The segment length $L = |\hat{\underline{a}}_{n,i}| = |\hat{\underline{b}}_{n,i}|$ affects the number of segments of each sequence and thus determines the number of key fragments ($I = \lfloor 1000/L \rfloor$).
2. **Number of patterns** M: M determines the accuracy of the segment representation by weight vectors and their dimensionality of the quantization space.
3. **Number of representation vectors** Q: Q defines the number of groups of weight vectors and the number of different symbols of which the cryptographic key consists.

We examine the influence of these parameters on the quality of the key generation algorithm by a systematic exhaustive search. We vary the respective parameters within a dedicated range, i.e. $L = 20, 25, \ldots, 150$, $M = 2, \ldots, 15$, and $Q = 2, \ldots, 15$. The objective of the exhaustive search is to find combinations of the three parameters which concurrently maximize the ratio of successfully generated equal keys and the average entropy of these keys. The results of the exhaustive search are illustrated in the Pareto chart shown in Fig. 6. The envelope function illustrates the boundary of the maximum average entropy per key (y-axis) which can be achieved for a certain ratio of successfully generated keys (x-axis). Each dot represents the outcome of the key generation algorithm for one specific setting of the three given parameters L, M, and Q.

Generally, the higher the entropy of a key, the lower the relative number of generated equal keys. The maximum entropy we can achieve with the proposed key generation algorithm is around 140 bits. Unfortunately, only one successful key could be generated from our test data for this selection of parameters. The Pareto chart also shows that there are parameters for which our key generation algorithm does not work properly, i.e. the algorithm always generates the same key regardless of the input sequence, which results in an entropy of 0 bits. In the majority of cases, however, there is a set-up of parameters which allows a robust and reliable key generation with reasonable entropy. In particular, we reach our intended objective of generating cryptographic keys with the same entropy as the Bluetooth PIN code (13bit/key) in about 80% of the cases with the parameter setting of $L = 75$, $M = 9$ and $Q = 12$. In this example, only 1.3% of the experiments from different shaking processes result in the same key.

5   Conclusion and Outlook

In this paper, we have assessed the idea of generating a cryptographic key by measuring acceleration data on small hand-held devices. The key is to be used during the pairing process and enables a secure connection between the devices. To this end, the two devices that shall initiate a secure connection are shaken together, so that both experience the same acceleration over time, from which the cryptographic key is generated locally without any communication between the devices.

We have introduced a key generation algorithm which is based on pairwise nearest neighbor quantization. Practical experiments assuming genie-aided synchronization and off-line computation have shown that with a success rate of about 80%, a key with an average entropy of 13 bits can be generated. This corresponds e.g. to the cryptographic strength of the Bluetooth PIN code.

Further work will be dedicated to synchronization and improved quantization algorithms.

References

1. Stajano, F.: Security for ubiquitous computing. John Wiley & Sons, Chichester (2002)
2. Cam, H., Özdemir, S., Muthuavinashiappan, D., Nair, P.: Energy-efficient security protocol for wireless sensor networks. In: IEEE VTC Fall Conference, vol. 5, pp. 2981–2984. IEEE, Los Alamitos (2003)
3. Bluetooth Spezial Interest Group: Specification of the Bluetooth System. Bluetooth, Version 1.1, vol. 1 (2001)
4. Bluetooth Spezial Interest Group: Specification of the Bluetooth System. Bluetooth, vol. 2, Version 1.1 (2001)
5. Muller, T.: Bluetooth security architecture. White Paper Version 1.0, Bluetooth (1999)

6. Diffie, W., Hellman, M.E.: New directions in cryptography. IEEE Transactions on Information Theory 22, 644–654 (1976)
7. Raymond, J.F., Stiglic, A.: Security issues in the Diffie-Hellman key agreement protocol. IEEE Transactions on Information Theory 22, 1–17 (2000)
8. Boyd, C., Mathuria, A.: Key establishment protocols for secure mobile communications: A selective survey. In: Boyd, C., Dawson, E. (eds.) ACISP 1998. LNCS, vol. 1438, pp. 3–540. Springer, Heidelberg (1998)
9. Bao, L.: Physical activity recognition from acceleration data under semi-naturalistic conditions. Master's thesis, Massachusetts institute of technology (2003)
10. Bao, L., Intille, S.S.: Activity recognition from user-annotated acceleration data. In: Ferscha, A., Mattern, F. (eds.) PERVASIVE 2004. LNCS, vol. 3001, pp. 1–17. Springer, Heidelberg (2004)
11. Hinkley, K.: Bumping objects together as a semantically rich way of forming connections between ubiquitous devices. In: Dey, A.K., Schmidt, A., McCarthy, J.F. (eds.) UbiComp 2003. LNCS, vol. 2864, Springer, Heidelberg (2003)
12. Lester, J., Hannaford, B., Borriello, G.: "Are you with me?" - Using accelerometers to determine if two devices are carried by the same person. In: Ferscha, A., Mattern, F. (eds.) PERVASIVE 2004. LNCS, vol. 3001, pp. 33–50. Springer, Heidelberg (2004)
13. Holmquist, L.E., Mattern, F., Schiele, B., Alahuhta, P., Beigl, M., Gellersen, H.W.: Smart-its friends: A technique for users to easily establish connections between smart artefacts. In: Abowd, G.D., Brumitt, B., Shafer, S. (eds.) Ubicomp 2001: Ubiquitous Computing. LNCS, vol. 2201, pp. 273–291. Springer, Heidelberg (2001)
14. Mayrhofer, R., Gellersen, H.: Shake well before use: Authentication based on acceleration data. In: Pervasive 2007: 5th International Conference on Pervasive Computing. LNCS, vol. 4480, pp. 144–161. Springer, Heidelberg (2007)
15. Huynh, T., Schiele, B.: Analyzing features for activity recognition. In: SocEUSAI, vol. 121, pp. 159–163 (2005)
16. Aylward, R., Lovell, S.D., Paradiso, J.A.: A compact, wireless, wearable sensor network for interactive dance ensembles. In: Proceedings of the International Workshop on Wearable and Implantable Body Sensor Networks (BSN'06), vol. 00, pp. 65–70. IEEE Computer Society Press, Los Alamitos (2006)
17. Shannon, C.: A mathematical theory of communication. Bell System Technical Journal 27, 379–423, 623–656 (1948)
18. Weigend, A.S., Gershenfeld, N.A.: Time series prediction: Forecasting the future and understanding the past, vol. 15. Addison-Wesley Publishing Company (1994)
19. Molgedey, L., Ebeling, W.: Local order, entropy and predictability of financial time series. In: The European Physical Journal B - Condensed Matter and Complex Systems, vol. 15, pp. 733–737. Springer, Heidelberg (2004)
20. Proakis, J.G., Manolakis, D.G.: Digital Signal Processing: Principles, Algorithms, and Applications, 2nd edn. Macmillan Publishing Company (1992) ISBN 0-02-396815-X
21. Haykin, S.: Adaptive filter theory, 4th edn. Prentice-Hall, Englewood Cliffs (2002)
22. Patterson, D.: Artificial neural networks, theroy and applications. Prentice Hall Inc., Englewood Cliffs (1996)

"Merolyn the Phone":
A Study of Bluetooth Naming Practices
(Nominated for the Best Paper Award)

Tim Kindberg[1] and Timothy Jones[2]

[1] Hewlett Packard Laboratories,
Filton Rd, Stoke Gifford, Bristol BS34 8QZ, UK
[2] University of Central England, Birmingham,
School of Social Sciences, Perry Barr, Birmingham, B42 2SU, UK
timothy@hpl.hp.com, Timothy.Jones@uce.ac.uk

Abstract. This paper reports the results of an in-depth study of Bluetooth naming practices which took place in the UK in August 2006. There is a significant culture of giving Bluetooth names to mobile phones in the UK, and this paper's main contribution is to provide an account of those Bluetooth naming practices, putting them in their social, physical and intentional context. The paper also uncovers how users have appropriated the ways in which Bluetooth, with its relatively short range of about 10-100m, operates between their mobile phones as a *partially embodied* medium, making it a distinctive paradigm of socially and physically embedded communication.

Keywords: Bluetooth, electronic identity, naming, mobile phones.

1 Introduction

This paper reports the results of an in-depth study of Bluetooth naming practices which took place in the UK in August 2006. There is a significant culture of naming phones and other devices in the UK [6], and this paper's contribution is to give an account of those Bluetooth naming practices, putting them in their social, physical and intentional context. This study reveals personal and social naming behaviours that go beyond the initial design of this *de facto* pervasive technology.

Bluetooth's overall popularity has been increasing markedly since it was integrated in mobile phones, especially in Europe. It was integrated in about half of all phones shipped in Western Europe in 2005; that figure is forecast to rise to about three quarters of mobile phones by 2008 [2]. Much of its use is relatively unremarkable, as a "cable replacement" for connecting phones to other devices such as wireless earpieces. However, a significant use of Bluetooth has emerged as an ad hoc channel for media sharing between users' phones when face-to-face, in places such as schools, pubs and transportation. Indeed, that usage is significant enough to have given rise to recent concerns about Bluetooth-equipped phones as a peer-to-peer channel for bringing pornographic material into schools [1]. This study shows that, in general, the sharing of media has led to an electronic projection of identity and presence through the Bluetooth channel, a presence which runs in parallel to the physical information

J. Krumm et al. (Eds.): UbiComp 2007, LNCS 4717, pp. 318–335, 2007.

flows within face-to-face engagements. Gary T. Marx writes, in reference to a discussion about privacy and anonymity [5]:

> "Some information is always evident in face-to-face interaction because we are all ambulatory autobiographies continuously and unavoidably emitting data for other's senses and machines. The uncontrollable leakage of some information is a condition of physical and social existence."

As this account will show, both controlled (intentional) and uncontrolled projections of our "ambulatory autobiographies" occurs through Bluetooth. Users deliberately project aspects of themselves in their Bluetooth names. At the same time, there is *spillage* of information that flows via Bluetooth within the immediate social group, and beyond it to or from others in the physical vicinity. Bluetooth, which has a relatively short range of about 10-100m, is a *partially embodied* medium. Bluetooth names of mobile phones can't always be matched unambiguously with their owners, who nonetheless are known to be nearby. Bluetooth between mobile phones thus lies somewhere between the wholly embodied medium of a face-to-face conversation, and the wholly disembodied medium of an internet chat between physically dissociated strangers. This paper documents how people make use of and react to the virtual-physical association and disassociation that occurs, as they match (or don't match) information between their sensory channels and their phones' Bluetooth channels.

2 Related Work

A previous project also studied how users appropriated an electronic naming feature, this time in the case of instant messaging (IM). Smale and Greenberg [11] captured the usage of IM clients which "include a feature that lets a person create and/or change their display name at any time". The study showed that users appropriated the field designed originally to display their name to other users. While many used it to identify themselves, others used the display field to provide information about themselves, or to broadcast messages, either instead of or in addition to their handle. Subsequent to that study (in 2005), IM clients began providing a dedicated field for a personal message to be shown to other users.

Several Bluetooth-based mobile phone applications have been designed for swapping profile information beyond a simple name, and exchanging messages with others nearby. Examples are Nokia Sensor [7], and MobiLuck (www.mobiluck.com). Even without Bluetooth, the phone is already a way of projecting one's identity. Skog [10] describes how the mobile phone "has become harnessed as part of many a teen's identity project". Similarly, Plant [8] describes its ostensive use as a physical prop to project something about the owner. For example, she describes "stage-phoning", where the phone's owner plays to an audience, for example on a train, in making a call. That language is redolent of Goffman's characterisation of action in social settings as taking place in regions of perceptability [3]: a "front region" where the actor deliberately projects a "performance"; and the "back region", not normally perceived by the same "audience", where that performance is prepared.

It is already established that Bluetooth also allows users to project their identity through their mobile phones, even without special software applications such as

Mobiluck. At least two projects have shown evidence of Bluetooth naming culture as an apparent performance of sorts. The current authors, in a 2005/2006 study [6], elaborated below, found a very rich set of Bluetooth names when automatically scanning in public places in the city of Bristol, UK. The Mobitip project [9] reported that in 2004 a remarkably high percentage of people's phones were discoverable by Bluetooth in Kista, Sweden, and that some users had changed the default Bluetooth names of their phones to interesting alternatives such as "Keep out!". But neither study established the context behind the names they discovered.

3 Background

We begin with an introduction to the essential features of Bluetooth communication needed to understand the findings of this study. Bluetooth, named after a 10th-century Viking king credited with unifying Denmark, is a short-range wireless networking technology used for several purposes, including connecting accessories such as earpieces and keyboards to devices such as computers, phones and PDAs; synchronizing mobile devices to computers; and, the use that features most in this paper, transferring content between mobile devices, principally phones. Devices connected by Bluetooth can exchange data at a nominal rate of 1 Mbps in the commonly implemented version 1.2 of the specification. That is enough to transfer media such as a sound file, image or short video clip within a few tens of seconds.

In practice, the devices being connected are typically at most a few metres apart. However, the typical range of a Bluetooth connection is about 10-100 metres, depending on the power of the radio transceivers in the devices and on whether there are obstructions in the environment. Bluetooth radio waves can travel through most obstructions such as walls found in buildings, although they are subject to attenuation. Users cannot control the radio range from their devices.

Often, a user needs to connect his or her device to a target device without the benefit of pre-established connection information. Rather than identifying the target device directly, the user has to select the target from the Bluetooth-enabled devices in range. The electronic process by which a device finds devices available for connection is known as *discovery*. Bluetooth's range may be relatively short, but many devices may be in range in urban settings such as pubs. We found tens of devices simultaneously present in some crowded places. Discovered devices appear by name, sometimes along with other information such as the type of the device (for example, a phone, a printer or a PC). By default, the name is set to the model of the device, e.g. "Nokia 6680". But the owners of devices such as phones with a means of user input can assign names of their choosing. A device name does not have to be unique. Although names of up to 248 characters are allowed by the specification, we found that user-chosen names are typically short – up to a few tens of characters, which is all that small devices tend to display of a name, anyway.

Discovery can take up to tens of seconds. Once one device has discovered another, a short-cut may be set up between them in the form of a long-term association called a *pairing*. Thenceforth, each device records the name of the other, together with other information necessary to make the connection. A user may connect the two simply by selecting the other from the pre-established list of paired devices, without the need for discovery.

Table 1. Names from automatic scans. Ellipses and asterisks replace characters given fully in the original.

Identifier	Association	Graffiti/T-Shirt	Direct Address
Adam J T*****	The Man From	4 a gay time call 07…	bonjour tutti!
Ami	Delmonte	BÃ©z	Call_me
Anna's phone	Biker chic	>>}Â¥{<<	Clear off!
x x carla x x	Bolton	Ho in training	F**k off u c**t
Chris 07…	Everton	Ima kettle	Jokes On U
Crown Jools	Pezza's girl	$LiK JiM	Porn please
Messy Dawg	Beer boy	MilkWasABad Choice	Tish-Send Me Stuff!
Snagglepuss	Madonna	M.C.F.C OK!	VIRUS ALERT!!

Finally, devices with Bluetooth enable their owners to control their own radio "presence". The user may switch Bluetooth off entirely while the device still functions. However, there is an intermediate state whereby Bluetooth is switched on, but the device is not discoverable by other devices. In that state, a user can send media to other devices, and other paired devices can send media to the user's device. But the user's device is "invisible" to other, unpaired devices in the radio sphere.

3.1 Study of Automatically Captured Names

In a previous study [6], we set up computers to scan continuously for the names of Bluetooth devices in three locations in the city of Bristol, UK: the university campus, a street in the city centre, and inside a pub in the city centre. We collected 1703 Bluetooth names: 771 from the city centre street, 307 from the pub and 625 from the campus. The great majority of these were names of mobile phones. We classified the names according to whether they were default names such as "Nokia 6680", or variations from those defaults that had been set by users. We found that 58% of discoverable devices had user-defined names in the city centre street; for the campus, the figure was 76%; and for the pub it was 88%.

We found that the vast majority of user-defined names fell into four categories (Table 1), when classified by their apparent meaning. *Identifiers* include full names, nicknames and pseudonyms. *Associations* are statements of the owner's interests, such as band names (The Man from Delmonte), football clubs (Bolton), and even a relationship to someone else (Pezza's Girl). *Graffiti/T-Shirt* includes text liable to be found on a wall, toilet door or a T-shirt. They include decorative forms of names (BÃ©z), jokes and surreality (MilkWasABad Choice) and the scatological (Ho in training). *Direct Address* includes exclamations that appear to address a person who has discovered the device. Examples include greetings (bonjour tutti!), invitations (Porn please), and insults (F**k off u c**t).

This *a priori* categorisation serves to broadly characterise the spread of names we found, and may seem uncontroversial in the case of many of the names we collected. But it was inadequate in several ways. Some of the names were ambiguous. For example, "Everton" is the name of a football club but it is also a boy's name. Some names could have been placed in more than one category. For example, "M.C.F.C OK!" refers to Manchester City Football Club but is commonly found as graffiti. But the deeper objection is that, since the exercise was based only on the names' apparent significance, it throws no light on the user's actual intentions or any other aspect of the context within which those names were chosen. What were the Bluetooth names in Table 1 intended to convey? To whom? And in what circumstances?

4 Methods

To answer our questions about Bluetooth naming practices and the context in which they take place, we gathered data through semi-structured interviews. Twenty-nine individuals were recruited to the study using a random sampling method and were eligible for inclusion providing they used Bluetooth. Participants were recruited in the daytime outside the Watershed Media Centre in Bristol, which is located adjacent to the recently redeveloped harbourside and includes a café, bar and cinema. It is worth noting however that the broader catchment of the harbourside is not limited to businesses with an interest in media. With local tourist attractions nearby, the area is frequented by a wide range of individuals, which was a major reason for choosing it.

To recruit participants, people walking by the Watershed were simply asked "Have you got Bluetooth?" As this study was not seeking to capture data on why individuals didn't have Bluetooth or didn't use it, individuals in those categories were not invited to participate. Individuals who used Bluetooth were invited to take part in the study through a recorded semi-structured interview conducted inside the Watershed's café. The interviews, which lasted up to about 30 minutes, were given in return for light refreshments and were subject to the interviewee signing a consent form. The two authors of this paper conducted the interviews, together at first so as to agree on the details of the procedure *in situ*, then separately.

Our introductory question served as a filter prior to the full interview. As no eligibility criteria were included, a wide range of people from different age, sex and ethnicity groups were approached to take part in the study. Age, sex and employment type of participants were recorded, however ethnicity was not recorded. Ten participants were female and 19 were male. The majority of the participants (19) were in the age range 15-25; nine were 26-35 and the remaining participant was 36-45. Twenty participants were in employment at least part-time; seven were students and the other two were unemployed.

The semi-structured interview had previously been piloted with five individuals (whose data are not reported as part of this paper) and minor amendments made. The initial section of the interview contained a series of socio-demographic questions relating to phone model, how often Bluetooth was used, what people did with Bluetooth, whether the participant changed Bluetooth discoverability and whether the participant was able to remember how to change the Bluetooth name of their mobile phone. Interestingly, although the filtering question didn't exclude other devices, all participants discussed Bluetooth use in relation to their mobile phone. Henceforth, Bluetooth is always taken in this paper to be used with mobile phones.

The second section of the interview concentrated on naming practices, including the Bluetooth names participants had selected for their mobile phone, the physical context in which the name was set (e.g. home, workplace or elsewhere), the social context (alone, friends, family or work colleagues etc.), the reason behind choosing a particular name and at least one occurrence of something that had happened when that name had been used (e.g. "I sent an image of my dog from my phone to my sister using Bluetooth").

The final section of the interview concentrated on what the participant thought about Bluetooth in general and what, if anything, they would like to change about it. It also captured data on other elements of context or naming practices not captured elsewhere.

Whilst less intrusive questions were asked initially to help guard against self-filtering and response-regulation by participants, it is unknown whether participants were reluctant to report on more provocative names such as some of those previously captured by automatic scanning. This highlights an important methodological consideration, particularly as the names reported in the results section below are not representative of the Bluetooth names in the *Direct Address* category, observed in the previous study [6].

5 Results

Results are presented for the 29 participants who were interviewed for this study and percentages are presented where applicable to highlight the points made. The percentages are presented, however, with the acknowledgement that a relatively small sample was interviewed.

5.1 Bluetooth and Media Sharing

Bluetooth was used primarily as a media-sharing tool on mobile phones, between family, friends and work colleagues and, much less frequently, between strangers. We now describe those media-sharing practices because they are the driving force behind the Bluetooth naming practices we shall go on to describe.

Pictures (both those taken with the phone camera and pictures from other sources) and music files are the most exchanged media between participants, with the majority of exchanges taking place between groups in highly social situations such as bars, cafes and at school or the workplace. Other media exchanged included contact information and videos although this was to a much lesser extent. Videos may be exchanged less often due to their size and the relatively slow speed associated with exchanging these files using Bluetooth.

Participants tended to send and receive media on a regular basis with 24% of participants sending at least one form of media on a daily basis and 10% of these sending several media files a day. Additionally, 48% of participants sent media at least once a week and 21% sent media every 2-3 days suggesting a high rate of media exchange between participants with Bluetooth. Receiving also occurs at a similar rate with 24% of participants receiving media files on a daily basis and 14% receiving multiple media files a day. Twenty-eight percent of participants received at least one media file a week and another 28% received at least one media file a month.

These figures suggest there is significant social value in media sharing between Bluetooth users. That was confirmed by the comments of some of our study participants. Sometimes the primary value of the exercise was not derived simply from the content, but also from the transaction itself. For instance, one participant described how he would play jokes on his friends by claiming, in one example he gave, to be sending them a "sexy girl" when what he actually sent was a not particularly attractive character from East Enders (a popular BBC "soap"). Another participant described media-sharing as a "good way to socialise", because it gave him and his friends "more to discuss". They listen to music on their friends' phones and then ask them to send the tracks they like. This corresponds to the physical exchange of camera phones for browsing, prior to exchanging selected images [4]. Overall, the combination of mobile phones and Bluetooth makes sharing very convenient, as our study participants commented: the mobility of the devices means that sharing can take place in socially convenient settings where people meet up with their acquaintances, and Bluetooth is free of charge and relatively efficient for exchanging small files.

5.2 The Bluetooth Names

Participants were asked to disclose up to three Bluetooth names that they had assigned to their current mobile phone. Only two of the 29 participants had never set their phone's name. Table 2 gives the 33 names we collected, of which six were second or third names from the same participant. The names were largely expressive of a personal or group identity, and indeed a stable identity: only five of the 29 participants had changed the name of their phone more than once, over an average of seven months for which the participants overall had possessed the phone.

The contexts in which participants named their phones confirmed there was an established awareness of Bluetooth in many cases. The initial naming of the mobile phones occurs largely when setting up the phone for the first time or browsing the features on the phone during an idle moment. About 70% of participants named their phone in those circumstances. The remaining 30% of participants named the phone when they were using Bluetooth to transfer files. Initial naming tends to occur when the participant is at home. Just over half of participants named their phone when at home; other places included work, during journeys, when out and about on the street, or in a venue such as a pub or fast-food restaurant. Overall, 57% of participants were with someone else (family member, friend or colleague) when they named the phone.

The contexts in which Bluetooth names were commonly set also suggest that naming the phone is an aspect of personalizing it in some general sense, and several participants described it in those terms. Equally, however, there was awareness that naming the phone had a practical purpose: to eliminate ambiguity when sharing media. In settings such as pubs, tens of phones may be simultaneously discoverable. There may, for example, be two phones with a default name such as "Nokia 6680". There is no way of distinguishing the phones without attempting to transfer media to one of them, which users are understandably reluctant to attempt. Participants who share media in public places therefore tend to re-name their device from the default to a less ambiguous name. Importantly, as will be shown, that new name is one which participants in their immediate social groups will recognise or respond to

Table 2. Participant names. Superscripts denote names of same participant. Asterisks replace letters given fully in the original. Names are in lower case irrespective of the original.

Name of my phone	Name for me (includes nickname or alias)		Statement about me	More like graffiti	Other
sami's phone	zoe	amon	caged_gardener[4]	lilla	nk83
	adamcall	popeye	caged_gardener@** *.co.uk[4]	soop	get your em out
	shell	smokey[2]	luddite[4]		merolyn the phone
	jasey	nokia ham	almost dr dee		leroy[3]
	ben's mobile	nkwile	the mac man		boop[1]
	james	star	blue army[5]		raspclart
	klc[1]	winston[3]	b.a. baracus[5]		
	ryan[2]	lady hype	optimus prime[5]		
		paulw810i	fuc***g bi**h		

Turning to the names themselves (Table 2), in order to understand the intention behind the choice of each name, participants were asked both why they had chosen that particular name and what type of name it was. On the basis of the prior study of automatically scanned names, participants were asked whether their name's type was one of the categories "Name of my phone", "Name for me", "Statement about me" or "More like graffiti". Alternatively, they could state that it was of an "other" type. Only a fifth (seven) of the total of 35 names belonged to the "other" category.

The answers to the questions "Why that particular name?" and "What type of name is this?" gave a consistent picture of the intentions behind each choice of name – which emerges as we consider the names of each type.

Name of my phone. Only one name, "sami's phone", was declared to be the name of the device itself; this participant expressed a functional view of the names he used. All but one of the other names ("nk83", discussed later) were connected with the identity of the owner in some way.

Name for me. The largest category, at just under half of the Bluetooth names, was that of a name of the phone's owner – including nicknames or other aliases. Some of these were part of the participants' bone fide names. A few first names appeared (zoe, ryan, james). The name "klc" is the owner's initials. The closest name to a full name is "adamcall", whose last four letters are the first of the participant's surname. Participants "klc" and "adamcall" were concerned to make their Bluetooth names unique but identifiable to their social groups, without fully identifying themselves to others. A similar motivation lay behind some hybrid names that also contained a reference to the device itself. Note that the owner of "ben's mobile" classified it as his own name, even though it is of the same form as "sami's phone"; similarly, "paulw810i", which contains the phone model, was in this category.

This category also includes participants' regular nicknames as used by their friends. As such, they have a variety of origins. For example, the names "amon" and "shell" are contractions of first names, and "ham" in "nokia ham" refers to the participant's last name, used as a nickname. The nickname "smokey" was adopted by a participant who is a runner and the name is in reference to his running pace.

Adoption of first names and nicknames as Bluetooth names enables familiars to recognise the name when sharing media, albeit with some possibility of ambiguity. An interesting special case is "jasey". His name is Jason but he also had a friend by the same name. To prevent ambiguity when receiving media from friends, he decided to adopt the name "jasey", although this was not a previously used nickname.

There were also a few cases where participants used an alias that was not a nickname used regularly by their acquaintances, and rather was more an expression of some aspect of their wider identity that they wanted to bring into the Bluetooth realm. Indeed, these participants' interview comments suggest that a classification under our category "statement about me" might also have been appropriate, despite the fact that they chose our category "name for me". "Lady hype" uses that name as a (hip-hop) MC name. "Nkwile" used that name as a contraction of the name "Wile-Kat" which he adopts widely in internet chat rooms ("nk" refers to his Nokia phone). A quite different example of an alias is "Winston". This Bluetooth name belongs to a black participant who chose the name as it reflected a stereotypical afro-carribean name. His explanation was that "it's kind of a mickey-take out of myself".

Statement about me. Names in this category express some aspects of the phone's owner. "Caged_gardener" chose a name that was reflective of his personal situation – he is a professional gardener living in the suburbs of Bristol and feels constrained by the suburban setting where he lives. That participant previously used his entire email address "caged_gardener@***.co.uk" as his Bluetooth name – as an invitation for others to contact him. This participant generally chose names to differentiate himself and gain a reaction from others; he formerly used "luddite", referring to his innate skepticism about technology, in order to "express an attitude that differentiated me from most people I know". "Almost dr dee" is a PhD student who is proud of his ambition to graduate with a doctorate. "The mac man" wanted playfully to distinguish himself from his colleagues, who use Windows PCs. The name "blue army" belongs to an Ipswich Town football fan. His other names "b.a. baracus" and "optimus prime" stem from his liking for 1980s TV series. Finally, "fuc***g bi**h" (without asterisks on her phone), adopted that name because "I think that's what I am".

More like Graffiti. The participant "soop" made up the name solely for his Bluetooth phone. He described that name as a kind of "handle", a term sometimes used as a synonym for "tag" in graffiti. The Bluetooth name "lilla" belongs to a participant who is in fact a graffiti artist and tags objects (buildings, walls, train carriages) using the name "Lilla".

Other. This category contains examples that are quite distinct from names in the other categories. First, the Bluetooth name "get your em out" is a unique case exemplifying the coupling of both social in-grouping and the inclusion of a participant's own identity. This participant chose a name of the form "get your _____ out" as it is a phrase used amongst her friendship group, but decided to include her name in place of any other more arbitrary object. Choosing such a Bluetooth name reinforces the participant's position of belonging to this particular friendship group (since this is an "in" phrase within the group), and in turn enables easy discovery by others in the group who may want to share media with the participant – since her real name "Em" is also included within the Bluetooth name. Another example of a group-specific choice of name was "Raspclart", which was offered spontaneously as a "funny" name by a friend of the participant – and where choosing "funny" names was part of the culture of the group.

In the rest of the "other" category, the participants used Bluetooth names not to express something about their true identity or that of their group, but for some other purpose. Two names are examples of concealment involving someone else's name in a Bluetooth name. "Leroy" is the real-world name of a friend of the person otherwise known in the Bluetooth realm as "winston". "Winston"/"leroy" actually changes his Bluetooth name according to the social context, and, in particular, according to which girlfriend he is with! A different participant also changed his Bluetooth name because of a girlfriend, but he did so long-term. This is the case of "merolyn the phone", where "merolyn" was the name of an ex-girlfriend that the participant spent considerable time with. Initially the Bluetooth name was simply "merolyn" but now the participant has a new girlfriend (who isn't called Merolyn), the participant changed the name to include the phrase "the phone", in order to remove the direct association with another girl's name.

The remaining names that participants placed in the "other" category were chosen spontaneously as distinctive identifiers, using whatever basis was conveniently to hand, but with quite different intentions. One participant chose "boop" because she wanted to hide her usual Bluetooth identity by way of a riddle to her friends, and had looked at Betty Boop merchandise in a shop that day. The final participant had a purely functional goal of unique identification in mind: he synthesised "nk83" as a hybrid "identifier" (his term) from the phone's manufacturer in the default name, Nokia, and his year of birth (83).

Turning to the collection of names as a whole, several themes emerge. First, the participants were largely naming their phones for the benefit of those they knew or directly encountered, not for strangers. It is unknown whether names such as "send me porn" in the *Direct Address* category of our previous study were addressed to strangers. (They might have been for the amusement of friends.) But, as we shall see, only two participants, "caged_gardener@***.co.uk" and "lilla", intended through their choice of name to obtain a reaction from strangers (by electronic means).

The second, overlapping, theme is that the social sphere constituted by the group and beyond often impinges on the choice of names. This is clearly true in respect of the participants' use of their own everyday names and nicknames. Indeed, when asked why they had chosen those names as their Bluetooth names, many responded "Because it's my (nick)name!" – as though it was obvious to transcribe it into the Bluetooth realm, and no further explanation was required. But some were names from somewhat more esoteric aspects of the participants' lives ("lilla" as a graffiti tag, "lady hype" as an MC name), and names used in the virtual world of electronic communication. "Lilla" was also used in online social communities (Microsoft Messenger and MySpace); "nkwile" derives from a chat name; and "caged_gardener" was first used in an email context.

In the latter cases, the participant specifically wanted to draw attention to his or her activities outside the use of Bluetooth. "Lilla" explained that the reason the same tagging name was used in a virtual world was to see if people would recognise this name and attempt to make contact, identifying the participant as an acknowledged graffiti artist in the physical world. This demonstrates how a participant was using a Bluetooth name to attract strangers and encourage communication and/or media sharing, rather than the participant declaring this aspect of his or her identity to others. "caged_gardener@***.co.uk" was curious whether anyone would contact him – and he reported that indeed someone emailed him to explain that he or she had encountered the address while scanning for Bluetooth devices. "Lady hype" wanted people around her to discuss her MC activities with her.

The desire for interaction in the foregoing examples is reflected throughout many of the remaining participants, especially those with Bluetooth names in the "statement about me" category. Participants in that category reported that they want their names to be noticed and to become a topic of conversation – for example, "almost dr dee" wanted "everyone to know" about his "ambition". As the examples show, Bluetooth enables people to express aspects of their identity in a relatively self-effacing way.

Finally, there is the observation that participants changed their Bluetooth names very little overall. Of the 27 participants in total who set the name at all on their current phone, only five did so more than once. That is arguably due to the reasons most had for choosing their names – such as making their phones easily identifiable as targets for media files – which themselves are quite stably connected with the participant's identity. Only one, "winston"/"leroy", changed his name regularly according to the social context – on the basis of which city he was in and which girlfriend he was with. His choice of Bluetooth names was somewhat ambiguous, being both playful and light-hearted on the one hand and used with more serious intent on the other. The other cases of name-changing are more definitely playful. "Klc" changed her Bluetooth name to "boop" during a football match when she was bored and wanted to send a file to her friends from an unknown source, to see their reactions. "Caged_gardner" changed his name as a result of projecting different aspects of his personality (he was previously "luddite"), and during a temporary experiment with his entire email address. And the participant known as "blue army" / "b.a. baracus" / "optimus prime" was playfully projecting whatever specific interest caught his imagination from time to time.

5.3 In-Group Conversations About Bluetooth Names

Just as the participants projected their own identity through their choice of Bluetooth names, they also showed interest in the Bluetooth-projected identities of others in their social groups. In addition to asking participants about their own Bluetooth names, we also asked about the Bluetooth names of their friends, family and colleagues. The majority of those interviewed were able to report at least one Bluetooth name of someone they knew from memory, and often several. The names that others had chosen were usually learned when sharing media. On occasion, learning someone's Bluetooth name resulted in further discussion and exploration of that name. Several examples appear above of participants choosing names that invite interaction from strangers; the same applies within their social groups.

Sometimes, to learn a Bluetooth name is to learn something surprising about the owner. "Almost dr dee" for example commented on his surprise when learning the Bluetooth name "mrs prince william" of his friend. He was surprised that she had this "fantasy" and he had not previously known anything about it. Similarly, "lilla" asked a friend about his Bluetooth name ("crisis") as he thought the name was "strange". His friend, who was a DJ, explained that when in Bristol he uses his real name but changes his name when in London to "crisis" as this is the DJ name he uses there. This is another example of name-changing in context with the social situation. "Fuc***g bi**h" was surprised and confused as to why someone she had known for a long time chose the name "rocking horse s**t". When questioned the friend explained that the name referred to the saying "as rare as rocking horse s**t", and as he liked the phrase he decided to adopt this as Bluetooth name. She first discovered his name when he was trying to send her an image from his mobile phone, supporting the notion that discussion of names occurs when media sharing is the primary activity.

Other participants also expressed surprise at the Bluetooth names of their friends and work colleagues, and sought to understand the reasoning behind the choice of name, suggesting that the culture of naming Bluetooth devices does lead to intrigue and occasional ambiguity even between familiar individuals. By the nature of Bluetooth discovery, sharing media with one individual usually entails becoming aware of other names around – names whose owner might not be known. For example, "amon" discovered the unfamiliar name "spongemonkey" when at the hotel where she works. The name baffled her but she felt able to ask the group of colleagues around her. A chef nearby responded that he used this Bluetooth name to reflect the fact that he makes the cakes.

As reported above, an interesting case where one participant deliberately created a conversation in her group about a Bluetooth name was "boop". She set her Bluetooth name to "boop" to hide her identity when sending files to her friends at a football match as a joke. She had the satisfaction of waiting until her friends had wondered who the sender was, before revealing herself.

Not all the interaction centred around Bluetooth name discovery was verbal. "The mac man" reports that because he is an Apple Macintosh user and has adopted this as part of his Bluetooth name, his friends have seen this as an opportunity to reflect the real-word rivalry between the two companies by sending him pictures of the Windows logo.

5.4 Interest in Bluetooth Names Beyond the Social Group

We have described the interest that some participants found in others' names within their social groups, and interactions that followed the discovery of those names. But some participants also showed interest in the names of strangers around them, and even interacted with them.

Participants were asked whether they ever browsed for Bluetooth names, and why they did so and in what circumstances. By "browsing" we mean the activity of a user setting his or her phone to discover all the Bluetooth names in range for the sake of doing so, rather than in the context of a specific goal such as media sharing. Almost three quarters of the 29 participants reported they sometimes browsed for Bluetooth names. Thirteen participants said that they did so about once a month or more, and

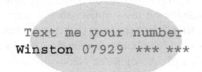

Fig. 1. Winston's image. Asterisks replace digits given fully in the original

seven browsed at least once a week. Browsing typically took place in leisure settings and places of dwelling, including pubs, concerts, trains and buses. Most said that they browsed only when bored, and that they did so for casual reasons including "out of curiosity", "to see how many people have it turned on" and "to see what people call themselves". Objects of particular interest in these cases were typically names that were, as two participants put it, "funny" or "strange".

Two participants had more focused interests when browsing. "Lilla", the tagger, looked for others who used their tags as Bluetooth names. "Popeye", who browsed at work during his lunch hour, was interested in the models of other people's phones: to "see what phones were out there" – he was not interested in the unusual names people had set for themselves.

5.5 Spillage

To assign a name and make a Bluetooth device discoverable is to project an electronic presence, but not all aspects of Bluetooth presence are under the user's control. This section describes ways in which Bluetooth presences "spill" both between social groups and between the virtual and physical worlds.

The people browsing for Bluetooth names in the previous section specifically looked for the names of strangers. But eight of the 29 participants used discovery only to find the device of an acquaintance, and were uninterested in the other names they observed. However, they had no choice in the matter: the presences of strangers "spill" into the discovery process even though they are looking for those of people they know. Given the public or semi-public contexts in which Bluetooth is typically used, the appearances of presences from beyond the immediate, known social group is not within the user's control. In most cases, this spillage of Bluetooth presences was of little importance. This type of spillage may be termed "overdiscovery", by analogy with overhearing – which is usually of little consequence. But two of those eight participants had concerns about it. One man said that he wanted to discover only friends' phones "because of security", although he wasn't able to elaborate on what he meant by that. The other said she was "shocked" at some of the "rude stuff" she saw: "what kind of person would call themselves that?" Her particular concern was that that "kind of person" must be nearby.

Her concern arises from a relationship between virtual Bluetooth presence and physical presence. Because Bluetooth is a short-range medium, there is a degree of correlation of this electronic presence with the device owner's physical presence: as the introduction stated, Bluetooth is in that sense a *partially embodied* form of communication. There are several ways in which these two forms of presence "spill" over into one another. In that respect, Bluetooth presence bears some similarity to WiFi presence. For example, an unfamiliar network observed when a user connects a laptop within the home must be nearby. Even on a wired network, there are presences of users known to be physically nearby. For example, the play-list discovered when running the iTunes application exists on the same subnet, and therefore belongs to someone nearby. But in both those cases, the environments in which the user discovers the other presence are well-known and relatively slow-changing – they are observed as belonging to our neighbours, colleagues or fellow students. As Bluetooth users move around urban places, they typically know less about the changing presences nearby.

Bluetooth presence is also comparable to online presence, such as in instant-messaging and chat rooms, which is normally wholly disembodied. In one respect, Bluetooth presence is more anonymous: beyond the Bluetooth name, there is no further information such as a picture or profile to identify the person. On the other hand, while a user may remain anonymous despite Bluetooth presence, the existence of correlated physical information channels may creates ways to break anonymity.

Some participants tried to varying extents to physically identify a person from his or her Bluetooth name. "Caged_gardener" tried to "match faces to names" – an act that went no further than his imagination. But three participants "Bluejacked" others: that is, having discovered their names, they sent them unsolicited content by Bluetooth. In each case, the goal was more than sending content *per se*: it was to have an effect on a recognizable person. One of these, "soop", sent a message to a stranger's device containing the text "phone will shut down". He did so using common Bluejacking practice, as a spurious "contact" message, which some phones accept automatically. Then he looked around to see who had received it. A person who receives such a message is liable to pick up his or her phone, and examine the contents. When it contains a phrase such as "phone will shut down", the recipient is liable to show concern or amusement, and to look around to see whether they can spot who sent it. In such circumstances, the sender may be able to identify the target with reasonable probability.

That identification doesn't necessarily work both ways. Another participant, "blue army", sent an image of Mr. T. (from "The A Team", a 1980s TV program) to a female-sounding name in a pub. He saw a girl pick up her phone. She sent back an image of a rock band, apparently without being able to see him – his intention was not to be identified himself.

The third example, of "Winston", was particularly interesting because his intention was to be identified, although he went about things in a way that stood little chance of success. He wanted to give his telephone number to women he felt attracted to. He constructed the image shown in Figure 1 with his telephone number for that purpose. On seeing a woman he liked, he would try to discover a Bluetooth name that he thought might be hers, and his plan was to send the image to her. But he never succeeded in discovering a name that he considered might belong to a woman he had spotted. If he had succeeded, he planned to make himself known when he observed the target receiving the image. He viewed Bluetooth as a "cool" way to introduce or project himself.

Some participants described spillage occurring the other way: that is, of others' attempts to contact them. "B.a.baracus" (also known as "blue army") once received an unsolicited image in a bar. He does not know whether the perpetrator identified him, but it gave him the idea of trying the same on someone else, as reported above. "Ryan" was identified in a very crude way: on a bus, a young woman he didn't know shouted "who's Ryan?", during a bout of Bluetooth activity between young people. He reports that he identified himself to the girl who had asked, even though he thought it was "pointless" of her. However, he remarked that he chose the name "smokey" not only because it was his nickname, but that, he felt, that "it's not really a name" and would "get fewer comments".

Sometimes the physical domain spills into the world of Bluetooth presences, as examples brought up by "amon" show. The first example is of the physical resolution of a problem with a Bluetooth transaction. She reports a situation when travelling on a bus of an unsolicited image being sent to her via Bluetooth. When she expressed surprise at receiving the image, the sender (also on the bus) overheard and apologized to her, stating that the file was intended for someone with the Bluetooth name "Amon3000". In the second example, the same participant answered a question from one of her colleagues, who did not know her personally, about her Bluetooth name. She wore a T-shirt bearing her nickname, Amon, and the colleague explained to her that he had previously known her only as a disembodied Bluetooth name.

5.6 Controlling Bluetooth Presence

Technically, Bluetooth can either be switched off entirely, or left on with discoverability turned off. The participants tended to be unclear about the difference.

Ten of the 29 participants said that they left Bluetooth on all the time; the remainder turned it "off" sometimes. Of those 19 who sometimes turned it off, 15 did so because of security considerations or because of Bluetooth's drain on battery life (or both), and were evenly divided between those issues; the remaining four gave other reasons or no definite response. Those concerned about battery life switched Bluetooth off when it was not needed, or when they noticed the battery getting low.

Of more interest here are the nine who mentioned security considerations. Their issues ranged from irritations such as erroneous headset connection attempts, to fear of "hacking". Four participants mentioned particular places where they turned Bluetooth off: at one participant's place of work (where viruses were quite common due to a high density of phones); at McDonald's restaurants, where "people always try and connect"; in "big crowds", where people might be able to "find who you are or get through to you"; and "in Birmingham" – the large city in the English Midlands, where the participant was generally suspicious of the crowds found there!

6 Discussion

This study has demonstrated (1) the significant culture around Bluetooth naming of mobile phones, which has emerged from what was designed simply as a mechanism for device association; and (2) the ways in which Bluetooth on mobile phones is a partially embodied medium, and how that plays into its use. Taking the culture first, a small but significant minority of people participate (about 10% of all people walking along a Bath street over various times had discoverable user-set names [6]), and we have shown that name-setting is rooted in a significant practice of media sharing: about half of our study participants (randomly chosen Bluetooth users) sent media files at least once a week. Media-sharing is a valuable social transaction in itself, but the names provide an additional channel for projecting facets of personal identity.

Our interview study provided an explanation for the names in most of our initial lexical categories from the automatic scans, which are now distinguishable by the intentions behind them. Those intentions go beyond the simple need to disambiguate. One is the *in-group* intention. Many are focused on their immediate social group. Nicknames are a popular choice, because they identify the user in such a way as to emphasise their belonging to the group. Nicknames do so without fully identifying them to anyone beyond, and so tend to maintain a degree of privacy. Some examples of in-group naming went a step further: "get your em out" involves an in-group phrase, and "raspclaart" shares an in-joke. We also found examples of *Statement about me* names that mirrored our former "association" category, but which we can now distinguish by intention. Those users tend to choose their Bluetooth names to prompt others to ask about them. Sometimes the intention is to *find commonality*: to directly find people with common interests, e.g. "blue army's" reference to the football team he supports. But sometimes people use the Bluetooth name with an *ask me* intention: as a prompt for others to find out more about them. They choose their name slightly cryptically ("almost dr dee", "caged_gardener") or even provocatively ("fuc***g bi**h"). A special case of that is the *alter ego* intention: users such as "lady hype" and "lilla" were drawing attention to identities they possess beyond their immediate social group, as a hip-hop MC and graffiti artist respectively. Finally, we found the *obfuscation* intention: in contrast to the preceding examples, the users with names "leroy" and "merolyn the phone" were using their names to obfuscate, respectively, a true identity and the significance of an ex-girlfriend's name. Similarly, "boop" was a deceptive Bluetooth identity chosen for a prank.

Some of the lexical classes of names from our initial scans are not represented in the interview study. Those include the *Direct Address* names such as "Porn please", and the more surreal or scatological *Graffiti/T-shirt* examples. That may be because the participants were reluctant to tell us about them. As a consequence, we have not been able to answer one of our original questions: what were the intentions behind those most provocative of names, and at whom were they directed? Both in-group amusement and out-of-group affect are plausible rationales. "Raspclaart" is an existence proof of the former. "Lilla" and "caged_gardener@***.co.uk" both sought interactions from people outside their immediate social group.

We now turn to what is perhaps the central question of this study: are Bluetooth names different from other types of electronic names? At first glance, the answer would seem to be 'no'. Many Bluetooth names are similar to those found online. Indeed "lilla" and "caged_gardener" were used online. As for the others, real-life names and nicknames found in the Bluetooth realm are not uncommon in instant messaging, where people message only their "buddies". Some Bluetooth pseudonyms, *Statement about me* names and graffiti-related names such as "lady hype" and "BÃ©z" seem redolent of online names in broader forums. Even the more scatological Bluetooth names might be found there. The only obvious difference from most online environments is that some Bluetooth names, such as "ben's mobile", mention phones.

However, we argue that Bluetooth naming is a distinct paradigm from other types of personal and electronic naming, not so much in the names themselves, as in the modes in which those names are used – particularly, the modes by which they are discovered and disclosed. That position is based on the other major finding of this study: that Bluetooth between mobile phones is what we have termed a *partially embodied* medium. At one extreme it is virtual or disembodied: one can communicate with a stranger who remains unknown. At the other extreme it is wholly embodied, in situations where the denotation of a Bluetooth name is unambiguous. For example, the "smokey" you have discovered is the Smokey you know at the same table, who is talking about the video you just sent to him. But there are important penumbral cases in which Bluetooth emanates from an unknown person who is known to be physically close, and may become known. That is often a cause of interest or even concern.

Indeed, we have shown that much may hinge on the discovery (or disclosure) that this Bluetooth name belongs to that person, in a way that is substantively different from other realms of interaction. Unlike the online realm, such a discovery is quite probable in many circumstances, and has physical immediacy. Unlike subnet-restricted broadcast of iTunes music, where the owners of network share names also may or may not become known, people carry their Bluetooth names into a variety of circumstances with new opportunities for discovery or disclosure. Unlike ordinary personal names learned in conversation, Bluetooth names are just latent enough to be put to interesting uses. People such as "almost dr dee" even base certain disclosures about themselves on that point of discovery. "Winston" wanted to impress women by discovering them. Moreover, some people play with the difficulty of making the association. "Boop" did that when she sent a file to her friends under an unknown name. "Blue army" could tell he had guessed correctly the Bluetooth name of a girl he saw in a pub, because she picked up her phone when he sent her an image. But she did not know who had sent it. If the pub was a stage, to follow Goffman [3], then this was dramatic irony. In general, its propensity for virtual-physical dissociation followed by a surprising or unwitting association make Bluetooth, used in this way between mobile phones, an *ironic* medium – a term chosen deliberately to emphasise how humans have appropriated the technology.

7 Conclusions

We have shown that Bluetooth between mobile phones represents a distinctive, partially embodied paradigm of identity projection in pervasive communication. It is integrated not simply into the physical world, but into the social world, in a sometimes ambiguous way; and that ambiguity itself plays into social practices.

There is further research to be carried out into the context behind some of the more provocative names found in our initial scans. In the meantime, however, what we have uncovered is not "how to design a better Bluetooth". Indeed, the only such implications the interviews clearly revealed was that users would, of course, prefer more bandwidth and lower battery drain, and some would prefer better security guarantees; otherwise, they were content with Bluetooth as it stands. Rather, this paper has provided a case study in how users have appropriated a pervasive system design. This is somewhat similar to the appropriation of SMS messages, also an exercise in squeezing significance into a small amount of text. However, this study shows how humans deal with an important difference: the partially embodied, relatively uncontrolled ways in which Bluetooth presence flows or 'spills' between people. In ongoing research, with a view to generating discussion about spillage and partial embodiment, we are constructing an application that will reveal scanned Bluetooth names on public displays, along with related scanned information about people's social networks and the locations where they were scanned.

Acknowledgments. The authors would like to thank Eamonn O'Neill, Vassilis Kostakos, the anonymous reviewers, and the Watershed Media Centre. This research is funded by the UK Engineering and Physical Sciences Research Council grant EP/C547683/1 (Cityware: urban design and pervasive systems).

References

1. Bell, R.: Love in the time of phone porn. The Guardian (January 30, 2007) http://education.guardian.co.uk/egweekly/story/0,2001171,00.html
2. Blaber, G., Brown, A., Bouchard, J.-P.: IDC Western European Mobile Phone Forecast and Analysis, 2005-2010 (2006)
3. Goffman, E.: The presentation of self in everyday life, Penguin (1959)
4. Kindberg, T., Spasojevic, M., Sellen, A., Fleck, R.: The ubiquitous camera: an in-depth study of camera phone use. IEEE Pervasive Computing 4(2), 42–50 (2005)
5. Marx, G.T.: What's in a Name? Some Reflections on the Sociology of Anonymity. The Information Society 15(2), 99–112 (1999)
6. O'Neill, E., Kostakos, V., Kindberg, T., gen, F., Schiek, A., Penn, A., Stanton Fraser, D., Jones, T.: Instrumenting the city: developing methods for observing and understanding the digital cityscape. In: Dourish, P., Friday, A. (eds.) UbiComp 2006. LNCS, vol. 4206, Springer, Heidelberg (2006)
7. Persson, P., Jung, Y.: Nokia Sensor: From Research to Product. In: proceedings Conference on Designing for User eXperience (DUX) (2005)
8. Plant, S.: On the Mobile: the effects of mobile telephones on social and individual life. Report commissioned by Motorola (2002)
9. Rudström, Å., Höök, K., Svensson, M.: Social positioning: Designing the Seams between Social, Physical and Digital Space. In: 1st International Conference on Online Communities and Social Computing, at HCII 2005, 24-27 July 2005, Las Vegas, USA (2005)
10. Skog, B.: Mobiles and the Norwegian teen: identity, gender and class. In: Katz, J.E., Aakhus, M. (eds.) Perpetual contact: mobile communication, private talk, public performance, pp. 255–273. Cambridge University Press, New York (2002)
11. Smale, S., Greenberg, S.: Broadcasting information via display names in instant messaging. In: Proceedings of the 2005 international ACM SIGGROUP conference on Supporting group work, pp. 89–98. ACM Press, New York (2005)

Why It's Worth the Hassle: The Value of In-Situ Studies When Designing Ubicomp
(Nominated for the Best Paper Award)

Yvonne Rogers[1,2], Kay Connelly[2], Lenore Tedesco[3], William Hazlewood[2], Andrew Kurtz[2], Robert E. Hall[3], Josh Hursey[2], and Tammy Toscos[2]

[1] The Open University, Computing Department
Milton Keynes, MK7 6AA, UK
`y.rogers@open.ac.uk`
[2] Indiana University, School of Informatics,
Bloomington, IN 47405, USA
`{connelly,whazlewo,ajkurtz,jjhursey,ttoscos}@indiana.edu`
[3] Indiana University~Purdue University, Indianapolis,
Center for Earth & Environmental Science Indiana 46202, USA
`{ltedesco,bhall}@iupui.edu`

Abstract. How should Ubicomp technologies be evaluated? While lab studies are good at sensing aspects of human behavior and revealing usability problems, they are poor at capturing context of use. In-situ studies are good at demonstrating how people appropriate technologies in their intended setting, but are expensive and difficult to conduct. Here, we show how they can be used more productively in the design process. A mobile learning device was developed to support teams of students carrying out scientific inquiry in the field. An initial in-situ study showed it was not used in the way envisioned. A contextualized analysis led to a comprehensive understanding of the user experience, usability and context of use, leading to a substantial redesign. A second in-situ study showed a big improvement in device usability and collaborative learning. We discuss the findings and conclude how in-situ studies can play an important role in the design and evaluation of Ubicomp applications and user experiences.

Keywords: In-situ studies, design, evaluation, user experience, usability, mobile learning.

1 Introduction

Evaluation is central to the design process when developing a new product, system or application. As ubiquitous computing technologies (aka Ubicomp) mature, it will become increasingly important that they, likewise, are evaluated to meet usability and user experience goals. However, Ubicomp applications are inherently difficult to evaluate due to their context of use. Traditional evaluation methods and metrics, designed for controlled laboratory settings, fail to capture the complexities and richness of the real world in which the applications are placed. For example, task completion times and usability errors say little about how an Ubicomp application

J. Krumm et al. (Eds.): UbiComp 2007, LNCS 4717, pp. 336–353, 2007.

engenders a novel user experience, such as collective story telling through distributed photography [27]. A new approach to capturing more of the context of use has been to create 'living' laboratories that attempt to simulate a particular environment, such as the home, that is instrumented to sense and measure all manner of human behaviors [e.g., 16,17].

An alternative paradigm has been to push the research out of the lab into the real world [see 29]. In-situ studies (also known as 'in the wild' studies) are beginning to appear that evaluate the situated design experience of Ubicomp, resulting in *understandings* of how novel pervasive technologies are appropriated in real world settings. These are quite different from the *results* of lab-based studies and include how: visitors engage with installations in museums [14]; people play mixed reality games in city streets and online [2, 4]; spectators record and communicate large-scale events [27]; biologists capture and analyze environmental field work observations [33] and students share and use a public display situated in their common room [7].

Kjeldskov et al., have argued, however, that in-situ studies provide *little added value,* being difficult and more expensive to conduct than lab studies and question whether "it is worth the hassle" [18]. While they can be labor-intensive and more costly to run than a lab study, it is increasingly accepted within the Ubicomp community that the rich and varied data that can be obtained *in situ* provide quite different insights into people's perceptions and their experiences of using, interacting or communicating through the new technologies in the context of their everyday and working lives. In addition, studies can be designed to obtain data about the usability of the technology, in terms of what functions are used, which are not and the difficulties encountered when used in a particular context.

The potential costliness and difficulty of running *in situ* studies, however, raises research questions as to how to make them effective. Utmost in many researchers' minds is how long should they last? Is a day, a week, a month or a year optimal? This obviously depends on the goals of a study, but the debate is most pertinent when evaluating mobile devices and applications that are explicitly designed to change people's habits that take time (e.g., exercising more [9, 31]) versus those that are designed to support and enhance an existing activity (e.g., brainstorming, scientific inquiry [25]). Another important issue is how much and what kinds of data to collect. Are *pervasive* methods, i.e., logging and sampling of events, enabled by the Ubicomp technologies, themselves, the most useful or are ethnographic methods, such as interviewing and videoing, more effective for capturing and analyzing changes in behavior? Or, is a hybrid approach feasible? A further debate is whether to represent *in situ* data as meaningful or significant: are bar charts, vignettes and quotes sufficient or are ANOVAs and regressions needed? Finally, having analyzed the data, how can the findings be fed back into the design process? In particular, how can they be used to improve both the design of the technology and the user experience?

Our research is concerned with explicating the methodological challenges and benefits of using *in situ* studies in the design process. We describe a case study that shows how an in-situ study informed the redesign of a mobile learning device, greatly improving both its situated use and usability. We describe the progression from initial user requirements to prototype design, to in-situ user study and analysis, to reflection and redesign, to a second in-situ evaluation that demonstrated substantial improvements. Section 2 provides the background to the evaluation methods being used in Ubicomp. Section 3 outlines the initial project goals and the first design iteration of the mobile learning tool. The first in-situ study is then described in Section 4, followed by the findings and analysis in Section 5. Section 6 shows how the user experience and usability problems were categorized and how we used these to iterate further our design. We present the findings from the second in-situ study in Section 7 before concluding with a discussion of the value (and challenges) of in-situ studies during the design process.

2 Background

Usability testing is the conventional approach to evaluating user interfaces that involves collecting data using a combination of methods (i.e., experiments, observation, interviews, questionnaires) in a controlled setting, usually a lab. The primary goal is to determine whether an interface is usable by the intended user population to carry out the tasks for which it was designed [11]. The approach has been extensively and successfully used to evaluate software applications running on PCs and other technologies where participants can be seated in front of them to perform a set of tasks.

Ubicomp applications that are used over a long period of time by people who are moving around and doing other things, however, present a new set of challenges. One approach is to adapt existing HCI methods, such as heuristic evaluation for analyzing ambient displays [21]. Another is to develop new intervention evaluation methods for collecting and sampling data, including cultural probes [12], photo blogging [23] and the experience sampling method [8]. Ethnographies that describe the work people do in their day-to-day activities have also become more popular. The focus has been on explicating the situated nature of the work or other practice with an emphasis on how existing technologies are used by people in places like the home, hospital or church [e.g., 1, 10, 30] with a view to the 'play of possibilities' for designing new Ubicomp-based systems.

A few ethnographically-based, evaluations of prototypes have been situated in physical spaces [6, 7, 26] or by following mobile users around [31, 20]. Based on the findings arising from these studies, various conceptual frameworks have been developed that prescribe or sensitize other researchers to design concerns. [e.g., 3, 5]. While such frameworks can inspire the early phases of Ubicomp development, they offer little guidance on how to iterate a design in order to improve its usability, efficacy and/or enhance the user experience. Alternatively, new conceptual measures have been proposed such as focus, adoption and interpretation [28]. Case studies, such as ours, that explicate the issues, design rationale and choices made in a project, can also elucidate the processes involved [32].

3 The Lilly ARBOR Case Study

Our case study addresses a problem identified as part of an ongoing educational program: how to augment field experiences to better engage students in scientific inquiry processes. A team of environmental scientists had observed that students performed limited analysis in the field, which was problematic since the program did not have a classroom component. The scientists asked if we could develop a mobile application that would provide the "right kind" of information to improve students' ability "to do more analysis" in the field. This premise was our starting point.

3.1 Overview of Lilly ARBOR Project

The Lilly ARBOR project is concerned with investigating ecological restoration of urban regions while also providing educational opportunities to a variety of students through hands-on learning activities. A one-mile stretch of riverbank in Indiana (US) was restored in 2000, using three of the most common methods for planting trees to restore native forests. The project site was divided into eight plots and over 1400 native trees were initially planted. The site is now evolving into a wildflower meadow and shrub/sapling habitat as the trees grow and other species gradually re-colonize the area.

Twice a year, teams of environmental scientists and students have conducted an assessment of the site, measuring the survival and growth of trees and noting things such as predator damage and the impact of the invasion of other trees and plants. Each team spends the day locating, identifying and measuring the surviving trees for a plot. The learning experience focuses on what is involved in being an environmental scientist: learning about wetland restoration and how to observe, collect, record and analyze data.

Assisted by the team leader, students perform two basic tasks for each tree originally planted at the site: locating and measuring. Students must first identify a particular tree from amongst the self-recruiting species now growing at the site. Once found, students measure the tree with specialized measuring tools. While seemingly straightforward, students need to learn how to hold the instruments and work out which part of the tree to measure, especially if it has multiple branches or has suffered damage. A paper-based chart is used to write down the measurements for each tree and any accompanying comments. It also shows the previous data and comments from the last measurement.

Interviews with the environmental scientists, who lead the student teams in the Lilly ARBOR project, revealed how the paper-based method of recording and looking up data can be laborious and susceptible to errors. In particular, they noted how the lack of space on the paper sheets restricts what information can be written down and revisited, having the effect of limiting exploration of observations and hampering hypothesis testing because previous data is not readily available on site. Instead, students have focused on the task of measuring the tree's dimensions, finding it difficult to reason subsequently about the implications of these with respect to environmental issues.

3.2 Requirements

In further discussions with the environmental scientists, we explored what kinds of contextually-relevant information might encourage students to reason more when conducting the measuring activities. Our aim was to replace the paper-based method of measuring with an electronic version that would enable the students to switch between observation, data collection and analysis. To this end, our primary design goals were categorized in terms of learning and usability, based on a combination of pedagogical objectives and usability design principles.

Learning (user experience) Goals. Students should be able to:
- use relevant digital information to understand more about their observations
- share and discuss their observations with other team members
- reflect upon their measuring activities and begin to make inferences about their findings with respect to the planting methods used in the various plots

Usability Goals. The mobile device should allow students to:
- enter measurements and observations into a database (ease of use)
- learn its functionality quickly (learnability)
- use it outdoors while on the move (ease of use)
- discover and locate information (findability)
- read its display in varying environmental conditions (readability)
- show, explain and relay relevant information to others in the team (shareability).

3.3   The Design of LillyPad 1.0

We designed the LillyPad application to provide three core functions: (i) a data entry feature for new measurements and comments, (ii) a historical overview feature showing previously recorded data for each originally-planted tree, and (iii) an information feature showing additional information about the various tree species present at the site. We used a simple and familiar 'tabs' metaphor of interaction, with three tabs representing the functions of data entry ('entry'), historical data ('stats') and additional information ('info'). Clicking on a tab results in a page for that function appearing on the screen (see Fig. 1). The tabs were always visible to enable easy tapping on and switching between. For example, a student could look at the stats page to see previously entered data for a particular tree, followed by tapping on the info tab to see what the leaf for the tree should look like. LillyPad has a page listing all of the trees planted in a given plot and their numbers as an anchor page. Clicking on a tree leads to the data entry page for that tree.

The entry tab page provides a dialog box; data is entered via a combination of checkboxes and a keypad, while comments are entered using a virtual keyboard that pops up at the bottom of the screen. The stats page shows the previous measurements recorded and comments made. This information was designed to help students both locate a tree, and reason about anomalies between the historic data and their current observations. The info tab provides information about the tree species in a small window, together with a thumbnail of professional sketches of the most common parts used to identify a tree (e.g., a leaf) taken from an environmental website (USDA). To see more detail, students could enlarge the sketches to the full screen by tapping on the thumbnails.

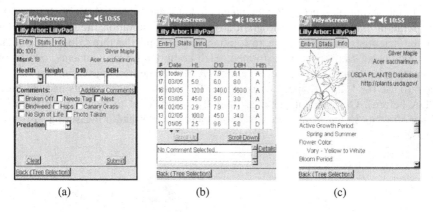

Fig. 1. Screen shots of a) data entry, b) stats and c) info pages for LillyPad 1.0

4 In-Situ Study I

4.1 Methodology

We collected both quantitative and qualitative data to evaluate whether the LillyPad application met our goals:

- logs of page clicks on PDAs throughout the measuring day
- focus group at end of measuring day with all team leaders reflecting on how their team used LillyPad
- commentary by students to roaming researchers throughout the day about their experiences with LillyPad
- vignettes selected from the video material recorded during the day

Having a mix of evaluation methods enabled us to obtain usage pattern data, elicit user feedback (primarily about usability aspects), and observe how LillyPad supported collaborative learning and analysis.

4.2 Procedure

Preliminary user testing of the LillyPad application was carried out by two environmental scientists. Their primary concerns were whether the application was accurate, understandable and easy to navigate. They checked that the database was up-to-date with the appropriate datasets for each plot and tried all functions. We subsequently trained the six scientists who would lead the teams on the measuring day how to use the device. Since technical support would take up to 15 minutes to arrive, they also went through the procedures for what to do when students pressed incorrect buttons or accidentally quit the application. We also designed an outdoor training session for the students, since they would not have the opportunity to become familiar with the application beforehand. Large posters of the most important screenshots were used as visual aids.

On the actual measuring day, eighteen students and eight volunteers from a local corporation that sponsors the program arrived at the restoration site at 8.00 a.m. One of the scientists introduced the restoration project and the three different planting methods used. Six teams were formed, each comprising three students, one or two volunteers and one of the trained scientists. A 10-minute training session was held on how to use the LillyPad application and the PDA (several participants had not used a PDA before). One student per team initially volunteered to be the PDA user. The other students in the team were each given another task and a measuring instrument to use.

Fig. 2. Teams measuring trees in the spring using LillyPad 1.0 and in the fall using LillyPad 2.0

The teams then began to systematically locate and measure the trees in their plot (see Fig. 2). As in previous years, team leaders used any unusual observations, such as if a tree appeared to be missing, as opportunities to probe the students to think about the likely causes. The field day lasted about 6 hours, with a lunch break when the teams had a chance to hear more about the Lilly ARBOR project. Throughout the day, team members switched between using the LillyPad application and the other measuring devices, which was encouraged by the team leader.

Given the physical scope of the project (i.e., a mile long stretch of land), it was impractical for the researchers to observe and record all teams. Instead, we asked a corporate volunteer to video their team's activities with a camcorder we provided. We instructed them to be selective in what they recorded, thereby allowing them to also participate in the group activity. This included videoing measuring the trees using the instruments, the use of and problems with the LillyPad application, and surrounding discussions that ensued. Three researchers roamed the site, staying with one team for an hour or so before moving on to another, while two others remained at base on call should any technical difficulties arise.

4.3 Findings

We analyzed the data in terms of descriptive usage patterns, team leader quotes, summaries of student comments and a detailed analysis of a poignant vignette. These were considered sufficient to assess the learning and usability goals.

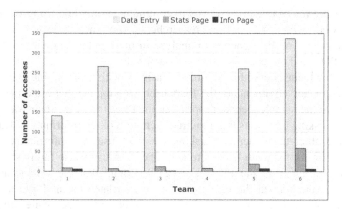

Fig. 3. Mean number of page clicks per team

Usage Patterns: Figure 3 summarizes the page clicks for each team. The number of accesses to the stats and info pages was relatively small, 10-60 for the stats page and less than 10 for the info page. In contrast, the data entry pages were accessed far more, varying between 140 and 330 times per team. This spread reflects, in part, the number of trees surviving in a plot and therefore the number of trees for which data was recorded per plot.

Team Leader Focus Group: All of the team leaders made positive comments about the potential of LillyPad, and said how successful it was for recording data entry. However, they noted that LillyPad was not used very often for other tasks. For example, one team leader pointed out how they *"only used it once but it was very important that one time."* Another pointed out how *"the real advantage was bringing up the stats page so that we could see what a tree was doing multiple times in the past. We found several trees that were missing, and with only the paper then it was missing with no data; but with the device it was very valuable for us to know that this was a beaver-eaten tree covered with reed-canary grass, and that two years ago it was 4cm in diameter."* Another mentioned how it made her change the types of questions she asked, knowing that the students could look up the information on the device that they could not do with the paper-based version.

Student Commentary: Most students learned how to enter data quickly. Several students commented on the difficulty of using the small keyboard to enter data and comments. Some also pointed out how the sketches were not very helpful for identifying trees, and having looked at a couple, they did not bother to access the info pages anymore.

Video Vignettes: In total we collected over 12 hours of video data (2-3 hours per team). The method of selecting certain activities from the total footage that exhibit routines, breakdowns and problems is typical of ethnographic field studies, acting "as a resource, as a set of alerting mechanisms, and as a means of orientation" [13]. One researcher watched all of the videos, marking down and transcribing events where (i) the teams used the PDA to look up information and do any subsequent analysis, and

(ii) there were noticeable breakdowns in communication while using LillyPad. These were viewed with two further researchers who then selected from them a representative set of 10 vignettes to analyze in more detail, showing different teams using the PDA and the problems they encountered.

For (i), the teams worked in an orderly fashion, with different members calling out measurements and comments to the PDA user, who tapped them into the application. We observed the team leaders appropriating the PDA to change their way of engaging students by asking questions that required them to look up information. Rarely did we observe the other team members asking the PDA user for information. It was far more common for the team leaders to ask. The PDA users also rarely showed or read aloud information from the PDA. For (ii) we found that the collaborative process sometimes overwhelmed the PDA user as she translated the multiple measurements called out by the team into numbers, comments and ticks, while simultaneously confirming the entries were correct. During these times, team members had to wait and sometimes repeat their measurement while she completed other parts of the entry task.

While the videos showed how the teams were able to enter data for each of the trees in their plot, the LillyPad application clearly did not meet our learning goals of enabling more analysis to take place whilst in the field measuring. We drilled down on three of the vignettes to explore why this might be the case. Transcribing the minutiae of a poignant moment of an activity, coupled with watching the vignette numerous times, can provide a richer account and interpretation of the interactions within the team, the physical environment and the technologies [15]. It also assists in framing specific recommendations for improving the design. We present one of the transcripts here that reveals the tensions that arose in one team when trying to do both data entry and analysis.

A portion of the vignette is presented in Table 1. The numbers in the text refer to the line in the table. The vignette starts with the team leader (T) noticing a tree that previously had been recorded as dead, re-appearing in the form of a bud (1). Two students (F1, F2) are measuring the height of the tree. A tree appearing to grow after being reported dead is a strange occurrence that warrants reasoning. T is excited and sees this as an opportunity to ask the PDA user (M1) to look up the stats data so they can reason about the tree's disappearance (8). M1 does not heed T's request, but continues to enter data while asking others to confirm what he is entering (3, 10, 13). It appears he is focused on the task and does not 'hear' T. T persists and repeats his request twice (9, 14), yet M1 continues to ignore him. Eventually, T stands up, walks to him, and forcefully gestures at the PDA telling M1 what to do. At this point, M1 does what is asked and brings up the stats page (15). T then reads aloud that the tree has been recorded as dead for the last five years. The other team members marvel and comment on how a tree that has been dead is now alive. M1 continues to be focused on the data entry and does not join in the discussion, only asking how he should record it (20).

It took several attempts by the team leader to access the information that would enable the team to reflect on the unusual sighting. The PDA user clearly focused on

Table 1. Transcript of the team measuring a tree presumed dead but which has grown a new bud

1. T *(team leader crouching next to budding tree holding measuring pole):* "It's come back! That clearly is an Ohio buckeye."
2. F1 *(female student crouching next to him, measuring the height of the tree against the pole):* "Now are we measuring the flower top or just the stem? I think it's about seven." *T and F1 look over to male student (M1) holding PDA standing 2 feet away.*
3. M1 "Seven point zero?"
4. T: "Yeah. And you can make an estimate for the width. Could be about half."
5. *F1 stands up.* "Yeah, yeah, that was what I was thinking." *F1 crouches down to test her prediction by measuring the diameter of the bud using the calipers.*
6. F2 *(another female student in the team looking on):* "It is a big flower!"
7. *F1 reads off her measurement:* "Point five zero"
8. T: "We're budding. Rejoice. The tree has resurrected. Let's look at the statistics in there and see how long it has been missing. Is it just one year?"
9. *T waits for a few seconds and then follows up his initial request by being more assertive:* "That will be the middle tab." *M1 still does not reply. T stands up and walks over to M1 and stands in front of him.*
10. *M1 does not look up but asks the others to confirm.* "It's budding you say?"
11. F2: "Yes it's budding"
12. M2 *(a student questions the observations)* "So, we want to figure out when it died?"
13. M1 *(puzzled by M2's comment)* "Once dead, now alive?"
14. *T looks at the PDA screen and points to the data entry accept button:* "Go ahead and accept that. And then look at the stats page." *(Points to the tab on the screen to click on)*
15. *M clicks on stats tab T reads off from stats page:* "Dead, dead, dead, dead, dead, dead, dead, dead. Our every measurement."
16. F2: "Wow, it's been dead?"
17. *M2 reading the screen over M1's shoulder:* "We got"
18. F1: "What a comeback!"
19. M1: "Should I say dead, now alive?" *(returns to task of adding comments)*
20. F1: "Planted and never to be seen for 5 years."

completing the data entry task, ignoring the repeated requests by the team leader. This suggests an inflexibility in our design that needed to be addressed. Specifically:

- data entry is successful but time-consuming
- the PDA user has difficulty multi-tasking when entering data
- the PDA user takes a more passive role during reasoning activities
- the PDA user does not share information from the PDA unless specifically asked.

5   Redesign: LillyPad 2.0

In light of the problems observed with LillyPad 1.0 in the in-situ study, our overarching goal for the redesign was to more fully support analysis *during the measuring activities*. The central objectives were to enable the PDA user to look up relevant data and information *when* it was deemed useful, and to *want* to share and reflect upon this data with the rest of the team. In essence, we wanted the PDA user to shift from a reactive to a proactive use of the application. We revised our learning and usability goals, accordingly:

- reduce the cognitive demands on the PDA user when entering data by making it less time-consuming and cumbersome
- redesign the stored information to make it more task-relevant and to encourage more active engagement
- include a new set of graphical representations to provide another way of supporting the analysis and reasoning about anomalies
- increase awareness of and reflection on what the other teams are discovering and measuring by enabling communication between teams located in different plots.

5.1 Reduced Cognitive Load

Our first priority was to reduce the data entry burden so that the PDA user can multitask when asked a question or when the team engages in an analysis. We endeavored to improve the interface to make data entry faster, and to make switching between data entry and other tasks easier (See Fig. 4).

Interface Enhancements: We redesigned the data entry page to make it easier and less demanding to fill in. We added white space and enlarged several of the interface widgets to make them easier to select. For example, we introduced a large customized pop-up keypad for easier entry of numerical measurements, reducing the risk of errors. We also included additional checkboxes, thereby reducing the need to type in common comments.

Increasing the size and spacing of the widgets comes at a cost of screen space. The checkboxes could no longer fit on one page, which meant adding sub-pages that appear as pop-up windows. While increasing the navigation path is typically frowned on in mobile application design, the benefits are to make data entry much less cumbersome, including reducing the need for typed comments which our in-situ study found to be particularly problematic in this setting. In addition, the new design should help the PDA users:

- deal with the rapid callouts from the other team members as they could more easily fill in the checkboxes in quick succession
- check that all of the necessary data has been entered in a systematic order
- manage the multiple inputs competently while feeling in control

Two PDAs per Team: We decided to provide half the teams with 1 PDA and the other with 2 PDAs to compare if more analysis would ensue if less work was required by the PDA user. In the 2 PDA condition, one student was assigned the role of 'data entry' and the other as 'information explorer' (i.e. they could view the data, but not enter it). This division of labor allows the data entry person to focus on their role while enabling the other student to look up and share relevant information with the team. We also considered providing each team member with their own PDA but that could have transformed the collaborative activity into individually-based tasks, when

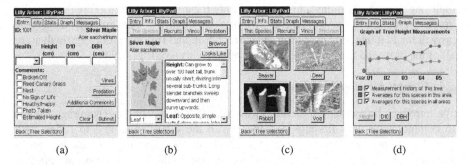

(a)   (b)   (c)   (d)

Fig. 4. Screenshots of LillyPad 2.0: revised (a) data entry, (b) info page, (c) new images of predation, and (d) graphical representation of average tree growth for tree, species and area

our goal was to encourage collaborative learning. Also they would have had to continuously switch between the various measuring activities and holding a PDA, which would have more likely increased cognitive load.

5.2 More Task Relevant Information

We completely rewrote the information pages to support the specific activities involved in tree identification for this particular restoration site. The description of the trees employed a more accessible and enjoyable form of prose. Distinguishing features used for identification appeared first. For example, the text for the Hawthorn begins with "Hawthorns are often affected by crown gall and witches brooms". In addition, we replaced the black and white sketches of the leaves and other identifying features with color photos taken from the Lilly ARBOR site during the fall. Given the next measuring day was scheduled for the fall (where the foliage is quite different from the spring) we wanted to enable them to make comparisons more readily between what they were seeing at the site (see Fig. 3) with what was stored on the Lillypad application (see Fig. 4b-c).

Further design sessions with the environmental scientists resulted in a revised ontology for structuring the information, which included new categories deemed to be more appropriate when identifying, measuring and analyzing. These included the categories of 'looks like', predators, vines and native recruits. Findability was improved by placing photos of the possible vines, trees, or predator damage side by side, so that they could be compared (see Fig. 4c). The rationale was that if a student noticed a tree that had been eaten, covered in a vine, or overtaken by an invasive recruit (e.g., grass), they could easily select a button to obtain relevant information for identifying the predator, vine, or recruit.

5.3 Graphical Representations to Support Analysis

We added a set of graphical representations to visualize the trends and patterns of tree growth over the five years. We thought they would encourage more analysis in situ, since it is easier to make inferences from explicit graphical representations as compared to equivalent numerical data [19]. We wanted the students to have the opportunity to interpret the significance of growth patterns over time in the context of their ongoing observations and measurements for a particular tree. Three simple line graphs were used to show: (i) the growth of a particular tree over time, (ii) the average growth for that tree species within the current plot, and (iii) the average growth across all of the plots and therefore all of the planting styles (see Fig. 4d).

5.4 Communication Between Teams

We introduced a messaging facility to the LillyPad application to encourage students to communicate their findings and ideas with the other teams and to reflect more globally about the planting method's effect on tree growth. The facility allows students to send short text messages to one another in the different plots at opportune times, such as when they noticed something unusual in their plot (e.g., the oak trees by the river not growing as well as expected). On receiving a message, the PDA users in the other plots could read it out to their team members, triggering the team to reflect upon it with respect to their own measurements (e.g., note if the oaks by the river in their plot were growing less or more). We provided a menu of partially completed messages to make it easy to send messages, such as "our <blank> are doing very well" and "we are seeing a lot of <blank>". We were able to create wi-fi coverage for just over half of the restoration site, using a number of access points and car batteries. Since we anticipated the data entry student to be focused on data entry tasks, we decided to only provide communication to teams with 2 PDAs.

6 In-Situ Study II

During the fall measuring day, a similar number, but different set, of students and volunteers took part. They were divided into teams and trained in the same way as before. However this time, half the teams were given two PDAs and half were given one PDA. The same evaluation methods were used as in the first study. For brevity, we highlight the most interesting results from the logged data, user feedback and video analysis.

Table 2. Average clicks per page types for versions 1 and 2 of the LillyPad application

Page Type	Version 1	Version 2
Data entry	247.5	268
Info	19	48
Stats	4.5	112
Graph	N/A	20

Usage Patterns: The logged data showed a big increase in the usage of pages for the redesigned LillyPad application compared with the first version, as shown in Table 2. To make the comparison fair, the totals were divided by two for the groups with two PDAs. As expected, there was no significant difference for the accesses to the data entry page because the two sets of teams were measuring approximately the same number of trees. However, teams using LillyPad 2.0 accessed the info and stats pages significantly more than teams using LillyPad 1.0 ($t = 4.3$, $P<0.002$ and $t = 2.8$,

P<0.01, respectively). There was very little difference between the teams with one and two PDAs for accessing data entry, stats and info pages. Users in both teams accessed the full range of pages, suggesting that improvements in the design of these pages encouraged greater use. The only significant difference between the one and two PDA teams was the number of graph pages accessed. Significantly more were looked at in the two PDA condition than in the one PDA condition (t = 6.001, P<0.004), and it was the info explorer who accessed most of them.

Contrary to our expectations, the messaging facility was rarely used. Table 3 shows the entire set of messages sent between the three teams using it, indicating they used it for only a short period. One function was to keep each other informed of progress (in terms of which tree they were on and that it was lunchtime). Another use was to report on unusual sightings. A confusion caused by a typo in a message sent by Area 8 became the topic of conversation for Team 6, where they mention having seen 'catalpzs' among their trees when they meant 'catalpas' (a catalpa is a native recruit, with showy clusters of white flowers, not often found in Indiana). Area 6 misread this and asks them have they seen 'caterpillars' in the trees. Area 8 then reads this as Area 6 having seen caterpillars and asks them on which trees. The video analysis later showed that this misunderstanding sparked a discussion within the team in Area 6 of whether it is possible for caterpillars to be around in the fall. The main reason that teams did not use the messaging facility is that they were too involved in their team's activities. The PDA users did not want to miss out on the discussions and activities that were going on and said that messaging interfered with that. It was considered too distracting; they did not want to be transported to another place, albeit momentarily, as they felt there was enough going on in their own teams.

Team Leader and Student Feedback: The team leaders pointed out that entering data was much easier and the checkboxes quicker to fill in compared with the first version. The students could not think of any problems when entering data or comments about a tree but instead volunteered what additional information could be added (e.g., other images). Some said that the PDA encouraged them to think more about what they were doing. For example, one student mentioned *"It was nice to be able to look up information about the trees, be able to identify it, plus the history, to be able to see if this tree is doing well because a lot of the time you can look at it and say wow that poor little tree has got a lot of competition ... So I think it really added to the experience of learning about what it was that we were looking at."* She also commented on the pleasure of interacting with the graphical and numerical data: *"The enjoyment was to look into the history to see what the tree was doing in the last six months, last year."*

Video Vignettes: The videos revealed far more instances of the PDA users sharing information with their team. They took the initiative to contribute to the ongoing activity, reading out information about a particular species, or showing a relevant image which often led to a teammate making a reasoned guess or hypothesis as to why a tree could not be located. This sometimes triggered a more general discussion about what the team was observing in the field and what they were finding out from the LillyPad application (e.g., why a particular species was not growing well close to the river).

Table 3. Text messages sent between the teams with 2 PDAS

10:57:52 I Area6 I bindweeds are dead
11:36:14 I Area7 I hi
11:41:12 I Area8 I we r seeing catalpzs in the trees
11:41:40 I Area8 I our bindweeds r dead as well
11:46:29 I Area6 I bindweed dead
11:48:13 I Area6 I catepillers
11:49:15 I Area6 I did you mean catepillers
12:00:13 I Area8 I we have a seedling cottonwood, Lenore is very excited!
12:02:55 I Area8 I on what are the caterpillers? and what kind?
12:13:41 I Area7 I is lunch ready
12:21:34 I Area7 I lunch is ready come get it
13:51:49 I Area6 I What tree are you on?
13:57:34 I Area8 I 8096

As with the first study, the team leaders tailored their questions in ways that the students could answer with information on the PDA, which sometimes led to more analysis. For example, a team discussed the different rates of growth with respect to the planting method. We saw between 5-10 examples per team of these types of analysis for the one PDA groups, and between 10-20 for the two PDA groups. Both the info explorer and data entry person took part. Illustrative examples of these have been transcribed and analyzed in terms of the interactions and inquiry processes that took place [24].

7 Discussion

This case study has shown how the findings from an in-situ study were used to understand and improve upon the usability and situated user experience of a mobile learning device. The first in-situ study showed the students not using the device other than for data entry and finding this to be time-consuming. Many of the interface changes that were subsequently made to the application led to enhanced usability and encouraged quite a different kind of user experience. The second in-situ study revealed the students enjoying entering data and finding information that in turn encouraged them to engage in more reflective processes. Being able to find pertinent information and share it with others at key moments resulted in discoveries and discussions that were rewarding. Team leaders also noted how the students' interactions with them and each other, together with their shared use of the device, were markedly different from the first version.

While the outcomes of our in situ studies were successful, they were costly in terms of the time and effort involved. Could we have not come up with a much cheaper form of discount usability engineering [22] and achieved the same or even better results by asking a team of experts to predict how it would be used? The answer is, simply, no. Our initial user testing with expert environmental scientists showed them all competently using the LillyPad application and not envisioning any usability problems. However, placing the device in the palms of students on a cold spring day revealed a whole host of unexpected, context-based usability and user experience problems.

Furthermore, the in-situ setting of our case study revealed how the environment can have a quite different impact on the user experience. In particular, the time of year and the accompanying changes in the foliage affected the way the two versions of LillyPad were used. In the spring the site was barren, making it easy to find trees but hard to identify them as they did not have the typical signs of life, e.g., bright foliage. In the fall, the opposite was true. The site was overgrown, making locating trees more difficult because they were often hidden by grasses, etc., while identifying them easier because of the presence of more identifiable features, e.g., leaves. The cold and clement conditions in the spring and fall, and the time of day also affected the well-being, moods and motivation of everyone. For example, most of the analyses in the second measuring day happened in the morning and very few in late afternoon, when the teams got into a routine and wanted to finish. The effects of and interactions between these situated experience factors made us think quite differently about how to change the design of LillyPad and also our criteria for what counted as successful learning.

Given that in-situ studies are inevitably costly and time-consuming, how do researchers decide upon which methods to use and which of the large amount of potential data they collect to focus on? We used a combination of methods, including logged device data, observations and interviews that enabled a range of data to be collected. A critical part of our analysis was the drilling down on a small number of video vignettes that enabled us to explore concretely the potential and problems experienced by a team when using the LillyPad application as they went about their measuring activities. This provided a 'contextual backdrop' against which to reflect upon the design of the user experience and the mobile device, sensitizing us to how LillyPad *would* (rather than should) be used in practice. It also provided a grounding with which to propose new functions, of which some proved to be successful (e.g. the graphing function) and others not (e.g., the messaging system). Further, this deeper understanding of the situated activities assisted us in explaining why some features were used and others were not.

Finally, it is impossible, and nor is it desirable, to capture everything when in situ. The key is to use various methods that reveal both hoped for and unexpected effects of the context of use. Identifying user experience and usability goals also provides a good framing reference from which to analyze the details of certain events.

Acknowledgments

We thank the Eli Lilly and Company Foundation, the Rotary Club of Indianapolis and the Pervasive Technology Labs, Indiana University for funding the project. Thanks also to Kara Salazar and Polly Baker at IUPUI and Allen Lee, CJ Fleck, Nick Gentille and Anne Stephenson at IUB for their various contributions. Finally, we thank all the team leaders, students and volunteers who participated in the measuring days.

References

1. Bell, G.: No More SMS from Jesus: Ubicomp, Religion and Techno-spiritual Practices. In: Dourish, P., Friday, A. (eds.) UbiComp 2006. LNCS, vol. 4206, pp. 141–158. Springer, Heidelberg (2006)
2. Bell, M., Chalmers, M., Barkhuus, L., Hall, M., Sherwood, S., Tennent, P., Brown, B., Rowland, D., Benford, S., Hampshire, A., Captra, M.: Interweaving mobile games with everyday life. In: Proc. of CHI, pp. 417–426 (2006)
3. Bellotti, V., Back, M., Edwards, K., Grinter, R., Henderson, A., Lopes, C.: Making sense of sensing systems: five questions for designers and researchers. In: Proc. of CHI, pp. 415–422 (2002)
4. Benford, S., Seager, W., Flintham, M., Anastasi, R., Rowland, D., Humble, J., Stanton, S., Bowers, J., Tandavanitj, N., Adams, M., Farr, J.R., Oldroyd, A., Sutton, J.: The error of our ways: the experience of self-reported position in a location-based game. In: Davies, N., Mynatt, E.D., Siio, I. (eds.) UbiComp 2004. LNCS, vol. 3205, pp. 721–730. Springer, Heidelberg (2004)
5. Benford, S., Schanädelbach, H., Koleva, B., Anastasi, R., Greenhalgh, C., Rodden, T., Green, J., Ghali, A., Pridmore, T., Gaver, B., Boucher, A., Walker, B., Pennington, S., Schmidt, A., Gellersen, H., Steed, A.: Expected, sensed, and desired: A framework for designing sensing-based interaction. Proc. of TOCHI, 12:1, 3–30 (2005)
6. Boucher, A., Gaver, W.: Developing the drift table. Interactions 13(1), 24–27 (2006)
7. Brignull, H., Izadi, S., Fitzpatrick, G., Rogers, Y., Rodden, T.: The introduction of a shared interactive surface into a communal space. In: Proc. of CSCW, pp. 49–58 (2004)
8. Consolvo, S., Walker, M.: Using the experience sampling method to evaluate Ubicomp applications. IEEE Pervasive Computing Mobile and Ubiquitous Systems 2(2), 24–31 (2003)
9. Consolvo, S., Everitt, K., Smith, I., Landay, J.: Design requirements for technologies that motivate physical activity. In: Proc. of CHI, pp. 457–466 (2006)
10. Crabtree, A., Rodden, T.: Domestic routines and design for the home. Computer Supported Cooperative Work: The Journal of Collaborative Computing 13(2), 191–220 (2004)
11. Dumas, J.S., Redish, J.C.: A Practical Guide to Usability Testing. Ablex, Norwood, NJ (1994)
12. Gaver, W., Dunne, T., Pacenti, E.: Cultural probes and the value of uncertainty. Interactions 11(5), 53–56 (2004)
13. Hughes, J.A., Randall, D., Shapiro, D.: Faltering from ethnography to design. In: Proc. of CSCW, pp. 115–122 (1992)
14. Hull, R., Reid, J., Geelhoed, E.: Creating experiences with wearable computing. IEEE Pervasive Computing 1(4), 56–61 (2002)
15. Hutchins, E., Klausen, T.: Distributed Cognition in an Airline Cockpit. In: Middleton, Engeström, Y. (eds.) Communication and Cognition at Work, pp. 15–34. Cambridge University Press, D. Cambridg (1996)
16. Intille, S., Larson, K., Tapia, E., Beaudin, J., Kaushik, P., Nawyn, J., Rockinson, R.: Using a live-in laboratory for ubiquitous computing research. In: Fishkin, K.P., Schiele, B., Nixon, P., Quigley, A. (eds.) PERVASIVE 2006. LNCS, vol. 3968, pp. 349–365. Springer, Heidelberg (2006)
17. Kidd, C., Orr, R., Abowd, G., Atkeson, C., Essa, I., MacIntyre, B., Mynatt, E., Starner, T.: The Aware Home: A Living Laboratory for Ubiquitous Computing Research. In: Streitz, N.A., Hartkopf, V. (eds.) CoBuild 1999. LNCS, vol. 1670, pp. 191–198. Springer, Heidelberg (1999)

18. Kjeldskov, J., Skov, M., Als, B., Høegh, R.: Is it worth the hassle? Exploring the added value of evaluating the usability of context-aware mobile systems in the field. In: Brewster, S., Dunlop, M.D. (eds.) MobileHCI 2004. LNCS, vol. 3160, pp. 61–73. Springer, Heidelberg (2004)
19. Larkin, J., Simon, H.: Why a diagram is (sometimes) worth ten thousand words. Cognitive Science 11, 65–99 (1987)
20. Lin, J., Mamykina, L., Lindtner, S., Delajoux, G., Strub, H.: Fish'n'Steps: Encouraging Activity with an Interactive Computer Game. In: Proc. of Ubicomp, pp. 261–278 (2006)
21. Mankoff, J., Dey, A., Hsieh, G., Kientz, J., Lederer, J., Ames, M.: Heuristic evaluation of ambient displays. In: Proc. of CHI, pp. 169–176 (2003)
22. Nielsen, J.: Usability engineering at a discount. In: Salvendy, G., Smith, M.J. (eds.) Human-Computer interaction on Designing and Using Human-Computer Interfaces and Knowledge Based Systems, pp. 394–401 (1989)
23. Olsen, A., Rogers, Y., Sharp, H.: The Snap Method. In: Workshop Proceedings, Designing Methods for New Users, Technologies, and Design Processes, CHI (2007)
24. Rogers, Y., Connelly, K., Tedesco, L., Hazlewood, W.R.: Mobile technologies for integrated scientific inquiry. Journal of Learning Sciences (submitted)
25. Rogers, Y., Price, S., Randell, C., Stanton-Fraser, D., Weal, M., Fitzpatrick., G.: Ubi-learning: Integrating outdoor and indoor learning experiences. Comm. of ACM 48(1), 55–59 (2005)
26. Rowan, G., Mynatt, E.: Digital Family Portrait Field Trial: Support for Aging in Place. In: Proc. of CHI, pp. 521–530 (2005)
27. Salovaara, A., Jacucci, G., Oulasvirta, A., Saari, T., Kanerva, P., Kurvinen, E., Tiitta, S.: Collective creation and sense-making of mobile media. In: Proc. of CHI, pp. 1211–1220 (2006)
28. Scholtz, J., Consolvo, S.: Toward a Framework for Evaluating Ubiquitous Computing Applications. Pervasive Computing 3(2), 82–88 (2004)
29. Sharp, H., Rogers, Y., Preece, J.: Interaction Design, 2nd edn. Wiley, Chichester
30. Taylor, A.S., Swan, L.: Artful systems in the home. In: Proc. CHI, pp. 641–650 (2005)
31. Toscos, T., Faber, A., An, S., Gandhi, M.: Chick Clique: persuasive technology to motivate teenage girls to exercise. In: Proc. of CHI, pp. 1873–1878 (2006)
32. Winograd, T.: Bringing Design to Software. Addison Wesley, Reading (1996)
33. Yeh, R., Liao, C., Klemmer, S., Guimbretière, F., Lee, B., Kakaradov, B., Stamberger, J., Paepcke, A.: ButterflyNet: a mobile capture and access system for field biology research. In: Proc. of CHI, pp. 571–580 (2006)

Locating Family Values:
A Field Trial of the Whereabouts Clock
(Nominated for the Best Paper Award)

Barry Brown[1], Alex S. Taylor[2], Shahram Izadi[2],
Abigail Sellen[2], Joseph 'Jofish' Kaye[3], and Rachel Eardley[4]

[1] UC San Diego, Dept. of Communications, San Diego CA, USA
Barry.AT.Brown@acm.org
[2] Microsoft Research Cambridge, Cambridge, UK
{ast,shahrami,asellen}@microsoft.com
[3] Information Science, Cornell University, Ithaca NY, USA
jofish@cornell.edu
[4] Skype, 711 Lexington St., London, UK
rachel.eardley@skype.net

Abstract. We report the results of a long-term, multi-site field trial of a situated awareness device for families called the "Whereabouts Clock". The Clock displayed family members' current location as one of four privacy-preserving, deliberately coarse-grained categories (HOME, WORK, SCHOOL or ELSEWHERE). In use, the Clock supported not only family co-ordination but also more emotive aspects of family life such as reassurance, connectedness, identity and social touch. This emphasized aspects of family life frequently neglected in Ubicomp, such as the ways in which families' awareness of each others' activities contributes to a sense of a family's identity. We draw further on the results to differentiate between location as a technical aspect of awareness systems and what we characterize as "location-in-interaction". Location-in-interaction is revealed as an emotional, accountable and even moral part of family life.

1 Introduction

The continued importance of positioning and location as core topics in Ubicomp should come as no surprise. We spend a great deal of our lives in transit, and location, of ourselves and others, is a common feature of conversation [15], highlighting the extent to which it is a fundamental concern in daily life. The technical problems involved in tracking individuals and devices has generated a rich body of research, with different radio signals in particular (GPS, wifi, GSM, FM radio) offering a range of trade-offs in location accuracy and performance (e.g. [4]). Alongside this research, user studies have explored what new applications might exist for tracking systems [5]. These applications, known broadly as "location-based services", tailor and deliver services based on a user's locale. Primary amongst such services has been the support for awareness of one's own and others' position, an area explored extensively in both commercial and research systems [8]. Studies of these systems have generated a range of issues for design, in particular how location awareness can conflict with privacy needs.

J. Krumm et al. (Eds.): UbiComp 2007, LNCS 4717, pp. 354–371, 2007.
© Springer-Verlag Berlin Heidelberg 2007

Despite this rich body of work, the commercial success of location awareness applications has been limited. One reason may be that we have yet to design systems that deliver compelling value for users, and that we have yet to gain a deep understanding of how location awareness is used in different social groups. In an effort to begin to address this, this paper presents the results from a long term trial of a distinctive location awareness system designed specifically for families called the "Whereabouts Clock" (or WAC). The WAC is a device intended to be situated in the home in the form of a clock that allows family members to see where other members of the family are in four broad categories ("home", "work", "school" and "elsewhere"). Family members are tracked using cell phones, with users choosing what geographical locations correspond to each category and thus what is displayed on the Clock at home. Following the design principle of "less is more", we deliberately designed the WAC to offer less functionality than existing systems – both communicating less about location than existing systems (essentially only two bits of information), and displaying information only within the home environment.

We present results from a trial of the Clock with five families (26 users) over a total period of six months. In practice we found that the particulars of its design successfully addressed any potential privacy concerns the families might have had. More important, however, was how the trial revealed aspects of location awareness previously neglected in the literature. Up until now, research has focused on how awareness systems can be used for the communication of location and activity, supporting coordination within social groups. However, for these families, location awareness was less about coordination and more about family members' emotional connection to one another. In other words, the WAC was not really about communicating geographical location or even activity. Rather it was about displaying information to support what families *already know* about each other and already share. More specifically, the value of the Clock came as much from the reassurance that knowing things are as one expects them to be than it did from dealing with exceptions or changing plans. This, we argue, is part and parcel of family life. Part of the "work" of being a family is to know what goes on, and to know how things are. With the WAC, we found that mothers in particular (but other family members too), used location as a way of demonstrating their care and attention to others.

Drawing on this we argue that the existing functionality of many location awareness systems fails to take into account how awareness is managed and monitored in family groups. Indeed, the current literature frequently presents an anodyne version of what position and location are, in practice, for end users. Location awareness can instead be understood for how it supports the routine and regular arrangement of family life – characterized by familiar events and familiar exceptions. Family members' positions are both *read* through these routines, but also *produced* with an awareness of that reading. In this way, the presentation of one's location is an "accountable" matter in that one can be called to account for where and why one is at certain places at certain times. In our trial, participants thought about and managed how their location appeared to others displaying sensitivity to how their location was seen. This leads to a number of implications: existing location awareness systems have been focused around supporting co-ordination between individuals, and accuracy of location has been a paramount concern. Instead this study shows how location awareness, as part of family life, is an emotional and moral affair rather than simply a tool for co-ordination or practicality. This opens up new technological possibilities for supporting home and family life.

2 Related Work

With regard to the underlying design of the technology, the WAC sits at the cross-section of location-based services and situated displays. As well as a longstanding research topic, there are now a number of commercial location-based services available in the marketplace, many of which provide a variety of ways of monitoring children and friends. For example, many cell phone service providers and operators are now leveraging location information as value-added services for their customers. Sprint's FINDME and Helio's Buddy Beacon [7] allow people to locate other cell phone users in the same network cell. Other systems, such as Dodgeball (www.dodgeball.com), which do not rely on operator support, have a fringe following of dedicated users, but are far from widespread. Many factors have impacted the broad adoption of these systems, including privacy concerns, technical issues, lack of a user base, and more general usability issues with the technology.

Location and user tracking are also prevalent areas of research in the Ubicomp and mobile computing literature. An early example was the Active Badge system, originally concerned with the ways in which the capture of real-time location information could support life within office buildings [8]. More recently, with the advent of wireless networks, many different kinds of applications have been developed, but more centered on the consumer than on the office or mobile worker. Some use location as a way of delivering context-sensitive information to tourists and shoppers [2]. Others are more properly called "tracking applications" in that they focus on the delivery of location information itself. Popular applications here include ways of supporting gaming, friendship and family [18]. Further, because of the potentially sinister connotations of "tracking" or "monitoring", much of this research is preoccupied with aspects of privacy [10]. Common to all of these applications is that location information is typically delivered to the same hand-held devices that generate that information (such as to cell phones or PDAs).

In contrast, the situated display literature reports an altogether different set of concerns, many of which have to do with the use of large displays designed to support community, whether it be in corporate life or urban settings [13]. A few have explored ways of presenting information about location, but these do not normally relate to real-time data, confining themselves instead to calendar-based information, where, for example, grandparents are offered views of events affecting their grandchildren [12].

The separation of these two literatures can be linked to the different affordances being leveraged in each case: for the location-based services literature it tends to be about the production and display of accurate information "on the hoof", where having that information in hand is paramount. For the situated display literature, the topic is how the persistent and "at-a-glance" display of information provides benefits in locations where the information is public or shared and is stable through time. In this research, the WAC brings these two sets of concerns together by combining the use of situated displays that afford persistent, at-a-glance access to information with the dynamic, real time production of that information.

3   Designing a Location Awareness System for the Family

In our own previous trials of prototype systems, as well as system trials more broadly, it is common for research prototypes to focus on providing robust functionality, with applications frequently designed by the programmers themselves. Little attention, as a result, is given to their usability and aesthetic design. In our own past experience, we have observed how shortcomings in design can impact on users' experiences and opinions of a system. In developing the WAC, we therefore sought to iterate through a number of different interfaces and physical forms in order to produce a prototype that families would be drawn to and want to have in their homes. An important step was an internal trial with an early version of the Clock that we tested with our own work group [16]. Another key step was to take early versions of the Clock home to try out over extended periods of time in our own households. As a result of this early testing, we made many refinements both to the underlying technology and the design. However, the essential nature of its design, including the use of the clock metaphor, remained unchanged. The idea of a clock displaying location rather than time, of course, is not new. In the Harry Potter books, the "Weasley" family has a magic clock with hands for each member of the family indicating their location or state. Yet using a clock as a situated device to display location information has some interesting properties, and guided many of our design decisions:

First, the WAC is a situated display designed to be located in a place in the home (like the kitchen) where it becomes part of the routine of family life, much as a clock does. The interface is designed to let families see information "at a glance"; that is, without time spent turning the device on, or changing the settings to view its status. This also means that the WAC's display is "always on", persisting in the periphery of vision in the way that information on a clock persists.

Again, as with a clock, the WAC is designed to broadcast information to anyone in sight of the device. This can be contrasted with a watch, for example, which is a personal device. However, although information is "publicly available" within the house, we decided that it should not be viewed remotely. This decision was one of our attempts to deal with the privacy issues that plague location-based systems. Since the WAC could only be seen when physically in the home, only people entitled to be in the home can see it. This acts as a crude, yet very straightforward, form of access control which we thought would help to allay families' concerns about privacy (even though, as we discuss later, this concern was perhaps overplayed in our design).

Lastly, the WAC displays only coarse-grained information (i.e., it shows only that a family member is at "home", at "work", at "school", or in an unlabelled region meaning "out" or "elsewhere"). We reasoned that for much of family life, precise location isn't necessary: planning a meal, knowing someone is on their way home, or being reassured a child is at school, can be done with a relatively crude indication of location. Precise information might also be more intrusive of people's privacy. While this aspect is not necessarily clock-like, we felt it to be an important aspect of its design. The WAC in a sense gives as *little* information about location as possible, rather than striving for accuracy or completeness.

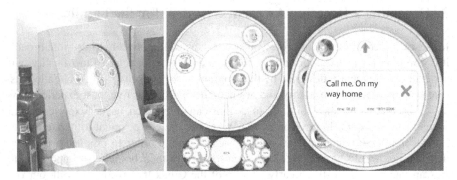

Fig. 1. Whereabouts Clock in case (a), interface (b), close-up of message window (c)

Figure 1 shows the final design of the WAC. The Clock itself is displayed on a tablet PC with touch input encased in a box made to look similar to that of a mantelpiece clock. The tablet is wirelessly connected via a GSM modem to a cellular network. In addition, a small physical "flap" hides softkeys for controlling both the volume of the Clock's chimes as well as the brightness of the display; a moving "pendulum" also showing signal strength. The Clock interface presents an animated representation of family location where members of the household are represented by icons linked to the location of their cell phones. Because we wanted engagement with the device to require minimal effort on the part of users from day to day, users have only to switch on their cell phones and the bespoke application starts running. When this happens, each user's icon appears bright and animated (appearing to "float" within each zone). If a user either switches off the application or the phone, their icon fades and becomes static. The WAC uses GSM cell ID available on cell phones to provide the location data. In this version, participants used Windows Mobile Smartphones running a custom client application (usually in addition to their own phones).

When at home, work or school, users need to first register or label these zones on their phones through a simple menu in the phone application. Upon registration, the Smartphone application records the underlying cell tower IDs within proximity for that particular zone. Whenever the phone is switched on, the application continually scans for cell towers in range, and maps the ID with strongest match onto a registered zone (indicating it as "out" if no zone has been registered for that ID). Updates are sent via SMS to the WAC display whenever the application determines that a person has moved from one registered zone to another. When this occurs, the Clock chimes to draw the attention to the move. After registering or labelling certain key locations using the phone as one of the three named zones, there is no further need to interact with the application. However, users were told that if they wanted they could change at any time what places they had set for the three different labels of "home", "work" and "school". For example, they could re-register any place as "school".

A final feature of the Clock was the ability for family members to send text messages from their cell phones to the Clock at home, a feature we added as a result of our initial trials. When a new text message arrives, the first couple of words rotate around the icon of the person who sent it and its arrival is signalled by the sound of a cuckoo clock. People at home can then touch the icon, and a window appears showing the whole message, time it was sent, and labelled location from which it was sent. With this window open, users can also look back at past messages, and delete unwanted ones. As a final part of the design, to include family members without cell phones (such as small children) we added icons which could be moved by hand, and which played random animations and sounds when touched.

4 Trial Methods

With a novel technology entering family life, we expected that it would take considerable time for a household to find its own uses for the Clock, and for these uses to stabilize. Therefore, rather than conduct short trials with a large number of families, we installed the Clock in five family homes for a period of at least one month with each family. Two of the families were particularly enthusiastic about the technology, so we left the Clocks with them for two months. In total, we ended up studying 26 family members with use ranging anywhere from 4 to 9 weeks. Households were selected from the local Cambridge area in which at least three members of the family owned cell phones, and which had established practice of 'texting' (or sending SMS messages) via their cell phones to each other. Families were informed prior to participation that we would have access not only to their location data but also to any messages sent to the Clock, but were reassured about the protection and privacy of their data. The households we selected cut across socioeconomic class, and were idiosyncratic in many respects (as we will discuss):

- **Household A** consisted of two parents with two boys, aged 11 and 13, and a lodger in his 20's. All had cell phones. The mother worked at a local school in Cambridge. The father, a vicar, lived 3 days a week in his parish vicarage in north London (an hour's drive away), but the main family home was in Cambridge. The youngest son was in boarding school during the week in Cambridge, coming home only on weekends. The other son attended the local secondary school. The Clock was installed in the Cambridge house.
- **Household B** consisted of two parents with two boys aged 11 and 18, and one daughter aged 17, all living at home. The mother worked in teaching support and part time for a local charity, and the father worked as an aerospace manager, having a long commute to and from work. The children were all at school. All three, but particularly the eldest two, were very active and relatively independent from the rest of the family.
- **Household C** consisted of two parents (a nurse and an IT consultant) and four children, a young boy aged 9, an older boy aged 12 (who lived with his mother outside the home we studied), a daughter aged 15 and a daughter aged 17 who had just started university in a different town, but who came home outside term time.
- **Household D** was a family of five: two parents, two daughters and one son (aged 13 and 15 years, and 10 months respectively). The father worked full-time in technical support at a small company and the mother part-time from home, welding parts onto circuit boards. Compared to the rest of the households, this family had the most unvaried routine. The daughters attended a nearby school and reported no

extracurricular activities. The mother spent most weekdays at home looking after her young son and housekeeping.

- **Household E** consisted of two retired parents and one 18 year-old son living at home. Two WAC enabled phones were also given to this family's 22 year-old daughter and her boyfriend, who lived together several miles away. The father spent much of his time at home, while the mother walked the household dog several miles each day and spent time gardening, either at home or in a garden allotment some distance from the house. The son was in the last year of high school and also worked part-time. The daughter worked locally and would visit several times a week after work and before returning to her boyfriend's. The boyfriend worked in a city 1 hour away by train and often returned home late.

On the first visit to the households, the WAC was installed and family members shown how to use it. In addition they were provided with an instruction and trouble-shooting sheet. Data were gathered through a series of interviews at approximately one week intervals which we scheduled with as many members of each family present as possible. On these visits, the families were asked questions about how they had used the Clock, how they felt about being tracked, and whether they had sent text messages to the Clock. In addition, printouts of the sent messages provided a focus for further discussion. Questions were also directed at how, if at all, the Clock and messaging facility interleaved with household activities and routines. In the final interview, we asked all family members to imagine different possibilities for a whereabouts device, seeking comments and criticisms and directions for novel design ideas. All interviews were audio-taped for later review and the interviews transcribed.

5 Uses and Values of the Clock

Generally, we found each household made substantial use of the Clock, although family members did at times forget to carry their extra cell phones with them or to keep them charged. On average, participants' phones were tracked on 72% of trial days, ranging from a minimum of 47% to a maximum of 80% of trial days. In addition, each family member sent on average 1.6 messages per week to the Clock during the trial. However, perhaps a better testament to the use of the Clock was some families' distress at losing the Clock at the end of the trial. As one family put it: "We're going to miss it" – the Clock had become an almost integral part of their routines. Despite this, all of the families also commented on various ways in which the design of the Clock could have been improved. For example, there was general agreement on how useful it would be to be able to send messages back *from* the Clock to individual people. In addition, the technology was not always as robust and reliable as we hoped – in particular sometimes family members were seen to move in and out of different zones due to technical problems. As we will discuss later, these problems sometimes caused needless anxiety. Nevertheless, from the interviews, it is clear that different patterns of use developed around the Clock in each household showing various ways in which it provided value within each family context.

We discuss these findings in three sections. In this section we give an overview of the uses of the Clock. This section describes not only the uses of the Clock for *co-ordination*, but also how it highlighted a set of values more emotive in nature. In particular, we will discuss the Clock as a tool for *reassurance, connectedness, identity* and lastly *social touch*. In the next section we discuss how the Clock's trial deepened our understanding of family life – revealing aspects of families frequently ignored in Ubicomp research. Lastly, in the final section we explore the implications for Ubicomp from this work. In particular we discuss how location-in-interaction, as supported by awareness technologies such as the WAC, differs from location as a technical feature of system design.

5.1 Co-ordination and Communication

The focus of most work on location awareness has been to support co-ordination and communication. By conveying information about their location and activity to one another, users can make decisions and better plan their activities. Support for co-ordination in this way was established early on in CSCW research, perhaps most classically with the Active Badge system [8], but also receiving more recent attention [5, 17]. Because of this, we fully expected the WAC to be used in the co-ordination and management of family activities. Indeed household members spoke of the ways in which they could better plan activities such as preparing meals by being able to see when someone was on their way home. In one case, a father reported how the WAC had informed him of his wife's early return home when he had expected her to miss dinner. This allowed him to offer an affectionate gesture by having dinner ready for her when she walked in the door. Households also made a number of references to what Household E called "put-the-kettle-on" movements on the Clock. Here, household members leaving a region or moving into HOME on the Clock (before they had physically arrived) would prompt those at home to put the kettle on for tea. Important here was an awareness of the household's rhythms: movements were "read" in different ways depending on the time of day and knowledge of the household routines. Trisha, the mother in Household E, captured this in describing an example of Clock use related to her son, Jon:

> A few times Jon has not left a message and around about quarter to six-ish I've seen his photo move up to HOME and I've thought "ooh, Jon is coming home," and I've had a cup of tea ready for him before he's even walked in the house.

Significantly, with the coarse granularity of position that the Clock communicated (not least to mention the underlying positioning algorithm), we noted that nearly all these readings of the Clock were 'fail safe' – in that if they were wrong the cost would be very low (such as a kettle boiled in vain). However, the messaging feature of the Clock was often used in coordination tasks when more precise information might be needed, or in order for someone to account for their location on the Clock. Messages such as: "Just at the train station. X"; "In a meeting 4 next few hours"; "M11 accident, taking back roads" and "Jus walkin down road now. Sum1 stick kettle on. ;-p" fell squarely in this category. The last of the messages above also illustrates that not only could people reading the Clock use this information to plan activities, but those sending messages home could try to direct other people's activities more explicitly. Thus with the messaging, we saw a number of "calls to action" such as "Mum phone"; "Shopping done help please"; and "Time for bed".

5.2 Reassurance

While co-ordination is perhaps the most obvious use of an awareness technology, the Clock was distinctive in that the most remarked upon benefit was the *reassurance* it provided for family members. Families regularly described, in both explicit and implicit ways, the Clock as reassuring:

> So I just come in and you know, 'yep, everybody's in the right place. All's right with the world', you know, just at a glance… It's just umm, it is just nice. It's not checking up on people. It's just a nice little reassurance. Everyone's where they should be and everything's right, or at least their phones are in the right place [laughs]. I mean, you know, you can take these things too far… but you're not using it as a security device like that.

The WAC invoked not simply a reassurance of family members being at the right place at the right time, but also an overriding sense that everything was *going to routine*, that *all was well*. As expressed above there is a sense "that everything's right" in looking at the Clock and seeing that everyone is where they should be. Rachel, the mother in Household C, expressed, evocatively, something similar in talking about her eldest daughter away at university:

> When you can't visualize where your offspring are, you have this ridiculous sense of anxiety that's just bubbling very quietly. […] I think in some way the Clock helps me think 'yes, they've definitely got there, and they're definitely there now, and they're on their way home.

The Clock, then, appears to put Rachel at ease, providing reassurance of her distant daughter's whereabouts. Again, it was not that the Clock did this by providing precise geographical coordinates. As Rachel put it, the Clock was simply an additional tool for visualizing – a means of gleaning just enough information, as it were. Something we had not expected was how the Clock's chimes also played into this sense of reassurance. The Clock would be glanced at or approached when it chimed to see who it was that had moved and where they had moved from and to. Indeed, families spoke of being drawn almost compulsively to the Clock because of the chimes it made— parents who spent large portions of their days at home felt particularly strongly about the chimes. Meg, for instance, chose to place the Clock in her living room so that she could easily glance over to it whenever it chimed:

> There's just some sort of thing where you've got to see what- you know, it makes that noise that someone's moved and you just have to look. I don't know why. You just have to look.

Whatever the underlying motivations, it appears reassurance came from being able to see the family as active and from seeing a family's movements, at a particular level of granularity, to be in keeping with known-about routines. The coarseness of the location *works*, so to speak, because the ways of seeing or reading the Clock are deeply enmeshed with what family members already know and indeed have rights to know. What we see through the use of the Clock is that family members are able to intuit a state of affairs using relatively crude types of information. It is unclear in the design of the Clock whether more detail or a higher level of accuracy in location would have provided a greater degree of reassurance. This led us to further explore location not purely as geographical coordinates, valued for how precise those coordinates can be, but rather how location fits into the "family geography" of where the family is or more particularly, where the family *should be*.

5.3 Connectedness and Togetherness

Tied closely to the sense of reassurance associated with the Clock was another salient theme that emerged from our interviews, that of *connectedness* and *togetherness*. Whilst having the Clock, family members spoke of how it helped them to feel connected to those out of the house. In Meg's glances at the Clock (noted above), for example, she gained a sense of what other family members were "up to" and, in turn, gained a sense of connection with them. For Trisha (mother in Household E), the persistently displayed information also provided a way of feeling connected to those who were out. In her words, "It just keeps you that little bit closer all the while."

Other households adopted a more purposeful approach to using the Clock as a means of connection. For Household A, distributed across three different "homes", the mother, Jo, expressed a particular sense of how the Clock allowed her to feel connected to her family even when they were apart. She talked about how seeing the family members together on the Clock presented everybody being in the same place even when they were not – a virtual sense of everybody together. The Clock explicitly connected family members who while at homes in different parts of the country, were still connected with what Jo saw as their *real* home.

This fleeting yet emotive aspect of the Clock was reiterated time and again in our interviews. In a fashion reminiscent of displayed family photos, the Clock provided a recurrent visual reminder of a family's togetherness. Indeed, the temporal rhythms that the Clock visualized brought out these moments of togetherness – particularly at poignant times such as dinnertime. As Dan, the father in Household C put it, seeing everybody "nestling" together at the top of the Clock each night (even though some of his children were in different homes), gave him a strong sense of family unity.

One issue was that the reverse was also true in that it could instill moments of anxiety and separation from family members. Householders reported feeling worried when others in the household appeared where they shouldn't be or moving when they should be in one place. These feelings were elevated when, on occasion, the positioning algorithm would find itself on an edge, and "flutter" between two different locations.

5.4 Expressing Identity

So far we have noted important ways in which household members came to see or "read" the WAC. We also found participants giving thought to how they were represented on the Clock to others. Common was the way in which households appropriated the Clock's three location labels, HOME, WORK and SCHOOL, to control how they were seen and to suit their particular needs. Household E (where neither parent worked) presented perhaps the most extreme example of this. All but the son, Jon, labeled places in unexpected ways; the daughter assigned both her boyfriend's house and family house as HOME, and the local train station, where she picked her boyfriend up after work, as SCHOOL. The mother, who wasn't working, used SCHOOL to refer to her walking the dog (registering several spots along her usual walk as SCHOOL). She also used WORK to refer to gardening either in the garden attached to the house or in the family's garden allotment some distance from their home. While at home, the retired father would regularly use his cell phone to register himself as either at WORK or HOME depending on what he was doing.

Striking, here, was the ease with which they incorporated these inflexible labels into their household routines. We gave only minimal instructions to families on how to assign different geographical locations to the three available labels. Even so, all but one of the households used the labels to designate something else, or assigned multiple geographical locations to one label, and did so with no apparent problems or need for technical assistance. These adaptations were often based on subtle use of geographical location. Registering two different gardens as the single label WORK, and an activity (dog walking) rather than a distinct place to SCHOOL seemed, if anything, a somewhat playful use of the Clock for Household E's mother, Trisha (a self-professed technophobe). It was also dealt with in stride by the rest of the family who knew what these labels meant and had no difficulty knowing where she was or what she was doing. Arguably, it was the coarseness of detail on the Clock that prevented the complexity from being overwhelming. It would seem the detail was sufficient to allow for a rough idea of location to be simply deduced. As several of our participants reported, if more detail was required, other channels of communication were available, such as a text message to the Clock.

Indeed, some family members went as far as to use their reported location as a way of identifying their activities and expressing them to others. The father in Household E, Ted, moved himself on the Clock between WORK and HOME – re-registering his location each time he moved from using his computer to watching television - not unlike the use of availability messages in Instant Messaging. However, it also actively asserted a sense of social position, or what might be termed, rather grandly, *identity*. Ted, if you like, was demonstrably composing his position *vis-à-vis* his family. This marking of social position in the home parallels the practice of *broadcasting identity* we have written about previously [17].

5.5 Social Touch

A final recurring use of the Clock worth noting amongst the households relates to what we have in the past referred to as "social touch", where technology is used as a channel through which family members express affection for one another [17]. In essence, many of the examples of coordination we have described have strong elements of this, such as having a cup of tea or a meal ready for someone when they come through the door. However, this showed itself most explicitly in the messages family members sent to the WAC. There were obvious examples such as "Good morning all ;-p" and "Nite nite every1. Cold nite here. B careful on the roads 2moro." In other cases, messages would be sent for some other purpose but would incorporate an element of social touch, a flourish, if you like, denoting one's thought for others. A particularly nice example of this was sent by Peter, the lodger staying at Household A. His message is to one of the family's young sons: "Harry, there's some hot chocolate in my cupboard if you'd like some. Hope you're not feeling too poorly, Peter". Peter is clearly making a thoughtful gesture in offering his hot chocolate to Harry. Interesting for us is his use of the Clock to do so. As with the 'fail-safe' use of the Clock for coordination, it appears such messages are not critical and have no immediate function. Instead, they simply add a distinct feel to a family and the relationships its members have with one another. From this perspective, it is worth noting that some of the households were far more emotionally demonstrative in their messaging on the Clock. Households A and E, for example, routinely sent messages appearing to supplement the "all is OK" status suggested by the display of people's whereabouts. On occasion, then, we saw the messaging via the Clock, perhaps unsurprisingly, weave its way into family relations, playing its part in the emotional repartee between family members; as with so many practical things in the home [19], the Clock came to offer a resource for playing out the social organization of home.

6   Understanding the Clock as a Family Device

Now that we have covered the basic ways in which the Clock was used, we move on to examine in more depth how the Clock found its place within family life. Our goals in running this trial were not simply to evaluate the success of the WAC but rather, through its adoption, we hoped to reflect anew upon location-centric technologies, and understand location as a feature of family life. We develop this analysis further in three main themes. First we discuss family attitudes toward privacy and their focus on sharing rather than intrusion. Second, we address the ways in which the Clock not only integrated into family life but supported what we will call 'the production of family life'. Lastly, we discuss the nature of location that the Clock supported, making a break from the technical notion of location prevalent in Ubicomp and arguing instead for the importance of understanding how location manifests itself for end users.

6.1 Privacy

If there has been a single topic that has dominated location awareness research it is privacy (e.g. [10]). In part, this is due to the growing concerns with the ways in which our lives are tracked electronically and considerable public worry about how such information could be abused. Privacy measures thus have featured prominently in location awareness prototypes. In the design of the WAC, we sought to address these concerns through both the fixed single location of the Clock, at home, and the limited coarse-grained information it shared.

At the very least, privacy concerns did not seem to inhibit the family's usage of the Clock. Indeed, despite repeated questioning, none of the families reporting being concerned about a loss of privacy. In part, participants' comments led us to believe that the coarse-grained resolution of the tracking information helped considerably. One teenager put it this way:

> Yeah, so a lot of my friends have said "So your parents are checking up on you" like. I said nah this is not that. It's not accurate enough. It doesn't tell you exactly where I am so I can go places and they won't know where I am.

But further than this, our repeated questioning around privacy was met with puzzlement by the families. As they explained, the Clock displayed information that they already shared. Thus the WAC was not seen as intruding any further into what they already knew or needed to know. Even questions about access to the Clock from outside the home failed to provoke worries about privacy. When asked about losing a phone that could display the Clock's information, Kris phrases this point well:

> Well you get over don't you? It's the same thing as losing your phone anyway. And anyway, would it really matter? They don't know who it is, they don't know what 'home' means, they don't, you know it doesn't bear any relation to anybody else that doesn't know.

It was only when we suggested radically more open designs – such as sharing location information with everybody on the Internet ("like MySpace" as one family put it) that we could get families to object. As for the possibility of hackers, or malicious access to the tracking information provided by the WAC, again it was pointed out to us that the level of detail the Clock provided was only something that really made sense to those who knew a household's routines; namely, close family and friends.

While not to downplay the tensions and pressures of family life, the reactions we received around privacy reflect the fact that family life is built, significantly, around shared awareness, without which much of the everyday co-ordination of the family (eating, driving children around, sharing costs and so on) would be impossible. As Martin [11] describes so astutely, the knowledge and control of a household's comings and goings are concerns continually being brokered, but, nevertheless, the very idea of home is built upon knowing and controlling just such matters. While it is possible that the families we studied were atypical, it could also be that privacy is more of a concern for us as researchers than it is of practical concern to families.

6.2 The Production of Family Life

In studying families, and looking at how technologies such as the WAC are used, it is all too easy to take the family for granted as an entity – to take the social arrangement or organization of a family as a given. With an eye on the technology, we can lose sight of the social phenomenon [3]. However, in many senses families are a "work in progress", with at times strenuous work needed to keep its members together, to keep in touch, and to maintain a common identity. In short, being in a family relies upon the work of its members to organize, in some recognizable fashion, itself as a social group. As we have already suggested, one aspect of this work – and something that family members undertake as a matter of course – is to know each other's whereabouts, what each other's routines are, and what each person's roles and accountabilities are (as it can be amongst other social and organizational groups). Sacks refers to one aspect of this as "private calendars" – the shared schedule of events both past and future [14] that families have in common. We can expand on this to describe our participants' "private geographies" – the shared, in-common knowledge of the different parts of their city, and what that meant for different family members. Naturally, particular members may fail at times in this organizational duty to the frustration of other family members. However, what is evident is that there is an obligation amongst family members, and particularly parents, to watch out and attempt to maintain their shared geography and calendar. Any family would be remiss, and crucially be seen as such, if it did not attend to such an obligation [9]. Here the WAC was readily incorporated into these practices: by revealing the routines of those distant, it helped to cement together each family's identity as not merely a group who share a living space, but who have an emotional bond of support and care.

Indeed, at one and the same time, the Clock revealed those practices to us – how a shared calendar can come to be demonstrably enacted as a feature of a household's organization *as a household*. So by presenting a view of the family through their locations, the Clock helped in letting family members monitor each other's behaviors and routines. It also enabled people (such as mothers and fathers) *to be seen* to monitor that activity. It was both the monitoring and its "performative" achievement that did the work of cementing family relations, contributing to the "production" of family, as it were [6]. We would not over-emphasize the role of technology, or the Clock, in this socially organizing work. Rather the use of the Clock foregrounded for us as researchers how the family is as much an *aspiration* or something that is worked toward, as it is a particular group of people. Likewise, home is not so much a place as it is *an idea*, an idea is bound up with being together, being cared for, and being safe.

6.3 From Location to Location-in-Interaction

As we discussed earlier, the majority of work on location awareness has focused on easily quantifiable – and thus comparable – performance measures of location-based systems, such as accuracy, resolution, coverage and so on. In these terms, the WAC was very limited – its resolution was crude, and its accuracy and coverage certainly no better (and on the whole worse) than many existing solutions. Yet the reception of the Clock by its users – and the important values it supported – led us to reflect again on how it is that location awareness plays out in use. That is to say, the WAC let us explore location not as a technical feature of a system, but as something interleaved with a family's interactions with each other. We would argue that the value of location technologies are seldom simply in their ability to track objects and people, but rather in how that tracking is, in the end, *used*. For location awareness, whether it is of family members or delivery trucks, this means *in interaction*. It is seldom the autonomous tracking of position that is important but what that tracking means to others involved – such as when a truck driver needs to explain to management the extra long route they took, or just a family member explaining why it took them so long to come home. Location, and thus location tracking systems, move from technical curiosities to valuable systems in how they support these activities. Our focus was therefore on *location-in-interaction*: how it is that location is used, read, viewed, and manipulated by groups, and what this can support. These activities are directly connected to the accuracy, resolution, or whatever, of a positioning system, but these technical aspects can only ever be a partial account of location's role. Our point is not that inaccuracy is unimportant – as we have mentioned, the inaccuracies of the WAC (or more specifically: its flutter) caused unnecessary distress. It is rather that it remains to be seen what accuracy is in a specific interactional situation, and we should not simply assume accuracy is a uniform concept.

For example, even the simplest glances at the Clock were informative in developing these ideas around location-in-interaction. When family members looked at the Clock to see another's whereabouts, they in a sense "read" what this meant about the recipient, taking into account what they knew and understood about that family member's context. In one example reported to us, the mother of Household A, Jo, cycled home after work over a bridge that crossed a local river. This area she had previously labeled as SCHOOL as this was the regular site where she practiced rowing. SCHOOL was therefore known by the family to mean "Mum is rowing". Yet as she cycled home that night, the brief appearance of her on the Clock as being in the region of SCHOOL was not interpreted by the rest of the family as rowing, but rather as where in particular she was on her route home from work. Through such examples, we see location as actively produced in interaction. Originally, we had worried about how an automatic tracking system might lead to confusion or undermine communication. Indeed, earlier work had gone as far as to argue that automatic functions are not desirable or useful in awareness systems [18]. Yet in practice, location generated by the WAC was flexibly read by participants taking into account its automatic nature. Location was understood, even at a glance, in the context of what that person ordinarily did, and their ordinary patterns and routines.

That people infer activity from location and do so as a matter of course has been discussed before in the literature [18]. However, on the basis of this research we want to develop this point further. Location for our study's families was not only meaningful in terms of their intimate knowledge of one another, it also had moral connotations. By this we mean that there were "right" places to be and "wrong" ones. Returning to the idea of location-in-interaction, we don't mean here that there were right or wrong geographical places to be. Rather, the use of the Clock revealed to us that, through location, judgments are made about whether others are doing what they should be; whether, in the case of family households, they are behaving appropriately as a member of the family. The most straightforward illustration of this is the way in which these families used the WAC to account for their actions. If they were late or made changes to their routine, they felt the need to explain these aberrations. This is something that the families used the text messaging features of the Clock to address: family members would text to say why they were late, and why the Clock showed they were in one place when it was expected they would be in another.

That location has a moral component means that one's status or activity has moral implications for others' view of oneself. The interesting use of the Clock's labels we wrote of in Section 5.4 is illustrative of this. By registering her gardening as WORK and re-registering his physical presence at home as WORK, Trisha and Ted were not merely appropriating the labels for convenience. Along with the use of these labels come certain rights of access and prescribed relations with others. Ted's re-registration, for instance, was redundant for all practical purposes; his computer desk where he worked at home was meters away from the Clock. What it achieved, however, was a social and moral positioning relative to the categories displayed on the Clock. Nigel, if you like, was demonstrably composing his position *vis-à-vis* his family, broadcasting his participation *in-work*. To say therefore that location is read as activity, or that it is activity that needs to be communicated rather than location, is to gloss over much of the complexity of what location means and how it is used in terms of family life and in the course of interaction.

7   Implications and Discussion

So far we have highlighted a number of differences between the results of this research and previous Ubicomp work on location and awareness. Certainly, through designing the Clock specifically as a family locating system, as well as one with a relatively simple design, the WAC and the results of the trial explore new issues for design, and uncover new values that users can derive from such systems. But the research also has some broader implications for Ubicomp, and in particular, how we conceive of and develop systems for location awareness.

One main implication of this work is that a deeper consideration of what location-in-interaction means for people may lead us not to simply optimize the underlying technology, but rather to optimize the fit between the technology and users' values and practices. This may lead us to develop different kinds of technical solutions, with new mechanisms and features. For example, the artful use of location labeling by our trial families suggests that this kind of mechanism may be as important a feature as accuracy in tracking. Recent work on qualitative location tracking is a relevant and insightful development here [1]. As another example, there has been a considerable body of work on optimizing tracking within buildings, as an extension to traditional GPS which on the whole only works well outside. Yet from a consideration of what location means in interaction, it may be that whether we are indoors or outdoors and what address we are at can be of more importance than our spatial location within a building. We might only want to know if one is inside a commercial establishment, waiting outside, or at a house next door. The importance and nature of a particular locating problem may be much transformed by considering what users want to know and why they want to know it. As our results have shown, location-in-interaction might be as much about emotion – reassurance, connection and the like – as it is about the communication of accurate information. The WAC deliberately offered a *lower* resolution of accuracy than was possible with the technology. As we discussed above (an established finding of design theory, if not Ubicomp), systems that provide value to end users can often feature less functionality rather than more.

A second implication of this work has to do with a different perspective on how we conceptualize the home, as it becomes a growing topic of concern for Ubicomp. Our research suggests we need to move beyond the notion of smart technologies, used in "smart home" visions and the like. The term implies technologies that do the work *for* people and, in the case of smart homes, the work of families. On the contrary, this research suggests that we develop technologies that *let people be smart*. In other words, when we look at how families derived value from the WAC, it is clear that this is a technology that helps *families* do the work of "being a family". This, then, we would claim, opens up the way for a different kind of design philosophy as well as a new research approach. This approach looks to support what people in homes *already do*, not to do it for them. It looks to provide families with new tools as resources for those already engrained activities. This not only takes us away from notions of predicting people's behavior or automating tasks, but also makes us think more deeply about what are the human values we want to support. These may not necessarily be about productivity and efficiency and getting tasks done. As we have seen, they might equally be about affection, reassurance, identity and togetherness.

On a final, broader note, this research provides a complementary contribution to existing research in other domains and with other types of social groups in Ubicomp. The settings and contexts in which we studied the use of the WAC are different from those of earlier studies exploring location systems. Perhaps for this reason, the importance of privacy was not echoed in our fieldwork experiences, and, unlike previous work, we found automatic locating technology to be both valuable and useful for the families we studied. Our findings have also touched on very different aspects of location – its emotional, accountable and even moral characteristics – than existing work. Rather than contradicting earlier work on locating technology, we suggest that our differences come from our different domain of enquiry (the family), the different nature of the prototype (as a situated, awareness device), as well as the different values and themes we have focused on in our study.

8 Conclusions and Future Work

In this paper we have focused on how a particular technology – the Whereabouts Clock – was integrated into family life. An extensive trial with the Clock in five households uncovered how it supported not just co-ordination and awareness, as commonly associated with location awareness systems, but rather reassurance, connectedness, expression of identity and social touch. These were not so much functional benefits of use as emotive ones – a feeling, as one of our participants put it, that "all is right with the world". The WAC supported these values without generating privacy concerns. It did this, in part, because of the coarse-grained information it communicated – an example of "less is more", offering enough functionality to fit with users' practices, but not more than they needed or were comfortable with.

More generally, we have argued that the use of the Clock helps to reveal practices around what we characterized as "location-in-interaction". We contrasted this with a focus on technical features of location systems (accuracy, resolution, coverage), and while they are of course interdependent, location as it plays out in interaction is more than simply a matter of technology. We suggest that understanding the value of location-in-interaction may lead to technical design distinct from optimizing the underlying technology, such as less accurate but more meaningful location information.

In our future work we plan to redesign the WAC to take into account the lessons of the trial. In particular, while our restricted set of location categories successfully dealt with privacy concerns, we suspect this was, if anything, an over-reaction to those concerns. Giving families more flexibility in labeling locations could have a number of interesting effects, particularly if labeled locations could be shared amongst family members. We are also exploring what it might mean to move from a clock to a watch – making the visualization portable and available on a user's phone. Again, this is potentially moving in a very different direction from the original design. However, broadening the design space will allow us to further explore the values supported by the WAC. More generally, further prototypes will allow us to understand how to best construct new technologies for the home. The complexities of family life are such that supporting it will involve technology embedded as much in the moral, emotional and caring aspects of family life as the functional or technical. It is here we see the most interesting set of new challenges.

Acknowledgments

We are indebted to the families who gave generously of their time for this study. We are also grateful to Richard Harper and Ken Wood for their valuable commentary and advice on the paper. In addition, one anonymous reviewer gave us the wittiest review we have ever received, reminding us why we do this job. Thank you.

References

1. Anderson, I., Muller, H.: Qualitative positioning for pervasive environments. In: Third International Conference on Mobile Computing and Ubiquitous Networking (ICMU 2006), London, UK, pp. 10–18 (2006)
2. Brown, B., Chalmers, M., Bell, M., Macoll, I., Hall, M.: Sharing the square: Collaborative leisure on the city streets. In: Brown, B., Chalmers, M., Bell, M., Macoll, I., Hall, M. (eds.) Procs. of ECSCW 2005, Paris, France, pp. 427–429. Kluwer, Dordrecht (2005)
3. Button, G.: The curious case of the vanishing technology. In: Button, G. (ed.) Technology in Working Order, Routledge, London (1993)
4. Chen, M.Y., Sohn, T., Chmelev, D., Haehnel, D., Hightower, J., Hughes, J., LaMarca, A.: Practical metropolitan-scale positioning for GSM phones. In: Dourish, P., Friday, A. (eds.) UbiComp 2006. LNCS, vol. 4206, pp. 225–242. Springer, Heidelberg (2006)
5. Consolvo, S., Smith, I., Matthews, T., LaMarca, A., Tabert, J., Powledge, P.: Location disclosure to social relations: Why, when, and what people want to share. In: Procs. CHI 2005, pp. 81–90 (2005)
6. Gubrium, J.: The family as project. Sociological Review (36), 273–296 (1988)
7. Hamilton, A.(2007). A wireless street fight. TIME Magazine (February 15th 2007)
8. Harper, R., Lamming, M., Newman, W.: Locating systems at work: Implications for the development of Active Badge applications. Interacting With Computers 4(3), 343–363 (1992)
9. Hogben, S.: Life's on hold. Time & Society 15(2-3), 327–342 (2006)
10. Iachello, G., Smith, I., Consolvo, S., Chen, M., Abowd, G.: Developing privacy guidelines for social location disclosure applications and services. In: SOUPS '05: Proceedings of the 2005 Symposium on Usable Privacy and Security, ACM Press, New York (2005)
11. Martin, B.: Mother wouldn't like it!': Housework as magic. Theory, Culture & Society 2(2), 19–35 (1984)
12. Mynatt, E., Rowan, J., Jacobs, A., Craighill, S.: Digital family portraits: Supporting peace of mind for extended family members. In: Procs. of CHI 2001, ACM Press, New York (2001)
13. O'Hara, K., Perry, M., Churchill, E., Russell, D. (eds.): Public and Situated Displays: Social and Interactional Aspects of Shared Display Technologies. Springer, Heidelberg (2003)
14. Sacks, H.: Lectures on Conversation: vol. 1, 2. Basil Blackwell, Oxford (1995)
15. Schegloff, E.: Notes on a conversational practice: Formulating place. In: Sudnow, D. (ed.) Studies in Social Interaction, pp. 75–119. Free Press, New York (1972)
16. Sellen, A., Eardley, R., Izadi, S., Harper, R.: The Whereabouts Clock: Early testing of a situated awareness device. In: Procs. of CHI, Extended Abstracts, ACM Press, New York (2006)
17. Sellen, A., Harper, R., Eardley, R., Izadi, S., Regan, T., Taylor, A.S., Wood, K.R.: HomeNote: Supporting situated messaging in the home. In: Procs of CSCW '06, pp. 383–392. ACM Press, New York (2006)
18. Smith, I.E., Consolvo, S., LaMarca, A., Hightower, J., Scott, J.: Social disclosure of place: From location technology to communication practices. In: Gellersen, H.-W., Want, R., Schmidt, A. (eds.) PERVASIVE 2005. LNCS, vol. 3468, pp. 134–151. Springer, Heidelberg (2005)
19. Taylor, A.S., Swan, L.: Artful systems in the home. In: Procs of CHI '05, pp. 641–650. ACM Press, New York (2005)

Safeguarding Location Privacy
in Wireless Ad-Hoc Networks

Tanzima Hashem and Lars Kulik

National ICT Australia
Department of Computer Science and Software Engineering
University of Melbourne, Victoria, 3010, Australia
{thashem,lars}@csse.unimelb.edu.au

Abstract. We present a novel algorithm that safeguards the location privacy of users accessing location-based services via mobile devices. Our technique exploits the capability of mobile devices to form wireless ad-hoc networks in order to hide a user's identity and position. Local ad-hoc networks enable us to separate an agent's request for location information, the query initiator, from the agent that actually requests this service on its behalf, the query requestor. Since a query initiator can select itself or one of the $k - 1$ agents in its ad-hoc network as a query requestor, the query initiator remains k-anonymous. In addition, the location revealed to the location service provider is a rectangle instead of an exact coordinate. We develop an anonymous selection algorithm that selects a query requestor with near-uniform randomness, which is a key component to ensure anonymity in an ad-hoc network. Our experiments show that a system can ensure a high quality of service and maintain a high degree of privacy in terms of anonymity and obfuscation while accessing location-based services.

1   Introduction

Mobile devices such as smartphones or GPS-enabled cars enable the access of location-based services from virtually anywhere at any time. Current location-based services are centered around the idea to continually sense a user's location in order to provide and update information services based on that location. If a user misses a turn following wayfinding instructions, a *location-based service provider* (LSP) that is continually monitoring a user's location can immediately respond and recalculate a modified set of instructions. As these devices will be permeating our daily lives they also hold privacy risks: an LSP that tracks the movement of a user automatically at all times with a high degree of spatial and temporal precision, is easily able to generate a complete user profile that does not only include a complete history of the user's movements but also reveals which type of information has been accessed where and when.

Over the last years a number of approaches have been suggested to safeguard the (location) privacy of nomadic users. They might have regulations or privacy policies in place, aim to dissociate a user's location from the user's identity, or actively hide a user's precise location. Nearly all approaches protecting privacy have the goal that users retain control over information about their locations when using an LSP. However, a lack in privacy-ensuring systems might inhibit the growth of location-based services [1].

J. Krumm et al. (Eds.): UbiComp 2007, LNCS 4717, pp. 372–390, 2007.

Currently, most location-based services that are accessed via mobile clients use the provided infrastructure of a cell phone network or connect wirelessly to the Internet. The location information and services are *centrally* processed by an LSP. If a user requests a location service such as the closest restaurant or the play times of a cinema close to the user, the LSP usually has to know the position and ID (often the IP or cell phone number) of the user's mobile device to deliver the requested information. To protect a user's location these approaches assume a centralized service such as a location anonymizer or trust the infrastructure provider such as the cellular operator.

We propose a decentralized approach to location privacy that does not need to trust any involved party, neither any of the involved peers nor the LSP (even if the LSP coincides with the cellular operator). Our approach exploits that current devices can form ad-hoc *wireless personal area networks* (WPANs), e.g., using Bluetooth. We call such a local ad-hoc network a *clique*. Cliques allow us to separate an agent's request for a location service from the agent that actually requests this service. Most systems assume that these two roles coincide: an agent that requires a location service, the *query initiator* [2], also requests this service, i.e, is the *query requestor*. We divide these roles and use cliques to anonymize a user's location: if k agents form an ad-hoc network then one of the agents can act as a query requestor on behalf of the query initiator. Even if the LSP has access to the information that currently k devices form an ad-hoc network, our algorithm will only permit the LSP to identify the query initiator as one of the k agents. This type of anonymity is called k-anonymity.

Our approach combines k-anonymity with obfuscation: each agent in a clique obfuscates (masks) its current position by providing a rectangle instead of a point as its location. If a query initiator requires a location service, it inquires those imprecise locations from other agents in the clique, computes the minimum bounding rectangle that includes its own rectangle and the rectangles of $k - 1$ other agents, and selects one of the agents to send its request along with the minimum bounding rectangle to the LSP (see Section 3). The request and the routing information are encrypted (see Section 4.4), i.e., agents do not know what services other agents in a clique request. Our proposed approach reveals as little information as possible: the identity or precise location of the agents involved in the service request is hidden from any member of the clique, and the replies from the LSP are only known to the query initiator.

A major challenge for an approach that requires no trust among its peers is the selection of an agent with uniform probability that it is more than one hop away from the query initiator. A simple selection scheme might request the IPs (or IDs) of nearby agents, but this would assume that the agents in the clique have to entrust the query initiator with their IP. In Section 4 we propose a new incremental algorithm that can select any agent in a clique with near-uniform randomness without knowing their IPs.

We show in Section 5 how an LSP can answer proximity queries (e.g., *what is the closest restaurant*), and analyze the quality of service for a decentralized model using anonymity and obfuscation. Our approach allows an agent to balance its need for privacy against its required quality of service. In general, there is little research how to evaluate the quality of a method for protecting location privacy. We propose proximity queries as the distance information can be used as a measure to assess the distances to the sought point of interests against the ones computed by a privacy-aware algorithm.

In summary, our approach

- combines anonymity and obfuscation in a decentralized manner,
- enables agents to act on the behalf of peers requiring a location-based service,
- does not require to trust any involved party, neither its peers not the LSP,
- balances the degree of privacy, required quality of service, and cost of the service,
- anonymizes the communication among the neighbors and the LSP,
- shows how an LSP can provide a high quality of service to an anonymous agent located at an imprecise location.

2   Related Work

Most research on location privacy for mobile agents assumes centralized approaches (e.g., see [3,4,5]). There are, however, a number of disadvantages of centralized approaches, such as a single point of failure, bottlenecks due to communication overhead between mobile agents and the LSP, and security threats as these systems store all information in a single place. A few decentralized approaches (e.g., see [6,7]) have been proposed to address these shortcomings.

To safeguard location privacy existing research efforts have suggested different strategies, in particular regulation [8], privacy policies [9,10], anonymity [3,5,7], and obfuscation [6,11]. Regulation and privacy policies are based on trust. Although they can prohibit the misuse of an agent's location, they might not be able to control malicious attacks to privacy for two reasons: (a) the rules and regulations may not anticipate the advancement of technology and (b) a hostile agent may not care about privacy policies while disclosing private information. Anonymity-based techniques aim to preserve the location privacy by separating the location information from the identity of individuals, nonetheless in some cases the identity may be revealed from the location information [12,13]. Obfuscation strategies degrade the quality of the location information in order to increase the degree of location privacy. They allow an individual's identity to be revealed. The idea of obfuscation was presented in [6,11]. Techniques that combine obfuscation with anonymity aim to ensure a higher degree of privacy than an approach based on anonymity or obfuscation alone.

The first decentralized approaches to location privacy are proposed in [2,7]. The communication with an LSP in both approaches is performed through a randomly selected query requestor from agents located in the anonymous region of the query initiator. While the query initiator hides its identity from the LSP, it may reveal its identity, the type of requested service as well as the answers from the LSP to a hostile agent, which may be one of the query requestors. To generate a cloaked area, the approach in [2] proposes that agents share their locations with their neighbors. Therefore, they rather trust a large number of other mobile agents than one centralized location anonymizer, and potentially creating more security threats.

Gruteser and Grunwald have introduced the idea of spatial and temporal cloaking [3] to protect location privacy. Gedik and Lu have proposed a personalized anonymization model [4], while Bettini et al. have introduced the concept of historical k-anonymity [14] for preserving privacy. Mokbel et al. have integrated both anonymity and obfuscation to protect privacy using a centralized system [5]. All of these approaches have used an intermediary centralized anonymizer. Kido *et al.*'s approach to preserve privacy is based on an anonymization technique using dummies [15], representing false locations along with the true locations to the LSP. This system has been criticized that it has a higher probability of malicious attacks due to the failure of generating realistic dummies and thus wasting resources in processing dummies [7]. This approach also assumes a direct communication with the LSP.

3 Computation of a *k*-Anonymous Imprecise Location

Our approach to privacy-aware location-based services is based on a decentralized ad-hoc network of mobile agents that combines anonymity and obfuscation. Each agent uses obfuscation to hide its precise location from other agents in a clique as well as from the LSP. We call this imprecise location a *locally cloaked area* (LCA). If an agent requires a service form a *location service provider* (LSP), it masks its current position by using not only its own LCA but also the LCAs of $k - 1$ other agents.

An ad-hoc clique might consist of n agents. To ensure k-anonymity an algorithm has to compute the smallest bounding box that contains the LCA of the query initiator and $k - 1$ LCAs of the $n - 1$ agents (see Section 3.2 if $k > n$). We call the minimum bounding box of the union of these k LCAs the *globally cloaked area* (GCA) of the agent. As a result the GCA provides obfuscation and k-anonymity at the same time. The GCA will be sent to the LSP for the query initiator's service request. As the GCA is the minimum bounding box, it ensures the highest possible quality of service given the privacy requirements of the query initiator in terms of k-anonymity and obfuscation.

A naive algorithm to compute the GCA is a *brute force-based computation* (BGC): we compute the minimum bounding rectangle for every k-subset of LCAs that contains the query initiator's LCA, and select the rectangle with the smallest area. A BGC is essentially an exhaustive search and computationally expensive as its time complexity is exponential. Therefore, we develop a greedy algorithm for the computation of the GCA that trades accuracy, i.e., computes a slightly larger minimum box than the optimal GCA, in turn for significant savings in computation time. The BGC serves as a benchmark against which we compare the *greedy-based GCA computation* (GGC) in Monte Carlo simulations in terms of accuracy and execution time. We first propose an algorithm for the computation of the LCA.

3.1 Generating the LCA

A mobile agent can specify its desired LCA via three constants: the constant c determines the ratio between the width and the length of the LCA, e.g., a long thin rectangle could hide where an agent is located in a street, and the constants c_1 and c_2 determine the minimum and maximum distance of the agent's position from the boundary of its LCA. If an agent A' provides its LCA to an agent A and some part of its LCA lies outside the communication range of agent A, then agent A can easily render a more precise location of A'. Restricting the position of A' via c_1 and c_2 to a smaller rectangle in the LCA ensures a larger obfuscated area for A' (Fig.1) compared to the case where the position of A' can be on (or close to) the boundary of its LCA. Algorithm 1 finds a random rectangle of the specified area representing the LCA.

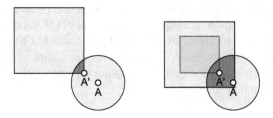

Fig. 1. The dark grey area shows the imprecise location of A' that can be computed by A. It can be smaller if A' is not restricted in its LCA (left) compared to the case where it is (right).

Algorithm 1. Find LCA

Input : An area A_{LCA} for the LCA, and the position (x, y) of the agent.
Output: Returns a rectangle defined by $(x_{\min}, x_{\max}, y_{\min}, y_{\max})$.

1.1 Let m be a random number between $1/c$ to c for a constant c, and x_l and y_l be the length in x and y direction, respectively;

1.2 $x_l := \sqrt{A_{LCA}/m}, \quad y_l := m \cdot x_l$;

1.3 Let n_x be a random number between x_l/c_1 to x_l/c_2 and n_y be a random number between y_l/c_1 to y_l/c_2, where c_1 and c_2 are constants;

1.4 Let l, and u be the distances to the left and up direction from (x, y) position, respectively;

1.5 Let l and u be random numbers between 0 to $x_l - n_x$ and 0 to $y_l - n_y$, respectively;

1.6 $x_{\min} := x - (l + n_x/2), \quad x_{\max} := x + (x_l - l - n_x/2)$;

1.7 $y_{\min} := y - (d + n_y/2), \quad y_{\max} := y + (y_l - u - n_y/2)$;

3.2   Generating the GCA

Each mobile agent periodically broadcasts its LCA to its neighbors in communication range. Similarly, each agent stores the LCAs of its neighbors. When an agent requires a service from the LSP, it queries its LCA database for the current number of LCAs of neighboring agents. If the number of records (the k-anonymity) is too small, it broadcasts to its 1-hop neighbors a request asking for the LCAs of their neighbors. A message consists of four parts: a unique message ID, a pseudonym (an encrypted IP address such as in Onion routing [16]), the request for the LCAs, and the maximum hop count, h_{max}. The pseudonym in the message determines the parent for the nodes receiving the message. Each agent receiving this message for the first time (1) decrements h_{max} by one in the message, (2) stores the message ID and its parents' pseudonym, and (3) broadcasts the message exchanging its parents' pseudonym with its own if h_{max} is greater than 0. This limited flooding continues until h_{max} is 0. Then, the agents recursively report their LCAs back to the previous agent using the stored parents' pseudonym. This technique does not lead to a flooding of the network as only the agent that can decrypt the pseudonym will relay the message to the next agent.

If the agent does not find any record in its database, then it has two options: (1) if an immediate service is required it sets its GCA to its LCA or (2) it waits until more agents are in its vicinity. This approach balances the agent's desired privacy level against the available time. In an automated system the agent could store a minimum rectangle for its GCA in its privacy profile.

The actual computation of the GCA is discussed in the next section.

3.3   The GGC Algorithm

We present a greedy algorithm to compute the GCA for an agent j. Assume that k is the desired anonymity level of j and n is the number of LCAs reported by its neighbors. For the computation of the GCA, we need to find the smallest rectangle r that encloses a k-subset (including j's LCA) from the n reported LCAs. The LCA of an agent i is described by $(x_{min_i}, x_{max_i}, y_{min_i}, y_{max_i})$. If the area of r is smaller than the minimum GCA size σ specified by the agent j, the area of r has to be randomly increased to σ.

We have developed a greedy-based GCA computation (GGC) with a time complexity of $\mathcal{O}(n \log n)$, where n is the total LCAs available to an agent; if the LCAs are sorted with respect to x_{min}, x_{max}, y_{min}, and y_{max}, the time complexity is linear. The GGC algorithm provides near-optimal results to compute the minimum bounding box. The algorithm removes at each iteration one rectangle of the n rectangles excluding the agent's rectangle r_j in a greedy manner. Each removal of a rectangle minimizes the size of the GCA. The algorithm continues until the number of remaining LCAs is equal to k. The greedy elimination process is based on a weighting of three different geometric criteria to minimize the area of the resulting GCA. In preliminary experiments we found that none of the criteria alone provides better results for computing a minimum GCA.

Assume that a set R of n LCAs is known by the agent j. The first criterion eliminates the rectangle whose edge has the greatest distance to the closest edge of the agent's rectangle r_j. More precisely, the metric $m_1(x_{min})$ for the first criterion is defined as $\max_{1 \le i \le n \wedge i \ne j}(x_{min_j} - x_{min_i})$. $m_1(x_{max})$, $m_1(y_{min})$, and $m_1(y_{max})$ are defined correspondingly and the rectangle which maximizes any of those 4 values is eliminated. The metric for the second criterion m_2 evaluates pairs of rectangles, those which have the first and second minimum for x_{min} and y_{min}, respectively, and the first and second maximum for x_{max} and y_{max}, respectively. We compute the distance for each pair and eliminate the most outward rectangle that maximizes the distance. The metric for the third criterion m_3 is similar to the second one but identifies the maximum area to be

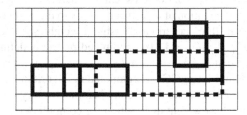

Fig. 2. A constellation where criterion 3 minimizes the GCA for $k = 3$

Algorithm 2. Find GGC

Input : A set R of LCAs, given by $(x_{\min_i}, x_{\max_i}, y_{\min_i}, y_{\max_i})$, an anonymity level k,
　　　　the agent j, and weights w_1, w_2, w_3

Output: A rectangle that covers k LCAs including the LCA of the agent j

2.1　Sort the lists $x_{\min_i}, y_{\min_i}$ in increasing order, the lists $x_{\max_i}, y_{\max_i}$ in decreasing order;

2.2　**while** $|R| > k$ **do**

2.3　　　Calculate $m(x_{\min})$, $m(x_{\max})$, $m(y_{\min})$, and $m(y_{\max})$;

2.4　　　Find the maximum from $m(x_{\min})$, $m(x_{\max})$, $m(y_{\min})$, and $m(y_{\max})$;

2.5　　　Delete the LCA from R which has the maximum value;

2.6　**return** A minimum rectangle covering the LCAs in R that are not eliminated;

Algorithm 3. Greedy-based GCA Computation

Input : A set R of LCAs, given by $(x_{\min_i}, x_{\max_i}, y_{\min_i}, y_{\max_i})$, an anonymity level k

Output: A rectangle tr that covers k LCAs including the LCA of the agent j

3.1　$tr \leftarrow \infty$;

3.2　**for** $i \leftarrow 0.1$ **to** 1 **step** 0.1 **do**

3.3　　　$w_1 \leftarrow i;\ w_2 \leftarrow (1-i)/2;\ w_3 \leftarrow (1-i)/2$;

3.4　　　$r \leftarrow$ **FindGGC**(R, k, j, w_1, w_2, w_3);

3.5　　　**if** $(\text{Area}(r) < \text{Area}(tr))$ **then** $tr \leftarrow r$;

3.6　**for** $i \leftarrow 0.1$ **to** 1 **step** 0.1 **do**

3.7　　　$w_2 \leftarrow i;\ w_1 \leftarrow (1-i)/2;\ w_3 \leftarrow (1-i)/2$;

3.8　　　$r \leftarrow$ **FindGGC**(R, k, j, w_1, w_2, w_3);

3.9　　　**if** $(\text{Area}(r) < \text{Area}(tr))$ **then** $tr \leftarrow r$;

3.10　**for** $i \leftarrow 0.1$ **to** 1 **step** 0.1 **do**

3.11　　　$w_3 \leftarrow i;\ w_1 \leftarrow (1-i)/2;\ w_2 \leftarrow (1-i)/2$;

3.12　　　$r \leftarrow$ **FindGGC**(R, k, j, w_1, w_2, w_3);

3.13　　　**if** $(\text{Area}(r) < \text{Area}(tr))$ **then** $tr \leftarrow r$;

3.14　**return** tr;

---

discarded from the current GCA. The idea of the second and third criterion is to minimize the "overhang" of the outward rectangles.

Figure 2 shows a case, where criterion 3 minimizes the area for $k = 3$. The dotted line shows the LCA for the agent j. The elimination of two further LCAs using criterion 1 or 2 lead to a GCA with a size of 40 unit squares, whereas criterion 3 leads to 36 unit squares. In general, a combination of all 3 criteria leads to the best greedy choice. Thus, we use for the metric all three criteria and assign a weight w_r, $r \in \{1, 2, 3\}$ to each criterion, such that $\sum_{1 \le r \le 3} w_r = 1$. The combined metric is defined as $m(x_{\min}) = w_1 \cdot m_1(x_{\min}) + w_2 \cdot m_2(x_{\min}) + w_3 \cdot m_3(x_{\min})$. $m(x_{\max})$, $m(y_{\min})$, and $m(y_{\max})$ are defined correspondingly. The GGC is computed in Algorithm 2.

In Algorithm 3 we first generate thirty combinations by varying the weight for the three criteria to find the best weight distribution for computing the minimum GCA. A higher number of combinations could produce more accurate results at the expense of a higher computation time.

3.4 Experimental Evaluation

We evaluate the BGC and the GGC in terms of accuracy and time. For the computation of the GCA we consider two scenarios: the agent computes its GCA as a k-subset first out of 10 then out of 25 LCAs. Higher values of n are difficult to investigate in experiments due to the exponential computation cost of the BGC. We compare the accuracy of the GGC with respect to the average deviation from the optimal solution given by the BGC. We generate the GCA from the available n LCAs (given by n agents), varying k from 1 to n, using both algorithms. Then we calculate the deviation of the GGC-generated GCA against the BGC-generated GCA. We perform 100 runs for these experiments and measure the average deviation from $100 \times n$ samples for each k. Figure 3 shows that the average error of the GGC increases from 0% to 3% until $k = 4$ in scenario 1 and increases from 0% to 5% until $k = 10$ in scenario 2, then again decreases in both scenarios for increasing values of k (Figure 3). We also computed the histograms and found that the GGC computes the optimal minimum bounding box in scenario 1 and 2 for 87% and 66% of the cases, respectively, and achieves at most 5% error in scenario 1 and 2 for 4% and 15% of the cases, respectively.

Figure 4 shows the average response times for computing the GCA for 10 and 25 LCAs using both approaches. The response time for the BGC, can increase significantly for different values k and n, as it performs an exhaustive search. The BGC is the best choice when n is small, as shown in Figure 4 (left) for $n = 10$. It does not only provide the fastest response but also computes the optimal result. However, when the value of n increases (i.e., $n = 25$ as in Figure 4 (right)), the GGC is significantly faster than the BGC, at least 10 times but often 1000 times faster (Figure 4 (right)). The response time

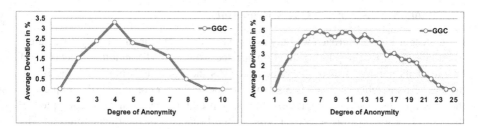

Fig. 3. Accuracy levels for k-subsets of 10 LCAs (left) and 25 LCAs (right)

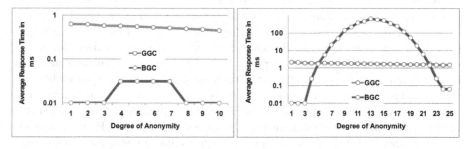

Fig. 4. Average response time for k-subsets of 10 LCAs (left) and 25 LCAs (right)

of the GGC is slightly affected by the anonymity level k for a given initial set of LCAs available to the agent. The response time decreases with the increase of k for a fixed initial set of LCAs and increases if the initial set of LCAs increases for a fixed k. In summary, the agent can balance its need for an optimal GCA against its available time for larger n. As the GCAs computed by the GGC are at most 4% larger (Figure 3), the GGC provides a good all-purpose algorithm. If the smallest GCA is required, the agent could opt for the BGC, although this is only possible for small values of n.

4   Accessing a Location Service

An agent that wishes to access a location service cannot directly contact the LSP if it wants to remain anonymous. Thus, it has to randomly select an agent (possibly itself) that requests the location service on its behalf. In contrast to other approaches, we develop a uniform selection algorithm that enables an agent, the query initiator, to select any other agent (the query requestor) on its behalf with equal probability, even those that are not in its communication range. We propose a lightweight algorithm that can work with localized information, that is, an agent only knows the IP of its neighbors in its communication range. To add a further level of security, in our algorithm an agent encrypts its IP before sending it to its neighbors. Our technique also restricts the broadcast of an agent's encrypted IP within its communication range to minimize the number of encrypted IPs available to an agent. The process to select a query requestor is independent from the computation of the GCA (see Section 3.3): an agent involved in the GCA computation may not be involved in the random selection process and vice versa.

4.1   Random Selection of a Query Requestor

In our decentralized approach we only assume that the agents are uniformly distributed. A mobile agent that requires a location service from an LSP randomly selects itself or one of its neighbors as a query requestor. As the agent does not know the IP addresses of its neighbors, it sends a simple broadcast with a hop count of 1 requesting the pseudonyms of its immediate neighbors. A pseudonym is simply an encrypted IP that is only known to the agent replying to the broadcast of the query initiator. The query initiator then randomly selects a pseudonym, i.e., determines the query requestor that should act on its behalf. If the total number of neighbors for the query initiator is N, then the probability for selecting a mobile agent is $1/(N + 1)$, which is uniform.

If the query initiator wants to increase its privacy level, it has to select the query requestor from a larger set of agents including those that are not its immediate neighbors. Since it does not know the IP addresses of the other agents, a naive solution is a recursive approach to selecting a query requestor with a hop count greater than 1: the query initiator randomly selects itself or one of its neighbors with equal probability, and the selected agent again selects itself or one of its neighbors with equal probability. The recursive selection process continues a number of times specified by the query initiator and the agent selected in the final step becomes the query requestor. However, this selection strategy leads to a non-uniform selection probability for an agent, and thus may be discovered by the LSP so that the query initiator could possibly be identified. If we

Table 1. Non-uniform selection probability (in %) for 25 agents and 49 agents

1.235	2.469	3.704	2.469	1.235
2.469	4.938	7.407	4.938	2.469
3.704	7.407	11.111	7.407	3.704
2.469	4.938	7.407	4.938	2.469
1.235	2.469	3.704	2.469	1.235

0.137	0.412	0.823	0.960	0.823	0.412	0.137
0.412	1.235	2.469	2.881	2.469	1.235	0.412
0.823	2.469	4.938	5.761	4.938	2.469	0.823
0.960	2.881	5.761	6.722	5.761	2.881	0.960
0.823	2.469	4.938	5.761	4.938	2.469	0.823
0.412	1.235	2.469	2.881	2.469	1.235	0.412
0.137	0.412	0.823	0.960	0.823	0.412	0.137

Table 2. Hop distance (left) and status for 81 agents (right)

4	4	4	4	4	4	4	4	4
4	3	3	3	3	3	3	3	4
4	3	2	2	2	2	2	3	4
4	3	2	1	1	1	2	3	4
4	3	2	1	*	1	2	3	4
4	3	2	1	1	1	2	3	4
4	3	2	2	2	2	2	3	4
4	3	3	3	3	3	3	3	4
4	4	4	4	4	4	4	4	4

1	2	3	4	4	4	3	2	1
2	1	2	3	4	3	2	1	2
3	2	1	2	3	2	1	2	3
4	3	2	1	1	1	2	3	4
4	4	3	1	*	1	3	4	4
4	3	2	1	1	1	2	3	4
3	2	1	2	3	2	1	2	3
2	1	2	3	4	3	2	1	2
1	2	3	4	4	4	3	2	1

assume a uniform distribution, and set for the sake of simplicity the value for the total number of neighbors to 8, then Table 1 shows the selection probabilities for a hop count h of 2 and 3 leading to a clique of 25 and 49 agents, respectively.

Let $d_h(A, A')$ be the hop distance between two agents A and A', and $N(A)$ the number of agents that are in communication range of A, i.e., $d_h(A, A') = 1$. If A is A' then $d_h(A, A') = 0$. The selection probability in the naive algorithm is only determined by the hop distance to the query initiator. We can recursively compute the selection probability at step t in the following way:

$$p^1(A) = 1/(N(A) + 1),$$

$$p^t(A) = \sum_{A': d_h(A, A') \leq 1} \frac{p^{t-1}(A')}{N(A') + 1}.$$

Table 1 shows that even the selection probability for agents with the same hop distance from the query initiator are different. Therefore, it is not possible to differentiate the selection probability based on the hop distance only. We need the concept of a status of an agent and will show that the status combined with the hop distance allows us to compute a close approximation of the uniform selection probability. Again for simplicity we compute the status of an agent assuming that all agents have 8 neighbors in their communication range. The status of an agent is characterized by the number of neighbors with a shorter or equal hop distance to the query initiator: an agent has status 1, if exactly one neighbor has a shorter hop distance; an agent has status 2, if exactly two neighbors have a shorter hop distance; an agent has status 3, if exactly three neighbors have a shorter hop distance and at least one neighbor has status 2 with the same hop distance; an agent has status 4, if exactly three neighbors have a shorter hop distance and no neighbor with status 2 has the same hop distance. An agent that is not the query initiator can have only one of the four statuses. Table 2 (left) shows an agent's hop distance to the query initiator and Table 2 (right) the status of the agents, where * is the query initiator.

4.2   Hop Distance and Status Generation

As highlighted above we need an algorithm so that each agent can compute its status (and hop distance) relative to the query initiator using the information of neighboring nodes only. The message includes three types of information, the maximum hop count $h_{\max}$ (decremented by 1 if a message is relayed), the current hop count c, i.e., the distance to the query initiator, and a unique encrypted message ID. A message ID has to be unique because some agents may be involved in more than one random selection process. An agent sets its status to 1, if it receives a message only once from a neighbor with a hop count c one less than itself. It sets its status to 2, if there are two neighbors of this type. If an agent receives the same message from three neighbors with a smaller hop distance, its status is either 3 or 4. It has to wait for some interval for a response of its neighbors with the same count and then requests the status from those agents. If the status of one of them is 2, it sets its status to 3, otherwise to 4. A message is only broadcast if the maximum hop count is greater than 0.

4.3   The Algorithm

We will present an algorithm that is able to compute a near-uniform selection probability, using only the hop distances and statuses of the agents. Agents that are further away from the query initiator are less likely to be selected if in each step an agent is always selected with the same probability (see Table 1).

To achieve a near-uniform selection process, we have to select agents with different probabilities. Algorithm 5 shows the algorithm for assigning the different probability values. It uses different procedures based on different criteria. Due to space constraints, we only show the procedure for agents with status 1 as an example in Algorithm 4. The status of an agent A and its minimum hop count to the query initiator are represented by $s(A)$ and $h(A)$, respectively. To enhance readability we assume $s(A) = s$ and $h(A) = h$ for agent A and $s(A') = s'$ and $h(A') = h'$ for agent A' in our algorithms. We also use N for $N(A)$. In our algorithms, $p(A)$ and $p_{\mathrm{prev}}(A)$ are the probabilities for an agent A at the current and previous step, respectively. The uniform selection probability, we call it target probability p_T, for an agent is $1/T(t)$, where $T(t)$ is the total number of agents involved in the selection process after t steps.

We assume that agents are uniformly distributed, i.e., we can partition the space into a grid-like structure such that each agent is within one grid cell and has $N = 8$ neighbors. If the query initiator selects itself or one of its neighbors for the first time, the total number of agents involved is $N + 1$; once the selected agent selects itself or one of its neighbors in the second step, the total number of involved agents increases to $1 + 3 * N$, and after t steps to a total of $T(t) = 1 + N * t * (t + 1)/2$ agents.

We explain the main idea of the algorithm for a status 1 and a status 2 agent. The first time, a status 1 agent can only be selected by another agent with status 1 or by the query initiator. Thus, the agent selecting a status 1 neighbor with a greater hop distance, has to select it with a probability equal to $p_T(t)$ after t steps. Similarly, an agent with status 2 can only be selected initially by 2 agents, with a target probability $p_T(t)/2$.

It is not possible to always follow all rules for $p_T(t)$ with increasing t, as the total required probability $p_T(t)$ for the neighbors and the selector itself may become greater than $p_{prev}(A)$ of the selector A for a larger t. As a result, it is not possible to achieve perfect uniformity for all agents. Table 3 shows the near-uniform selection probability for 25 and 49 agents after 2 and 3 steps, respectively.

However, our selection scheme is close to uniform and significantly better than the naive selection strategy. Table 4 compares the naive algorithm with our selection strategy for a maximum hop distance h_{max} ranging from 1 to 5. For example, the improvement is nearly 1000% for 121 agents ($h_{max} = 5$). It is also possible to refine the computation and distinguish between more statuses. However, for most practical purposes (around 100 peers) our experiments show that the computation of a status of up to 4 is sufficient to select a query requestor with near uniform randomness. The near-optimal selection probability makes it difficult for a hostile agent (or the LSP) to identify a query requestor, in particular as the selection probability does not follow a specific pattern. Although there may be some local skewness in the selection probabilities if the number of 1-hop neighbors varies for an agent, i.e., is greater or less than $N = 8$, this deviation will only have a small impact on the overall performance: the key

---

Algorithm 4. AssignByStatusOne(A, A', h, h', s')

Input : An agent A and its hop distance to the query initiator h, an agent A' (for which a probability will be computed) and its hop distance h' and status s'

Output: $p(A')$

4.1 $p_T(h + 1) = 1/T(t)$;
4.2 **if** $h' > h$ **then**
4.3   **if** $s' = 1$ **then**
4.4   **if** $(p_T(h + 1) <= p_{prev}(A))$ **then**
4.5 $p(A')+ = p_T(h + 1)$;
4.6   **else**
4.7 $p(A')+ = p_{prev}(A)$;

4.8   **else if** $s' = 2$ **then**
4.9   **if** $(p_T(h + 1) <= (p_{prev}(A) - p_T(h + 1)))$ **then**
4.10 $p(A')+ = p_T(h + 1)/2$;
4.11   **else if** $((p_{prev}(A) - p_T(h + 1)) > 0)$ **then**
4.12 $p(A')+ = (p_{prev}(A) - p_T(h + 1))/2$;

4.13   **else**
4.14   **if** $(p_T(h + 1) * 2/3 <= (p_{prev}(A) - (2 * p_T(h + 1))))$ **then**
4.15 $p(A')+ = p_T(h + 1)/3$;
4.16   **else if** $((p_{prev}(A) - (2 * p_T(h + 1))) > 0)$ **then**
4.17 $p(A')+ = (p_{prev}(A) - (2 * p_T(h + 1)))/2$;

Algorithm 5. AssignProbability(A, h, s)

Input : An agent A, its hop distance to the query initiator h and its status s

5.1 **if** $h = 0$ **then**

5.2   **for** *each A' with $d_h(A, A') \leq 1$* **do**

5.3 $p(A') + = p_{\text{prev}}(A)$;

5.4 **else if** $h = 1$ **then**

5.5   **for** *each A' with $d_h(A, A') \leq 1$* **do**

5.6   **AssignByLevelOne** (A, A', h, h', s');

5.7 **else if** $s = 1$ **then**

5.8   **for** *each A' with $d_h(A, A') \leq 1$* **do**

5.9   **AssignByStatusOne** (A, A', h, h', s');

5.10 **...**

5.11 **else if** $s = 4$ **then**

5.12   **for** *each A' with $d_h(A, A') \leq 1$* **do**

5.13   **AssignByStatusFour** (A, A', h, h', s');

Table 3. Near uniform selection probability (in %) for 25 agents (left) and 49 agents (right)

4.000	4.000	4.000	4.000	4.000
4.000	4.000	4.000	4.000	4.000
4.000	4.000	4.000	4.000	4.000
4.000	4.000	4.000	4.000	4.000
4.000	4.000	4.000	4.000	4.000

2.041	2.000	2.014	1.953	2.014	2.000	2.041
2.000	2.041	2.452	1.813	2.452	2.041	2.000
2.014	2.452	2.141	2.111	2.141	2.452	2.014
1.953	1.813	2.111	2.041	2.111	1.813	1.953
2.014	2.452	2.141	2.111	2.141	2.452	2.014
2.000	2.041	2.452	1.813	2.452	2.041	2.000
2.041	2.000	2.014	1.953	2.014	2.000	2.041

Table 4. Ratio between the maximum and minimum values of the selection probability of a non-uniform and a near-uniform algorithm

Number of Agents	Non-uniform Algorithm	Near-uniform Algorithm
9	1	1
25	8.997	1
49	49.431	1.353
81	366.8	1.6
121	2202.5	2.568

aim is to ensure that agents close to the query initiator do not have a higher selection probability.

If a query initiator requires an anonymity degree k that involves agents in the selection process that are not its immediate neighbors, finding the query requestor is a two stage process that consists of two messages, M_Q and M_R. The query initiator broadcasts a message M_Q to its one-hop neighbors querying each agent for its hop distance, its status and its pseudonym (e.g., an encrypted IP). The responding agents return this information in the format *<hop distance, status, pseudonym>*. The hop distance and the status of the agents for this step are always 1. The query initiator then uses the selection scheme specified in Algorithm 5 to select an agent. Afterwards the query initiator sends a message M_R including the service request encrypted using the public key of the LSP, its public key, the maximum hop distance $h_{\max}$, the probability value with which the agent is selected and the pseudonym of the selected agent in the format *<encrypted service request, public key, $h_{\max}$, probability value, pseudonym>*. If $h_{\max}$ is greater than 0, then the selected agent decrements $h_{\max}$ by one in M_R, repeats the selection process including M_Q, and forwards M_R to the new selected agent. The process continues until $h_{\max}$ is 0 and an agent discovers itself as the query requestor.

4.4 Secure Communication with LSP Provider

After the selection of the query requestor, the query requestor communicates with the LSP on behalf of the query initiator. It sends the message M_R to the LSP excluding $h_{\max}$ and the pseudonym in the format *<encrypted service request, public key>*. Only the LSP can decipher the requested service. The LSP decrypts the message with its private key and encrypts the requested information using the public key of the query initiator. Then, the LSP broadcasts the encrypted message in the GCA of the query initiator. Although all agents in the GCA can receive the message, only the query initiator can decrypt it. We assume that the query initiator remains in the GCA as its service request is based on its current location. This ensures it can receive the requested service. In this sense, our approach also enables dynamic queries as long as the query initiator stays within the GCA.

5 Experimental Results

Our approach is based on the idea that mobile agents requesting location services neither disclose their exact locations nor their identity to an LSP. There are no restrictions for the agents' positions: they could be located in a street, an office building, a shopping mall, or public place. The LSP, however, knows the precise locations of points of interests (POIs) such as restaurants, hospitals, or train stations. These places are public and have an interest in being advertised. In our experiments, we will evaluate the impact of obfuscation and anonymity against the quality of service (QOS) the LSP can provide under these constraints. To measure the QOS, we will consider proximity queries that select the m closest relevant POIs, for example the five closest pharmacies. Our algorithm can also deal with several requests from the same (or different) agents but it is not optimized for continuous queries.

5.1 Estimating the QOS by the LSP Using Hausdorff Distances

As the agent's location is not known precisely to the LSP, an LSP could simply provide all answers to the agent. This option, however, is not economically viable (data is valuable to the LSP) nor is it practical due to the high communication load. Thus, we assume that the LSP returns a small subset of m POIs that is closest to the GCA of the query initiator, because it does not know the agent's precise position.

In our model the LSP measures proximity using Hausdorff distances. Two point sets have the Hausdorff distance d iff d is the smallest distance such that for every point in one set there is a point in the other set within distance d. In our case, the LSP measures the Hausdorff distance between the rectangle representing the GCA and the exact location (x, y) of the POI. Since the GCA is a rectangle, the Hausdorff distance can be computed as the maximum Euclidean distance from (x, y) to the 4 corner points of the rectangle.

We could simply use the Euclidean distance instead of the Hausdorff distance in our approach. However, in this case we would loose an important aspects of the Hausdorff distance: it is even applicable, if the locations of the POIs have to be kept private as well, i.e., if their location is given by a rectangle (or more generally a set) instead of a coordinate. Although we assume that POIs are public places, our approach would also work for POIs requiring location privacy.

5.2 Experimental Setup

To determine the QOS of an LSP, we analyze nearest neighbor queries, more specifically m-nearest POI queries. If m is equal to one, we simply search for the closest POI. However, we expect that greater values of m are beneficial in two ways: they do not only have the potential to increase the accuracy of the answer of an LSP but also provide an agent with the option to receive a higher QOS. For example, an agent that agrees to pay a higher price for a 3-subset of POIs, could select the closest POI from this subset, if it knows its position using a GPS-enabled mobile device. In return for a higher price, an agent can maintain both, a higher level of privacy and accuracy.

We have designed our experiments to evaluate the QOS against the level of privacy, which is determined by the degree of k-anonymity and the size of the agent's obfuscated area, i.e., its GCA. We measure the obfuscation level using the size of the GCA. We call the *total search area*, in which the agent is interested in the POIs, the TSA. An agent might be interested in French restaurants in walking distance, for example in a square of 1 km^2. In order to make our comparison independent from the absolute size of the search space, a pedestrian might have different requirements than the driver of a car, we measure the GCA relative to the TSA. The *obfuscation level* is simply defined as the size of the GCA divided by the size of the TSA. If the GCA is equal to the TSA, the obfuscation level is 100%. Although an obfuscation level of 1% appears to ask for a low level of privacy, the agent is actually requesting a high level of privacy, as the agent's imprecise location (its GCA) could be a $100 \text{ m} \times 100 \text{ m}$ square in a TSA of 1 km^2.

We expect (and verified) that a small decrease of the obfuscation level does not affect the QOS significantly. Hence, we decrease in the first experiment the area of the GCA recursively, halving it in each step, to investigate the impact of its size on the QOS. We vary for the first experiment the total number of POIs. In the second experiment, we vary the k-anonymity to study its impact on the QOS, changing k from 1 to the total available LCAs, i.e., to the total numbers of agents forming a clique. We run the second experiment for different maximum values of k, i.e., the total number of available LCAs.

In the first and second sets of experiments, we compute 100 randomly distributed GCA samples for each obfuscation level and for each degree of anonymity, respectively. The POIs are randomly distributed in the TSA. We calculate the actual nearest

POIs from the query initiator using the Euclidean distance. To compute the relative error, we determine the POIs returned by the LSP based on the Hausdorff distance (see Section 5.1). We perform 10 runs for each set of parameters and measure the QOS in terms of average relative error. The relative error is the ratio of the Euclidean distance of the query initiator from the actual m-closest POIs and the Euclidean distance of the query initiator from the m-closest POIs returned by the LSP. For all experiments we have varied m from 1 to 5 as $m = 5$ provides already a high degree of accuracy.

5.3   Effect of the Obfuscation Level

We evaluate the impact of the size of the obfuscated area on the QOS of the LSP. Our expectation is that the relative error decreases as the size of the GCA decreases. Figure 5 also shows that the accuracy increases with decreasing obfuscation levels and the accuracy increases with increasing values for m, ranging from 1 to 5. If the agent increases m from 1 to 3, it can enlarge its GCA by an average factor of 4 for an error less of than 10% and by an average factor of 2 for an error less than 1%. Increasing m from 3 to 5, the GCA is on average 2 and 4 times larger for errors less than 1% and 10%, respectively. We also analyze the performance varying the number of total POIs from 10 to 100, in steps of 10. Due to space limitations, we show the details for 10 POIs.

Figure 6 (left) shows that the relative error decreases with a decreasing total number of POIs for the closest POI. Thus, an agent can expect a better QOS, if it issues a

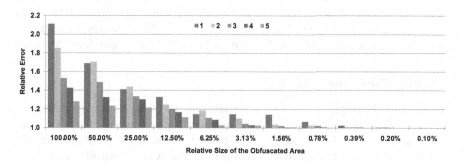

Fig. 5. Impact of the obfuscation level

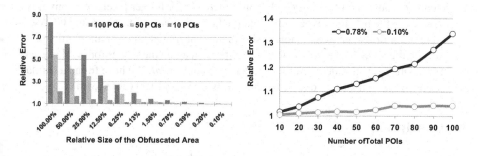

Fig. 6. Impact of the total POIs

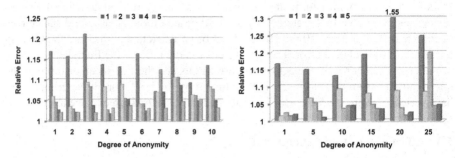

Fig. 7. Impact of the degree of anonymity for k-subsets of 10 LCAs (left) and 25 LCAs (right)

selective query that limits the number of POIs to search from. For example, a tourist can receive a more accurate response from the LSP if it specifies the type of restaurant instead of searching for all restaurants. We limit the presentation in Figure 6 (left) for 10, 50, and 100 POIs and in Figure 6 (right) for 0.78% and 0.10% obfuscation levels.

For realistic values, such as an obfuscation level around 1%, we see in Figure 6 (right) that for an obfuscation level of 0.78%, the accuracy for the closest POI increases from 92.4% to 98.3%, if the total number of POIs is reduced from 30 to 10. This provides a good compromise of a high degree of privacy, QOS and total POIs. If the agent is not willing to sacrifice the QOS (96.7%–99.3% average accuracy), it could request the 3 closest POIs but also paying more for a larger subset. In general, an agent has three options: (1) requesting larger values of m (but paying more) and selecting the closest POIs from the result set, (2) reducing the size of the GCA and thereby sacrificing its privacy in return for a higher QOS, (3) sacrificing the QOS for a higher level of privacy.

5.4   Effect of the Anonymity Level

We also study the impact of the anonymity level on the QOS. As the computation of the POIs by the LSP is not related with the number of agents involved in the GCA, we expect that the QOS does not change significantly with varying degrees of anonymity. If the agents are close to each other, the size of the GCA can be small even for high degrees of anonymity, but if the agents are far away from each other, the GCA can be large even for low degrees of anonymity. We did not consider a uniform distribution of the agents, because the resulting GCA would increase for higher levels of anonymity; we know from the previous experiment that the QOS decreases for increasing GCAs.

Figure 7 confirms our expectation. It shows that varying degrees of anonymity have no effect on the QOS. The numbers for 1 to 5 represent again the values for m. However, the error probability also decreases for increasing values of m. We have found a similar performance for a maximum degree of anonymity of 50 and 100 (not shown).

6   Conclusions

In this paper, we have introduced an approach that combines obfuscation and anonymization to ensure both location and anonymity privacy for mobile agents in a distributed wireless ad-hoc network. We show in our experiments that a decentralized architecture can successfully combine a high QOS with a high level of location privacy.

Our approach does not require any central trusted party and, more importantly, agents even do not need to disclose their exact position or identity to the LSP or their neighbors. Agents can specify separate privacy levels for their GCA generation and random query requestor selection process. In our system, agents have the option to increase their required levels of privacy and their expected QOS from the LSP in exchange for a higher service cost. We exploit the wireless advantage that all agents in communication range can overhear a message in order to anonymize the communication among agents. This allows us to eliminate the need for a trusted party such as an intermediary centralized anonymizer.

We have proposed a greedy algorithm for computing the GCA. Experimental results show that our heuristic approach achieves a good accuracy; on an average in more than 77% of all cases it provides the optimal result. Furthermore, our approach is of orders of magnitudes faster than the brute force approach.

Using our proposed algorithm for the random selection process, the selection probabilities for the agents in the process are near uniform. The slight deviation does not follow any specific pattern. Therefore, it is not possible for a hostile agent to predict the position of the query initiator. Since the information for the requested service to the LSP is encrypted, no agent is able to discover that information. Furthermore, there is no third party involved while receiving the result sets for the service requested, and thus only the query initiator can interpret the result. We have assumed a homogeneous distribution of the agents to recursively compute the selection probability. We plan to develop a more general selection scheme that overcomes this limitation.

We have shown that it is possible to combine high levels of privacy with a high QOS and that agents can balance their requirements for privacy, QOS, and service cost. Our experimental evaluations reveal that for nearest POI queries, an agent can obtain a higher level of privacy and accuracy by requesting a k-subset of nearest POIs instead of just requesting a single POI, at the expense of a higher service cost.

We did not address two concerns often pointed out for anonymity-based approaches: anonymity can present a barrier to authentication and billing. Two promising solutions are digital cash [17] and zero knowledge proofs [18]. Digital cash enables an agent to anonymously pay for a service. Similarly, zero knowledge proofs allow an agent to prove that it is authorized to access information without revealing its identity.

References

1. Muntz, R., Barclay, T., Dozier, J., Faloutsos, C., Maceachren, A., Martin, J., Pancake, C., Satyanarayanan, M.: IT Roadmap to a Geospatial Future. The National Academies Press, Washington, DC (2003)
2. Ghinita, G., Kalnis, P., Skiadopoulos, S.: PRIVÉ: Anonymous location-based queries in distributed mobile systems. In: Proceedings of the 16th International World Wide Web Conference, pp. 371–389 (2007)
3. Gruteser, M., Grunwald, D.: Anonymous usage of location-based services through spatial and temporal cloaking. In: Proceedings of MobiSys, pp. 31–42 (2003)

4. Gedik, B., Liu, L.: Location privacy in mobile systems: A personalized anonymization model. In: ICDCS '05: Proceedings of the 25th IEEE International Conference on Distributed Computing Systems, pp. 620–629. IEEE Computer Society Press, Los Alamitos (2005)

5. Mokbel, M.F., Chow, C.Y., Aref, W.G.: The new casper: query processing for location services without compromising privacy. In: Proceedings of VLDB, pp. 763–774 (2006)

6. Duckham, M., Kulik, L.: A formal model of obfuscation and negotiation for location privacy. In: Gellersen, H.-W., Want, R., Schmidt, A. (eds.) PERVASIVE 2005. LNCS, vol. 3468, pp. 152–170. Springer, Heidelberg (2005)

7. Chow, C.Y., Mokbel, M.F., Liu, X.: A peer-to-peer spatial cloaking algorithm for anonymous location-based services. In: 14th ACM International Symposium on Geographic Information Systems, ACM-GIS 2006, pp. 171–178. ACM Press, New York (2006)

8. Langheinrich, M.: Privacy by design—principles of privacy-aware ubiquitous systems. In: Abowd, G.D., Brumitt, B., Shafer, S. (eds.) Ubicomp 2001: Ubiquitous Computing. LNCS, vol. 2201, pp. 273–291. Springer, Heidelberg (2001)

9. Kaasinen, E.: User needs for location-aware mobile services. Personal and Ubiquitous Computing 70(1), 70–79 (2003)

10. Görlach, A., Terpstra, W.W., Heinemann, A.: Survey on location privacy in pervasive computing. In: Proceedings of SPPC (2004)

11. Duckham, M., Kulik, L.: Simulation of obfuscation and negotiation for location privacy. In: Cohn, A.G., Mark, D.M. (eds.) COSIT 2005. LNCS, vol. 3693, pp. 31–48. Springer, Heidelberg (2005)

12. Beresford, A., Stajano, F.: Location privacy in pervasive computing. IEEE Pervasive Computing 2(1), 46–55 (2003)

13. Duri, S., Gruteser, M., Liu, X., Moskowitz, P., Perez, R., Singh, M., Tang, J.-M.: Framework for security and privacy in automotive telematics. In: Proceedings of WMC, pp. 25–32. ACM Press, New York (2002)

14. Bettini, C., Wang, X.S., Jajodia, S.: Protecting privacy against location-based personal identification. In: Proceedings of SDM, pp. 185–199 (2005)

15. Kido, H., Yanagisawa, Y., Satoh, T.: An anonymous communication technique using dummies for location-based services. In: Proceedings of ICPS, pp. 88–97 (2005)

16. Reed, M., Syverson, P., Goldschlag, D.: Anonymous connections and onion routing. IEEE Journal on Selected Areas in Communications 16(4), 482–494 (1998)

17. Brands, S.: Untraceable off-line cash in wallet with observers. In: Stinson, D.R. (ed.) CRYPTO 1993. LNCS, vol. 773, pp. 302–318. Springer, Heidelberg (1994)

18. Fiat, A., Shamir, A.: How to prove yourself: practical solutions to identification and signature problems. In: Odlyzko, A.M. (ed.) CRYPTO 1986. LNCS, vol. 263, pp. 186–194. Springer, Heidelberg (1987)

Haggle: Seamless Networking for Mobile Applications

Jing Su[1,2], James Scott[1,*], Pan Hui[1,3,4], Jon Crowcroft[3], Eyal de Lara[2],
Christophe Diot[4], Ashvin Goel[2], Meng How Lim[1], and Eben Upton[1]

[1] Intel Research Cambridge
[2] University of Toronto
[3] Cambridge University
[4] Thomson

Abstract. This paper presents Haggle, an architecture for mobile devices that enables seamless network connectivity and application functionality in dynamic mobile environments. Current applications must contain significant network binding and protocol logic, which makes them inflexible to the dynamic networking environments facing mobile devices. Haggle allows separating application logic from transport bindings so that applications can be communication agnostic. Internally, the Haggle framework provides a mechanism for late-binding interfaces, names, protocols, and resources for network communication. This separation allows applications to easily utilize multiple communication modes and methods across infrastructure and infrastructure-less environments. We provide a prototype implementation of the Haggle framework and evaluate it by demonstrating support for two existing legacy applications, email and web browsing. Haggle makes it possible for these applications to seamlessly utilize mobile networking opportunities both with and without infrastructure.

1 Introduction

Advances in computing technology have had a profound impact on the capabilities of portable devices such as smart-phones, notebooks, and personal digital assistants. Today these devices provide a rich computing environment and multiple communication methods based on different radio technologies such as short-range Bluetooth, medium-range 802.11 and longer-range cellular radios.

Users expect ubiquitous access to applications such as messaging and information browsing on these powerful devices. Unfortunately existing applications are often unable to take advantage of the mobility and connectivity options that may be present because they are written to a software abstraction that is deeply intertwined with the underlying networking architecture. This is illustrated by the fact that applications must currently be responsible for establishing all bindings necessary to perform communication. This requirement causes applications to assume the implicit design, conventions, and operating modes of the underlying networking. As a result, applications are difficult to adapt to new communication mechanisms. For example, email and web addresses implicitly assume a naming structure which requires the use of highly available DNS servers.

---

* Now at Microsoft Research Cambridge.

J. Krumm et al. (Eds.): UbiComp 2007, LNCS 4717, pp. 391–408, 2007.

We believe that the user experience should be that of applications adapting to changing network conditions with devices responsive to different available connectivity options, protocols, and communication environments. For instance, email should be sent peer-to-peer if the sender and recipient are in close proximity, browsers should be able to search neighbours for possible matching content if the Internet is not reachable, and devices should be able to utilize the connectivity of peers willing to provide a bridge to the Internet. Currently, it is non-trivial to add the decision logic into applications to handle these different usage models, and furthermore, if each application makes the decisions individually, the overall system may perform poorly [5,4].

In this paper, we present Haggle, a novel framework that enables seamless network connectivity and application functionality in dynamic mobile environments. At its core, Haggle allows separating application logic from the underlying networking technology. Applications delegate the task of handling and communicating data to Haggle, which in turn adapts to the current network environment using the best available connectivity and protocol for the situation and user-specified policies that allow trading speed, cost and power constraints.

Haggle employs three main ideas to achieve its goals (Section 3). First, it is able to adapt to its mobile environment by delaying network connectivity interface and protocol selection until the moment of data transmission, a technique also known as late-binding. This approach allows operating across multiple interfaces (possibly concurrently), protocols and applications. Second, applications can share their data and meta-data with Haggle, which allows localized data search and sharing, such as browsers being able to search neighbours for matching content. Third, Haggle provides a unified mechanism for managing these shared data and network resources centrally on each device, according to user preferences and expectations.

These Haggle concepts are realized in an architecture for which we have developed a freely available open-source prototype implementation (Section 4). The prototype currently supports existing email and web applications, allowing them to seamlessly operate across environments with and without infrastructure (Section 5). We also present experimental evaluations demonstrating Haggle's ability to allow these applications to function seamlessly in highly dynamic mobile environments (Section 6).

2   Motivation

We begin with a motivating example for the problem with current networking state and why it is lacking. Alice and Bob are in a train heading towards the city. Alice wishes to forward Bob a discussion thread containing a document for review. However, the email may be difficult to send due to absence of any Internet connectivity, or slow and expensive to send as the mail is sent over a cellular link to an email server and then retrieved from the server by Bob's device.

For users Alice and Bob it is not intuitively obvious why it is so difficult or slow to send the email and attachment. Ideally the contents should be sent over a fast mutually supported peer-to-peer technology such as Bluetooth or 802.11 in ad hoc mode. However, even if Alice and Bob mutually configured an ad hoc network between their devices, their email programs would still not be able to communicate across this ad hoc network since email protocols assume the presence of infrastructure services.

Our second motivating example considers Charlie who wants to read some news to pass time in the train, but is either outside of the cellular coverage area or subject to high roaming charges. Currently, Charlie would not even try to use his web browser to read news since he knows there is no connection. However, since reading news is a popular activity in the train, it is highly likely that other people around him will have some reasonably matching cached content available. Unfortunately this information is not available to him.

We observe that the current networking framework is not flexible enough to support applications and mobile users in an intuitive and simple way. The problem is that we need a smart method for selecting the connectivity method, protocols and name bindings appropriate for the connectivity method, and a mechanism for managing the device's communication resources across the various applications on a device. For example, in the case of Alice and Bob, the non-intuitive reason why their email programs won't communicate over an ad hoc link with each other is because email clients assume the availability of DNS services to look up MX records for the domain portion of email addresses, and expect to contact the mail server found in the MX record – both of which are not available in a local ad hoc network. Our goal in Haggle is to provide a networking framework for applications and users that enables these usage models and provides an intuitive mechanism for specifying policies and preferences.

3   The Haggle Approach

The key insight in Haggle's approach is that applications should not have to concern themselves with the mechanisms of transporting data to the right place. Instead, this should be left to the networking architecture. Providing this separation of concerns not only simplifies the application logic, but allows them to automatically adapt to new mobile environments and technologies. To achieve this separation, Haggle uses a data-centric network architecture [2] that internally manages the task of handling and propagating data. Applications can then be automatically adapted to dynamic network environments using the best connectivity channel for the situation. Below, we identify three principles that are critical to our approach.

Just-in-Time Binding of Interfaces, Protocols, and Names: At the hardware interface level, mobile devices provide different (and often multiple) connectivity interfaces of varying characteristics depending on their intended usage situations. Networking technologies can differ in many aspects, ranging in physical characteristics such as power and range, communication characteristics such as latency and cost, and peering characteristics such as ad hoc and neighbour discovery. We aim to support and embrace the use of many different networking technologies at the same time. To achieve this flexibility, we use late-binding (or just-in-time binding) of the connectivity interface to use, balancing the interface characteristics with user and application supplied preferences.

In mobile environments, depending on the interface that is selected and the connection context, the necessary protocols for performing networking operations can vary.

For example, the SMTP protocol is needed for sending mail messages to a server, but a peer-to-peer protocol should be used for sending to the recipient in close proximity. Haggle allows supporting multiple routing protocols such as peer-to-peer and intentional naming [1], and late binding to these protocols in different environments to automatically adapt applications.

In order to identify services, devices, or individuals, it is necessary to support a naming system that is flexible enough for the different networking environments. Specifically, it is not possible to resolve DNS names in ad hoc environments when infrastructure is absent. Furthermore, different entities along the delivery path may have different name resolution mechanisms. Thus it is necessary to have a flexible and semantically rich naming system which can support late-binding specification of services, individuals, or devices.

While late binding has been explored in several contexts [22, 1], Haggle is unique in allowing late binding at the three levels described above.

Exposure of Persistent Data and Metadata: To facilitate the correct searching, sharing, and opportunistic use of data, it is necessary to employ the help of applications since much of the metadata context is embedded in the application logic. For example, in order to answer queries for keyword-matching web pages in the local cache, we must have metadata for the browser's cache of pages, images, related links, and relative freshness.

Providing support for data-driven network operations requires exposure of data and metadata context outside of the application logic. We provide two classes of metadata: attribute tags and relationships. Data objects can be tagged with arbitrary sets of attribute key/value pairs, and relationships between objects can be established using directed edges. Relationships can have many different semantic meanings, established by attribute values on the edges themselves. In this paper, we consider two distinct relationships: ownership and dependency. We elaborate on the details of our use of these two relationships when we describe, in Section 5, the applications we use in our experiments.

Centralized Resource Management: Haggle manages the use of networking resources on the device centrally to ensure that the behaviour of the mobile device conforms to the expectations and preferences of the user. On a user's mobile device, there may be many applications running, each with varying types of simultaneous requests. Assuming that applications are "smart" and internally support all of the features described above, it is likely that the selfish actions of some applications will result in poor and unmanageable system behaviour. In Haggle, all requests for manageable resources are issued as *tasks* to a centralized module which dictates which actions are allowed to proceed, in accordance with current context and user-specified policies.

4   Haggle Architecture and Prototype

Haggle is internally composed of six managers organized in a layerless fashion (Figure 1) in contrast to the stacked approach of TCP/IP. The managers are each responsible for a key modular component or data structure (shown in italics in the diagram) - this provides flexibility e.g. allowing for many protocols (e.g. SMTP and HTTP) and connectivities (e.g. 802.11 and Bluetooth) to be instantiated simultaneously. The managers and modules all have well-defined APIs, and each manager (and internal component) may use the API of any or all of the other managers. This novel architecture provides necessary and useful flexibility over a layered architecture in which each layer may only talk to the two APIs above and below.

Externally, the application layer API is a subset of the interfaces provided by the individual modules. For more details, please see the technical report [23]. The remainder of this section describes how this architecture supports the core concepts of just-in-time binding, data management and resource scheduling.

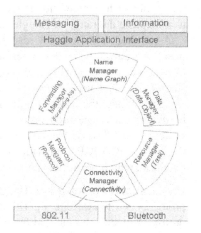

Fig. 1. Architecture overview

4.1   Just-in-Time Binding

Connectivity Interfaces: Haggle aims to embrace the use of many different networking technologies at the same time. Networking technologies can differ in many aspects, including range, latency, bandwidth, cost, availability, power, and so on. It is therefore appropriate for different connectivity interfaces to be used depending on the particular type of data being sent.

For each network interface on a node, we construct a connectivity instance. For example if there were two 802.11 interfaces there would be two connectivity objects, one for each interface. This is because a connectivity is regarded as a schedulable resource which can consume network time, battery power, monetary costs, etc. As a scheduled resource, all operations that result in network activity, including operations initiated by the connectivity itself, must be delegated for scheduling.

Connectivity objects in Haggle must support a well-defined interface including functionality for neighbour discovery, opening/using/closing communications channels, and estimating the costs (in terms of money, time and energy) of performing network operations. Each connectivity must interface with the underlying driver and hardware to provide this functionality.

Neighbour discovery can take various forms, depending on the connectivity. In 802.11, any node with reception turned on can see beacons from access points which announce their existence. For Bluetooth, neighbour discovery is an active (and time-consuming) process. For GPRS, neighbour discovery is implicit in that when base station coverage is present the Internet is accessible. Delegating the initiation of such operations is an important design approach which enables Haggle to manage multiple interfaces with respect to user defined policies.

The prototype implementation of Haggle focuses on using the 802.11 connectivity because it is a widely used wireless access network and is available for a range of devices from laptops to mobile phones. It also offers both neighbourhood and infrastructure connections (through ad hoc mode and infrastructure mode respectively) which allow us to explore the range of Haggle capabilities using a single connectivity type.

As a schedulable network resource, 802.11 interfaces must provide a cost function, which we currently model in terms of time-on-network cost. For data transfers, the time-on-network cost is calculated per byte, taking into account the bandwidth and size of data. We used a lower bandwidth estimate for AP mode than ad hoc mode since we expect the access link to be the bottleneck in AP mode. This would ideally be dynamically measured on a per-AP basis rather than statically estimated. When switching to AP mode from ad hoc, there can be a delay of a number of seconds due to the latency of DHCP to provide an IP address. We model this as a 5 second switching overhead, which we have experimentally determined to be fairly typical.

Protocols and Forwarding: Haggle encapsulates the late-binding of communication protocols and forwarding algorithms necessary for transporting data. Communication protocols specify the method for point-to-point communication, both for transmitting data as well as opening and receiving connections. For example, the HTTP protocol specifies how to connect to a web server and request objects, while the peer-to-peer protocol specifies how to connect to and receive connections from peers.

When connecting to peer or infrastructure endpoints, the most appropriate protocol is selected just-in-time to perform the necessary initializations as well as transformations and translations in order to send and receive. For protocols which must accept incoming connections, such as a peer-to-peer protocol, the protocol must provide sufficient information to the connectivity interface so that incoming connections can be redirected and properly handled by the protocol.

Forwarding algorithms determine the suitability of a next hop for transmission of application and user-level messages. The suitability is presented as a benefit value which enables Haggle to select the just-in-time binding for the forwarding algorithm, communication protocol and connectivity interface. Forwarding algorithms can be active entities, generating and receiving network messages required for maintenance and routing in an overlay or ad hoc network. Such messages, like all network use operations, must also be delegated for scheduling.

Haggle's flexible architecture allows many forwarding algorithms to be in use *simultaneously*. Possible algorithms can range from epidemic [24] to MANET algorithms such as geographic [15] or distance-vector [16], as well as store-and-forward [20, 26] or mobility based [10, 14, 13]. Delegating the proposed actions essentially allows the forwarding algorithms to compete for action. The most applicable algorithm for a given environment will prevail.

We implemented two forwarding algorithms so far, namely "direct" and "epidemic". The direct algorithm only proposes to deliver messages to their destinations if the destination is reachable by direct communication. As a result, the direct forwarding algorithm will always propose a delivery benefit of 100%. The epidemic algorithm proposes to send messages to all immediately reachable destinations. Because the epidemic algorithm cannot be certain if flooding will reach the destination, it will propose a lower delivery benefit value.

Names: Current networking architectures require early-binding of names as nested headers found in the front of physical-layer packets. Current dynamic name resolution

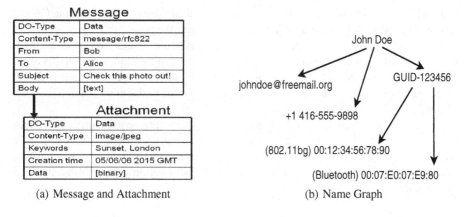

Message

DO-Type	Data
Content-Type	message/rfc822
From	Bob
To	Alice
Subject	Check this photo out!
Body	[text]

Attachment

DO-Type	Data
Content-Type	image/jpeg
Keywords	Sunset, London
Creation time	05/06/06 2015 GMT
Data	[binary]

(a) Message and Attachment

(b) Name Graph

Fig. 2. Example Data and Name Object Graphs

systems such as DNS still require eager resolution of human-readable names to routable addresses, which then must be bound to the physical address of the transmission interface. Unfortunately this paradigm does not work well in mobile environments where infrastructure services such as DNS might not be available at the moment of the application's request, or the connectivity interface has different resolution semantics such as Bluetooth discovery.

Haggle presents a general form of naming notation that allows late-binding of many user-level names, independent of the lower-level addressable name, as proposed in i3 [22]. We achieve this by using *name graphs*, inspired by INS [1], which are hierarchical descriptions of many known mappings from a user-level endpoint to lower-level names (which may imply particular protocols/connectivity methods). Name graphs are used as recipient identifiers for messages as well as identifying the source node and any intermediate nodes. This late-binding approach contrasts with the existing network architecture were names are only meaningful at particular layers of the protocol stack.

What's in a Name? An example name graph, which illustrates the provision of many deliverable addresses for communication endpoints is shown in Figure 2(b). The figure illustrates how one individual, John Doe, can have many different addressable identities, reachable using different connectivity methods. Name graphs span from top-level nodes such as personal names through to leaves comprising persistent methods of reaching them, such as email addresses, but not transient addressing data such as the IP address for the email server. The choice of this partition [12] stems from the feature that any "name" in Haggle can also be an "address" if there exists a suitable protocol which understands that name. For example, an SMS-capable device regards a phone number name as an address, but a non-SMS capable device would not. As a message moves between nodes, different methods of mapping names to transmission methods can become available. Transient names such as looked-up IP addresses are not valid "names" since they do not provide useful identity information for another node.

Haggle's design allows it to take advantage of any number of existing name management schemes that have been explored in previous work, such as Persistent and Personal

Names [9]. In the prototype, we utilize a hierarchical name graph construction. On first startup, Haggle nodes create a GUID name to identify the node itself. Then, the MAC addresses of the node's interfaces are also created as names under the root name. New names can also be learned from applications. For example the names and emails of the sender can be captured from an outbound email and added to the name graph as part of the person's identity. This identity graph is then linked to the node graph to indicate ownership of the device by the individual.

In the prototype implementation, Haggle nodes actively request tasks to contact newly visible names which have no associated node or user identity information. If the peer responds with identity information, it is merged into node's knowledge-base of names. In this way peer nodes can learn identity information even if infrastructure is not available.

4.2   Data Management and Data Objects

Haggle exports an interface for applications to manage persistent data and metadata explicitly. Haggle's data format is designed around the need to be *structured* and *searchable*. In other words, relationships between application data units (for example, a webpage and its embedded images) should be representable in Haggle, and applications should be able to search both locally and remotely for data objects matching particular useful characteristics. We draw inspiration from desktop search products (e.g. Google Desktop) which have changed the way that many users file and access their data [7], allowing us to avoid having to methodically place data in a directory structure. We propose that applications can use a combination of structured data and search, with the former providing the kind of capabilities expected of a traditional file-system, and the latter allowing applications to easily find and use data that they themselves did not store.

Data Objects: A Data Object comprises many *attributes*, each of which is a pair consisting of a *type* and *value*. Types and values are typically strings, though some values may also be binary packed representations. We encourage and expect applications to expose as much *metadata* as possible about an item, including application data. Two examples are shown in Figure 2(a), representing a message from Bob to Alice, and a photo of sunset. Note that we do not require users to enter more metadata about their objects than applications would require themselves; the value of exposing metadata is in the ability to search and organize data.

Links Between Data Objects: Data objects can be linked into a directed graph to either represent prerequisite dependencies or ownership information. For example, a photo album's metadata can link to the set of photos in the album, a webpage can link to its embedded objects, or an email can link to its attachments. This explicitly exposes the structured relationship between data objects more richly than directory hierarchies. Applications can also express an "ownership claim" over objects by linking its application object to the desired data objects. For example, a web browser may lay claim over cached objects, and an email reader may claim stored emails.

Since Haggle allows many applications to claim objects, it does not have a "delete" call. Instead, Haggle implements lazy garbage collection, to allow searching for unreferenced objects and delay space reclamation until it is needed.

Object Filters: To facilitate searching, the data manager supports searching for objects using a filter object which comprises of a set of regular-expression-like queries over the attributes. For example, a query might include: $(mimetype = text/html \land news \in keywords \land timestamp >= (yesterday))$ Filters can be one-time searches, or made persistent to "watch" for new or incoming matches. Filters can also be made local or remote, effectively providing a "subscription" mechanism.

4.3 Scheduling and Managing Just-in-Time Resources

Network interfaces are shared mediums which consume device and user resources, in terms of time, energy, and cost. To manage and schedule multiple network interfaces, requests for network use from components and applications are delegated to the resource manager. The resource manager considers the set of outstanding tasks and determines which tasks are allowed to execute by evaluating whether it is beneficial and cost effective when taking into account the user's preferences and policies. The centralized resource management design enables Haggle to schedule network resources in a manner coherent with the user's policies and behave in a manner understandable by the end user.

Because certain operations are time or sequence critical, there are two types of tasks supported by Haggle: asynchronous and immediate. Asynchronous tasks can be delayed or scheduled by the resource manager at any arbitrary time. Immediate tasks are evaluated right away and a decision for whether or not to execute a task is based only on the current context.

Due to the dynamic scheduling of tasks and potentially changing mobile environment, the benefits and costs of asynchronous tasks can also vary over time. For example, an email checking task is less beneficial if email was last checked 1 minute ago, but more beneficial if over an hour has elapsed. Similarly, as the connectivity environment changes, the costs for operations can dynamically change.

Once a task is being executed, the resource manager can also be asked for an extension on the resource use if the scope of the work being done by the task needs to be increased beyond the initial cost/benefits specified. This is useful for circumstances such as email checking, where we may find a large attachment waiting for download.

The task model is in marked contrast to the traditional network stack, where networking operations proposed by applications or operating system functions are always attempted. The centralization of decision-making about what tasks are worth doing at all, and which are more important at any time, allows Haggle to have a number of advantageous features. First, Haggle can easily and intuitively manage the use of multiple connectivity interfaces. Haggle's support for late-binding protocols and names allows it to manage which subset of connectivity interfaces to use and what kinds of tasks are allowed on those interfaces. Second, Haggle can easily enable dynamic scheduling and prioritizing of tasks. For example, instead of checking email at fixed intervals, the checks can be more often when bandwidth and energy are abundant, and less often otherwise or when there are more important tasks. Similarly, applications are free to request operations of varying priorities, including speculative operations, which are often not possible or worthwhile, but automatically executed when the right opportunity arises.

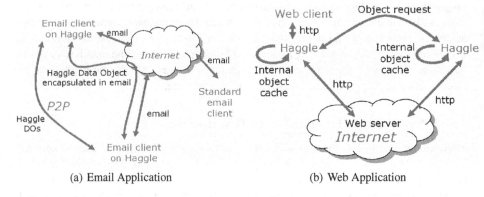

(a) Email Application   (b) Web Application

Fig. 3. Haggle Email and Web Applications

The current prototype implementation only considers costs in terms of time-on-network, which provides an estimate of energy consumption. We do not yet support costs in terms of monetary charges per byte or quota limits. Ideally the network interface card or driver would provide power consumption estimates since they have a greater knowledge of their radio characteristics and medium state. We currently assume all nodes are cooperative, and are not using policies which limit interactions with peers.

5 Support for Existing Applications

Based on our introductory motivating examples, we have chosen to target email and web as our prototype applications. To be clear, by "email" and "web" we mean the applications, rather than the protocols that underlie them.

Both of these applications enjoy significant support from the pre-existing infrastructure deployment of servers and content. It is a crucial feature of Haggle that we can take advantage of this infrastructure as well as providing new functionality. This makes Haggle much more compelling to existing users of that infrastructure, and the value added by Haggle provides motivation for its deployment.

To provide legacy support for existing email and web applications, we implement localhost SMTP/POP and HTTP proxies as Haggle-native applications. This allows users to keep using the same applications they habitually use (we have tested Outlook Express, Thunderbird, Internet Explorer and Firefox) with only minimal reconfiguration. We will first describe how Haggle provides support for email, followed by the description of web support.

5.1 Email

Supporting email in Haggle consists of two components: an SMTP/POP proxy for interfacing with email clients, and SMTP and POP Protocols inside Haggle that communicate with email servers.

The SMTP proxy accepts emails provided by the user's email client and translates them into linked data objects using Haggle's API. The proxy uses the recipient field of the email header to search for an appropriate *name* which describes the intended recipient, as illustrated in Figure 2(b). The proxy then creates a forwarding request to send the mail object to the individual described by the name object. Haggle now will dynamically decide when the message will get delivered, the protocol to use, and over which network interface.

Similarly, when the user's email client checks for new mail, the POP proxy uses the data manager to search for newly arrived messages. New messages are reconstructed as email messages (including attachments) and returned to the email client.

When infrastructure connectivity to the Internet is available and the recipient is not nearby, Haggle will use the existing email infrastructure to deliver the email message. This is possible when the 802.11 connectivity reports that it has access to the Internet. The direct forwarding algorithm and SMTP protocol plugin will both report their ability to resolve the name graph to a deliverable end-point. The resource manager will then determine if there is sufficient benefit to execute the delivery. If so, the direct forwarding algorithm will use the email protocol to transform the message object and use the SMTP protocol to deliver the email using 802.11 connectivity.

If Haggle decides to use a peer-to-peer connection, whether due to lack of infrastructure availability or to improve throughput, the two peers rendezvous to form an ad hoc network. The sending node then establishes a peer-to-peer connection to the receiver, and sends the message as a Haggle object, complete with all necessary links and meta-data.

5.2 Web

The Haggle web proxy operates as a normal web proxy when Internet connectivity is available. As requests are retrieved and returned to the browser, the web proxy stores the information in the Data Manager, including link and object relationships. The mechanism for resolving web addresses and retrieving web objects is similar to the description for the email application, except instead of email protocols, the web plugin is able to understand URL addresses as names and communicate HTTP protocols. If Internet connectivity is not available or too expansive to use, then the proxy creates a filter subscribing to the URL. A notice page is returned to the browser notifying the user that Haggle is attempting to service the request. This page refreshes itself occasionally so that the webpage will be displayed automatically when it arrives.

If a peer has matching cached content, the requested URL and linked embedded objects are sent back to the requester. If a peer is willing or has an incentive [3] to bridge the request to the Internet, the HTTP protocol first downloads the requested URL, parses it to look for embedded content, and downloads the necessary objects. The linked object is then sent back to the requester.

6 Experiments and Results

In this section we describe several experiments using the motivating applications described earlier. We provide qualitative results showing the new capabilities that Haggle enables, in addition to quantitatively demonstrating that Haggle's implementation, although not optimized, has acceptable overheads.

The Haggle implementation has been developed using Java J2ME CDC, which means it is compatible with PC and notebook platforms (e.g. Windows, Linux) as well as mobile platforms (e.g. Windows Mobile, Nokia tablets running Linux). This development has been conducted using sourceforge.net, under the GNU General Public License (GPL), available at http://sourceforge.net/projects/haggle.

We conducted the experiments on two laptop computers, which we will call *node1* and *node2*. Both are running Windows XP. Node1 is equipped with an Intel 3945 mini-PCI 802.11 interface, and node2 is equipped with an Intel 2200 802.11 interface. For infrastructure connectivity, the nodes connect via wireless 802.11g to an access point with access to the Internet.

Email: For the email experiments we created several accounts using the Google Mail (GMail) service. GMail provides POP and SMTP services over an encrypted and authenticated SSL link. This allows us to have one configuration which works from within any network that allows Internet access. However, there are limitations with using the GMail service. Though there is no limit for the size of email received, GMail restricts the size of outbound emails to be 10 megabytes or less.[1]

For the quantitative experiments we send emails of varying sizes, ranging from 10 bytes (no attachment) up to a 10 megabyte attachment, from node1 to node2. For each size increment seven unique emails are sent over a 3 Megabit download / 800 Kilobit upload DSL link. An automated script is used to send an email from node1 to node2, with node2 configured to check its inbox once every 5 seconds. The script ensures that for every email that node1 sends, node2 must receive it first before node1 sends the next email. This eliminates any congestion effects in the results.

Figure 4(a) shows the latencies for end-to-end delivery of various-sized emails under different network connectivity conditions, both with and without Haggle. The *no haggle* and *haggle infra* clusters provide a comparative baseline between email clients as normal versus using Haggle forced to use infrastructure connectivity, respectively. The results show that Haggle imposes a low overhead.

The most important result is shown in the *haggle adhoc* cluster, which shows Haggle sending and receiving emails without infrastructure present. This operation is not possible using the email client alone and would have corresponding graphs of infinite height. The ad hoc transmission of emails, shown by the *haggle adhoc* bars, is fastest since it uses a direct transmission in ad hoc mode. The other modes of operation require use of the access point link, which includes going out the DSL line, through the Internet for both transmitting the email as well as retrieving. We note that having ad hoc transmission ability can also overcome limitations of infrastructure based services, as seen in the 10Mb attachment test. Gmail places a size limit on the mail size, which prevents large emails from being sent.

The *haggle both* bar shows Haggle performing in an environment that has infrastructure access but Haggle has the option to communicate in ad hoc mode when appropriate. Ideally, the *haggle both* performance would be close to the *haggle adhoc* performance.

---

[1] Limit raised to 20 megabytes at time of publication.

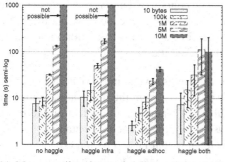 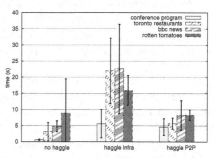

(a) Mean email end-to-end delivery times. Individual bars indicate attachment size.

(b) Mean webpage retrieval times.

Fig. 4. Email and web experiment performance. Both graphs show standard deviations as error bars. Lower values are better. Note that in 4(a) for both *no haggle* and *haggle infra* cases it was not possible to send 10M emails due to server limitations. 4(b) does not show *no haggle P2P* because it is not possible to access web pages using existing software.

This is not so (though it is still comparable with *no haggle*) and there is a larger variance in the numbers. This is due to interaction between the 802.11 connectivity and the POP protocol. Because an Internet neighbour is visible in this scenario, the POP protocol is requesting tasks to check the email account. This is additional work that Haggle is not doing in the *haggle adhoc* case. Added to this is the significant overhead incurred by 802.11 in switching between ad hoc and AP modes due to lost DHCP request packets. This overhead is not inherent to Haggle, but rather a limitation in the current implementations of 802.11 which can be overcome using techniques such as MultiNet [6].

Web: In our web experiments we focus on the retrieval of static and dynamic pages from content providers. We chose four different webpages to cover a range of complexities, sizes, and scenarios. All of these sites represent classes of content which users would like to look up and, in the right mobile context, have a reasonable expectation that other users around might have similarly matching content.

– Conference Program: This page is for a conference's technical program, which is relatively simple consisting mostly of text and no dynamic content, with a transfer size of 64Kb. Attendees at the conference are likely to request this page frequently to see what is on next; however, wireless networks at conferences can frequently encounter connectivity failures [11].
– City Life is a popular city life and culture site with moderately complex layout. The transfer size is 500Kb, sent as 380K of gzip-enabled web traffic.
– BBC news is a relatively complex website with frequently updated content. The transfer size is 370Kb, sent as 100Kb of gzip-enabled web traffic. This page is highly viewed, so there is a reasonable likelihood of a copy being present in a group of users.

– Rotten Tomatoes is a movie review site which contains a dense layout with dynamic content. The transfer size is 834Kb, sent as 230Kb of gzip-enabled web traffic. This might be looked for at a cinema while deciding what to watch, with a reasonable expectation that others in the area already looked it up.

For each of the experiments we retrieve the contents seven times, each time clearing all caches. We measure the end-to-end time as starting from the moment of request at the browser until the browser finishes loading and rendering all content on the page, using the Firefox web browser with the FasterFox plugin since it contains a built-in page load timer (we turned off all other functionality that FasterFox offers).

Figure 4(b) shows the performance results for retrieving the above described webpages with and without Haggle. Between *no haggle* and *haggle infra* the comparison is less favourable than for the email case. We attribute this to the overheads of (a) the time taken to parsing the HTML pages to determine linked data objects, (b) the overhead in the proxy approach, since the web client opens and closes multiple socket connections to inform Haggle of different objects it requires, (c) inefficiencies in our Data Manager implementation in that the webpages are stored data persistently before they are transmitted to the web client.

For each web object retrieved from the Internet, the web proxy attempts to reconstruct its relation with other objects it was linked from. Because web browsers make multiple simultaneous connections to the proxy and use each pipe in parallel, we must examine the headers of the objects returned in order to properly associate objects to webpages. To do this the web proxy examines the referrer tag of the HTTP response message for the retrieved object to determine from which other object the current was requested from. After finding the originating object, the web protocol creates a link from it to the newly retrieved web object. This search and link requires queries to the data manager in Haggle which adds overhead time to each web object retrieved, visible in the comparison between *no haggle* and *haggle infra*.

For the *haggle P2P* experiments, we have node1 configured to enable access to the access point as well as communicate in ad hoc mode. The four webpages described are then visited using the web client on node1 so that it has a cache of data objects representing those pages and embedded objects. At this time, the access point is turned off, modelling node1 being moved to an infrastructure-free location. Node2 is only able to communicate in ad hoc mode, and is placed near node1. We request a webpage on node2 (clearing the cache each time an experiment is run); since node2 does not have Internet connectivity, it sends a filter requesting the webpage to node1, who returns the matching webpage with embedded objects. This last experiment shows fundamentally new functionality enabled by Haggle for the web browser, in that it can now operate even when there is no infrastructure Internet connectivity..

7   Discussion and Future Work

Haggle's architecture enables new applications to be created easily, taking advantage of the flexibility that Haggle provides. One interesting application that we are targeting for future work is in the area of "resource-friendly media sharing". We observe that humans collect ever more media (photos, music, videos, etc) and wish to (a) share them easily with friends, and (b) have them transferred seamlessly between their devices, both mobile devices and those fixed at various locations.

In current networks, it is not possible for an application to easily express "all photos taken on my mobile phone should be sent to my home server for backup" without being at risk of consequences such as large GPRS bills when their phone transmits holiday snaps over a foreign carrier, and the phone running out of batteries since it performs transfers even if there is scarce power. With Haggle, these concerns can be easily expressed, and persistent remote filters provide a simple yet powerful publish-subscribe mechanism for this kind of application.

Another feature easily enabled using Haggle is the predictive and prefetching download of content. For example, web clients can ask for low-priority predictive downloads of webpages that users might need because they are often-viewed or linked form the currently viewed page. Such predictive requests are easily expressed in Haggle using lower application benefit levels. Haggle is able to automatically allow or disallow these predictive operations based on the user's policies of energy and cost constraints.

A further interesting avenue of research is to investigate how users will perceive the networking world with Haggle. We observe that users currently have a simple mental model of mobile networking. When they have an IP connection, their apps work, otherwise they don't. Haggle breaks this model for the good, as it provides more functionality. How will users mentally model this flexibility? How will they understand what works under Haggle and what fails? One possible way in which users can be trained is to consider if they can see what they need in the environment. If a user can see the person that they are messaging, or they can see others who have data that they want, then they should expect that Haggle might deliver that message or find that data.

With the growing popularity of web service applications such as web-based office suites, many applications are being re-developed on the client side to take advantage of these services. However, despite the growing availability of affordable broadband-speed cellular services, request latency [5] requires clients to use smart local caching and prefetching strategies to give users a smooth experience. Haggle provides a simple networking model for creating these client-side applications while simultaneously enabling significant support for utilizing peer-provided resources.

7.1 Future Work for the Haggle Prototype

The currently experimental prototype for Haggle matches for web objects based on exact URL addresses. As motivated by our example, users seeking information often use search functionality and are happy to receive results from any number of different websites. Because Haggle already supports regular expression matching of attribute contents, we expect adding basic searching capability for neighbourhood cached content to be a powerful new feature. In addition, for nodes willing to bridge search queries to the Internet, we plan to add protocols which interface with search engines to perform queries and retrieve the first few query results.

We also plan to extend the prototype to support additional interfaces such as Bluetooth, cellular, and even ultra-wideband connectivity. Many other research projects have explored the problems of heterogeneous network interfaces [21], and struggled with how this can be done sensibly using IP routing. Haggle offers a new approach to this problem, complementing existing IP-based approaches [25].

A limitation of the current Resource Manager is that it is reactive only, and does not attempt to predict future connectivity options (e.g. as OCMP [19]). For example, currently Haggle may epidemically send a message to a remote host when, in five minutes, the user will arrive at their place of work and have free broadband connectivity. A related feature is to enable streaming support by adding reservation capabilities in cooperation with connectivity predictions to provide smoother experiences.

We do not use monetary costs or energy consumption in our current decision process, however these are key issues in device connectivity today, as they impact battery life and the potentially high cost staying "always-on". Particularly when we have multiple connectivity interfaces, we will likely be faced with situations where we have to choose between connectivity options which trade off forwarding benefit against monetary cost or energy consumption.

7.2 Security and Privacy

In the current version of Haggle, security and privacy have not been addressed as key concerns in order to narrow the scope of the problem. We intend to introduce security primitives as a core concern in future versions of Haggle. In the following discussion we have made an initial analysis of the potential security threats that Haggle raises.

Many data security issues in Haggle can be handled using standard security techniques such as encryption, access control, and data signing. Haggle merely makes it more feasible to launch a man-in-the-middle attack. One proviso is that many security techniques rely on access to a trusted third party, e.g. a certificate signing authority. This access may be available less often when using Haggle. One interesting approach would be to accept data which is signed but unverified and taint it as "untrusted" (both internally and to the user) until the signature can be checked and verified.

There are particular security and privacy issues in the use of name graphs. A name graph can contain sensitive information, e.g. a user's email address and/or phone number, or the number and type of a user's devices. A possible solution is to restrict trust of certain names to particular groups of users, such as circle of friends or known personnel of a company. Tackling this problem is left for future work.

8   Related Work

Many previous efforts have individually addressed late-binding interfaces or names to provide flexibility across dynamic environments. This work extends previous efforts [18] in providing a novel node architecture for applications by providing a clear resource delegation model for late binding interfaces, protocols, and names.

Late-binding interfaces allow devices to make better use of their available connectivities, utilizing their strengths and minimizing the impacts of their weaknesses. Horde [17] presents a middleware system which can stripe across different wireless radios according to user specified profiles. Wang [25] presents a policy based hand-off system which allows users to specify the best wireless communication system to use.

Late-binding name systems allow applications and services to rendezvous based on descriptive names over a self-organizing overlay network. Decoupling naming from the physical addressing provides a clean abstraction for supporting dynamic and mobile nodes in the network topology as well as routing based on new metrics such as location and domain specific contexts. The i3 [22] system hashes the name identifier space into a DHT overlay network, allowing applications and services to rendezvous at the same overlay node, independent of node mobility. INS [1] allows applications to specify names as trees of key-value pairs expressing the desired service or device. Each node participating in the routing overlay network can perform matching functions to determine where best to forward the request in order to find a matching destination.

Other projects such as OCMP [19] have similar goals in providing a node architecture for supporting applications. However these efforts are mostly focused on routing, particularly for challenged environments [8]. Haggle provides a more general node architecture for the provisioning, scheduling, and late-biding of network resources independent of applications.

9   Conclusions

Haggle is a new node architecture for mobile devices that enables seamless network connectivity and application functionality in mobile environments. By separating the networking concerns from the application, Haggle enables delegating network operations to a central resource manager on the device which can effectively select the right just-in-time bindings for network interfaces, protocols, and names in accordance with user-defined policies. We demonstrate the effectiveness of Haggle's approach using existing email and web applications on a Haggle prototype. Our experiments showcase the ability to dynamically select the best network operating mode when transferring emails and function even when disconnected from infrastructure. This allows people to use the same application across different connectivity scenarios, something that today would at best require manual configuration, and at worst be impossible.

References

1. Adjie-Winoto, W., Schwartz, E., Balakrishnan, H., Lilley, J.: The design and implementation of an intentional naming system. In: Proceedings of SOSP 1999 (1999)
2. Aguilera, M.K., Strom, R.E., Sturman, D.C., Astley, M., Chandra, T.D.: Matching events in a content-based subscription system. In: Proceedings of PODC '99 (1999)
3. Ananthanarayanan, G., Padmanabhan, V., Thekkath, C., Ravindranath, L.: Collaborative downloading for multi-homed wireless devices. In: HotMobile 2007 (2007)
4. Balakrishnan, H., Rahul, H.S., Seshan, S.: An integrated congestion management architecture for internet hosts. SIGCOMM Comput. Commun. Rev. 29(4), 175–187 (1999)
5. Chakravorty, R., Clark, A., Pratt, I.: Gprsweb: optimizing the web for gprs links. In: Proceedings of MobiSys, ACM Press, New York (2003)
6. Chandra, R., Bahl, P., Bahl, P.: MultiNet: Connecting to Multiple IEEE 802.11 Networks Using a Single Wireless Card. In: Proceedings of IEEE Infocomm 2004, IEEE Computer Society Press, Los Alamitos (2004)

7. Cutrell, E., Dumais, S.T., Teevan, J.: Searching to eliminate personal information management. Commun. ACM 49(1) (2006)
8. Fall, K.: A delay-tolerant network architecture for challenged internets. In: Proceedings of SIGCOMM 2003 (2003)
9. Ford, B., Strauss, J., Lesniewski-Laas, C., Rhea, S., Kaashoek, F., Morris, R.: Persistent personal names for globally connected mobile devices. In: Proceedings of OSDI (2006)
10. Hui, P., Chaintreau, A., Scott, J., Gass, R., Crowcroft, J., Diot, C.: Pocket Switched Networks and human mobility in conference environments. In: Proceedings of WDTN 2005 (2005)
11. Jardosh, A.P., Ramachandran, K.N., Almeroth, K.C., Belding-Royer, E.M.: Understanding congestion in ieee 802.11b wireless networks revised. In: Proceedings of IMC 2005 (2005)
12. Karsten, M., Keshav, S., Prasad, S.: An axiomatic basis for communication. In: Proceedings of HotNets 2006 (2006)
13. Leguay, J., Friedman, T., Conan, V.: Dtn routing in a mobility pattern space. In: Proceedings of WDTN 2005, ACM Press, New York (2005)
14. Lindgren, A., Doria, A., Schelen, O.: Probabilistic routing in intermittently connected networks. In: Proc. SAPIR (2004)
15. Mauve, M., Widmer, A., Hartenstein, H.: A survey on position-based routing in mobile ad hoc networks. Network 15(6) (November 2001)
16. Perkins, C., Belding-Royer, E., Das, S.: Ad hoc on-demand distance vector routing. RFC3561 (2003)
17. Qureshi, A., Guttag, J.: Horde: separating network striping policy from mechanism. In: Proceedings of MobiSys 2005, ACM Press, New York (2005)
18. Scott, J., Hui, P., Crowcroft, J., Diot, C.: Haggle: a networking architecture designed around mobile users. In: Proceedings of IFIP WONS 2006 (2006)
19. Seth, A., Kroeker, D., Zaharia, M., Guo, S., Keshav, S.: Low-cost communication for rural internet kiosks using mechanical backhaul. In: Proceedings of MobiCom 2006 (2006)
20. Shah, R.C., Roy, S., Jain, S., Brunette, W.: Datamules: Modelling a three tiered architecture for sparse sensor networks. In: IEEE SNPA 2003, IEEE Computer Society Press, Los Alamitos (2003)
21. Sorber, J., Banerjee, N., Corner, M.D., Rollins, S.: Turducken: hierarchical power management for mobile devices. In: Proceedings of MobiSys 2005 (2005)
22. Stoica, I., Adkins, D., Zhuang, S., Shenker, S., Surana, S.: Internet indirection infrastructure. In: Proceedings of SIGCOMM 2002 (2002)
23. Su, J., Scott, J., Hui, P., Upton, E., Lim, M.H., Diot, C., Crowcroft, J., Goel, A., de Lara, E.: Haggle: Clean-slate networking for mobile devices. Technical report, University of Cambridge, UCAM-CL-TR-680 (2007)
24. Vahdat, A., Becker, D.: Epidemic routing for partially connected ad hoc networks. Technical report, Duke University, CS-200006 (2000)
25. Wang, H.J.: Policy-enabled handoffs across heterogeneous wireless networks. Technical Report CSD-98-1027, 23 (1998)
26. Zhao, W., Ammar, M., Zegura, E.: A message ferrying approach for data delivery in sparse mobile ad hoc networks. In: Proceedings of MobiCom 2004 (2004)

Exploiting Social Interactions in Mobile Systems

Andrew G. Miklas[1], Kiran K. Gollu[1], Kelvin K.W. Chan[2], Stefan Saroiu[1],
Krishna P. Gummadi[3], and Eyal de Lara[1]

[1] University of Toronto
[2] Google
[3] MPI for Software Systems

Abstract. The popularity of handheld devices has created a flurry of research activity into new protocols and applications that can handle and exploit the defining characteristic of this new environment – user mobility. In addition to mobility, another defining characteristic of mobile systems is user social interaction. This paper investigates how mobile systems could exploit people's social interactions to improve these systems' performance and query hit rate. For this, we build a trace-driven simulator that enables us to re-create the behavior of mobile systems in a social environment. We use our simulator to study three diverse mobile systems: DTN routing protocols, firewalls preventing a worm infection, and a mobile P2P file-sharing system. In each of these three cases, we find that mobile systems can benefit substantially from exploiting social information.

1 Introduction

Recent news articles are reporting a dramatic increase in the use of battery-powered, mobile, lightweight, handheld devices often equipped with wireless interfaces [13,4]. Examples of such ubiquitous devices include cell-phones and PDAs, music players like Zune, and gaming devices like PSP. The number of mobile systems for these devices is also quickly growing. Their key challenge is providing functionality in a dynamic and often unreliable network environment. This need has led to a flurry of research on the design and implementation of new protocols and applications that can handle (and perhaps exploit) the primary characteristic of this new environment – user mobility.

In addition to user mobility, another defining characteristic of mobile systems is user social interaction. A variety of new applications focus on facilitating social activities in pervasive systems. For example, new Internet dating services allow clients to use their cell-phones' Bluetooth radios to detect when they are in the proximity of a person that matches their interests [18]. Other companies are offering file-sharing software for mobile phones that allows users to share ring-tones, music, games, photos, and video [28,17]. In these new mobile systems, information exchange is driven by the users' social interactions: friends use their cell-phones to share photos or song collections; strangers with similar dating profiles are notified when they are near each other.

In this paper, we examine how these mobile systems could exploit people's social relations to make more informed decisions, potentially leading to substantial performance gains and higher query hit rates. We start by classifying social interactions in two categories. One category is interactions between friends, that is people who meet

J. Krumm et al. (Eds.): UbiComp 2007, LNCS 4717, pp. 409–428, 2007.

more regularly and for longer periods of time. The other category is interactions between strangers, that is people who meet sporadically, by passing each other by. Note that in practice, the spectrum of social interactions is quite complex. For instance, a pair of people could be classified as "familiar strangers" [22] – two people encountering regularly without ever interacting or forming an explicit relationship of a social nature. Nevertheless, in this paper, we classify all relationships only as friends or as strangers; based on our simple definitions, we classify familiar strangers as friends. We leave a more complex social classification to future work.

We investigate the potential of incorporating social information in three mobile systems with diverse characteristics. First, we study the performance of routing protocols in delay tolerant networks (DTNs) when a sender and a receiver are friends, and when they are strangers. Our findings show that incorporating social information in routing decisions significantly improves the performance of several DTN routing protocols. Second, we examine whether firewalls that discriminate between traffic sent by friends and traffic sent by strangers can slow down the propagation of a worm or virus in a mobile network. We find that worms spread significantly slower if a small fraction of nodes reject traffic sent by strangers. Third, we examine the performance of file exchange protocols in a P2P file-sharing application. We find that sharing files only among friends drastically reduces the rate of successful requests in such systems. To maintain a high query hit rate, mobile P2P systems must allow their users to exchange content with strangers. In summary, we show that separating people's interactions only as friends and strangers leads to a more efficient routing protocol, a more effective security measure, and a higher query hit rate in a mobile application.

We build a trace-driven simulator that enables us to re-create the behavior of mobile systems in a social environment. Our simulator recreates all encounters between a large population of mobile users. To build our simulator, we analyze a 101-day trace of encounters between people equipped with Bluetooth-enabled cell-phones collected by the "Reality Mining" project at the MIT Media Lab [23]. To generate encounters between friends, we use a well-known social networking model – the Watts-Strogatz model [33]. To generate encounters between strangers, our simulator uses a heavy-tailed model inspired from the well-known preferential attachment model [3]. By combining encounters between friends and encounters between strangers, we can accurately simulate how social information can lead to performance gains and higher query hit rates in our three mobile systems.

The paper is organized as follows. Section 2 presents our trace-based analysis of people encounters. Section 3 uses our observations and analysis to develop a social networking-based simulator of people encounters. In Section 4, we use our simulator to study the effect of incorporating social information to three mobile systems: DTN routing, the spread of worms in a mobile network, and the performance of file-sharing applications. Section 5 summarizes our results and presents conclusions.

2   Characterizing People's Encounters

To perform an evaluation of using social information in mobile systems, we need a data trace of a mobile environment together with information about the social relationship among the participants. Unfortunately, we are unaware of any such previously gathered

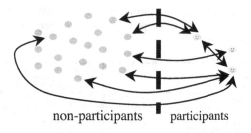

non-participants   participants

Fig. 1. The type of encounters present in the trace. One arrow represents one encounter. Each pair of people could have more than one encounter. Encounters between non-participants are not captured in the trace.

traces. Instead, we perform a social-based analysis of a trace of Bluetooth activity to annotate it with the required information. For this, we use a 101-day trace of encounters between people equipped with Bluetooth-enabled cell-phones collected by the "Reality Mining" project at the MIT Media Lab [23]. By studying the frequency of encounters, we can annotate this trace with social information by classifying pairs of people who encounter frequently as "friends", whereas pairs of people encountering sporadically are classified as "strangers". The Reality Mining group has also used this trace to infer social relationships between participants. Their analysis is focused on identifying different contexts in which social relationships are formed. Instead, our goal is to characterize the key temporal and social parameters of people's encounters from this trace.

2.1   Trace Description

Gathering a suitable trace to analyze the properties of people encounters is very challenging. Such a trace requires tracking many people simultaneously while recording all interactions among them. Collecting the data must not inconvenience the individuals being monitored and tracked. The privacy concerns raised by such experiments makes it particularly difficult to gather the data at scale. For all these reasons, very few large-scale traces of people encounters are available.

We use a trace collected by the Reality Mining project at the MIT Media Lab [23]. This project equipped 100 students with Bluetooth-enabled cell-phones. The phones were instrumented to probe and discover all nearby Bluetooth devices every five minutes. Data was collected for the entire 2004 – 2005 academic year producing a trace with over 285,000 Bluetooth-to-Bluetooth contacts.

We use this data as a rough approximation of people encounters since most of the Bluetooth-to-Bluetooth contacts involve people encounters. Many participants used the instrumented devices as their primary cell-phones. Consequently, these cell-phones were able to capture these individuals' encounters across a broad range of their day-to-day activities; the trace is not limited to the time that participants spent on campus or in their lab only.

While the trace captures all encounters between participants themselves, the majority of encounters present in the trace are between participants and non-participants. A non-participant appears in the trace whenever their cell-phone responded to Bluetooth

Table 1. Summary statistics for trace of people encounters, 09/08/2004 to 12/17/2004. Each participant encounters other people, either participants or non-participants. One pair of people can encounter each other multiple times.

data source	Bluetooth cell-phones
trace length	101 days, 0 hours, 49 mins
participants	88
non-participants	10,739
total # of encounters	155.321
# of pairs of people encountering	28,166
median # encounters per participant	1,970

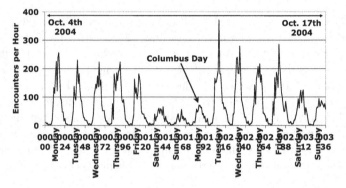

Fig. 2. The number of encounters over a two week period. Encounters show diurnal and weekly patterns. This two week period includes a U.S. statutory holiday.

probes from a participant's instrumented phone. This data gives us only a partial view into the behavior of non-participants: we lack additional information on how they encounter each other. While all encounters with non-participants are included in the study, our analysis's findings are restricted to the set of participants only. Figure 1 illustrates the type of encounters present in the trace.

The use of only one trace in our analysis restricts the applicability of our conclusions to the general population. This problem is further exacerbated by the limited scope of the sample population; it consists entirely of students, professors, and other academic staff. We hope to validate our findings with larger scale traces conducted in a variety of contexts as they become available.

2.2   High-Level Trace Statistics

In all our analysis, we use a trace of people encounters that spans the Fall school term only. Table 1 shows the summary statistics of the trace we used. The trace contains over 155K encounters made by 88 participants over 101 days. On average, there is one encounter every 7 seconds. The peak rate of encounters in the trace is 370 encounters over 10 minutes, while the longest period with no encounters reported is 4 hours and 24 minutes.

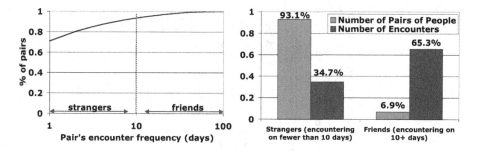

Fig. 3. There are two types of pairs of people: friends and strangers. (a) CDFs of number of pairs of people as a function of the pairs' encounter frequency, and (b) number of pairs and number of encounters as a function of the pairs' encounter frequency, split in two groups.

Figure 2 shows the number of encounters per hour for a typical two week period. As expected, encounters show diurnal and weekly patterns. The two week period shown includes a statutory U.S. holiday (Columbus Day) that shows the same level of activity as a typical day on a week-end. We checked the MIT school calendar; the school is officially closed during Columbus Day.

2.3   Two Types of People Encounters: Friends and Strangers

We would like to investigate how people's social relations affect their encounters. For this, we use the number of days on which two people encounter as a first-degree approximation of their social relation. Intuitively, people encountering on many different days are likely to have a strong social relation (i.e., they are friends) as opposed to people who rarely encounter (i.e., they are strangers).

Figure 3a shows the percentage of pairs of people with encounters as a function of their encounters frequency. The graph shows that most pairs of people (71%) encounter on only one day. Less than 7% of pairs encounter on 10 or more days. We classify encounters into two groups: between pairs of people who encountered on fewer than 10 days in our trace, and between pairs of people who encountered on at least 10 days. We chose the value 10 days as a reasonable lower bound for the number of days on which two friends encounter in the trace if they were to meet weekly. Our trace spans 14 full weeks.

Figure 3b shows the number of pairs and the number of encounters broken down by their types: friend versus stranger encounters. While only 6.9% of pairs of people were friends, these pairs account for two-thirds (65.3%) of all encounters in the trace. This demonstrates that while most pairs of people encountering are strangers having no social relation, most encounters made are between friends. Thus, if our concern is to propagate information quickly across a mobile network, we need to focus on stranger encounters since they are rare opportunities for different people to exchange information. However, if our concern is to provide more stable and predictable network links for an application, then we must focus on friend encounters.

The stark difference between friend encounters and stranger encounters lead us to study their properties independently for much of the analysis that follows.

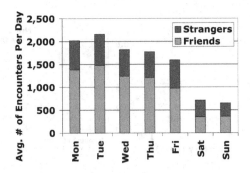

Fig. 4. Daily encounters. The average number of encounters per day broken down by day-of-the-week. People have more encounters during week days than week-end days. Two thirds of the daily encounters are with friends.

2.4   Weekly and Diurnal Patterns

As previously shown in Figure 2, people encounters present weekly and daily patterns. In this subsection, we take a closer look at the day-of-the-week and time-of-the-day effects present in the trace.

Figure 4 shows the average number of daily encounters broken down by the day-of-the-week when they occur. While more encounters occur on week days than on week-end days, the number of encounters is roughly the same across all week days. This suggests that people's behavior is consistent across each day of the week and across each day of the week-end. Figure 4 also separates friend encounters from stranger encounters. For each day of the week, two thirds of encounters (between 61 and 68%) are friend encounters and one third are stranger encounters. Over the week-end, this behavior is more balanced, only 50 to 55% of encounters are friend encounters.

We also examine the number of daily encounters by hour-of-the-day for both week days and week-end days (these results are not graphed for lack of space.) We find that most people's encounters occur on afternoons during week days with a peak at 4:00pm. There are 50% more encounters on afternoons (2-5pm) compared to mornings (9am-12pm). The diurnal pattern of week-end days is different than that of week days: week-ends have high activity during late afternoons and even late nights, but relatively little activity during mornings.

To understand whether people's encounter rates are predictable, we first calculated each participant's rate of encounters for each hour of the day. For each individual, we measured how consistent their encounter rate is during the same hour across all week days and across all week-end days. For example, we measure how often the number of encounters between 1pm and 2pm on Monday through Fridays change. We consider Saturday and Sunday separately since week-ends have a different dynamic of how people encounter. For each pair of consecutive hour slots, we compute the difference in the number of events for each individual.

Figure 5 shows the distribution of the differences of an individual's number of encounters for the same hour-of-the-day for week days and week-end days. From this graph, we can see that people's encounter rates are predictable. On average, an

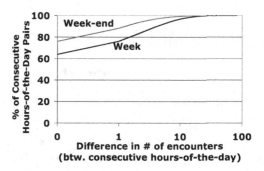

Fig. 5. CDF of the differences of each individual's number of encounters for the same hour-of-the-day for week days and week-end days. People's encounter rates are predictable. An individual's number of encounters per hour remains the same 64% of the time Monday through Friday and 76% of the time on Saturdays and Sundays.

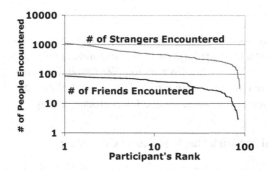

Fig. 6. Distribution of the number of friends and the number of strangers for each participant, on a log-log scale. These curves appear to follow a power-law distribution, suggesting that the friend and the stranger network graphs are scale-free. Many social networks have been previously found to be scale-free [2].

individual's encounter rate remains the same during two consecutive hour slots 64% of the time Monday through Friday and 76% of the time on Saturdays and Sundays. Also, the changes in the rate between consecutive hour slots are very small; this rate changes by more than 5 encounters less than 7% of the time. These results show that people's encounter rates are very predictable during the same hour of the day.

2.5 The Friend and the Stranger Networks Are Scale-Free

Many social networks have been previously found to be scale-free [2]. One of the distinguishing characteristics of scale-free networks is that their node degree distribution follows a power-law relationship $P(k) = k^{-\gamma}$. In power-law networks, a small number of nodes are highly connected, while most nodes have low connectivity.

Figure 6 shows the distributions of the number of friends and the number of strangers encountered by the 88 participants on a log-log scale. Both curves appear to follow a

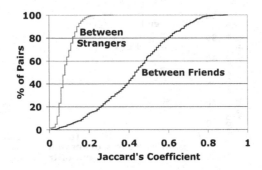

Fig. 7. Distribution of Jaccard's coefficients between the neighbor sets of the friend and the stranger networks, respectively. We use the Jaccard's coefficient to measure the similarity between the encounter sets of two people. The data shows that the friend network has more similar neighbor sets than the stranger network. This suggests that the friend network is more clustered than the stranger network.

similar power-law distribution for most participants (a power-law distribution appears as a straight line on a log-log plot). We further examined these curves' tails since they do not seem to follow a power-law distribution. We found that many of these participants are not fully active over the entire trace duration; we believe that their lack of activity makes them encounter fewer friends and fewer strangers, respectively.

2.6   The Friend Network Has High Local Clustering

Many social networks have been shown to have a high local clustering coefficient [2]. In this section, we examine whether the friend and the stranger networks are highly clustered.

Unfortunately, the trace methodology prevents us from measuring the clustering co-efficient in both the friend and the stranger networks. While we have full information about participants, we lack complete information about their friends or their strangers. Instead, we measure the similarity of the participants' neighbor sets in these two networks. We use the Jaccard's coefficient to measure similarity as a first order approximation of the degree of clustering present in these networks. The Jaccard's similarity coefficient of two sets is the size of their intersection divided by the size of their union $- J(A, B) = |A \cap B|/|A \cup B|$. Two identical sets have a Jaccard's coefficient of 1, and two completely disjoint sets have a coefficient of 0.

Figure 7 shows the distribution of the Jaccard's coefficient for all pairs of friends and strangers in our data. The data suggests that there is a substantial difference between these two networks. In the friend network, the neighbor sets appear similar, with a median Jaccard's coefficient of 0.43, over five times higher than the median Jaccard's coefficient of the stranger network (0.08). In the friends graph, over 90% of all pairs have more similar neighbor sets than almost all (95%) pairs of strangers.

2.7 Summary

This section used trace data to identify key properties of people encounters. From this data, we find several important observations:

- While most pairs of people encounter sporadically, most encounters are generated by pairs of people encountering often. This suggests the presence of two types of encounters in the data: encounters between friends and encounters between strangers.
- People encounters are driven by diurnal and weekly cycles. Once we account for time-of-day and day-of-the-week effects, the number of encounters of an average person is consistent. People's encounter rates are predictable during the same hour of the day for week days and week-end days.
- Both the friend and the stranger graphs are scale-free. The node degree distribution in these networks follow a power-law distribution, suggesting that while few nodes have many friends (or strangers), most nodes have few friends (or strangers, respectively).
- In the friend network, the participants' neighbor sets are similar, where in the stranger network, they are not. This suggests that the friend network has a high degree of clustering.

3   A Social Networking-Based Simulator of People's Encounters

The premise of our work is that the performance of mobile applications and protocols can improve if they incorporate information about people's social relations. This section presents a simulator of a mobile environment that enables us to explore our premise. Our simulator captures key social and temporal aspects of mobile environments, such as friend encounters, stranger encounters, and how the number of encounters varies with the time-of-the-day and the day-of-the-week. From these parameters, it produces a large-scale synthetic trace of people encounters over time.

3.1 Simulator Description

As previously discussed, a person's friend encounters are different from their stranger encounters in important ways. To capture this distinction, our simulator uses two different models to generate friend and stranger encounters. We use the Watts-Strogatz small-world model [33] when generating encounters between friends, while we use a version of the Barabasi scale-free model [3] when generating encounters between strangers.

The Watts-Strogatz small-world model captures the high clustering property specific to the friend social networks. A clustered friend graph preserves the transitive nature of friendships: an individual's friends must be related to each other in a realistic manner. Our simulator captures this transitive nature of friendships: if A and B are friends, and B and C are friends, then the probability of A and C being friends is higher than a random chance. This transitivity property of friendships is important to the flow of information in social networks [9].

Table 2. Simulator structure and notation. These parameters' settings reflect the values seen in the trace we analyzed.

Symbol	Meaning	Base value
N	# of nodes	20,000
f	# of friends per node (Watts-Strogatz)	20
α	Zipf parameter for stranger encounters' distribution	1.129
p	probability of encountering a friend	63.1%
$\lambda_{week\ day}$	hourly rate of encounters (vector with 24 values one for each hour of a week day)	(0.1, 0.06, 0.06, 0.04, 0.05, 0.06, 0.03, 0.02, 0.07, 0.5, 1.03, 0.97, 1.58, 1.37, 1.52, 1.73, 1.76, 1.37, 1.62, 0.76, 0.46, 0.37, 0.24, 0.15)
$\lambda_{week\text{-}end\ day}$	hourly rate of encounters (vector with 24 values one for each hour of a week-end day)	(0.15, 0.15, 0.09, 0.03, 0.02, 0.03, 0.02, 0.02, 0.05, 0.06, 0.08, 0.16, 0.19, 0.3, 0.34, 0.34, 0.33, 0.31, 0.19, 0.29, 0.26, 0.25, 0.2, 0.18)

The Watts-Strogatz model places N nodes on a ring and connects each with K of its neighbors ($K/2$ on each side). To randomize the graph, each edge is rewired to a random node with a small probability. The resulting graph has a small average path length and a high clustering coefficient relative to a completely random graph with the same number of nodes and edges, as desired [33]. When the simulator generates a friend encounter, it selects a node at random and then selects another node at random from the first node's set of friends. An encounter will then be generated between these two nodes. Each node's friend set remains fixed over the course of the simulation, since the friend network is not altered once the simulation begins to run.

This model's main limitation is that the nodes' degree distribution is not a power-law, but more similar to that of a regular graph. Several extensions to this model address this limitation [15,11,8; we plan to examine more sophisticated small-world models in future work. However, since friends on average compose less than 7% of each individual's unique contacts, the overall degree distribution of the encounter network is driven almost entirely by stranger encounters.

We generate stranger encounters using an approach inspired by the preferential attachment model proposed by Barabasi et al. [3]. Barabasi's model grows a scale-free network by adding one node at a time. Each new node attaches itself to a fixed number of existing nodes with a probability proportional to each existing node's degree. Although each node enters the network with a fixed number of edges, the node may acquire additional edges as new nodes link to it when they are added to the network. One side-effect of Barabasi's model is that the last opportunity for two nodes to be linked by an edge is when the second node of the pair is added to the network. Once added without a link between them, two existing nodes can never encounter each other.

Our simulator makes a small modification to this model. Instead of growing the network one node at a time, it assumes a closed population. Each node is pre-assigned a Zipf-based popularity score that determines the probability of selecting this device when generating stranger encounters. The Zipf law is a type of a power-law commonly found in nature. To generate a stranger encounter, the simulator randomly selects two nodes with a probability proportional to their respective Zipf scores. An encounter will then be generated between these two devices. The simulator is careful not to pick a pair of friends when generating a stranger encounter.

Our method of generating stranger encounters ensures that at any time, the probability of two nodes meeting each other in a stranger encounter is non-zero, except

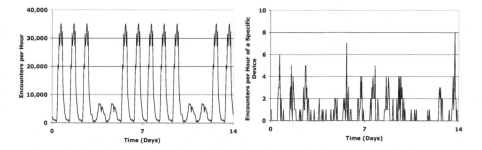

Fig. 8. Encounters produced by our simulator. The number of encounters per hour for all 20,000 people on the left, and the number of encounters for one specific person on the right. Since the number of encounters per hour is fixed (based on the hour of the day), each week day and each week-end day appear indistinguishable on the left. However, individual persons do not have cyclical behaviors. On the right, we show how an average person's number of encounters per hour varies.

when the two nodes are friends. While in the long-run this violates the power-law property of nodes' degrees, we believe that it captures adequately the behavior of a closed population: in a fixed set of people, everybody eventually meets everybody else. However, we never experience this saturation regime in any of our simulations.

Table 2 summarizes the parameters used in our simulations. We use our simulator to generate a two week synthetic trace of encounters. We chose parameter values from a two week period of the MIT Reality Mining trace. We do not simulate the encounters' durations and we assume a fixed number of people in the system. Our simulator generates requests as follows. On average, 63.1% of a person's daily encounters are with friends and 36.9% with strangers. To generate an encounter, our simulator creates a friend encounter with probability 0.631 and a stranger encounter with probability 0.369. We hypothesize that the underlying stranger popularity is driven by Zipf's law. We estimated the Zipf's parameter from a two week portion the trace to be $\alpha = 1.129$. The encounter rates vary according to the time-of-the-day and the day-of-the-week. Since the number of encounters remains constant on an hourly basis, we use 24 hourly rates during a week day and another 24 hourly rates during a week-end day.

Despite our ability to estimate many of the input parameters from the trace data, it is not possible to directly estimate N (the number of people) with any confidence. For that reason, we leave N as a free parameter, adjusting it to obtain as tight a correspondence between the simulator and the data trace as possible. Figure 8 illustrates the encounter patterns captured by our simulator.

3.2 Simulator Validation

Our simulator's main goal was to capture the specific characteristics of friend and stranger encounters. Many of these properties are built-in: the rate of encounters, the fraction of friend versus stranger encounters, the heavy-tailed distribution of friend and stranger popularities, and the heavy clustering of the friend network. We validated our model by measuring the speed of information propagation in our synthetic trace and

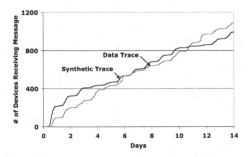

Fig. 9. Predicted versus measured flow of information in a restricted trace. The speed of information flow in the network is reflected in the curves' slopes. The synthetic curve's characteristics are close to the real data trace's characteristics.

comparing it to the data trace. The data trace is restricted; it does not capture encounters between non-participants. In contrast, our synthetic trace captures all encounters between all people. To match the data trace's environment, we selected a set of nodes from our synthetic trace to serve as our instrumented participants. We matched the number of participants selected to the two week Reality Mining trace we used to parameterize our model. We did not choose the participants randomly. Instead, we chose a subgraph in the friend network and we marked all nodes as participants in our validation experiment. In this way we ensured that participants have strong friendship ties among them, similar to the the data trace's participants, who come from a single environment and are likely to be socially related.

Next, we removed all encounters between unselected nodes in our synthetic trace since these correspond to encounters between non-participants. Thus, we were able to produce a synthetic trace with an experimental restriction similar to the original trace. We used the number of encounters in our restricted synthetic trace to calibrate how to scale up the rate of encounters in our simulator. Initially, we scaled up the rate of encounters linearly with the size of the population. However, this led to an unrealistically high number of encounters. Instead, we calibrated the scaling factor so that the number of encounters in the restricted synthetic trace matches the number of encounters in the real trace. The same scaling factor also led to an accurate distribution of encounters between participant-to-participant and participant-to-non-participant encounters.

Figure 9 shows how information propagates through our restricted synthetic trace and through the original trace. For this, we simulated how a message sent by a random participant spreads through the network over time. When the total number of people in the simulation (N) is set to 20,000, the rate of information propagation in the synthetic network is close to the real trace.

4   Exploiting Social Interactions in Mobile Systems

In this section, we use our social networking-based simulator to investigate the potential benefits of using social networking information to three mobile systems: (1) the performance of DTN routing protocols, (2) slowing down the propagation of mobile worms, and (3) improving the query hit rate of a mobile file-sharing application. We examine each of these applications in turn.

4.1 Routing in Delay Tolerant Networks (DTN)

In this section, we examine the performance of DTN routing protocols from a social networking perspective. After presenting a brief primer on DTN routing protocols, we study their performance in the presence and in the absence of social information. Our findings will show that, by using social information, routing protocols can achieve substantial performance gains.

A Brief Primer on DTN Routing

Various DTN routing protocols make different assumptions about the knowledge available to network nodes. While some assume that nodes have no knowledge about the state of the network, others assume that nodes have access to different types of information, such as the topology of the network, the average time between successive encounters of two nodes, who the congested nodes are, or the network traffic matrix [14].

Most protocols assuming no knowledge about the network are based on epidemic routing [14,31,26]. These algorithms are optimal – they *always* deliver the message over the *shortest* available path. They are also well-understood and relatively easy to implement and deploy. Although optimal, epidemic routing is expensive and unscalable since a message can potentially reach all nodes in the network.

To control the flooding of packets, epidemic protocols typically associate a time-to-live field with each packet or they restrict their forwarding decisions. For example, in the First Contact protocol [14], a node only forwards along the first available link. While these techniques reduce the cost of epidemic routing, they also reduce the protocols' performance, and they sometimes fail to deliver the packet. In fact, the First Contact protocol has been known to perform poorly in general since the chosen next-hop is essentially random [14]. In summary, the DTN routing protocols that assume no knowledge about the network perform poorly: they are either unscalable in practice (uncontrolled epidemic routing) or their delivery success rates are low (first contact routing) [16].

Other DTN routing protocols assume some knowledge about the state of the network [19,14,16,30]. All these protocols try to compute shortest paths to the destination assuming that certain network information is available. Some assume little extra information, such as the average waiting time until the next contact for an edge, while others assume that all nodes know the entire network topology at all times. The performance of these DTN routing protocols varies depending on the amount of information available and the network dynamics. A comprehensive evaluation of these protocols for several DTN scenarios is presented in [14].

Incorporating Social Networking in DTN Routing

Social information is another type of information that is often readily available to nodes in a DTN scenario. This information can help DTN routing protocols make more informed decisions to whom to forward a specific message. For example, when routing

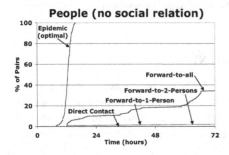 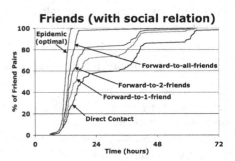

Fig. 10. The performance of DTN routing protocols. In the "direct contact" protocol, the sender does not forward the message to any intermediary; instead it waits to encounter the destination. In "forward-to-k-persons/friends", the sender forwards the message to the first k persons (or friends). The sender and the intermediaries do not subsequently forward the message unless they encounter the destination. "Forward-to-all" forwards to all persons encountered by the sender. Epidemic routing floods the message to all nodes. On the left, the distribution of a message's delivery times between 100 pairs of random people is shown. On the right, the same distribution between 100 pairs of friends is shown; in this experiment, all forwarding decisions are restricted to friends only. The routing protocols perform significantly better in the presence of social information.

between friends, a protocol could prefer selecting intermediaries who are friends with either the source or the destination. Friends are more likely to be clustered and to encounter one another. To quantify the performance of incorporating social networking in DTN routing, we used our simulator to evaluate several protocols in the presence and in the absence of social information.

While we evaluated a suite of DTN protocols, in this paper, we present only four protocols: "direct contact", "forward-to-1-person", "forward-to-2-persons", and "forward-to-all" [32]. In "direct contact", the sender does not forward the message to any intermediary; instead it waits to encounter the destination. In "forward-to-1-person", the sender forwards the message only to the first person encountered. There is no subsequent forwarding; the message is delivered only when the sender or the intermediary encounters the destination. The "forward-to-2-persons" works similarly, the sender forwarding to the first two persons encountered. Finally, in "forward-to-all" the sender forwards the message to all persons it encounters. Note that this is different than epidemic routing, since in "forward-to-all", none of the intermediaries forward to any nodes other than the destination. We also implemented the optimal, epidemic routing protocol to serve as a baseline of comparison.

On the left, Figure 10 shows the distribution of delivery times of 100 messages sent between 100 pairs of people randomly chosen. With epidemic routing, all messages are successfully routed in less than 16 hours. However, the cost of epidemic routing is immense: over half a million messages are being forwarded throughout the network. On the other hand, the other four DTN routing protocols perform very poorly. In two weeks, "direct contact" is unable to deliver even one single message.

On the right, Figure 10 shows how these routing protocols perform in the presence of social information. For this, the simulator selected 100 random pairs of friends and it restricted all the protocols to only forward to a friend of the source or the destination. To capture the optimal delivery times, we left the epidemic routing protocol to forward to any person. As Figure 10 shows, "direct contact" delivers 50% of the messages in less than 19 hours, taking only an extra 7 hours over the optimal epidemic routing protocol. Forwarding to one friend reduces the delivery times of half of the messages by two hours and 45 minutes, and forwarding to two friends adds an additional two hours of savings to the delivery times. By forwarding the message to all friends of the source or the destination, 98% of all messages are delivered in less than 17.5 hours. These routing protocols' performance is close to optimal without the huge overhead of flooding the entire network – each message is forwarded a small number of times only, at most on the order of the number of friends of the source and the destination. We also evaluated these protocols when routing between people with no social relation and forwarding to the source or the destination's friends; the protocols' performance is much more modest.

In summary, our findings show that social information leads to substantial performance gains for DTN routing protocols. While our experiments only separated friend from stranger encounters, we believe that a more refined treatment of social information (e.g., identifying social groups and social behavior) is likely to further improve these protocols' performance. We plan to investigate this in future work.

4.2 Slowing the Spread of Worms

In this section, we examine whether firewalls that discriminate between traffic sent by friends and traffic sent by strangers can slow down the propagation of a worm in a mobile network. We use the propagation speed of a worm infection as a lens to measure the effectiveness of firewall rules based on social networking.

The research community has already started to investigate the feasibility and the propagation dynamics of worms in mobile networks [5,6,34,29]. While no large-scale mobile worm outbreak has been reported so far, several reports of worms spreading over the Bluetooth protocol in a cell-phone environment exist [7,12]. The consequences of a malicious program infecting a large number of cell-phones can be disastrous. For example, such a worm could launch a DoS attack by overloading a segment of the cellular network. Similarly, a spyware program infecting cell-phones could collect personal information. By slowing the propagation of a worm in a mobile network, security experts can have more time to create and distribute a software patch repairing the vulnerability exploited by the worm.

An effective way of slowing the propagation of a worm is to firewall devices to prevent them from receiving traffic from all other devices. While such a measure would be very effective, this solution is also unappealing – it will prevent devices from using their radio interfaces for legitimate applications. Instead, a firewall that allows traffic only from a select set of devices could greatly slow the spread of a worm but allow many applications to function normally. For example, a firewall that accepts traffic only from friends would not prevent people from using their devices to exchange data with people they know. In this way, several applications, such as exchanging chat messages or files with friends, can still function in the presence of such firewalls.

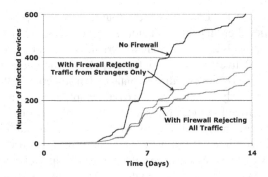

Fig. 11. The propagation of a mobile worm over time. In this experiment, 5% of devices (out of 20,000) are vulnerable. The rate of infection is presented when no firewalls are present in the system and when 30% of vulnerable nodes (1.5% of the entire population) are firewalled. We show the results when running a firewall rejecting all traffic and when running a firewall rejecting traffic from strangers only. The two firewalls are almost as effective suggesting that social based firewalls can provide a good compromise between preventing a worm from infecting devices and allowing some network applications to still function.

We use our simulator to investigate the effectiveness of such firewalls in a mobile network. In our experiments, a worm outbreak occurs by initially infecting one randomly chosen node. We randomly select 5% of the population to be vulnerable; our fraction of vulnerable devices is low since the most virulent known worms, such as Internet worms, only infected a relatively small fraction of all Internet nodes [25,24]. We select 30% of the vulnerable devices (1.5% of the entire population) to be equipped with a social networking firewall. We measure the number of infected devices with and without social networking firewalls.

Figure 11 shows our results. Without a firewall, a worm can infect half of the vulnerable devices in 9.5 days. While the worm does not propagate very quickly for the first five days, over 30% of vulnerable devices are infected in one week. The rate of propagation is also influenced by the network's temporal properties – the worm "slows-down" during nighttime, but it then resumes a quick infection pace on the next day.

Even when a small fraction of devices (1.5%) turn on a social networking firewall, the worm infection slows down significantly. Only a small fraction of vulnerable devices (10%) are infected in the first week of the outbreak. It takes over two weeks to infect half of the vulnerable devices, a delay of over five days when compared to the time it takes to infect half of the population in the absence of such firewalls. The effectiveness of the social networking firewall is almost close to optimal – a perfect firewall would only prevent an additional 27 devices from becoming infected in one week.

These results suggest that social networking firewalls can slow down the spread of a worm allowing for extra time to distribute a patch to the uninfected but still vulnerable devices. At the same time, devices running such firewalls can continue to use the network to communicate with their friends. These findings show that social networking firewalls can provide an attractive solution to both users and security experts in the face of a large-scale worm outbreak.

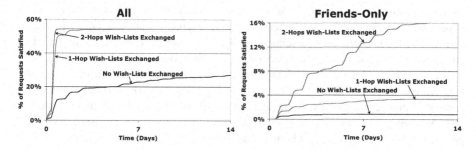

Fig. 12. The fraction of successful requests over time in mobile P2P systems. We implemented three file exchange policies: "no wish-lists exchanged", "1-hop wish-lists exchanged", and "2-hops wish-lists exchanged". A peer downloads a file if either it wants it or it has previously received a wish-list containing this file. On the left, content is exchanged between all peers. On the right, content and wish-lists are exchanged between friends only. When restricting content exchanges to friend encounters only, the rate of successful requests decreases drastically.

4.3 File-Sharing in Mobile P2P Systems

Recently, several companies have started to offer file-sharing software for mobile phones that allow users to share ring-tones, music, games, photos, and video [28,17]. In mobile P2P systems, content exchange is driven by the users' social interactions – people encounter each other in social settings and they use their cell-phones to exchange content. To understand these systems' behavior, we need to understand to what extent content propagation is driven by friend versus stranger encounters. In this section, we examine the performance of several file exchange protocols in a mobile P2P file-sharing system from a social networking perspective.

P2P systems must provide incentives for participants to upload and share content. In the absence of such incentives, many peers offer little or no data to the system. Such peers are known as "free-riders" [1]. Creating a suitable incentive mechanism in a P2P system and enforcing it in a decentralized manner is a challenging problem and an active area of research [21,20,27]. On the other hand, much of the content exchange in a mobile network occurs in social settings: friends share content among themselves. Such environments offer a natural set of incentives: friends are likely to share data or even forward data on each other's behalf. If exchanging content between friends, without involving strangers, can satisfy most people's requests, the need for an explicit incentive mechanism design is greatly diminished.

To examine whether content exchange is driven by friend encounters or by stranger encounters in a mobile P2P system, we performed the following experiment. We started with a trace of P2P file exchanges in Kazaa, a popular Internet P2P system, collected at the University of Washington [10]. Each of the 24,578 nodes in this trace has a "wish-list" and a "have-list". The wish-list corresponds to all of the files that the node downloads from its peers over the course of the trace, while the have-list is the set of all files that this node is willing to provide to its peers. From this trace, we selected 20,000 peers and we mapped them to the 20,000 people whose encounters are generated by our simulator. The mapping is done according to peers' popularities: the peer having the largest have-list is mapped to the participant with the highest number of encounters in our simulator. When two peers encounter, a file-exchange policy dictates which files and wish-lists the peers should exchange. Since our simulator does not capture contact durations, we assume that file transfers occur instantaneously.

We implemented three file-exchange policies by varying the number of hops wish-lists are exchanged in the network. In the first policy, "no wish-lists exchanged", a content exchange occurs only if one peer wants a piece of content present on the other peer. No content is downloaded on behalf of others. In the "1-hop wish-lists exchanged" policy, wish-lists are exchanged between neighbors only (wish-lists are flooded with a time-to-live (TTL) of 1.) A peer downloads a file if either it wants it, or it has previously received a wish-list containing this file. In this way, content is replicated on peers who have previously encountered someone wanting the file. The "2-hops wish-lists exchanged" policy behaves similarly, except the wish-lists' TTL is set to 2.

To evaluate whether peers can find content among their friends, we conducted two sets of experiments: one in which all peers share content among themselves, and one in which content sharing is restricted to friend encounters only. Figure 12 shows our findings. On the left, we show the fraction of requests satisfied over time when all peers exchange content. In two weeks, only 27% of requests are satisfied when no wish-lists are exchanged. On the other hand, if wish-lists are exchanged between neighbors, 54% of requests are satisfied. Exchanging wish-lists between peers can substantially improve the users' query hit rate in the system.

On the right, Figure 12 shows the fraction of requests satisfied over time when only friends exchange content. In two weeks, less than 1% of requests are satisfied when wish-lists are not exchanged. Even if wish-lists are exchanged along two hops, only 15% of requests are satisfied over two weeks. These findings suggest that restricting content exchange only to friend encounters drastically reduces the rate of successful requests. In our experiments, peers find three times fewer files when restricting their content exchange to friend encounters only.

Our findings illustrate that mobile P2P systems cannot rely on friend encounters to deliver content to their users. Although such a scheme could provide a natural set of incentives to a system, it would significantly penalize the users' query hit rate. Instead, like the file-sharing systems present on the Internet, P2P systems in mobile environments must rely on developing alternate incentive schemes to ensure that peers contribute their content.

5   Conclusions

In this paper we used social networking-based simulations to show how three mobile systems can exploit people's social relations to improve performance and query hit rate. We first showed that simple DTN routing protocols that avoid forwarding to strangers work very well when routing between friends. Next, we found that firewalls allowing traffic from friends while rejecting traffic from strangers are effective at slowing down the spread of worms in mobile environments. Finally, we showed that mobile P2P file-sharing systems must rely on strangers to exchange content to satisfy their users' requests.

Acknowledgments. We would like to thank Mostafa Ammar for his encouragement to pursue our ideas. We gratefully acknowledge the use of Bluetooth data from Nathan Eagle at MIT. Finally, we wish to thank the anonymous reviewers for their comments and feedback.

References

1. Adar, E., Huberman, B.: Free riding on Gnutella. First Monday 5(10) (October 2000)
2. Albert, R., Barabasi, A.-L.: Statistical mechanics of complex networks. Reviews of Modern Physics 74(1), 47–97 (2002)
3. Barabasi, A.-L., Albert, R.: Emergence of scaling in random networks. Science 286(5439), 509–512 (1999)
4. CNET News.com. Mobile browsing becomes mainstream (2006),
   http://news.com.com/Mobile+browsing+becoming+mainstream/
   2100-1039_3-606 2365.html
5. Cole, R.G.: Initial Studies on Worm Propagation in MANETS for Future Army Combat Systems (2004), http://stinet.dtic.mil/oai/
   oai?&verb=getRecord&metadataPrefix=html&iden tifier=ADA431999
6. Cole, R.G., Phamdo, N., Rajab, M.A., Terzis, A.: Requirements of Worm Mitigation Technologies in MANETS. In: Principles of Advanced and Distribution Simulation (2005)
7. ComputerWorld. Cabir Worm Wriggles into U.S. Mobile Phones (2005), http://
   www.computerworld.com/securitytopics/security/virus/story/
   0,10801,999 35,00.html
8. Ebel, H., Davidsen, J., Bornholdt, S.: Dynamics of social networks. Complexity 8(2), 24–27 (2002)
9. Granovetter, M.S.: The strength of weak ties. The American Journal of Sociology 78(6), 1360–1380 (1973)
10. Gummadi, K.P., Dunn, R.J., Saroiu, S., Gribble, S.D., Levy, H.M., Zahorjan, J.: Measurement, modeling, and analysis of a peer-to-peer file-sharing workload. In: 19th ACM Symposium on Operating Systems Principles (SOSP), Bolton Landing, NY, USA, October 2003, ACM Press, New York (2003)
11. Holme, P., Kim, B.J.: Growing scale-free networks with tunable clustering. Physical Review E 65(026107), 1–4 (2002)
12. InfoSyncWorld. First Symbian OS Virus to Replicate over MMS Appears (2005), http://www.infosyncworld.com/news/n/5835.html
13. InfoWorld: More mobile Internet users than wired in Japan (July 2006), http://
   www.infoworld.com/article/06/07/05/HNjapannetusers_1.html
14. Jain, S., Fall, K., Patra, R.: Routing in a delay tolerant network. In: Proceedings of ACM Sigcomm, Portland, OR, USA (2004)
15. Jin, E.M., Girvan, M., Newman, M.E.J.: The structure of growing social networks. Physical Review E 64(046132), 1–8 (2001)
16. Jones, E.P., Li, L., Ward, P.A.S.: Practical routing in delay-tolerant networks. In: Proc. of ACM Sigcomm Workshop on Delay-Tolerant Networking, Philadelphia, PA, USA (2005)
17. JuiceCaster. Share your mobile life with juicecaster (2007),
   http://www.juicecaster.com
18. Kangourouge. Proxidating, the first ever Bluetooth dating software for mobile phones (2007), http://www.proxidating.com
19. Lindgren, A., Doria, A., Shelen, O.: Probabilistic routing in intermittently connected networks. In: Proceedings of ACM Mobihoc, Annapolis, MD, USA (2003)

20. Liogkas, N., Nelson, R., Kohler, E., Zhang, L.: Exploiting bittorrent for fun (but not profit). In: Proceedings of Proceedings of 5th International Workshop on Peer-to-Peer Systems (IPTPS), Santa Barbara, CA, USA (2006)

21. Locher, T., Moor, P., Schmid, S., Wattenhofer, R.: Free riding in bittorrent is cheap. In: Proceedings of HotNets, Irvine, CA, USA (2006)

22. Milgram, S.: The Familiar Stranger: An Aspect of Urban Anonymity. Addison-Wesley, Reading (1977)

23. MIT Media Lab: Reality Mining. http://reality.media.mit.edu/

24. Moore, D., Paxson, V., Savage, S., Shannon, C., Staniford, S., Weaver, N.: The Spread of the Sapphire/Slammer Worm. Technical Report CAIDA, ICSI, Sillicon Defense, UC Berkeley EECS and UC San Diego (January 2003)

25. Moore, D., Shannon, C., Brown, J.: Code-red: a case study on the spread and victims of an internet worm. In: 2002 Internet Measurement Workshop (November 2002)

26. Niculescu, D., Nath, B.: Trajectory based forwarding and its applications. In: Proceedings of Mobicom, San Diego, CA, USA (2003)

27. Piatek, M., Isdal, T., Anderson, T., Krishnamurthy, A.: Do incentives build robustness in bittorrent. In: Proceedings of 4th Usenix Symposium on Networked Systems Design and Implementation (NSDI), Cambridge, MA, USA (2007)

28. Pogo. Pogo browser (2007), http://www.pogo42030.co.za

29. Su, J., Chan, K.K.W., Miklas, A.G., Po, K., Akhavan, A., Saroiu, S., de Lara, E., Goel, A.: A preliminary investigation of worm infections in a bluetooth environment. In: 4th Workshop of Recurring Malcode (WORM), Fairfax, VA, USA (2006)

30. Su, J., Goel, A., de Lara, E.: An empirical evaluation of the student-net delay tolerant network. In: 3rd International Conference on Mobile and Ubiquitous Systems: Networks and Services (MOBIQUITOUS), San Jose, CA, USA (2006)

31. Vahdat, A., Becker, D.: Epidemic routing for partially-connected ad hoc networks. Technical Report CS-200006, Department of Computer Science, Duke University (April 2000)

32. Wang, Y., Jain, S., Martonosi, M., Fall, K.: Erasure-coding based routing for opportunistic networks. In: WDTN '05: Proceeding of the 2005 ACM SIGCOMM workshop on Delay-tolerant networking, pp. 229–236. ACM Press, New York (2005)

33. Watts, D.J., Strogatz, S.H.: Collective dynamics of 'small-world' networks. Nature 393(6684), 440–442 (1998)

34. Yan, G., Eidenbenz, S.: Bluetooth worms: Models, dynamics, and defense implications. In: 22nd Annual Computer Security Applications Conference, Miami Beach, FL, USA (2006)

Rapidly Exploring Application Design Through Speed Dating

Scott Davidoff, Min Kyung Lee, Anind K. Dey, and John Zimmerman

Carnegie Mellon Human-Computer Interaction Institute + School of Design
{scott.davidoff,mklee,anind,johnz}@cmu.edu

Abstract. While the user-centered design methods we bring from human-computer interaction to ubicomp help sketch ideas and refine prototypes, few tools or techniques help explore divergent design concepts, reflect on their merits, and come to a new understanding of design opportunities and ways to address them. We present Speed Dating, a design method for rapidly exploring application concepts and their interactions and contextual dimensions without requiring any technology implementation. Situated between sketching and prototyping, Speed Dating structures comparison of concepts, helping identify and understand contextual risk factors and develop approaches to address them. We illustrate how to use Speed Dating by applying it to our research on the smart home and dual-income families, and highlight our findings from using this method.

Keywords: Design methods, need validation, user enactments, Speed Dating Matrix, future breaching experiments, sketching, prototyping, reflection.

1 Introduction

For many years, design teams in the human-computer interaction (HCI) community have employed a user-centered design (UCD) approach to develop interactive products and services. In these traditional contexts, UCD provides many tools and techniques that help teams move from abstract concept to deployed system or artifact. As more and more researchers and developers begin to explore the possibilities of ubiquitous computing, they often adopt the tools and techniques inherited from UCD. Critical differences, however, differentiate ubicomp from these traditional contexts.

First, more than thirty years and millions of commercial products have produced mature design patterns [2] that provide design teams insight into how users might react to new products and interaction methods. Ubicomp, however lacks a similar commercial foundation while at the same time is tasked with breaking new ground in highly-contextualized, social environments. Second, the high cost of ubicomp development forces teams to quickly converge on a single concept to prototype, while the complex nature of the social environments in which ubicomp is typically deployed are best addressed by a flexible approach that compares many possible and diverse prototypes. Traditional UCD, however, offers no methods that directly support these critical differences, making it difficult and risky to directly apply them to ubicomp.

J. Krumm et al. (Eds.): UbiComp 2007, LNCS 4717, pp. 429–446, 2007.

UCD provides many sketching methods [5] that support generating ideas, and prototyping methods that help foreground usability [27] and support implementing an idea [5]. But few methods help design teams transition from ideation to iteration, to explore a diverse collection of early-stage concepts, to reflect on their merits [25], to check their assumptions of user behaviors and needs, and to reinterpret opportunity areas while evolving an understanding of users at the same time. Ultimately, progress in ubicomp is retarded because important contextual factors are not discovered until after a single system has been deployed.

To address this challenge, we introduce a new design method that we call Speed Dating. Like its romantic namesake[1], Speed Dating (SD) supports low-cost rapid comparison of design opportunities and situated applications by creating structured, bounded, serial engagements. SD helps teams contextualize multiple applications as well as critical aspects of individual applications, quickly foregrounding potential "showstopper" issues before any implementation. By structuring comparison, SD also injects time to reflect upon issues [25], practices and opportunity areas, helping teams to reform their hypotheses and produce more adept understanding both of user needs and ways to meet them. We used SD to explore over 100 design concepts, prototyping 27 application variations over the course of two weeks. SD helped us identify showstopper issues, and reflect that certain needs *not seen as critical* during our user research were actually much richer opportunity areas for technical interventions.

In this paper we describe how Speed Dating works and report on our experience using it to investigate the role a smart home should play in the lives of dual-income families, and report on the insights it provided. We situate SD within other design methods regularly used in HCI and ubicomp, and we provide a discussion of the strengths and weaknesses of our approach.

2   How to Use Speed Dating

As we move from ideation to iteration, designers necessarily narrow the solution space and compare design alternatives with the goal of identifying and refining a single system. During this narrowing, teams inevitably compare applications at two different levels. First, they compare broadly across many potential applications or design opportunities, and select a small subset of applications to iterate. Then they compare deeply within this smaller application subset, and examine various implementation strategies for each, before selecting a single system to implement. Instead of focusing on a small subset of prototypes using a single design method, Speed Dating structures multiple lightweight comparisons between widely-different application strategies, or multiple varieties of a single contextualized application. By exposing participants to varieties of interventions, the design team gains insight into the social and contextual factors that most strongly influence a situation, helping them understand more about their user needs in the face of this potential intervention. This comparison also helps designers revise their understanding of the needs they identified, ultimately helping to turn identified needs into opportunities, and defining new ways to meet those opportunities.

---

[1] Speed Dating is a technique to help busy single professionals meet many potential partners in a series of pre-screened, timed engagements. See http://en.wikipedia.org/wiki/Speed_dating.

Speed Dating consists of two main stages – *need validation* and *user enactments*. In need validation, teams first present a variety of paper storyboards to a set of target users to synchronize the design opportunities researchers found with the needs users perceive. These storyboards help designers prioritize user needs, more clearly map spaces for innovation, and use that focus to narrow the design space for potential applications. Teams then conduct user enactments, which evolved from the broad set of methods that make up experience prototyping [3]. Design teams create a matrix of critical design issues and write short dramatic scenarios that address the permutations of these issues. Researchers then ask participants to enact a specific role they regularly play (like mother or father) as they walk through the scenarios, within an inexpensive, low-fidelity simulation of the target environment. The following sections describe how to perform each part of Speed Dating using illustrative examples.

2.1 Need Validation Helps Focus on Broad Opportunity Areas

Need validation has evolved from the concept validation method invented by the myInfo team at Philips Research [31] and through our repeated application [10][17][19]. The myInfo team recognized that when interactive products were designed that met needs researchers *observed* in users, but that the users did not *perceive* in themselves, that users had trouble recognizing the value of the innovation. Concept validation was invented to discover where observed and perceived needs align in order to better guide technical innovation. Need validation intends to synchronize this alignment, helping teams focus technical innovation on areas where users both have a need and are aware of that need. We intentionally renamed this method because we find that even experienced designers find themselves focus on validating individual concepts rather than on discovering the overlap between observed and perceived needs.

Need validation asks target users to react to concepts represented as paper storyboards. Since a more complete discussion of paper scenarios is available [6][29], we focus on the steps of need validation, what distinguishes it from storyboards, and how the data generated feeds into a new understanding of design opportunities.

1. Focus concepts on user needs. Teams generate and cluster concepts around the needs identified in fieldwork. Since generating concepts can reveal new needs, teams revisit key user research findings repeatedly. Teams then identify needs for which no concepts exist and generate concepts until all needs have been addressed with several concepts. Teams prioritize a critical subset of needs and then select and/or hybridize concepts in order to have a small set that match the prioritized needs.

Rather than have participants speculate on the social mores of imagined future situations and how technology could modify them – which often challenges users – Speed Dating instead deliberately focuses on creating scenarios that fall on both sides of boundaries the design team has speculated on. After Garfinkel [11], we call these *future breaching experiments*. In previous use of concept validation [10][17][19] we have found that presenting users with scenarios that push social boundaries helps to uncover where these boundaries actually lie.

2. Develop Materials. Teams produce storyboards that document how each need arises in daily life, and how the concept intervenes to improve the quality of life. Scenarios focus on situations where it is easy for participants to imagine themselves.

Storyboards show people in specific contexts interacting with the proposed system; however, the storyboards should downplay specific technical solutions that distract users from the focus on the need and unintentionally dominate conversations. In addition to the storyboard, the team authors a *lead question* to direct conversation towards the underlying need documented in the scenario.

3. *Conduct Session.* Teams conduct sessions with small groups of target users, presenting boards serially and following each with a lead question. Conversation should focus on the need – what triggers it and how important it is to address. If participants focus on the technology, the conversation is redirected back to needs.

4. *Debrief + Reflect.* The design team discusses reactions to concepts, prioritizing needs that appear strongly in both user research and validation sessions. This discussion should not focus on the details of the existing scenarios, but instead help to reveal new design opportunities. The places where perceived needs do not perfectly align with observed needs become opportunities for invention.

Need validation is not intended to be a Darwinian fitness comparison. Many techniques already support the ranking of existing ideas. Instead, design teams should reflect on their misunderstanding(s), and redefine both what they see as user needs and how to meet them. Doing this across many storyboards produces insight both within and across opportunity areas. Teams gain additional clarity not in confirming the merits of any single idea but through the comparison of many ideas [27].

Need Validation in Action. In our work on supporting the activity management of dual-income families we used affinity diagrams to group more than 100 concepts [19] produced through a process of brainstorming, bodystorming [3], and a review of our fieldwork [9]. These clustered into 21 categories. We then created scenarios for each category that described a need found in our fieldwork and a technical intervention that addressed the need. In order to increase the empathic connection between participants and our scenarios we developed a fictional, persona-like family consisting of two parents and two children – Johnny, 13 and Annie, 7 – in many enrichment activities. We conducted a series of 2-hour sessions with dual-income parents, where we presented our storyboards.

The "Safety Net" storyboard provides a good example of how to address challenges of presenting ubicomp scenarios (see Figure 1). This scenario focuses on the anxiety parents experience about forgetting or not being able to pick up their children. In this scenario, Dad is stranded and cannot pick up his daughter. The storyboard shows that the smart home arranges to have her picked up. With respect to reducing discussion about the underlying technology, in this scenario we show only a mobile phone in Dad's hand. The storyboard does not address how the smart home reasons about the situation, or how it selects and communicates with neighbors. Instead, the entire communication process is reduced to concentric circles. With respect to social boundaries, the smart home potentially oversteps its bounds by communicating directly with people outside of the family, asking them for favors.

To form the basis for more objective comparison between opportunities, we asked participants to rank our depictions of their needs, and the potential interventions depicted. Our top-ranked storyboard depicted the "Snack Day at School" opportunity

Fig. 1. "Safety Net" storyboard: dad is stranded and cannot pick up his daughter

Fig. 2. Parents strongly identified with the "Snack Day at School" concept

(Figure 2). The scenario depicts days when parents need to provide a snack for their child's class. Parents reacted strongly to the story of this responsibility, which because of its infrequency, falls outside of the daily routine, increasing the chances for breakdowns. One mother commented, "It is very hard to keep track of future events and their impact." A father shared that failure has very high costs in disappointing his children; "It's devastating to the kids when we forget."

2.2 User Enactments Concretize Abstract Contextual Risk Factors

Storyboards help design teams identify the overlap between observed needs and perceived needs, and through that experience, redefine the opportunities for technical interventions. User enactments, in which subjects serially-enact invented scenes, build on this outcome, helping teams explore a critical set of design issues within the earlier-identified subset of opportunity areas, and provide further structure to reflect on their both their understanding of the opportunity and a strategy to address it.

To begin, researchers place the design issues (or problem dimensions they wish to explore) on the axes of a Speed Dating Matrix, articulating points of interest along those dimensions (see Table 1). Matrix cells are populated with fictional scenes that address the intersection of issues described by column and row labels. The team constructs a simulated physical location in which to situate the enactments, and adds whatever low-fidelity props and prototypes the enactment requires. The team then asks participants to enact a familiar role and walk through a subset of the scenarios. Like experience prototyping [3], by engaging users as they carry out tasks, enactments bypass opinions based on the imagined fiction of storyboards and instead activate response to real-time engagements.

User enactments provide a structure to explore social mores surrounding situations that stretch our understanding of user needs in two ways. First, they provide a setting for users to experience future breaching experiments. And second, by combining wide exploration via multiple structured engagements, user enactments provide a broad perspective to analyze the impact of risk factors.

User enactments in action. Our fieldwork and storyboard sessions identified three principal dimensions of family activity management to explore: activity lifecycle, activity type, and system proactivity.

Family needs vary as activities evolve through their lifecycle. The first day of hockey practice presents different needs from the middle of the season, when families have established successful routines. Days when kids forget their skates and force deviations from a routine also present very different needs. Different activities also provide families with varied needs. The first day of school suggests a more permanent schedule change and ritual shopping, while soccer practice requires more episodic requirements and special equipment. We selected the type of activity as an axis to vary (*e.g.*, soccer, ballet, school). System proactivity is also an important dimension to explore. By proactivity we mean the degree of initiative that an intelligent system might take based on its understanding of the needs of the family. We recognize that different levels of proactivity might be appropriate for different kinds of activities or different kinds of needs, among other factors.

Many other issues rounded out our list of dimensions: location within the home (*e.g.*, kitchen, living room, bedroom), time of day (morning rush, evening rush, evening chill), type of chore (making lunch, picking up clothes), could all influence how a family might perceive the benefits of a particular technology. Using our top 3 as row and column labels, we created a 3x3x3 Speed Dating Matrix (Table 1).

From matrix cells to user enactments. In conducting our own user enactments, we again leveraged a fictional family and asked participants to enact the role of the mom or dad. Sixteen individual dual-income parents participated. Each parent "play acted" 9 user enactments over the course of two hours. Parents walked through three scenes for each activity (Soccer, Ballet, School) with different combinations of proactivity and at different points in the lifecycle for each. In all, each user enactment was performed by at least 5 participants.

We asked parents to walk through simulated daily routines (*e.g.*, dressing and feeding children), and each user enactment required them to complete additional tasks. The Soccer (activity) Beginning (lifecycle) enactments, for example, situate parents before soccer season begins, and asks them to arrange a carpool. The smart home either: (1) entirely automates the setup (High Proactive); (2) polls candidate driver families and informs parents who might be available, automatically confirming with the family of their choice (Medium Proactive); or (3) simply informs the family who might be available. To simulate extreme time pressure we asked participants to

Table 1. A compact representation of our Speed Dating Matrix for kids' activities. Concept dimensions form the row and column labels. Cells outline the content of user enactments, which juxtapose specified risk factors with social situations defined in the table structure. SH here refers to the "smart home." An extra row is added to explain deviation circumstances.

	Proactive	**Soccer**	**Ballet**	**School**
Begin	**High**	SH auto arranges carpool, interrupts to inform parent	SH auto adds lessons to calendar, interrupts to highlight conflict with doctor + reschedules	SH purchases supplies online, and prompts for optional items
	Medium	SH finds carpool availability, interrupts to inform parent	SH prompts to add to lessons to calendar, then highlights conflict and prompts to reschedule	SH auto adds supplies to shopping list and prompts to schedule shopping
	Low	SH informs parent when on phone with friend they could be driver	SH highlights schedule conflict when lessons are added manually	Constant ambient reminder via embedded picture frame
Routine	**High**	SH interrupts parent to inform that shin guards are not in bag	SH tells parent "you must" pick up your daughter from ballet	SH passes task from spouse to make lunch
	Medium	SH highlights bag as parent passes, indicating missing shin guards	SH tells parent "you should" pick up your daughter from ballet	SH adds lunch task to to-do list
	Low	Constant ambient reminder via embedded picture frame	SH asks parent to pick up daughter from ballet as favor to other parent	Constant ambient reminder via embedded picture frame
Deviate		What: Last-minute meeting and parent can't drive to soccer	What: Mom's away, and Dad needs a reminder of what to bring and when	What: Parents need to bring cookies for a school play in 2 weeks
	High	SH arranges new ride home for kid and informs parent	SH rearranges schedule and provides list of needed items	SH auto adds items to shopping list, auto schedules shopping
	Medium	SH asks friends for favor and relays their reply	SH suggests new schedule and suggests list of needed items	SH auto adds items to shopping list and prompts to schedule
	Low	SH asks friends for availability	Constant ambient reminder via embedded picture frame	SH prompts to add items to shopping list

complete these tasks within a short time window. When actual routines deviated from scripted scenes, parents were afforded an opportunity to draw on their real experiences and engage with the scenario.

Speed Dating advocates highly-disposable creations to support these user enactments. We simulated our smart house (Figure 3) out of 6'x4' white foam-core, drew appliances on a wall of a whiteboard, and filled the environment with enough physical trappings to suggest a home: magazines on a den table, coffee pot on the kitchen table, and a laundry basket partially blocks a hallway. After each enactment we probed participant reactions, digging past observed behavior towards its root cause. We conducted semi-structured interviews after participants completed 3 enactments for each activity (exploring one dimension fully), and a more elaborate interview after completing all 9 enactments.

Fig. 3. Our simulated smart home for Speed Dating. Foam core walls organize the "smart home" prototype into rooms. The refrigerator and washer-dryer are drawn on a wall of whiteboard (emphasis added for photo). A confederate is shown interacting with the fridge.

3 Insights Provided by Speed Dating

Speed Dating evolved our understanding of both the needs of dual-income families and how smart homes might help them in important ways. First, SD helped us identify that supporting kids' activities presents a major opportunity for ubicomp to positively influence home life. Next, Speed Dating helped us explore the many ways in which we might choose to support kids' activities. The wide and structured exploration provided when looking across need validation and user enactments helped us re-learn the kind of support that families really need, and has pushed our work in unexpected directions. We describe two of these directions.

First, Speed Dating evolved our perspective of how to address the opportunity of managing kids' activities. It helped us realize that the work surrounding kids' activities actually sits within the much larger, principal task of the home – raising kids. Though our early applications focused largely on kids' activities, SD revealed that applications cannot decouple support for kids' activities from the fundamental act of parenting. In other words, parenting and kids' activities are contextually bound, and applications expecting to focus on one necessarily will need to be aware of the other in order to deliver appropriate assistance.

Second, Speed Dating helped us realize that we could not support communication to facilitate the work of the home without considering communication's other roles. It revealed that communication plays an important social role when it occurs between members of different households, and that it can play a more utilitarian role when it occurs between members of the same household. Any application that supports communication within and between homes, will have to balance a desire for utilitarianism with the need for maintaining social protocol. In this section, we discuss these issues in greater detail.

3.1 Need Validation and Kids' Activities

Several storyboards presented parents with scenes depicting recurring deviations from routines and the need for parental role shift, two problems that our fieldwork brought

Mom's on a business trip. Dad has to take Annie to ballet. Mom always packs Annie's bag, so Dad has no idea what she needs or where to find it.

The smart home shows Dad what Annie needs, and where it's hiding.

The home spotlights the objects when Dad goes into each room.

On the way out, the house reminds Dad he forgot Annie's water bottle. He grabs it from the kitchen and they head out the door.

Fig. 4. Parents strongly favored this storyboard, validating our observation of the need to support the process of remembering activity-related objects. Testing in context also revealed that this service directly competes with kids learning responsibility.

to light many times. One storyboard depicting "Where are the Ballet Shoes" (Figure 4) explores both of these issues through a particularly stressful example of kids' activity management. When Mom, who normally manages the responsibilities surrounding ballet lessons, is away on business, Dad assumes Mom's responsibilities. Dad has no idea what gear his Daughter needs or where they put these things in their house. One mother observed, "My husband would love this. He never knows how to dress our daughter." The storyboard also helped elaborate the consequences of failure to meet even these seemingly simple needs. One father described that "it's very stressful for me. I feel like I failed as a parent when I forget what my kids need.

A tension emerges between efficiency and parenting. While storyboards such as this showed much potential in supporting kids' activities, other storyboards brought to light critical considerations that would impact *how* a smart home might support these activities. During fieldwork, many parents frustratingly described the stress of the morning rush. Part of that morning stress involved parents having to constantly persuade or nag younger kids to get them to comply with the parents' wishes. In "Annie Dresses Herself" (see Figure 6), the smart home limits Annie's TV consumption, and then helps her pick clothes on her own.

Though designed to help Annie feel more independent, and offload some of the morning struggle onto the smart home, the storyboard also revealed contextual factors: some more complex and subtle dimensions of the morning struggle that were less visible during our earlier fieldwork. For example, one mother asked "What's the parents' job, and what's the house's job? Is Annie going to listen to her Mom, or to the house?" This concept surfaced the fact that while dressing children creates stress for parents, it also creates opportunities for parents to feel like good parents, and to teach their kids skills and independence, and provides moments for meaningful interaction. Through concepts like this, we recognized that we should focus our attention on how to support the work of parenting, but also saw early evidence that we had to be careful not to reduce opportunities for meaningful interaction that occur through that work.

" MOM SAID 10 MINUTES MAX. "
The smart home shuts off the TV.
Annie goes to get dressed.

" IT'S SNOWING. WHAT SHOULD YOU WEAR?"

Annie picks a sweater and boots.
Her "cyber pet" meows with joy.

Mom's downstairs making breakfast.
She hears the cat's meow, and knows
that Annie's dressed.

Fig. 5. Parents reported that dressing younger children often injected stress into the morning. To alleviate stress and encourage independence, the smart home helps the daughter choose her own clothes. Parents resisted this system, suggesting that, while challenging, dressing children also forms a pleasurable part of their morning and helps them feel like good parents.

3.2   User Enactments and Contextual Factors in Parenting

Through the use of user enactments, we were able to witness richer evidence of the contextual factors found in need validation. Here, we describe three factors relating to our emerging view of the complexity between kids' activities and parenting.

Parents want support focusing on the big picture. One future breaching experiment explored potential emotional support from the smart home. The smart home interrupts a busy parent during the dinnertime rush, and presents them with a naked compliment, "You're very very busy. But no matter how busy you are, you always do everything you have to." We expected distracted parents to dismiss this empty sentiment. But interestingly, over three quarters of parents responded positively, saying "thank you." Half stopped their activity to express an almost shocked gratitude.

We do not interpret this to mean that smart homes should literally emotionally serve their occupants. Instead, in looking to understand an emotional connection with a home, our future breaching experiment actually uncovered a much deeper emotional need between the occupants of the home. Parents were so starving for attention and gratitude from their children and each other, that they accepted a compliment from a computer system that could hardly grasp the truth of the statement or invest in it with any real emotional significance.

Supporting activity means being a parent. As part of the user enactments, fictional Son Johnny keeps all his soccer gear in a dedicated bag to avoid having to remember each needed item individually. Johnny's strategy breaks down whenever an item is separated from the bag. Muddy cleats that stay outside or a clean uniform in the dryer breaks this system down. These kinds of breakdowns can impact both kids, who need the gear to participate, and parents, who feel the stress when their kids can't participate in their activities, and sometimes rescue them with emergency deliveries.

The Soccer Routine Enactment explores an opportunity to avoid this potential disaster. As a parent passes a dryer containing a forgotten uniform, the smart home tells the parent about the dryer contents. Interestingly, parents strongly objected to this system. One father said that this felt "weird that the smart home is telling me something that I don't have to do. It should be telling Johnny directly." Another even said "I don't want to do it for Johnny." Even though the application supports an observed and validated need, and if used could help avoid a potentially stressful situation, parents instead describe that the needs of parenting supercede our earlier identified need to avoid the stress surrounding the potential breakdown.

Speed Dating illustrated that a smart home cannot simply view its mission as one to prevent errors. Errors form part of the critical pedagogical mission of parents to raise kids who understand the consequences of their actions. And to raise kids to be responsible, successful adults, parents do not want to prevent their kids from making every mistake, or doing any work. In fact, doing work and making mistakes are important parts of being a child. The smart home has to approach support for these situations not just as failures but as important didactic opportunities.

Other user enactments went on to add further layers of nuance to this contextual risk factor. For example, parents strongly favored having the smart home tell them to deliver their daughter's forgotten lunch to school, as part of the School Routine Enactment. Through this comparison, we see the same didactic needs of parenting now strongly interacting with parents' desire to protect their child. A forgotten uniform presents modest consequences when compared to a hungry child. One parent noted, "Vital stuff. No problem. Without lunch...kids don't eat. It's reassuring. I wouldn't be as worried and stressful knowing somebody is watching."

Essentially, user enactments foregrounded contextual factors that the storyboard under-emphasized, forcing us to redefine our understanding of what we saw as similar situations, and by extension, applications we could design to address them, and ultimately helped to expand our understanding of the role of the smart home. Where we could have interpreted parents' responses to the earlier "Ballet Shoes" storyboard to mean that we should build applications that support "gathering items for activities," the first user enactments actually demonstrate that unconditionally supporting this need interferes with another equally compelling need to teach responsibility to children. But, by comparing the results from these user enactments to the user enactment on lunch delivery (School-Routine), we realized that this particular issue of parenting was much more nuanced than we first expected. Without user enactments and without the structured comparison that they offer, these nuances would not have been evident. We discuss the implications of this finding in Section 4.

3.3 User Enactments and Contextual Factors in Communication

Communication proved to be another contextual risk factor that offered a layer of nuance affecting application development. Parents were very uncomfortable when automated support messages from the smart home sought help outside the family. In contrast, parents tolerated the efficiency of extremely abrupt, bordering on rude communication from the smart home when seen as coming from their spouse.

Parents resist support for external communication. In the Soccer Deviation Enactment, a last-minute meeting traps a participant at work unable to complete her responsibility to transport her Son to his impending soccer game. With her husband also unavailable, the smart home: (High Proactive) automatically arranges a new ride;

(Medium Proactive) communicates directly with candidate drivers on parents' behalf; or (Low Proactive) presents mom with a list of candidate drivers and availability.

Despite the stress and work dictated by the situation, and the convenience automated support could provide, many parents placed social factors above convenience. "I would want to talk to the parents [asked] and see how they feel. I would have to connect and talk to people. I want there to be a person behind the name and to make sure they'd be comfortable when my kids are involved." Parents described that automated communication simply smothers critical highly-social characteristics of human expression. One parent notes, "I would never say no to my friends without personal contact." Automation would smother explanation or opportunities for coercion. "I would want to know why [he said no]. I might try to push if he could go," says one mother.

Efficiency predominates discussion of internal coordination. Coordination within the home reflects a different standard for utility than external coordination. Here, the primacy of efficiency prevails. In the School Routine Enactment, a parent is asked to negotiate with their spouse about who will pick up their daughter. The smart home either: (1) assigns the task to them; (2) passes them the task from their spouse; or (3) relays them a voice message from the spouse.

Parents realized that they appreciated the expediency afforded by the smart home, and gave little consideration to the same requisite subtlety they rallied for when communicating outside the home. One father prefers automatic coordination when in his busy office environment. "I don't like to be called at work during the day. It's better to be like a quick message. It normally takes a lot to get somebody on the phone but this is more thoughtless." Some parents wanted even more automation: one wants "[the] smart home to make the call on my behalf. It's better for the system to automatically tell me to pick up [my daughter] so I don't have to make a call. I would feel comfortable with smart home automatically determining who has more time."

User enactments redefine communication opportunity areas. Fieldwork and need validation both provided evidence that kids' activities impose heavy communication costs on families. But user enactments showed us that families feel uncomfortable mapping the binary nature of automated communication with the social factors embedded in human contact, and that the work saved would not outweigh the potential risks of handling social needs without their requisite subtlety. In this way, user enactments helped us refocus our efforts on the work of supporting communication within the home.

4   Moving from Ideation to Iteration

In the previous sections, we have described the method of Speed Dating, illustrated how we applied it to our research on smart homes and dual-income families, and highlighted key results from its application. Here, we contextualize Speed Dating within the available set of user-centered and participatory design tools and techniques.

Design ideation and iteration have been the focus of ongoing invention and discourse in the HCI community, resolving two principal forces at work – sketching

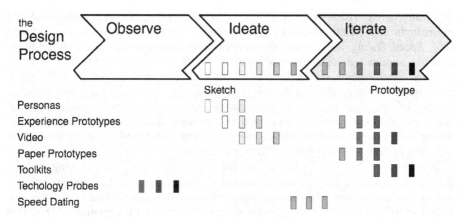

Fig. 6. Sketching and prototyping form a continuum that spans the design process. Lightweight sketching techniques support ideation, helping explore multiple concepts early in the design process. Prototyping , however, more directly supports iteration of a specific idea.

and prototyping (see Figure 6). At the beginning of the design process, teams create a large number of ideas through processes that we describe, after Buxton, as sketching – any process where the output is quick, timely, inexpensive, disposable, plentiful and ambiguous [5]. Sketching helps designers explore rather than confirm [27].

UCD provides many tools and techniques to help design teams sketch ideas across various media. Paper naturally supports abundant sketching of interface elements, scenarios [6] that depict users or personas [8] interacting with technology in a context. Informance (informative performance) [4] techniques like experience prototyping [3] use the contextually-rich felt experience of role play to inspire design ideation. Video also capably supports sketching concepts [30].

UCD also provides a rich tradition of tools and techniques that support prototyping. Prototypes use paper [24][26] or video [20] to quickly discover "showstopper" issues [27] before making too large an investment in a single direction, Higher-fidelity prototypes can rely on sophisticated toolkits to simulate functioning screens [18], physical tools [14], or aspects of user experience [15], and helps teams find the "right design" [5] to accomplish a decided-upon direction.

Lower-cost prototypes have more flexible uses. For example, they can function as ethnographic stimuli. When users discovered new purposes for technology probes [16], the researchers gained new insight into user needs and goals. These robust prototypes function more like a single engagement than SD's many short flirtations. Other prototypes are more exploratory. Simulating a distributed information system with paper [7], a sound transcription system by following users [21], or telephone interviews to simulate activity recognition [23], "Wizard of Oz" simulations [12] help teams provide low-cost exploration of ideas.

But even where prototypes help teams explore ideas, there is a need for tools and techniques to support the transition between sketching and prototyping. Speed Dating could provide for this need in two important ways. First, earlier techniques focus on the simulation of single systems, while evidence from both early-stage sketches [27] and deployed systems [1][28] shows that multiple systems provide more perspective into both the value of an idea and the user reaction to it. Sketching functions best when alternative visions encourage designers to explore, compare, understand and evaluate an opportunity space and gain insight into the space through that reflection [25]. Speed Dating helps lower the cost of simulation enabling teams to compare multiple application instances, and provides a structure to explore those multiple versions. And second, earlier techniques were applied in areas where there was a fundamental understanding of the role a particular service would play, and often the design of their devices and interactions could follow well-formed cultural conventions. Speed Dating would help in domains that lack similar conventions, where teams might have trouble choosing between them, and are unaware of how users might react to mores surrounding the technology.

Participatory Design [22] approaches many of these same issues, asking users to participate in the design process from start to end. Instead of focusing on what is wrong with a proposed solution, techniques like user sketches [27] encourage users to reflect on what they want, helping designs co-evolve with the opportunity [13]. Our research with busy dual-income families limited our exposure to families' time, so we focused on a more user-centered approach.

5 Discussion

In the previous section, we placed Speed Dating in the larger context of an overall design process. Here, we discuss benefits of the method including: its focus on sampling actual user experiences, its usefulness in identifying important contextual risk factors early in the process, and how structured examination of applications reveals larger themes across those applications. We discuss each point in turn.

Speed Dating samples user experience, not opinion. We gained valuable insights about our concepts without putting subjects into a position that ubicomp research often places them in, when asking them what they would do or how would they respond to some future technology without contextualization. Speed Dating was able to expose their real current needs in context of this imagined future technology, but did not place the burden on the imagination of the user.

Speed Dating surfaces insights early in the research process. It would not have represented a departure from standard practices to deploy an application after our fieldwork and need validation. We could easily have invested heavily in an application that could have delivered some benefits to families, but as Speed Dating showed, would have simply overlooked parents' larger needs to teach their kids responsibility. A field study of such an application could have revealed this insight. But instead, Speed Dating brought this important contextual factor forward before investing in any implementation. Moving forward with this knowledge, we argue that Speed Dating will make it more likely that the applications we build will both target the correct needs and be designed in a way that is respectful towards the important contextual factors that it helps identify.

Future breaches force reevaluation of invalid hypotheses. One future breaching experiment showed us that everyday stress often leaves parents starving for gratitude. Interestingly, this enactment was included largely to disconfirm a desire for emotional connection with a smart home. Instead, the situation destabilized our understanding of parents' needs, and how a smart home might meet them. We do not interpret this literally as evidence that a smart home should provide emotional support. Instead, we were forced to go back and reinterpret some core parent needs and how they affect fundamental application goals. Knowing that parents are filled with so much need to do damage control, a smart home could potentially help parents focus not on the day-to-day chores, but instead on the larger perspective of raising successful kids, and the activities that help them support that larger goal.

Larger themes emerge and revise design strategy. It is important to distinguish the Speed Dating Matrix from the structured comparisons used in controlled experiments. A controlled experiment manipulates single dimensions while at the same time strictly controlling all other potential variables, enabling researchers to make a measured statement of causality with respect to an explicit hypothesis. Instead of precise control, the Speed Dating Matrix facilitates *exploration*. Speed Dating is not designed for, and cannot provide, experimental discrimination or predictive power. Instead, looking across grid cells, researchers should observe that larger and potentially-unexpected themes emerge. This variety of themes then allows researchers to iteratively refine how they interpret the original design opportunity.

Our early research, for example, interpreted kids' activity-related failures as stressful problems to be solved by delivering the right information at the right time. But user enactments showed us that, while stressful, these problems are literally necessary parts of raising responsible kids. A smart home that removed these didactic opportunities in the name of "fixing problems" would also interfere with an important aspect of parental responsibility, and by showing an insensitivity to an important aspect of family life, risk rejection by parents.

This added nuance presents important implications as we move forward with our current research agenda, and shows how careful exploration of contextual risk factors can help effectively reformulate application design, opening previously overlooked opportunities. Instead of delivering information to parents to help them *prevent mistakes* their kids might make, we could instead create systems that give parents a choice about when to get involved, and that gives kids the tools to learn good decision-making without replacing their existing responsibilities. This would mean creating moments for kids to learn responsibility, and to involve parents in that dialog.

Exploring what we believed was a firm understanding of a single need instead exploded a different need. Instead of learning that parents want an emotional connection with their smart home, we looked back at our fieldwork and storyboards and found much evidence that parents are focused on the day-to-day activities. This evidence forced us to go back and reinterpret what we see as parents' core needs. We used this information to reinterpret one of our fundamental goals, and we now see that one of the potential role of the smart home could potentially be to help parents focus not on the day-to-day chores that they so easily fall into, but on the larger perspective that they want to raise successful kids.

Whatever the experiment might suggest about a potential relationship between families and a smart home, it also revealed significant nuance to our understanding of the social needs of families. The stress of the everyday work to support activity often leaves parents starving for gratitude. The smart home cannot simply focus on making the home more efficient by taking over appropriate parenting responsibilities. Instead, it should play an active role in helping parents feel like good parents.

Match design process to project needs and domain knowledge. We see Speed Dating as an opportunity to explore both a variety of approaches and new and undefined opportunities. Because Speed Dating helps foreground contextual factors, it seems appropriate to domains where models of users are less well-defined, or researchers suspect their understanding may contain assumptions they wish to explore. We chose to apply Speed Dating to domestic technology because while researchers have observed that the home will likely produce needs that differ from the workplace, few models have arisen that can demonstrate successful alternative models of applications for the home. By adding 2 weeks to a project timeline to perform Speed Dating, we argue that the risks are minimal in proportion to the rewards. Projects that utilize Speed Dating will likely require further prototyping to explore critical widget-level decisions. Though Speed Dating can help explore poorly-defined design spaces, foregrounding critical contextual factors, designers still face the question of how to implement the systems that it gives them the confidence to say are valuable, including interaction metaphors, timing, transitions and appropriate feedback levels.

Did Speed Dating provide insight about what specifically to design? SD, like all other design processes, can guarantee no output. The output rests most heavily with the creativity of the design team. It answered some but not all of our questions. For example, while it helped us see that the desired amount of proactivity interacts with other variables (*e.g.* location, activity), it did not tell identify an optimal proactivity level. And SD provided little insight toward some matrix dimensions, leaving us to wonder if the issues are less critical than imagined, or if SD did not reflect their actual importance. For example, by focusing more carefully on the fidelity of the services represented during SD, would SD be able to discern how proactive a system should be? In our future work, we plan to explore the kinds of questions for which SD can provide sufficient discrimination to deliver insight, and at what point issues are more appropriately addressed through prototyping.

6 Conclusion

The paper offers three contributions. First, we present Speed Dating, a method for helping researchers move in a structured manner from ideation to iteration as part of a larger design process. By combining need validation and user enactments, researchers can select concepts worth pursuing, explore dimensions of those concepts in a structured and low-cost manner, and reveal subtle contextual risk factors that can impact application success. By structuring exploration and foregrounding user needs, SD helps design teams reflect upon the opportunity for technical intervention, reinterpret their strategy. and create more appropriate and innovative solutions.

Second, we illustrate how to use Speed Dating by applying it to our research on the smart home and dual-income families. Third, we share our novel results from the application of Speed Dating to the smart home domain. Speed Dating enabled us to rapidly identify managing the stress of kids' activities as a key parental need, and to rapidly identify contextual factors such as the interplay between kids' activities and parenting, and the dynamic role of communication within and between households.

To continue the romantic metaphor, Speed Dating is not about finding the best person, but through the process of comparing, learning what aspects of others are (in-) compatible with your likes and dislikes.

Acknowledgments. We thank the 52 families who have taken over 250 hours from their busy lives to inform and inspire our research, smart home summer class students Bryan Crowe, Elena Kim, Ben Koh, K.C. Oh and Ray Su who helped us invent and come to understand Speed Dating, and the myInfo [31] team at Philips Research.

References

1. Abowd, G.D.: Classroom 2000: An Experiment with the instrumentation of a living educational environment. IBM Systems Journal 38(4), 508–530 (1999)
2. Alexander, C., Ishikawa, S., Silverstein, M.: A Pattern language. Oxford University Press, New York (1977)
3. Buchenau, M., Fulton Suri, J.: Experience prototyping. In: Proceedings of DIS 2000, pp. 424–433 (2000)
4. Burns, C., Dishman, E., Verplank, W., Lassiter, B.: Actors, hairdos & videotape— informance design. In: Proceedings of CHI 1994, pp. 119–120 (1994)
5. Buxton, B.: Sketching users experiences: getting the design right and the right design. Morgan Kaufman, San Francisco (2007)
6. Carroll, J.: Making use: Scenario-based design of Human-Computer Interaction. MIT Press, Cambridge (2000)
7. Carter, S., Mankoff, J., Klemmer, S., Matthews, T.: Exiting the cleanroom: On Ecological validity and Ubiquitous Computing. Human-Computer Interaction (in press)
8. Cooper, A., Reimann, R.: About Face 2.0: The essentials of Interaction Design. Wiley, New York (2003)
9. Davidoff, S., Lee, M.K., Yiu, C.M., Zimmerman, J., Dey, A.K.: Principles of smart home control. In: Dourish, P., Friday, A. (eds.) UbiComp 2006. LNCS, vol. 4206, pp. 19–34. Springer, Heidelberg (2006)
10. Forlizzi, J., DiSalvo, C., Zimmerman, J., Mutlu, B., Hurst, A.: The SenseChair: The lounge chair as an intelligent assistive device for elders. In: Proceedings of DUX (2005)
11. Garfinkel, H.: Studies in Ethnomethodology. Polity, Cambridge (1967)
12. Gould, J., Conti, J., Hovanyecz, T.: Composing letters with a simulated listening typewriter. Communications of the ACM 26(4), 295–308 (1983)
13. Halloran, J., Hornecker, E., Fitzpatrick, G., Weal, M., Millard, D., Michaelides, D., Cruickshank, D., De Roure, D.: Unfolding understandings: Co-designing UbiComp in situ, over time. In: Proceedings of DIS, pp. 109–118 (2006)
14. Hartmann, B., Klemmer, S.R., Bernstein, M., Abdulla, L., Burr, B., Robinson-Mosher, A., Gee, J.: Reflective physical prototyping through integrated design, test, and analysis. In: Proceedings of UIST 2006, pp. 299–308 (2006)
15. Hartmann, B., Doorley, S., Kim, S., Vora, P.: Wizard of Oz sketch animation for experience prototyping. In: Dourish, P., Friday, A. (eds.) UbiComp 2006. LNCS, vol. 4206, Springer, Heidelberg (2006)
16. Hutchinson, H., Mackay, W., Westerlund, B., et al.: Technology probes: Inspiring design for and with families. In: Proceedings CHI 2003, pp. 17–24 (2003)

17. Kim, J., Zimmerman, J.: Cherish: Smart digital photo frames. In: Proceedings of Design and Emotion 2006 (2006)
18. Landay, J.A., Myers, B.A.: Sketching storyboards to illustrate interface behaviors. In: Proceedings of CHI 1996 Extended Abstracts, pp. 193–194 (1996)
19. Lee, M.K., Davdoff, S., Zimmerman, J., Dey, A.K.: Smart homes, families and control. In: Proceedings of Design & Emotion 2006 (2006)
20. Mackay, W.E., Ratzer, A.V., Janacek, P.: Video artifacts for design: Bridging the gap between abstraction and detail. In: Proceedings of DIS 2000, pp. 72–82 (2000)
21. Matthews, T., Carter, S., Pail, C., Fong, J., Mankoff, J.: Scribe4Me: Evaluating a mobile sound transcription tool for the deaf. In: Dourish, P., Friday, A. (eds.) UbiComp 2006. LNCS, vol. 4206, pp. 159–176. Springer, Heidelberg (2006)
22. Muller, M.J.: Retrospective on a year of participatory design using the PICTIVE technique. In: Proceedings CHI 1992, pp. 455–462 (1992)
23. Mynatt., E.D, Rowan, J., Jacobs, A., Craighill, S.: Digital family portraits: Supporting peace of mind for extended family members. In: Proceedings of CHI 2001, pp. 333–340 (2001)
24. Rettig, M.: Prototyping for tiny fingers. Communications of ACM 37(4), 21–27 (1994)
25. Schon, D.A.: The reflective practitioner. Basic Books, New York (1983)
26. Snyder, C.: Paper Prototyping: The fast and easy way to design and refine user interfaces. Morgan Kaufmann, San Francisco (2003)
27. Tohidi, M., Buxton, B., Baecker, R., Sellen, A.: User sketches: A quick, inexpensive, and effective way to elicit more reflective user feedback. In: Proceedings of NordCHI 2006, pp. 105–114 (2006)
28. Trevor, J., Hilbert, D.M., Schilit, B.N.: Issues in personalizing shared ubiquitous devices. In: Borriello, G., Holmquist, L.E. (eds.) UbiComp 2002. LNCS, vol. 2498, pp. 56–72. Springer, Heidelberg (2002)
29. Truong, K.N., Hayes, G.R., Abowd, G.D.: Storyboarding: an empirical determination of best practices and effective guidelines. In: Proceedings of DIS 2006, pp. 12–21 (2006)
30. Zimmerman, J.: Video Sketches: Exploring pervasive computing interaction designs. IEEE Computing 4(4), 91–94 (2005)
31. Zimmerman, J., Dimitrova, N., Agnihotri, L., Janevski, A., Nikolovska, L.: Interface design for MyInfo: A personal news demonstrator combining Web and TV content. In: Proceedings of INTERACT, pp. 41–48 (2003)

Addressing Mobile Phone Diversity in Ubicomp Experience Development

Chris Greenhalgh[1], Steve Benford[1], Adam Drozd[1], Martin Flintham[1],
Alastair Hampshire[1], Leif Oppermann[1], Keir Smith[2], and Christoph von Tycowicz[3]

[1] Mixed Reality Lab, University of Nottingham
[2] University of New South Wales
[3] Hochschule Bremen
{cmg,sdb,asd,mdf,axh,lxo}@cs.nott.ac.uk,
keirs@cse.unsw.edu.au

Abstract. Mobile phones are a widely-available class of device with supporting communications infrastructure which can be appropriated and exploited to support ubicomp experiences. However mobile phones vary hugely in their capabilities. We explore how a single dimension of *phone application type* embodies the critical trade-off between capability and availability, i.e. between what can be done and the fraction of potential participants' phones that can do this. We describe four different mobile phone ubicomp experiences that illustrate different points along this continuum (SMS, WAP/Web, and J2ME, Python and native applications) and the common software platform/toolkit, EQUIP2, that has been co-developed to support them. From this we propose four development strategies for addressing mobile phone diversity: prioritise support for server development (including web integration), migrate functionality between server(s) and handset(s), support flexible communication options, and use a loosely coupled (data-driven and component-based) software approach.

1 Introduction

A researcher who wishes to deploy a ubicomp experience outside of a lab setting has two options for technology platform: they can either deploy their own devices and infrastructure, or they must appropriate and build upon existing devices and infrastructure. The mobile phone is an excellent – and popular – example of such an existing device and supporting infrastructure.

In this paper, we describe the trade-offs which must be made when targeting mobile phones as a technology platform for ubicomp experience development. We illustrate these trade-offs through four different mobile phone experiences and the common software platform/toolkit, EQUIP2, that has been co-developed with them. From this we identify and reflect on four development strategies for effectively exploiting mobile phones.

We begin by considering the attractions of the mobile phone as a platform for ubicomp experiences. In section 3 we suggest that *handset application type* is the primary dimension for characterising handset capability, and identify some of the key

J. Krumm et al. (Eds.): UbiComp 2007, LNCS 4717, pp. 447–464, 2007.

trade-offs inherent in targeting different points along this dimension. In section 4 we introduce the four proposed strategies for addressing mobile phone diversity in system and experience development. We then introduce four mobile-phone based ubicomp experiences and EQUIP2, the common supporting software platform that has been co-developed with these experiences (section 5). From these, in section 6, we reflect on the four strategies and their impact on EQUIP2 and the experience projects. Finally, section 7 presents our conclusions.

2 Background and Motivation

Perhaps the most compelling argument made in favor of using a mobile phone platform is its almost ubiquitous status in many countries today. For example, in 2006 in the UK mobile phones were owned by 85% of the adult population [1], were present in 90% of households [2, p.157] (the same fraction as have fixed line telephones) and had coverage across 99.9% of the country (2G) [2, p. 17]. For many users their mobile phone is an important and integral part of their everyday life: in the UK in 2005 73% of mobile users rated their mobile phone as "essential", while 31% of all telecoms users used their mobile as the main method of making calls (up from 21% in 2004) [2, p.158].

We can identify two main ways in which ubicomp researchers can – and do – build upon and exploit mobile phones as a technology platform. The first approach uses the mobile phone as a system component which is readily available and relatively cheap (due to the large market). For example [3] uses mobile phones as personal interfaces to an augmented card-playing table, while [4] uses a mobile phone as a mobile client/interface for a mobile mixed-reality game. In each case the handsets are programmed and provided as part of a complete system and lent to users or provided in situ.

The second approach uses – or seeks to use – people's own mobile phones as the technology platform. For example ContextPhone [5] augments users' smart phones with a context-sensing software platform to support (e.g.) augmented contact management and tagged media sharing and [6] trials a location-based reminder application on mobile phones. Using people's own mobile phones reduces the resources to be supplied by the ubicomp researcher, offers the possibility of a very large-scale deployment and means that the device is already part of a user's everyday activities and routines.

However mobile phone handsets are extremely diverse, varying widely in display, input, memory capacity, processor speed, support for downloaded applications and networking. Many of the current projects which target mobile phones as a "ubiquitous" infrastructure actually target a very specific subset of handset capabilities. For example, [5] and [6] both require smart phones running a custom application (native or J2ME), and also (like many phone-based location-sensitive applications) require access to GSM cell ID which is only available via a native application on a particular range of operating systems.

In practice this restricts a project to some combination of: a small minority of current handset owners; giving or lending suitable handsets to participants; or a possible future in which those handset capabilities will dominate the market. In the first case the handset is still part of the user's own everyday routine, however the potential scale of the deployment is limited, and some areas of research are almost impossible (e.g. "viral" recruitment of social contacts who have different handsets). In all cases the potential scale of any current practical deployment (and therefore of any non-simulation evaluation) is quite limited.

3   Characterising Mobile Phone Diversity

We have been involved in designing and developing a number of ubicomp experiences based on mobile phone platforms, including those described in section 5. The most significant choice that has had to be made in each experience has been the type of handset application to be used within the context of the experience. The main trade-off is between the potential numbers of users on the one hand and the richness of functionality and interaction supported on the other hand. Figure 1 summarises the main options and trade-offs associated with this dimension of choice, and the remainder of this section considers each option in turn. We expect that the handset market will continue to maintain this diversity of capabilities, e.g. to reflect variations in user preference as well as the cost-sensitivity of the market.

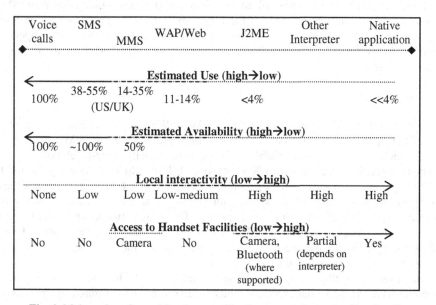

Fig. 1. Main options for mobile phone application type and associated trade-offs

3.1   Voice Calls

Voice telephony is the only universally available service on mobile phones. However the use of voice telephony in ubicomp experiences appears to be limited to direct communication between players/participants without system mediation, e.g. [7]. Richer experiences could be supported by integrating VoIP (Voice over IP) functionality into the system more generally, or by using phone operator location services which are available commercially on an explicit opt-in basis.

3.2 SMS/Text Messaging

After voice telephony, SMS or text messaging is the next most widely available option for incorporating mobile phones into a ubicomp experience. However availability and take-up varies worldwide, for example use of text messaging in the UK in 2006 was 85% of mobile phone subscribers but only 38% in the US [8]. Compared to voice, text messaging is much easier to integrate into a complete system (via one of the many commercial SMS gateway service providers).

A further sub-option here is MMS or photo messaging. On a phone with integrated camera this provides a richer capture capability for user content and context, or for interaction and location when used with server-based glyph reading technologies (as in CONQWEST [9]). However, take-up of picture messaging is substantially lower than for text messaging, with about 30.7% of UK subscribers and 14.5% of US subscribers in 2006 having used it [8] (36% and 38% of the numbers using text messaging in the UK and US, respectively). About 50% of subscribers actually have a handset with an integrated camera [10].

SupaFly [11] is one example of an experience (a pervasive game) based on SMS communication with players. Day of the Figurines (section 5.3) relies solely on SMS for mobile phone interaction, while LoveCity (section 5.4) uses SMS plus operator location as its "mass" participation option. SMS is also mentioned for direct player interaction in [7].

3.3 WAP/Web Browser

The next step up in capability is dynamic WAP/Web pages accessed via a (pre-installed) mobile phone browser. The main sub-options here are WML over WAP [12], which is more widely available on handsets (especially entry-level handsets) but limited in graphical richness, and XHTML over HTTP, which is currently limited to more capable (often smart phone) handsets but gives full HTML functionality and composition options. WAP/Web-based interfaces allow more complete interactive applications to be delivered via mobile phones. On some networks and contracts this may also be cheaper than using SMS. WAP/Web interfaces can be combined with WAP push/SMS to push new experience elements to the user, and can also be combined with operator location services.

However, as well as requiring a sufficiently capable handset, they require a contract which includes data services which often has to be configured by the user (at least selecting the correct "access point"). They also require reasonable network connectivity throughout the interactive session (each exchange with the server, which may be every page) and interaction latency is generally high (of the order of 3-5 seconds for even simple pages). The take-up of WAP/web-based services is much lower than for text messaging, with 14.4% of UK subscribers and (relatively higher) 11.7% of US subscribers using their mobile phone to browse news and information in 2006 [8].

Of the experiences described below Prof. Tanda (section 5.5) uses XHTML/HTTP as its main mobile phone interface, although in that case it is supported by an additional Python "trigger" application also running on the handset.

3.4 J2ME

The majority of ubicomp experiences on mobile phone platforms have a custom application running on the handset. Compared to the previous options, this can support richer interaction, reduce interaction time, give more complete access to the phone's facilities (e.g. camera) and support peer-to-peer (e.g. Bluetooth) and disconnected operation. J2ME appears to be the most widely available platform for running applications on mobile handsets at the present time. In 2004 penetration of J2ME on 3G handsets was predicted to reach 75% this year [13], and 50% on 2.5G handsets. In the UK at the end of 2005 8.0% of households had a 3G handset/service [2]. In 2006, 4.2% of UK subscribers and 3.2% of US subscribers had actually downloaded a game (not necessarily J2ME-based) to their phone [8].

However J2ME is not a single option but rather a set of options. The minimal (most widely compatible) "profile" for J2ME is CLDC1.0/MIDP1.0, which is quite limited. Further sub-options include CLDC1.1 (adds floating point types), MIDP2.0 (adds better UI and more networking options), Bluetooth, Media (adds camera access) and so on. J2ME development also suffers from several complications, including buggy and inconsistent virtual machine and package implementations (see [14] and [15]). It is also not possible to access native APIs directly from J2ME applications; where this is required a separate native application must be deployed on the phone that can be communicated with via (e.g.) local HTTP (for example, ContextPhone [5] and PlaceLab [16] support such local interfaces).

[3] and [6] both use J2ME phone applications, which in [6] is also combined with a small native application (to obtain phone cell ID). The phone client for MobiMissions (section 5.6) is implemented in the same way.

3.5 Other Cross-Platform Interpreters

There are also a number of non-Java scripting engines or interpreters available for mobile phones (in particular, smart phones). In general these are native applications which, once installed, allow other content and applications to be downloaded and run. Current options include a Python interpreter (for Nokia Series 60 phones), Flash Lite (a cut-down version of Adobe Flash, available for Symbian and BREW) and Nokia's MUPE multi-user application development platform [17] (the interpreter for which is a J2ME application).

These have the advantage of (generally) simpler development than for native applications, but typically require a large installation of the interpreter on the phone first, and (like J2ME) have more limited access to native phone facilities than a native application. LoveCity (section 5.4) has a Python-based smart phone client option, while Prof. Tanda (section 5.5) has a Python-based "trigger" application which runs in the background on the phone.

3.6 Native Application

As well as the general advantages of running a custom client, native applications are often essential to access the widest possible range of handset information. However, this also narrows the compatibility to very specific platforms and handsets. [14] and [15] deal at some length with issues of native application development and capability. At this level handsets are more diverse and less compatible than the common profiles of J2ME. The main platforms at present are Symbian (although the Nokia and Sony Ericsson UI layers differ), Windows Mobile and BREW (which is strictly a cross-platform development/deployment environment) (see [15]).

As already noted native helper applications are used in [6] and MobiMissions. The applications in [4] and [5] are realized as native applications.

Note that installing a native or J2ME application raises additional barriers to participation: the download may be slow (and expensive over the air), the user may not trust the application provider, or the user may not be familiar with this aspect of their phone's capabilities.

4 Introducing the Development Strategies

The following section introduces four strategies for addressing this diversity of mobile phones in the development of ubicomp experiences. These strategies respond to the characteristics and constraints of working with mobile phones as a hardware platform, and have shaped the development of the EQUIP2 software platform/toolkit introduced in section 5. We revisit these strategies in section 6 to explore *how* and they have influenced EQUIP2 and its applications and *how effectively* this has been.

Note that these strategies are primarily concerned with the software design and development process, rather than particular run-time capabilities. We have focused on strategies of this kind for a number of reasons. First, we are doubtful that a single run-time platform or set of run-time facilities can be applied to all possible types of mobile phone-based application/experience. Second, even if it were possible, developing such an all-encompassing solution would be a huge undertaking, beyond the scope of many research and development activities. Third, a single comprehensive software solution or framework can be a major barrier to use, requiring a broad range of skills and a large amount of up-front learning from any potential developer. Fourth, the resource-constrained nature of many mobile phones requires that optimizations (e.g. identifying and assembling minimal subsets of facilities) can be performed *before* deployment on a particular device, and dynamic code loading is not available on many phone platforms (e.g. J2ME CLDC). Finally, by reflecting on the choices and trade-offs made during development on practical projects we may identify new or critical elements to be incorporated in any future platform development or run-time infrastructure.

4.1 Prioritise Strong Server Support

At the present time the only truly mass-scale applications available and used on mobile phones are voice and SMS/text messaging. In both cases all custom application functionality must exist off the handset, normally on one or more "server" machines which together comprise the "engine" for the experience. Even with J2ME or native phone applications many experiences still have a large server element, for example for communication and coordination.

In addition, many experiences of this kind have a web-based component (accessed from regular PCs) in addition to the phone-based component of the experience. This is true of all four experiences described here (and of others such as [11]). A standard web-based interface can provide richer and more extensive content than the phone interface (e.g. larger screen, various plug-in options), and is also useful "behind the scenes" for management, monitoring, authoring and "orchestration" of the experience (as in [18]).

Consequently we argue that a platform to support development of experiences delivered on mobile phones should prioritise support for server development.

4.2 Migrate Functionality from the Server to More Capable Handsets

It is relatively difficult and slow to develop applications on mobile phones, for example due to limited debugging support, inconsistencies and errors in virtual machines and libraries, and slow development cycles (see [14], [15]).

Consequently, especially given good support for server development (section 4.1), we argue that it is a good strategy to develop initial functionality on the server and then to migrate that functionality to higher-capability mobile phone client applications as required. This also allows the initial server-based version(s) to be used with less capable handsets.

Different kinds of functionality can potentially be migrated in different ways and at different times. At one extreme mobile code or agent approaches such as that of LIME [19] allow run-time migration of functionality between mobile devices. However this is contingent on the underlying platform's support for code hosting and mobility which is absent in most mobile phone application types (including J2ME CLDC) and this is therefore not a general solution for mobile phone-based applications. At the other extreme – as described above – functionality can be migrated by the developers during the development, testing and deployment process. The challenge in this case is to make this migration as easy as possible, for example maximizing opportunities for re-use between server-based and phone-based versions.

4.3 Support Very Flexible Communication

We argue that a software platform to support ubicomp experience development for mobile phones needs to support very flexible communication in at least three respects.

First, any server(s) may need to communicate with different types of phone client including SMS, WAP/Web, J2ME and native application.

Second, in the case of custom applications running on the handset, it must be possible to carefully structure and optimize the communication between that client and the server. There are several reasons for this: communication with mobile phones is relatively high latency and low bandwidth; it may be expensive for the user; and there may be repeated or extended periods when a connection cannot be obtained or maintained. All of these can have a profound impact on the user's experience, which may need to be designed to explicitly account for them and reflect them to the user.

Third, the server may also need to communicate with diverse other clients in addition to mobile phones, for example public and web clients as in Day of the Figurines and LoveCity (sections 5.3 and 5.4).

We argue that as a result there will be no single best solution for communication in these kinds of experiences. Consequently, a supporting platform should provide help with realizing and integrating communication options, rather than a specific solution (or a closed set of solutions).

4.4 Use a Loosely Coupled (Data-Driven and Component-Based) Software Approach

The last strategy that we argue for is a software system design approach which is data-driven and component-based, creating a loosely coupled and flexible system. This is not specific to mobile phone development, but rather is a general strategy which can enable reconfiguration and reuse of software elements within an application or family of applications. This is particularly important for mobile phone-based experiences because of their potential diversity and in order to effectively support the previous three strategies with limited development resources. There are three potentially complementary elements to such an approach.

First is an emphasis on starting with the key data structures (object classes, tuples, or whatever) to be used within the application. These provide a common language for design and development without the assumption of direct invocation (local or remote) implicit in an API, method or procedure call definition. This makes it closer to defining Data Transfer Objects than Domain Objects [20], and reflects the limited and variable connectivity experienced by many mobile phone-based experiences.

Second is the adoption of indirect communication and coordination models where possible. Options here include publish-subscribe event systems [21] and tuple-spaces and similar approaches [22]. Both support indirect multi-party communication through pattern matching, which in the case of tuple spaces has an additional element of statefulness, decoupling communication in time.

Third is the adoption of component-based software design and re-use wherever possible [23]. This differs from object-oriented design by a greater emphasis on re-use, in particular by configuration and assembly as against subclassing and inheritance. This avoids some of problems of fragility and framework buy-in common to object-oriented approaches.

5 Introducing EQUIP2 and the Experience Projects

This section introduces the EQUIP2 platform/toolkit and four mobile phone-based ubicomp experiences that have been co-developed with it. Section 6 then explores the ways in which the strategies suggested in section 4 have been reflected in and supported by EQUIP2, and based on a developer evaluation of EQUIP2 also characterizes the perceived utility of those strategies as embodied in EQUIP2.

5.1 From EQUIP Version 1 to EQUIP2

EQUIP version 1 was developed and used to support a number of ubicomp experiences, primarily interactive installations, spaces and artefacts, for example in [24]. At the heart of EQUIP version 1 was a "dataspace" API, i.e. a tuple-space [22] which stores strongly typed (programming language) objects rather than untyped tuples. As the name implies a dataspace can be thought of as an information space into which objects can be placed and from which they can be retrieved or removed. Most retrieval/removal operations on a dataspace (or tuple-space) are based on pattern matching (i.e. "find objects like this..."). A single application may have one or many dataspaces, and each can be regarded as a sharable *model* in the sense of the Model-View Controller pattern/paradigm [25].

In this way EQUIP version 1 supported part of our fourth strategy: the dataspace approach supports loosely-coupled, data-driven communication. However EQUIP 1 was a substantial software framework for Java and C++, requiring extensive use and extension of framework classes, requiring a high level of buy-in from the developers and creating framework specific (less reusable) code. It also used a subset of CORBA IDL for language-independent type definition and had its own build system which were alien to most developers.

With regard to the strategies proposed here for mobile phone development EQUIP version 1 had many short-comings. First, there was no particular support for web-oriented server development (although there was some support for LAN-based servers, e.g. through multicast discovery and distributed dataspace facilities). Second, there was no support for J2ME or mobile phone operating systems such as Symbian, and therefore no way to migrate EQUIP elements to a handset. Third, the EQUIP version 1 dataspace had one built-in distribution protocol which worked well on LAN, wired broadband and local WiFi networks, but which did not cope well with intermittent or limited bandwidth connectivity (as with GPRS, Bluetooth or mobile WiFi).

EQUIP2 was developed to combine the best element(s) of EQUIP 1, in particular the dataspace approach, with support for experiences having mobile phone-based elements. Specifically, it was developed initially in tandem with and to support the Day of the Figurines and MobiMissions experiences described in sections 5.3 and 5.5.

5.2 EQUIP2 Overview

As with version 1, the core of EQUIP2 is a dataspace API (redesigned in some of its details compared to version 1). The dataspace API has two main parts. The first is a synchronous data storage and query interface which is very similar to an object database, and which (in EQUIP2) was inspired in part by the Hibernate open source Java Object/Relational mapping system. Like Hibernate, and unlike previous versions of the platform, the objects placed in the dataspace do not have to support particular (Java) interfaces or extend particular base classes. In most cases they are simple JavaBeans or "Plain Old Java Objects" (POJOs), and tend to be entirely passive data holders (with no internal threads or overridden methods).

The second part of the dataspace API is an asynchronous pattern-based notification facility, which allows sections of code to register an interest in certain kinds of objects being placed into, changed or removed from the dataspace. This provides facilities comparable to a content-based publish-subscribe event system such as ELVIN [21], but tightly integrated with the dataspace's state management facilities: the "published" events are actually all changes made to the dataspace.

EQUIP2 is written in Java, using language features and classes common to both J2ME (for use on mobile phones) and J2SE (for use on more capable devices and server machines). Consequently it cannot make use of J2SE reflection facilities (which Hibernate does) since these are not present in J2ME, but has to provide its own simple reflection-like facilities (through a system of dynamically loaded "helper" classes). Similarly, it has to provide its own object marshalling framework (J2SE object serialization is again dependent on reflection), which currently supports XML and binary encoding options. The dataspace API is common across J2ME and J2SE, but different dataspace implementations are available on each platform. An experimental Java-to-C++ translator is used to generate the C++ version of EQUIP2 from a subset of the Java version, and currently supports Windows (MSVC++) and Linux (GCC/g++), with partial support for Symbian.

All of the experiences presented have an EQUIP2-based server component, which is based on a common template web application for use in a J2EE (Java 2 Enterprise Edition) servlet container such as Apache Tomcat. As illustrated in figure 2, this combines: a persistent EQUIP2 dataspace based on Hibernate over a relational database (in these cases, MySQL); an EQUIP2 Java Server Pages taglib for dataspace access from JSPs; a set of generic form views for browser-based viewing and editing the dataspace content; and forms for bulk XML and binary upload and download of the dataspace content. This also uses the Java Spring Framework [26] for declarative application composition and web-based MVC support.

The template web application provides a common starting point for each experience, which is then specialized by defining experience-specific data classes, followed by iterative development of experience-specific user interfaces (for participants, authors, operators and analysts) and application logic. Client applications can be developed concurrently as server capability matures, making use of EQUIP2 where appropriate (e.g. as in the MobiMissions J2ME client).

The remainder of this section briefly describes four experiences that been developed and deployed over the past two years using EQUIP2 and in collaboration with three different user groups: Blast Theory for Day of the Figurines and Prof Tanda; Active Ingredient for Love City; and FutureLab for MobiMissions.

5.3 Day of the Figurines (DoF)

DoF [27] is a role playing game for mobile phones that employs text messaging in order to be widely accessible to large numbers of players who can use their own mobile phones. The game follows twenty four hours in the life of a small virtual town which are mapped onto twenty four days of real time. It is therefore a long-term, slow-paced game that unfolds in the backgrounds of players' lives, requiring them to send and receive just a few messages each day. Players join the game by visiting a physical venue where they register their details and choose a plastic figurine to represent them. After they leave the venue, players control their figurine by sending and receiving SMS text messages.

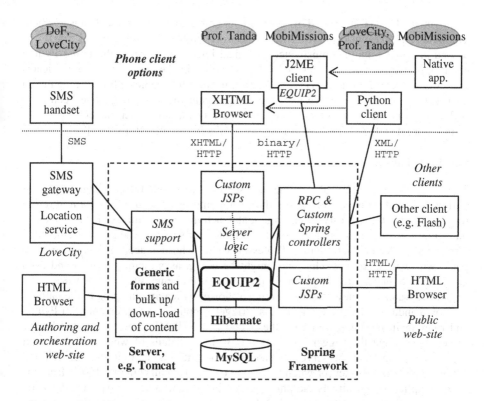

Fig. 2. **Common** and *optional* elements of the EQUIP2 server platform

As well as the SMS interaction with players' phones there is also a public spectator interface where human game operators move the players' figurines around a large physical game board that models the virtual city. A player can also view their figurine's state and messages sent and received on a game web site.

As part of a process of iterative development, DoF has so far been deployed in London (85 players), Barcelona (160 players), Berlin (145 players) and Singapore (141 players). In its most recent outing in Singapore, players sent a total of 12,685 messages to the game, received a total of 21,767 from it, and 75% of the 24 who responded to a questionnaire said that they would play again.

5.4 Love City

Love City [28] is a location-based game for mobile phones that connects three different physical cities with and through a single virtual city. Players' movements through their local physical cities are mapped to their location in the virtual Love City, enabling them to encounter one another. A player is given one chance to send a message of love – an anonymous text message – to each other player that they meet who may then choose to accept or reject it.

The implementation of Love City includes two different mobile phone clients. The first uses SMS messaging only on the handset in order to address as wide an audience as possible. This is supported by network operator location of the handset where available (on three out of the four major networks in the UK in the initial trial). The second provides a more sophisticated graphical interface delivered through a Python client application. This utilises cell ID positioning in the client and communicates with the game server over HTTP. A central website enables players to gain an overview of the state of Love City including recent messages that have been sent, "offspring" that have been created and the virtual locations of other players.

For more details of Love City, including results from initial trials, see [28].

5.5 Prof. Tanda

Prof. Tanda is a mixture of a game and survey and is intended to engage players during their daily routines, providing them with amusement and information in return for data about their lifestyle, environmental actions and attitudes. Prof. Tanda is played up to twice each day for about ten minutes per session. The game is embodied through a quirky character called Professor Tanda who contacts the player, tries to guess where they are and what they might be doing, asks them questions and even gets them to undertake simple activities and experiments such as measuring the amount of water that they use when taking a shower by leaving the plug in the bath.

Prof. Tanda is currently realized as a "trigger" application implemented in Python and running in the background on the phone and XHTML pages generated by the server. Each night the trigger application downloads details of when it should next trigger a session from the server. It then monitors the time and current cell ID, and when the condition is met (or when the player explicitly "calls" the Professor from the trigger application) it directs the phone's web browser to a session-specific URL on the server, which generates the XHTML pages for the player's interaction with the Professor during that session.

This initial implementation of Prof. Tanda has recently been trialed by 20 players for two weeks. In general, they reported enjoying their interactions with the central character in the game, especially the way in which it engaged them in local activities, an aspect of the game that they would like to see extended in future versions.

5.6 MobiMissions

MobiMissions [29] is a game in which players use camera smart phones to create, complete and document real-world missions. The content and purpose of missions is left open-ended for players to define for themselves, each mission being defined by up to five photographs and/or five sections of text. Missions are located based on the player's mobile phone cell ID. As a player carries out a mission they document their progress by capturing up to five photographs and adding short text annotations. They also rate how good the mission was.

The MobiMissions phone client is implemented in J2ME, specifically CLDC1.1, MIDP2.0 and the media API (for camera access). Communication with the game server is over HTTP. Cell ID is determined using the Placelab server (a native Symbian application) that runs on the handset [16], limiting the experience to Symbian Series 60 phones. The mobile game is supported by a website which allows players to browse missions and responses, rate other players' responses to a mission and leave comments.

An initial trial of MobiMissions has been conducted with a group of seventeen 16-18 year old users who created 75 missions which generated 123 responses over a period of five weeks (see [29]). Feedback through participant diaries and interviews showed that these players generally enjoyed the experience.

6 Discussion

We have now briefly described four ubicomp experiences which employ mobile phones in various ways and the EQUIP2 software platform/toolkit that has supported and been co-developed with them. From this, the following section returns to the four strategies identified in section 4 and assesses their impact on EQUIP2 and the development of these experience projects.

In addition to drawing on our own direct experience of development we have also surveyed the five core developers who worked on these four experiences using an optionally anonymous web-based questionnaire. These developers were not primary developers of EQUIP2 itself, and it was made clear to all respondents that an impartial response was desired, and that responses would be treated anonymously and used only for evaluation and planning for future extensions to the software platform.

6.1 Prioritise Strong Server Support

This has been a major area of development in EQUIP2, in particular the template web application and associated reusable elements (taglib, forms, Hibernate-based dataspace implementation, SMS support). All of the experiences developed with EQUIP2 have had substantial web-based elements, including public web pages and operator pages (based on the JSP taglib) and authoring and monitoring pages (based on the generic forms).

All of the respondents to our developer survey thought that the use of EQUIP2 made experience monitoring and orchestration faster than it would have been with alternative technologies, and three of the five respondents reported that the generic database forms were one of the best elements of using EQUIP2.

6.2 Migrate Functionality from the Server to More Capable Handsets

In MobiMissions all possible user interaction has been migrated to the J2ME phone client to integrate access to the phone's camera, minimize communication with the server and support play in areas of poor network coverage. This client application is built around a persistent EQUIP2 dataspace running on the phone, which caches information from the server (missions) to minimize communication with the server. The phone dataspace also accumulates new information and images (captured with the phone camera) as the user performs those missions, which can be uploaded to the server at a later time. The developer who worked on the phone client for MobiMissions rated the use of EQUIP2 for this as faster, less complicated and more flexible than using J2ME without EQUIP2.

In Prof. Tanda the trigger application represents a migration of one key function to the handset: monitoring certain aspects of user context (time and cell ID) in order to trigger a new interactive session. At present other phone interactivity is provided by the server-generated XHTML pages, however the server implementation of this uses Java over the standard EQUIP2 API and is designed so that in a future version this could be run directly within a J2ME MIDlet on the phone, similar to MobiMissions. The same approach allows (non-UI) EQUIP2-dependent code intended for a phone-based (J2ME) application to be initially developed and tested within desktop J2SE applications.

6.3 Support Very Flexible Communication

EQUIP2 reflects this strategy because, unlike its predecessor, it has no fixed communication mechanism (e.g. no single built-in distributed dataspace protocol). Instead it provides a number of supporting facilities that can be assembled and tailored in different ways.

For example, in DoF there are a set of data classes and supporting web interfaces for linking to commercial SMS gateways which have been reused in LoveCity. DoF and LoveCity also use EQUIP2's object marshalling framework with a simple generic (reflection-based) RPC server skeleton to support interaction with public Flash-based visualization clients.

In MobiMissions the protocol used between the J2ME phone client and the server again exploits the marshalling framework (this time the binary encoding, for performance). However the protocol has been carefully crafted in tandem with the user interface and interaction. For example, it is relatively common for the upload of a completed mission to fail part way through. If the user then goes to the server web site they may see the mission as completed, or not, depending on whether the failure occurred during the final acknowledgement phase of the upload. Consequently the protocol, data model, user views and user interaction all reflect the fact that a mission upload may have succeeded, definitely failed, or be in an unknown state.

All respondents to our developer survey rated EQUIP2 as making networking development more or much more flexible compared to alternative technologies they might have used, and two respondents rated it as much less complicated and much faster than the alternatives (of the other two respondents to these questions one rated both neutrally and one – who worked on with the very first release of EQUIP2 – more complicated/slower). One respondent reported speed of networking development as a main reason for using EQUIP2 in the future.

6.4 Use a Loosely Coupled (Data-Driven and Component-Based) Software Approach

We have already argued that the dataspace approach (and other indirect communication approaches) can support loosely coupled application development and code re-use. For example, the SMS "component" from DoF effectively forms a link between a dataspace and an external SMS gateway. However it does not "care" (or need any re-coding to deal with) how the data objects corresponding to incoming and outgoing text messages are processed or generated within the rest of the application – it just adds a new received message object to the dataspace when a SMS arrives, and requests the sending of a new message by the SMS gateway when a new message request object appears in the dataspace.

A number of other aspects of EQUIP2 also reflect this strategy. First, the integrated notification facility, which is present in a subset of tuple-space systems, provides additional support for decoupled but timely coordination. Indeed, four of the five respondents to our survey identified this as one of the best elements of using EQUIP2. Second, the build process for the template web application encourages the application developer to begin by defining the data types (object classes) to be used in the application. This was put forward by two of the five respondents as an important element. Third, the template web application makes extensive use of the Spring Framework [26], which in turn embodies a particular approach to component-based software development called "dependency injection", which makes it relatively easy to separate and then reuse the components (objects) that make up an application, without sub-classing or re-coding. Note also that the consistency of the EQUIP2 API across different platforms and implementations makes it easy to create unit tests (e.g. using JUnit) against test dataspaces without the overhead of creating and populating dummy relational databases or J2ME record stores.

6.5 Related Platforms and Toolkits

As we argued in section 4 our strategies – and priorities in EQUIP2 – reflect development-time concerns more than run-time facilities. EQUIP2 does provide a number of common run-time facilities (e.g. local dataspaces and marshalling) and so may be regarded as a run-time platform. However "out of the box" it is not a *distributed* platform for mobile phone application development, at least in its current form. This can be contrasted with specifically distributed tuple space systems such as MobiSpaces [30]. We plan to add some distributed dataspace options to EQUIP2 but these will only be applicable to particular deployment situations and handset application types. This mix and match approach gives EQUIP2 its toolkit character.

As discussed in section 3 there are several different platforms for (smart) phone applications, including J2ME, BREW, Symbian, Python and ContextPhone. In addition OSGi [31] (and JSR 232) supports modular application development and management, including for mobile devices, but requires the Java CDC profile rather than the CLDC profile normally found on mobile phones. The scope of EQUIP2 in terms of supported handset(s) is broader than any one of these, both in that the C++ version of EQUIP2 targets Symbian as well as J2ME (and potentially also Python through a suitable wrapper), and also in that the web server and SMS support is an integral element of EQUIP2 as a whole.

MUPE combines smart phone client development with server support, but the phone client is limited to J2ME and the server support is limited to communication with MUPE clients (for multi-user experience development) and has no particular support for web development or linking to other kinds of handset. Some other platforms or services such as BREW and SnapMobile [32] provide similar combinations of smart phone client support (as a library) and complementary server support for developing multi-user applications. But these are all adjuncts to smart phone client development on particular platforms, and do not offer support for other kinds of handsets or migration of functionality. None of the other ubicomp experiences considered in this paper identify a supporting platform or toolkit.

7 Conclusions and Future Work

The mobile phone is a very attractive existing device with a supporting infrastructure on which to deploy ubicomp experiences. However mobile phones are extremely diverse in their capabilities, so that an experience designer must choose which handset application type(s) they will target for any particular deployment, for example SMS, WAP, J2ME MIDlet or native application. This forces them to make a trade-off between the functionality of the handset application (e.g. interactivity and access to phone facilities) and the potential number of users having a compatible handset.

We have suggested four strategies which can ease development for mobile phone-based experiences given this trade-off: prioritise support for server development (including web integration), migrate functionality between server(s) and handset(s), support flexible communication options, and use a loosely coupled (data-driven and component-based) software approach. These strategies have shaped the development of the EQUIP2 software platform/toolkit, which underlies and has been co-developed with the four phone-based ubicomp experiences described in section 5. As we have argued, these are primarily development-time strategies. The experiences presented and the feedback from the experience developers suggest that these strategies, as supported and partially embodied by EQUIP2, have been effective in developing experiences across a range of handset application types, both in different projects and within the same project.

EQUIP2 is still under active development and being used in other projects and activities. It is freely available under the "new" BSD open source license: see the SourceForge project 'equip'[1]. To date we have chosen not to provide any particular distributed dataspace facilities. However the experience with MobiMissions in particular points to issues of communication uncertainty and scheduling which should be considered by any such facility.

Acknowledgements

With many thanks to our collaborators on these experiences. This work has been carried out for the EPSRC/DTI funded Participate project (grant EP/D033780/1). The development of EQUIP2 and the described experiences have also been supported by the EPSRC through the EQUATOR IRC (grant GR/N15986/01), by the EU IST programme though the Integrated Project on Pervasive Gaming (FP6 - 004457), and by Futurelab, the Arts Council England, the European Regional Development Fund and the East Midlands Development Agency.

---

[1] equip.sourceforge.net/equip2/

References

1. TimesOnline: Mobile madness consumes the UK (2006), http://technology.timesonline.co.uk/article/0,19510-2189680.html
2. Ofcom (Office of Communications): The Communications Market 2006 (2006), http://www.ofcom.org.uk/research/cm/cm06/main.pdf
3. Floerkemeier, C., Mattern, F.: Smart Playing Cards – Enhancing the Gaming Experience with RFID. In: Proc. PerGames, pp. 27–36 (2006)
4. Cheok, A.D., Sreekumar, A., Lei, C., Thang, L.N.: Capture the flag: mixed-reality social gaming with smart phones. Pervasive Computing 5(2), 62–69 (2006)
5. Raento, M., Oulasvirta, A., Petit, R., Toivonen, H.: ContextPhone - A prototyping platform for context-aware mobile applications. Pervasive Computing 4(2), 51–59 (2005)
6. Sohn, T., Li, K.A., Lee, G., Smith, I., Scott, J., Griswold, W.G.: Place-Its: A Study of Location-Based Reminders on Mobile Phones. In: Beigl, M., Intille, S.S., Rekimoto, J., Tokuda, H. (eds.) UbiComp 2005. LNCS, vol. 3660, pp. 232–250. Springer, Heidelberg (2005)
7. Smith, I., Consolvo, S., Lamarca, A.: The Drop: Pragmatic Problems in the Design of a Compelling, Pervasive Game. ACM Computers in Entertainment 3(3), 1–14 (2005)
8. Metrics, M.: M:Metrics Unveils Industry's First Definitive Mobile Marketing Metrics (2006), http://www.mmetrics.com/press/PressRelease.aspx?article=20061003-sms-shorttext
9. CONQWEST. http://homepages.nyu.edu/~dc788/conqwest/
10. M:Metrics: Captured By Camera Phomes (2006), http://www.mmetrics.com/press/PressRelease.aspx?article=20060807-photo-messaging
11. Jegers, K., Wiberg, M.: Pervasive gaming in the everyday world. IEEE Pervasive Computing 5(1), 78–85 (2006)
12. Kumar, V., Parimi, S., Agrawal, D.P.: WAP: present and future. IEEE Pervasive Computing 2(1), 79–83 (2003)
13. Sun Microsystems: Sun in Telecom (2004), http://www.sun.com/aboutsun/media/presskits/ctia2005/Sun_Telecom_External_V2.pdf
14. Huebscher, M., Pryce, N., Dulay, N., Thompson, P.: Issues in developing ubicomp applications on Symbian phones. In: Proc. Future Mobile Computing Applications, International Workshop on System Support, pp. 51–56 (2006)
15. Coulton, P., Rashid, O., Edwards, R., Thompson, R.: Creating entertainment applications for cellular phones. Comput. Entertain. 3, 3 (2005)
16. LaMarca, A., Chawathe, Y., Consolvo, S., Hightower, J., Smith, I., Scott, J., Sohn, T., Howard, J., Hughes, J., Potter, F., Tabert, J., Powledge, P., Borriello, G., Schilit, B.: Place Lab: Device Positioning Using Radio Beacons in the Wild. In: Gellersen, H.-W., Want, R., Schmidt, A. (eds.) PERVASIVE 2005. LNCS, vol. 3468, pp. 116–133. Springer, Heidelberg (2005)
17. Suomela, R., Räsänen, E., Koivisto, A., Mattila, J.: Open-Source Game Development with the Multi-user Publishing Environment (MUPE) Application Platform. In: Entertainment Computing – ICEC, pp. 308–320 (2004)
18. Crabtree, A., Benford, S., Rodden, T., Greenhalgh, C., Flintham, M., Anastasi, R., Drozd, A., Adams, M., Row-Farr, J., Tandavanitj, N., Steed, A.: Orchestrating a mixed reality game 'on the ground'. In: Proc. CHI, pp. 391–398 (2004)
19. Murphy, A.L., Picco, G.P., Roman, G.-C.: Lime: A Coordination Middleware Supporting Mobility of Hosts and Agents. ACM Transactions on Software Engineering and Methodology (TOSEM) 15(3), 279–328 (2006)

20. Fowler, M.: Patterns of Enterprise Application Architecture. Addison Wesley Professional, Reading (2002)
21. Segall, B., Arnold, D., Boot, J., Henderson, M., Phelps, T.: Content Based Routing with Elvin4. In: Proc. AUUG Winter Conference, AUUG2K, June 2000, Canberra, Australia (2000)
22. Gelernter, D.: Generative Communication in Linda. ACM Transactions on Programming Languages and Systems 7, 80–112 (1985)
23. Szyperski, C.: Component Software: Beyond Object-Oriented Programming, 2nd edn. Addison-Wesley Professional, Boston (2002)
24. Humble, J., Crabtree, A., Hemmings, T., Åkesson, K.-P., Koleva, B., Rodden, T., Hansson, P.: Playing with the Bits - User-configuration of Ubiquitous Domestic Environments. In: Dey, A.K., Schmidt, A., McCarthy, J.F. (eds.) UbiComp 2003. LNCS, vol. 2864, Springer, Heidelberg (2003)
25. Reenskaug, T.: The Model-View-Controller (MVC): Its Past and Present, http://heim.ifi.uio.no/trygver/2003/javazone-jaoo/MVC_pattern.pdf
26. Spring Framework, http://www.springframework.org/
27. Flintham, M., Smith, K., Benford, S., Capra, M., Green, J., Greenhalgh, C., Wright, M., Adams, M., Tandavanitj, N., Row Farr, J., Lindt, I.: Day of the Figurines: A Slow Narrative-Driven Game for Mobile Phones Using Text Messaging. In: Proc. PerGames (2007)
28. Oppermann, L., et al.: Love City: A Text-Driven, Location-Based Mobile Phone Game Played Between 3 Cities. In: Magerkurth, C., Röcker, C. (eds.) Pervasive Games - Concepts & Technologies (2007)
29. Grant, L., Benford, S., Hampshire, A., Drozd, A., Greenhalgh, C.: MobiMissions: The Game of Missions for Mobile Phones. In: Proc. PerGames (2007)
30. Fongen, A., Taylor, S.J.: Mobispace - A Distributed Tuplespace for J2me Environments. In: 17th IASTED International Conference on Parallel and Distributed Computing and Systems (2005)
31. OSGi Alliance: http://www.osgi.org/
32. Nokia: SNAP Mobile, http://snapmobile.nokia.com/

Sensor Networks or Smart Artifacts?
An Exploration of Organizational Issues of an Industrial Health and Safety Monitoring System

Gerd Kortuem[1], David Alford[2], Linden Ball[2], Jerry Busby[3], Nigel Davies[1],
Christos Efstratiou[1], Joe Finney[1], Marian Iszatt White[3], and Katharina Kinder[3]

[1] Computing Department, InfoLab21, Lancaster University, Lancaster, LA1 4WA, UK
{kortuem,nigel,efstrati}@comp.lancs.ac.uk, finneyj@v6testbed.net
[2] Department of Psychology, Lancaster University, Lancaster, LA1 4YF, UK
{d.alford,l.ball}@lancaster.ac.uk
[3] Management School, Lancaster University, Lancaster, LA1 4YX, UK
{j.s.busby,m.iszattwhite,k.kinder}@lancaster.ac.uk

Abstract. Industrial health and safety is an important yet largely unexplored application area of ubiquitous computing. In this paper we investigate the relationship between technology and organization in the context of a concrete industrial health and safety system. The system is designed to reduce the number of incidents of "vibration white finger" (VWF) at construction sites and uses wireless sensor nodes for monitoring workers' exposure to vibrations and testing of compliance with legal health and safety regulations. In particular we investigate the impact of this ubiquitous technology on the relationship between management and operatives, the formulation of health and safety rules and the risk perception and risk behavior of operatives. In addition, we contrast sensor-network inspired and smart artifact inspired compliance systems, and make the case that these technology models have a strong influence on the linkage between technology and organization.

Keywords: ubiquitous computing, sensor network, smart artifact, workplace support, occupational health and safety, safety culture, risk management, compliance architecture, organizational fit, privacy.

1 Introduction

Industrial workplaces such as construction sites, factories and plants pose enormous risks for workers and operatives. The International Labor Organization has estimated that some two million people die every year from work-related accidents and diseases worldwide [1]. An estimated 160 million people suffer from work-related diseases, and there are an estimated 270 million fatal and non-fatal work-related accidents per year. In economic terms, this means that 4% of the world's annual GDP is lost as a consequence of occupational diseases and accidents. Lowering occupational risks has long been the focus of legal authorities and industrial firms. It is an interesting and important question to ask if and how ubiquitous computing can play a role in making industrial workplaces safer.

J. Krumm et al. (Eds.): UbiComp 2007, LNCS 4717, pp. 465–482, 2007.
© Springer-Verlag Berlin Heidelberg 2007

Ubiquitous tracking and monitoring technologies are now routinely used in industrial environments [2,3], but very rarely with the goal to improve occupational health and safety. Research in ubiquitous computing has shown promise in health-related domains such as hospitals [4], elder care [5] and emergency rescue [6], yet applications in industrial settings are few. Over the last 1 ½ year, we have explored ubiquitous computing technologies for industrial workplaces, with a special focus on health and safety. In particular, we developed a sensor-based system designed to reduce the number of incidents of "vibration white finger" (VWF) at construction sites [7]. The system monitors workers' exposure to vibrations when using heavy-duty equipment such as pneumatic drills, tests compliance with legal health and safety regulations in real-time and creates detailed data records of worker's vibration exposure.

An industrial organization is a complex socio-technical system that is characterized by the formal and informal practices, rules and habits that influence interactions between people and groups in the organization. Designing technology, such as our vibration monitoring system, to fit established work practices and to function properly within an existing organization is a difficult task. Novel technology may disturb the balance between the various players and result in unintended and unforeseen consequences. To minimize the risk of failure it is essential that we assess a system's potential impact on work practices and identify an appropriate linkage between technology and organization as early as possible in the design process. This problem has been widely researched in the information systems community [8,9], but is just beginning to receive attention with regard to ubiquitous computing [10].

In the context of the previously mentioned vibration monitoring case study this paper makes two specific contributions: First, we identify work-organizational issues that are relevant for ubiquitous health and safety systems. According to Doherty and King [11] organizational issues are issues that need to be treated during the systems development process to ensure that the individual human, wider social, and economic impacts of the resultant technical system are likely to be desirable. In particular we investigate the representation of health and safety rules, the relationship between operatives and management, and operatives' risk perception and risk behavior. We argue that these issues need to be understood to enable successful introduction of ubiquitous health and safety technology in industrial environments.

Second, we define two fundamental architectural alternatives for a ubiquitous health and safety system and illuminate the architecture's influence on organizational issues. The first architecture is based on the concept of sensor networks and the second is built around the notion of smart everyday objects. Both models represent archetypes that have a great influence in ubiquitous computing research. We discuss how these models differ with respect to centralization and locality and how they may impact in different ways on safety behavior, accountability and formulation of health and safety rules. In essence we argue that system architecture is not neutral, but plays a crucial part in shaping work-organizational factors and thus influences the overall success or failure of a ubiquitous computing system in an organization.

The research reported in this paper is part of the interdisciplinary NEMO project. In previous publications we identified research challenges of ubiquitous health and safety system [12], reported our experiences in building and field-testing technology prototypes [7], explored safety culture and risk management at participating industrial firms [13,14], and studied human reasoning about health and safety rules [15]. In contrast, this paper focuses on the interplay of technology and organization.

In the remainder of the paper we start our discussion with a description of the "vibration white finger" case study (Section 2). This is followed by a discussion of methodological considerations when developing technologies to fit organizations (Section 3). Next we explore the sensor network and smart artifact models as two opposing alternatives for designing a ubiquitous health and safety system (Section 4). This lays the basis for an in-depths discussion of organizational issues and especially the linkage between system architecture and organization (Section 5).

2 Case Study: Controlling Hand-Arm Vibrations

Most industrial organizations do their utmost to reduce the risks associated with work activities and to provide a safe and healthy work environment. The reasons for this can be attributed to economic, legal and social pressures. As a matter of fact, health and safety compliance has today become a strategic objective for many large companies [16]. To prove compliance, organizations need to provide evidence that appropriate controls are in place – and that they work. While this can be done in several ways, it commonly involves data collection and record keeping, a process that is time consuming and costly. As a result of the mounting legislative pressure and the increasing need to prove compliance, companies have started to look for innovative ways to ensure workplace safety and are increasingly using enterprise-wide health and safety management systems. We believe that ubiquitous computing technology and embedded wireless systems offer a great potential for improving health and safety processes. Similarly, industrial safety exposes important new research challenges for ubiquitous computing [12].

As part of the NEMO project we have teamed up with major industrial firms to identify health and safety scenarios and to study technology in-situ through field trials and workplace studies. One of the first scenarios to come out of this project relates to the potential damage caused by vibrations when operating hand machinery such as hydraulic drills and breakers. Long-term exposure to hand arm vibration (HAV) can lead to serious health conditions known as "vibration white finger" (VWF) and in extreme cases to life-long disability. VWF is triggered by prolonged use of vibrating machinery, and causes the fingers to become numb and to begin turning white. In a progressive stadium the disease is irreversible; the person suffers increasingly frequent painful attacks at any time and may even lose their fingers. In order to understand how companies deal with this problem we investigated legal requirements and observed work practices at a major road construction and service company (referred to in this paper as *Safe*-company). The following provides a summary of our key observations.

2.1 Vibration-Related Health and Safety Regulations

Extensive health and safety regulations exist to limit workers' exposure to HAV. For example, in 2005 the UK Parliament introduced the Control of Vibration at Work Regulations [17]. The guidelines place a responsibility on employers to assess every employee's risk and to consider the specific individual working conditions of each employee. The damage caused by exposure to vibration is a combination of both the frequency of the vibrating tool and the duration of the exposure [18]. Using a tool that vibrates slightly for a long time can be as damaging as using a heavily vibrating tool for a short time. Thus regulations introduce action and limit values for hand-arm vibration [19]:

- Exposure action value of $2.5m/s^2$ A(8) at which level employers should introduce technical and organizational measures to reduce exposure.
- Exposure limit value of $5.0m/s^2$ A(8) which should not be exceeded in all circumstances.

These values are defined in terms of the average daily exposure dose A(8) which is specific to each equipment and provided by manufacturers. In practice an operative's vibration exposure can be estimated from three parameters: the equipment type, the duration of use and the surface hardness (soft, medium, hard).

2.2 Safety-Related Work Practices

2.2.1 Methodology
In order to understand how organizations address vibration-induced health concerns we conducted an ethnographic study of work practices at *Safe*-company (see also [13,14]). The organization itself saw its emphasis on safety as a unique selling point in tendering for new business, and its ability to publicize its involvement with a major research project in this area as contributing to its safety conscious image. The fieldwork for the study consisted of a number of semi-structured interviews with operatives and supervisory and management staff, aimed at drawing out 'sensitizing concepts' to inform the later stages of the fieldwork, followed by the extended observation of operatives, together with the collection of documents and other artifacts, with the aim of developing a rich understanding of the setting, including working practices, safety and audit culture perceptions, and concerns in relation to technology. A coding template [20] was then developed to structure the analysis of interview/fieldwork data, including the theorizing of links between various levels of coding, and the location of the template in the existing literature. The findings from this process were used to inform the technology design and implementation process on an ongoing basis. In total, the study involved more than 40 people from *Safe*-company (including high-level management, supervisors and operatives), spanning over 18 months and 6 different work sites.

As part of the interview phase, the interviewees were asked to grant access to others within the specific contracts on which they worked, in order to construct the subsequent program of fieldwork. The fieldwork observations included participation in safety training, observation of a wide range of on-site activities, attendance at safety-related meetings (for example, at a number of multi-level, multi-disciplinary Safety Action Group meetings), and informal discussions with site operatives. The latter took place both in one-to-one situations (for example, whilst observing them at their work or driving with them in their vehicles) and in small groups, usually when operatives were eating their lunch in the site mess rooms. A range of organizational and sector-related documents were also obtained.

2.2.2 Work Practices

Our investigations at *Safe*-company focused on smallish maintenance work, rather than new construction. Such work is usually carried out by two-men crews that drive to the location of defects to carry out repair work prescribed in work orders. The work requires the use of heavy-duty pneumatic drills for breaking open tarmac, saws for cutting square holes in the tarmac surrounding potholes, and wacker plates for compacting new tarmac. Such equipment can only be operated by one worker at a time, but workers frequently switch, passing the tool between them. With regard to pneumatic drills our observations revealed that drilling tends to happen in bouts of 1-5 minutes at a time, with 2-3 bouts per patch, but on occasion may take up to about half an hour. Operatives often interrupt work for brief moments to turn or place the drill. A crew may do 5-20 patches per day depending on the size of the patches and the distance they have to travel between them. For example, one crew did six patches of between 30 cm^2 and one square meter, with quite a lot of driving around in between, while another one had a row of nine small patches to do within 100 yards of each other, each one about 30 cm^2.

2.2.3 Current Compliance Practice

Workers are advised about safety procedures and the dangers of VWF in so-called toolbox talks. These are a weekly events that cover a variety of topics, most of them safety related. They often only last 10-15 minutes, are conducted in lunch breaks or out on site, and are repeated 2-3 times in the course of the day until everyone has attended a session. To minimize health damage, the company requires workers to wear ear protectors, safety glasses and gloves. Vibration exposure data is manually recorded by operatives on paper sheets, where exposure times and the type of tool used are noted (surface conditions are usually ignored and assumed to be 'hard'). Workers hand these sheets to their supervisors at the end of the day or week and the data in processed in the backend, often in a central database at the company headquarters. Supervisors will often (but not always) advise workers on the cumulative amount of exposure.

The system relies on workers diligently recording their exposure times and handing back records to supervisors on time. In practice we observed that this could be difficult since throughout a day a worker may use various vibrating tools at several work sites. Exposures were hand timed by operatives and entered on a paper record sheet. This record was often made retrospectively (for example, all exposures for the morning working hours were 'calculated' and entered on the sheet whilst sitting in the truck having lunch) and the process of hand timing was little more than guesswork. Thus the current practice raises serious concerns with respect to completeness, accuracy and consistency of captured data.

2.2.4 Risk Perception

The dangers posed by vibrations can be classified as 'invisible risks', i.e. risks with a loose or delayed linkage between the risk and its outcomes. Invisible risks, even if appropriately assessed and documented at an organizational level, are often underestimated or viewed as insignificant by operatives. Asking operatives about the risks of hand arm vibration (HAV) was regularly met with a variation of 'well, I've been doing this job for twenty years and I haven't had any problems with it'. Whilst everyone seemed to know someone who had suffered from vibration white finger, this was insufficient to make the risk appear 'real' in relation to their own conduct. Most accidents in the industry happen through trips, slips and falls, and the most prominent danger to the workers' lives is posed by road accidents involving cars driving by the work sites. In comparison to this, operatives seem to neglect or disregard a long-term risk such as vibration white finger as a less immediate danger. Managers and supervisors, in contrast, tended to be well aware of invisible risks and of the problems associated with conveying this risk to operatives.

We observed that the lack of recognition of vibration as a serious risk was exacerbated by the imprecise and low-key method of collecting exposure data. Operatives viewed the system as impractical in relation to actually getting the work done – i.e. timing and adding up a series of short bursts would be very disruptive to the work itself – and its low-key nature suggested to them that it was not important enough to attempt to do more accurately.

2.3 Real-Time Compliance Monitoring as an Opportunity for Ubiquitous Computing

A wide variety of IT solutions for managing health and safety compliance exist, yet with respect to hand-arm vibrations our investigations have identified a distinctive lack of tailored solutions. The current practice can be improved using mobile data entry solutions based on handheld wireless computers. Yet, while mobile solutions reduce the need for paper forms, they still suffer from the fact that they rely on human information gathering and recording in the field.

Whereas audits are often seen as one-off events, compliance-related legislation and regulation increasingly contains requirements for ongoing and real-time monitoring of the level of compliance. This opens an opportunity for sensor-based ubiquitous systems to improve health and safety compliance. Technologies such as wireless sensor network and wearable sensors can be designed to extract salient information from the workplace, recognize work activities and interpret them (possibly in real-time) with regard to health and safety regulations. In particular we see three beneficial uses of ubiquitous technologies: 1) Improving the quality of recorded health and safety data. 2) Providing timely, personalized notices to workers and operatives about health and safety risks. 3) Improving the understanding of company-wide health and safety risks.

3 Designing Technologies to Fit Organizations: Methodological Considerations

To minimize project risks, organizational issues should be considered from the very beginning of the development process, starting with idea generation and market assessment. In reality, however, this is rarely the case. A study exploring to what extent organizational issues are proactively managed in design processes of ubiquitous computing technologies found that (a) wider organizational aspects are perceived to be less of less importance than user centered issues and those directly related to the effective functioning of the technologies, and that (b) even those organizational issues that are considered to be of importance do not actually influence the design process [10].

Designing technologies for industrial organizations requires an understanding of the roles, needs and expectations of a variety of stakeholders. In our case study we are concerned with legal authorities, insurance companies, management, supervisors and operatives. Not every stakeholder has the same influence on the design process and the resulting system might benefit one stakeholder (for example management) to the detriment of another (for example operatives). Such a situation can lead to conflicts that negatively impact the functioning of the overall organization and, in our case, could mean a worsening of the company's health and safety record.

There is a particular danger that development is driven by technology visions, rather than by a grounded understanding of the organization and its business environment. On the other hand, in order to innovate we cannot always wait until we have a full understanding of these issues. Many questions will only come to light once we had a chance to try things out in the real world. Thus, we are faced with a methodological problem: how can we design technology if we do not fully understand the organizational environment, and how can we assess a technology that has not yet fully materialized and that has not yet been deployed within the organization? This is a problem that is common to technology innovation but especially profound for ubiquitous computing technologies that have the potential to fundamentally alter established principles and practices. A similar problem is described in [21]. To solve this methodological problem we use an approach combining five elements:

- Development of technology-driven demonstrators
- Field trials of technology prototypes
- Observational work place studies
- Lab-based human studies
- Comparative studies of prior technology deployments

The observational studies are described above. We use lab-based studies to explore questions of human perception, understanding and interaction with technology (see [15] for some results). Studies of prior technology deployments are concerned with similar technologies deployed within other companies and different technologies deployed within the same organization. For example, we investigated *Safe*-company's use of GPS technology for tracking vehicles. This technology was introduced by the management a few years prior to our investigations and was often used as a reference point by operatives and management.

4 Architectural Models for Ubiquitous Health and Safety Systems

In this section we identify two fundamental alternative system models for a ubiquitous compliance system. The first is based on the concept of sensor networks and the second is built around the notion of smart everyday objects. Both models represent archetypes that are intuitively understood by ubiquitous computing researchers, even though their technical realization may be less well defined. Their importance lies in the fact that they lead to highly diverging compliance regimes. These models inspired the construction of a prototype vibration monitoring system that was tested during a 2-week long field trial at *Safe*-company ([7], see also Section 4.3). Section 5 then explores the divergent impact of these system models on organizational issues.

4.1 The Sensor Network Approach

The concept of wireless sensor-networks (and smart dust) originally arose in the context of military applications and since then has been extended to civilian applications. Wireless sensor networks are beginning to be used in the industrial sector for manufacturing control [2], equipment monitoring and control [3], and structural health monitoring [22]. Wireless sensor networks are composed of low-power embedded sensor nodes that are connected through self-forming, self-healing wireless networks with flexible topologies. Nodes are distributed throughout the target environment, sometimes at random, sometimes attached to or embedded in objects. Traditionally, sensor networks have a small number of gateway nodes for streaming sensor data off the network or for interrogating the network state.

A ubiquitous compliance system based on the sensor network model can be build by scattering wireless nodes throughout the work site or by attaching nodes to work-related objects and people. To measure vibration we need nodes with vibration sensors or accelerometers, attached to vibrating equipment and/or people. While placing sensor nodes on people would allow direct measurement of vibrations experienced by operatives, such a set-up might run into usability and acceptance problems. Attaching sensors only to machinery would still make it possible to estimate human vibration exposure, similar to the way exposure is currently estimated using knowledge about surface conditions and equipment characteristics.

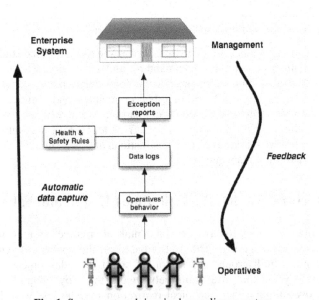

Fig. 1. Sensor-network inspired compliance system

A gateway node would connect the sensor network to a back-end enterprise system, which can be located in the company's central IT facilities. This enterprise system would permanently store sensor data and provide means for analyzing and summarizing data.

A compliance system based on a sensor network model creates a top-down compliance regiment as visualized in Figure 1. Data about operatives' behavior is captured in the field using sensors. Sensor data is streamed into a wired compliance infrastructure where it is stored in the form of data logs in a database. Data logs are then analyzed and compared against digitized health and safety regulations. If compliance violations are detected they are reported in the form of exception reports, which are forwarded to management on a regular weekly or monthly basis. The information contained in the exception reports provides indications in which way operatives violate health and safety regulations. This information is fed back to operatives, for example in the form of tailored training measures or through enforcement measures such as penalties. In that way, a sensor-network inspired compliance system is similar in character to the paper-based system that is currently in place. It improves the quality of the data that is available to the management (completeness and accuracy), while at the same time reducing the need for operatives and supervisors to manually keep track of work activities. It could be said that a sensor-network based compliance system improves the overall efficiency of the compliance monitoring process, but does not fundamentally change its character. This is in contrast to the smart artifact approach, which we describe next.

4.2 The Smart Artifact Approach

One of the key themes of ubiquitous computing is the vision of smart everyday objects, sometimes also called smart artifacts [23,24,25] or physical-digital object systems [26]. Such smart artifacts are objects of our everyday lives, augmented with information technology and equipped with sensing, computation, and communication capabilities, that are able to perceive and interact with their environment and with other smart objects. Smart artifacts retain their original use and appearance while computing supports a new quality of interaction and behavior. The vision of smart artifacts entails the notion of autonomy and self-directed actions based on previously collected information and knowledge about users. For example, a smart tool might adapt to its user's usage pattern and stop operating in harmful situations. In contrast, some researchers stress a people-orientated approach by postulating that smart artifacts should make people 'smarter' and empower them to make decisions and take actions as mature and responsible people [27]. According to this interpretation, the overall design rationale should aim to keep the user engaged and in control whenever possible [28].

The technological foundation for smart artifacts and sensor networks is very similar. In fact, researchers often build smart artifacts by placing sensor network nodes inside everyday objects, or by attaching nodes to the object. The difference between the sensor network approach and the smart artifact approach cannot be found in the technology but in the relation between technology and human. A sensor networks is an instrument for collecting data from the real world; it is not designed to be interacted with and is thus virtually invisible to humans. Smart artifacts, on the other hand, retain their physical nature and are conceptualized by humans in terms of the familiar everyday object they are based on.

Using smart artifacts, a compliance system can be realized in a completely different fashion (Figure 2). In the centre of the artifact-based compliance system is the smart artifact with a capability to observe the operative's behavior, to create a personalized health and safety record and to provide context-sensitive notices to the operator. Notices may be shown on a small embedded display and relate to the operator's state with regard to health and safety regulations, for example, if the operator exceeds the allowed daily exposure limits. In order to work, the smart artifact must have embedded knowledge about relevant health and safety regulations and the capability to interpret behavior with respect to these regulations (a partial technical solution was described in [29]). An artifact-inspired compliance system creates a feedback loop that enables the operator to watch and - if necessary - to adjust his behavior. This empowers the operative and puts him in control of his own health. It can be speculated that having real-time information about their health and safety status and being able to observe the impact of their actions promotes responsible behavior in individuals and encourages compliance with health and safety regulations. On the other hand, an artifact-based compliance system does not provide direct means for management to test compliance and to prove it to auditors, because compliance data is created and managed locally.

The two models described above represent opposing poles of a continuous design spectrum. Of course they can be combined and systems can be built that exhibit features of both.

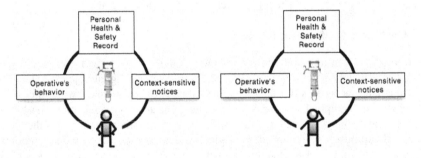

Fig. 2. Smart artifact inspired compliance system

4.3 The Prototype System

It is clear that neither the sensor-network approach nor the artifact approach alone is able to satisfy the needs of all stakeholders. The sensor-network approach captures data with the intention to satisfy audit requirements, but imposes a rigid top-down approach on the organization and overly emphasizes enforcement. The smart artifact approach supports a bottom-up approach to safety and emphasizes operators' responsibility, yet it does not address the management's need for centralized record keeping.

We have developed a sensor-based vibration monitoring system that falls somewhat between the sensor-network and the artifact model. It consists of a heavy-duty pneumatic drill augmented with a wireless sensor node, and a wireless dosimeter that is worn by operators on top of their protective clothing (Figure 3). The drill measures vibrations using accelerometers, and the dosimeter records how often and

Fig. 3. Sensor-based vibration monitor system with wireless drill & dosimeter (reproduced from [7])

how long an operative uses a drill. The dosimeter shows the user's current vibration exposure on a small display. Vibration exposure is estimated in cooperation between drill and dosimeter using information about the drill type and the duration of use. Dosimeters are personal devices: each operator uses his or her own device, yet the drill is shared among workers.

At the end of a workday, exposure data is uploaded to a backend database using a wireless communication gateway installed in vehicles. The database can be used by management to create compliance reports for each individual operative or for the whole workforce. We have tested the entire system in a 2-week long field trial at one of Safe-company's work sites and were able to estimate vibration exposure with an error of less than 8%. Details about the implementation, experiences with the technical system and a report about the field trial can be found in [7].

5   The Interplay Between Technology and Organization

A ubiquitous compliance system automates large parts of the compliance process. Actions and responsibilities that previously were in the hands of people are now taken on by technology. Such a system produces information about people, work activities and regulatory compliance at a level of detail that previously has not been available to the organization. It can be expected that the system and the information it produces will be appropriated by the various players to reshape how the organization works. Much of this reshaping will be unexpected and unintentional but we can assume that the effects will be profound.

A full assessment of these effects is not possible until after technology has been deployed on a large scale over a longer period of time. However, based on our observations and theoretical insights we are able to identify key organizational issues that will be affected by the introduction of ubiquitous compliance technology. These issues are captured by the 'compliance triangle' in Figure 4, which highlights three areas: (1) power and control, (2) rule formulation and (3) risk perception and risk behavior. In the following, we will explore these issues in more detail. Furthermore we will argue that the underlying system architecture of a compliance system will

Fig. 4. Compliance triangle

have a profound effect on how a system fits in the organizational context and how it will be appropriated.

In general, the relationship between rules and responsibility emerged as a key theme in our work. This relationship represents a double-edged sword for both management and operatives: For the latter, rule following without heedfulness may be irresponsible and potentially dangerous. At the same time, not complying with a rule – even when there appears to be a good reason for doing so – is potentially a disciplinary offence. For the former, rule writing which is abstracted from the realities of the rule application setting runs the risk of creating 'forced violations' – i.e. where operatives believe they have no choice but to break a rule in order to address specific local working conditions, or just to get the job done - and thus being wholly or partially ineffective in mitigating the underlying risks.

5.1 Formulating and Representing Rules

An organization must create an internal control system in order to comply with external health and safety regulations. The internal control system is a combination of explicit rules ("You must wear vibration gloves"), informal guidelines, work routines and business processes, with explicit rules representing only a small part of the overall control system. Yet a ubiquitous compliance system requires a digital representation of health and safety rules that is precise and unambiguous. In the case of vibration-related regulation the translation of external regulations into internal rules is straightforward because legislation is already formulated in very precise language, yet in other health and safety areas this is not necessarily the case. While this may limit the scope of a ubiquitous compliance system it also increases the burden for the organization to formulate effective and precise internal rules. On the other hand, it can be expected that technology progress will have an influence on how legal regulations are formulated in the first place.

A more immediate concern for operatives is the abstraction of *rule writing* from *rule application*. In our interviews we discovered strong reactions from operatives towards rules that had been formulated by management seemingly without comprehension of the consequences for operatives on the ground, including the predictable resentment at management enforcing rules that they themselves do not have to operate under (such as wearing full protective equipment on hot days whilst working with tarmac). There is also considerable frustration at 'blanket' rules that fail to recognize the variations in specific working conditions. We assume that the contrast between rule writing and rule application will be exacerbated by ubiquitous compliance technology as it increases the need for more precise and less flexible rules.

5.2 Power and Control

An issue that is often brought up in the context of ubiquitous computing and its impact on social interactions relates to privacy and surveillance. As Mark Weiser already pointed out, this issue is really about control [30]. In addition to health and safety purposes, information produced by a ubiquitous compliance system can be used by management to increase control over operatives, for example by creating more accurate logs of workers' activities. Even if the system is not used in that way by the management, operatives may *perceive* it in that sense. Similarly, a ubiquitous compliance system may be used in the future for purposes other than health and safety. From that point of view concerns about surveillance and control are understandable.

We found evidence for perception of control in how operatives view the GPS system deployed by *Safe*-company for tracking vehicles. The GPS system had originally been introduced to bring down insurance costs as vehicles had been stolen and is now occasionally used to locate people to send them to the nearest work site. At first, GPS units were installed inside vehicles, visible to drivers and operatives. Yet after some incidents where GPS units were damaged (possibly on purpose), units are now installed under the vehicles, with no indication when the unit is activated and able to track the vehicle. Operatives do not know much about this system apart from the fact that it is 'there'; they often do not even know whether this system works when the ignition is off. One operatives' perception of this technology is made clear by this statement: *"It's a double edged sword, its good and its bad. We had a case last year, [...] one of our drivers knocked a lad down, and because the GPS was running, it recorded everything. And he was found ... he was under the speed limit so ... he was in the clear [...]. But we also had a case recently where two lads were pulled up for dangerous driving and speeding, yeah? [...] the dangerous driving bit was dropped, erm, but he went into an argument about the speeding, because the GPS recorded, [...] but it doesn't tell you where he was speeding (in relation to specific speed limits). So we had a situation where we were arguing here – backwards and forwards, backwards and forwards [...] but they (management) ended up saying [...] 'well, we know its speeding, but we can't say where', which to me, doesn't mean a thing."*

This example highlights both a perceived lack of trust and a lack of effective, two-way communication between management and operatives within *Safe*-company. Whilst there appears to be willingness on both sides, it is insufficient to ensure that management reasoning concerning the formulation and purpose of rules, and operatives' experience and expertise in the specifics of the setting, are effectively communicated to 'the other side'. The resultant lack of trust operates both in terms of management seeking to control the activities of operatives rather than trusting their common sense, and operatives ascribing less than altruistic motives to management in their imposition of rules, with self-preservation in a litigious environment or the desire to maximize profits seen as the 'real' motives behind them.

It is thus obvious that a ubiquitous health and safety system that follows the sensor-network model with its implied top-down approach may exacerbate this situation and may lead to a pronounced conflict between management and operatives. If workers feel their privacy is violated, they can feel humiliated and depressed, and it is an open question how much an organization will benefit or lose from close surveillance of its employees. On the other hand, a ubiquitous health and safety system that follows the smart artifact approach and focuses on increasing operative's awareness does not directly intervene in the management–operative relationship. Indirectly such an approach may lead to a better understanding of health and safety issues on the operatives' part and facilitate communication. The generally positive attitude operatives shown towards the wearable dosimeters can be explained by the fact that in contrast to the GPS system the dosimeter design emphasizes awareness and personal control, rather than surveillance. In the word of one project manager: "*I don't think people would object if you were clamping something onto them because they've got this view of safety [...] as long as you're clear that its not about measuring productivity. (So if for example the display that was on the machine - they could see what was being measured, they would feel comfortable with that, would they?) Yes, I think so. Yes, there's not a problem, it's a bit like all sorts of devices like that that often on sites and fork lift trucks and all that sort of stuff, but they wouldn't object. But the only thing they'd object is if its being used as I say linked to some sort of pay. Anything else they'd be fine.*"

Perception of technology is not only shaped by reality (what a technology is actually used for in an organization), but also by the narratives, stories and metaphors used to talk about it [31] In this context, it is interesting to note that operatives favorable compared the wearable dosimeters to mobile phones, again emphasizing the personal nature of the device and their control over it, rather than to GPS units (to which they bear a closer technical resemblance).

5.3 Risk Perception and Risk Behavior

As outlined at the beginning of the paper, there is a distinct lack of risk awareness among operatives, especially in connection with invisible risks. Mitigating invisible risks may require the suspension of ones own judgment in favor of compliance with prescribed organizational rules, such as wearing the required personal protective equipment. In this instance, a sense of self-efficacy – of feeling that one can work safely without following the rules or that the possible effects of this type of risk simply 'won't happen to me' – needs to be overridden by trust in the efficacy and applicability of organizationally devised rules and practices [32,33]. A ubiquitous health and safety system that exhibits features of the artifact-based approach may be able to support this process by raising the awareness of risks and aiding the understanding of organizational rules. This, however, is only possible when information is made available in situ, i.e. to operatives in the field while they are working.

Going one step further, a ubiquitous health and safety system could be designed to protect workers by automatically shutting down the drill whenever an operative reaches his or her exposure limit. While we did not test this feature in the field trial, we found support for both design options (warning-only and shutting down) among operatives and management. The argument for shutting down a tool is that it is the best way to enforce compliance with existing regulations. The arguments against is are that it will disturb work too much (for example if a job could be finished with another 30 seconds of drilling, but the tool will not allow it), that people will always find ways to work around technology (for example by swapping dosimeter tags) and that it takes control away from operatives instead of empowering them.

The latter point relates to the ongoing discussion about behavior-based safety [34,35]. The theory of behavior-based safety argues against the enforcement style approach to safety and emphasizes that employees need to take an ownership of their own safety as well as unsafe behaviors. Its purpose is to identify safe and at-risk behaviors, communicate the risk and help to identify safer solutions. The behavior-based approach is fundamentally a data-driven decision-making process that relies on operatives as the basic source of expertise of behavioral change. Behavior-based approaches are controversial as they shift responsibility for health and safety to the workers without at the same time requiring significant change in the work processes. Nevertheless, an artifact centric compliance system could be able to empower operatives to observe and interpret their own behavior with respect to existing regulations, and to motivate them to modify their behavior if necessary.

While the extent to which an artifact-based system is able to support behavior-based safety is mostly speculation at this point, we did observe initial signs of collaborative safety behavior. At more than one occasion, operatives would show their dosimeter tags to each other to discuss the meaning of the data and the level of their exposure. This can be interpreted as collaborative learning process that may lead to improved safety behavior.

5.4 Dealing with Well-Intentioned Violations

The underlying assumption of a ubiquitous compliance system is that any violation of health and safety rules is bad. While this is true in theory, we discovered that it is not true in practice. The term 'rule violation' may conjure up visions of deliberate sabotage, malicious damage or willful disobedience: in the vast majority of cases, however, the reality is far more mundane. A so-called 'violation' may be a habitual short-cut to a familiar procedure, a lax interpretation of a rule on the basis of perceived self-efficacy or experience, or a genuine attempt to get the job done in adverse circumstances (for example, in the absence of the proper equipment). Such violations are concerned with mismatches between rules and reality, and may be as simple as a worker not wearing anti-vibration gloves because he finds them uncomfortable. It is also clear from our data that routine rule violations are often condoned – implicitly or explicitly – by management, sometimes with a resultant perception by operatives of double standards and/or mercenary motives. In some cases, management 'turning a blind eye' may be viewed quite benignly, even when adverse consequences ensue. So, for example, one working foreman, who developed white finger syndrome through over-exposure to hand arm vibration whilst bringing a tree-clearing contract back on target, talked about the fact that management praised him for bringing the contract back on track even though they knew he was the only person with a chain saw ticket on the contract, and that he must have been going over the exposure limit. He did not blame them for this behavior, and, in fact, praised them for their responsiveness to the situation once he brought it to their attention. For others, their perception of such condoning is clearly part of a much more generalized, cynical perception of management as wanting to maximize profits or minimize the likelihood of being sued by workers in the event of accidents.

A ubiquitous compliance system that automatically records rule violations runs counter to such established practices, especially in the case of a sensor-network inspired system. If we accept that rule violations can be good - or at least that not all rule violations are bad - then a ubiquitous compliance system creates a potential problem for the organization in that it may make it impossible to circumvent the rules even if this is in the common interest of management and operatives An artifact-based system with its focus on local rather than global awareness does not pose the same problem, as it does not make information globally available.

6 Conclusion

Industrial health and safety is an important but as of yet largely unexplored application area for ubiquitous computing technologies. Our ubiquitous compliance system for controlling "vibration-white-finger" is one of the first examples of a ubiquitous health and safety system for industrial workplaces. The underlying architectural model of such a system has a strong influence on the linkage between technology and organization. A sensor-network model inspired system best supports a top-down compliance regiment that may exacerbate the already strained relationship between management and operatives because it promotes information imbalance, discourages workers' active participation in promoting and ensuring health and safety. A smart artifact inspired system, however, with a focus on raising operatives' awareness and control lends itself to a behavior-based safety approach in which health and safety policies emerge from the bottom up in the interplay between management and operatives. Other significant differences between these models can be identified in their influence on risk perception and risk behavior.

These models represent system archetypes that are helpful for exploring organizational issues. Any actual concrete system is most likely a mix of these models, inheriting advantages and disadvantages of both. While we can make some assertions about the possible impact of this technology on power relationships, perception and safety behavior it is too early to answer the crucial 'big' question, if the organization as a whole becomes more or less compliant as result of this technology, and if the technology actually contributes to a safer and healthier work environment. Answering these questions will require more technology development, field tests and observational studies.

Acknowledgements

This work has been supported by the UK Engineering and Physical Science Research Council (EPSRC) project NEMO (EP/C014677/1) and the EU project CoBIs (IST 004270). We would like to thank Daniel Boos (ETH Zurich) and Joe McCarthy (Nokia Research) for their helpful comments and suggestions.

References

1. Yearbook of Labour Statistics 2006, 65th issue. International Labour Organization (2006)
2. Ota, N., Wright, P.: Trends in Wireless Sensor Networks for Manufacturing. International Journal of Manufacturing Research 2006 1(1), 3–17 (2006)
3. Krishnamurthy, L., Adler, R., Buonadonna, P., Chhabra, J., Flanigan, M., Kushalnagar, N., Nachman, L., Yarvis, M.: Design and deployment of industrial sensor networks: experiences from a semiconductor plant and the north sea. In: Proceedings of the 3rd Int. Conference on Embedded Networked Sensor Systems, November 2-4, 2005, San Diego, Ca (2005)
4. Bardram, J.E.: Applications of context-aware computing in hospital work: examples and design principles. In: Proceedings of the 2004 ACM Symposium on Applied Computing (2004)
5. Stanford, V.: Using Pervasive Computing to Deliver Elder Care. IEEE Pervasive Computing 1(1), 10–13 (2002)
6. Lorincz, K., Malan, D.J., Fulford-Jones, T.R.F., Nawoj, A., Clavel, A., Shnayder, V., Mainland, G., Welsh, M., Moulton, S.: Sensor networks for emergency response: challenges and opportunities. IEEE Pervasive Computing 3(4) (October-December 2004)
7. Efstratiou, C., Davies, N., Kortuem, G., Finney, J., Hooper, R., Lowton, M.: Experiences of Designing and Deploying Intelligent Sensor Nodes to Monitor Hand-Arm Vibrations in the Field. In: Proceedings of The 5th International Conference on Mobile Systems, Applications, and Services (MobiSys 2007), 11-14 June 2007, Puerto Rico (2007)
8. Clegg, C.W., Coleman, P., Hornby, P., McClaren, R., Robson, J., Carey, N., et al.: Tools to incorporate some psychological and organizational issues during the development of computer-based systems. Ergonomics 39(3), 482–511 (1996)
9. Heller, T.: If only we'd known sooner: developing knowledge of organizational changes earlier in the product development process. IEEE Trans. on Eng. Man. 47(3), 335–344 (2000)
10. Günter, H., Grote, G., Boos, D.: Organizational issues in ubiquitous computing. In: Paper presented at 22nd EGOS Colloquium, Subtheme 14: Technology, Organization and Society: Recursive Perspectives, July 06-08, Bergen
11. Doherty, N.F., King, M.: An investigation of the factors affecting the successful treatment of organisational issues in systems development projects. European Journal of Information Systems 10(3), 147–160 (2001)
12. Davies, C., Efstratiou, C., Finney, J., Hooper, R., Kortuem, G., Lowton, L.: Sensing Danger – Challenges in Supporting Health and Safety Compliance in the Field. In: Proceedings of The 8th IEEE Workshop on Mobile Computing Systems and Applications (HotMobile 2007), Tucson, Arizona, February 26-27, 2007, IEEE Computer Society Press, Los Alamitos (2007)
13. Iszatt White, M.: Catching Them At It? An Ethnography of Rule Violation. In: Symposium on Current Developments in Ethnographic Research in the Social and Management Sciences, 13th-14th September 2006, Liverpool, UK (2006)
14. Busby, J., Iszatt White, M.: Pushing the Boundaries of HRO Thinking: Non-complex and Uncoupled but still Deadly. In: SRA Annual Meeting - Risk Analysis in a Dynamic World: Making a Difference, 3rd-4th December 2006, Baltimore, Maryland (2006)
15. Ball, L.J., Alford, D.: What determines the acceptability of deontic health and safety rules? In: Proceedings of the 29th Annual Conference of the Cognitive Science Society, Nashville, Tennessee, August 1-4, 2007, Sheridan Printing, Alpha, NJ (2007)
16. Power, M.: The Audit Society: rituals of verification. OUP, Oxford (1997)

17. The Control of Vibration at Work Regulations 2005. Statutory Instrument 2005 No. 1093 The Stationery Office Limited (2005) ISBN 0110727673
18. Bovenzi, M., Griffin, M., Hagberg, M.(eds.): Proceedings of the 2nd International Workshop on Diagnosis of Injuries Caused by Hand-Transmitted Vibration. Goteborg, Sweden, 6-7 September 2006. Report no 14, Occupational and Environmental Medicine, ISSN 1650-4321
19. Health and Safety Executive. Control the risks from hand-arm vibration. Advice for employers on the Control of Vibration at Work Regulations 2005 (2005)
20. King, N.: Template Analysis. In: Symon, G., Cassell, C. (eds.) Qualitative Methods and Analysis in Organizational Research: A Practical Guide, Sage, London (1998)
21. Hilty, L.M., Som, C., Köhler, A.: Assessing the Human, Social, and Environmental Risks of Pervasive Computing. Human and Ecological Risk Assessment 10, 853–874 (2004)
22. Kim, S., Pakzad, S., Culler, D., Demmel, J., Fenves, G., Glaser, S., Turon, M.: Wireless sensor networks for structural health monitoring. In: Proc. of the 4th international Conference on Embedded Networked Sensor Systems, October 31-November 3, 2006, Boulder, Colorado (2006)
23. Beigl, M., Gellersen, H.W., Schmidt, A.: Mediacups: experience with design and use of computer-augmented everyday artifacts. Computer Networks 35(4), 401–409 (2001)
24. Siegemund, F.: A Context-Aware Communication Platform for Smart Objects. In: Proceedings of the 2nd Int. Conference on Pervasive Computing, April 18-23, 2004, Linz, Austria (2004)
25. Mattern, F.: From Smart Devices to Smart Everyday Objects. In: Proceedings of Smart Objects Conference 2003, May 2003, Grenoble, France (2003)
26. Nelson, L., Churchill, E.F.: User Experience of Physical-Digital Object Systems: Implications for Representation and Infrastructure. In: Smart Object Systems Workshop, in cojunction with Ubicomp 2005, September 2005, Tokyo (2005)
27. Streitz, N.A, Rocker, C., Prante, T., van Alphen, D., Stenzel, R., Magerkurth, C.: Designing Smart Artifacts for Smart Environments. IEEE Computer 38(3) (March 2005)
28. Rogers, I.: Moving on from Weiser's Vision of Calm Computing: Engaging UbiComp Experiences. In: Proceedings of the 8th International Conference of Ubiquitous Computing, 17-21 September 2006, California, USA (2006)
29. Strohbach, M., Gellersen, H., Kortuem, G., Kray, C.: Cooperative Artefacts: Assessing Real World Situations with Embedded Technology. In: Davies, N., Mynatt, E.D., Siio, I. (eds.) UbiComp 2004. LNCS, vol. 3205, Springer, Heidelberg (2004)
30. Weiser, M.: The computer for the 21st century. Sci. Am. 265, 94–104
31. Kendall, J.E., Kendall, K.E.: Metaphors and their Meaning for Information Systems Development. European Journal of Information Systems 3(1), 37–47 (1994)
32. Rebecca, L.: Not Working to Rule: Understanding Procedural Violations at Work. Safety Science 28, 2, 77–95
33. Hale, A.R., Heijer, T., Koornneef, F.: Management of Safety Rules: The Case of Railways. Safety Science Monitor 7, 1, 1–11 (2003)
34. Scott, E.: Geller, Behavior-Based Safety and Occupational Risk Management. Behavior Modification 29(3), 539–561 (2005)
35. Hopkins, A.: Lessons from Longford: the Esso Gas Plant Explosion. In: CCH, Canberra (2000)

A Long-Term Evaluation of Sensing Modalities for Activity Recognition

Beth Logan[1], Jennifer Healey[1], Matthai Philipose[2],
Emmanuel Munguia Tapia[3], and Stephen Intille[3]

[1] Intel Digital Health, One Cambridge Center 11FL,Cambridge MA 02139, USA
Beth.Logan@intel.com
http://www.intel.com/healthcare/
[2] Intel Research Seattle, 1100 NE 45th Street, Seattle WA 98105, USA
[3] MIT House_n, One Cambridge Center 4FL, Cambridge MA 02142, USA

Abstract. We study activity recognition using 104 hours of annotated data collected from a person living in an instrumented home. The home contained over 900 sensor inputs, including wired reed switches, current and water flow inputs, object and person motion detectors, and RFID tags. Our aim was to compare different sensor modalities on data that approached "real world" conditions, where the subject and annotator were unaffiliated with the authors. We found that 10 infra-red motion detectors outperformed the other sensors on many of the activities studied, especially those that were typically performed in the same location. However, several activities, in particular "eating" and "reading" were difficult to detect, and we lacked data to study many fine-grained activities. We characterize a number of issues important for designing activity detection systems that may not have been as evident in prior work when data was collected under more controlled conditions.

1 Introduction

Computer sensor systems able to reliably identify activities of daily living would enable novel ubiquitous computing applications for health care, education, and entertainment. For example, in long term home health monitoring, automatic detection of activity may allow people to receive continuous care at home as they age, thus reducing health care costs, improving quality of life, and enabling independence. Recent work on automatic detection of activities in the home setting has shown promising results using machine learning algorithms and data from embedded sensors (e.g., with RFID tags[3] or switch sensors[2]), mobile devices (e.g., accelerometers[5]), or combinations of these[7].

In this paper, we extend these prior results by studying activity detection from sensor data generated by subjects living for a relatively long period in a real but highly instrumented home. Our experiment studied a married couple living for 10 weeks in this home. We annotated and then analyzed a 104 hour sub-set of the data, comprised of data collected on 15 separate days. Neither of the participants was affiliated with the authors, and the ground truth video annotations were

J. Krumm et al. (Eds.): UbiComp 2007, LNCS 4717, pp. 483–500, 2007.
© Springer-Verlag Berlin Heidelberg 2007

provided by a third party also not part of the research team. Only the activities of the male subject were annotated, due to financial constraints and the original intent of our experiment as discussed in Section 6.5.

We report on: (1) the impact on recognition performance when several different types of sensors are considered (wired switches, RFID tags, wireless object usage detectors, electrical current and water flow detectors, etc.), and (2) difficult cases that were encountered when doing this work that impact how one might design a home activity recognition system. In addition, we highlight some evaluation issues that arose when testing algorithms and that may be of interest for others studying home activity recognition inference systems. Finally, we describe some of the challenges we encountered as we extended previously reported lab experiments (e.g. [11]) to more realistic, real-world conditions.

2   Related Work

Although there are different commercial systems available for activity monitoring in the home, such as Quiet Care Systems[13] and e-Neighbor[14], these provide only a limited analysis of activity. So-called "smart" appliances such as the Japanese "i-pot"[15] only detect one activity.

In this paper we examine methods of monitoring many activities within the home using dense object-based sensing with low cost sensors. In particular, we focus on work using object usage (motion) detectors placed on large objects and furniture [1], body-worn accelerometers [5,4], magnetic reed switches [6,2], water/power system monitors [10] and wrist-worn RFID readers [8]. Prior work shows promising results for these methods. However, it is difficult to extrapolate from reported experiments how these sensors would perform under more real-world conditions for the following reasons.

First, in some cases, test data was generated by having the researchers who developed the system or their affiliates perform activities. Although such data are often sufficient as an early proof of concept for a system, there exists the obvious problem of potential bias. A researcher who knows how the system works may perform an activity in a manner favoring the recognition system. We address this problem by using subjects completely unaffiliated with any of the researchers.

Second, in many cases, the techniques are evaluated on datasets collected when subjects are asked to perform activities collected in short recording sessions, where subjects repeatedly perform random sequences of activities. In each case, the data may not represent the variety of ways in which a subject may perform activities outside of these artificial conditions over a long period of time. For instance, a single subject may ordinarily eat in many locations around the home, but in a time-bounded experiment he or she may always do so at the dining table. In our study, we collect data over a period of 10 weeks and draw our evaluation set from a 15 day subset of this. Additionally, unlike many previous long-term studies, we record full video and audio for annotation rather than relying on self-reporting.

Third, the techniques are often evaluated on data collected in lab settings that are intended to mimic the home, but are not the actual residence of the subjects. In the unfamiliar confines of a lab setting, subjects will likely perform activities in much more restricted ways. For instance, it is unlikely that a subject will sprawl on a couch and eat dinner over a few hours in a lab setting. Although in this work our participants moved into an instrumented home that is not their own, they lived in the home for 10 weeks, allowing time for them to acclimate to the environment.

Fourth, much prior work focuses on proving the effectiveness of one particular type of sensor. Further, each technique is validated on a data set that may be (unintentionally) biased toward the capabilities of the sensor type selected. As a result, it is difficult to gage the relative efficacy of the sensors for recognizing activities. In this work, we employ a number of sensors simultaneously in a single apartment. Our goal is not to introduce interesting new sensors, but rather to allow comparison of previously proposed sensors using a common baseline.

Finally, in most cases, labeling of the data was performed by researchers and their affiliates. Such self-labeling may be unfairly biased towards the system being tested since researchers may favor labels that they expect their system to produce. For instance, when the subject eats in short spurts over a period of hours, there may be a temptation to label the whole period as a single long period of eating. To avoid biases stemming from self-labeling, we employ a professional coder to label our data.

To summarize, we describe in this paper a carefully constructed experiment to compare recently proposed sensors for activity recognition while avoiding a number of limitations in their evaluations. We believe that such apples-to-apples analyses are essential if activity recognition sensor technology is to move beyond the "interesting concept prototype" stage.

3   Description of the Experiment

The aim of our study was to provide guidance for the development of home activity recognition systems by testing under more realistic conditions than may have been achieved in past work. We did this by exploiting an instrumented home environment that permitted multiple modes of sensor data to be collected simultaneously.

3.1   Sensing Environment

We obtained access to the PlaceLab, an instrumented home environment operated as a shared research facility [9], and collected and analyzed data from a couple who lived at the home for a period of 10 weeks. The home is a custom built condominium instrumented with several hundred sensors, including an audiovisual recording system that captures ground truth of the participants' activities. The environment contains the following built-in wired sensors that were used in this work: 101 reed switch sensors installed on doors, cabinets, drawers and windows, electrical current flow sensors on 37 residential circuits, 36 temperature sensors, 10 humidity sensors, 6 light sensors, 1 barometric pressure sensor, 1 gas sensor and 14 water flow sensors. We also used 277 wireless object usage (motion) detection sensors [1] of three types: 265 "stick-on" object usage sensors that measure when objects move, 2 3-axis accelerometer sensors that are worn on limbs and measure limb movement at 20+Hz, and 10 wireless infra-red motion sensors that detect when there is motion in various regions of the condominium. The object usage sensors were placed on nearly all objects that might be manipulated ranging from doors and cabinets to remote controls for appliances. In some cases these were redundant with wired sensors. The 3-axis accelerometer sensors were worn on the dominant wrist and dominant hip of the male subject. The infra-red motion detector sensors were placed around the apartment to cover each room.

The home's audio-visual recording infrastructure was used to record the behavior of the participants as they lived in the home. The audio-visual record shows all views of the apartment except for the bathrooms, with a limited view of the bedroom. All data is relayed to a central processing and storage facility in the apartment where it is time-stamped on arrival. Figure 1 shows an image of the living room of the home. Despite the ubiquity of the sensor infrastructure, the majority of sensors are embedded in cabinetry or hidden from sight.

Fig. 1. View of the PlaceLab living room taken before the participants moved in

We further augmented the existing sensors in the home by installing 435 RFID tags. We obtained access to an RFID reader in a bracelet form factor [8] and requested that the male subject wear it whenever he was awake and in the home. Ideally, we would have had the female subject wear a bracelet also, but lack of hardware and financial resources for annotation of her activities prevented this.

Readings from the RFID bracelet were sent wirelessly to the central processing and storage facility for logging. Three types of 13.56MHz RFID tags were used: 309 55mmx55mm stickers, 78 86mmx54mm "credit card" style tags and 48 22mm diameter "button" tags. These different form factors trade off parameters such as range, obtrusiveness, cost and durability. Tags were placed on all objects in the home that could be tagged without impacting use of the object in an obvious way and that appeared to permit the tag to be read if the object was handled normally. Tags were placed on food items, on major kitchen objects such as handles of cooking knives, on appliances and devices (computer mousepad/keyboard), under shelf paper at the edge of shelves, inside couch armrests and pillows, inside the front cover of books, etc. In some cases, due to the shape of objects, the makeup of the objects (e.g., metal), or the usage of objects (i.e., might be put in the microwave), it was not possible to place tags. Examples where RFID tags were not placed include the television remote, metallic kitchen appliances, and cups and plates which might be put in the microwave. Once a week when the participants were at work, researchers entered the apartment and added tags to new objects found in the apartment, such as food and magazines.

We believe this is one of the largest and richest continuous datasets collected of its kind, and certainly it is the only one that combines embedded sensors such as switch and flow meters with wearable accelerometer data and RFID readings and contains full video and audio. It is our intent to release as much of this dataset as possible without violating privacy. Researchers interested in using this dataset should contact the authors.

3.2   Participants and Data Collection

A major goal of our experiment was to analyze behavioral data that was as natural as possible. We recruited our participants from a pool of individuals who had responded to advertisements for a study on how to make technology easier to use in the home. The participants were a married couple: a woman, age 31, working in the publishing industry, and a man, age 29, a high school science teacher. Although they both worked in science-related fields, they did not have advanced knowledge of computer science or sensor technology.

The participants were encouraged to maintain as normal a routine as possible. They went to work, had visitors over, cooked meals, and worked on projects and leisure activities according to their own preferences. They brought objects such as small appliances, clothing, bedding, boxes of books and audio tapes, and food from their own home when they moved in. Although they were living away from home, the relatively long duration of the experiment allowed the residents to acclimate to the apartment.

Both participants were interviewed together after the study about the experience of living in the home; the interview was audio recorded and transcribed. Identity-masked interview transcripts are available from the authors. The post study interviews with these and other participants who have lived in the facility indicate that after a few days the sensors do not impact most of the residents' everyday behavior. For example, the male subject reported that, "We weren't as conscious as I thought we would be, it was actually kind of natural being here ... I didn't notice some things as much as I thought I would, like the cameras." The female felt similarly stating, "I wasn't bothered by it, really at all, I thought I might get weirded out every once in a while, but there were very few times where I was totally tired of being in the project, and I felt pretty comfortable here." The participants were asked to wear sensors, which obviously impacted behavior, but study of the video suggests that the activities that our team was interested in, such as eating, hygiene and grooming, are performed in a natural way. Additional institutional review board procedures and options for deletion of sensitive data may have also helped the participants to feel comfortable in the sensorized environment. Over a ten week period, data was collected for several experiments in addition to this one.

3.3   Data Annotation

At the conclusion of the experiment, an anthropology student unaffiliated with the investigative team was hired to perform annotation. A custom tool was used to annotate the data using the audio and video record. The annotator averaged about 1.5 hours of real-time annotated for each hour of effort. Within our financial constraints, 104 hours of data could be annotated.

Since only the male was wearing the RFID bracelet, only his activities were annotated, and we chose data from a series of days where he was in the instrumented home for the longest periods of time. Data was used from 15 days in total. These days consist of 4 days preceding and 11 days following a 10 day vacation in the middle of the experiment. The first day begins after the couple had been living in the home for 3 weeks, hopefully allowing them time to acclimatize to the environment.

A detailed activity ontology was used for labeling and is available from the authors on request. The activity information is quite fine-grained. For example, activities include "sweeping", "folding laundry" and "brushing teeth". The annotator was given instructions to make reasonable judgments about the start and end times of the activities. In some cases, "foreground" and "background" activities were labeled. For example, "actively watching tv" occurred when the subject appeared to be paying attention, while "watching tv in background" occurred when the TV was on but was only being selectively attended to. The annotator was extremely precise, for instance labeling a "misc. hygiene" activity each time the male subject wiped his face with a napkin during eating. While spot checking the annotator's work, no errors have been found.

3.4   Limitations

Our data collection process has several limitations, some mentioned above that we reiterate here. The instrumented home was not the participants' real home, and although the experiment was much longer than most in prior work, ideally a longer time-frame would be observed and annotated. As mentioned shortly, our dataset is missing some activities and has only limited data on others. Due to the tedious and therefore costly nature of annotation, our results use a 104 hour subset of the collected data. The full bathroom, powder room, and part of the bedroom were not observable by the annotator, so many activities of potential interest related to sleep, personal hygiene, and grooming are not labeled. Finally, the subjects were participating in other experiments that may have made them somewhat more conscious of the sensors, because, for instance, they were wearing sensors on their bodies. Nevertheless, in comparison with data collection methods and lengths of observation time reported in prior work, the data we collected may be more natural and, as will become apparent, may be more challenging to analyze.

4   Characterization of Data Collected

In this section, we present some initial statistics of our dataset. Unless otherwise stated, this and all subsequent sections will refer only to the 104 hours of data that has been annotated.

4.1   Activity Frequency and Length

We first examined which activities were most common by time and by number. Our ontology contains 98 different activities which cover most aspects of home life. In our dataset, we only have examples of 43 of these. There were no annotations for many of the cleaning, laundry, cooking or yard-work tasks. These tasks were either not performed, or were performed by the subject's spouse whose activities were not annotated because she did not wear an RFID bracelet.

Widely varying amounts of data were collected for each activity. Table 1 shows the amount of data collected for the 5 most and least often observed activities by cumulative time. We see that the amount of sensor data available for each activity can be severely limited by how often the activity is performed and the typical length of the activity. Additionally, we see that several of the infrequently observed activities likely take place in the bedroom or bathroom where we have limited or no video for annotations. Table 1 illustrates that even the 104 hours of data annotated in this work may be too little to build data-driven models of some activities of interest.

Table 1. Most and least often observed activities performed by the male subject

Activity	Total cumulative time (min)
using a computer	1866
listening to music or radio in the background	813
actively watching tv or movies	732
sleeping deeply	728
reading paper/book/magazine	359
preparing a snack	0.74
leaving the home	0.70
making the bed	0.56
washing hands	0.40
drying dishes	0.10

4.2   Statistics of Activities Studied

For the remainder of this paper we will focus on activities or groupings of activities for which we have at least 10 minutes of data. We studied a range of activities that may be useful input to a home health monitoring system. In some cases, this meant defining the activity at a higher level of our ontology. Table 2 lists various statistics of the activities studied. This table highlights the detail of our annotations. For example, there are 197 instances of the "eating" activity. This does not mean the subjects had 197 meals. Rather, there were 197 bouts of eating or drinking instances.

Table 2. Mean, variance, total time and number of instances of the activities studied with sub-activities in italics if applicable. Time units are in minutes unless otherwise noted. The number of instances of sub-activities is shown in parentheses.

Activity	Mean Time	Var Time	Total Time	Number Instances
actively watching tv or movies	33.29	2613	732	22
dishwashing	23s	820s^2	11	30
-putting away dishes (0), loading the dishwasher (1),				
hand washing or rinsing dishes (28), drying dishes (1),				
dishwasher on in the background (0), soaking dishes (0),				
unloading the dishwasher (0), dishwashing misc (0).				
eating	1.58	25	311	197
- eating a meal (11), eating a snack (35) , drinking (151).				
grooming	1.05	4.4	50	48
- drying hair (0), brushing hair (0), shaving (0),				
getting undressed (25), applying makeup (0), putting up				
clothes (0), getting dressed (23), grooming misc (0).				
hygiene	3.05	36	116	38
-brushing teeth (2), washing hands (2), flossing (0),				
washing face (0), bathing or showering (2), toileting (1),				
hygiene misc (31).				
meal preparation	27s	2954s^2	59	132
- cooking or warming food on microwave (3),				
retrieving ingredients/cookware (39), measuring (0),				
chopping/slicing/grating food (1), preparing a drink (54),				
preparing a snack (4), preparing a meal (2),cooking				
or warming food on stove-top (0), preparing a meal in				
background (0), cooking or warming food on oven (0)				
mixing/stirring food (10), combining/adding (15),				
washing ingredients (0), meal preparation misc (4).				
reading book/paper/magazine	14.36	443	359	25
using a computer	19.24	1068	1866	97
using a phone	2.02	23	204	101

4.3 Complex Behavior

Video footage reveals various complexities in the way activities are performed. Here we describe an episode of the "hand washing or rinsing dishes". We originally watched this sequence to investigate the performance of the RFID reader so the description contains a number of references to tag firings.

The male starts in the office using the computer for a few minutes and apparently wants a drink. The RFID tag under the keyboard fires. The male turns out the light and goes to the kitchen, where he opens the cup cabinet with his right hand (wearing bracelet), but reaches in with the left hand. The tags under the shelves usually fire when the bracelet reaches in, but the participant used the "wrong" hand to grab his cup. Cups don't have tags because of the microwave. He puts the cup on counter and opens the fridge with his right hand. No tags are on the front of the fridge because they did not work due to the metal surface. He reaches in with his right hand and a tag on one of the shelves fires. He grabs a bottle, which is untagged because it was recently purchased, and puts it on counter next to the cup. He leaves the fridge door open and walks out of kitchen into the hallway to speak to his spouse. He comes back and closes the fridge with his right hand and then walks to the living room to get a key chain that has a bottle opener on it. He reaches down to the table with his right hand, at which time a tag for another object on the table might have fired if he were just centimeters closer. He returns to the kitchen, opens the bottle and pours a glass. He takes the bottle to the untagged metal sink and rinses several times holding the bottle in his right hand, without using the tagged soap. He takes a drink and then puts the glass down and carries the bottle down the hall to the recycling area. A tag could fire at the recycle bin, but the area is large and even with 2 tags nearby, his hand does not get sufficiently close. He walks back to the living room and starts cleaning up, leaving the full cup in the kitchen. His spouse is in the apartment activating other sensors the entire time.

The example behavior above is not atypical, and it only takes a few minutes of watching any sequence of the video to encounter examples of behavior that either defy common assumptions about how people will behave or create difficult activity labeling and detection challenges. Examples include eating dinner in several different locations in the home that are not the dining room table, brushing teeth while walking all around the home, eating and snacking for extended lengths of time in front of the television with no clear start and end time, and multiple behaviors that are very similar in how they appear to the sensor stream (e.g. eating vs. watching TV).

These examples and others we have identified highlight several complexities in our dataset that may not be present in datasets collected in less natural conditions: interruptions (e.g. talking to spouse while fridge is open), task abandonment (e.g. leaving the cup on the counter while going to do another task), lack of location specificity for many activities (e.g. eating dinner at the office computer), and interleaved multi-tasking and overlapping multi-tasking (e.g. snacking, doing laundry, watching TV and talking at the same time).

Also common is having two people in the same space, both doing independent activities but also cooperating on activities. Finally, although the RFID sensors that fire are person-specific, the rest of the sensors in the unit fire due to the actions of either of the participants, creating a data analysis challenge. We will return to such challenges as we discuss our results.

5   Activity Classification

Having made some initial observations about the dataset, we now investigate how well we can recognize a set of common activities. We follow standard activity classification procedure and convert the data to a series of feature vectors, each covering a fixed period of time. We then conduct a series of "activity" vs. "the rest of the world" experiments. We use binary classifiers for each activity rather than considering all activities together because very few of the activities are mutually exclusive. We report results for the three main sensor categories studied: RFID, "built-in", which covers all the wired sensors, and "motion", which covers the on-body and on-object accelerometers and the infra-red sensors.

5.1   Data Preparation

We converted the sensor data to a series of vectors formed by concatenating all of the data observed in 30s windows overlapped by 15s. All but three of the activities studied have average durations on the order of a minute.

Different types of sensors require different processing to convert them to features. We assigned one component of the feature vector to each sensor input. For all sensor types, if readings were observed during the time window, we stored the average value. If no readings were observed, for the RFID and motion sensors, we set the sensor value to zero. For the remainder of sensors such as continuous valued sensors (e.g., current flow, water flow) and switches with an on/off state (wired switches in cabinets), if a sensor value was not seen in the current window we used the value from the previous window, assuming that the state of the sensor had not changed. The three sensor types, built-in, motion and RFID, generated 206, 281 and 435 component feature vectors respectively. Experiments involving all sensor types use 926-dimensional feature vectors.

5.2   Label Assignment

We assigned each feature vector to Class 0 or Class 1 according to whether the activity of interest occurred at any time during the 30s window covered. We thus took a very conservative approach to annotation. For activities with typical durations of less than 30s, we expect some error in the class assignments.

5.3   Classification Results

We experimented with two types of static classifiers, naive Bayes and C4.5 decision trees, using the implementations in the WEKA [16] software package. The decision tree classifiers had consistently superior performance so we restrict our discussion to these in the interest of space. Decision trees have the added advantage of relative transparency of which sensors inputs contribute to classification.

We conducted "leave one day out" cross validation-experiments for each activity using the various input sensor categories. Using folds of one full day of data was chosen as the best method for generating reasonably independent test data that would best reflect a classifier's real world performance. In the discussion section, we address how more simplistic sampling methods for choosing folds can lead to over-fitting. In our method, we designate one day's worth of data as testing and train on data from all the other days in our dataset. Because the training sets were highly unbalanced for many activities, we balanced them by uniformly sampling features from Class 0 (i.e. times when the activity was not being performed) to match the number of features in Class 1. We did not balance the test sets.

Our figure of merit was area under the ROC curve for each cross validation experiment averaged over all the folds. This was chosen as the best overall figure of merit because it gives a measure of goodness at all possible thresholds of a binary classifier and is invariant to class skew. An ROC curve plots the true positive rate vs. the false positive rate. Figure 2 (a) shows an ideal classifier with area 1.0, where every "operating point" on the curve gives only true positives and no false positives. Figure 2 (b) shows a worthless classifier with area 0.5. This is comparable to pure chance where every operating point gives an equal number of false positives for every true positive. A good rule of thumb states that any classifier with ROC area less than 0.7 is poor while any classifier with ROC area greater than 0.9 is excellent (e.g. [17]). Note though that ROC area is an overall measure of goodness. An application can choose to operate at any point on the curve. For example, if false positives are more costly than false negatives, an operating point toward the left hand side would be chosen.

For each activity, we calculated the ROC area over each of the cross-validation tests and averaged the result. Figure 2 (c) shows the curves for classifying the "eating" activity using all sensors. The average curve is shown in bold. This experiment yielded poor performance with an average ROC area of 0.587. Conversely, Figure 2 (d) shows the curves for classifying the activity "dishwashing" using only motion sensors. In this case the average classifier resembles the ideal and has an ROC area of 0.937. Space limitations preclude showing the many ROC curves and detailed analysis generated by all the classifiers studied. We therefore instead report the area under each ROC curve averaged over all the folds/days for each experiment. Figure 3 shows results for the activities and sensor input subsets studied.

A few trends stand out. First, for every activity except "actively watching tv" and "reading," motion-based sensors, which comprise on-object and on-body accelerometers and infra-red sensors, are the best sensor category. In fact, except for "actively watching tv", motion sensors outperform the classifier that results from combining all sensors. This indicates that we have insufficient data to learn how the other sensors contribute to detecting most activities. Thus in most

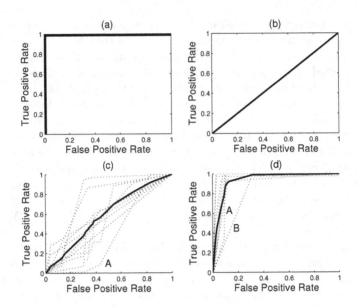

Fig. 2. ROC curves for different classifiers: a) ideal b) worthless and each cross-validation for c) "eating" using all sensors and d) "dishwashing" using only motion-based sensors with the average curve in bold. Labeled curves are discussed in the text.

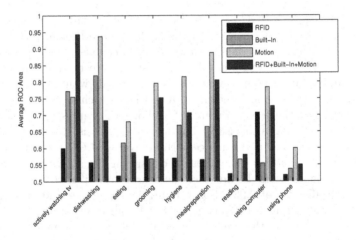

Fig. 3. "Leave one day out" cross validation results for decision tree classifiers for various sensor categories: RFID, built-in (wired switches, current flow etc), motion (object motion, on-body accelerometers and infra-red) and all sensors.

cases, the other sensors add little to motion sensors for this dataset. When motion sensors are outperformed by any other kind of sensor, it is not by a great deal. Except for "reading" and "using phone", motion sensors yield ROC areas greater than 0.7; they are therefore not just better performers than the other

other sensors, but at least moderately good performers according to the rule of thumb mentioned above. For the "dishwashing" activity, the performance is excellent. Given the set of sensors we used and the activities we observed, motion-based sensors appear to be the most promising. We discuss the reasons for this in Section 6.1.

Second, RFID has less than acceptable performance on every activity except "using computer". This can be explained by data sparsity. Examination of the data collected showed that there were relatively few RFID firings. On average, a typical five minute time slice contained less than 1 tag firing. Fewer than 10% of all episodes yielded *any* RFID data. We discuss the reasons for this in Section 6.2.

Third, although built-in sensors perform better than RFID sensors, for the most part they fail our 0.7 rule of thumb. This is likely because many of the wired sensors, such as cabinet doors, are not tied to specific objects but rather groups of objects.

6   Discussion

To determine the causes of success and failure of our experiments, for many outlier cases, we watched the video ourselves. Our analysis highlighted a number of considerations that we discuss below.

6.1   Why Motion-Based Sensors Perform Well

Figure 4 shows the performance of the different kinds of motion-based sensors. It is clear that the infra-red detectors have the best performance for almost every activity. The only exceptions are "eating", where on-body accelerometers achieve acceptable performance, and "reading" and "using phone" for which no motion-based sensor, or indeed any sensor, succeeds.

Looking closer at our list of activities, it is clear why the infra-red sensors are so successful; There is a one-to-one mapping between activities we detect acceptably using infra-red sensors and the location where they are almost always performed in the house: "watching tv" happens in the couch area, "dishwashing" in front of the sink, "grooming" in the bed room, "hygiene" in the bathroom, "meal preparation" in the kitchen, but not in front of the sink, and "using computer" in the study. Conversely, the three activities with no fixed location, "eating", "reading" and "using phone" fare poorly with motion sensors.

Overall, it seems that if the performance of activities is strongly correlated with locations in the home and since these locations do not overlap, a few infra-red sensors at these locations can yield excellent performance.

6.2   Why RFID Performs Poorly

The primary reason RFID proved to be a poor sensor was that for most activities, it detected very few objects being touched. For example, during the "eating and meal preparation" activity, only 26 distinct tags were ever observed to fire in

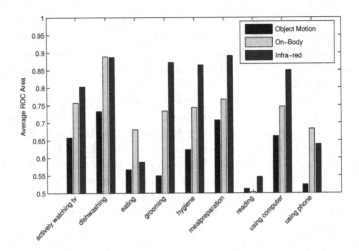

Fig. 4. 'Leave one day out' cross validation results for decision tree classifiers for the different kinds of motion sensors

the kitchen despite 205 tags being installed there. For the "hygiene" activity, only 7 distinct tags of the 50 installed in the bathroom and powder room were ever observed to fire. This lack of tag firing means that even using a temporal classifier ([11]) does not improve the results since there is simply too little data for training.

In order to understand why the bracelet detected so few tags, we identified 10 activity episodes where we expected objects to be used, but did not see any tag firings. These spot-checked activities checked included "hand washing or rinsing dishes", "hygiene miscellaneous" and "using phone". In each case, we examined video of the episodes. An example of our notes was described in Section 4.3.

Our findings from the video may be summarized as follows:

1. Some activities,(e.g., sleeping), do not involve interactions with objects
2. Many activities (e.g., dishwashing) involve objects that could not be tagged because of the object is metallic or went in the microwave.
3. Some activities involve objects that were too small to tag, and
4. Some activities involved tagged objects that were missed because the bracelet was on the opposite hand.
5. For certain activities (e.g., toileting aspects of hygiene), the bracelet was removed, according to followup interviews.

In this work we tagged as many objects as we could, doing our best to place tags so they would fire during normal object use but not impede normal usage of a device or be too visibly noticeable. Based on our results, however, that strategy was insufficient. Instead, it may be more useful to ensure that a few specific objects of interest have one or more tags that will definitely fire under normal use. Objects may require either multiple tags, highly visible tags, or even changes to the objects themselves (e.g., metal to plastic) to overcome some of the limitations of RFID technology. In practice, it may be useful to observe subjects performing activities before attaching RFID tags. Improving bracelet range and requiring bracelets on both arms may also improve RFID performance.

6.3   Cross-Validation and Over-Fitting

Initially, we conducted a series of 10-fold cross validation tests in which for each fold, we constructed the testing and training sets by assigning every 10th positive and negative data point to the positive and negative test sets respectively. Since little variability is seen across the adjacent time slices, we observed good results. Indeed, the average ROC area for all sensor types was close to or above 0.9 except for RFID which again performed poorly due to data sparsity. However, analysis of the "excellent" decision trees learned showed that they were over-fitted, evidenced by deep trees with little overlap between the sensors used for decisions between folds. This highlights an important issue to consider when building statistical models for home activities. Data is often collected in one session, but lack of variability in the way activities are performed and the lack of major changes in the environment may promote algorithm over-fitting, locking on to possibly spurious features that just happened not to change much. As more sensors are used, the chance of modeling a sporadic correlation may increase. For instance, if a sensor is on a kitchen appliance that happens to be near another sensorized appliance, firings from both appliances might be built into a model. But the minute one appliance is moved that correlation will no longer exist and the model will fail. We believe we have reduced this problem by using one day cross-validation and that these results are a more robust estimate of real world performance.

6.4   Performance vs. the Marginal Model

To illustrate the benefits of our classifiers over more naive schemes, we compared one of our classifiers to the marginal model classifier that takes maximum advantage of the unbalanced set. Specifically we chose the example of dishwashing where a classifier that always chose "not dishwashing" would be correct nearly 100% of the time (0.003% error). Table 3 compares this classifier to our trained "dishwashing"classifier for day "9-11-2006," shown as curve A in Figure 2(d). We see that at the (0,0) operating point, the trained classifier has the same accuracy. However this is a useless operating point since no dishwashing events are ever reported. By operating at 90% accuracy our model is able to report all instances of dishwashing with only 10% false positives.

6.5   Other Considerations

In addition to the lessons learned about the various sensor types, our experiments highlighted the following points that are of interest to anybody designing or experimenting with home activity recognition systems.

Table 3. Performance of a "dishwashing" classifier trained on motion-based sensor data vs. the marginal model that always chooses "not dishwashing"

Classifier	True Positive Rate	False Positive Rate	Accuracy
Trained	1.00	1.00	0.00
	1.00	0.90	0.11
	1.00	0.10	0.90
	0.33	0.09	0.91
	0.00	0.00	1.00
Marginal	0.00	0.00	1.00

Lack of Data. Despite annotation of 104 hours of the male's activity, we experienced two types of lack of data. The first is a lack of sufficient number of observed examples of specific activities to use for training. We have less than a minute's worth of data for activities such as "drying dishes" and "making the bed" which is likely unreasonable for training feature vectors of length $O(100)$ or $O(1000)$, given the observed variability in the way that some activities are performed. The second type of lack of data is the number of sensors of particular types that fired within each bout of activity. The RFID example in Section 6.2 highlights this problem; despite a very high density of RFID tags, a sufficient number of tags was not detected for most activities.

Data at Transitions. A related problem to lack of sensor data within a bout is that for some activities and types of sensors, sensor firings may cluster at the beginning and end of the activity, with a sparse or non-existent signal throughout the activity itself. An example is eating, when RFID tags or object motion detectors may fire during food preparation, but then once the participants sit down on the couch to eat and watch television, no more eating-related sensors may fire until they go back to the kitchen to wash dishes. Those that might fire (e.g., an RFID sensor on a remote control) may only indicate another activity, such as television watching.

Multiple Subjects and Incomplete Annotations. The presence of a second subject whose actions were not annotated in our ground truth was a definite source of error. For example, we attempted to train a "cooking or warming food on microwave" classifier using only the 5 sensors directly related to the microwave (outlet current, object motion sensor on the microwave etc) and tested it against our ground truth. Contrary to common sense, the results showed that this classifier performed poorly. This is due to the fact that the times when the female used the microwave were not marked as true positives. Similarly, when we examined video to understand why classifier labeled B in Figure 2(d) performed relatively poorly, we saw that the this was due to the female subject using the sink to wash objects. Although we had originally intended to conduct experiments using only RFID data and thought that only the male's activities would be of interest, this assumption failed as soon as we took all sensors into account. The main reason the results were reasonable for many activities is that often the couple did things together in the same location.

Annotating Events with Privacy Concerns. Although we had the luxury of full video and audio for annotating purposes in much of the instrumented home, these facilities were limited for privacy reasons in the bedroom and bathroom. Unfortunately though, many health-related activities take place in these rooms. Our annotator had only the audio to guide her here, so she was unable to annotate many of these activities. For example, 31 of the 38 observed "hygiene" activities are labeled "hygiene misc".

Behavioral Factors. We cannot stress enough that this experiment highlighted that the way people behave when they live somewhere for a while is likely very different from the way they might simulate an activity in the lab or self-report how they perform it. We saw many examples of interrupted activities and multitasking in our dataset. Eating, in particular, was performed in several places and in a variety of ways but usually not at the dining room table. For example, we examined the video for the worst eating classifier, labeled A in Figure 2(c). On this day, "eating" consisted of the subjects "grazing" on food for several hours in front of the television. Differentiating "eating" from "non-eating" in this scenario is difficult because the sensor firings are practically identical for both classes.

7 Conclusions

In this paper, we described experiments performed on 104 hours of annotated activity data collected from a person living in a home instrumented with over 900 sensor inputs. These included built-in wired sensors, motion-detection sensors and RFID tags. The subject wore an RFID reader in a bracelet form factor. Neither the subject nor the annotator were affiliated with the authors.

We found that 10 infra-red motion detectors outperformed the other sensors on many of the activities studied, especially those which were typically performed in the same location. However, several activities, in particular "eating" and "reading" were difficult to detect and will likely require the use of additional sensors and improved algorithms We may have found different results had we had sufficient data to analyze fine-grained activities.

Although some of our classifiers may be sufficiently good for development of some ubiquitous computing applications, on the whole we found this dataset to present a challenge for automatic activity recognition. Some of the problems that we have characterized may not have been as evident in prior work when data was collected under more controlled conditions. This work highlights the importance of studying real-world behavior in home settings when proposing and evaluating home-based activity recognition algorithms.

References

1. Munguia Tapia, E., Intille, S.S., Lopez, L., Larson, K.: The design of a portable kit of wireless sensors for naturalistic data collection. In: Fishkin, K.P., Schiele, B., Nixon, P., Quigley, A. (eds.) PERVASIVE 2006. LNCS, vol. 3968, pp. 117–134. Springer, Heidelberg (2006)
2. Munguia Tapia, E., Intille, S., Larson, K.: Activity recognition in the home using simple and ubiquitous sensors. In: Ferscha, A., Mattern, F. (eds.) PERVASIVE 2004. LNCS, vol. 3001, pp. 158–175. Springer, Heidelberg (2004)
3. Philipose, M., Smith, J.R., Jiang, B., Mamishev, A., Roy, S., Sundara-Rajan, K.: Battery-free wireless identification and sensing. IEEE Pervasive Computing 4(1), 37–45 (2005)
4. Lester, J., Choudhury, T., Kern, N., Borriello, G., Hannaford, B.: A hybrid discriminative/generative approach for modeling human activities. In: IJCAI, pp. 766–772 (2005)
5. Bao, L., Intille, S.S.: Activity recognition in the home setting using simple and ubiquitous sensors. In: Ferscha, A., Mattern, F. (eds.) PERVASIVE 2004. LNCS, vol. 3001, pp. 1–17. Springer, Heidelberg (2004)
6. Wilson, D.H., Atkeson, C.G.: Simultaneous tracking and activity recognition (STAR) using many anonymous, binary sensors. In: Gellersen, H.-W., Want, R., Schmidt, A. (eds.) PERVASIVE 2005. LNCS, vol. 3468, pp. 62–79. Springer, Heidelberg (2005)
7. Wang, S., Pentney, W., Popescu, A.-M., Choudhury, T., Philipose, M.: Common sense joint training of human activity recognizers. In: Proceedings of IJCAI 2007 (2007)
8. Fishkin, K.P., Philipose, M., Rea, A.D.: Hands-On RFID: Wireless wearables for detecting use of objects. In: ISWC, pp. 38–43 (2005)
9. Intille, S.S., Larson, K., Munguia Tapia, E., Beaudin, J.S., Kaushik, P., Nawyn, J., Rockinson, R.: Using a live-in laboratory for ubiquitous computing research. In: Fishkin, K.P., Schiele, B., Nixon, P., Quigley, A. (eds.) PERVASIVE 2006. LNCS, vol. 3968, pp. 349–365. Springer, Heidelberg (2006)
10. Fogarty, J., Au, C., Hudson, S.E.: Sensing from the basement: a feasibility study of unobtrusive and low-cost home activity recognition. In: UIST, pp. 91–100 (2006)
11. Patterson, D., Fox, D., Kautz, H., Philipose, M.: Fine-Grained Activity Recognition by Aggregating Abstract Object Usage. In: ISWC (2005)
12. Placelab Data website. Available: architecture.mit.edu/house_n/data/PlaceLab/PlaceLab.htm
13. Quiet care systems. Available: www.quietcaresystems.com
14. E-Neighbor system from Healthsense. Available: www.healthsense.com
15. i-pot from Zojirushi Corporation. Available: www.mimamori.net
16. Witten, I., Frank, E.: Data Mining: Practical machine learning tools and techniques. Morgan Kaufmann, San Francisco (2005)
17. Streiner, D.L., Cairney, J.: What's under the ROC? An introduction to receiver operating characteristic curves. Canadian Journal of Psychiatry 52(2) (2007)

Cooperative Augmentation of Smart Objects with Projector-Camera Systems

David Molyneaux[1], Hans Gellersen[1], Gerd Kortuem[1], and Bernt Schiele[2]

[1] Computing Department, Lancaster University, England
{d.molyneaux,hwg,kortuem}@comp.lancs.ac.uk
[2] Computer Science Department, Darmstadt University of Technology
schiele@informatik.tu-darmstadt.de

Abstract. In this paper we present a new approach for cooperation between mobile smart objects and projector-camera systems to enable augmentation of the surface of objects with interactive projected displays. We investigate how a smart object's capability for self description and sensing can be used in cooperation with the vision capability of projector-camera systems to help locate, track and display information onto object surfaces in an unconstrained environment. Finally, we develop a framework that can be applied to distributed projector-camera systems, cope with varying levels of description knowledge and different sensors embedded in an object.

Keywords: Cooperative Augmentation, Smart Objects, Projector-Camera Systems.

1 Introduction

The interest in embedding sensing, communication and computation in everyday physical artefacts is growing. Such smart objects are expected to bridge the gap between the physical and digital world, and become part of out lives in economically important areas such as retail, supply chain or asset management [29,30,31] and safety critical situations in work places [10]. A challenge for the design of such smart objects is to preserve their original appearance, purpose and function, thus exploiting natural interaction and a user's familiarity with the object [12]. Consequently adding output capability to objects is difficult, as embedding displays would fundamentally change an objects appearance. Mobile objects are also typically constrained in terms of power, weight and space availability. However, the recent availability of small, cheap and bright video projectors makes them practical for augmenting objects with non-invasive displays. By adding a camera and using computer vision techniques, a projector system can also dynamically detect and track objects [2,4], correct for object surface geometry [2,4,16,18], varying surface colour and texture [19] and allow the user to interact directly with the projected image [1,30].

We can imagine an unconstrained environment in the future containing many smart objects. In this environment new objects can arrive, move around or be manipulated by users and leave. If we assume projector-camera systems are installed ubiquitously in this environment offering a display service, the smart objects can request use of the

J. Krumm et al. (Eds.): UbiComp 2007, LNCS 4717, pp. 501–518, 2007.

projection capability to obtain a display on its surface and solve its output problem. To realise this vision we have to address the two challenges of how the object can make use of the projector-camera system capability to be a). Located and tracked, and b). Projected on so the display is undistorted and visible to the user.

In this paper we investigate a new approach to these challenges by using spontaneous cooperation between the smart object and projector-camera system. In particular, we investigate how capabilities of the smart object (such as knowledge storage and sensing) can assist projector-camera systems in the object detection, tracking and projection tasks.

In cooperative augmentation there is a division of labour between the projector-camera system and smart object as follows:

- The objects themselves are self-describing. They carry information about themselves (such as knowledge of their appearance) that is vital to the detection process. We call this information the Object Model.
- The projector-camera system provides a display service that can be used by any smart object in the vicinity. The projector-camera system display service is generic, as it holds no knowledge about any of the objects. Consequently, it could be used by any type of smart object, for example, smart cups [9], smart chemical containers [10] or smart tables [11].
- The Object Model is transmitted to the projector-camera system whenever the object enters proximity of the projector-camera system.

The projector-camera system uses the Object Model to dynamically tailor its services to the object. In contrast to traditional vision-based detection approaches where all object knowledge is held in the detection system, no user intervention is required to configure the detection and projection system for new objects. Objects bring all information with them so system configuration happens automatically in response to the Object Model. The object detection task is also made simpler and faster as the projector-camera system need not maintain and search a large database of object information. With the registration process the cooperative augmentation system always knows which smart objects exist in the environment.

The cooperative augmentation approach is flexible as the dynamic configuration process caters for varying amounts of knowledge stored in the object. The projector-camera system can also use its camera in a learning process to extract more appearance knowledge about the object over time and re-embed it within the object.

The main contribution of the cooperative augmentation approach is a flexible framework to allow smart objects to spontaneously use projection capability in an environment for output. Our approach can locate and track mobile objects in the environment, determine suitable areas for projection and finally align the projection with the object's surfaces so it appears undistorted, as shown in Figure 1.

In section 2 we compare our approach to related work. Section 3 follows with an analysis of the cooperative augmentation process in detail, with reference to a real world example. Sections 4 and 5 explain the visual detection process and projection process in more detail. Section 6 validates our concept using an example implementation of the cooperative augmentation concept. Finally, section 7 discusses the concept evaluation and lessons learned.

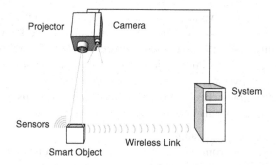

Fig. 1. Cooperative Augmentation of Smart Objects with Projector-Camera Systems

2 Related Work

The question of how to augment mobile objects with projected displays was investigated by Bandyopadhyay et al. in [1]. Objects with planar surfaces were equipped with a magnetic and infra-red tracking system. Static projectors were used to augment the objects in real-time. However, this work suffered from two key problems of latency and limited working volume due to the tracking systems used. Our approach uses a projector-camera system with a vision-based object detection system. This allows augmentation of objects anywhere within the field of view of the system at camera frame-rates, without relying on separate tracking hardware. The use of a camera also allows direct interaction with the projection, for example, by visual detection and tracking of the user's fingertips as described by Kjeldsen et al. in [30].

Although there is an enormous body of work on detection and location of mobile non-smart objects using a camera, there is little work which uses the capabilities of smart objects themselves. For example, vision-based detection and tracking approaches have been taken by Ehnes et al. in [2], using AR Toolkit fiducial markers [3] to track and project on mobile planar surfaces. Borkowski et al. also demonstrate a mobile projected interactive display screen object tracked by its black border in [4]. However, both these systems rely on modifying or engineering the external appearance of a non-smart object to enable detection. In contrast, our approach uses features of the natural appearance of a smart object for detection.

The sensing capabilities of smart objects were used by Raskar et al. in [7] to detect the location and orientation of static smart objects relative to a handheld projector. Here embedded light sensors detected the projection of gray codes (which encode a spatial location by changes in brightness over time) onto the object's surface to directly locate the object in the projector's frame of reference. Projection onto mobile planar smart objects was addressed using the same techniques by Summet and Sukthankar in [6] and Lee et al. in [5] where a 12Hz location update rate was achieved. For these techniques a minimum of one un-occluded light sensor is required to be in the view of the projector to enable detection. 3D location and orientation of an object can be calculated from a static projector location with three light sensors in view of the projector, however, 3D or self-occluding objects require many more light sensors to guarantee correct pose calculation. For example, cubical objects require at least 3 sensors per face (18 total) to detect all poses.

In contrast, our cooperative augmentation approach does not require a minimum number of light sensors to operate. Instead, we use appearance knowledge stored in the object to visually detect the object with algorithms that offer robustness to partial occlusion. Movement sensor information is used to further constrain the detection task and distinguish between objects with similar appearances.

There exist many implementations of projector-camera systems – for example, we can decompose existing systems into three categories with respect to display mobility:

1. Static projector-camera systems
2. Steerable projection from static system with pan and tilt hardware
3. Mobile, handheld and wearable projector-camera systems

All types of projector-camera system have been used for augmenting objects with projection, however, static [1], mobile, handheld [7] or wearable [15] projector-camera systems can only opportunistically detect and project on objects passing through the field of view of the projector and camera.

In contrast, projector-camera systems in the second category with computer controlled steerable mirrors or pan and tilt platforms [16][2][4][17] allow a much larger system field of view and the ability to track objects moving in the environment.

Levas et al. first presented a framework for steerable projector-camera systems to project onto objects and surfaces in their Everywhere Display framework [8]. However, although supporting a distributed architecture, this framework was limited to creating displays on static surfaces in locations pre-calibrated by the user. Our cooperative augmentation approach enables spontaneous displays on the surfaces of mobile smart objects without user intervention or calibration.

3   Cooperative Augmentation

This section expands the concept behind cooperative augmentation by explaining the three areas of cooperative augmentation:

1. The Object Model representation of the smart object.
2. The projector-camera system.
3. The cooperative augmentation process.

3.1   Object Model

The Object Model is a description of the object and its capabilities, allowing the projection system to dynamically configure its detection and projection services for each object at runtime. We assume the Object Model knowledge is embedded within the object during manufacture.

The model consists of five components:

1. Unique Object Identifier
   This allows an object to be uniquely identified on the network as a source and recipient of event messages and data streams.

2. Appearance Knowledge

This knowledge describes the appearance of the smart object. The description is specific information extracted by computational methods from camera images of the object. For example, colour histograms, an image of the object itself, or locations of features detected on the object.

3. 3D Model

A 3D model of the object is required in VRML representation to allow the projector-camera system to compute the object's pose.

4. Sensor Knowledge

The sensor model is a description of the data delivered by the object's sensors. The data type is classified into three groups with regard to the originating sensor: movement sensor data, light sensor data and others. The data is further classified into streaming or event-based, depending on the way sensor data is output from the smart object. The model contains associated sensor resolutions, and sensor range information to allow the projector-camera system to interpret sensor events.

5. Location and Orientation of the Object

When an object enters an environment, it does not know its location and orientation. The projector-camera system provides this information on detection of the object to complete the Object Model.

3.2 Projector-Camera Systems

A projector-camera system consists of a co-located projector and camera. We assume they are mounted so the respective projection and viewing frustums overlap, allowing objects detected by the camera system to be projected on by the projector.

In this work we use an intelligent steerable projector-camera system, composed of a computer-controlled pan and tilt platform on which the projector and camera are mounted. This platform is ceiling mounted for a greater view of the environment and can rotate the projector-camera system hardware in two dimensions – horizontal (pan) and vertical (tilt) about the centre of projection.

The projector-camera system has six main capabilities:

1. To provide a service allowing smart objects to register for detection and projection.
2. To search an environment for smart objects by automatically rotating the pan and tilt platform.
3. To detect smart objects in the camera images and calculate their location and orientation based on the knowledge and sensing embedded in the object, as explained in section 3.3.
4. To track detected objects by automatically rotating the pan and tilt platform to centre the detected object.
5. To project an image onto an object in an area specified by the smart object, or choose the area most visible to the projector. This image is geometry corrected so that the image appears to be attached to the object's surface and is undistorted.
6. To further correct an image before projection for variations in an object's surface colour and texture so that the image appears more visible.

3.3 Cooperative Augmentation Process

To illustrate the cooperative augmentation process in action, we can imagine a goods warehouse scenario, in which objects are stored for distribution. In this scenario the objects are augmented with computing, giving them knowledge of their contents and sensors allowing them to monitor themselves and the local environment to ensure integrity and to maintain the authenticity of the goods [20]. Such sensing allows them to detect rough handling based on sensed movement and automatically report their position and status wirelessly for goods tracking and inventory purposes.

We can decompose the cooperative augmentation of an object such as a chemical container into five steps:

1. Registration

As the container enters the warehouse it detects the presence of a location and projection service through a service discovery mechanism. The object sends a message to the projector-camera system requesting registration for the projection service to display messages. On receipt of the registration request, the projector-camera system requests the Object Model from the smart object.

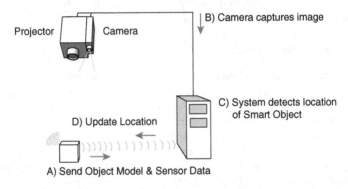

Fig. 2. Detection Sequence Diagram

2. Detection

Following registration, the object begins streaming sensor data to the projector-camera system, as shown in Figure 2 (A). This data is used in combination with the Object Model to constrain the visual detection process and generate location and orientation hypotheses (B and C). When an object is located with sufficient accuracy, the 3D location and orientation hypothesis is returned to the smart object (D). This process is explained in more detail in section 4.

3. Projection

When an object has knowledge of its location and orientation it can request a projection onto its surfaces. For example, if it detects it has been dropped, it can request a message is projected onto it requesting employees visually inspect it for damage. This projection request message contains both the content to project and location description of where on the object to project the content, as shown in

Figure 3 (A). The projector-camera system automatically corrects the projection of the message for the object's geometry based on the 3D model stored in the Object Model and the calculated object location and orientation, so that it appears undistorted (B). The projection is also corrected for the surface colour of the object to make it more visible to the user [19]. The projector system starts displaying the corrected content on the objects surfaces immediately on receipt of the request, if the object is in view and the projector system is idle (C).

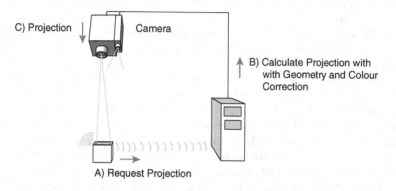

Fig. 3. Projection Sequence Diagram

4. Manipulation of Smart Object

A requested projection is active as long as the object is detected, including during movement or manipulation of the object. Consequently, smart objects can give direct feedback to the user in response to the manipulation or movement of the object by changing their projection. For example, as the projector sends location information to the object, if an employee places an object in the wrong storage area of the warehouse it could request a warning message is projected until moved to the correct location.

5. Update Appearance

If an object does not enter the environment with much appearance knowledge (see Table 1 in section 4), additional knowledge about the appearance of its surfaces is extracted once the object has been detected and its pose calculated. As part of the cooperative process this new knowledge can be re-embedded into the Object Model for faster and more robust detection on next entry to an augmented environment.

4   Visual Object Detection

The projector-camera system dynamically configures its visual object detection processing based on the type of appearance knowledge in the Object Model, and the sensors the object possesses.

Objects in the real world have appearances that vary widely, for example, in colour, texture, shape and the features that appear on their surfaces. Their appearance can also be easily changed by influences in the surrounding environment such as lighting conditions (including changes in intensity, colour and direction of lighting) or scene changes (such as partial occlusion by other objects or background changes). An object's appearance also changes with the relative location and orientation of the object to the viewer.

To cope with these changes we use four different detection algorithms:

i.) Colour Histograms

Swain and Ballard [27] first proposed the use of colour histograms to describe an object by its approximate colour distribution. Objects can be detected by matching a colour histogram from a camera image region to a histogram from a training sample of the object using histogram intersection and statistical divergence measurements such as chi-square (χ^2). Colour histograms offer a simple and fast object recognition method which has been shown to be robust to many transformations of an objects appearance, such as orientation, scale, partial occlusion and even shape. However, colour histograms are sensitive to changes in light intensity and colour.

ii.) Multidimensional Receptive Field Histograms

As many objects cannot be described by colour alone (for example, black objects), the histogram approach has been generalised by Schiele and Crowley [28] to multidimensional receptive field histograms. The histograms encode a statistical representation of the appearance of objects based on vectors of joint statistics of local neighbourhood operators such as image intensity gaussian derivatives (Dx,Dy) or gradient magnitude and the local response of the laplacian operator (Mag-Lap). Experimental results show the histograms are robust to partial occlusion of the object and are able to recognise multiple objects in cluttered scenes in real-time using the probabilistic local-appearance hashing approach proposed by Schiele and Crowley.

iii.) Shape Context

Shape detection compares the silhouette contours of an object to a pre-computed database of object appearances with the object in different poses. The database of object appearances can be calculated directly from the 3D model of the object stored in the Object Model by rendering the model in different poses and extracting the silhouette contour using the Canny edge detection algorithm. We use the Shape Context descriptor described by Belongie et al. in [29] to enable scale and rotation invariant matching of the contours.

iv.) Local Features

Local feature based detection algorithms aim to uniquely describe (and therefore detect) an object using just a few key points. To extract features, training images of an object are searched for a set of interest points (such as corners, blobs or lines) that can be repeatably detected under transformations of an objects appearance. The local image area immediately surrounding these interest points can then be used to calculate a feature vector which we assume serves to uniquely describe and identify that point. The feature descriptor can be a simple colour histogram of the local area, or as complex as the gaussian derivative histogram based SIFT algorithm, described by Lowe in [22]. Object detection now becomes a problem of matching a feature set between the training image and camera images. A comparison of different feature detection and descriptor algorithms can be found in [21].

The different detection methods are shown in Table 1, corresponding to different aspects of an objects possible appearance.

Table 1. Appearance knowledge levels and detection methods with associated processing cost

Appearance Knowledge	Detection Method	Discriminative Power	Cost in Time
Colour	Colour histogram comparison	Low	Medium
Texture	Multidimensional Receptive Field Histograms	Medium	Medium
Shape	Contour detection and Shape Context	Medium	Medium
Local Features	Interest point detection and feature descriptor comparison	High	High

These methods form a flexible layered detection process that allows an object to enter the environment with different levels of appearance knowledge. As we descend the table, the power of the detection methods to discriminate between objects with similar appearances increases, however, at the cost of increased processing time. We consider higher discriminative methods to hold more knowledge about the object.

Where an object holds more than one piece of appearance knowledge, one of two strategies can be followed. The first is using the most discriminative (least abstract) information to increase the probability of an accurate detection. The second strategy is to fuse the results of multiple detection methods to make the detection more robust. However, detection method selection is always a trade-off, as both the use of multiple methods and the more discriminative individual methods (such as local features) share the cost of increased processing requirements.

Our cooperative augmentation method can also serendipitously use any movement sensors the object possesses to constrain the detection process. Common sensors that can be used for movement detection on objects are accelerometers, ball-switches and force sensors which detect pick-up and put-down events. If an object is moving, we use visual differences generated between the camera image and a gaussian-mixture model of the background [14] to provide a basic figure-ground segmentation for the detection algorithms, increasing the probability of correct detection.

Maintaining a background model also allows us to take the object's context into account when performing the method selection step, for example, we can compare the object's colour histogram to the global environment colour histogram and if they are too similar we would not use the colour method as the probability of detection is low.

The detection method selection step forms part of the visual detection pipeline shown in Figure 4. Here, following each camera frame acquisition the method selection step is performed based directly on the appearance knowledge embedded in the object. If the object is successfully detected a 2D location result is generated. This can take the form of correspondences between extracted image features and features in the Object Model, or a 2D image region in which the object has been detected,

Following 2D location of the object in the camera image, a pose computation step is performed. The object pose is calculated either directly from matched local feature correspondences or by fitting the 3D model to edges detected in the 2D image region from the detection step. RANSAC is used for robust model parameter estimation [26] and eliminates incorrectly matched correspondences. Typically the pose computation

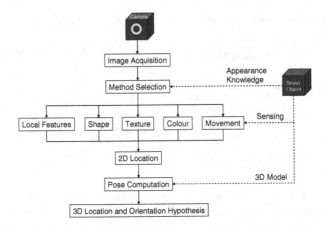

Fig. 4. Detection method selection based on smart object knowledge

step achieves a mean location error under 5mm in the X and Y axes, 2cm in distance to object and mean orientation error under 1 degree with an object at 3m distance.

Sensing can also be used in the pose computation step if a smart object contains 3D accelerometer sensors. Here the sensed gravity vector can be directly used to constrain the number of 3D model poses that must be tested to match the edges detected in the 2D image region from the detection step.

5 Object Projection Processing

When the smart object requests a projection its message includes both the content to project (which can be images, text or video or a URL where content can be found) and the location to project it. We can project onto any object surface visible to the projector. The location description refers to the projection location abstractly or specifically. Abstract locations refer to faces of the object's 3D model. For example, a projection can be requested on the top or front face. A more specific location can also be specified as coordinates in the 3D model coordinate system, allowing exact placement and sizing of the projection on an object.

There are cases where projection cannot begin immediately, such as where the system is busy, the object is occluded or the object is out of the field of view of the projector. Here the display requests are cached at the projector-camera system and the projection commences when the object is in view and the projector is available. Projection requests are displayed sequentially and can be ended by the object requesting a null content projection. Simultaneous projection onto multiple objects can be accomplished if all are detected within the field of view of the projector-camera system.

A rectangular image projected on to a non-perpendicular or non-planar surface exhibits geometric distortion. We compensate for this distortion by warping our projected image if we know both the surface geometry of the object and the orientation angle of the surface with respect to the projector. We obtain the

Table 2. Projection geometric correction methods based on object geometries [18]

Object Geometries	Correction Method
Planar	Planar Homography
Rectilinear	
Cylindrical	Quadric Image Transfer
Spherical	
Irregular	Discretised Warping

orientation of the object from the object detection step, and the surface shape from the geometric 3D model contained within the Object Model. The surface shape directly configures the projection geometric correction method [18], as shown in Table 2.

The projector-camera system uses a real-time colour correction algorithm developed by Fujii et al. [19] to correct for the colour of the object's surface and make the projection more visible. This entails an initial one-time projection of four colour calibration image frames (red, green, blue and grey) to recover the reflectivity response of the surface followed by calculation of the adaptation algorithm for each frame to be projected.

6   Concept Validation

This section uses the scenario outlined in section 3 to present a concrete detection and projection process for two smart chemical containers in a warehouse.

6.1   Registration

Objects enter proximity of the projector-camera system; detect the presence of a projection service and register. This process transfers Object Model knowledge from the smart object to the projector-camera system. Here, an employee enters the environment with two smart chemical containers, as seen in Figure 5.

The projector-camera system registers the objects, and returns a confirmation message to the containers. On receipt of this message the containers begin sending sensor events to the projector-camera system. In this case, they are being carried by the employee so embedded accelerometer sensors generate movement events.

6.2   Detection

The registering objects trigger the detection process in the projector-camera system. Here the challenge is to simultaneously detect mobile or static objects and distinguish between objects with similar appearances.

The steerable projector now rotates from its current position to search the environment. As the objects have just entered, the system does not know their location. Consequently, the projector system uses a creeping line search pattern with a horizontal major axis to thoroughly search the whole environment.

The projector uses the appearance knowledge embedded in the Object Model and the sensor events to configure its detection process. In this case the containers store

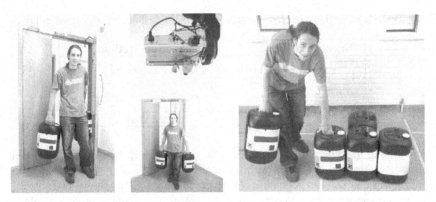

Fig. 5. Left: New objects arrives in environment, Centre: An employee walks with containers, Right: The employee places one object on the floor

knowledge of a colour histogram, and sense they are moving. This knowledge triggers the method selection step to choose colour and movement detection processes. The movement process generates a motion mask which is used by the colour detection process to constrain its search for the object by masking the back-projection result of the object's colour histogram.

As the two chemical containers look identical, two possible objects are identified in the image. It is not currently possible for the camera to distinguish between the objects. Consequently the steerable projector tracks the moving areas in the camera image by centring their centre of gravity.

Both objects generate movement event messages while they are being carried by the employee. However, when an employee places one of the containers on the floor (see Figure 5) the container's movement sensors stop sending movement events. The projector-camera system now only detects one moving area and the system can differentiate between the objects directly based on sensing. A 3D location and pose is now calculated and sent wirelessly to the containers, completing the Object Model.

6.3 Projection

Once an object's 3D location and orientation is calculated by the projector-camera system, objects can request projection of content on their surfaces. Here the challenge

Fig. 6. Left: Warning message projection on two chemical containers, Right: Scale and rotation invariant local features detected on chemical containers

is to correct the projection for the orientation of the object, and variations in its surface colour to ensure the most undistorted and visible projection.

The container detects it was put down in the wrong storage area based on the location it was sent and requests a warning message is projected (see figure 6). The projector-camera system projects the warning message on the front surface of the container objects so as to appear undistorted by drawing the text and images with the calculated transformations applied.

6.4 Manipulating the Object

When projecting onto objects, the object can respond to sensed manipulation or network events by dynamically modifying the projected content. The challenge here is to keep the projection aligned with the object as it is manipulated or moved.

The employee sees the projected message and picks up the object. The detection process continues to track it and generate 3D location and pose information. Consequently, the message appears to remain fixed to its surface as long as the surface is visible to the projector system. When the object is in the correct area it requests the projection stops. The employee puts down the container when they see the message disappear. The projector-camera system keeps tracking the objects.

6.5 Knowledge Updating

If objects enter the environment with only partial knowledge of their appearance, their knowledge can be increased over time by performing extra detection processes and re-embedding the result into the Object Model. The challenge is how to make the knowledge extraction accurate, given that the initial knowledge was incomplete.

The two containers entered the environment only with knowledge of their colour, so the projector-camera system extracts more appearance knowledge over time. In this case, the SIFT algorithm [22] is used to detect scale and rotation-invariant features on the object just put down, as shown in Figure 6. The SIFT descriptors are calculated on small image patches around the detected interest points. The resulting 128 value feature vectors are mapped to locations on the object's 3D model using the known 3D location and orientation of the container.

If the object is manipulated so it is rotated from its original pose new features will be detected as they come into view. The projector-camera system manages the Object Model local feature database to merge new features or update the database if the object appearance is changed. The new local feature appearance knowledge is sent to the smart containers to be embedded in the Object Model and used for faster, more accurate detection in future.

6.6 Objects Departing the Environment

When objects depart the proximity of the projector-camera system, their virtual object representation is removed by the projector system and the projector is free to track other objects. Here, the employee moves to the exit with the container that was never

Fig. 7. A container leaves the environment with the employee

put down. This container continues to generate motion events. As there are no other moving objects or projections active, the projector system tracks the carried object, as shown in Figure 7.

As the employee exits through the door with the object, the system looses sight of the object and it no longer responds to messages from the projector-camera system. The system assumes it has departed the environment after a short time-out.

The projector-camera system then returns to the last-known position of the other container objects. If no objects can be detected the projector system begins an expanding square search pattern centred on their former locations.

7 Discussion

This section discusses issues arising from the concept validation in terms of the five cooperative augmentation steps presented in section 6.

7.1 Registration

Currently, smart object registration and communication is performed over a wireless network, implemented using Smart-Its sensor nodes [23]. The wireless network bandwidth requirements for smart objects depend on where the sensor data is abstracted to events. If a sensor node is not powerful enough to perform this processing then raw sensor data must be streamed to another device on the network. Due to the 13ms timeslots used for each node with the Smart-Its AwareCon protocol [23], only a maximum of 2 smart devices can stream sensor data simultaneously and remain synchronised with a 30Hz (33.3ms) camera refresh rate.

The use of active smart objects with sensing provides three benefits over passive technologies such as RFID:

1. Active sensing (such as movement or light sensing) can constrain the detection process to make it more robust and differentiate between objects.
2. Objects whose appearance or geometry changes can update the projector-camera system dynamically with new appearance knowledge. (For example, if a user opens a smart book the appearance is updated and tracking is un-interrupted).

3. The object itself can be modelled as a state machine which requests projections based on sensed changes in its environment, location or direct interaction with the projection. (For example, a message about how to assemble two smart objects can be projected only when they are moved together into the same location).

7.2 Detection

It has been reported by Brooks in [24] that users of projector based interactive systems routinely accept total system latencies of 150ms. There are three main sources of latency in the detection and projection framework – camera frame acquisition, image processing for object detection and projection. For a camera running at 30Hz the frame acquisition takes up to 33.3ms, while for a 60Hz projector a frame is projected every 16.7ms. Maximum latency before image processing is 50ms; consequently, the object detection step should be performed below 100ms.

The use of complex or multiple computer vision methods in the object detection step is CPU intensive. For example, a CPU optimised version of the SIFT local feature algorithm takes approximately 333ms to detect a single object in a 640x480 pixel image [22]. Our approach is to make use of the ability of the Graphics Processing Unit (GPU) on the graphics card to process pixels in parallel, allowing our system to achieve detection and augmentation of objects in near real-time.

7.3 Projection

As we do not change the appearance of smart objects, their surfaces can present a challenge to projection. Generally, a smooth, diffuse, light coloured object is ideal for projection; however, few objects exhibit these characteristics. Certain combinations of projected content and object surface colour can make the projection almost invisible to the human eye. For example, when projecting a yellow font on a deep red background. Conversely, with a smooth, diffuse, light coloured object, projection illumination on the object can significantly alter its appearance, causing the object detection step to fail.

Consequently, the use of colour correction techniques in the projection step was chosen, as it goes part way to solving these competing problems. Colour correction algorithms can change the projected image to correct for non-uniform and non-white surface colours. An image of the object without projection can also be calculated as part of this process and used for object detection.

Despite the large body of work on photometric correction, the algorithm by Fujii et al. [19] was chosen for this step as it is the only algorithm demonstrated to perform in real-time. However, this correction does have the cost of a one camera frame delay to allow the camera image to be used in the algorithm. The algorithm also cannot completely correct very saturated surfaces, as the dynamic range of typical projectors is not sufficient to invert the natural surface colour.

7.4 Manipulation of Objects

The maximum speed a smart object can move is limited by the camera frame rate and object detection step processing time. For an average camera acquisition and processing step of 133.3ms and a typical human walking speed of 5kph a handheld object could move 18cm. As the lack of projection would be very obvious to a user during a move of this distance, we can de-couple the projection from the detection step. By using a Condensation algorithm particle filter [25] to predict the 3D location and orientation of the smart objects between detections we can exploit the faster frame rate of the projector. The benefit of using a particle filter over a Kalman filter is that it allows us to model multiple alternative hypotheses; it can integrate detection results from multiple distributed cameras and better suits the non-linear movement typically seen in handheld objects.

7.5 Knowledge Updating

When the projector-camera system updates or merges new knowledge about an object, constraints on smart object sensor node memory limit the amount of knowledge that can be stored in a smart object. For example, the particle Smart-Its sensor node [23] currently only has 512KB of flash memory which can be used for Object Model storage. Our solution for larger models is to only store a URL link to the actual Object Model in the smart object (which assumes a network connection).

8 Conclusion

In this paper we have presented the concept of cooperative augmentation and validated our approach with an implementation using a warehouse scenario. We discussed issues arising from the implementation and the lessons learned.

Our contribution is a new approach to augmenting smart objects with a display capability without changing their natural appearance, by using projector-camera systems. Our approach can locate and track mobile objects in the environment, align the projection with the object's surfaces and correct for surface colour so the display appears undistorted and visible to a user.

The main challenges in our approach are real-time visual detection of smart objects, keeping the projection synchronised when the object is moved or manipulated and correcting the projection for non-ideal surface colours and textures.

More research is required in how different levels of knowledge change the detection performance, what impact sensing has on the robustness of detection and which computer vision algorithms are best suited to detecting the objects. Open questions remain in the area concerning location of projections on an object. Specifically, how can we determine the best strategy to ensure the most visible, readable and useable projection location on an object's surfaces for the user? Also, if an object is in view of multiple distributed projector-camera systems, what is the best strategy to decide which system should project onto each object surface?

Acknowledgements

This research is supported by the EPSRC, the Ministry of Economic Affairs of the Netherlands through the BSIK project Smart Surroundings under contract no. 03060 and by Lancaster University through the e-Campus grant.

References

1. Bandyopadhyay, D., Raskar, R., Fuchs, H.: Dynamic Shader Lamps: Painting on Movable Objects. In: Proc. IEEE and ACM Int. Symposium on Augmented Reality, New York (2001)
2. Ehnes, J., Hirota, K., Hirose, M.: Projected Augmentation – Augmented Reality using Rotatable Video Projectors. In: Third IEEE and ACM International Symposium on Mixed and Augmented Reality (ISMAR'04), September-October 2004, Arlington, VA, USA (2004)
3. Kato, H., Billinghurst, M.: Marker Tracking and HMD Calibration for a video-based Augmented Reality Conferencing System. In: Proceedings of the 2nd International Workshop on Augmented Reality (IWAR 99), October 1999, San Francisco, USA (1999)
4. Borkowski, S., Riff, O., Crowley, J.: Projecting Rectified Images In an Augmented Environment. In: IEEE International Workshop on Projector-Camera Systems (PROCAMS-2003), October 12, 2003, Nice, France (2003)
5. Lee, J.C., Hudson, S.E., Summet, J.W., Dietz, P.H.: Moveable Interactive Projected Displays Using Projector Based Tracking. In: Proceedings of the ACM Symposium on User Interface Software and Technology (UIST), October 23-26, 2005, Seattle, WA, pp. 63–72 (2005)
6. Summet, J., Sukthankar, R.: Tracking Locations of Moving Hand-held Displays Using Projected Light. In: Gellersen, H.-W., Want, R., Schmidt, A. (eds.) PERVASIVE 2005. LNCS, vol. 3468, Springer, Heidelberg (2005)
7. Raskar, R., Beardsley, P., van Baar, J., Wang, Y., Dietz, P., Lee, J., Leigh, D., Willwatcher, T.: RFIG Lamps: Interacting with a Self-Describing World via Photosensing Wireless Tags and Projectors. In: Proceedings of SIGGRAPH 2004, Los Angeles, USA (2004)
8. Levas, A., Pinhanez, C., Pingali, G., Kjeldsen, R., Podlaseck, M., Sukaviriya, N.: An Architecture and Framework for Steerable Interface Systems. In: Dey, A.K., Schmidt, A., McCarthy, J.F. (eds.) UbiComp 2003. LNCS, vol. 2864, Springer, Heidelberg (2003)
9. Gellersen, H., Beigl, M., Krull, H.: The MediaCup: Awareness Technology embedded in an Everyday Object. In: Gellersen, H.-W. (ed.) HUC 1999. LNCS, vol. 1707, pp. 308–310. Springer, Heidelberg (1999)
10. Strohbach, M., Gellersen, H.-W., Kortuem, G., Kray, C.: Cooperative Artefacts: Assessing Real World Situations with Embedded Technology. In: Davies, N., Mynatt, E.D., Siio, I. (eds.) UbiComp 2004. LNCS, vol. 3205, Springer, Heidelberg (2004)
11. Schmidt, A., Strohbach, M., Van Laerhoven, K., Friday, A., Gellersen, H.-W.: Context Acquisition based on Load Sensing. In: Boriello, G., Holmquist, L.E. (eds.) Proceedings of Ubicomp 2002, September 2002. LNCS, vol. 2498, pp. 333–351. Springer, Gothenburg, Sweden (2002)
12. Schmidt, A., Strohbach, M., Van Laerhoven, K., Gellersen, H.W.: Ubiquitous Interaction - Using Surfaces in Everyday Environments as Pointing Devices. In: 7th ERCIM Workshop "User Interfaces For All (23 - 25 October, 2002)
13. Strohbach, M., Gellersen, H.-W., Kortuem, G., Kray, C.: Cooperative Artefacts: Assessing Real World Situations with Embedded Technology. In: Davies, N., Mynatt, E.D., Siio, I. (eds.) UbiComp 2004. LNCS, vol. 3205, Springer, Heidelberg (2004)
14. Stauffer, C., Grimson, W.E.L.: Adaptive background mixture models for real-time tracking. Computer Vision Pattern Recognition, 246–252 (1999)

15. Karitsuka, T., Sato, K.: A Wearable Mixed Reality with On-board Projector. In: Second IEEE and ACM International Symposium on Mixed and Augmented Reality (ISMAR2003), 7-10 October 2003, Tokyo, Japan (2003)

16. Pinhanez, C.: The Everywhere Displays Projector: A Device to Create Ubiquitous Graphical Interfaces. In: Abowd, G.D., Brumitt, B., Shafer, S. (eds.) Ubicomp 2001: Ubiquitous Computing. LNCS, vol. 2201, Springer, Heidelberg (2001)

17. Butz, A., Schneider, M., Spassova, M.: Searchlight: A Lightweight Search Function for Pervasive Environments. In: Ferscha, A., Mattern, F. (eds.) PERVASIVE 2004. LNCS, vol. 3001, pp. 21–23. Springer, Heidelberg (2004)

18. Bimber, O., Raskar, R.: Spatial Augmented Reality Merging Real and Virtual Worlds. A K Peters LTD (publisher), ISBN: 1-56881-230-2

19. Fujii, K., Grossberg, M.D., Nayar, S.K.: A Projector-Camera System with Real-Time Photometric Adaptation for Dynamic Environments. In: IEEE Conference on Computer Vision and Pattern Recognition (CVPR), vol. 1, pp. 814–821 (2005)

20. Decker, C., Beigle, M., Krohn, A., Robinson, P., Kubach, U.: eSeal – a system for enhanced electronic assertion of authenticity and integrity. In: Ferscha, A., Mattern, F. (eds.) PERVASIVE 2004. LNCS, vol. 3001, Springer, Heidelberg (2004)

21. Mikolajczyk, K., Schmid, C.: Scale and Affine invariant interest point detectors. International Journal of Computer Vision (IJCV) 60(1), 63–86 (2004)

22. Lowe, D.: SIFT: Distinctive image features from scale invariant keypoints. International Journal of Computer Vision (IJCV) 60(2), 91–110 (2004)

23. Decker, C., Krohn, A., Beigl, M., Zimmer, T.: The Particle Computer System, IPSN Track on Sensor Platform, Tools and Design Methods for Networked Embedded Systems (SPOTS). In: Proceedings of the ACM/IEEE 4th International Conference on Information Processing in Sensor Networks (IPSN05), April 2005, Los Angeles, pp. 443–448 (2005)

24. Brooks Jr., F.P.: What's Real About Virtual Reality? IEEE Computer Graphics and Applications 19(6), 16–27 (1999)

25. Isard, M., Blake, A.: CONDENSATION – conditional density propagation for visual tracking. International Journal of Computer Vision (IJCV) 29(1), 5–28 (1998)

26. Fischler, M.A., Bolles, R.C.: Random sample consensus: a paradigm for model fittingwith applications to image analysis and automated cartography. Communications of the ACM 24, 6, 381–395 (1981)

27. Swain, M.J., Ballard, D.H.: Color indexing. International Journal of Computer Vision (IJCV) 7(1) (1991)

28. Recognition without Correspondence using Multidimensional Receptive Field Histograms. International Journal of Computer Vision (IJCV) 36(1), 31–50 (2000)

29. Belongie, S., Malik, J., Puzicha, J.: Matching Shapes. In: Proceedings of International Conference on Computer Vision (ICCV'01) (2001)

30. Kjeldsen, R., Pinhanez, C., Pingali, G., Hartman, J., Levas, T., Podlaseck, M.: Interacting with Steerable Projected Displays. In: Proc. of the 5th International Conference on Automatic Face and Gesture Recognition (FG'02), May 20-21 2002, Washington (DC) (2002)

Author Index

Lecture Notes in Computer Science

Sublibrary 3: Information Systems and Application, incl. Internet/Web and HCI

For information about Vols. 1– 4270
please contact your bookseller or Springer

Vol. 4519: E. Franconi, M. Kifer, W. May (Eds.), The Semantic Web: Research and Applications. XVIII, 830 pages. 2007.

Vol. 4518: N. Fuhr, M. Lalmas, A. Trotman (Eds.), Comparative Evaluation of XML Information Retrieval Systems. XII, 554 pages. 2007.

Vol. 4508: M.-Y. Kao, X.-Y. Li (Eds.), Algorithmic Aspects in Information and Management. VIII, 428 pages. 2007.

Vol. 4506: D. Zeng, I. Gotham, K. Komatsu, C. Lynch, M. Thurmond, D. Madigan, B. Lober, J. Kvach, H. Chen (Eds.), Intelligence and Security Informatics: Biosurveillance. XI, 234 pages. 2007.

Vol. 4505: G. Dong, X. Lin, W. Wang, Y. Yang, J.X. Yu (Eds.), Advances in Data and Web Management. XXII, 896 pages. 2007.

Vol. 4504: J. Huang, R. Kowalczyk, Z. Maamar, D. Martin, I. Müller, S. Stoutenburg, K.P. Sycara (Eds.), Service-Oriented Computing: Agents, Semantics, and Engineering. X, 175 pages. 2007.

Vol. 4500: N.A. Streitz, A. Kameas, I. Mavrommati (Eds.), The Disappearing Computer. XVIII, 304 pages. 2007.

Vol. 4495: J. Krogstie, A. Opdahl, G. Sindre (Eds.), Advanced Information Systems Engineering. XVI, 606 pages. 2007.

Vol. 4480: A. LaMarca, M. Langheinrich, K.N. Truong (Eds.), Pervasive Computing. XIII, 369 pages. 2007.

Vol. 4471: P. Cesar, K. Chorianopoulos, J.F. Jensen (Eds.), Interactive TV: A Shared Experience. XIII, 236 pages. 2007.

Vol. 4469: K.-c. Hui, Z. Pan, R.C.-k. Chung, C.C.L. Wang, X. Jin, S. Göbel, E.C.-L. Li (Eds.), Technologies for E-Learning and Digital Entertainment. XVIII, 974 pages. 2007.

Vol. 4443: R. Kotagiri, P.R. Krishna, M. Mohania, E. Nantajeewarawat (Eds.), Advances in Databases: Concepts, Systems and Applications. XXI, 1126 pages. 2007.

Vol. 4439: W. Abramowicz (Ed.), Business Information Systems. XV, 654 pages. 2007.

Vol. 4430: C.C. Yang, D. Zeng, M. Chau, K. Chang, Q. Yang, X. Cheng, J. Wang, F.-Y. Wang, H. Chen (Eds.), Intelligence and Security Informatics. XII, 330 pages. 2007.

Vol. 4425: G. Amati, C. Carpineto, G. Romano (Eds.), Advances in Information Retrieval. XIX, 759 pages. 2007.

Vol. 4412: F. Stajano, H.J. Kim, J.-S. Chae, S.-D. Kim (Eds.), Ubiquitous Convergence Technology. XI, 302 pages. 2007.

Vol. 4402: W. Shen, J.-Z. Luo, Z. Lin, J.-P.A. Barthès, Q. Hao (Eds.), Computer Supported Cooperative Work in Design III. XV, 763 pages. 2007.

Vol. 4398: S. Marchand-Maillet, E. Bruno, A. Nürnberger, M. Detyniecki (Eds.), Adaptive Multimedia Retrieval: User, Context, and Feedback. XI, 269 pages. 2007.

Vol. 4397: C. Stephanidis, M. Pieper (Eds.), Universal Access in Ambient Intelligence Environments. XV, 467 pages. 2007.

Vol. 4380: S. Spaccapietra, P. Atzeni, F. Fages, M.-S. Hacid, M. Kifer, J. Mylopoulos, B. Pernici, P. Shvaiko, J. Trujillo, I. Zaihrayeu (Eds.), Journal on Data Semantics VIII. XV, 219 pages. 2007.

Vol. 4365: C. Bussler, M. Castellanos, U. Dayal, S. Navathe (Eds.), Business Intelligence for the Real-Time Enterprises. IX, 157 pages. 2007.

Vol. 4353: T. Schwentick, D. Suciu (Eds.), Database Theory – ICDT 2007. XI, 419 pages. 2006.

Vol. 4352: T.-J. Cham, J. Cai, C. Dorai, D. Rajan, T.-S. Chua, L.-T. Chia (Eds.), Advances in Multimedia Modeling, Part II. XVIII, 743 pages. 2006.

Vol. 4351: T.-J. Cham, J. Cai, C. Dorai, D. Rajan, T.-S. Chua, L.-T. Chia (Eds.), Advances in Multimedia Modeling, Part I. XIX, 797 pages. 2006.

Vol. 4328: D. Penkler, M. Reitenspiess, F. Tam (Eds.), Service Availability. X, 289 pages. 2006.

Vol. 4321: P. Brusilovsky, A. Kobsa, W. Nejdl (Eds.), The Adaptive Web. XII, 763 pages. 2007.

Vol. 4317: S.K. Madria, K.T. Claypool, R. Kannan, P. Uppuluri, M.M. Gore (Eds.), Distributed Computing and Internet Technology. XIX, 466 pages. 2006.

Vol. 4312: S. Sugimoto, J. Hunter, A. Rauber, A. Morishima (Eds.), Digital Libraries: Achievements, Challenges and Opportunities. XVIII, 571 pages. 2006.

Vol. 4306: Y. Avrithis, Y. Kompatsiaris, S. Staab, N.E. O'Connor (Eds.), Semantic Multimedia. XII, 241 pages. 2006.

Vol. 4302: J. Domingo-Ferrer, L. Franconi (Eds.), Privacy in Statistical Databases. XI, 383 pages. 2006.

Vol. 4299: S. Renals, S. Bengio, J.G. Fiscus (Eds.), Machine Learning for Multimodal Interaction. XII, 470 pages. 2006.

Vol. 4295: J.D. Carswell, T. Tezuka (Eds.), Web and Wireless Geographical Information Systems. XI, 269 pages. 2006.

Vol. 4286: P.G. Spirakis, M. Mavronicolas, S.C. Kontogiannis (Eds.), Internet and Network Economics. XI, 401 pages. 2006.

Vol. 4282: Z. Pan, A. Cheok, M. Haller, R.W.H. Lau, H. Saito, R. Liang (Eds.), Advances in Artificial Reality and Tele-Existence. XXIII, 1347 pages. 2006.

Vol. 4278: R. Meersman, Z. Tari, P. Herrero (Eds.), On the Move to Meaningful Internet Systems 2006: OTM 2006 Workshops, Part II. XLV, 1004 pages. 2006.

Vol. 4277: R. Meersman, Z. Tari, P. Herrero (Eds.), On the Move to Meaningful Internet Systems 2006: OTM 2006 Workshops, Part I. XLV, 1009 pages. 2006.

Vol. 4276: R. Meersman, Z. Tari (Eds.), On the Move to Meaningful Internet Systems 2006: CoopIS, DOA, GADA, and ODBASE, Part II. XXXII, 752 pages. 2006.

Vol. 4275: R. Meersman, Z. Tari (Eds.), On the Move to Meaningful Internet Systems 2006: CoopIS, DOA, GADA, and ODBASE, Part I. XXXI, 1115 pages. 2006.

Vol. 4273: I. Cruz, S. Decker, D. Allemang, C. Preist, D. Schwabe, P. Mika, M. Uschold, L. Aroyo (Eds.), The Semantic Web - ISWC 2006. XXIV, 1001 pages. 2006.